THE ✺ TIMES

Good University Guide 2010

WITHDRAWN

John O'Leary

with
Patrick Kennedy
Dr Nicki Horseman

TIMES BOOKS

Published in 2009 by Times Books

HarperCollins Publishers
77–85 Fulham Palace Road
Hammersmith
London
W6 8JB

www.collins.co.uk

First published in 1993 by Times Books. Sixteenth edition 2009

ISBN 978-0-00-731348-8

Patrick Kennedy and Dr Nicki Horseman have been lead consultants for Exeter Enterprises Limited, which has compiled the main university league table and the individual subject tables for this guide on behalf of The Times/HarperCollins.

Please see chapters 2 and 3 for a full explanation of the sources of data used in the ranking tables. The data providers do not necessarily agree with the data aggregations or manipulations appearing in this book and are also not responsible for any inference or conclusions thereby derived.

Project editor: Christopher Riches
Design, editorial and additional research: Edenside Computing Services Ltd

Printed and bound in Great Britain by Clays Ltd, St Ives plc.

Mixed Sources

Product group from well-managed
forests and other controlled sources
www.fsc.org Cert no. SW-COC-1806
© 1996 Forest Stewardship Council

FSC

FSC is a non-profit international organisation established to promote the responsible management of the world's forests. Products carrying the FSC label are independently certified to assure consumers that they come from forests that are managed to meet the social, economic and ecological needs of present and future generations.

Find out more about HarperCollins and the environment at
www.harpercollins.co.uk/green

Contents

About the Author   4

Acknowledgements   4

How to Use this Book   5

Introduction   7

1. What and Where to Study   15

2. The Top Universities   37

3. The Top Universities by Subject   48

4. Making Your Application   175

5. Finding Somewhere to Live   186

6. Finding Out About University Sport   198

7. The Cost of Studying   210

8. What Parents Should Do   232

9. International Students   237

10. Oxbridge   248

11. University Profiles   282

Colleges of Higher Education   525

Index   529

About the Author

John O'Leary is a freelance journalist and education consultant. He was the Editor of *The Times Higher Education Supplement* from 2002 to 2007 and was previously Education Editor of *The Times*, having joined the paper in 1990 as Higher Education Correspondent. He has been writing on higher education for nearly 30 years and established the World University Rankings, published by *Times Higher Education* and QS. He now edits *Policy Review* and is the author of *Higher Education in England*, published in 2009 by the Higher Education Funding Council for England. He has a degree in politics from the University of Sheffield.

Acknowledgements

We would like to thank the many individuals who have helped with this edition of *The Times Good University Guide*. We are particularly indebted to Alexandra Frean, Education Editor of *The Times*, for her support; to Patrick Kennedy and Dr Nicki Horseman the lead consultants for Exeter Enterprises Limited, which has compiled the main university league table and the individual subject tables for this Guide on behalf of *The Times* and HarperCollins Publishers; to the members of *The Times Good University Guide* Advisory Group for their time and expertise: Ben Chisnall, Planning Officer, Imperial College, London, Jim Galbraith, Senior Strategic Planner, University of Edinburgh, Sue Hybart, Director of Planning, Cardiff University, Fidelma Hannah, Director of Planning, Loughborough University, and Janet Isaac, Head of Corporate Information, University of Plymouth; Jonathan Waller of HESA for his technical advice; Susannah Attwell of University and College Sport and Kit Martin for the provision of the table of sports facilities in chapter 6; and Tony Tysome, Murad Ahmed and Patrick Foster for their contributions to the book. We also wish to thank Sodexo for permission to use material taken from the *Sodexo University Lifestyle Survey 2008* (a summary of the survey can be found on their website: **www.sodexo.co.uk**), the NatWest Bank for material taken from the *NatWest Student Living Survey 2008*, and all the university staff who assisted in providing information for this edition.

How to Use this Book

The Times Good University Guide 2010 will help you to select the subject and university of your choice and to guide you through the whole process of getting to university. The answers to the questions below will help you to get the most out of the information we offer.

How do I choose a course?

- The first half of chapter 1 provides advice on what you should consider when choosing a subject area and relevant courses within that subject.
- Chapter 3 provides details for 62 different subject areas (as listed on page 50).
- For each subject there is a league table that provides our assessment of the ranking of all universities offering courses in the particular subject area.
- For each subject we also provide some background information, details of employment prospects and selected websites where you can find out more about the subject.
- Specific advice for international students is given in chapter 9.

How do I choose a university?

- The second half of chapter 1 provides advice on choosing a university.
- Central is the main *Times League Table* on pages 40–47. This ranks the universities by assessing their quality not just according to student satisfaction (drawn from the National Student Survey) but also through seven other factors, including research quality, the spending on services and facilities, and graduate employment prospects. This table gives an indication of the overall performance of each university.
- The second half of the book contains two pages on each university, giving a general overview of the institution as well as data on student numbers, how to contact the university, the accommodation provided by the university, and the fees payable and the bursaries available.
- In addition, chapter 6 provides information on sport and sporting facilities across all the universities.
- For those considering Oxford or Cambridge, details of admission processes and of all the colleges can be found in chapter 10.
- Specific advice for international students is given in chapter 9.

How do I apply?

- Chapter 4 outlines the application procedure for university entry.
- It starts by advising you on how to complete the UCAS application, and then takes you step-by-step through the process that we hope will lead to your university place for autumn 2010.
- Specific information about applying to Oxford and Cambridge is given in chapter 10.

Can I afford it?

- Chapter 7 outlines the costs of studying at university (including the payment of fees) as well as sources of funds (including student loans, grants and bursaries).
- Chapter 5 provides advice on where to live while you are there.
- Accommodation charges for each university are given in the university profile in chapter 11.

How do I find out more?

- *The Times Good University Guide* website **www.timesonline.co.uk/gug** will keep you up to date with developments throughout the year and contains further information and online tables.
- In each university profile (chapter 11) contact details are given (including e-mail addresses and websites), so you can obtain more information on any university you are interested in.
- At the end of each chapter, a selection of useful websites is given.
- A further listing (pages 525–27) provides contact details for Higher Education Institutes and Colleges that are not covered elsewhere within the book.

Introduction

Higher education pundits long ago marked out 2010 as a potential watershed for universities. It would be the year in which top-up fees were increased, or even deregulated, and the Government moved on (and probably up) from its target of 50 per cent participation in higher education. It still promises to be a turning point for universities, but for different reasons. The recession has already prompted Government restrictions on student numbers that have prevented universities from responding to a spike in demand for places, and higher education is preparing for a period of austerity, whichever party is in power.

The good news for students seeking degree places in 2010 is that they are unlikely to face fee rises above the rate of inflation – and not even that in Scotland, where graduate charges have been abolished. The bad news is that competition for places seems certain to be stiffer than for many years. The number of 18- to 20-year-olds is peaking at a time when a bleak jobs market has made university an even more attractive proposition.

It is a combination of factors that will make choosing the right course more important than ever for those hoping to start a degree in 2010. There will be a place somewhere for most students with basic qualifications, but many courses that traditionally struggle to recruit students are expected to be turning weaker candidates away. As in 2009, those who achieve higher grades than the top offer they are holding will be able to make use of a five-day Adjustment Period immediately after A-level results day in which to 'trade up' to more selective universities. Unfortunately, many of the top universities will be full by then, as will the most popular degrees at many other institutions, so it may be an exercise in frustration for a lot of candidates. However, there will be openings for those who had anticipated low grades and whose new target is a course where the pressure on places is not intense.

For some universities, there will be the added complication of the new A* grade at A level, introduced to sort the real high-fliers from the merely excellent. The development is a response to the ever-increasing numbers achieving three As, but it is one that many universities did not want. At the time of writing, only Cambridge had announced that it would use the new grade for selection in its first year, expecting candidates to have at least one A*. A handful of others may follow suit, but the signs are that most universities will wait to see the system bed in before including the new grade in entry requirements, as the Government has recommended.

Getting into the most popular universities is going to take a well-targeted application, as well as good grades. That is where this *Guide* – identified by a Government-funded review as the most influential of its type – can help. Choosing the right course at the right university is a personal decision, influenced by family circumstances, relationships, outside interests and geography, as much as by academic reputation. Often an intangible feeling will tip the balance one way or another. But the evidence collected here about the relative quality of universities and their courses should help to whittle down the list of potential destinations.

Early in 2009, applications were up by almost 9 per cent and there was no sign of the trend reversing, in spite of the downturn in graduate employment. No one can predict the eventual impact of the credit crunch, but few good judges expect the outcome to be an economy in which a degree is less of an advantage than it has been in recent years. International surveys continue to show the salary premium enjoyed by UK graduates over those who choose not to go to university as among the highest in the world. And with more and more jobs requiring a degree, the financial case for going to university remains compelling, even without the wider benefits of an undergraduate education.

In the longer term, this may have to be balanced against higher fees for UK and EU students. But, while the promised review of top-up fees may have reported before the start of the 2010–11 academic year, the recommendations are unlikely to affect those beginning courses then. The requirement for any change to be agreed by both Houses of Parliament and the further lead time needed to include new rates in university prospectuses make an above-inflation increase unlikely before 2013, even if the political will exists to sanction one. In any case, previous increases have never applied to those already on courses.

Universities and league tables

League tables are seldom popular with those being measured, and the review commissioned by the Higher Education Funding Council for England (HEFCE) contained criticisms of all university rankings. But the rankings at the heart of this *Guide* have stood the test of time, after 16 years of publication, and are quoted frequently by universities themselves and by those with an interest in higher education, both at home and abroad.

Indeed, favourable results invariably appear prominently on universities' websites. Professor David Eastwood, now the Vice-Chancellor of Birmingham University and chief executive of HEFCE at the time of the review, reminded universities at a conference to discuss its findings that they often "deplore league tables one day and deploy them the next". He said the tables had become part of the higher education landscape and one of the sources to which prospective students would refer when choosing where and what to study.

However, this *Guide* contains far more than league tables. There are chapters on choosing a course and a university, the application process, managing your money as a student, where to live and what to expect in terms of sport. There are also special sections for overseas applicants and for parents, as well as profiles of every university and Oxbridge college.

This year's outlook

The pattern of applications in 2009 makes it hard to predict with any certainty where the peaks and troughs of demand will be in the coming year. Most universities and most subjects have enjoyed increased demand for places, but not all. And those that have seen their popularity grow have tended not to be those at the top of the league tables or the most job-related subjects.

Not surprisingly, given the economic picture, one discernible pattern appears to be renewed growth in home-based study. The longstanding British preference for studying away from home had begun to reassert itself among those who can afford it, after a move in the opposite direction when top-up fees were introduced in 2006. Now, it may be that a change of culture will become established. Several of the big city post-1992 universities, such as Birmingham City and Portsmouth, saw the biggest growth in applications in 2009.

There is no such pattern of subject choices, however. For several years, students have been more conscious of the need for a marketable qualification to service growing levels of debt among graduates. But the initial rush away from pure academic subjects towards the vocational has not persisted. While some job-related degrees, including most branches of engineering, continue to prove attractive, subjects such as politics, with no direct link to employment, have again increased their popularity in 2009. Yet others such as finance and building do appear to have been affected by the recession. It may simply be that prospective students recognise that the majority of graduate jobs are open to any discipline.

What has not changed in 2009 is the growing tendency for UK students to remain within national borders. More Scots have applied to Scottish universities, where they will no longer pay the graduate endowment; more Welsh are applying to study in Wales, where they are eligible for reduced fees; and more English are chasing places at universities in England, with fewer looking further afield.

One incentive for English students is a Government grant of almost £3,000, available in full to those from families with a combined income of less than £25,000, and in part where family income reaches up to £50,000. Although the thresholds were reduced in 2009 and fewer students will qualify as a result, ministers still hope that, combined with university bursaries, the scheme will boost participation among working-class students. The changes will limit the number of beneficiaries from middle-class backgrounds.

So far, top-up fees have seen a slight increase in working-class participation in higher education, although far less than the Government is seeking. Indeed, the fee changes have not all been bad news for students: the requirement to pay fees of £1,000-plus upfront has gone and grants, bursaries and scholarships made available to bring down the cost for those from poor backgrounds. The institutional profiles in this year's *Guide* include a section detailing the (sometimes complex) arrangements at each university.

Finding a place

In 2010, as in previous years, there will be a place somewhere in the higher education system for virtually every candidate with the basic qualifications for a course at this level, whether those are A levels, Highers or relevant vocational qualifications. There have been 1.3 applications per place in higher education for the last six years, and this is unlikely to alter significantly in the coming year, whatever the squeeze on places. Many of those who do not find a place drop out of the process of their own accord, while others defer for a year while they travel or work to finance their studies. More than 90 per cent of those with two A-level passes go on to higher education each year, and almost all of the remainder choose a different career path, rather than being rejected.

Commentators on higher education distinguish between "selecting universities" and "recruiting universities", but these labels underestimate the complexity of the choices facing today's applicants. There are very few universities where all the courses are heavily selective – there are simply not enough well-qualified candidates to go around in some subjects – and most so-called recruiting universities have areas in which they excel and can attract a strong field of applicants. The *Guide* uses the ratings of academics and students, plus entry standards and graduate employment rates, to differentiate between universities in 62 different subject areas.

When *The Times Good University Guide* first appeared almost 16 years ago, it helped to explode the myth that any British degree was as good as any other. Since then, the statistics behind the tables have confirmed significant variations in performance within British higher education. Charles Clarke, Labour's former Education Secretary, was prepared to cite this *Guide* as evidence to demolish what he termed the "emperor's clothes idea that all universities are broadly the same".

The changes that Mr Clarke was advocating and that his successors have pursued – chiefly the introduction of variable tuition fees, but also the encouragement of greater specialisation – are creating a new pecking order in higher education, albeit one with familiar names at the top. Employers already distinguish between universities as well as individuals. The need to know the standing of a university, both as an institution and in the various subjects it offers, can only become more important as time goes on.

This year's tables

Unlike most of the rankings that have sprung up in recent years, *The Times Good University Guide* has maintained as much consistency as possible in the methods used to compare universities. The indicators and weightings used in the overall ranking of universities are the same as last year. However, the first official assessments of research at UK universities for seven years mean that there will be fresh data in all eight of the measures used in the main League Table for the first time since the 2003 *Guide*.

Like last year, entry scores have been calculated using grades from A levels and Highers alone. This was done to maintain a fair basis for comparison when it emerged that the scores of some Scottish universities contained UCAS tariff points for qualifications that were not included in the returns of other institutions.

Two minor changes in the subject tables involve the addition of a separate ranking for sports science to serve the large numbers of candidates now choosing a degree in this area. And there is an additional table for medicine, showing the scores achieved in different specialisms in the 2008 Research Assessment Exercise.

The other change that seems to occur every year is in the number of universities. Two more have been created since the last edition was published: the University for the Creative Arts, which has bases in Kent and Surrey, and Glyndŵr University, the former North East Wales Institute of Higher Education, in Wrexham. Both are comparatively small and may climb the tables as they begin to feel the benefits of university status.

The number of institutions in this year's tables has increased by only one because a fourth university – the West of Scotland – has instructed the Higher Education Statistics Agency not to release its data. It joins Swansea Metropolitan, London Metropolitan and Liverpool Hope universities in blocking the release of data in order to avoid appearing in league tables. Other published statistics suggest that all four would have been in the lower reaches of *The Times* League Table, but prospective applicants can only guess at their actual standing.

The first *Times* ranking, 16 years ago, effectively produced a dead heat between Oxford and Cambridge, with the light blues a fraction of a point ahead. After several years of Cambridge domination, changes in methodology saw the roles reversed in the 2003 edition and Oxford subsequently extended its lead. The current table sees Oxford maintain its leadership, despite playing second fiddle to Cambridge in most of the subject tables. Cambridge has the better record on student satisfaction, research, entry standards, completion and graduate destinations, but Oxford's lead in staffing levels, degree classifications and particularly in spending on libraries and other student facilities makes the difference. Accurate comparisons of the two are difficult because of the mix of college and central university responsibilities, but Oxford appears to include more college spending in its submission. Cambridge remains well ahead of Imperial

College and St Andrews, the top university in Scotland. Cardiff is well clear in Wales.

For most readers, however, the scramble over a handful of points at the top of the overall ranking of universities will be literally academic. The key information is contained in the subject tables, which now cover every area of higher education. One of the strengths of this *Guide*, and others like it, has been to highlight the quality of previously underestimated universities such as York and Bath, and to celebrate the achievements of centres of excellence, such as the social sciences at Essex.

Universities' own research suggests that well over half of all applicants use newspaper guides, and this year's review predicts that league tables will become increasingly influential as fees rise further. Candidates have already become more selective about the courses they choose, as top-up fees have been introduced and the financial pressures on students and their families have grown.

The new hierarchy

Higher education has seen other important changes with the introduction of incentives to extend access to a wider share of the population, and much more selective allocation of research funds. The Government still wants half of all young people to experience higher education by the time they are 30, many of them taking two-year Foundation degrees rather than the traditional honours. The result is a gradual return to the hierarchical system that seemed to have been abandoned when the polytechnics acquired university status; only this time there are more than two tiers. Although one or two new universities appear above one or two older foundations in this year's table, the divisions remain stark.

At the top of the pile, in terms of funding and prestige, is a group of little more than 20 universities, which attract 90 per cent of the resources available for research and also take the lion's share of money for teaching, partly because they offer expensive subjects such as medicine and engineering. A middle group, composed mainly of traditional universities, has been recruiting more undergraduates – especially overseas – while trying to compete on research. The remainder have stayed buoyant mainly by expanding, or at least maintaining student numbers, while interacting with local companies.

Universities in the last group have been feeling the squeeze since several of the most popular institutions have taken the opportunity to expand their numbers and move into less traditional subjects. But fears have also been expressed for some of those in the middle, which miss out not only on the Government's boost for leading research but also on the rewards for widening access to higher education.

Uncertainty over sixth-form qualifications continues to complicate the picture. The future of A levels is uncertain, with the Government championing a new range of vocational (and eventually academic) diplomas. And even the current range of qualifications is treated differently by different types of university. Most of the leading institutions continue to frame their offers in terms of A-level grades, but the majority of others now use the UCAS tariff to set a points requirement. Whichever system is used, every grade may help in the race for selection. The right choice of course remains vital. This book should help in the process of choice for, unlike other guides, its emphasis is on the quality of education.

The university explosion

At first sight, choosing a university appears to have become simpler over the past decade. The distinction between universities and polytechnics was swept away in 1992, and the number of places expanded to the point where far more young (and not-so-young) people could benefit from higher education. Although the parties may differ in the 2010 election about the scale of expansion, consensus has grown among politicians and business leaders that, quite apart from the benefits to the individual, a modern economy needs mass higher education. Countries such as the United States and Japan reached the same conclusion long ago but a combination of factors – not all of them planned – has seen Britain making up for lost time at a rate that has prompted concerns about the quality of some courses.

More than a third of 18-year-olds are now going on to higher education, compared with one in seven in 1980, while a much higher proportion will take a higher education course at some point in their life. Yet, paradoxically, by ridding Britain of its elite university system, the last Conservative Government sowed the seeds of a different form of elitism. The very process of opening up higher education ensured the creation of a new hierarchy of institutions. The old certainties could not survive in a nation of more than 100 diverse universities and a growing number of degree-providing colleges.

As student numbers have gone through the roof, however, general higher education budgets have been squeezed and the funding gap has widened. Beneath the veneer of a unified higher education system, it was inevitable that greater specialisation would arrive eventually. There is no need for formalised divisions like the American Ivy League because the market – and Government policy – is already taking the university system in that direction.

The benefits of information

There always was a pecking order of sorts. Oxford and Cambridge were world leaders long before most British universities were established, and parts of the University of London have always enjoyed a high status in particular fields. But few outside the higher-education world could discriminate between Keele and Kent, for example.

Employers, careers advisers, even academics, had their own ideas of which were the leading universities, but there was little hard evidence to back their conclusions. Often they were based on outdated, inaccurate impressions of distant institutions. The expanded higher education system has made such judgements more scientific as well as more necessary. Employers of graduates and those who commit their money to student sponsorship or funding research are comparing institutions department by department. This has become possible because of a new transparency in what a former Higher Education Minister described as the "secret garden of academe". Official demands for more and more published information may have taxed the patience of university administrators, but they have also given outsiders the opportunity to make more meaningful comparisons. The **unistats.com** website represents the latest attempt to bring together the statistics relevant to applicants. But many readers value the more concise nature of guides such as this one, which distil the information displayed on such sites into a more manageable form.

Why university?

Particularly in a recession, some will be tempted, once the cost of living has been added to the fees burden and the attractions of university life balanced against loss of potential earnings, to write off higher education. There are plenty of self-made millionaires who still swear by the University of Life as the only training ground for success. Yet even by narrow financial criteria it would be rash to dismiss higher education. With so many more competing for jobs, a degree will never again be an automatic passport to a fast-track career. But graduates' financial prospects remain much brighter than school leavers', as do their prospects in other important areas, such as health.

Even for those who cannot or do not wish to afford three or more years of full-time education after leaving school, university remains a possibility. The modular courses adopted by most universities enable students to work through a degree at their own pace, dropping out for a time if necessary, or switching to part-time attendance. Distance learning is another option, and advances in information technology now mean that some nominally full-time courses are delivered mainly via computers.

For many – perhaps most – students, therefore, the university experience is not what it was in their parents' day. There is more assessment, more crowding, more pressure to get the best possible degree while also finding gainful employment for at least part of the year. The proportion of students achieving first-class degrees has risen significantly, while an upper second (rather than the previously ubiquitous 2:2) has become the norm. Research shows that the classification has a real impact in the labour market.

An uncertain future

The 2004 Higher Education Act and the White Paper that preceded it ensured that the pace of change in universities would accelerate. The Government's new "Framework" for higher education and the fees review that will follow it may alter parts of the system, but seem unlikely to change the long-term direction of travel. In the future it is likely that more students will begin their degrees at further education colleges, more will opt initially for two-year courses and the range both of subjects and teaching methods will grow still further. Some predict the rise of the "virtual university" or the demise of the conventional higher-education institution, as companies customise their own courses. However, universities have demonstrated enduring popularity and show every sign of weathering the current turbulence.

Overall competition for places should ease over the coming decade, as the population of 18-year-olds begins to decline, as long as further restrictions are not placed on universities' ability to recruit. But numbers will remain more buoyant among the socio-economic groups that provide the bulk of university students than in the population as a whole, so the effects of demographic change may be less dramatic than many commentators have predicted. Especially in traditional universities, many arts and social science courses will remain oversubscribed and some science degrees, too, will continue to command high entrance requirements. There may be institutional casualties, particularly if public spending is tightened to the extent that many in universities predict. However, the value of higher education to society and to the economy is now generally acknowledged. There may be difficult times ahead for universities, but most are strong enough to survive.

What and Where to Study

Choosing where and what to study are life-shaping decisions. The outcome will help determine your career and personal life far beyond the next three or four years (and they are important enough). Many graduates end up living and working near their university; they may make their closest friends in their student days and may even meet their future partner there. So finding the right university demands serious thought and research, and this *Guide* may play an important part.

The current outlook

This year, of all years, career prospects will be uppermost in the mind of anyone considering a higher education course. How could it be otherwise, with graduate unemployment rising rapidly and the cost of going to university continuing to grow? But there are good reasons not to let fear of the future squeeze out all other considerations. As David Lammy, the Higher Education Minister, said: "A degree is for life, and so are the better prospects that go with it."

No one knows which subjects will be in demand when the recession ends, but graduates will almost undoubtedly be in a stronger position than those who choose not to invest in better qualifications. In any case, the majority of graduate jobs are not subject-specific – employers value the transferable skills that higher education confers. Rightly or wrongly, however, most employers are influenced by which university a graduate attended, so the choice of institution remains as important as ever.

Some students may cut their costs by taking a part-time course; others by enrolling on a two-year foundation degree, which can be converted into an honours degree later. But, at a time of low employment generally, logic suggests that it would be a false economy to dismiss higher education entirely.

Those who want to add value to their degree in the jobs market will find that growing numbers of universities are offering employment-related schemes. In many cases, this will involve work experience or extra activities organised by the careers service. Some universities, such as Leicester, now run certificated employability programmes, while others, such as Liverpool John Moores, have built such skills into degree programmes. Such programmes are highlighted in the institutional profiles in Chapter 11 and should be described in detail on university websites.

Is higher education for you?

Before you start, there is one important question to ask yourself: what do you want out of higher education? The answer will make it easier to choose where (and whether) to be a student. With more than a third of school-leavers going on to university, it is easy to drift that way without much thought, opting for the subject in which you expect the best grades and looking for a university with a reasonable reputation and a good social life. Your career will look after itself – you hope.

With graduate debt soaring, however, and job prospects varying widely between subjects, now is the time to look at your own motivation. Love of a subject is perhaps the best reason for taking a degree, and one that allows you to focus almost exclusively on the search for a course that corresponds with your passions. If, on the other hand, higher education is a means to an end, you need to think about career ambitions and look carefully at employment rates for any courses you might consider.

Key reasons for going to university

To improve job opportunities	74%
To improve salary prospects	60%
To improve knowledge in an area of interest	58%
To specialise in a certain subject / area	47%
To obtain an additional qualification	46%
Essential to my chosen profession	43%
To experience a different way of life	41%
It's the obvious next step	40%
To have a good social life	31%
My parents expected me to	24%
I didn't want to get a job straightaway	23%
I didn't know what else to do	18%
All my friends were going	14%
Can live at home and still go to university	9%

Sodexo University Lifestyle Survey 2008

Many graduates look back on their student days as the best years of their lives, and there is nothing wrong with wanting to have a good time. Remember, though, that you will be paying for it later (literally) and there will be more studying than partying. If you have not enjoyed sixth-form or college courses, you may be better off in a job and possibly becoming one of the hundreds of thousands each year who return to education later in life.

Narrowing down the choices

Once you have decided that higher education is for you, the good news is that, as long as you start early enough, finding the right university need not be stressful. Media attention focuses on the scramble for places on a relatively small proportion of courses where competition is intense, but there are plenty of places at good universities for candidates with the basic qualifications – it's just a matter of finding the one that suits you best. For older applicants, relevant work experience and demonstrable interest in a subject may be enough to win a place.

If anything, the problem is that of too much choice. Students prepared to move away from home will have more than 100 universities and numerous specialist colleges to consider, most with hundreds – even thousands – of course combinations on offer. Institutions come in all shapes and sizes, so there is work to do at the outset narrowing down your options.

Deciding what you want to study may reduce the field considerably – only seven institutions offer veterinary medicine for example, although the total is closer to 100 in subjects such as law and English. By the time you have factored in personal preferences about the type or location of your ideal university, the list of possibilities may already be reduced to manageable proportions.

After that, you can take a closer look at what the courses contain and what life is really like for students. Prospectuses and university websites will give you an accurate account of course combinations, and important facts like the accommodation available to new students, but it is their job to sell the university. To get a true picture, you need more – preferably a visit not just to the university, but to the department where you would be studying. If that is not possible, there are plenty of other sources of objective information, such as the National Student Survey (which is available online, with a range of additional data about each institution, at **www.unistats.com**).

Many students' unions publish alternative prospectuses, giving a "warts and all" view of the university, and those that do not provide this service may be able to arrange a

GCE AS/ AS VCE	GCE AS Double Award	GCE A level/ AVCE	A level with additional AS (9 units)	GCE/AVCE Double Award	Points	Advanced Higher	Higher	Int 2
				A*A*	280			
				A*A	260			
				AA	240			
				AB	220			
			A*A	BB	200			
			AA	BC	180			
			AB		170			
				CC	160			
			BB		150			
		A*	BC	CD	140			
					130	A		
	AA	A	CC	DD	120			
	AB		CD		110	B		
	BB	B		DE	100			
	BC		DD		90	C		
	CC	C	DE	EE	80		A	
					72	D		
	CD				70			
					65		B	
A	DD	D	EE		60			
B	DE				50		C	
					42			A
C	EE	E			40			
					36		D	
					35			B
D					30			
					28			C
E					20			

GCE/VCE Qualifications — **Points** — **Scottish Qualifications**

International Baccalaureate

Points for the International Baccalaureate (IB) are awarded to candidates who achieve the IB Dip. The scores have been reduced for 2010 entry.

IB Dip	Points	IB Dip	Points	IB Dip	Points	IB Dip	Points
45	720	39	589	33	457	27	326
44	698	38	567	32	435	26	304
43	676	37	545	31	413	25	282
42	654	36	523	30	392	24	260
41	632	35	501	29	370		
40	611	34	479	28	348		

brief discussion with a current student, either by phone or email. Your school or college may put you in contact with someone who went to a university that you are considering. Guides and collections of statistics may give you valuable information about a course or a university, but there is no substitute for personal experience.

What to study?

Most people seeking a place in higher education start by choosing a subject and a course, rather than a university. If you take a degree, you are going to spend at least three years immersed in your subject. It has to be one you will enjoy and can master – not to mention one that you are qualified to study. Many economics degrees require maths, for example, while some medical schools demand chemistry or biology. The UCAS website (**www.ucas.com**) contains course profiles, including entrance requirements, which is a good starting point, while universities' own sites contain more detailed information. In chapter 3, we describe 62 subject areas and provide league tables for each of them.

Your school subjects and the UCAS tariff

The official yardstick by which your results will be judged is the UCAS tariff (see page 17), which gives a score for each grade of every type of UK qualification considered relevant for university entrance, as well as for the International Baccalaureate (IB). This tariff has become more controversial as more subjects and types of qualifications have been included in it. Top scores in the new vocational diplomas, for example, will attract more points than a full set of A grades at A level, while the most successful IB students

---

A-level subjects only acceptable as a third or fourth subject at Cambridge (Camb) and London School of Economics (LSE) and **International Baccalaureate (IB) subjects** only acceptable as a third or fourth subject at Cambridge

A levels		IB
• Accounting (Camb, LSE)	• Information and	• Business and Management
• Art and Design (Camb, LSE)	Communication Technology	• Design and Technology
• Business Studies (Camb, LSE)	(Camb, LSE)	• Information Technology in a
• Communication Studies (Camb, LSE)	• Law (LSE)	Global Society
• Dance (Camb)	• Leisure Studies (Camb)	• Theatre Arts
• Design and Technology (Camb, LSE)	• Media Studies (Camb, LSE)	• Visual Arts
• Drama/Theatre Studies (Camb, LSE – some departments)	• Music Technology (Camb, LSE)	
• Film Studies (Camb)	• Performance Studies (Camb)	
• Health and Social Care (Camb)	• Performing Arts (Camb)	
• Home Economics (Camb, LSE)	• Photography (Camb)	
	• Physical Education (Camb)	
	• Sports Studies (Camb, LSE)	
	• Travel and Tourism (Camb, LSE)	

General Studies and Critical Thinking A levels will only be considered as fourth A level subjects and will not therefore be accepted as part of a conditional offer.

already earn considerably more points. If this process continues, it is likely that more of the leading universities will abandon the tariff, as some have done already.

The latest change is good news for those awarded high grades in Scottish qualifications. A review has resulted in the number of points awarded for grade A Highers increasing from 72 to 80 points, while an A in Advanced Highers will rise from 120 to 130 points – ten points more than a grade A at A level. Grades B and C will also be worth more, although a D in an Advanced Higher will stay at 72 points and a Higher grade D will actually drop from 42 to 36 points.

"Soft subjects"

There is a separate issue for some of the top universities about the subjects studied at A level. The variety of A-level courses now available includes many subjects that they do not consider on a par with traditional academic subjects. For many years, a minority of universities have refused to accept General Studies as a full A level for entrance purposes (although even some in the Russell Group of top universities do). The growth of supposedly "soft" subjects, such as media studies and photography, has prompted a few to produce lists of subjects that will only be accepted as a third, or fourth, A level. The Cambridge list (see opposite) includes no fewer than 20 A levels, including business studies, dance and home economics, and five International Baccalaureate (IB) subjects.

For most courses at most universities, there are no such restrictions, although those choosing A levels would be wise to bear the list in mind in case more of the leading universities move in this direction. At the very least, it is an indication of the subjects that admissions tutors may take less seriously than the rest. Although only Cambridge and the London School of Economics identify those subjects publicly, others may adopt less formal weightings.

Diplomas

This also applies to the new diplomas, just as it has to vocational qualifications down the years. Although there has been university involvement in designing the diplomas, there remains confusion about which will be accepted by leading universities – especially for admission to degree courses outside the direct scope of the diploma. The engineering diploma has now won near-universal approval (for admission to engineering courses and possibly some science degrees), but some of the other diplomas are in fields that are not on the curriculum of the most selective universities. Regardless of the points awarded under the tariff, it is essential to contact universities direct to ensure that a diploma will be an acceptable qualification for your chosen degree.

Use of tariffs

While the majority of universities use the tariff to make offers of places, those that are heavily oversubscribed will tend to demand particular grades even at A level, often naming the subjects in which the highest grades are required. There are no set rules about using the tariff. Some universities will give credit for qualifications in key skills, for example, while others exclude them from candidates' points totals. In certain universities, some departments, but not others, will use the tariff to set offers. The university's prospectus or website should show which does what. In addition, some universities now require applicants to take an entrance test. The details are listed on page 20.

Making a choice

Choosing a subject to study at university is not always as straightforward as it sounds. Your A levels, or Scottish Highers, may have chosen themselves, but the range of subjects across the whole university system is vast. Even subjects that you have studied at school

Admissions Tests

Some courses now have additional entrance tests. The most significant are listed below. A few other courses may also require tests, so check the course details on the UCAS website.

BioMedical Admissions Test (BMAT): for entry to medicine and veterinary medicine at Cambridge, Imperial College London, Oxford, Royal Veterinary College, University College London. Standard closing date for 2010 admissions is 30 September 2009. (**www.bmat.org.uk**)

English Literature Admissions Test (ELAT): for entry to English at Oxford. (**www.elat.org.uk**)

Graduate Medical School Admissions Test (GAMSAT): for graduate entry to medicine and dentistry at Keele, Nottingham, Peninsula College of Medicine and Dentistry, St. George's University of London, Swansea. Closing date for registration is 14 August 2009. (**www.gamsatuk.org**)

Health Professions Admissions Test (HPAT): for certain medical courses at Ulster.

History Aptitude Test (HAT): for entry to history or a joint honours degree involving history at Oxford. (**www.history.ox.ac.uk/prosundergrad/applying**)

National Admissions Test for Law (LNAT): for entry to law courses at Birmingham, Bristol, Cambridge, Durham, Exeter, Glasgow, King's College London, Nottingham, Oxford, University College London. (**www.lnat.ac.uk**)

Modern and Medieval Languages Test (MML): for entry to modern and medieval languages at Cambridge. (**www.mml.cam.ac.uk/prospectus/undergrad/applying/test.html**)

Thinking Skills Assessment (TSA) Oxford: for entry to Philosophy, Politics and Economics (PPE) and Economics and Management (E&M) courses at Oxford. (**www.tsa.cambridgeassessment.org.uk/ppe**)

Sixth Term Examination Papers (STEP): for entry to mathematics at Cambridge and Warwick. (**www.admissionstests.cambridgeassessment.org.uk/adt/step**)

Thinking Skills Assessment (TSA) Cambridge: mainly for computer science, economics, engineering, land economy, natural sciences and social and political sciences at most Cambridge colleges. (**www.admissionstests.cambridgeassessment.org.uk/adt/tsacambridge**)

Thinking Skills Assessment (TSA) UCL: for entry to European Social and Political Studies at University College London. (**www.admissionstests.cambridgeassessment.org.uk/adt/tsaucl**)

UK Clinical Aptitude Test (UKCAT): for entry to medical and dental schools at Aberdeen, Brighton and Sussex Medical School, Barts and the London School of Medicine and Dentistry, Cardiff, Dundee, Durham, East Anglia, Edinburgh, Glasgow, Hull York Medical School, Keele, King's College London, Imperial College London (graduate entry), Leeds, Leicester, Manchester, Newcastle, Nottingham, Oxford (graduate entry), Peninsula College of Medicine and Dentistry, Queen's University Belfast, Sheffield, Southampton, St Andrews, St George's University of London, Warwick (graduate entry). Candidates for 2010 entry must have taken the test by 9 October 2009. (**www.ukcat.ac.uk**)

may be quite different at degree level – some academic economists actually prefer their undergraduates not to have taken economics A level because they approach the subject so differently. Other students are disappointed because they appear to be going over old ground when they continue with a subject that they enjoyed at school. Universities now publish quite detailed syllabuses, and it is a matter of going through the fine print.

The greater difficulty comes in judging your suitability for the many subjects that are not on the school or college curriculum. Philosophy and psychology sound fascinating (and are), but you may have no idea what degrees in either subject entail – for example, the level of statistics that may be required. Forensic science may look exciting on television – more glamorous than plain chemistry – but it may open fewer doors if the type of work portrayed in *Silent Witness* or *Raising the Dead* is not available.

Vocational subjects

The introduction of top-up fees has encouraged more students into job-related subjects, rather than traditional academic disciplines, in the hope of improving their employment prospects. This is understandable and, if you are sure of your future career path, possibly also sensible. But much depends on what that career is – and whether you are ready to make such a long-term commitment. Some of the programmes that have attracted public ridicule, such as surf science or golf course management, may narrow graduates' options to a worrying extent, but there is nothing wrong with their employment records. Jibes about so-called "Mickey Mouse" courses have become less frequent, although there are some who are yet to accept that the higher education curriculum has moved into new areas since they were students.

Many vocational courses are tailored to particular professions. If you choose one of these, make sure that the degree is recognised by the relevant professional body (such as the Engineering Council or one of the institutes) or you may not be able to use the skills that you acquire. Most universities are only too keen to make such recognition clear in their prospectus; if no such guarantee is published, contact the university department running the course and seek assurances.

Even where a course has professional recognition, bear in mind that a further qualification may be required to practise. Both law and medicine, for example, demand additional training to become a fully qualified solicitor, barrister or doctor. Nor is either degree an automatic passport to a job: only about half of all law graduates go into the profession and the UK is now training more medical students than the National Health

Top Ten Most Popular Subjects by Applications		The Ten Most Popular Subjects by Acceptances	
1 Business & administration	91,453	1 Business & administration	55,892
2 Law	78,581	2 Creative arts & design	49,188
3 Psychology	73,317	3 Subjects allied to medicine	43,275
4 Pre-clinical medicine	71,430	4 Biological sciences	35,598
5 Nursing	54,475	5 Social studies	35,146
6 English studies	53,614	6 Maths and computer sciences	26,472
7 Management studies	50,643	7 Engineering	23,519
8 Training teachers	45,499	8 Law	21,196
9 History by period	45,057	9 Sciences with social sciences or arts	20,149
10 Economics	44,750	10 Physical sciences	16,523
UCAS 2009 (number of applicants to 15 January 2009)		UCAS acceptances in 2008	

Service can afford. Both law and medicine also provide a route into the profession for graduates who have taken other subjects. Law conversion courses, though not cheap, are increasingly popular, and there is a growing number of graduate-entry medical degrees.

One way to ensure that a degree is job-related is to take a "sandwich" course, which involves up to a year in business or industry. Students often end up working for the organisation which provided the placement, while others gain valuable insights into a field of employment – even if only to discount it. The drawback with such courses is that, like the year abroad that is part of most language degrees, the period away from university inevitably disrupts living arrangements and friendship groups. But most of those who take this route find that the career benefits make this a worthwhile sacrifice.

Academic or vocational courses?

Employers' organisations calculate that more than half of all graduate jobs are open to applicants from any subject, and recruiters for the most competitive graduate training schemes often prefer traditional academic subjects to apparently relevant vocational degrees. Newspapers, for example, often prefer a history graduate to one with a media studies degree; computing firms take a disproportionate number of classicists. A good degree classification and the right work experience are more important than the subject for most non-technical jobs. But it is hard to achieve a good result on a course that you do not enjoy, so scour prospectuses, and email or phone university departments to ensure that you know what you are letting yourself in for. Their reaction to your approach will also give you an idea of how responsive they are to their students.

If you are not sure whether you will be suited to a particular subject, you can take an online aptitude test through the UCAS website. The "What to study" section gives you access to the Stamford Test, which uses an online questionnaire to match your interests and strengths to possible courses and careers (**www.ucas.com/students/beforeyouapply/ whattostudy/stamfordtest**).

Studying more than one subject

You may find that more than one subject appeals, in which case you could consider Joint Honours – degrees that combine two subjects – or even Combined Honours, which will cover several related subjects. Such courses obviously allow you to extend the scope of your studies, but they should be approached with caution. Even if the number of credits suggests a similar workload to Single Honours, covering more than one subject inevitably involves extra reading and often more essays or project work.

However, there are advantages. Many students choose a "dual" to add a vocational element to make themselves more employable – business studies with languages or engineering, for example, or media studies with English. Others want to take their studies in a particular direction, perhaps by combining history with politics, or statistics with maths. Some simply want to add a completely unrelated interest to their main subject, such as environmental science and music, or archaeology and event management – both combinations that are available at UK universities.

At most universities, however, it is not necessary to take a degree in more than one subject in order to broaden your studies. The spread of modular programmes ensures that you can take courses in related subjects without changing the basic structure of your degree. You may not be able to take an event management module in a single-honours archaeology degree, but it should be possible to study some history, or a language. The number and scope of the combinations offered at many of the larger universities is extraordinary. Indeed, it has been criticised by academics who believe that "mix-and-match" degrees can leave a graduate without a rounded view of a subject. But for those who seek breadth and variety, close scrutiny of university prospectuses (whether online or on paper) is a vital part of the selection process.

What type of course?

Once you have a subject, you must decide on the level and type of course. Most readers of this *Guide* will be looking for full-time degree courses, but higher education is much broader than that. You may not be able to afford the time or the money needed for a full-time commitment of three or four years at this point in your life.

Part-time courses

Tens of thousands of people each year opt for a part-time course – usually while holding down a job – to continue learning and improve their career prospects. It can be exhausting, unless your employer gives you time off to study, and any financial support you receive from the Government will not be the same as that provided for full-time students. However, if you have the stamina for a course that will usually take twice as long as the full-time equivalent, this route may make a degree more affordable. Part-time students tend to be highly committed to their subject, and many claim that the quality of the social life associated with their course makes up for the quantity of leisure time enjoyed by full-timers.

Distance learning

Another option, if you are confident that you can manage without regular face-to-face contact with teachers and fellow students, is distance learning. Courses are delivered mainly or entirely online or through correspondence, although some programmes offer a certain amount of local tuition. The process might sound daunting and impersonal, but students of the Open University (OU), all of whom are educated in this way, are the most satisfied in the country, according to the results of the annual National Student Survey. Attending lectures or oversized seminars at a conventional university can be less personal than regular contact with your tutor at a distance. Of course, not all universities are as good at communicating with their distance-learning students as the OU, or offer such high-quality course materials, but this mode of study does give students ultimate flexibility to determine when and where they work. Distance learning is becoming increasingly popular for the delivery of professional courses, which are often needed to supplement degrees. The OU now takes students of all ages, not just mature students.

Foundation degrees

Even if you are set on a full-time course, you might not want to commit yourself for three years. Growing numbers are taking two-year Foundation degrees – vocational courses which the Government would like to be the main source of expansion in universities and colleges. Even more students take longer-established two-year courses, such as Higher National Diplomas or other diplomas tailored to the needs of industry or parts of the health service. Those who do well on such courses usually have the option of converting their qualification into a degree with further study, although many achieve their goal without immediately staying on for a further two or more years.

What Graduates Do by Subject Studied

	Times Subject (ranked by the total of the first three columns on the right)	Employed in Graduate Job	Employed in Graduate Job and Studying	Studying and Not Employed	Employed in Non-Graduate Job and Studying	Employed in Non-Graduate Job	Unemployed
1	Medicine	88%	7%	5%	0%	0%	0%
2	Dentistry	81%	18%	0%	0%	0%	1%
3	Veterinary Medicine	91%	4%	2%	0%	1%	1%
4	Nursing	86%	8%	2%	0%	3%	2%
5	Architecture	59%	20%	14%	1%	4%	2%
6	Pharmacology and Pharmacy	65%	16%	11%	1%	6%	2%
7	Civil Engineering	71%	13%	7%	0%	5%	2%
8	Building	75%	12%	3%	1%	6%	4%
9	Town and Country Planning and Landscape	52%	15%	19%	3%	9%	3%
10	Land and Property Management	58%	20%	7%	1%	11%	3%
11	Chemical Engineering	63%	6%	16%	1%	8%	6%
12	Social Work	69%	7%	5%	2%	12%	5%
13	Other Subjects Allied to Medicine	66%	8%	7%	1%	14%	4%
14	Education	65%	5%	10%	2%	16%	3%
15	Chemistry	34%	7%	39%	2%	13%	6%
16	General Engineering	59%	9%	10%	2%	15%	5%
17	Mechanical Engineering	60%	7%	12%	1%	14%	7%
18	Law	21%	5%	47%	6%	18%	3%
19	Celtic Studies	31%	3%	42%	2%	20%	4%
20	Mathematics	35%	15%	25%	2%	18%	5%
21	Physics and Astronomy	28%	9%	38%	2%	17%	7%
22	Economics	44%	15%	15%	2%	19%	5%
23	Electrical and Electronic Engineering	53%	7%	14%	2%	17%	7%
24	Geology	44%	4%	27%	1%	18%	7%
25	Food Science	55%	3%	14%	1%	21%	5%
26	Aeronautical and Manufacturing Engineering	52%	7%	13%	2%	19%	8%
27	Theology and Religious Studies	29%	6%	33%	4%	24%	3%
28	French	41%	5%	23%	3%	24%	4%
29	Anatomy and Physiology	26%	5%	37%	3%	23%	5%
30	German	42%	5%	22%	3%	24%	4%
31	Russian	40%	5%	24%	2%	21%	8%
32	Middle Eastern and African Studies	33%	3%	25%	10%	25%	4%
33	Computer Science	55%	4%	9%	2%	20%	10%
34	Accounting and Finance	35%	22%	7%	5%	24%	7%
35	Iberian Languages	44%	6%	18%	2%	25%	5%

Times Subject (ranked by the total of the first three columns on the right)	Employed in Graduate Job	Employed in Graduate Job and Studying	Studying and Not Employed	Employed in Non-Graduate Job and Studying	Employed in Non-Graduate Job	Unemployed
36 Biological Sciences	31%	5%	30%	3%	25%	6%
37 Music	35%	6%	24%	4%	26%	5%
38 Classics and Ancient History	30%	5%	29%	5%	27%	4%
39 Materials Technology	51%	5%	12%	1%	25%	7%
40 East and South Asian Studies	45%	4%	15%	3%	24%	8%
41 Librarianship and Information Management	56%	4%	5%	2%	24%	8%
42 Geography and Environmental Sciences	35%	6%	22%	3%	29%	5%
43 Anthropology	34%	6%	22%	5%	29%	5%
44 Business Studies	49%	7%	7%	3%	29%	6%
45 Politics	36%	4%	21%	3%	29%	6%
46 Sports Science	36%	7%	18%	4%	32%	3%
47 Archaeology	37%	3%	20%	3%	29%	7%
48 Italian	40%	6%	16%	2%	31%	5%
49 Linguistics	34%	4%	21%	4%	33%	3%
50 Philosophy	30%	4%	23%	4%	31%	6%
51 English	31%	4%	23%	4%	32%	6%
52 Agriculture and Forestry	42%	11%	7%	3%	32%	5%
53 History	28%	4%	25%	4%	32%	6%
54 History of Art, Architecture and Design	30%	4%	22%	4%	34%	5%
55 Art and Design	47%	3%	7%	3%	32%	9%
56 American Studies	33%	4%	17%	5%	34%	6%
57 Psychology	31%	6%	17%	5%	37%	5%
58 Social Policy	30%	6%	15%	5%	38%	6%
59 Communication and Media Studies	45%	2%	6%	3%	36%	7%
60 Drama, Dance and Cinematics	39%	3%	9%	3%	38%	8%
61 Sociology	33%	4%	13%	4%	40%	5%
62 Hospitality, Leisure, Recreation, and Tourism	38%	3%	6%	3%	44%	5%
Overall	**45%**	**6%**	**16%**	**3%**	**24%**	**5%**

See Job prospects section on page 28 for further explanation of this table. The table is ranked by the sum of "positive destinations" – Employed in Graduate Job, Employed in Graduate Job and Studying, and Studying and Not Employed – that is, activities that require a degree. The individual lines of information may not precisely summed to 100% due to presentational rounding.

Source: HESA 2006–07 DLHE return

What Graduates Earn by Subject Studied

	Subject	Graduate Employment or Self Employment	Non-graduate Employment or Self Employment
1	Medicine	£28,900	*
2	Dentistry	£28,813	*
3	Chemical Engineering	£26,366	£16,553
4	Economics	£25,101	£17,316
5	Veterinary Medicine	£24,762	*
6	General Engineering	£23,876	£15,349
7	Mechanical Engineering	£23,572	£17,426
8	Middle Eastern and African Studies	£23,414	£17,692
9	Civil Engineering	£23,387	£15,444
10	Social Work	£23,354	£15,572
11	Aeronautical and Manufacturing Engineering	£22,965	£16,489
12	Building	£22,941	£19,484
13	Mathematics	£22,904	£16,171
14	Land and Property Management	£22,883	*
15	Electrical and Electronic Engineering	£22,579	£16,486
16	Physics and Astronomy	£22,249	£16,234
17	Russian	£21,835	£17,202
18	Computer Science	£21,714	£16,370
19	Philosophy	£21,466	£15,312
20	Geology	£21,400	£15,563
21	Business Studies	£21,081	£16,172
22	Nursing	£20,967	£15,434
23	Politics	£20,877	£15,364
24	Accounting and Finance	£20,586	£16,614
25	Iberian Languages	£20,473	£15,865
26	French	£20,425	£16,012
27	Town and Country Planning and Landscape	£20,320	£17,110
28	Italian	£20,201	£16,636
29	Education	£20,135	£13,818
30	German	£19,971	£15,364
31	Librarianship and Information Management	£19,958	£15,904
32	East and South Asian Studies	£19,821	£16,316
33	Law	£19,805	£15,693
34	Chemistry	£19,799	£15,121
35	Food Science	£19,765	£15,345
36	Geography and Environmental Sciences	£19,591	£14,886
37	Social Policy	£19,550	£14,079
38	Anthropology	£19,485	£15,619
39	Classics and Ancient History	£19,422	£16,078
40	Other Subjects Allied to Medicine	£19,418	£14,750
41	History	£19,197	£14,651
42	Theology and Religious Studies	£19,115	£14,461

Subject		Graduate Employment or Self Employment	Non-graduate Employment or Self Employment
43	Anatomy and Physiology	£19,008	£15,400
44	History of Art, Architecture and Design	£18,975	£15,749
45	Pharmacology and Pharmacy	£18,944	£14,422
46	Materials Technology	£18,871	£14,764
47	American Studies	£18,757	£14,534
48	Agriculture and Forestry	£18,755	£14,604
49	Biological Sciences	£18,689	£13,917
50	Architecture	£18,624	£15,357
51	Hospitality, Leisure, Recreation and Tourism	£18,621	£15,236
52	Sports Science	£18,572	£14,159
53	English	£18,499	£14,272
54	Sociology	£18,339	£14,548
55	Psychology	£18,110	£13,995
56	Linguistics	£17,681	£14,535
57	Communication and Media Studies	£17,549	£14,474
58	Art and Design	£17,297	£14,059
59	Music	£17,157	£14,204
60	Drama, Dance and Cinematics	£17,130	£14,249
61	Archaeology	£17,065	£14,473
62	Celtic Studies	£16,604	*
Overall		**£20,790**	**£15,010**

See Job prospects section on page 28 for further explanation of this table.
* Indicates a suppressed mean salary based on 7 or fewer graduates
Source: HESA 2006–07 DLHE return

Other short courses

A number of universities have experimented with two-year degrees, squeezing more work into an extended academic year. The so-called "third semester" makes use of the summer vacation for extra teaching, so that mature students, in particular, can reduce the length of their career break. But the pattern has really only caught on at the University of Buckingham, the UK's only established private university, where it has had a small but enthusiastic following for more than 30 years.

Other short courses – usually lasting a year – are designed for students who do not have the necessary qualifications for a degree in their chosen subject. Foundation courses in art and design have been common for many years, and are the chosen preparation for a degree at leading departments, even for many students whose A levels would win them a degree place elsewhere. Access courses perform the same function in a wider range of subjects for students without A levels, or for those whose grades are either too low or in the wrong subjects to gain admission to a particular course. Entry requirements are modest, but students have to reach the same standard as regular entrants if they are to progress to a degree.

Yet more choice

No single guide can allow for personal preferences in choosing a course. You may want one of the many degrees that incorporate a year at a partner university abroad, or to try a six-month exchange on the Continent through the European Union's Erasmus Programme. Either might prove a valuable experience and add to your employability. You might prefer a January or February start to the traditional autumn start – there are plenty of opportunities for this, mainly at new universities. In some subjects – particularly engineering and the sciences – the leading degrees may be Masters courses, taking four years rather than the norm (in England) of three.

Job prospects

Even before the recession, job prospects were the key element in choosing a subject for many (probably most) students. The tables on pages 24–27 are the obvious starting point in assessing whether your prospective course will pay off in career terms. Although they date from well before the downturn in graduate employment, there is no reason to believe that the pattern of success rates will have changed.

The Higher Education Statistics Agency (HESA) collects data both on what graduates do straight after graduation (sometimes called graduate destinations) and their average salaries. But the results are to be treated with caution because they represent only the first six months of a graduate's career – not even that if he or she has gone on to postgraduate study – and they make no allowances for the variety of entry routes into different areas of employment. Dentists, for example, have been virtually guaranteed a job if they complete a degree successfully, whereas those going into art and design know that periods of freelance and/or casual work may be an occupational hazard at the start of their career.

Non-academic factors considered when choosing a university	
Good impression from open days	51%
Friendly atmosphere	46%
Attractive university environment	42%
Active social life and good social facilities	31%
Campus university	31%
Close to transport links	28%
Living away from home, but sufficiently close if support needed	27%
City centre university	26%
Recommendation from friends	23%
Quality of accommodation	22%
Close to home/able to live at home	21%
Internet research favourable to university	18%
Advice from teachers	16%
Low cost of living	14%
Cost of accommodation	13%
Advice from parents	11%
Good sporting facilities	10%
Opportunities for part-time jobs	8%

Sodexo University Lifestyle Survey 2008

This type of table can mislead. We use classifications developed at the universities of Warwick and the West of England to distinguish between "graduate-level" work and jobs that do not normally require a degree. Subjects are ranked on "positive destinations", which include postgraduate study and other forms of training, whether or not they are combined with a job. Some similar tables do not make a distinction between different types of job – thus giving universities and subjects uniformly high employment rates.

The second table, on pages 26–27, gives average earnings six months after graduation. It contains interesting – and in some cases surprising – information about early career pay levels. Few would have placed social work and nursing among the top dozen fields for graduate pay, for example, while business studies and accounting do not make the top 20. Those positions underline the differences between starting salaries and long-term prospects in different jobs.

By three years after graduation, the figures are significantly different, according to recent research. HESA found that by then, overall unemployment had dropped from 5 per cent, six months after graduation, to 2 per cent, while 80 per cent were in graduate occupations, compared with 71 per cent in the initial survey of the same group. Corresponding differences emerged when the sample was broken down by subject.

Where to study

Once you have decided what to study, there are still several factors that might influence your choice of university or college. Obviously, you need to have a reasonable chance of getting in, you may want reassurance about the university's reputation, and its location will probably also be important to you. On top of that, most applicants have views about the type of institution they are looking for – big or small, old or new, urban or rural, specialist or comprehensive. You may surprise yourself by choosing somewhere that does not conform to your initial criteria, but working through your preferences is another way of narrowing down your options.

Entry standards

Unless you are a mature student or have taken a gap year, your passport to your chosen university will be a conditional offer based on your predicted grades, previous exam performance, personal statement and school or college reference. A lucky few may get an offer that is so low that success is a foregone conclusion – because the university considers them outstanding and needs no further evidence of their potential. But only those who already have their grades receive unconditional offers.

Supply and demand dictate whether you will receive an offer, and that is influenced both by the university and the subject. A few universities (but not many) at the top of the league tables are heavily oversubscribed in every subject; others will have areas in which they excel, but may make relatively modest demands for entry to other courses. Even in many of the leading universities, the number of applicants for each place in languages or engineering is not high. Conversely, three As at A level will not guarantee a place on one

Top Increases in Applications 2009 over 2008		Top Decreases in Applications 2009 over 2008	
1 Birmingham City	35.0%	1 Bolton	−7.7%
2 Buckinghamshire New	33.7%	2 Cardiff, UWIC	−5.1%
3 Portsmouth	25.1%	3 West of Scotland	−4.5%
4 Hull	25.0%	4 Sussex	−4.4%
5 Gloucestershire	19.8%	5 SOAS	−4.2%
6 Kent	19.2%	6 Wolverhampton	−3.9%
7 Exeter	19.0%	7 Bristol	−3.5%
8 Loughborough	19.0%	8 East London	−2.8%
9 Glamorgan	18.4%	9 Durham	−2.3%
10 Keele	18.2%	10 Leeds	−2.0%
UCAS applications to 15 January 2009		UCAS applications to 15 January 2009	

of the top English or law degrees, but there are enough universities running courses to ensure that three Cs will put you in with a chance somewhere.

University prospectuses and the UCAS website will give you the "standard offer" for each course, but in some cases this is pitched deliberately low in order to leave admissions staff extra flexibility. The standard A-level offer for medicine, for example, is usually two As and a B, but nearly all successful applicants have three As or more.

The average entry scores in our subject tables give the actual points obtained by successful applicants – many of which are far above the offer made by the university, but which give an indication of the pecking order at entry. The subject tables (in chapter 3) are, naturally, a better guide than the main table (in chapter 2), where average entry scores are influenced by the range of subjects available at each university.

Location

The most obvious starting point is the country you study in. Most degrees in Scotland take four years, rather than the UK norm of three. It is possible, but not normal, for A-level candidates to go straight into the second year of a Scottish degree course. Otherwise, four years obviously cost more than three, especially given the loss of the year's salary you might have been earning after graduation. A later chapter will go into the details of the system, but suffice to say that students from Scotland pay no fees, while those from the rest of the UK do. Nevertheless, Edinburgh and St Andrews remain particularly popular with English students and more than 1,000 students from Northern Ireland entered Scottish universities in 2007.

Close to home

Far from crossing national boundaries, however, growing numbers of students choose to study near home, whether or not they continue to live with their family. This may be to cut costs or for personal reasons, such as family circumstances, a girlfriend or boyfriend, continuing employment, or religion. Some simply want to stick with what they know. But the trend for full-time students who do go away to study, is to choose a university within about two hours' travelling time. The assumption is that this is far enough to discourage parents from making unannounced visits, but close enough to allow for occasional trips home to get the washing done and have a decent meal. The leading universities recruit from all over the world, but most still have a regional core.

Top Universities for Living at Home			Ten Most Popular Universities by Applications		
1	Wolverhampton	8,900	1	Manchester	54,021
2	Glasgow Caledonian	7,845	2	Leeds	51,110
3	Ulster	7,210	3	Edinburgh	45,476
4	London Metropolitan	6,800	4	Bristol	42,532
5	Westminster	6,635	5	Manchester Metropolitan	39,377
6	Manchester Metropolitan	6,505	6	Nottingham	38,123
7	Glasgow	6,170	7	Birmingham	36,776
8	Northumbria	6,080	8	Warwick	33,123
9	Kent	6,040	9	Cardiff	30,978
10	Glamorgan	5,905	10	Kingston	30,939
HESA 2008			UCAS applications to 15 January 2009		

City universities

The most popular universities, in terms of total applications, are nearly all in big cities – generally with other major centres of population within that two-hour travelling window. For those looking for the best nightclubs, top sporting events, high-quality shopping or a varied cultural life – in other words, most young people, and especially those who live in cities already – city universities are a magnet. The big universities also, by definition, offer the widest range of subjects, although that does not mean that they necessarily have the particular course that is right for you. Nor does it mean that you will actually use the array of nightlife and shopping that looks so alluring in the prospectus, either because you cannot afford to, because student life is focused on the university, or even because you are too busy working.

Campus universities

City universities are the right choice for many young people, but it is worth bearing in mind that the National Student Survey shows that the highest satisfaction levels tend to be at smaller universities, often those with their own self-contained campuses. It seems that students identify more closely with institutions where there is a close-knit community and the social life is based around the students' union rather than the local nightclubs.

Few UK universities are in genuinely rural locations, but some – particularly among the latest group to be promoted from college status – are in relatively small towns. Several longer-established institutions in Wales and Scotland also share this type of setting, where the university dominates the town.

Importance of Open Days

The only way to be certain if this, or any other type of university, is for you is to visit. Schools often restrict the number of open days that sixth-formers can attend in term-time, but some universities offer a weekend alternative. The full calendar of events is available at **www.opendays.com** and on universities' own websites. Bear in mind, if you only attend one or two, that the event has to be badly mismanaged for a university not to seem an exciting place to someone who spends his or her days at school, or even college. Try to get a flavour of several institutions before you make your choice.

The Top Ten Universities for Student Satisfaction with Courses		The Top Universities Targeted by the Top 100 Employers 2008–9	
1 Buckingham	96%	1 Manchester	
2 Open University	94%	2 London	
3 St Andrews	93%	3 Warwick	
4 Cambridge	93%	4 Cambridge	
5 Oxford	92%	5 Oxford	
6 East Anglia	92%	6 Bristol	
7 Birkbeck College, London	92%	7 Durham	
8 Leicester	92%	8 Nottingham	
9 Exeter	91%	9 Bath	
10 Aberdeen	91%	10 Leeds	

National Student Survey 2008

The Graduate Market in 2009, published by High Fliers.

How many universities to pick?

When that time comes, of course, you will not be making one choice but five; four if you are applying for medicine, dentistry or veterinary science. (Full details of the application process are given in chapter 4.) Tens of thousands of students each year eventually go to a university that did not start out as their first choice, either because they did not get the right offer or because they changed their mind along the way. UCAS rules are such that applicants do not list universities in order of preference anyway – indeed, universities are not allowed to know where else you have applied. So do not pin all your hopes on one course; take just as much care choosing the other universities on your list.

Until recently, it was normal for applicants to include at least one "insurance" choice on that list – a university or college where entry grades were significantly lower than at their preferred institutions. This practice has been in decline, presumably because candidates expecting high grades think they can pick up a lower offer either in Clearing or through UCAS Extra, the service that allows applicants rejected by their original choices to apply to courses that still have vacancies after the first round of offers.

The recent switch from being able to choose six courses to only being able to apply for five may cement this change but, if you are at all uncertain about your grades, including an insurance choice remains a sensible course of action. The main proviso, as with all your choices, is that you must be prepared to go and take up that place. If not, you might as well go for broke with courses with higher standard offers and take your chances in Clearing, or even retake exams if you drop grades.

Reputation

A university's reputation is something intangible, often built up over a long period and sometimes outlasting reality. Before universities were subject to external assessment and the publication of copious statistics, reputation was rooted in the distant past. League tables are partly responsible for changing that, although employers are often influenced by the pecking order of higher education when they were students.

The fragmentation of the British university system into groups of institutions is another factor: the Russell Group (**www.russellgroup.ac.uk**) represents 20 research-intensive universities, nearly all with medical schools; the 1994 Group (**www.1994group.ac.uk**) a similar number of smaller research universities; and the Million + Group (**www.millionplus.ac.uk**) containing many of the former polytechnics and newer universities. In addition there is Guild HE (**www.guildhe.ac.uk**), an organisation mainly for specialist colleges, but including five of the newest universities.

Many of you will barely have heard of a polytechnic, let alone be able to identify which of today's universities had that heritage, but you will know which of two universities in the same city has the higher status. While that should matter far less than the quality of a course, it would be naïve to ignore institutional reputation entirely if that is going to carry weight with a future employer. Some big firms restrict their recruitment efforts to a small group of leading universities, for example, and, however short-sighted that might be, it is something to bear in mind if a career in the City or a big law firm is your ultimate aim.

Cost

Critics of top-up fees feared that the fees, introduced in 2006, would add cost to the list of factors driving students' choice of university. But only Leeds Metropolitan University pitched its fees significantly below the original £3,000 maximum, opting for £2,000 and leaving them at that level until at least 2009–10. Other than in Oxford and Cambridge, where there is an additional college fee (not paid by those paying the standard UK tuition fee), cost differences are restricted to rents and the general cost of living in different parts of the country. Some cities – notably London – are notoriously expensive for students and non-students alike. But even these comparisons can be complicated by the availability of part-time employment – an important factor for a growing number of students today. One survey rated London as one of the cheapest places in the UK to study once earning opportunities were taken into account. If you intend to take part-time employment while studying, check that your chosen university has a "job shop", or some other organisation to help students find reasonably paid work.

Accommodation costs listed alongside the university profiles in this *Guide* are probably the nearest proxy for a cost-of-living indicator. The *Guide* also includes a summary of the bursaries available at each university. The size of bursaries varies enormously, as do the rules governing eligibility. Most bursaries are available only to students who qualify for at least some Government support, but scholarships are awarded for other achievements, regardless of family income.

Facilities

Universities compete for the best students not only through their courses but, increasingly, also through non-academic facilities. Accommodation (see chapter 5) is the main selling point for those living away from home, but sports facilities (see chapter 6),

---

Going Abroad

While most British students stay in their own country, a small, but steadily increasing band is venturing overseas – mainly to the United States, but also to Australia and some parts of Europe. This trend is being actively encouraged by American Ivy League universities, which promote generous scholarships on recruiting visits to independent schools, and it may well accelerate if tuition fees are allowed to rise significantly.

For the moment, however, travel costs and longer degree courses make the American experience an expensive one at most universities. The Fulbright Commission runs "College Day" in London and Edinburgh for those who would like to talk through the possibilities.

Fees are still low, or non-existent in most of Europe, although British students tend to be nervous of the language barrier. A halfway house is to choose a course with the option of a year at a partner university, or to apply for a six-month exchange under the European Union's Erasmus Programme.

Further information is available from:

Association of Commonwealth Universities	www.acu.ac.uk
College Board (USA)	www.collegeboard.com
Education Ireland	www.educationireland.ie
Erasmus Programme (EU)	www.britishcouncil.org/erasmus
Finaid (USA)	www.finaid.org
Fulbright Commission	www.fulbright.co.uk
Study in Australia	www.studyinaustralia.gov.au
Study in Canada	www.studyincanada.com

libraries and computing equipment also play an important part. Even campus nightclubs have become part of the facilities race that has coincided with the introduction of top-up fees.

Many universities guarantee first-year students accommodation in halls of residence or university-owned flats. But it is as well to know what happens after that. Are there enough places for second or third-year students who want them, and if not, what is the private market like? Rents for student houses vary quite widely across the country and there have been tensions with local residents in some cities. All universities offer specialist accommodation for disabled students – and are better at providing other facilities than most public institutions. Their websites give basic information on what is provided, as well as contact points for more detailed inquiries.

Special-interest clubs and recreational facilities, as well as political activity, tend to be based in the students' union – sometimes knows as the guild of students, especially in Scotland. In some universities, the union is the focal point of social activity, while in others the attractions of the city seem to overshadow the union to the point where facilities are underused. Students' union websites are included with the information found in the university profiles (see chapter 11).

Sources of information

With more than 100 universities to choose from, the Unistats and UCAS websites, as well as guides such as this one, are the obvious places to start your search for the right course. But once you have narrowed down the list of candidates, you will want to go through undergraduate prospectuses. Most are available online, where you can select the relevant sections rather than waiting for an account of every course to arrive in the post. Beware of generalised claims about the standing of the university, the quality of courses, friendly atmosphere and legendary social life. Stick, if you can, to the factual information, which is generally accurate.

If the material that the universities publish about their own qualities is less than objective, much of what you will find on the internet is equally unreliable, for different reasons. A straightforward search on the name of a university will turn up spurious comparisons of everything from the standard of lecturing to the attractiveness of the students. These can be seriously misleading and are usually based on anecdotal evidence, at best. Make sure that any information you may take into account comes from a reputable source and, if it conflicts with your impression of a university, try to cross-check it with this *Guide* and the institution's own material.

Checklist

Choosing a subject and a place to study is a major decision. Make sure you can answer these questions:

Choosing a course:
- What do I want out of higher education?
- Which subjects do I enjoy studying at school?
- Which subject or subjects do I want to study?
- Do I have the right qualifications?
- What are my career plans and does the subject and course fit these?

Choosing a university:
- What type of university do I wish to go to: campus, city or smaller town?
- How far is the university from home?
- Is it large or small?
- Is it specialist or general?
- Does it offer the right course?
- How much will it cost?
- Have I arranged to visit the university?

Useful websites

The following websites will help you find out more about the topics discussed in this chapter. The best starting point is the UCAS website. On the site there's lots of information on courses, universities and the whole process of applying to university.

www.ucas.com
Within the UCAS site, useful but not immediately obvious pages include:
The Stanford Test
www.ucas.com/students/beforeyouapply/whattostudy/stamfordtest
The UCAS tariff (and especially its use with vocational courses)
www.ucas.com/students/ucas_tariff/tarifftables

As a source of statistical information which allows limited comparison between universities (and for full details of the National Student Survey), visit:
www.unistats.com

Foundation degrees: Foundation Degrees Forward
www.findfoundationdegree.co.uk

HERO, an official site covering many aspects of higher education, from applying to research. The site includes an interactive location map of universities.
www.hero.ac.uk

UK Course Finder
www.ukcoursefinder.co.uk

Unofficial Guides to universities
www.unofficial-guides.com

Woody's Web-Watch, an independent website for students, parents and careers advisers, with a wide selection of useful links.
www.woodyswebwatch.com

For a full calendar of university and college open days
www.opendays.com

Students with disabilities: SKILL National Bureau for Students with Disabilities
www.skill.org.uk

Studying overseas
Association of Commonwealth Universities
www.acu.ac.uk
College Board (USA)
www.collegeboard.com
Education Ireland
www.educationireland.ie
Erasmus Programme (EU)
www.britishcouncil.org/erasmus
Finaid (USA)
www.finaid.org
Fulbright Commission
www.fulbright.co.uk
Study in Australia
www.studyinaustralia.gov.au
Study in Canada
www.studyincanada.com

University groupings
1994 Group, a group of medium and small research-intensive universities
www.1994group.ac.uk
GuildHE, a group of higher education colleges, specialist institutions and some universities:
www.guildhe.ac.uk
Million + Group, a group of newer universities
www.millionplus.ac.uk
Russell Group: a group of large research-intensive universities:
www.russellgroup.ac.uk

The Top Universities

What distinguishes a top university? And who is to say that one course is better than another – especially when the university system is so reluctant to make any such comparison?

Higher education now publishes copious statistics, but resists combining them in a way that might answer applicants' questions. Critics of league tables insist that this is because every university has different priorities, and every course different ways of approaching a subject. Students must choose the one that suits them best.

So they must. However, the sheer range of universities and courses in the UK is such that most applicants need some help paring down the options to create a shortlist for their five application choices. For 16 years, *The Times Good University Guide* has been assisting students and their parents with that process, using the statistics that universities themselves employ to measure their own performance.

Every element of the table in this chapter has been chosen for the light it shines on the undergraduate experience and a student's future prospects. The selection of these eight measures and the way in which they are combined give a particular view of universities' overall strengths, but it is one that has stood the test of time. Unlike some others, *The Times Good University Guide* has placed a premium on consistency, confident that the measures are the best available for the task.

Some changes have been forced upon us. Universities stopped assessing teaching quality subject by subject, when this was the most heavily weighted measure in the table. Spending on libraries, which was a measure in virtually all university league tables, is no longer collected separately from that relating to museums, galleries and observatories. There have been new developments, too, such as the National Student Survey, which could not be ignored.

The basic information that applicants need, however, in order to judge universities and their courses does not change. A university's entry standards, staffing levels, completion rates, degree classifications and graduate employment rates are all vital pieces of intelligence for anyone deciding where to study. And research grades, while not directly involving undergraduates, bring with them considerable funds and enable a university to attract top academics. Leading researchers in any subject may deliver the most inspiring lectures.

Most of the measures in *The Times Good University Guide*'s table have been used since it was first published and, while any element can be discounted by the individual, the package has struck a chord with readers. The ranking is the most-quoted of its type both in Britain and overseas, and has built a reputation as the most authoritative arbiter of changing fortunes in higher education.

The measures used in the ranking are kept under review by a group of university administrators and statisticians, which meets annually. The raw data that go into the table in this chapter and the subject tables in chapter 3 are all in the public domain and are sent to universities for checking before any scores are calculated.

Indeed, while the various official bodies concerned with higher education do not publish league tables, several produce system-wide statistics in a format that encourages comparison. The Higher Education Funding Councils' Research Assessment Exercise was one early example of this, with universities trumpeting their successes almost as soon as the grades had been announced. The Higher Education Statistics Agency (HESA), which supplies most of the figures used in our tables, also publishes annual "performance indicators" on everything from completion rates and research output to the proportion of under-represented social groups at each university.

Any scrutiny of league table positions is best carried out in conjunction with an examination of the relevant subject table – it is the course, after all, that will dominate your undergraduate years and influence your subsequent career.

How *The Times* League Table works

The table is presented in a format that displays the raw data, wherever possible. In building the table, scores for Student Satisfaction and Research Quality were weighted by 1.5; all other measures were weighted by 1. The indicators were combined using a common statistical technique known as Z-scores, to ensure that no indicator has a disproportionate effect on the overall total for each university, and the totals were transformed to a scale with 1000 for the top score.

For Entry Standards, Good Honours and Graduate Prospects, the score was adjusted for subject mix. It is accepted that engineering, law and medicine graduates will tend to have better graduate prospects than their peers from English, psychology and sociology courses. Comparing results in the main subject groupings helps to iron out differences attributable simply to the range of degrees on offer. This subject-mix adjustment means that it is not possible to replicate the scores in the table from the published indicators because the calculation requires access to the entire dataset.

The Z-score technique makes it impossible to compare universities' total scores from one year to the next, although their relative positions in the table are comparable. Individual scores are dependent on the top performer, so a university might drop from 60 per cent of the top score to 58 per cent but still have improved, if the leading university had done better still.

Only where data are not available from HESA are figures sourced directly from universities. Where this is not possible – for example, in the case of those Scottish universities that are not part of the National Student Survey – scores are generated according to a university's average performance on other indicators.

The organisations providing the raw data for the tables are not involved in the process of aggregation, so are not responsible for any inferences or conclusions we have made. Every care has been taken to ensure the accuracy of the tables and accompanying information, but no responsibility can be taken for errors or omissions.

Student satisfaction

This is a measure of students' views of the quality of their courses. The National Student Survey (NSS) was the source of this data. The NSS is an initiative undertaken by the Funding Councils for England, Northern Ireland and Wales. It is designed, as an element of the quality assurance for higher education, to inform prospective students and their advisers in choosing what and where to study. The survey encompasses the views of final-year students on the quality of their courses. Data from the surveys published in 2007 and 2008 were used.

- The National Student Survey covers six aspects of a course: teaching, assessment and feedback, academic support, organisation and management, learning resources and personal development, with an additional question gauging overall satisfaction. Students answer on a scale from 1 (bottom) to 5 (top) and the measure is the percentage of positive responses (4 and 5) in each section, averaged to produce the final score.
- The survey is based on the opinion of final-year students rather than directly assessing teaching quality. Most undergraduates have no experience of other universities, or different courses, to inform their judgements. Although all the questions relate to courses, rather than the broader student experience, some types of university – notably medium-sized campus universities – tend to do better than others.
- Scottish universities were not automatically included in the survey, although nine out of 14 have so far opted in.
- Where a university did not have sufficiently high response rates to publish results for one of the two years used to compile this measure, a single year's data have been used.

Research quality

This is a measure of the quality of the research undertaken in each university. The information was sourced from the 2008 Research Assessment Exercise (RAE), a peer-review exercise used to evaluate the quality of research in UK higher education institutions undertaken by the UK Higher Education funding bodies. Additionally, academic staffing data for 2007–08 from the Higher Education Statistics Agency have been used.

- A research quality profile was given to every university department that took part. This profile used the following categories – 4* *world-leading*, 3* *internationally excellent* and 2* *internationally recognised* (with another two lower categories). The Funding Bodies decided only to fund research in the higher 3 categories, and directed more funds to the very best research by applying weightings – 4* receiving 7 times the funding for 2*, and 3* receiving 3 times the funding for 2*. These weightings have been used in the tables.
- Universities could choose which staff to include in the RAE, so, to factor in the depth of the research quality, each quality profile score has been multiplied by the number of staff returned in the RAE as a proportion of all eligible staff.
- Technically, the maximum score possible in the main table is 7 – which would be achieved if a university submitted all of its staff, and all its research was world-leading, i.e. 4*. Because the highest proportion of 4* research in any one university was about 35 per cent (not surprisingly given the demands of the *world-leading* standard), and because even the best ranked universities generally submitted less than a full complement of their academic staff, the highest score seen is 3.7 (Cambridge), well below the theoretical maximum. A low score may be a function of low submission rates as well as of lower research quality – the subject tables give the picture of quality within each department.
- Estimations of the eligible staff for each university were made drawing from publicly available data that have been quality assured by universities themselves. The eligible staff data include all staff directly responsible for teaching and research, with an adjustment made to remove more junior staff on research-only contracts. An adjustment has also been made to reflect patterns of staffing in those institutions which carry out further education as well as higher education.

Estimation was necessary because, as you will see from the note on page 41, HESA decided not publish data on numbers of staff in university departments who were eligible to be submitted in the RAE. The proportion of staff entered by each university was considered sufficiently important to be included in the grades used in every previous RAE to give an indication of the ethos and overall quality of departments. The methodology used in *The Times* League Table attempts to replicate that process as accurately as possible, given the restrictions imposed by HESA.

Entry standards

This is the average score, using the UCAS tariff (see page 17), of new students under the age of 21 who took A and AS Levels, Highers and Advanced Highers. It measures what new students actually achieved rather than the entry requirements suggested by the universities. The data comes from HESA for 2007–08. The original sources of data for this measure are data returns made by the universities themselves to HESA.

- Using the UCAS tariff, each student's examination results were converted to a numerical score. HESA then calculated an average for all students at the university. The results have then been adjusted to take account of the subject mix at the university.
- A score of 360 represents three As at A level. Although all of the top 30 universities in the table have entry standards of at least 360, it does not mean that everyone achieved such results – let alone that this was the standard offer. Courses will not demand more than three subjects at A level and offers are pitched accordingly. You will need to reach the entry requirements set by the university, rather than the scores represented here.

Student–staff ratio

This is a measure of the average number of students to each member of the academic staff, apart from those purely engaged in research. In this measure a low score is better than a high score. The data comes from HESA for 2007–08. The original sources of data for this measure are data returns made by the universities themselves to HESA.

- The figures, as calculated by HESA, allow for variation in employment patterns at different universities. A low value means that there are a small number of students for each academic member of staff, but this does not, of course, ensure good teaching quality or contact time with academics.
- Student–staff ratios are usually low for medicine and this will influence the scores of universities with medical schools.

Services and facilities spend

The expenditure per student on staff and student facilities, including library and computing facilities. The data comes from HESA for 2005–06 and 2006–07. The original data sources for this measure are data returns made by the universities to HESA.

- This is a measure calculated by taking the expenditure on student facilities (sports, grants to student societies, careers services, health services, counselling, etc.) and library and computing facilities (books, journals, staff, central computers and computer networks, but not buildings) and dividing this by the number of full-time-equivalent students. Expenditure is averaged over two years to even out the figures (for example, a computer upgrade undertaken in a single year).

Completion

This measure gives the percentage of students expected to complete their studies (or transfer to another institution) for each university. The data comes from the HESA performance indicators, based on data for 2006–07 and earlier years.

- This measure is a projection, liable to statistical fluctuations.

Good honours

This measure is the percentage of graduates achieving a first or upper second class degree. The results have been adjusted to take account of the subject mix at the university. The data comes from HESA for 2007–08. The original sources of data for this measure are data returns made by the universities themselves to HESA.

- Four-year first degrees, such as an MChem, are treated as equivalent to a first or upper second.
- Scottish Ordinary degrees (awarded after three years of study in Scotland) are excluded.
- Universities control degree classification, with some oversight from external examiners. There have been suggestions that since universities have increased the numbers of good honours degrees they award, this measure may not be as objective as it should be. However, it remains the key measure of a student's success and employability.

Graduate prospects

This measure is the percentage of the total number of graduates who take up graduate-level employment or further study. The results have been adjusted for subject mix. The data come from HESA for 2007 graduates.

- HESA surveys graduates six months after graduation to find out what they are doing and the data are based on this survey.

Statement from the Higher Education Statistics Agency (HESA) regarding the use of staffing data in looking at Research Assessment Exercise performance:

> *This analysis of the results of the Research Assessment Exercise 2008 makes use of contextual data supplied under contract by the Higher Education Statistics Agency (HESA). It is a contractual condition that this statement should be published in conjunction with the analysis.*
>
> *HESA holds no data specifying which or how many staff have been regarded by each institution as eligible for inclusion in RAE 2008, and no data on the assignment to Units of Assessment of those eligible staff not included. Further, the data that HESA does hold is not an adequate alternative basis on which to estimate eligible staff numbers, whether for an institution as a whole, or disaggregated by Units of Assessment, or by some broader subject-based grouping.*

	Student satisfaction (%)	Research quality	Entry standards	Student–staff ratio	Services and facilities spend per student (£)	Completion (%)	Good honours (%)	Graduate prospects (%)	Total
Max score	100.0	7.0	n/a	n/a	n/a	100.0	100.0	100.0	1000
1 Oxford	85	3.5	524	10.8	3396	97.7	91.1	82.3	1000
2 Cambridge	86	3.7	539	11.6	2385	99.0	87.0	85.5	968
3 Imperial College	75	2.7	489	10.3	3518	97.1	68.5	88.4	859
4 St Andrews	84	2.5	468	12.4	1423	94.2	85.1	77.8	792
5 University College London	77	2.7	452	8.9	1784	92.0	80.4	82.9	775
6 Warwick	77	2.4	463	13.1	2118	96.0	79.7	79.2	772
7 London School of Economics	73	2.8	483	13.3	1699	96.5	76.0	90.6	768
8 Durham	79	2.5	459	14.8	1578	96.7	77.5	78.3	749
9 Exeter	85	2.5	394	17.5	1378	94.8	79.4	71.7	723
10 Bristol	74	2.6	447	13.1	1657	95.6	81.5	82.0	722
11 York	79	2.5	434	13.1	1534	96.0	74.9	69.4	711
12 King's College London	76	2.0	415	11.4	1821	92.3	72.8	83.2	709
13 Bath	78	2.0	440	15.0	1358	95.7	75.1	81.9	705
14 Edinburgh	74	2.8	447	12.4	1511	90.4	80.6	76.9	704
15 Leicester	84	1.9	360	14.7	1489	93.0	71.6	76.2	693
16 Southampton	78	2.0	407	13.9	1562	93.7	74.6	76.5	692
17 Loughborough	85	2.1	368	17.0	1340	91.3	67.7	75.7	691
18 Sheffield	78	2.4	406	14.2	1191	92.1	74.5	79.1	684

University									
19 Glasgow	79	2.2	412	13.2	1377	86.6	71.3	75.4	671
20 Nottingham	76	2.1	408	13.7	1402	95.7	74.3	76.3	668
21 Newcastle	77	2.0	405	14.9	1504	92.2	72.2	79.4	664
22 Birmingham	78	2.1	403	14.9	1552	93.6	70.9	72.7	663
23 Lancaster	79	2.4	388	13.7	1407	93.3	69.6	64.3	661
24 Manchester	73	2.4	412	13.6	1489	91.6	70.4	73.8	641
25 Aston	80	1.2	365	16.5	1507	91.0	63.6	78.1	631
26 Cardiff	77	1.8	394	14.7	1177	92.4	66.8	77.6	630
27 Leeds	76	2.0	392	13.9	1143	91.9	73.4	71.1	627
=28 Liverpool	76	1.8	387	12.2	1273	91.2	68.8	72.5	622
=28 East Anglia	83	1.8	361	17.1	1231	85.4	70.1	71.9	622
30 Royal Holloway	75	2.3	365	14.5	1308	92.9	70.3	69.8	617
31 Reading	79	2.1	347	16.7	1062	91.7	75.4	68.7	612
32 Queen's Belfast	78	1.7	358	15.2	1362	85.0	69.0	78.3	611
=33 Aberdeen	81	1.9	363	15.1	1194	77.3	67.6	74.4	607
=33 School of Oriental and African Studies	72	1.7	378	10.8	1829	82.6	73.2	73.5	607
35 Sussex	74	2.2	378	15.5	1117	90.1	81.7	70.6	606
36 Queen Mary, London	76	2.0	346	13.0	1161	88.5	64.2	77.3	600
=37 Surrey	76	1.8	352	16.8	1202	88.8	65.1	80.0	596
=37 Strathclyde	76	1.6	394	19.1	1344	83.1	73.9	78.1	596
39 Kent	81	1.4	317	17.1	1148	87.8	61.7	71.8	566
40 Heriot-Watt	75	1.7	350	15.6	1183	80.3	65.5	76.2	558
41 Dundee	78	1.5	371	14.0	1124	71.4	65.8	75.6	554
42 Keele	77	1.2	319	14.3	1148	89.1	64.4	70.4	552
43 Essex	76	1.8	302	13.7	1385	87.4	61.0	62.7	550
44 Hull	81	1.1	285	18.7	1096	87.0	57.7	73.2	530
45 Goldsmiths College	72	2.1	318	12.7	806	85.7	65.2	69.0	529

	Student satisfaction (%)	Research quality	Entry standards	Student–staff ratio	Services and facilities spend per student (£)	Completion (%)	Good honours (%)	Graduate prospects (%)	Total
Max score	100.0	7.0	n/a	n/a	n/a	100.0	100.0	100.0	1000
46 Aberystwyth	81	1.7	310	17.6	1047	87.5	61.1	53.0	522
47 Brunel	72	1.6	319	17.8	1576	86.4	64.9	67.9	516
48 Stirling	76	1.3	288	14.2	958	81.5	64.3	69.8	512
49 City	72	1.2	316	17.8	993	84.3	66.6	81.4	511
50 Swansea	78	1.5	304	14.7	1122	87.3	50.3	62.5	506
51 Robert Gordon	..	0.6	332	18.0	1102	81.8	53.2	84.1	504
52 Oxford Brookes	77	0.6	301	18.4	997	83.9	66.1	73.0	496
53 Bradford	75	1.0	270	15.0	1176	82.3	62.8	70.4	492
54 Ulster	75	1.0	268	15.9	1548	77.4	61.4	65.0	487
55 Bangor	77	1.5	283	18.9	998	83.9	55.7	67.8	480
56 Portsmouth	79	0.5	271	18.7	1158	86.1	52.4	63.9	463
57 Nottingham Trent	74	0.4	276	17.1	1144	86.2	55.7	74.1	462
58 Bournemouth	74	0.4	289	20.8	1059	85.2	58.9	75.5	450
59 Chichester	81	0.2	234	18.3	851	89.2	49.3	64.0	445
60 Glasgow Caledonian	75	0.3	328	21.0	933	76.8	66.5	68.8	443
61 Queen Margaret Edinburgh	..	0.4	328	20.0	885	78.5	65.3	69.2	442
62 West of England	76	0.5	275	19.2	995	78.8	63.2	66.1	436
63 Plymouth	75	0.7	268	15.7	955	84.3	61.5	58.0	435

University									
64 Northumbria	76	0.3	291	20.0	1063	80.3	54.1	73.0	434
65 Edinburgh Napier	..	0.4	291	18.2	895	72.6	62.4	72.9	430
=66 Hertfordshire	73	0.3	244	14.4	1593	82.3	47.3	65.3	424
=66 De Montfort	77	0.6	248	17.0	882	81.5	51.1	65.7	424
68 Gloucestershire	74	0.3	239	16.5	1190	82.1	56.2	64.2	421
69 Sheffield Hallam	73	0.4	268	18.1	937	83.8	61.3	64.2	420
70 Brighton	74	0.8	278	20.0	800	84.7	58.5	65.3	417
=71 Coventry	75	0.3	280	19.1	1122	75.2	61.0	67.5	414
=71 Bedfordshire	75	0.2	215	15.6	1431	75.1	47.8	66.7	414
73 Winchester	77	0.4	261	17.2	867	85.6	55.7	55.6	411
=74 Staffordshire	76	0.1	232	17.5	1092	78.1	53.0	69.0	410
=74 Bath Spa	77	0.4	287	21.6	615	87.0	67.7	59.0	410
76 UWIC, Cardiff	74	0.4	261	19.9	1205	83.2	51.8	61.5	401
77 Birmingham City	72	0.2	258	16.5	1217	75.5	57.3	65.7	393
78 Central Lancashire	76	0.4	252	20.2	1083	72.9	49.3	70.1	392
79 Lampeter	74	1.0	252	14.6	482	82.7	52.8	61.8	391
80 York St John	75	0.2	288	20.0	1042	84.5	52.9	58.8	390
=81 Worcester	76	0.1	236	20.0	869	83.9	48.4	68.2	389
=81 Teesside	77	0.2	257	19.3	808	72.7	52.4	67.3	389
83 Cumbria	70	0.1	256	14.9	741	84.2	48.8	71.4	384
=84 Salford	73	0.9	253	18.6	987	76.4	55.1	62.7	383
=84 Sunderland	77	0.5	226	16.1	775	75.6	50.2	59.3	383
86 Lincoln	75	0.5	266	23.7	865	85.0	57.1	60.4	381
87 Huddersfield	74	0.2	265	16.1	897	81.2	51.9	56.9	378
88 Edge Hill	78	0.1	248	19.8	1082	79.2	46.1	56.8	373
89 Kingston	73	0.4	236	19.1	1012	79.4	60.1	61.0	372
90 Manchester Metropolitan	72	0.5	266	19.7	972	79.0	57.2	63.8	371

	Student satisfaction (%)	Research quality	Entry standards	Student–staff ratio	Services and facilities spend per student (£)	Completion (%)	Good honours (%)	Graduate prospects (%)	Total
Max score	100.0	7.0	n/a	n/a	n/a	100.0	100.0	100.0	1000
91 Chester	73	0.2	267	18.3	753	78.2	54.8	65.1	365
=92 Roehampton	71	0.8	251	18.4	1242	78.5	51.0	56.8	362
=92 Northampton	75	0.2	233	20.4	853	81.3	53.7	59.5	362
94 Glamorgan	74	0.4	263	18.3	1103	69.1	52.4	60.4	361
95 Abertay	..	0.4	279	19.8	1603	70.1	48.3	53.3	353
96 University of the Arts, London	62	1.0	322	21.7	849	85.5	61.6	63.6	339
97 Glyndŵr	72	0.2	212	19.7	996	70.1	50.6	69.3	338
98 Canterbury Christ Church	73	0.2	238	18.3	633	80.2	49.7	59.0	334
99 Liverpool John Moores	73	0.4	244	19.6	979	76.1	45.7	58.8	327
100 Westminster	69	0.5	249	16.4	800	77.5	51.5	54.1	321
101 Leeds Metropolitan	68	0.2	257	21.1	975	82.1	53.0	59.9	315
102 Wolverhampton	72	0.3	204	19.0	1078	73.4	44.6	60.9	313
103 Anglia Ruskin	68	0.2	257	19.7	773	74.3	55.5	66.2	309
104 Derby	72	0.1	231	19.8	1091	76.5	46.6	54.9	307
105 Middlesex	70	0.5	194	23.4	1645	64.7	50.8	64.4	296
106 Greenwich	73	0.3	212	22.9	829	75.8	44.9	59.6	289
107 UWCN, Newport	73	0.3	229	25.8	922	72.1	54.8	55.8	284
=108 Bolton	75	0.3	213	19.0	697	56.0	53.5	59.1	282

=108	East London	70	0.4	191	21.6	1257	71.5	44.4	62.7	282
110	Thames Valley	73	0.2	197	20.6	827	63.6	50.4	59.7	273
111	Southampton Solent	70	0.1	211	21.4	1054	74.5	45.7	56.6	272
112	Buckinghamshire New	68	0.1	210	20.3	1110	79.8	46.3	50.9	263
113	London South Bank	71	0.3	179	25.2	829	69.4	53.7	63.2	253
114	University for the Creative Arts	66	0.5	247	24.3	1033	85.3	51.2	58.2	243

Liverpool Hope, London Metropolitan, Swansea Metropolitan and the University of the West of Scotland have refused to allow the release of data, and so do not appear in this year's League Table.

Useful websites

The main League Table is available on *The Times* website **www.timesonline.co.uk/gug**. There is the facility there to compare selected universities. The subject tables are also available to view on this site.

For more information on the data collected by HESA and a detailed explanation of the HEFCE performance indicators, visit the HESA site: **www.hesa.ac.uk**

Information on the 2008 Research Assessment Exercise can be found at: **www.rae.ac.uk**

3 The Top Universities by Subject

Knowing where a university stands in the pecking order of higher education is a vital piece of information for any prospective student, but the quality of the course is what matters most. As the latest Research Assessment Exercise (RAE) confirmed, the most modest institution may have a centre of specialist excellence, and even famous universities have mediocre departments. This section offers some pointers to the leading universities in a wide range of subjects.

Since last year, the subject tables in this *Guide* have included scores from the National Student Survey (NSS). These distil the views of final-year undergraduates on several aspects of their course, including teaching quality, assessment and feedback, and the level of resources. They have been added to the three measures used in previous editions: research quality, students' entry qualifications and graduate employment prospects. None of the measures has been weighted.

The tables also include the first new research grades for six years, drawn from the deliberations of expert assessors in the 2008 RAE. The exercise adopted a different grading system, so the scores are not directly comparable with previous years'. No data have been released on the proportion of academics entered for assessment, for example, so it has not been possible to mirror the approach adopted in the main institutional ranking (see page 39).

Data supplied by the Higher Education Statistics Agency (HESA) are used to calculate average entry qualifications and the employment prospects of graduates. The prospects information draws a distinction between different types of employment: graduate employment, where a degree is normally required, and non-graduate employment. The tables give the percentage of "positive destinations" by adding those undertaking further study to the total in graduate employment.

Many subjects, such as dentistry or sociology, have their own table, but others are grouped together in broader categories, such as subjects allied to medicine, which includes such specialisms as physiotherapy and radiology. There is one new category this year: sports science, which has been extracted from the broader group of subjects that includes hospitality and tourism. There is also a separate set of tables covering research in the different medical specialisms.

Not all universities in Scotland participate in the National Student Survey, so to qualify for inclusion in the table a university has to have data for at least two of the other measures. Scores are not published where the number of students is too small for the outcome to be statistically reliable. In the NSS, a 50 per cent response rate is required from a minimum of 30 students.

Cambridge is again by far the most successful university. It tops 35 of the 62 tables. Oxford has the next highest number of top places with eight.

The subject rankings demonstrate that there are "horses for courses" in higher education. Thus the London School of Economics is more than a match for its rivals in social science, while Imperial College remains a force in engineering. In their own fields, table-toppers such as Loughborough in sports science, Warwick in American studies, and Reading in agriculture, are equally well-known. But the tables contain less obvious success stories, such as Sheffield in social work and Bath in accounting and finance.

Research quality

This is a measure of the quality of the research undertaken in the subject area. The information was sourced from the 2008 Research Assessment Exercise (RAE), a peer-review exercise used to evaluate the quality of research in UK higher education institutions, undertaken by the UK Higher Education Funding Bodies.

For each subject, a research quality profile was given to those university departments that took part, showing how much of their research was in various quality categories. These categories were 4* *world-leading*, 3* *internationally excellent* and 2* *internationally recognised*, with another two lower categories. The funding bodies decided to fund only research in the three top categories, and directed more funds to the very best research by applying weightings: 4* receiving seven times the weight of 2*, and 3* receiving three times the weight of 2*. These weightings have been used in the tables.

Technically, the maximum score possible in the main table is 7 – which would be the case if all a department's research was *world-leading*, i.e. 4*. In fact the highest score seen in any subject table is 5.3 (London School of Economics, for economics), with that score having 60 per cent of research at 4* and the remainder in 3* and 2*, which is not surprising given the demands of the *world-leading* standard. Perhaps what is most useful is to look within each subject and compare RAE scores for the universities in that subject.

Staffing data to show how many of a department's academics were submitted in the RAE are not currently available. Some research ratings shown could relate to a relatively low proportion of the academic staff in the department.

Entry standards

This is the average UCAS tariff score for new students under the age of 21, taken from HESA data for 2007–08. Each student's examination grades were converted to a numerical score using the UCAS tariff that then applied (at A level A = 120, B = 100, etc; for Scottish Highers A = 72, B = 60, etc) and added up to give a total score. HESA then calculated an average score for each university.

Student satisfaction

This measure is taken from the National Student Survey results published in 2007 and 2008. A single year's figures are used when that is all that is available, but an average of the two years' results is used in all other cases. The score for each university represents the percentage of final-year undergraduates declaring themselves satisfied or very satisfied with their course, averaged over the seven sections of the survey.

Graduate prospects

This is the percentage of graduates undertaking further study or in a graduate job, in the annual survey by HESA six months after graduation. Two years of data (2006 and 2007 graduates) are aggregated to make the data more reliable. A low score on this measure does not necessarily indicate unemployment – some graduates may have taken jobs that are not categorised as graduate work. The averages for each subject are given at the bottom of the relevant subject table in this chapter and in a table in chapter 1 (see pages 24–25).

The Education table uses a fifth measure: teaching quality, as measured by the outcomes of Ofsted inspections of teacher training courses.

The subjects listed below are covered in the tables in this chapter:

Accounting and finance

Aeronautical and manufacturing engineering

Agriculture and forestry

American studies

Anatomy and physiology

Anthropology

Archaeology

Architecture

Art and design

Biological sciences

Building

Business studies

Celtic studies

Chemical engineering

Chemistry

Civil engineering

Classics and ancient history

Communication and media studies

Computer science

Dentistry

Drama, dance and cinematics

East and South Asian studies

Economics

Education

Electrical and electronic engineering

English

Food science

French

General engineering

Geography and environmental sciences

Geology

German

History

History of art, architecture and design

Hospitality, leisure, recreation and tourism

Iberian languages

Italian

Land and property management

Law

Librarianship and information management

Linguistics

Materials technology

Mathematics

Mechanical engineering

Medicine

Middle Eastern and African studies

Music

Nursing

Other subjects allied to medicine
(see page 145 for included subjects)

Pharmacology and pharmacy

Philosophy

Physics and astronomy

Politics

Psychology

Russian and East European languages

Social policy

Social work

Sociology

Sports science

Theology and religious studies

Town and country planning and landscape

Veterinary medicine

Accounting and Finance

Bath enters the accounting and finance ranking for the first time in top position, with good scores on three of the four indicators but not leading on any of them. Only Cardiff had a better research grade in the 2008 assessments, but the LSE, Glasgow and Warwick (last year's leader) all have higher entry standards.

Second-placed Exeter had by far the most satisfied students in the National Student Survey results published in 2008. Only Lincoln, in 36th place, and Thames Valley, in 59th, came anywhere near Exeter's 95 per cent satisfaction level.

Robert Gordon's graduates again had most cause to be satisfied, 97 per cent of them finding graduate-level jobs or starting further training within six months of finishing their course. The achievement left Robert Gordon as the top new university for the second successive year. Only Bristol came close to matching its employment score.

Compiled from data extracted from the Business Studies statistics to reflect the growth of accountancy and finance degrees, the table has two more entries than last year. Applications for accounting were up by 6.5 per cent at the start of 2009, leaving it just outside the 20 most popular subjects, although the finance area saw a small decline.

Even long before the recession was on the horizon, when these employment data were collected, accounting and finance were not surefire bets for a graduate job. The subjects were outside the top 30 on this measure, with an above-average unemployment rate, although average salaries of more than £20,500 for those who did get graduate jobs placed them close to the top 20.

Strathclyde has overtaken Edinburgh to become the top university in Scotland, while Cardiff remains comfortably ahead in Wales. Robert Gordon is the only new university in the top 25 places, with Northumbria next at 30th.

Entry scores are widely spread among the 76 universities in the table, ranging from close to 500 points at the LSE to less than 150 at Southampton Solent. The grades show a similar pattern to last year, with a dozen universities averaging more than 400 points and eight less than 200. Almost three graduates in ten started their careers in low-level jobs and in several universities, more than half of the graduates were in this position

- Actuarial Profession: **www.actuaries.org.uk**
- Association of Chartered Certified Accountants: **www.accaglobal.com**
- Careers in accounting: **www.careers-in-accounting.com**
- Chartered Institute of Public Finance and Accountancy: **www.cipfa.org.uk**
- Institute of Chartered Accountants: **www.icaew.co.uk/students**
- Institute of Chartered Accountants of Scotland: **www.icas.org.uk**
- Institute of Financial Services: **www.ifslearning.ac.uk**

Accounting and Finance	Research quality/7	Entry standards	Student satisfaction %	Graduate prospects %	Overall rating
1 Bath	3.6	452	81		100.0
2 Exeter	2.5	389	95	77	99.0
3 Strathclyde	3.3	444	83	83	98.5
4 Loughborough	2.8	406	87	84	97.9

Accounting and Finance cont.

	Research quality/7	Entry standards	Student satisfaction %	Graduate prospects %	Overall rating
5 London School of Economics	3.6	485	74	91	97.8
6 Warwick	3.5	457	76	89	96.9
7 Glasgow	2.1	460	84	90	96.4
8 City	2.6	395	85	79	94.4
9 Nottingham	3.2	399	79	84	94.1
10 Manchester	3.3	408	80	77	93.9
11 Queen's, Belfast	2.7	392	82	83	93.3
12 Lancaster	3.5	389	78	76	93.0
13 Cardiff	3.8	376	79	68	92.3
14 Edinburgh	2.3	449	78	84	92.0
15 Reading	2.3	385	80	88	91.8
16 Birmingham	2.8	392	80	76	91.6
17 Southampton	2.6	406	76	86	90.8
=18 Kent	2.5	316	82	82	89.9
=18 Newcastle	2.3	412	77	84	89.9
=20 Leeds	3.2	412	72	76	89.1
=20 East Anglia	2.2	351	82	77	89.1
22 Robert Gordon	1.3	342		97	88.3
=23 Bangor	2.9	259	84	71	88.0
=23 Bristol	2.4	430	68	95	88.0
25 Queen Mary, London	2.6	332	76	81	87.4
26 Durham	2.7	351	75	80	87.1
27 Sheffield	2.8	348	75	76	86.8
28 Aberdeen	2.0	346	80	73	85.7
29 Heriot-Watt	2.2	354	75	75	84.4
30 Northumbria	1.1	315	84	73	83.4
31 West of England	2.0	270	81	71	83.0
32 Hull	2.0	265	77	83	82.9
33 Nottingham Trent	1.6	268	79	83	82.4
34 Ulster	1.8	286	81	68	82.1
35 De Montfort	1.9	248	83	65	81.8
36 Lincoln		267	92	69	81.0
37 Surrey	2.3	358	72		80.9
38 Portsmouth	1.6	253	86	57	80.7
=39 Dundee	1.8	337	74	71	80.6
=39 Brighton	2.4	244	80	60	80.6
=39 Bournemouth	1.5	279	82	65	80.6
=39 Central Lancashire	1.5	266	84	63	80.6
43 Liverpool	2.3	347	75	59	80.5
44 Stirling	1.8	284	78	66	79.8
45 Keele	2.1	267	73	73	79.1
=46 Essex	2.5	291	71	69	79.0
=46 Bradford	2.4	238	79	57	79.0

48 Glasgow Caledonian	1.0	327	78	64	77.6
49 Manchester Metropolitan	1.7	260	76	63	76.6
50 Sheffield Hallam	1.4	256	79	60	76.3
51 Salford	1.5	293	78	55	76.2
52 Glamorgan	1.2	289	76	66	75.8
53 Edinburgh Napier	0.9	269		74	75.7
54 Oxford Brookes		302	77	74	74.0
55 Greenwich	1.2	194	84	48	73.6
56 Aberystwyth	1.5	276	79	41	73.5
57 Birmingham City	1.2	227	77	62	73.2
58 Gloucestershire		250	76	76	72.4
59 Thames Valley		152	91	52	72.2
60 Liverpool John Moores	0.6	244	78	59	71.8
61 Hertfordshire	1.7	235	74	52	71.7
62 Kingston		231	81	61	71.1
63 Coventry		274	72	73	70.3
64 Northampton		221	82	53	69.7
65 Plymouth	1.6	254	72	45	69.2
66 Huddersfield	1.4	244	75	34	67.7
67 East London		156	84	46	66.4
68 Leeds Metropolitan		269	75	50	66.2
69 Bedfordshire		228	82	37	66.0
70 Staffordshire		233	72	63	65.9
71 Middlesex		162	76	60	64.9
72 Derby		191	75	57	64.8
73 London South Bank	1.1	165	72	43	64.0
74 UWIC, Cardiff		248	76	40	63.9
75 Wolverhampton		181	70	55	61.4
76 Southampton Solent		148	67	65	60.6

Employed in graduate job:	35%	Employed in non-graduate job and studying:	5%
Employed in graduate job and studying:	22%	Employed in non-graduate job:	24%
Studying:	7%	Unemployed:	7%
Average starting graduate salary:	£20,586	Average starting non-graduate salary:	£16,614

Aeronautical and Manufacturing Engineering

Most of the courses in this table focus on aeronautical or manufacturing engineering, but it includes some with a mechanical title. To add to the confusion, manufacturing degrees often go under the rubric of production engineering (see General Engineering and Mechanical Engineering). The number of institutions in the ranking has stabilised after a period of decline, but there were still four more when the 2006 *Guide* appeared.

Cambridge remains well clear of the field, with by far the highest entry grades and the best performance in the latest Research Assessment Exercise (RAE), when some of the university's work in this field was submitted in other engineering categories. However, it has been overhauled by Surrey this year on the student satisfaction and graduate employment indicators. Outstanding scores on both measures allow Surrey to leap from

Aeronautical and Manufacturing Engineering cont.

14th place to second – and even then fifth-placed Newcastle has a better graduate employment record.

Bristol is the other leading university to move up the table this year after good research grades. Imperial did even better in the RAE but was let down, as was Manchester, by an unusually low student satisfaction rate. The West of England is the only new university in the top half of the table, while Swansea is the leader in Wales and Strathclyde in Scotland.

A one-off decline in applications for aerospace engineering last year, after four successive increases, had been reversed at the start of 2009, when the demand for degree places had grown by 20 per cent. Many graduates go on to further study or training to meet professional requirements and – particularly for aeronautical engineering graduates – employment prospects are bright. The subjects are just outside the top ten for graduate salaries, with an average of almost £23,000 for those in graduate jobs. Surprisingly, even though more than half go straight into graduate jobs, the unemployment rate of 8 per cent is among the highest for any subject area. Entry grades have been rising, with Cambridge posting a particularly high average, but three Cs at A level (and another at AS level) will secure a place at most universities outside the top 20.

- Manufacturing Institute: **www.makeit.org.uk**
- Royal Aeronautical Society: **www.aerosociety.com**
- Why Aeronautical engineering?:

www.science-engineering.net/aeronautical_engineering.htm

Aeronautical and Manufacturing Engineering	Research quality/7	Entry standards	Student satisfaction %	Graduate prospects %	Overall rating
1 Cambridge	4.6	564	85	94	100.0
2 Surrey	3.1	355	90	95	89.6
3 Bristol	3.6	464	78	94	88.8
4 Southampton	2.8	451	86	79	85.4
=5 Sheffield	3.7	376	79	85	84.9
=5 Newcastle	2.9		78	96	84.9
7 Bath	2.5	460	82	86	84.2
8 Imperial College	3.8	490	68	84	83.3
9 Loughborough	3.2	383	81	80	82.8
10 Nottingham	3.5	391	78	72	81.2
11 Queen's, Belfast	2.9	342	76	82	78.5
12 Aston	2.0	306	87	74	76.8
13 Liverpool	3.1	373	71	70	75.1
14 Leeds	3.3	358	70	69	74.7
=15 Swansea	2.3	318	78		73.6
=15 Manchester	3.2	414	63	73	73.6
17 Strathclyde	2.4	397	70	69	72.6
18 Brunel	2.3	361	69	77	72.0
19 West of England	2.4	261	75	72	71.2
20 Queen Mary, London	2.1	298	76	70	71.1
21 Glasgow	2.2	374	66	73	70.1

=22 Hertfordshire	2.4	247	78	61	69.6
=22 De Montfort	2.1		73	71	69.6
24 Portsmouth	2.0	222	81	67	69.5
25 Sheffield Hallam	1.7	279	72	77	68.3
26 Salford	2.3	279	67	73	67.2
27 Brighton	2.6	223	69		65.6
28 Coventry	1.0	231	75	72	64.4
29 Kingston	1.4	254	73	67	64.3
30 Bradford	2.1	221	70		63.8
31 City	2.2	237	73	50	63.5
32 Liverpool John Moores	2.9	183	70	49	62.9
33 Ulster		196	72	90	61.8
=34 Sussex		361	70	67	61.0
=34 Manchester Metropolitan	1.5	259	67	62	61.0
36 Plymouth	1.3	202	76	41	58.0
37 London South Bank	2.4	132	64	51	56.5
38 UWIC, Cardiff		309		54	56.3
39 Northampton		250		53	53.1

Employed in graduate job:	52%	Employed in non-graduate job and studying:	2%
Employed in graduate job and studying:	7%	Employed in non-graduate job:	19%
Studying:	13%	Unemployed:	8%
Average starting graduate salary:	£22,965	Average starting non-graduate salary:	£16,489

Agriculture and Forestry

Only a low research score prevented Harper Adams University College, in Shropshire, from taking over the leadership of the ranking for agriculture and forestry. It has by far the most satisfied students and the best graduate employment record in this year's table, but none of the research it entered for the 2008 assessments was considered world-leading.

Reading, with the highest entry standards, takes over top position from Newcastle, which has slipped to fourth. Nottingham – often the leader in previous years, returns to the table in third place, eclipsed only by seventh-placed Aberdeen, on research. Aberdeen is the only university in Scotland to offer agriculture or forestry, while Aberystwyth has overtaken Bangor in Wales.

The number of institutions in the ranking has dropped from 20 to 16 since last year. The demand for places had grown by 7 per cent at the start of 2009, but there were still only 2,400 applications for degree courses in agriculture. Foundation degrees in the subject continue to grow in popularity and are likely to have more than 1,000 applicants by the summer. Forestry is a much smaller area, with only 120 degree applications by the official deadline for courses starting in 2009, although this represented a big increase on last year.

A quarter of those enrolling for degrees in agriculture and more than a third in forestry do so without A levels, often coming with relevant work experience. About one in seven arrives through the clearing system. This shows in comparatively low entry grades, although only one university averages less than 200 points.

The definition of a graduate job does no favours to agriculture or forestry in the employment statistics, but the figures are still low in several universities. In half of the

Agriculture and Forestry cont.

institutions in the table, fewer than half of the leavers had graduate jobs or training courses within six months.

More than a third of graduates start in lower-level jobs. The subjects are never going to lead to big starting salaries, but they not in the bottom ten this year.

- Institute of Chartered Foresters: **www.charteredforesters.org**
- Royal Agricultural Society of England: **www.rase.org.uk**
- Royal Forestry Society: **www.rfs.org.uk**
- Royal Scottish Forestry Society: **www.rsfs.org**
- Sector Skills Council for the Environmental and Land-Based Sector (LANTRA): **www.lantra.co.uk**

Agriculture and Forestry	Research quality/7	Entry standards	Student satisfaction %	Graduate prospects %	Overall rating
1 Reading	2.2	345	83	65	100.0
2 Harper Adams	1.2	298	88	82	98.3
3 Nottingham	2.8	336	80	55	97.4
4 Newcastle	2.0	295	84	71	97.2
5 Queen's, Belfast	1.7	296	82	63	92.2
6 Aberystwyth	2.3	322	85	38	92.0
7 Aberdeen	2.9			38	89.9
8 Bangor	2.0	284		54	89.0
9 Greenwich	1.6	241		55	81.9
10 Royal Agricultural College	0.7	296	79	47	81.4
11 West of England	2.0	286	67	48	80.9
12 Nottingham Trent		297	74	48	75.3
13 Sheffield Hallam		303	77	38	75.2
14 Lincoln	1.0		67	54	74.1
15 Plymouth	0.9	217	75	40	71.9
16 Salford		186	76	46	67.6

Employed in graduate job:	42%	Employed in non-graduate job and studying:	3%
Employed in graduate job and studying:	11%	Employed in non-graduate job:	32%
Studying:	7%	Unemployed:	5%
Average starting graduate salary:	£18,755	Average starting non-graduate salary:	£14,604

American Studies

American studies has seen a surge in popularity this year, perhaps because of the huge interest in the election of Barack Obama. The 22 per cent increase was one of the biggest in any subject, although there were still only 2,500 applications. About 550 students started degree courses in 2008.

Warwick retains top place in the ranking, sharing the lead for research quality and student satisfaction, while boasting by far the highest entry standards. Manchester was the other research star in the 2008 assessments, while Hull matched Warwick's score in the National Student Survey.

Sussex was the only university to see three quarters of graduates go straight into graduate-level jobs or continue their studies, although Goldsmiths came close. This success and a good showing on all the other indicators moved Sussex up from eighth place to second. Portsmouth is the top-rated new university and the only one to enter the latest Research Assessment Exercise. Swansea is the only Welsh representative and Dundee the only one from Scotland.

Entry scores are more bunched than in many subjects, with only Warwick averaging more than 400 points and no university slipping below 200. Nine out of ten students taking American Studies have A levels or equivalent qualifications and there is an impressive level of firsts and 2:1s. The downside is in the employment statistics, with four universities reporting success rates in the graduate jobs market of less than 40 per cent. The subject is in the bottom ten overall for graduate employment rates, although it does a little better in the salaries table.

- British Association for American Studies: **www.baas.ac.uk**

American Studies	Research quality/7	Entry standards	Student satisfaction %	Graduate prospects %	Overall rating
1 Warwick	3.7	448	89	70	100.0
2 Sussex	3.4	395	79	75	92.4
3 Lancaster	3.5	346	80	68	88.8
4 Leicester	2.8	323	88	69	88.0
5 Manchester	3.7	359	74	57	85.3
=6 East Anglia	2.7	370	80	59	83.8
=6 Hull	2.4	268	89	68	83.8
8 Nottingham	2.7	367	76	59	82.3
9 Kent	3.4	271	79	54	80.9
10 Essex	2.5	286	80	65	80.3
=11 Birmingham	2.6	379	75	49	79.4
=11 King's College London	2.3	386	73	58	79.4
13 Liverpool	2.0	344	80	52	77.4
14 Portsmouth	2.3	286	76	53	74.7
15 Goldsmiths College		348	75	74	71.1
16 Swansea	1.7	297	77	43	69.8
17 Keele		318	77	60	66.7
18 Dundee		325	82	37	63.9
19 Plymouth		229	81	48	61.2
20 Winchester		253	83	33	59.8
21 Canterbury Christ Church		239	79	39	58.4
22 Liverpool John Moores		272	74	36	57.2
23 Ulster		208	56	45	47.7

American Studies cont.

Employed in graduate job:	33%	Employed in non-graduate job and studying:	5%
Employed in graduate job and studying:	4%	Employed in non-graduate job:	34%
Studying:	17%	Unemployed:	6%
Average starting graduate salary:	£18,757	Average starting non-graduate salary:	£14,534

Anatomy and Physiology

Anatomy, physiology and pathology have recovered their popularity after a big drop in applications in 2008. It was already a competitive field, with more than six applications for every place, although average entry scores at the five new universities in this year's table remain below 300 points. At Oxford – and probably at Cambridge, which does not collect separate entry scores for these subjects – the average is more than 500 points. Grades are boosted by the fact that the subjects are often a fall-back for candidates whose real targets are medical schools.

Oxford, which has moved up six places this year, achieved much the best grades in the 2008 Research Assessment Exercise, but Cambridge still regains the leadership with better scores for student satisfaction and graduate employment. In fact, East London has by far the best employment record, with all of the leavers going straight into graduate-level work or continuing their studies. The most satisfied students were at fourth-placed Edinburgh, last year's leader and the top university in Scotland.

Scores in the National Student Survey were generally high, with only four universities registering less than 70 per cent satisfaction among final-year undergraduates.

Employment prospects throughout the 27 universities in the ranking are close to the average for all subjects. More than a third of the students go on to postgraduate training – one of the highest proportions for any group of subjects. Average earnings in graduate jobs are below average, but had risen to more than £19,000 in the latest statistics.

This ranking covers degrees in cell biology, neurosciences and pathology, as well as anatomy and physiology. Universities often demand at least two science subjects at A level – usually biology and chemistry, although some new universities will accept just one science qualification.

- Anatomical Society of Great Britain and Ireland: **www.anatsoc.org.uk**
- British Association of Clinical Anatomists: **www.liv.ac.uk/HumanAnatomy/BACA.html**
- Physiological Society: **www.physoc.org**

Anatomy and Physiology	Research quality/7	Entry standards	Student satisfaction %	Graduate prospects %	Overall rating
1 Cambridge	2.9		86	85	100.0
2 Oxford	3.8	510	70	73	98.4
3 University College London	3.0	424	78	87	97.3
=4 Loughborough	2.9	368	90	74	95.8
=4 Edinburgh	2.6	434	91	69	95.8
6 Dundee	3.2	391	81	74	94.9
7 Bristol	2.6	425	81	78	94.0
8 Manchester	3.1	418	83	63	93.3

9 Aberdeen	1.8	415	90	78	92.2
10 Leeds	2.8	383	88	63	91.8
11 Cardiff	2.6	407	79	71	90.4
12 Liverpool	2.4	400	85	65	89.5
=13 King's College London	2.8	380	77	71	89.4
=13 Newcastle	2.7	393	82	64	89.4
15 Nottingham	1.9	418	83	75	88.9
16 Sussex	2.8	364	79	67	88.0
17 Glasgow	2.6	384	78	61	86.0
18 Salford	1.7		84	69	82.5
19 Leicester		378		80	77.4
20 Bradford	1.8	256	84	59	77.3
21 Nottingham Trent	2.7	254	69	62	76.9
22 Sheffield		392	80	72	74.2
23 Queen's, Belfast		340	83	72	73.4
24 East London		281	64	100	70.1
25 Northampton		219		83	67.8
26 Ulster		285	69	82	67.1
27 Westminster		235	69	41	53.4

Employed in graduate job:	26%	Employed in non-graduate job and studying:	3%
Employed in graduate job and studying:	5%	Employed in non-graduate job:	23%
Studying:	37%	Unemployed:	5%
Average starting graduate salary:	£19,008	Average starting non-graduate salary:	£15,400

Anthropology

The relatively small numbers taking anthropology – fewer than 700 started degrees in 2008 – make for substantial swings in average performance. The subject had the highest unemployment rate in last year's *Guide*, for example, but is back down to the average of 5 per cent in this edition. Nearly a quarter of all graduates go on to take a higher degree or some form of postgraduate training and the proportion in non-graduate jobs has improved considerably.

Cambridge has resumed its accustomed place at the head of the ranking, having lost it to Oxford last year. It has the highest entry standards in the country and ties with Kent and St Andrews for the top score on student satisfaction. The London School of Economics (LSE), in third place, eclipsed both of the ancient universities in the 2008 Research Assessment Exercise, with 40 per cent of its work judged to be world-leading. The LSE also has the best employment record, but its students were the least satisfied in the table.

Anthropology tends to be the preserve of old universities, but Roehampton is the highest-placed of three new universities in this year's table. Only the top three saw more than two thirds of leavers go straight into graduate-level jobs or further study. Entry standards are high: eight of the 21 universities in the table averaged more than 400 points.

There was a small rise in applications at the beginning of 2009, continuing a positive

Anthropology cont.

trend that was interrupted in the previous year. Clearing usually accounts for a significant share of the places in anthropology. There are no subject-specific requirements at most universities.

- Royal Anthropological Institute: **www.therai.org.uk**

Anthropology	Research quality/7	Entry standards	Student satisfaction %	Graduate prospects %	Overall rating
1 Cambridge	3.6	504	88	75	100.0
2 Oxford	3.0	499	82	75	93.7
3 London School of Economics	3.9	429	66	81	90.1
4 University College London	3.3	438	81	66	89.7
5 School of Oriental and African Studies	3.6	414	76	65	88.1
6 St Andrews	3.0	438	88	54	87.6
7 Sussex	3.0	368	77	64	83.4
8 Durham	2.7	388	76	65	82.4
9 Aberdeen	3.1	321	87	46	81.5
10 Kent	2.5	328	88	54	81.0
11 Goldsmiths College	3.0	312	73	65	79.6
=12 Glasgow	2.0	411	76	63	78.9
=12 Queen's, Belfast	3.3	337	79	45	78.9
=14 Edinburgh	3.1	441	68	52	78.8
=14 Hull	2.1		81	62	78.8
16 Brunel	2.7	311	73	61	77.0
17 Roehampton	3.2	232	75	56	75.9
18 Manchester	2.7	394	70	45	73.9
19 Oxford Brookes	1.6	291	78	56	71.2
20 Lampeter	2.5	215		57	70.2
21 Liverpool John Moores	2.1	270	74		69.4

Employed in graduate job:	34%	Employed in non-graduate job and studying:	5%
Employed in graduate job and studying:	6%	Employed in non-graduate job:	29%
Studying:	22%	Unemployed:	5%
Average starting graduate salary:	£19,485	Average starting non-graduate salary:	£15,619

Archaeology

Cambridge holds on to first place in archaeology, although the indicator for entry standards is the only one in which it leads. Durham has the best record for research, with three quarters of its work rated as world-leading or internationally excellent in 2008. It is just pipped by Robert Gordon for the best graduate employment score, while three universities – Reading, York and Exeter – tie for the distinction of having the most satisfied students.

Unusually among the subject tables, the top five for archaeology remain the same as last year. Sheffield has made the most progress in the top half of the table, breaking into the top ten. Glasgow remains the top university in Scotland, Cardiff the leader in Wales, while Robert Gordon is the only new university in the top 20.

The number of universities in the ranking continues to grow by leaps and bounds – the 2005 *Guide* contained only 25 institutions, compared with this year's 45. New universities are mainly responsible, their numbers growing from three to 18 over the same period. The change has had the effect of spreading out entry scores, which now range from little more than 200 points to over 500.

Archaeology has produced consistently high levels of satisfaction. Only four universities in the ranking failed to satisfy at least two thirds of their final-year undergraduates in the results published in 2008. The subject appeared to be one of the victims of top-up fees – perhaps because of the uncertain employment prospects and relatively low salaries for those who make a career in the subject – with applications dropping for two years after the change was introduced. But there had been a recovery at the start of 2009, with almost 2,000 applications representing a 10 per cent increase. The broader category of forensic and archaeological science was also up. Unemployment six months after graduation remains higher than average, at 7 per cent, and only Celtic studies has a lower average starting salary for graduate-level jobs. At five universities, fewer than half of the graduates in the latest survey found graduate-level work or went on to further study within six month of completing their course.

- Council for British Archaeology: **www.britarch.ac.uk**
- TORC (Training Online Resource Centre for Archaeology): **www.torc.org.uk**

Archaeology	Research quality/7	Entry standards	Student satisfaction %	Graduate prospects %	Overall rating
1 Cambridge	3.4	504	88	75	100.0
2 Durham	3.9	416	86	77	98.0
3 Oxford	3.6	469	79	73	94.5
4 University College London	3.3	395	88	71	93.2
5 Reading	3.8	312	90	67	91.1
6 York	3.1	389	90	63	89.9
7 Sheffield	3.1	375	84	70	89.4
8 Exeter	2.9	363	90	57	85.6
9 Leicester	3.2	353	82	60	84.8
10 Glasgow	2.3	362	86	66	84.6
11 Queen's, Belfast	3.1	289	83	64	82.7
12 Liverpool	3.3	352	78	55	81.5
=13 Bristol	2.5	404	75	61	81.1
=13 Nottingham	2.9	339	77	61	81.1
15 Southampton	3.2	316	84	50	79.9
16 Manchester	2.7	321	78	59	79.1
17 Edinburgh	2.9	415	75	48	78.9
18 Dundee		405	86	69	77.9
19 Robert Gordon		332		78	77.7
20 Cardiff	2.6	334	79	54	77.6
21 Birmingham	2.4	367	76	55	77.0
22 Bradford	2.7	260	74	66	76.7
23 Newcastle	2.5	335	76	54	75.8

Archaeology cont.

	Research quality/7	Entry standards	Student satisfaction %	Graduate prospects %	Overall rating
24 Central Lancashire	1.3	283	81	68	75.4
25 Hull		295	88	71	74.3
26 Kent	1.2	301	77	68	73.9
27 Lampeter	2.5	268	72	58	72.4
28 Bournemouth	1.9	249	79	59	72.3
29 Nottingham Trent	1.6	248	69	68	70.0
30 West of England		268	86	64	69.9
31 Staffordshire		249	82	61	66.4
32 Lincoln		286	78	60	66.3
33 Glamorgan		297	73	64	66.1
34 Swansea		344	75	48	63.4
35 Glasgow Caledonian		316	71	53	61.9
36 Chester		238	77	55	61.7
37 Anglia Ruskin		355	58	61	61.4
38 Liverpool John Moores		241	71	60	61.3
39 Derby		227	73	58	60.6
40 Teesside		262	73	53	60.4
41 De Montfort		219	59	74	59.9
42 Winchester	1.2	204	77	36	58.5
43 Wolverhampton		206	65	59	56.8
44 Canterbury Christ Church		220	68	41	52.6
45 Kingston		218	63	44	50.9

Employed in graduate job:	37%	Employed in non-graduate job and studying:	3%
Employed in graduate job and studying:	3%	Employed in non-graduate job:	29%
Studying:	20%	Unemployed:	7%
Average starting graduate salary:	£17,065	Average starting non-graduate salary:	£14,473

Architecture

With more than six applications for every place, architecture is one of the most competitive of the major subjects. Entry grades at the leading universities reflect this, with almost a dozen averaging over 400 points. Some universities ask candidates to produce a portfolio of work if they have not taken an art or design based A level. Cambridge averages more than 500, but still does not make the top four places in this year's table.

Bath takes over from Cardiff at the head of the ranking, with the most satisfied students and good scores on the other indicators. University College London, which had the best research grades in the latest assessments, also overtakes Cardiff, as does Sheffield.

Training in architecture is a long haul – usually seven years, in which the first degree is but one step on the way – but the graduate employment rate is some compensation. Only 2 per cent are unemployed six months after graduation – a rate bettered only by medicine, dentistry and veterinary studies. Three universities – Kent, Ulster and Queen's, Belfast –

had 100 per cent success rates and only 13 out of the 43 in the ranking slipped below 90 per cent.

Strathclyde is the top university in Scotland and Ulster outperforms Queen's, Belfast, in Northern Ireland. New universities take up more than half the places in the ranking, with Sheffield Hallam the highest-placed of five in the top 20.

A third of all undergraduates enter architecture degrees with qualifications other than A level or Advanced Highers. A series of increases in applications continued at the start of 2009, when there was another rise of almost 7 per cent, making a total more than 24,000. Satisfaction rates are high at undergraduate level and beyond – three years into their careers, architects were among the least likely of all graduates to say that they wished they had taken a different degree or chosen a different profession.

This cannot be a matter of money: architecture is not far outside the bottom ten subjects for graduate starting salaries. But nine out of ten graduates still go on to complete their professional training, either with further study or within a job.

- Commission for Architecture and the Built Environment: **www.cabe.org.uk**
- Royal Institute of British Architects: **www.architecture.com**

Architecture	Research quality/7	Entry standards	Student satisfaction %	Graduate prospects %	Overall rating
1 Bath	3.4	509	87	97	100.0
2 University College London	3.9	471	83	94	97.9
3 Sheffield	3.6	484	77	96	95.8
4 Cardiff	3.0	477		97	95.1
5 Cambridge	3.8	515	80	86	94.0
6 Newcastle	3.1	467	75	97	93.4
=7 Liverpool	3.7	409	65	95	89.1
=7 Ulster	2.9	265	76	100	89.1
9 Sheffield Hallam	1.9	303	83	97	88.3
10 Edinburgh	3.4	444	69	89	88.2
11 Nottingham	2.1	444		93	87.7
=12 Strathclyde	1.8	404	70	99	86.7
=12 Northumbria	2.1	320	77	96	86.7
14 Brighton	3.6	351	66	92	86.1
15 Salford	3.2	214	74		84.5
16 West of England	2.0	322	72	96	84.4
17 De Montfort	2.8	278	67	96	84.2
18 Manchester Metropolitan	2.1	341	65	97	83.8
19 Manchester		401	75	97	82.6
20 Bolton	1.9	211	81		82.3
21 Kent		347	75	100	82.1
22 Westminster	2.9	344	69	85	81.9
23 Oxford Brookes		371	78	94	81.3
24 Dundee	1.7		70	93	81.1
25 Liverpool John Moores	2.8	272	71	86	81.0
26 Robert Gordon	1.7	349		90	80.7

	Research quality/7	Entry standards	Student satisfaction %	Graduate prospects %	Overall rating
27 Birmingham City		293	82	93	80.2
28 Plymouth	2.3	349	62	89	79.8
29 Lincoln	1.6	285	69	92	79.3
=30 Queen's, Belfast		349	66	100	79.0
=30 Nottingham Trent	1.3	330	72	88	79.0
32 Wolverhampton	2.3	190	71		78.3
33 Portsmouth	0.8	299	78	83	77.0
34 Greenwich	2.0	249	64	85	75.1
35 East London		235	68	93	73.7
36 Leeds Metropolitan		308	68	88	73.3
37 Huddersfield		270		89	72.5
38 Derby		234		91	72.2
39 UWIC, Cardiff		226	60	96	71.8
40 University for Creative Arts		219	70	88	71.7
41 London South Bank		206	64	93	71.3
42 Kingston		349	61	86	70.9
43 Southampton Solent		216	61	73	61.6

Employed in graduate job:	59%	Employed in non-graduate job and studying:	1%
Employed in graduate job and studying:	20%	Employed in non-graduate job:	4%
Studying:	14%	Unemployed:	2%
Average starting graduate salary:	£18,624	Average starting non-graduate salary:	£15,357

Art and Design

There were 215,000 applications for courses in art and design in 2008 and, with design alone showing an increase of more than 11 percent, that figure is bound to rise this year. The demand for places has continued to rise, despite employment rates and average starting salaries that are both in the bottom ten for all subjects. Artists and designers accept that they are likely to have a period of self-employment early in their career while they find a way to pursue their vocation, but two thirds of those surveyed three years after graduation said they would make the same choice again.

Only computer science had a higher unemployment rate than the 9 per cent for art and design in the latest survey. Half of all leavers went straight into graduate-level jobs, but only 7 per cent went on to take another course – one of the lowest proportions for any subject.

Most courses in art and design are at new universities – often in former art colleges – but the top 13 places in this year's ranking are all filled by older institutions. Oxford is back in first place even though little more than half of the graduates in the latest statistics were in graduate-level work or further study six months after completing a degree. Oxford's Fine Art degree is taught at the Ruskin School of Drawing, where student satisfaction is the highest in the country.

Surprisingly, both Glasgow and Edinburgh have higher entry grades than Oxford. Second-placed University College London, the leader for the last two years, shares the top research grades with Kent, Newcastle and Reading. Students at UCL attend the Slade School of Fine Art. By far the best employment rate is at Bangor where, for the second year in a row, all the leavers went straight into graduate-level jobs or further courses. Only Edge Hill came within 20 percentage points of this achievement.

Glasgow, in third place, has overtaken Edinburgh to become the top university in Scotland. Nottingham Trent is the leading new university, with Falmouth University College only three places below it. Brighton, Bournemouth and Edinburgh Napier also made the top 20. Low entry grades and research scores count against many of the new universities and colleges, although most artists would argue that these are of less significance than in other subjects.

- Design Council: **www.designcouncil.org.uk**
- National Society for Education in Art and Design: **www.nsead.org**
- Sector Skills Council for the Audio Visual and Publishing Industries: **www.skillset.org**
- Sector Skills Council for Fashion and Textiles: **www.skillfast-uk.org**

Art and Design	Research quality/7	Entry standards	Student satisfaction %	Graduate prospects %	Overall rating
1 Oxford	3.4	422	92	54	100.0
2 University College London	3.7	384		65	96.5
3 Glasgow	3.0	450	76	67	96.3
=4 Loughborough	3.5	367	81	58	93.4
=4 Brunel	1.5	374	84	75	93.4
6 Kent	3.7	301	76	72	91.9
7 Lancaster	3.6	381	73	62	91.4
8 Edinburgh	2.8	437	78	52	91.2
9 Newcastle	3.7	387	69	63	90.5
10 Bangor		262	82	100	88.5
11 Goldsmiths College	3.1	300	74	67	87.0
12 Dundee	3.3	345	76	48	85.3
13 Heriot-Watt	2.3	336	65	78	85.0
14 Nottingham Trent	1.6	323	73	73	84.3
15 Leeds	3.1	371	65	59	84.2
16 Reading	3.7	321	65	59	83.3
17 Falmouth	1.7	297	78	65	83.1
18 Brighton	3.6	272	73	55	82.6
19 Bournemouth	3.0	273	65	70	82.0
20 Edinburgh Napier	1.1	319		71	81.7
21 West of England	2.5	288	77	53	81.5
22 Northumbria	2.2	281	70	67	81.3
23 UWIC, Cardiff	2.8	288	75	51	80.9
24 Coventry	1.8	313	70	65	80.8
25 Robert Gordon	1.8	321		59	80.4
26 University of the Arts London	2.8	330	62	58	78.5

	Research quality/7	Entry standards	Student satisfaction %	Graduate prospects %	Overall rating
27 Edge Hill		243	69	91	78.2
28 Birmingham City	3.2	271	71	47	78.0
29 Norwich University College of the Arts	1.8	284	74	53	77.2
30 Manchester		354	72	62	76.6
31 Kingston	1.4	253	73	62	76.5
32 De Montfort	1.8	275	71	56	76.2
33 Ulster	2.5	238	68	57	75.3
34 Portsmouth	0.8	277	78	53	75.1
35 Teesside		261	86	51	75.0
36 Lincoln	1.1	283	74	52	74.6
37 Glamorgan		290	70	67	73.5
38 Manchester Metropolitan	2.1	262	67	53	73.4
39 Southampton	1.5	377	57	55	73.3
40 Newport	2.8	229	64	55	73.1
41 Aberystwyth		337	76	46	72.9
42 Westminster	3.3	246	67	40	72.7
43 Chester	0.2	288	77	51	72.4
44 Bath Spa	1.5	271	68	53	72.2
45 Greenwich		219	73	68	71.8
=46 Oxford Brookes	2.2	217	73	44	71.6
=46 Salford	1.4	212	73	54	71.6
48 Middlesex	1.5	220	70	55	71.5
49 Staffordshire	0.5	236	77	54	71.3
50 Central Lancashire	0.7	230	70	60	70.5
51 Wolverhampton	2.0	214	70	48	70.3
52 Plymouth	2.3	224	65	48	69.2
=53 Leeds Metropolitan	1.1	222	70	52	69.0
=53 Sunderland	1.8	191	69	52	69.0
=53 University for Creative Arts	1.5	221	65	57	69.0
=56 Sheffield Hallam	2.5	270	66	35	68.7
=56 Northampton	0.4	265	70	51	68.7
58 Buckinghamshire New	1.5	230	65	52	68.4
59 Gloucestershire	1.1	251	68	48	68.3
60 Huddersfield		272	70	53	68.2
61 Thames Valley	0.9	223	65	60	67.8
62 Southampton Solent	1.3	211	65	56	67.6
=63 Hertfordshire	2.5	238	55	54	67.4
=63 Derby	1.4	230	69	44	67.4
65 Glasgow Caledonian		345		39	67.1
66 Liverpool John Moores	1.5	217	65	50	66.8
67 Bolton	0.3	247	74	43	66.7
68 East London	2.1	162	65	50	66.0
69 Canterbury Christ Church		290	71	40	65.8

	Research quality/7	Entry standards	Student satisfaction %	Graduate prospects %	Overall rating
70 Cumbria	0.6	159	71	55	65.1
71 Anglia Ruskin	1.5	232	58	48	63.4
72 Glyndŵr	0.6	258	53	55	61.5
73 Essex		194	73	38	60.8
74 Chichester		210	71	36	59.7
75 York St John		241	59	48	59.3
76 Bedfordshire		173	58	54	56.9

Employed in graduate job:	47%	Employed in non-graduate job and studying:	3%
Employed in graduate job and studying:	3%	Employed in non-graduate job:	32%
Studying:	7%	Unemployed:	9%
Average starting graduate salary:	£17,297	Average starting non-graduate salary:	£14,059

Biological Sciences

While other science subjects have struggled to attract applicants in recent years, biological subjects have thrived. The various combinations all registered increases at the start of 2009, when the main subject of biology remained well ahead of chemistry and physics. Two thirds of all entrants arrive with A levels or their equivalent, and more than half of the undergraduates are awarded firsts or 2:1s. Well over a third go on to take postgraduate courses, either full or part-time.

Cambridge has maintained its lead over its rivals, with the best graduate employment record and some of the highest entry grades in any subject – the equivalent of four As at A level and another at AS level. Only Oxford comes close, although Manchester achieved the best grades in the 2008 Research Assessment Exercise and Ulster, in 37th place, has the most satisfied students.

Imperial College has moved up to third, while St Andrews continues to lead in Scotland and Cardiff remains well clear of the competition in Wales. The University of the West of England is the only new university in the top 30.

Entry standards have been rising: in addition to Oxford and Cambridge, where successful candidates average more than 500 points, another 12 universities average 400 or more. Like last year, only four universities have an average below 200 points, even though a relatively high proportion of the entrants (11 per cent) win places through Clearing.

Graduate employment prospects nationally are slightly below average for all subjects. Starting salaries are in the bottom 20 and are the lowest for any subject, at less than £14,000, for those who fail to find a graduate-level job.

- Biochemical Society: **www.biology4all.com**
- British Society for Cell Biology: **www.bscb.org**
- Institute of Biology: **www.iob.org**
- Society for Experimental Biology: **www.sebiology.org**

Biological Sciences	Research quality/7	Entry standards	Student satisfaction %	Graduate prospects %	Overall rating
1 Cambridge	2.9	557	86	85	100.0
2 Oxford	3.2	518	85	79	97.7

Biological Sciences cont.

	Research quality/7	Entry standards	Student satisfaction %	Graduate prospects %	Overall rating
3 Imperial College	3.0	466	78	84	92.8
4 York	3.1	449	86	69	92.6
5 Sheffield	3.2	415	85	69	91.1
6 Bristol	2.7	442	81	78	91.0
7 Surrey	3.0	343	81	84	90.5
8 Manchester	3.3	432	82	66	90.1
9 St Andrews	2.4	445	86	69	89.8
10 University College London	3.0	435	78	75	89.0
11 Leicester	2.2	383	86	72	88.0
12 Bath	2.3	428	79	78	87.6
13 Durham	2.3	475	77	75	87.4
14 Edinburgh	2.7	429	79	66	85.9
=15 Lancaster	3.0	363	81	66	85.8
=15 Sussex	2.3	363	83	70	85.8
=17 Glasgow	2.6	380	85	60	85.6
=17 Dundee	3.2	384	84	53	85.6
19 Warwick	2.3	416	80	68	85.4
20 Nottingham	2.6	359	78	74	85.3
21 Birmingham	2.3	400	82	65	85.2
=22 Cardiff	2.6	393	80	66	85.1
=22 Newcastle	2.7	368	79	69	85.1
24 East Anglia	2.3	379	84	63	85.0
25 King's College London	3.0	384	76	68	84.8
26 Southampton	2.9	382	78	65	84.4
27 Exeter	2.3	351	80	72	84.1
28 Royal Holloway	3.0	308	76	76	83.9
29 West of England	2.5	257	86	64	83.5
30 Aberdeen	2.6	314	81	66	83.2
31 Leeds	2.8	355	79	62	83.0
32 Aston	2.5	312	78	72	82.4
33 Liverpool	2.1	365	78	67	81.3
34 Nottingham Trent	2.7	213	74	84	81.0
35 Portsmouth	2.4	242	83	65	80.8
36 Kent	1.7	294	82	68	80.4
=37 Queen's, Belfast	1.6	338	80	69	80.2
=37 Ulster		265	87	84	80.2
39 Reading	1.7	333	81	64	80.0
40 Essex	1.9	278	81	69	79.9
=41 Strathclyde	2.6	345	70	67	78.1
=41 Queen Mary, London	1.9	326	78	63	78.1
43 Heriot-Watt	1.8	318	79	60	77.5
44 Keele		308	83	75	77.0
45 Robert Gordon		300		78	76.5

=46 Abertay	2.2	247		63	75.9
=46 Brunel	1.4	322	72	73	75.9
=48 Glasgow Caledonian	1.6	318	80	54	75.2
=48 Salford	1.7	207	79	66	75.2
50 Hull	1.2	277	82	57	75.0
51 Sheffield Hallam	1.2	235	77	71	74.4
52 Edinburgh Napier	1.1	264		69	73.6
53 Brighton	1.9	243	72	66	73.4
54 Teesside		233	82	73	73.2
55 Northumbria	1.5	264	71	70	73.1
56 Huddersfield	1.3	237	81	57	73.0
57 Bradford	1.8	256	77	55	72.9
58 Stirling	2.0	276	77	48	72.7
59 Plymouth	1.7	302	76	49	72.2
60 Swansea	1.2	316	73	60	71.6
=61 Bangor	1.5	278	71	62	71.0
=61 UWIC, Cardiff	1.0	255	76	61	71.0
63 Chester	0.8	249	77	62	70.9
64 Hertfordshire	1.7	244	67	70	70.6
65 Glamorgan	0.6	272	76	61	70.5
66 Liverpool John Moores	1.5	247	77	50	70.4
67 Manchester Metropolitan		252	80	63	70.3
68 Canterbury Christ Church		206	76	70	68.4
69 Kingston	1.4	207	69	64	68.1
=70 Central Lancashire		271	66	81	67.9
=70 Greenwich		201	78	65	67.9
=72 Staffordshire		197	82	56	67.8
=72 Roehampton	0.5	188	74	67	67.8
74 Edge Hill		219	76	65	67.6
75 Aberystwyth		298	81	46	67.4
76 Oxford Brookes	1.3	260	68	59	66.9
77 Bournemouth		218	77	59	66.6
78 Leeds Metropolitan		247	70	69	66.3
79 Worcester		201	78	57	65.9
80 Bath Spa	0.2	265	82	40	65.8
81 Coventry		255	76	55	65.7
82 Bolton		167	76	62	65.0
83 Wolverhampton		207	69	70	64.4
84 Sunderland		231	77	50	64.3
85 Anglia Ruskin		217	81	39	63.1
86 Westminster		215	73	55	62.6
87 East London		173	69	57	60.1
88 Derby	0.8	235	69	39	59.5

Employed in graduate job:	31%	Employed in non-graduate job and studying:	3%
Employed in graduate job and studying:	5%	Employed in non-graduate job:	25%
Studying:	30%	Unemployed:	6%
Average starting graduate salary:	£18,689	Average starting non-graduate salary:	£13,917

Building

It remains to be seen what damage the recession has done to the employment prospects of graduates with building degrees, but they were in the top ten for all subjects when the last statistics were published. Almost nine out of ten were in graduate-level jobs, leaving only 4 per cent unemployed and another 6 per cent in lower-level work. Although not quite in the top ten for starting salaries, an average of nearly £23,000 was still a good return for a subject where entry grades are comparatively modest. There were fewer than four applications to the place in 2008.

Loughborough has stretched its lead at the top of the building table, with the most satisfied students and good scores on the other indicators. Wolverhampton, in 27th place, came close to matching Loughborough's score in the National Student Survey, although Glasgow Caledonian is the leading new university and top in Scotland.

Aston is the top performer in an almost universally good set of employment scores, with all its leavers finding graduate-level work or starting another course within six months. University College London achieved the best grades in the 2008 Research Assessment Exercise, but missed second place because of comparatively low scores for student satisfaction and employment. Instead, Reading moves up to second place. Fourth-placed Nottingham has highest entry grades.

Not surprisingly since the applications season coincided with unrelenting bad news about the construction industry, the demand for places on building degrees had dropped by more than 7 per cent at the official deadline for courses beginning in 2009. But this followed some big increases in recent years and there were still 12,000 applications. The subject has been one of the best prospects for a place in Clearing and may be so again if places in other subjects are restricted. Almost half of all building students come with qualifications other than A level.

- Chartered Institute of Building: **www.ciob.org.uk**

Building	Research quality/7	Entry standards	Student satisfaction %	Graduate prospects %	Overall rating
1 Loughborough	3.5	348	85	98	100.0
2 Reading	3.4	331	77	99	95.9
3 University College London	3.9	375	76	73	91.2
4 Nottingham	2.1	376			90.5
5 Salford	3.2	262	74	93	88.6
6 Aston	2.0	305		100	87.7
7 Glasgow Caledonian	2.7	333	71	88	87.0
8 Ulster	2.9	283	67	96	86.4
9 Northumbria	2.1	284	77	90	85.2
10 Heriot-Watt	2.5	326	68	89	85.1
11 West of England	2.0	282	77	91	84.5
12 Edinburgh Napier	1.7	283		95	82.6
13 Plymouth	2.3	259	71	88	81.2
14 Robert Gordon	1.7	309		88	81.0
15 Glamorgan	2.3	222		93	80.8

16 Brighton	1.7	278	68	92	79.9
17 Liverpool John Moores	2.8	243	66	84	79.7
18 Sheffield Hallam	1.9	266	65	92	79.4
19 Nottingham Trent	1.3	257	69	96	79.1
20 Westminster	2.9	256	61	84	78.7
21 Bolton	1.9	198	81	81	77.9
22 Greenwich	2.0	204	67	87	75.6
23 Central Lancashire	1.8	220	66	86	74.7
24 Birmingham City		229	77	94	74.5
25 Anglia Ruskin		334	59	94	72.7
26 Coventry		285		88	72.5
27 Wolverhampton	2.3	165	84	61	72.2
28 Kingston		275	67	91	71.6
29 Oxford Brookes		246	76	84	71.3
30 Leeds Metropolitan		266	60	92	69.0
31 London South Bank		187	61	88	63.8
32 Southampton Solent		134	60	73	55.6

Employed in graduate job:	75%	Employed in non-graduate job and studying:	1%
Employed in graduate job and studying:	12%	Employed in non-graduate job:	6%
Studying:	3%	Unemployed:	4%
Average starting graduate salary:	£22,941	Average starting non-graduate salary:	£19,484

Business Studies

Taken together, the various branches of business and management represent by far the most popular area of higher education. Even without the many dual or combined honours degrees that are common for both of the main areas, there were nearly 95,000 applications by the official deadline for courses beginning in 2009. That represented a modest increase on the previous year for management and more than 5 per cent growth in business studies. The subjects are the biggest recruiters in many of the new universities, although some of the most famous business schools are absent from this ranking because they do not offer undergraduate courses.

Oxford has regained first place from Cambridge this year, with by far the highest entry standards and nearly the best employment score. Neither Cambridge's Judge School of Management, nor Oxford's Said Business School qualify for the table, which assesses the universities on courses offered by other colleges. Third-placed Imperial produced the best research score in the 2008 assessments, while Exeter, in fifth place, has much the most satisfied students.

The London School of Economics is the top performer in a surprisingly varied set of employment scores. Its record of 95 per cent graduate-level employment or further study contrasts with 36 per cent at London South Bank and only 26 per cent at Bolton.

Overall, the subjects are in the bottom half of the employment table, even though more than half of those completing courses go straight into graduate-level jobs.

However, those who do find graduate-level work enjoy average starting salaries of more than £21,000 that are only just outside the top 20 for all subjects.

Business Studies cont.

St Andrews has maintained its position as the top university in Scotland, while Cardiff remains the clear the leader in Wales. More than half of the institutions in one of the biggest tables in the *Guide* are new universities, of which Robert Gordon is the highest-placed, just outside the top 30. Bournemouth and Brighton are also in the top 40.

About 10 per cent of those securing places in business and management do so through Clearing. Entrance qualifications vary widely, with 18 universities averaging more than 400 points and 11 less than 200. Satisfaction levels have been improving in the last National Student Survey, but few are in the top range displayed in the top subjects on this measure.

- Chartered Management Institute: **www.managers.org.uk**
- Confederation of British Industry: **www.cbi.org.uk**
- Institute of Management Consultancy: **www.imc.co.uk**

Business Studies	Research quality/7	Entry standards	Student satisfaction %	Graduate prospects %	Overall rating
1 Oxford	3.6	530	83	94	100.0
2 Cambridge	3.9			90	99.2
3 Imperial College	4.1	448		74	94.9
4 Bath	3.6	459	81	89	94.7
5 Exeter	2.7	401	92	81	93.7
6 London School of Economics	3.6	470	75	95	93.2
7 Loughborough	2.8	392	88	84	92.2
8 Warwick	3.5	450	79	82	91.3
9 St Andrews	2.6	430	84	82	89.9
10 Lancaster	3.5	415	80	72	88.4
11 Aston	2.8	405	83	76	88.1
12 Strathclyde	3.3	417	81	70	87.7
13 King's College London	3.6	421	71	85	86.8
14 City	2.6	394	81	79	86.5
15 Nottingham	3.2	407	74	79	85.5
16 Leicester	2.6	316	87	72	84.8
=17 Manchester	3.3	418	72	73	83.6
=17 Cardiff	3.8	383	76	62	83.6
19 Durham	2.7	367	76	79	83.2
20 Southampton	2.6	402	74	80	83.1
21 Leeds	3.2	410	71	71	82.2
22 Birmingham	2.8	411	75	66	82.0
23 Kent	2.4	302	81	77	81.8
24 Sussex	2.6	362	78	71	81.6
25 Sheffield	2.8	365	76	71	81.4
26 Newcastle	2.3	391	72	81	81.2
27 East Anglia	2.2	331	82	70	81.1
28 Glasgow	2.4	392	80	60	80.9
=29 Queen's, Belfast	2.7	330	79	63	79.1
=29 Reading	2.3	347	78	67	79.1

31 Robert Gordon	1.7	318		78	78.2
32 Hull	2.0	259	83	70	78.1
33 Surrey	2.3	347	71	76	77.4
=34 Edinburgh	2.3	441	69	65	77.3
=34 Royal Holloway	2.7	377	66	76	77.3
36 Heriot-Watt	2.2	345	72	73	77.1
37 Bournemouth	1.5	312	78	74	76.9
38 Keele	2.1	291	74	76	76.7
39 Brighton	2.4	262	76	72	76.4
40 Aberdeen	2.0	337	75	68	76.3
41 Oxford Brookes	1.4	311	80	68	76.0
42 Queen Mary, London	2.6	331	72	65	75.9
43 Swansea	2.1	294	75	69	75.4
44 York	2.3	338	69	72	75.3
=45 Bangor	2.9	264	70	71	74.8
=45 Stirling	2.0	275	75	72	74.8
=47 Nottingham Trent	1.6	269	73	81	74.4
=47 Liverpool	2.3	359	71	62	74.4
49 Northumbria	1.1	304	76	77	74.3
50 De Montfort	1.9	228	83	58	73.8
51 Portsmouth	1.6	258	78	68	73.7
52 University College London		396	73	80	73.4
53 Sheffield Hallam	1.4	271	78	63	72.3
54 West of England	1.5	267	75	67	71.9
55 Edinburgh Napier	0.9	286		75	71.7
=56 Central Lancashire	1.5	250	76	67	71.5
=56 Glamorgan	1.2	281	82	53	71.5
58 Lincoln	1.0	255	79	65	71.2
59 Plymouth	1.6	259	76	60	70.6
60 Brunel	2.1	306	68	61	70.4
61 Salford	2.1	261	72	59	70.3
62 Bradford	2.4	231	73	57	70.1
63 Aberystwyth	1.5	290	79	47	69.8
64 Dundee		359	74	68	69.5
65 Ulster	1.8	250	78	49	69.2
66 Kingston	2.2	214	76	52	69.1
67 Manchester Metropolitan	1.7	256	71	62	68.5
68 Essex	2.5	301	66	54	68.4
69 Harper Adams		286		70	68.3
70 Bath Spa		245	84	58	68.0
=71 Northampton	1.0	208	79	56	67.3
=71 Chichester		203	87	53	67.3
=71 Teesside	1.3	214	79	51	67.3
74 Coventry	1.0	283	75	53	67.2
75 Staffordshire	1.5	219	73	60	67.1
76 Hertfordshire	1.7	235	70	57	66.2
77 Glasgow Caledonian	1.3	309	71	49	66.0

Business Studies cont.	Research quality/7	Entry standards	Student satisfaction %	Graduate prospects %	Overall rating
78 York St John		332	74	54	65.2
79 Gloucestershire	0.7	235	71	65	65.0
80 Winchester		230	79	58	64.8
=81 Huddersfield	1.4	260	73	42	64.2
=81 Bedfordshire	0.9	159	81	47	64.2
83 Worcester		221	76	62	64.1
84 St Mary's College		205	80	55	63.7
85 Westminster	1.5	232	70	48	63.4
86 Birmingham City	1.2	218	71	52	63.2
=87 Liverpool John Moores	0.6	230	72	57	62.7
=87 Edge Hill		227	81	43	62.7
89 Greenwich	1.2	177	73	51	62.5
90 Sunderland		227	76	54	62.4
91 Leeds Metropolitan	1.1	261	64	58	62.0
92 Southampton Solent		187	74	60	61.4
93 Royal Agricultural College		248	70	59	61.1
94 Cumbria		218	71	59	60.7
95 Abertay	0.8	277		43	60.6
96 Canterbury Christ Church		195	78	47	60.5
97 Chester		235	66	67	60.3
98 Glynd r		231		55	60.0
99 London South Bank	1.1	142	77	36	59.5
100 UWIC, Cardiff	0.6	245	67	51	59.4
101 Middlesex	1.6	160	67	44	58.6
102 Roehampton		198	70	56	58.4
103 Queen Margaret Edinburgh	0.4	279		41	58.1
104 Derby		227	70	48	57.9
105 Buckinghamshire New	1.0	196	67	46	57.8
106 Wolverhampton	1.2	178	66	48	57.5
107 Anglia Ruskin		234	67	51	56.8
108 East London		161	70	43	53.9
109 Bolton	0.6	193	65	26	50.6
110 University of the Arts London		250	56	44	50.1

Employed in graduate job:	49%	Employed in non-graduate job and studying:	3%
Employed in graduate job and studying:	7%	Employed in non-graduate job:	29%
Studying:	7%	Unemployed:	6%
Average starting graduate salary:	£21,081	Average starting non-graduate salary:	£16,172

Celtic Studies

There were only 553 applications for places on Celtic studies degrees in 2008, but the chances of success were still close to the average for all subjects. Most of the 131 students who took up places had good A levels, or equivalent qualifications. Only one of the nine universities in the table averaged less than 300 points and Cambridge's average was close to 500 points.

Cambridge has reclaimed the lead it lost last year to Aberystwyth, when there were not enough students to compile scores for some of the measures used in the ranking. As well as boasting by far the highest entry grades, Cambridge produced extremely good results in the 2008 Research Assessment Exercise, when almost half of its submission was judged to be world-leading.

Second-placed Aberystwyth tied with Cambridge for the highest levels of satisfaction, but only one university satisfied fewer than 80 per cent of its students. Ironically, that was Ulster, which also had the lowest entry grades, but again produced the top employment score. That achievement enabled Ulster to overhaul neighbouring Queen's, Belfast. Glasgow is the only Scottish university in the ranking.

The small numbers play havoc with the employment data. Celtic studies appears in this year's top 20 for graduate employment, with nearly half of the leavers going on to take postgraduate courses. Only 4 per cent are unemployed, although 20 per cent start their career in lower-level employment. However, Celtic Studies remains rock bottom of the earnings league with average starting salaries of only £16,600 in graduate jobs. There were not enough graduates in lower-level jobs to compile a reliable average.

- Intute Celtic Studies portal: **www.intute.ac.uk/artsandhumanities/celtic**

Celtic Studies	Research quality/7	Entry standards	Student satisfaction %	Graduate prospects %	Overall rating
1 Cambridge	4.3	494	88		100.0
2 Aberystwyth	3.2	361	88	80	84.4
3 Cardiff	2.6	372	80	87	81.2
4 Glasgow	2.5		86	79	80.4
5 Bangor	2.4	356	83	80	78.9
6 Swansea	3.1	305	82	68	75.5
7 Ulster	3.9	274	56	89	73.6
8 Queen's, Belfast	1.7	341	80	69	71.0
9 Liverpool	2.4	325	80	48	67.6

Employed in graduate job:	31%	Employed in non-graduate job and studying:	2%
Employed in graduate job and studying:	3%	Employed in non-graduate job:	20%
Studying:	42%	Unemployed:	4%
Average starting graduate salary:	£16,604	Average starting non-graduate salary:	*

Chemical Engineering

Cambridge tops the chemical engineering table for the eighth year in a row, with much the highest entry standards and one of the two top research scores. Second-placed Imperial College London matched Cambridge's rating for research, both universities having 30 per cent of their work rated as world-leading.

Chemical Engineering cont.

The most satisfied students were at Aston, only four places off the bottom of the table, while Surrey was again the only university to see all its chemical engineers go straight into graduate-level work or further study. All but five of the 20 universities in the table registered "positive destinations" for at least 80 per cent of those graduating.

Edinburgh has overtaken Heriot-Watt to become the highest-placed Scottish institution, while Swansea is the only representative of Wales. London South Bank is the only new university left in the ranking.

Chemical engineering is one of the smaller branches of engineering, but an 18 per cent surge in applications at the start of 2009 took the total to more than 8,500, including process and energy engineering. The appeal of the subject has been growing for several years and there were more than five applications for every place in 2008 – the highest ratio for any branch of engineering.

The fact that only medicine and dentistry enjoy higher average starting salaries may have something to do with it. Chemical engineers in graduate jobs six months into their career averaged more than £26,300. Almost 70 per cent of students go straight into graduate jobs, although the 6 per cent unemployment rate is just average for all subjects.

Four out of five students have A levels or equivalent qualifications, and average entry grades are the highest for any engineering subject. This helps produce engineering's largest proportion of firsts and 2:1s. Most courses offer industrial placements in the final year and leading to Chartered Engineer status.

- Institution of Chemical Engineers: **http://cms.icheme.org**
- Royal Society of Chemistry: **www.rsc.org**

Chemical Engineering	Research quality/7	Entry standards	Student satisfaction %	Graduate prospects %	Overall rating
1 Cambridge	3.9	541	85	97	100.0
2 Imperial College	3.9	482	82	87	93.8
3 Manchester	3.7	460	75	87	89.3
4 Surrey	3.1	316	80	100	88.5
5 Leeds	3.4	358	80	88	87.4
6 Newcastle	2.6	400	78	97	87.1
7 Loughborough	3.2	393	85	79	86.8
8 Sheffield	2.7	400	79	94	86.6
9 Nottingham	3.5	363	72	86	83.7
10 Birmingham	3.1	410	73	83	83.0
11 Edinburgh	2.7	421	75	84	82.8
12 Heriot-Watt	2.8	380	77	83	82.5
=13 Strathclyde	1.8	392	78	89	81.0
=13 Queen's, Belfast	2.1	356	76	91	81.0
15 University College London	3.1	376	74	77	80.4
16 Bath	2.5	430	75	77	80.3
17 Aston	2.0	294	87	80	80.1
18 Aberdeen	2.8	397	70		79.3

19 Swansea	3.2	272	74	75	77.2
20 London South Bank	2.4	163	64	69	64.1

Employed in graduate job:	63%	Employed in non-graduate job and studying:	1%
Employed in graduate job and studying:	6%	Employed in non-graduate job:	8%
Studying:	16%	Unemployed:	6%
Average starting graduate salary:	£26,366	Average starting non-graduate salary:	£16,553

Chemistry

The number of universities in the chemistry ranking dipped below 50 for the first time following a much-publicised series of closures last year and is down again this year. Applications were down slightly at the start of 2009, but the decline followed a succession of increases that took the total over 20,000 for the first time for many years. Forensic science has become an attractive alternative to the pure subject but, for many, chemistry remains the classic science. There are now five applications for every place.

Cambridge remains well clear of Oxford at the top of the table, with the highest entry standards and the best research grades. Both universities had average entry scores of more than four As at A level, and 40 per cent of Cambridge's research was rated world-leading. St Andrews has moved up to third from outside the top ten with high scores on every measure.

Keele and Surrey – neither university in the top 20 – have the best employment records. But there were good scores throughout the ranking. Chemistry is in the top 20 subjects for employment, with more than half of all graduates continuing their studies, either full or part-time. Loughborough – only just in the top 20 – has the most satisfied students and is the only university to reach a satisfaction level of 90 per cent.

Chemistry is old university territory, with Nottingham Trent the only former polytechnic in the top 30. Plymouth is not far behind but only eight of the 46 institutions in the table are from that part of the sector.

Almost nine out of ten undergraduates have A levels or their equivalent, but entry requirements are not far above the average for all subjects. Starting salaries are just below average for all subjects, at £19,800.

- European Association for Chemical and Molecular Sciences: **www.euchems.org**
- Royal Society of Chemistry: **www.rsc.org**
- Society of Dyers and Colourists: **www.sdc.org.uk**

Chemistry	Research quality/7	Entry standards	Student satisfaction %	Graduate prospects %	Overall rating
1 Cambridge	4.2	559	86	85	100.0
2 Oxford	3.7	544	85	88	98.1
3 St Andrews	3.6	444	85	89	95.6
4 Durham	3.1	508	87	83	94.7
5 York	3.1	413	89	82	93.2
6 Sheffield	3.0	406	86	87	92.3
7 Bristol	3.5	436	83	83	91.9

Chemistry cont.

	Research quality/7	Entry standards	Student satisfaction %	Graduate prospects %	Overall rating
8 Southampton	2.6	402	89	85	91.7
9 Imperial College	3.3	465	77	88	90.2
10 Glasgow	2.8	393	82	89	89.5
11 Warwick	3.1	426	81	82	89.3
12 Strathclyde	2.8	397	84	82	88.7
13 Nottingham	3.9	370	79	78	88.4
14 Liverpool	3.2	358	80	88	88.0
15 Sussex	2.4	411	81	87	87.2
16 Aberdeen	2.0	348	83	92	87.1
=17 Leeds	3.2	390	77	84	86.9
=17 Bath	2.4	403	81	85	86.9
=19 Loughborough	1.5	315	90	87	86.7
=19 University College London	2.9	425	80	78	86.7
21 Surrey	3.0	301	77	94	85.9
22 Leicester	2.0	343	85	83	85.8
23 Nottingham Trent	2.7	218	83	91	85.7
24 Cardiff	2.6	363	79	84	85.1
=25 Edinburgh	3.6	448	75	70	85.0
=25 Hull	2.2	238	87	85	85.0
27 Manchester	3.1	412	76	76	84.5
28 Heriot-Watt	2.4	339	80	83	84.3
29 East Anglia	2.3	357	83	68	82.0
30 Queen's, Belfast	2.1	339	81	77	81.9
31 Birmingham	2.6	365	75	80	81.8
32 Bradford	2.6	245	74	87	79.7
33 Newcastle	2.1	324	77	75	79.0
34 Plymouth	1.7	235	77	88	78.8
35 Queen Mary, London	2.1	284	80	72	78.7
36 Bangor	2.2	258	79	70	77.5
37 Keele		284	80	94	77.4
38 Reading	1.4	307	77	79	77.1
39 Northumbria	1.5	279	78	73	75.9
40 Sheffield Hallam	1.2	194	76	80	73.1
41 Huddersfield	1.3	209	78	65	70.6
42 Aston	2.0	283		54	70.1
43 Brighton	1.9	213	71	61	68.2
44 Manchester Metropolitan	1.3	203	76	58	67.8
45 Liverpool John Moores		221	73	74	66.7
46 Abertay		254		60	64.1

Employed in graduate job:	34%	Employed in non-graduate job and studying:	2%
Employed in graduate job and studying:	7%	Employed in non-graduate job:	13%
Studying:	39%	Unemployed:	6%
Average starting graduate salary:	£19,799	Average starting non-graduate salary:	£15,121

Civil Engineering

Civil engineering is in the top ten subjects both for employment levels and graduate starting salaries. Only 2 per cent of graduates were unemployed in the last survey, with another 5 per cent in non-graduate jobs. Those in graduate-level employment were paid average starting salaries of more than £23,000. Four universities – Nottingham Trent, Bradford, Wolverhampton and Liverpool John Moores – achieved full employment at graduate level, but none reaches this year's top 20.

Cambridge has stretched its lead in civil engineering after two years at the top. The university enjoys a predictably enormous lead over the rest on entry standards and has the top research grades. Imperial College London has moved up to second place with high scores across the board, as one-time leader Cardiff has slipped down the table.

Kingston, just outside the top 30, ties with Cambridge for the highest satisfaction levels, but Nottingham Trent is the top-placed new university. Dundee is the year's top university in Scotland.

Entry scores have been rising, with only two universities averaging less than 200 points this year. Almost a dozen average more than 400 points, although only four out of ten undergraduates are admitted with A levels or equivalent qualifications. Applications were up by nearly 10 per cent at the start of 2009, the latest in a series of increases stretching back several years. There were five applications for every place in the previous year.

Some of the top courses in civil engineering are four-year courses leading to an MEng degree; others are sandwich courses incorporating a period at work. The leading departments will expect physics and maths A levels, or their equivalent.

- Engineering and Technology Board: **www.etechb.co.uk**
- Institute of Civil Engineers: **www.ice.org.uk**
- Institution of Structural Engineers: **www.istructe.org**

Civil Engineering	Research quality/7	Entry standards	Student satisfaction %	Graduate prospects %	Overall rating
1 Cambridge	4.6	564	85	94	100.0
2 Imperial College	4.5	477	73	97	92.7
3 Sheffield	3.5	432	82	98	92.6
4 Bristol	3.6	461	81	95	92.4
5 Cardiff	3.8	425	82	91	91.0
6 Loughborough	2.8	381	87	96	90.9
7 Dundee	3.3	409	82	96	90.6
8 Bath	3.4	434	82	92	90.3
9 Southampton	3.6	431	78	94	90.0
10 Nottingham	3.7	375	81	91	88.9
11 Swansea	4.3	320	78	94	88.7
12 Queen's, Belfast	3.3	377	77	99	88.4
13 Manchester	3.2	414	79	92	87.9
14 Newcastle	3.6	355	79	93	87.7
15 Surrey	3.1	343	79	96	87.0
16 Edinburgh	2.7	417	76	96	86.8

Civil Engineering cont.	Research quality/7	Entry standards	Student satisfaction %	Graduate prospects %	Overall rating
17 University College London	2.7	432	80	90	86.4
18 Birmingham	2.7	372	74	93	83.5
19 Leeds	2.5	354	76	90	81.9
20 Liverpool	2.8	364	73	89	81.3
21 Nottingham Trent	1.3	234	82	100	80.9
22 City	2.2	293	73	97	80.5
23 Heriot-Watt	2.2	349	77	86	80.1
24 Aberdeen	2.8	369	70	86	79.3
25 Bradford	2.2	269	69	100	79.2
=26 Portsmouth		273	81	98	77.5
=26 Glasgow	2.5	387	67	86	77.5
=28 Strathclyde	1.7	395	63	94	76.4
=28 Wolverhampton	2.3	192	67	100	76.4
30 Plymouth	2.4	250	76	83	76.3
=31 Northumbria	2.1	275	68	91	75.2
=31 Kingston	1.4	176	85	84	75.2
33 Salford	3.2	223	71	78	74.0
34 Liverpool John Moores		297	70	100	73.9
35 Brighton	1.7	283	69		72.4
36 Greenwich	1.6	200	75		72.1
37 Ulster		239	72	96	71.7
38 Glamorgan	2.3	210	62	89	70.9
39 Coventry	1.0	274	75	73	68.9
40 Edinburgh Napier	1.6	245		79	68.8
41 Abertay		261		83	67.1
42 Leeds Metropolitan		201	68	82	63.9
43 Teesside		260	77	65	63.6

Employed in graduate job:	71%	Employed in non-graduate job and studying:	0%
Employed in graduate job and studying:	13%	Employed in non-graduate job:	5%
Studying:	7%	Unemployed:	2%
Average starting graduate salary:	£23,387	Average starting non-graduate salary:	£15,444

Classics and Ancient History

Oxford and Cambridge have been locked together at the top of the classics table since it was first published six years ago, when their scores were identical. Cambridge maintains a slim lead in the latest ranking with the best scores in the table for both graduate prospects and research quality. Oxford has the highest entry standards at any university, although still within three points of Cambridge.

The most satisfied students in a subject of generally high satisfaction levels are at seventh-placed Exeter, as they were last year. St Andrews, the clear leader in Scotland, has moved up four places to third. There are now no new universities left in the ranking.

Several universities teach the subjects as part of a modular degree scheme, but not as a degree in its own right. A-level grades in classics are among the highest for any group of subjects – no university averages less than 300 points in this year's table. But most universities offering classics teach the subject from scratch, as well as to more practised students.

The subjects' reputation for attracting analytical high-fliers helps in the jobs market, but relatively few (35 per cent) go directly into graduate jobs. The 4 per cent unemployment rate six months after graduation is below average for all subjects, but the proportion in non-graduate work is relatively high. The subjects have slipped down the salaries table since the last edition of the *Guide*. The average starting salary of less than £19,500 is £500 below last year's figure. A 10 per cent rise in applications at the start of 2009 almost compensated for a big drop in the previous year. There are more than five applications for every place.

- Classical Association: **www.classicalassociation.org**
- Society for the Promotion of Roman Studies: **www.romansociety.org**

Classics and Ancient History	Research quality/7	Entry standards	Student satisfaction %	Graduate prospects %	Overall rating
1 Cambridge	4.2	518	87	84	100.0
2 Oxford	4.0	521	89	79	98.7
3 St Andrews	2.8	479	85	82	91.9
4 King's College London	3.4	413	86	70	88.6
5 University College London	3.5	459	77	77	88.2
6 Durham	3.3	461	78	77	87.9
7 Exeter	3.3	395	90	61	87.4
8 Bristol	2.9	439	70	81	82.5
9 Warwick	3.3	430	77	57	81.9
10 Glasgow	1.7	422	85	54	79.0
11 Birmingham	2.7	359	83	48	77.8
12 Edinburgh	2.2	441	71	65	77.2
13 Royal Holloway	1.9	351	82	59	76.6
14 Nottingham	2.4	387	78	53	76.3
15 Leeds	1.6	354	80	64	75.7
16 Manchester	3.0	399	72	49	75.2
17 Reading	2.3	320	82	50	74.2
18 Newcastle	2.2	398	71	57	73.6
19 Liverpool	2.3	348	83	36	72.8
=20 Swansea	1.5	311	81	47	69.7
=20 Lampeter	1.2		74	59	69.7
22 Kent	1.2	305	79	49	67.9

Employed in graduate job:	30%	Employed in non-graduate job and studying:	5%
Employed in graduate job and studying:	5%	Employed in non-graduate job:	27%
Studying:	29%	Unemployed:	4%
Average starting graduate salary:	£19,422	Average starting non-graduate salary:	£16,078

Communication and Media Studies

Controversy has raged over the currency in the employment market of the subjects in this ranking, but nothing has dampened students' enthusiasm for them. Media studies saw another increase in applications of almost 10 per cent at the start of 2009, while the growth in journalism was 24 per cent. Together, they attracted almost as many applications as mathematics.

The division of jobs into graduate and non-graduate fields of employment hits communication and media studies harder than any other group of subjects. Only three sets of subjects has a lower proportion of "positive destinations". Academics in the field argue that it is normal for students completing media courses to take "entry level" work that is not classified as a graduate job. Nevertheless, the unemployment rate is above average and the subjects are in the bottom six for graduate starting salaries.

Communication and media studies are mainly the preserve of the new universities, but older universities have been moving in and now fill the top 14 places in a table that contains five more institutions than last year. Warwick has taken over at the top after an outstanding performance in the 2008 Research Assessment Exercise. The university, which also has the highest entry standards, achieved one of the highest grades in any subject for its film and television studies. Westminster matched Warwick's 60 per cent of world-leading research in media studies, but was restricted to 18th place by low scores for student satisfaction and graduate employment.

Sheffield, last year's leader, takes second place with the most satisfied students and by far the best record in the graduate jobs market. Almost 40 of the 88 institutions in the table saw fewer than half of their leavers find graduate-level jobs or continue their studies within six months of graduation. However, the latest survey did not repeat the low employment levels reported in last year's *Guide*, when only a quarter of the graduates at three universities had "positive destinations".

Nottingham Trent is the highest-placed new university this year, in 15th place, just ahead of Central Lancashire. Third-placed Cardiff remains the top university in Wales, while Strathclyde has taken over from Stirling as the leader in Scotland. Only four universities average more than 400 points at entry, while four average less than 200 points.

- Broadcast Journalism Training Council: **www.bjtc.org.uk**
- Chartered Institute of Journalists: **www.cioj.co.uk**
- National Union of Journalists: **www.nuj.org.uk**
- Sector Skills Council for the Audio Visual and Publishing Industries: **www.skillset.org**

Communication and Media Studies	Research quality/7	Entry standards	Student satisfaction %	Graduate prospects %	Overall rating
1 Warwick	5.2	430	85	58	100.0
2 Sheffield	2.0	404	87	81	96.0
3 Cardiff	4.3	391	78	67	93.5
4 Loughborough	2.7	374	82	69	90.7
5 Queen Mary, London	3.3	337	75	75	88.9

6 Leeds	2.6	374	74	72	87.3
7 Leicester	3.8	312		64	87.1
8 Goldsmiths College	4.4	349	71	61	86.4
9 Bournemouth	2.5	355	73	74	86.2
10 East Anglia	4.8	339	78	42	85.3
11 Strathclyde		401		68	84.5
12 Southampton	3.2	398		45	84.0
13 Lancaster	3.5	339	82	43	83.3
14 Brunel	2.1	303	76	74	83.1
15 Nottingham Trent	3.3	307	72	66	82.9
16 Royal Holloway	3.3	368	71	56	82.8
17 Central Lancashire	2.0	316	71	76	81.9
=18 Stirling	2.8	302		60	80.9
=18 Westminster	5.2	338	66	44	80.9
20 Sussex	3.1	353	71	52	80.1
21 Birmingham City	3.2	311	71	57	79.4
22 Lincoln	3.0	283	77	51	78.8
23 Liverpool		387	80	54	77.5
24 Manchester		410		49	76.8
25 Surrey	1.6	321	68	67	76.6
=26 Keele		309	75	74	76.5
=26 Glasgow Caledonian	1.9	351	74	48	76.5
28 Roehampton	1.9	262	82	50	76.0
29 De Montfort	3.1	250	77	47	75.9
30 Robert Gordon		321		63	75.4
31 Nottingham	1.9			57	74.7
32 Birmingham		363	76	53	74.2
33 Sunderland	2.9	240	77	46	74.1
=34 Portsmouth	1.8	292	79	43	73.9
=34 Edinburgh Napier		301		63	73.9
36 West of England	2.8	269	76	40	73.5
37 King's College London		403	71	50	73.3
=38 Hertfordshire	1.7	244	74	59	73.2
=38 Hull	2.4	266	75	45	73.2
=40 Staffordshire	1.3	250	78	54	73.0
=40 Salford	2.5	300	63	57	73.0
42 Queen Margaret Edinburgh	2.2	297		46	72.5
43 Derby	2.7	233		52	71.8
44 Oxford Brookes		321	78	47	71.3
45 Brighton	1.7	307	68	49	71.2
=46 Swansea	1.7	262	77	44	71.1
=46 Northumbria	2.2	299	68	46	71.1
48 Ulster	2.9	267	69	43	70.7
49 Lampeter	0.9	265		59	69.9
50 Wolverhampton	1.1	204	81	49	69.5
51 Plymouth	1.7	273			69.0
52 Bath Spa	1.3	261	74	45	68.9

Communication and Media Studies cont.

	Research quality/7	Entry standards	Student satisfaction %	Graduate prospects %	Overall rating
53 Sheffield Hallam	2.0	268	65	52	68.8
54 Middlesex	1.6	226	67	59	68.6
55 Leeds Metropolitan	2.6	261	62	51	68.4
=56 Kingston	1.2	260	68	55	68.3
=56 Coventry	2.2	270	60	55	68.3
58 City		315	64	63	68.2
=59 Greenwich	0.8	240	79	42	67.6
=59 Aberystwyth		250	76	53	67.6
=61 Liverpool John Moores		276	73	52	67.4
=61 Bedfordshire	2.4	188	81	31	67.4
=63 St Mary's College		239	79	48	67.1
=63 Anglia Ruskin		257	82	40	67.1
65 Winchester	1.8	252	77	30	67.0
66 Chichester		235	85	36	66.2
67 Southampton Solent		249	69	58	65.7
68 Worcester		243	76	48	65.6
69 University of the Arts London		297	62	60	65.4
=70 Falmouth		265	66	60	65.3
=70 East London	3.4	192	65	40	65.3
72 Manchester Metropolitan	1.7	211	67	50	65.2
73 Queen's, Belfast		324	66	45	64.7
74 York St John		270	78	33	64.0
75 Glamorgan	1.8	267	62	40	63.3
76 Canterbury Christ Church		211	76	45	63.2
=77 London South Bank	2.3	195	63	45	62.6
=77 Edge Hill		262	74	37	62.6
79 Gloucestershire	0.2	260	64	51	62.1
80 Bradford	1.0	244			61.7
81 Chester		245	62	53	60.5
82 UWIC, Cardiff		229	73	35	59.7
83 Teesside		220	77	30	59.6
84 Thames Valley	0.9	182	66	46	59.4
85 Essex		234	61	51	59.0
86 Northampton		218	71	34	57.5
=87 Buckinghamshire New		203	64	46	57.2
=87 Huddersfield	0.2	284	58	39	57.2

Employed in graduate job:	45%	Employed in non-graduate job and studying:	3%
Employed in graduate job and studying:	2%	Employed in non-graduate job:	36%
Studying:	6%	Unemployed:	7%
Average starting graduate salary:	£17,549	Average starting non-graduate salary:	£14,474

Computer Science

Computer science, once seen as the guarantee of a lucrative career, has the highest unemployment rate of any subject in this year's *Guide*, at 10 per cent. However, it is not all bad news in the computing world: the subject is still among the top 20 for graduate salaries and nearly 60 per cent of those completing degrees do go straight into graduate-level jobs.

Eight universities have joined the ranking this year and applications for degree places were up by more than 8 per cent at the start of 2009 – the best figure since a prolonged decline set in early in this decade. With nearly 40,000 applications, computer science remains among the 20 most popular degree choices.

Cambridge remains well clear of Oxford at the top of the table, with the best research grades and by far the highest entry scores. Cambridge's computer scientists average nearly five As at A level, one of the highest scores in any subject, while 45 per cent of the university's research was considered world-leading in the 2008 assessments.

Third-placed Imperial College London has the best employment record, with an impressive 97 per cent of graduates in graduate-level jobs or further study six months after completing a degree. Greenwich, in 57th place, had the most satisfied undergraduates in the 2008 National Student Survey, with Loughborough and Royal Holloway close behind. Three years after graduation, more than a quarter of computing students said they would be "very likely" to choose a different course if they had their time again – the second-highest total among 19 groups of subjects.

Glasgow's leap of six places up the table has taken it ahead of Edinburgh to become the top Scottish university. With St Andrews also performing strongly, three of the top seven universities are now in Scotland. Cardiff remains the leader in Wales. Only three new universities, headed by Robert Gordon, feature in the top 50. The others are Glyndŵr, on its debut as a university, and Plymouth.

Entry standards are spread more widely than in any other subject, average scores on the UCAS tariff ranging from nearly 600 points to only 125, the equivalent of two Es at A level. A dozen universities average more than 400 points, while 21 have an average of less than 200.

- British Computer Society: **www.bcs.org**

Computer Science	Research quality/7	Entry standards	Student satisfaction %	Graduate prospects %	Overall rating
1 Cambridge	4.6	591	82	93	100.0
2 Oxford	4.0	510		88	96.0
3 Imperial College	4.1	467	82	97	95.4
4 Southampton	4.1	405	84	82	90.8
5 Glasgow	3.8	369	85	85	90.0
6 Edinburgh	4.1	441	78	86	89.9
7 St Andrews	2.8	443		89	88.1
8 Royal Holloway	3.2	292	87	89	87.4
9 Warwick	2.9	464	83	78	87.1
10 York	3.5	430	76	89	86.8
=11 Bath	3.5	412	79	79	85.5
=11 Bristol	3.6	448	74	84	85.5

Computer Science cont.	Research quality/7	Entry standards	Student satisfaction %	Graduate prospects %	Overall rating
13 Loughborough	2.6	316	87	85	85.3
14 University College London	4.0	404	75	81	85.2
15 Newcastle	3.2	325	84	81	85.0
16 Leeds	3.6	345	79	80	84.0
17 Strathclyde	2.5	381	82	83	83.9
18 Aberdeen	3.2	341	78	86	83.5
19 Birmingham	3.7	372	79	73	83.4
20 Surrey	2.2	350	81	91	83.3
21 Sheffield	2.9	367	74	90	82.5
22 Manchester	3.9	356	72	80	82.0
23 Dundee	2.9	360	84	67	81.9
24 Cardiff	3.2	325	77	81	81.4
25 East Anglia	3.1	299	83	73	81.0
26 Lancaster	3.6	319	78	72	80.9
=27 Bangor	2.5	267		93	80.6
=27 Durham	3.1	409	67	90	80.6
29 Exeter	2.8	318	80	78	80.4
30 Nottingham	3.8	310	74	78	80.3
=31 Essex	2.9	308	81	72	79.8
=31 King's College London	2.8	350	75	81	79.8
33 Leicester	3.1	278	79	78	79.5
34 Heriot-Watt	2.7	347	81	69	79.4
35 Kent	2.9	305	75	82	78.8
36 Swansea	3.4	309	74	76	78.6
37 Liverpool	3.7	321	76	62	77.6
38 Sussex	3.2	340	72	74	77.4
39 Aberystwyth	3.4	241	80	67	77.2
40 Queen's, Belfast	2.7	325	71	82	77.0
41 Reading	1.6	332	78	79	76.4
42 Hull	1.8	249	81	80	75.8
43 Robert Gordon	2.0	298		81	75.5
44 Glynd r	1.9			82	75.1
45 Plymouth	3.5	207	75	65	73.7
46 Aston	2.0	320	74	72	73.5
47 Queen Mary, London	3.5	276	67	69	72.5
48 Bournemouth	1.8	241	73	83	72.3
=49 West of England	2.2	252	72	77	71.9
=49 Brighton	2.6	246	70	75	71.9
=49 Brunel	2.7	302	72	64	71.9
=52 City	2.6	223	68	80	71.1
=52 Ulster	2.4	230	76	64	71.1
54 Oxford Brookes	2.5	206	72	76	71.0
55 Stirling	2.0	261		70	70.5

56 De Montfort	2.2	187	78	65	70.3
57 Greenwich	1.1	169	88	61	70.1
58 Portsmouth	1.4	242	74	71	68.9
59 Keele		262	81	73	68.6
=60 Glamorgan	1.8	256	76	58	68.3
=60 Teesside	2.4	281	73	54	68.3
=62 Central Lancashire		213	80	78	67.9
=62 Edinburgh Napier	1.4	265		69	67.9
=64 Nottingham Trent	1.5	217	68	82	67.7
=64 Glasgow Caledonian	1.0	300	78	55	67.7
66 Salford	2.7	179	72	63	67.6
=67 Liverpool John Moores	2.2	195	69	72	67.4
=67 Hertfordshire	2.5	191	72	63	67.4
69 Northumbria		238	81	68	67.0
70 Staffordshire	1.4	207	72	73	66.6
71 Coventry	1.6	280		60	66.4
72 Goldsmiths College	2.9	219	67	59	66.2
=73 Lincoln	2.5	243	71	51	65.7
=73 Manchester Metropolitan	1.7	222	71	64	65.7
75 Newman		156		86	65.3
76 Huddersfield	1.5	246	70	63	65.2
=77 Kingston	1.7	198	72	62	64.9
=77 Cumbria		277	74	70	64.9
=79 Sheffield Hallam	1.3	223	68	66	63.4
=79 Chester		244	73	70	63.4
81 Chichester		272		65	63.1
82 Bedfordshire	1.4	148	74	60	63.0
83 Abertay		314		56	62.0
=84 Bradford	2.0	229	63	61	61.9
=84 Gloucestershire		179	75	69	61.9
=86 Middlesex	1.9	144	67	57	60.4
=86 Derby		234	68	70	60.4
88 Sunderland	1.3	191	69	55	59.9
89 Wolverhampton		172	77	56	59.7
90 Worcester		178	72	67	59.6
91 Anglia Ruskin		240	71	59	59.2
92 Northampton		202	71	61	58.9
93 London South Bank	1.6	125	76	38	58.6
94 Edge Hill		228	67	63	58.0
=95 East London		171	71	62	57.8
=95 Westminster	1.5	161	68	50	57.8
97 UWIC, Cardiff		184		61	57.4
98 Canterbury Christ Church		150	74	57	57.3
99 Southampton Solent		173	70	61	57.0
=100 Roehampton		155	73	55	56.8
=100 Buckinghamshire New		167	72	55	56.8
=102 Leeds Metropolitan		207	64	56	53.8

Computer Science cont.	Research quality/7	Entry standards	Student satisfaction %	Graduate prospects %	Overall rating
=102 Newport		210	62	58	53.8
104 Birmingham City		211	67	47	53.5
105 Thames Valley	0.9			51	53.0

Employed in graduate job:	55%	Employed in non-graduate job and studying:	2%
Employed in graduate job and studying:	4%	Employed in non-graduate job:	20%
Studying:	9%	Unemployed:	10%
Average starting graduate salary:	£21,714	Average starting non-graduate salary:	£16,370

Dentistry

Only medicine tops dentistry's 99 per cent graduate employment rate. In all but four of the 13 undergraduate dental schools, every leaver was in a graduate job or studying six months after finishing the course when the latest survey was carried out. As a result, not even medicine can match the level of competition for places in dentistry: almost nine applications to the place in 2008. The demand for places is still growing, with another increase in applications of nearly 9 per cent at the start of 2009 taking the total to more than 11,500.

Dentistry is not a subject for academic slouches: entrants to every one of the schools averages at least 430 points on the UCAS tariff. Most demand chemistry and may give preference to candidates who also have biology A level.

Scores in the subject are so close that the ranking changes frequently. Glasgow has taken over the leadership this year, with the highest entry standards and the second-highest student satisfaction score. But Newcastle could hardly be closer and both Manchester and Sheffield are only a fraction of a point behind.

Queen's, Belfast, last year's leader, slips into the bottom half of the table, despite registering the most satisfied students. Third-placed Manchester was the most successful school in the 2008 Research Assessment Exercise, with 30 per cent of its work considered world-leading.

Cardiff offers the only dentistry degree in Wales and there are no new universities in the ranking. However, that will change when there are data for Central Lancashire, which opened a purpose-built dental school in 2007. Another has opened at the Peninsula Medical School, in Plymouth and Exeter.

Most degrees last five years, although several universities offer a six-year option for those without the necessary scientific qualifications. The average starting salary of more than £28,800 is second only to that enjoyed by doctors. The number of places is growing to tackle shortages in the profession.

- British Dental Association: **www.bda.org**
- Dental Practitioners Association: **www.uk-dentistry.org**

Dentistry

Dentistry	Research quality/7	Entry standards	Student satisfaction %	Graduate prospects %	Overall rating
1 Glasgow	2.7	502	87	100	100.0
2 Newcastle	2.8	488	86	100	99.6
3 Manchester	3.7	451	78	100	99.1
4 Sheffield	3.0	452	87	100	99.0
5 Leeds	2.9	445	80	100	98.2
6 Cardiff	2.9	452	76	100	98.1
7 Queen's, Belfast	2.5	430	89	100	98.0
8 Bristol	3.0	456	71	100	97.9
9 King's College London	3.6	470	69	99	97.7
10 Liverpool	2.2	459	76	100	97.5
11 Dundee	2.3	463	80	99	97.3
12 Birmingham	2.5	438	86	99	97.2
13 Queen Mary, London	3.5	446	67	98	96.5

Employed in graduate job:	81%	Employed in non-graduate job and studying:	0%
Employed in graduate job and studying:	18%	Employed in non-graduate job:	0%
Studying:	0%	Unemployed:	1%
Average starting graduate salary:	£28,813	Average starting non-graduate salary:	*

Drama, Dance and Cinematics

The top two universities for drama, dance and cinematics swap places this year, with Glasgow overtaking Warwick without leading the table on any of the four measures. Bristol, in seventh place, has the highest entry standards, while the best graduate employment record is at the Central School of Speech and Drama, which is part of the University of London.

For the second year in a row, the most satisfied students are at Bishop Grosseteste University College, in Lincoln, which again recorded 92 per cent satisfaction in the National Student Survey. Third-placed Queen Mary produced the best results in the 2008 Research Assessment Exercise, with half of its submission rated world-leading. Roehampton's research in dance achieved an even higher score, but it was not sustained over the whole group of subjects in this category.

Queen Margaret University, in Edinburgh, is the only post-1992 university in the top 20, while Middlesex is the leading new university in England. This is another table where the gulf in qualifications between entrants to new and old universities is evident, although for drama and dance in particular, this is unlikely to be the main criterion for selection. Entry standards have been rising: only one of the universities in the ranking averages less than 200 points and this year six have averages of more than 400 points. But the overall tariff score remains the lowest in any of the subject tables.

Drama, dance and cinematics is off the foot of the employment table this year, but it remains among the bottom three. Almost half of all graduates were unemployed or in non-graduate jobs at the time of the latest survey. The subjects are in the same low position in the salaries league, but freelancing and periods of temporary employment are common throughout the performing arts. This does not seem to put off prospective students: drama

Drama, Dance and Cinematics cont.

is in the top 20 subjects in terms of applications, with an 8 per cent increase producing a total of 40,000 at the start of 2009. There were more than six applications to the place in 2008, as there were for dance. Competition for places is less stiff in other performing arts, but applications have remained generally buoyant.

- The Stage: **www.thestage.co.uk**
- UKP-Arts: **www.ukperformingarts.co.uk**

Drama, Dance and Cinematics	Research quality/7	Entry standards	Student satisfaction %	Graduate prospects %	Overall rating
1 Glasgow	4.2	413	82	63	100.0
2 Warwick	3.9	430	82	57	97.9
3 Queen Mary, London	4.8	391	84	51	97.1
4 Exeter	3.9	396	87	50	95.3
5 Central School of Speech and Drama	2.6	324	76	85	93.9
6 Royal Holloway	3.9	388	76	60	93.2
7 Bristol	4.3	459	59	59	91.9
8 Birmingham	2.8	415	75	63	91.7
9 Manchester	4.5	400	66	57	91.2
10 Kent	3.7	334	81	58	91.0
11 Loughborough	2.3	387	76	64	89.0
12 Surrey	2.8	360	67	74	88.9
13 Nottingham	2.7	330	82		88.0
14 Goldsmiths College	3.0	381	69	61	87.0
15 Lancaster	3.6	382	74	46	86.4
16 Reading	3.2	328	82	44	84.5
17 East Anglia		404	82	63	84.0
18 Queen Margaret Edinburgh	0.2	359		75	83.4
19 Hull	2.5	277	77	62	82.9
20 Aberdeen	2.9	310		54	82.2
21 Middlesex	2.7	254	70	69	81.7
22 Leeds	3.1	356	63	55	81.4
23 Aberystwyth	3.2	300	78	44	80.7
24 UWIC, Cardiff		248	81	80	80.2
25 De Montfort	2.6	261	75	57	79.6
26 Queen's, Belfast	2.6	327	69	52	79.0
27 Essex	2.5	300	72	48	76.8
28 Roehampton	3.7	297	69	39	76.6
29 Brunel	2.3	303	73	48	76.5
30 Bishop Grosseteste		180	92	68	76.4
31 Coventry	2.2	291	76	45	76.1
32 Plymouth	2.0	297	77	45	75.9
=33 Brighton	3.6	261	68	43	74.8
=33 Manchester Metropolitan	1.7	241	76	56	74.8
35 University of the Arts London		360	65	63	74.0

36 Birmingham City		291	74	64	73.9
37 Nottingham Trent		301	66	69	72.5
38 Chichester	1.7	248	70	55	72.4
39 Sussex		387	56	64	71.8
40 Glamorgan	1.6	262	69	54	71.6
41 Bath Spa		293	74	57	71.4
42 Liverpool John Moores		285	75	56	71.2
=43 Portsmouth	0.8	289	77	44	70.9
=43 Huddersfield		302	80	47	70.9
45 Staffordshire	1.3	228	83	39	69.8
46 Falmouth		248	79	52	69.1
=47 Hertfordshire	1.1	233	69	56	69.0
=47 Cumbria		204	82	55	69.0
=49 Chester	1.8	268	63	49	68.9
=49 Winchester	1.8	250	74	39	68.9
=51 West of England		283	82	41	68.7
=51 York St John	1.6	311	60	47	68.7
=53 Salford	1.4	245	67	51	68.3
=53 St Mary's College		253	75	53	68.3
55 Kingston	1.6	243	72	42	67.9
56 Northampton	1.2	251	73	44	67.8
57 Oxford Brookes		300	74	45	67.7
=58 Bedfordshire	2.4	209	69	39	66.6
=58 Gloucestershire		230	77	50	66.6
60 Westminster		280	69	48	65.3
61 Worcester		247	79	36	63.7
62 Wolverhampton		212	72	52	63.6
63 Lincoln	1.1	265	58	49	63.4
64 Ulster		240	72	45	62.9
=65 Sunderland	1.2	203	71	40	62.5
=65 London South Bank		242	71	44	62.5
67 University for Creative Arts		252	63	52	62.4
68 Northumbria		253	57	58	61.8
69 Edge Hill		268	67	42	61.5
=70 East London	1.8	228		35	61.3
=70 Canterbury Christ Church		267	73	35	61.3
72 Thames Valley		224	56	63	61.1
73 Sheffield Hallam		212	76	38	60.8
74 Anglia Ruskin		261	70	34	59.6
75 Newman		224		46	59.5
76 Central Lancashire		223	61	50	59.2
77 Southampton Solent		224	67	43	59.0
78 Newport		227	64	45	58.7
79 Glynd r		242	52	51	56.7
80 Derby		222	64	29	53.0
81 Buckinghamshire New		206	66	29	52.7
82 Leeds Metropolitan		256	34	42	45.9

Drama, Dance and Cinematics cont.

Employed in graduate job:	39%	Employed in non-graduate job and studying:	3%
Employed in graduate job and studying:	3%	Employed in non-graduate job:	38%
Studying:	9%	Unemployed:	8%
Average starting graduate salary:	£17,130	Average starting non-graduate salary:	£14,249

East and South Asian Studies

The number of universities in the East and South Asian studies ranking is down by one since last year, but is still more than the total three years ago, when these subjects were identified as officially "vulnerable". Universities come in and out of the table because small numbers of students mean that reliable averages cannot always be compiled, even though courses are still running.

Numbers may well grow in future years, with the clamour for more interaction with China and India. However, as yet fewer than 4,000 students take the languages at any level of higher education. Yet around half those completing degrees go straight into graduate jobs. Starting salaries had dropped below £20,000 in the latest survey but such fluctuations are common with small subject groups.

Japanese is still the biggest draw, with a near 30 per cent increase bringing the number of applications to more than 1,200 by the official deadline for courses beginning in 2009. Chinese also enjoyed an increase of almost 11 per cent and, with more schools teaching Mandarin, numbers are expected to rise further in the foreseeable future.

Cambridge remains clear of Oxford at the top of the table, with the most satisfied students and the best employment record. Cardiff, which enters the ranking in third place, has the best research score, while Oxford has the highest entry qualifications.

Four out of five students enter with tariff scores that are above average for all subjects, so degree classifications are also high. Most undergraduates learn their chosen language from scratch, although universities expect to see evidence of potential in other modern language qualifications.

- Association of South-East Asian Studies (UK): **http://aseasuk.org.uk**
- British Association for Chinese Studies: **www.bacsuk.org.uk**
- British Association for Japanese Studies: **www.bajs.org.uk**
- British Association for Korean Studies: **www.baks.org.uk**
- British Association for South Asian Studies: **www.basas.org.uk**
- Royal Asiatic Society: **http://royalasiaticsociety.org**
- Royal Society for Asian Affairs: **www.rsaa.org.uk**

East and South Asian Studies	Research quality/7	Entry standards	Student satisfaction %	Graduate prospects %	Overall rating
1 Cambridge	2.4		88	79	100.0
2 Oxford	3.0	548	81	64	97.6
3 Cardiff	3.8	361	78		93.6
4 School of Oriental and African Studies	3.4	394	72	72	91.2
5 Nottingham	1.7	381	70	77	85.2

	1.5	386	77	72	84.9
6 Sheffield	1.5	386	77	72	84.9
7 Manchester	1.9	385	69		81.2
8 Edinburgh	1.7	441	56	65	78.4
9 Leeds	2.0	369	73	57	78.1

Employed in graduate job:	45%	Employed in non-graduate job and studying:	3%
Employed in graduate job and studying:	4%	Employed in non-graduate job:	24%
Studying:	15%	Unemployed:	8%
Average starting graduate salary:	£19,821	Average starting non-graduate salary:	£16,316

Economics

Competition for places in economics is among the stiffest in any subject, with more than six applications for every degree place. There will be no let-up in 2009, following a 15 per cent increase in applications for a subject that was already among the ten most popular. Economics is also in the top four for graduate starting salaries, reflecting the value that employers place on a subject that they see combining the skills of the sciences and the arts.

Indeed, many prospective students underestimate the mathematical skills required for an economics degree. Many universities demand maths at A level, or its equivalent, as part of offers that are consistently high. Entry standards in this year's table reflect that, with the top three universities all averaging over 520 points – the equivalent of more than four As at A level. Another nine universities have averages of at least 450 points, while only five of the 67 institutions in the ranking average less than 200 points.

Oxford tops the table for the first time, having been out of the top ten only five years ago. A much-improved performance in the 2008 Research Assessment exercise, when 40 per cent of its submission was rated world-leading, is partly responsible. The third-placed London School of Economics and University College London, in fourth, won even higher research grades.

Cambridge, which has dropped to second place, has the highest entry standards and the best employment score. East Anglia, just outside the top ten, had the most satisfied undergraduates in the 2008 National Student Survey, with Exeter close behind.

St Andrews is the leading university in Scotland, having moved into the top ten this year, while Cardiff remains the leader in Wales. Nottingham Trent is the highest-placed new university and the only one, apart from Brighton, in the top 40.

Economics is not the sure-fire bet for a good job that many assume it to be: more than a quarter of all leavers are in non-graduate jobs or unemployed after six months, leaving the subject outside the top 20 in the employment table. But starting salaries in the latest survey averaged more than £25,000 for graduate-level jobs and the £17,300 average for other types of employment is also among the highest for any subject.

- Economics and Business Education Association: **www.ebea.org.uk**
- Royal Economic Society: **www.res.org.uk**
- Why Study? Economics: **www.whystudyeconomics.ac.uk**

Economics

Economics	Research quality/7	Entry standards	Student satisfaction %	Graduate prospects %	Overall rating
1 Oxford	4.5	538	85	89	100.0
2 Cambridge	3.7	554		93	99.3
3 London School of Economics	5.3	523	75	90	96.4
4 University College London	5.1	488	72	89	93.0
5 Warwick	4.5	499	73	89	92.3
6 Exeter	3.3	386	87	76	89.3
7 Durham	2.7	491	79	88	89.2
8 St Andrews	2.7	475	81	84	88.8
9 Nottingham	3.9	468	74	84	88.5
10 Birmingham	2.9	403	85	79	88.1
11 Bristol	3.9	457	70	86	86.5
12 Bath	3.6	454	70	86	85.5
13 East Anglia	2.9	332	89	70	85.3
14 Glasgow	3.5	414	79	71	85.1
15 Aston	2.8	351	83		84.7
=16 Kent	3.1	306	85	75	84.3
=16 Surrey	2.9	329	82	79	84.3
=16 Essex	4.5	325	76	74	84.3
19 Southampton	3.4	422	74	80	84.2
=20 Leicester	3.2	320	83	72	83.7
=20 Edinburgh	3.4	450	70	81	83.7
22 Strathclyde	3.3	442	79	66	83.6
23 York	3.2	457	74	72	83.3
24 Loughborough	2.1	378	83	76	83.2
25 Lancaster	3.5	423	76	69	82.9
26 Sheffield	3.0	372	79	74	82.7
27 Royal Holloway	3.4	370	73	81	82.6
28 Queen Mary, London	3.9	370	71	76	81.8
29 Sussex	2.6	345	81	71	81.3
30 Cardiff	3.8	398	75	64	81.2
31 Newcastle	2.3	417	73	80	80.8
=32 Leeds	3.2	418	72	72	80.5
=32 Aberdeen	3.1	344	80	64	80.5
=34 Hull	2.0	283	80	80	79.4
=34 Swansea	2.8	277	80	72	79.4
36 Liverpool	2.3	385	74	77	79.2
37 Nottingham Trent	1.6	264	83	74	77.9
38 Manchester	3.6	408	69	65	77.6
39 Heriot-Watt	2.2	328	73	76	76.4
=40 Brighton	2.4	251	80		76.3
=40 School of Oriental and African Studies	2.0	390	71	75	76.3
42 Aberystwyth	1.5	249	86	61	75.0
43 Queen's, Belfast	2.7	355	70	63	73.7

44	Keele	2.1	284	68	82	73.6
45	Reading	2.3	348	72	64	73.3
46	Portsmouth	1.6	249	79	67	73.1
47	West of England	1.5	248	79	68	73.0
48	City	2.5	328	66	72	72.6
49	Coventry		245	85	70	72.4
50	Stirling	2.8	279	75	55	72.1
51	Dundee	2.1	337	73	59	72.0
52	Northumbria	1.1	274	73	74	71.2
53	Brunel	2.6	311	67	65	70.8
54	Bradford	2.3	239	78	55	70.7
55	Plymouth	1.6	241	79	51	68.5
56	Ulster		254	78	67	68.3
=57	Salford	1.5	249	75	56	67.2
=57	Manchester Metropolitan	0.8	259	72	66	67.2
59	Liverpool John Moores	0.6	221	77	61	66.4
60	Staffordshire	1.5	199	72		65.1
61	Hertfordshire	1.7	233	69	57	64.5
62	Oxford Brookes		289	70	62	63.7
63	Middlesex		167	74	68	63.6
64	Leeds Metropolitan		278	71	60	63.2
65	East London		193	80	52	63.1
66	Greenwich	1.2	191	77	43	62.6
67	Kingston	1.4	191	71	51	61.9

Employed in graduate job:	44%	Employed in non-graduate job and studying:	2%
Employed in graduate job and studying:	15%	Employed in non-graduate job:	19%
Studying:	15%	Unemployed:	5%
Average starting graduate salary:	£25,101	Average starting non-graduate salary:	£17,316

Education

Education is the only ranking that still contains teaching scores – because teacher training assessments by Ofsted remain current. East Anglia enters the table in second place with the best performance in those assessments, although it still does not have scores for student satisfaction or graduate employment. Cambridge remains in first place, with the best performance among the universities in the table in the 2008 Research Assessment Exercise and average entry grades that are almost 100 points ahead of its nearest challengers.

Huddersfield is the only university to register 100 per cent positive destinations, although both Aberdeen and Glasgow are within a single percentage point of this feat and nearly a dozen others reach the 90 per cent mark. Education is high up the employment table, with 80 per cent of graduates going straight into schools or continuing to study and only 3 per cent unemployed. However, the average starting salary of just over £20,000 is only just in the top 30 for all subjects.

Employment scores at different universities reflect to some extent the variations in demand for new staff in primary and secondary schools and in different parts of the UK.

Education cont.

But even in the bottom ten, there are universities where at least eight out of ten leavers went straight into graduate jobs or further study.

The most satisfied students are at Aberystwyth. Satisfaction levels are high generally, not only among the final-year undergraduates who complete the National Student Survey, but also in the early stage of careers. Three years after graduation, those with education degrees were among the most satisfied at work and least inclined to wish they had taken a different subject.

Some of the leading universities are absent from the education table because they offer only the postgraduate courses that have become the normal route into secondary teaching and an increasingly popular choice for those wanting a career in primary schools. As such, they are not included in the National Student Survey for the subject and neither entry scores nor graduate destinations are comparable. The University of London's Institute of Education, which achieved the top grades in the 2008 research assessments, is one example; Oxford and King's College London, which ran it close, are others.

Low entry scores have been a concern in the past, but only three universities average less than 200 points in the latest table, while most score more than 250. Teacher training courses have become more selective of late and there are now more than five applications to the place – more than the average for all subjects. The demand for places was growing at the start of 2009, when it remained among the ten most popular subjects.

- Education Institute of Scotland: **www.eis.org.uk**
- Graduate Teacher Training Registry (GTTR): **www.gttr.ac.uk**
- NAS UWT: **www.nasuwt.org.uk**
- National Union of Teachers: **www.teachers.org.uk**
- TeacherNet: **www.teachernet.gov.uk**
- Training and Development Agency for Schools: **www.tda.gov.uk**

Education	Research quality/7	Teaching quality/5	Entry standards	Student satisfaction %	Graduate prospects %	Overall rating
1 Cambridge	3.4	3.7	474	83	93	100.0
2 East Anglia	2.5	4.0	249			90.8
3 Stirling	2.6		297	82	94	88.7
4 Exeter	2.9	3.7	333	84	65	88.4
5 Aberdeen	1.4		363	76	99	86.9
6 Dundee	1.2		349	81	94	86.7
7 Edinburgh	2.3		379	69	94	86.2
8 Brighton	1.8	3.5	301	80	91	85.8
9 Reading	1.7	3.3	313	81	94	85.3
10 Durham	2.8	3.0	379	73	89	85.1
=11 Manchester	2.8	3.5	308	81	59	83.6
=11 Glasgow	1.7		349	68	99	83.6
=11 Canterbury Christ Church	1.8	3.7	304	69	91	83.6
14 Cardiff	3.0		337	73	70	83.2
15 Strathclyde	1.5		369	71	88	82.9
16 Brunel	1.0	3.2	317		93	81.9

=17 Oxford Brookes	1.5	3.2	304	82	76	81.2
=17 Warwick	2.9	3.5	285	71	69	81.2
=19 Huddersfield	1.2	3.0	231	85	100	81.0
=19 Manchester Metropolitan	2.8	3.3	284	69	82	81.0
21 Bangor	1.5		274	81	79	80.5
22 Winchester	1.7	3.3	289	75	79	80.0
23 Leeds	3.0	3.0	342	74	60	79.6
24 York	2.7	3.3	331	70	61	79.5
25 Birmingham City	1.4	3.3	249	79	83	79.4
26 Ulster	1.7		252	79		79.2
=27 Hull	1.4	3.2	245	79	85	78.9
=27 Wolverhampton	1.2	3.7	220	78	74	78.9
29 Northumbria		3.7	303	79	67	78.7
30 Sunderland	1.1	3.3	230	77	90	78.6
31 Aberystwyth			269	86	76	78.5
32 UWIC, Cardiff	0.3		269	81	85	78.1
33 Hertfordshire	1.0	3.0	284	82	77	77.8
34 Edge Hill	0.4	3.3	273	78	84	77.7
=35 Kingston	1.0	3.0	260	81	82	77.5
=35 Plymouth	1.7	3.3	247	76	72	77.5
37 York St John	0.2	3.3	290	79	77	77.2
38 Newman	1.1	3.2	212	80	83	77.1
=39 Northampton	1.1	3.3	252	78	74	76.9
=39 Roehampton	1.6	3.2	279	75	68	76.9
41 Birmingham	2.1	3.2	335	73	52	76.7
42 St Mary's College	0.5	3.0	278	77	88	76.5
43 De Montfort			234	81	85	76.0
44 Bishop Grosseteste	0.5	2.5	270	83	95	75.8
45 Newport	0.3		254	78	85	75.6
46 Keele		3.0	301	80	77	75.3
=47 Glyndŵr	0.4		231	82	77	74.9
=47 West of England	1.2	3.2	271	71	74	74.9
=49 Goldsmiths College	1.6	2.8	245	73	87	74.8
=49 Southampton	1.9	3.0		70		74.8
51 Bedfordshire		3.3	249	71	90	74.7
52 Cumbria	0.4	3.3	263	70	83	74.5
=53 Chichester		3.0	239	83	81	74.4
=53 Bath Spa	0.8	2.7	279	81	77	74.4
=53 Gloucestershire	1.6	2.8	240	75	83	74.4
56 Sheffield Hallam	1.3	3.0	277	71	74	73.9
=57 Nottingham Trent		3.0	281	80	72	73.8
=57 Worcester		3.2	250	77	78	73.8
59 Liverpool John Moores	1.0	3.3	234	73	71	73.7
60 Marjon, Plymouth	0.3	3.2	222	75	81	73.3
61 Chester	0.9	3.0	257	74	73	73.0
62 Central Lancashire	0.4		258	75	75	72.9
63 Leeds Metropolitan	1.0	3.0	253	71	76	72.4

Education cont.	Research quality/7	Teaching quality/5	Entry standards	Student satisfaction %	Graduate prospects %	Overall rating
64 Middlesex		3.2	193	64	96	70.2
65 Greenwich	1.0	3.0	217	65	83	70.0
66 Derby		3.0	219	81	61	69.8
67 Anglia Ruskin		3.0	252	58	83	66.8
68 East London	1.3	3.0	174	62	70	66.0
69 Essex			218	63	69	63.3
70 University College Birmingham			194	70	59	63.2

Employed in graduate job:	65%	Employed in non-graduate job and studying:	2%
Employed in graduate job and studying:	5%	Employed in non-graduate job:	16%
Studying:	10%	Unemployed:	3%
Average starting graduate salary:	£20,135	Average starting non-graduate salary:	£13,818

Electrical and Electronic Engineering

Cambridge has again extended its lead over Southampton in electrical and electronic engineering, with by far the best research grades and a lead of approaching 100 points on entry standards. It is also one of the four universities with the most satisfied students and is joint second only to Loughborough on graduate recruitment. There are few subjects with a bigger gap between the leading university and the rest.

Three universities have dropped out of the table since last year. Applications have been declining nationally, although they were recovering at the start of 2009, when there was a 6 per cent increase. In its heyday at the start of the decade, electronic and electrical engineering used to attract far more applications than civil or mechanical engineering, but it is now the least popular of the three.

The three universities that matched Cambridge in the 2008 National Student Survey are Surrey, Loughborough and York, all of which appear in the top ten. Edinburgh remains the top university in Scotland, while Cardiff again takes the honours in Wales. The West of England is the leading new university and the only one in the top 30 of a table where old universities predominate.

Employment rates vary considerably among the 64 universities in the ranking. Most of those in the top half of the table see at least 80 per cent of leavers go straight into graduate jobs or further training, but the proportion dropped below half at several of the institutions in the bottom half.

About half of the students – more in electrical engineering – come with qualifications other than A levels. Yet it is electrical engineering which has the higher proportion of firsts and 2:1s. Almost three quarters of the leavers nationally go straight into graduate jobs or continue their studies, but the unemployment rate is above average, at 7 per cent. For those who do find graduate work, the average starting salary of over £22,500 is in the top 15 of all subjects.

- Institute of Electrical and Electronic Engineers: www.ieee.org
- Institution of Engineering and Technology: www.theiet.org

Electrical and Electronic Engineering	Research quality/7	Entry standards	Student satisfaction %	Graduate prospects %	Overall rating
1 Cambridge	4.6	564	85	94	100.0
2 Southampton	3.3	468	81	92	88.8
3 Imperial College	3.3	475	82	84	88.3
4 Surrey	3.6	374	85	85	87.6
5 Loughborough	2.8	334	85	95	85.4
6 Edinburgh	2.7	425	77	92	83.0
7 Sheffield	2.9	346	82	85	82.9
8 Bristol	2.7	413	77	94	82.7
9 York	2.4	398	85	78	82.4
10 Essex	2.9		80	84	82.1
11 Bath	3.1	375	78	84	81.9
12 Glasgow	3.1	403	79	75	81.7
13 Queen's, Belfast	2.9	344	80	84	81.3
14 Leeds	3.8	373	75	76	81.1
=15 University College London	3.2	427	72	84	80.6
=15 Strathclyde	2.5	420	78	82	80.6
=17 Manchester	3.4	384	72	78	79.5
=17 Heriot-Watt	3.1	336	77	82	79.5
19 Newcastle	2.7	348	75	89	79.0
20 Nottingham	2.7	363	75	86	78.9
21 Cardiff	2.4	343	78	84	77.8
22 Aberdeen	2.8			75	76.4
23 Kent	2.3	282	78	86	76.2
24 King's College London	1.8	339	78	85	75.9
25 Birmingham	2.5	300	77	80	75.6
26 Queen Mary, London	2.5	263	80	76	75.3
27 Liverpool	2.6	382	73	70	74.7
28 Lancaster	2.4	278	70	92	73.8
29 Reading	1.8	365	74	79	73.4
30 West of England	2.4	256	75	83	73.3
31 Brunel	2.2	303	77	69	72.8
32 Sussex	2.6		70	72	70.3
33 Aston	2.0	290	73	73	70.1
34 Northumbria	2.1	236	75	72	69.6
35 Portsmouth	1.4	206	81	75	69.3
36 Swansea	1.7	255	73	79	69.1
37 Hull	1.8	235	75	75	68.8
38 Robert Gordon		336		84	68.7
39 Coventry	2.0	248	75		68.4
40 Liverpool John Moores	2.9	222	71	61	68.3
41 Bangor	3.6	200		48	68.0
=42 Plymouth	1.3	221	83	60	67.6
=42 Central Lancashire	1.4		78	63	67.6

Electrical and Electronic Engineering cont.	Research quality/7	Entry standards	Student satisfaction %	Graduate prospects %	Overall rating
44 Bradford	0.8	276	75	76	66.5
45 Salford	2.7	230	71	57	66.4
46 Hertfordshire	2.4	178	75	57	65.7
47 Aberystwyth		259		79	63.5
48 Huddersfield	1.8	265	72	50	63.2
49 Manchester Metropolitan	1.5	202	72	61	62.3
50 Sheffield Hallam	1.7	200	68	65	61.4
51 City	2.2	202	63	64	61.0
52 Westminster	0.9	178	78	53	60.8
=53 Teesside		257	78	54	60.0
=53 Glasgow Caledonian		302	68	72	60.0
55 Ulster		210	73	74	59.9
56 De Montfort	1.7	201	73	42	59.8
57 Staffordshire	2.1	147	68		59.6
58 Bolton		212	76	62	59.0
59 Oxford Brookes		249	70	66	58.0
60 Greenwich		238	71	63	57.6
=61 Glamorgan	2.0	266	62	32	55.4
=61 Derby		241	68	60	55.4
63 Birmingham City		244	65	62	54.2
64 London South Bank	2.4		63	33	54.0

Employed in graduate job:	53%	Employed in non-graduate job and studying:	2%
Employed in graduate job and studying:	7%	Employed in non-graduate job:	17%
Studying:	14%	Unemployed:	7%
Average starting graduate salary:	£22,579	Average starting non-graduate salary:	£16,486

English

Nothing, it seems, can dent the popularity of English as a degree subject. It is not in the top 50 for employment levels or starting salaries, but it remains among the top five choices by applicants. The number of applications had risen again, by more than 6 per cent at the start of 2009. Rising entry grades reflect this, with 25 universities averaging more than 400 points in the latest survey and none dropping below 200. Only seven of the 98 institutions in the ranking average less than 250 points on the UCAS tariff.

The old order has been restored in this year's table, after a year in which neither Oxford nor Cambridge appeared in the top two places. Now both do, with Cambridge taking the lead for the first time. Cambridge had the highest entry standards, while York produced the best results in the 2008 Research Assessment Exercise, with three quarters of its work judged to be world-leading or internationally excellent.

Bishop Grosseteste University College, in Lincoln, had the most satisfied students and the best of a generally mediocre set of employment scores. Only one of the lowest research scores prevents the college from breaking into the top 20, where no university comes close to its record of 85 per cent of English graduates going straight into graduate-level jobs or continuing their studies.

Durham, leader for the last three years, slips to fourth in the new ranking, behind University College London. St Andrews pips Glasgow to the title of top university in Scotland, while Cardiff remains the leader in Wales. De Montfort is the leading new university, outside the top 30 but still above Birmingham and Manchester in the table.

Almost a third of English graduates continue their studies, either full or part-time – almost as many as go into graduate-level jobs. The subject is in the bottom ten for starting salaries, with an average of £18,500 in graduate-level jobs and less than £14,300 for those who are self-employed or in lower-level work.

However, English has produced consistently good scores in the National Student Survey. In the results published in 2008, only four universities out of 98 failed to satisfy at least 70 per cent of the final-year undergraduates.

- Alliance of Literary Societies: **www.allianceofliterarysocieties.org**
- Poetry Society: **www.poetrysociety.org.uk**
- Royal Society of Literature: **www.rslit.org**
- Society of Authors: **www.societyofauthors.org**
- Society for Editors and Proofreaders: **www.sfep.org.uk**
- Teaching English as a Foreign Language: **www.eflweb.com**

English	Research quality/7	Entry standards	Student satisfaction %	Graduate prospects %	Overall rating
1 Cambridge	3.8	514	90	70	100.0
2 Oxford	3.9	504	87	70	98.1
3 University College London	3.4	480	84	77	96.6
4 Durham	3.3	489	83	73	94.8
=5 York	4.3	496	78	71	94.5
=5 Exeter	4.0	427	87	65	94.5
7 Warwick	3.7	474	79	71	92.5
8 Queen Mary, London	4.0	366	85	67	91.9
=9 Leeds	3.7	444	83	65	91.8
=9 St Andrews	3.7	458	81	66	91.8
11 Glasgow	3.7	425	83	63	90.6
=12 Southampton	3.2	419	86	61	90.0
=12 Leicester	2.8	383	87	68	90.0
14 Edinburgh	4.0	446	79	60	89.5
15 Bristol	3.2	464	74	76	89.4
16 Loughborough	2.3	367	90	66	89.3
17 Cardiff	3.5	432	81	61	88.8
=18 Aberdeen	3.5	325	87	63	88.6
=18 Kent	3.4	336	84	68	88.6
20 Royal Holloway	3.4	413	78	68	88.1
=21 Nottingham	3.8	460	75	63	87.8
=21 Bishop Grosseteste	0.8	258	93	85	87.8

	Research quality/7	Entry standards	Student satisfaction %	Graduate prospects %	Overall rating
23 Sheffield	3.3	438	78	64	87.6
=24 Liverpool	3.5	422	81	58	87.2
=24 East Anglia	3.1	405	81	64	87.2
26 Queen's, Belfast	3.6	346	81	61	85.9
=27 Newcastle	3.4	445	72	66	85.2
=27 King's College London	3.0	452	74	66	85.2
29 Hull	2.4	318	82	70	84.8
30 Dundee	2.2	354	86	59	84.6
31 Lancaster	2.9	409	80	57	84.1
32 De Montfort	3.8	251	83	61	83.9
33 Reading	3.2	359	84	51	83.8
34 Birmingham	3.2	417	73	62	83.1
35 Keele	2.4	327	77	71	82.3
=36 Manchester	3.7	430	71	56	81.9
=36 Stirling	2.4	313	79	67	81.9
=36 Goldsmiths College	2.8	359	76	64	81.9
39 Bolton	0.6		90	60	81.6
40 Oxford Brookes	2.0	330	79	67	81.1
41 Essex	2.5	319	79	63	81.0
=42 Aston	1.3	339	85		80.6
=42 Nottingham Trent	2.4	285	82	61	80.6
44 Sussex	2.9	418	67	66	80.3
45 Aberystwyth	2.2	332	84	49	79.2
46 Swansea	2.5	310	83	48	78.9
=47 Strathclyde	2.4	378	74	59	78.7
=47 Middlesex	1.8	205	79	78	78.7
49 Brunel	2.4	306	80	54	78.4
50 Kingston	2.1	263	82	58	78.2
51 Portsmouth	2.3	304	81	51	77.7
52 Chester	1.3	293	85	54	77.4
=53 Birmingham City	1.4	266	81	64	77.2
=53 Bath Spa	1.6	316	80	57	77.2
55 Sunderland	2.1	232	82	57	77.1
56 Hertfordshire	2.2	256	78	62	76.9
57 West of England	1.7	294	79	59	76.6
58 Coventry	1.0	289	84		76.4
59 Bangor	2.5	326	77	49	76.2
60 Northumbria	1.5	302	80	54	75.9
61 Central Lancashire	1.1	292	78	64	75.6
62 Newman		238	76	83	75.1
63 Roehampton	2.0	291	72	64	74.9
64 Anglia Ruskin	2.8	284	69	62	74.8
65 Bedfordshire	2.1	210	81		74.5

66 Salford	2.0	283	82	43	74.1
67 Edinburgh Napier	1.4	322			73.7
=68 Ulster	1.8	250	83	45	73.5
=68 Gloucestershire	1.7	264	82	45	73.5
70 Worcester	1.3	251	80	54	73.0
71 Manchester Metropolitan	2.2	309	76	46	72.9
72 Edge Hill	0.9	249	83	50	72.2
73 St Mary's College	1.4	264	81	46	71.8
74 Cumbria	0.7	283	67	75	71.1
=75 Winchester		281	83	49	71.0
=75 Marjon, Plymouth	0.4		81	51	71.0
77 Sheffield Hallam	1.7	296	76	44	70.7
78 Huddersfield	1.3	305	75	47	70.5
=79 Brighton	1.7	301	67	57	69.7
=79 York St John	0.6	281	76	53	69.7
81 Westminster	1.0	266	74	55	69.5
=82 Plymouth	1.7	305	73	43	69.0
=82 Staffordshire	1.3	257	74	51	69.0
84 Glamorgan	2.3	266	76	34	68.8
=85 Newport		251		58	68.4
=85 Lampeter	0.9	238	72	59	68.4
87 Liverpool John Moores	1.6	250	78	38	68.3
88 Bradford	1.5	235			68.2
89 Teesside		262	81	45	68.0
90 Northampton	1.0	227	78	44	67.7
91 Falmouth		299	73	53	67.1
92 Lincoln		286	74	51	66.7
93 Greenwich	1.0	256	72	47	66.3
94 Wolverhampton		232	79	48	66.1
95 Canterbury Christ Church	0.9	255	75	43	65.8
96 Chichester	1.2	272		40	65.6
97 Leeds Metropolitan		281	73	49	65.3
98 Derby		250	75	44	63.6

Employed in graduate job:	31%	Employed in non-graduate job and studying:	4%
Employed in graduate job and studying:	4%	Employed in non-graduate job:	32%
Studying:	23%	Unemployed:	6%
Average starting graduate salary:	£18,499	Average starting non-graduate salary:	£14,272

Food Science

King's College London has taken over from Surrey at the top of the food science table, thanks to the best grades in the 2008 Research Assessment Exercise, when two thirds of its submission in nutritional sciences was considered world-leading or internationally excellent. King's was also within a whisker of second-placed Surrey for entry standards. The two universities were the only ones in the table where entrants averaged more than 400 points on the UCAS tariff.

Food Science cont.

Leeds Metropolitan and Bath Spa shares the distinction of having the most satisfied students, with University College Birmingham only a percentage point behind. Easily the best employment score is at third-placed Nottingham, where 87 per cent of the leavers went straight into graduate-level work or continued their studies.

Both of Northern Ireland's universities are in the top ten, with Queen's, Belfast the highest-placed institution outside England. Robert Gordon is the top university in Scotland, while UWIC is the only representative of Wales. The majority of the 29 institutions in the ranking are new universities, although higher entry standards and research grades ensure that their older counterparts fill the top five places. Brighton is the most successful of the new universities, while Greenwich and Coventry are also in the top ten.

Entry standards have been rising – no university in this year's ranking averages less than 200 points – but there were still only three applications per place in 2008. Almost a third of entrants to food science courses arrive with alternative qualifications to A levels. The subjects attracted big increases in the number of applications earlier in the decade, but had been in the doldrums for two years before recovering at the start of 2009, when there was 6 per cent growth in applications.

Career prospects are good, with almost three quarters of graduates going straight into graduate-level work or further study – a proportion that placed food science in the top 25 subjects in the employment table. It is just in the bottom half of the graduate salaries league, with an average starting rate close to £20,000.

- Institute of Food Science and Technology: **www.ifst.org**
- Society of Food Hygiene and Technology: **www.sofht.co.uk**

Food Science	Research quality/7	Entry standards	Student satisfaction %	Graduate prospects %	Overall rating
1 King's College London	3.4	413		80	100.0
2 Surrey	3.0	415	74	82	91.9
3 Nottingham	2.8	349	80	87	90.7
4 Reading	2.2	336	81	74	84.9
5 Queen's, Belfast	1.7	316	79	81	82.3
6 Brighton	1.8			73	80.6
=7 Greenwich	1.6		82	70	80.4
=7 Coventry		370		79	80.4
9 Newcastle	2.0	387	83	46	80.1
10 Ulster	1.6	298	81	73	79.7
11 Leeds	2.8	375	66	56	78.2
=12 Robert Gordon		367		73	77.9
=12 Leeds Metropolitan		300	88	80	77.9
14 Bath Spa		297	88	74	76.0
15 Liverpool John Moores	1.4	243	81	71	75.2
16 Manchester Metropolitan	1.3	311		64	74.1
17 Northumbria	1.5	288	80	52	72.2
18 Plymouth	0.9		68	80	71.7

=19 Sheffield Hallam		276	81	74	71.6
=19 Glasgow Caledonian		329	80	65	71.6
21 Queen Margaret Edinburgh		330		64	71.0
22 UWIC, Cardiff	1.0	232	80	67	70.9
23 Oxford Brookes		311	72	66	67.5
24 Chester	0.8	357	58	63	66.7
25 University College Birmingham		260	87	48	66.5
26 Bournemouth		241	68	75	64.5
27 Huddersfield		253	83	39	61.8
28 Roehampton		207		65	60.5
29 St Mary's College		253	73	48	59.8

Employed in graduate job:	55%	Employed in non-graduate job and studying:	1%
Employed in graduate job and studying:	3%	Employed in non-graduate job:	21%
Studying:	14%	Unemployed:	5%
Average starting graduate salary:	£19,765	Average starting non-graduate salary:	£15,345

French

French at degree level has weathered the problems that have afflicted the teaching of modern languages in secondary schools: there are more applications and more places than there were five years ago. Applications showed a small increase at the start of 2009, suggesting no let-up in the competition for places. A ratio of five applications for every place in the previous year was well above average for all subjects and is reflected in the usual high entry grades. Entrants to two of the bottom ten universities in this year's table averaged more than 400 points, as did all but four of the top 20.

Oxford has replaced Cambridge as the top university for French, thanks to the best performance in the 2008 Research Assessment Exercise, when 30 per cent of its submission were rated world-leading. Cambridge is a fraction of a point behind, with the highest entry grades and a share in the best employment score. Lancaster was the only other university to see more than 80 per cent of its leavers go straight into graduate-level jobs or continue their studies.

Leicester again has the most satisfied students, but unusually low research grades and one of the lowest employment scores consign the university to the bottom half of the table. Third-placed St Andrews has made the most progress in the upper reaches of the table and is now easily the top university in Scotland for French. Swansea has overtaken Cardiff to become the narrow leader in Wales. Oxford Brookes is the leading new university and one of only two in the top 40, the other being Nottingham Trent.

French still attracts twice as many degree applications as any other language, although there were still fewer than 4,000 at the start of 2009. Nine out of ten undergraduates enter with A levels or their equivalents, almost 10 per cent securing their place in Clearing.

Seven out of ten of those completing a degree in French go on to graduate jobs or further study within six months and the 4 per cent unemployment rate is better than average for all subjects. No university came close to dipping below the 50 per cent success mark for graduate destinations. Starting salaries improved considerably in the latest survey and were above average, at more than £20,000 when the figures were collected.

French cont.

- Alliance Française: **www.alliancefrancaise.org.uk**
- Chartered Institute of Linguists: **www.iol.org.uk**
- National Centre for Languages (CILT): **www.cilt.org.uk**
- Society for French Studies: **www.sfs.ac.uk**

French	Research quality/7	Entry standards	Student satisfaction %	Graduate prospects %	Overall rating
1 Oxford	3.4	516	86	79	100.0
2 Cambridge	2.8	534	88	81	99.4
3 St Andrews	2.6	483	83	79	93.8
4 Durham	2.5	497	86	74	93.5
5 Warwick	3.1	466	83	71	92.8
6 Southampton	3.2	433	88	66	92.5
7 Portsmouth	2.3		88	74	91.1
8 King's College London	3.2	419	75	74	89.0
=9 Exeter	2.5	415	82	74	88.6
=9 Sheffield	2.9	404	81	71	88.6
11 Bath	2.2	418	84	75	88.4
12 Aberdeen	2.8	373	84	68	87.4
13 Leeds	2.6	404	84	66	87.3
14 University College London	2.4	433	76	75	86.8
15 Birmingham	2.1	416	85	69	86.7
=16 Nottingham	2.8	409	75	72	85.9
=16 Lancaster	1.8	358	83	81	85.9
=18 Royal Holloway	2.3	361	82	72	85.3
=18 Heriot-Watt	1.7	391	88	69	85.3
=20 Newcastle	2.5	433	72	75	85.0
=20 Edinburgh	2.4	468	68	78	85.0
22 Kent	2.6	297	87	66	84.1
23 Queen's, Belfast	2.0	366	80	74	83.6
24 Queen Mary, London	2.4	326	80	72	83.1
25 Leicester	1.4	358	93	61	82.7
26 Glasgow	2.4	425	82	56	82.6
27 Bristol	1.7	438	73	74	82.4
28 Aston	1.3	364	85	71	81.9
29 Manchester	2.5	419	74	63	81.4
30 Swansea	1.8	314	81	74	81.2
=31 Cardiff	2.3	405	79	58	80.8
=31 Stirling	1.6	311		79	80.8
33 Hull	2.4	314	87	55	80.7
34 Liverpool	2.3	356	78	62	79.6
35 Strathclyde		387	81	80	78.3
36 Reading	2.6	303	80	56	77.6
37 Oxford Brookes	1.7	321	75	66	75.8

38 East Anglia		338	80	78	75.2
39 Nottingham Trent	1.4	260	79	69	74.6
40 Sussex		401	76	71	73.7
41 Salford	1.5	334	74	57	72.2
42 York		450	77	59	72.1
43 Bangor		374	85	57	71.7
44 Aberystwyth		306	84	64	71.0
45 Northumbria		288	77	72	69.7
46 Ulster	1.3	298	72	55	68.5
47 Manchester Metropolitan	1.1	266	75	57	68.2
48 Liverpool John Moores		292	68	69	65.0

Employed in graduate job:	41%	Employed in non-graduate job and studying:	3%
Employed in graduate job and studying:	5%	Employed in non-graduate job:	24%
Studying:	23%	Unemployed:	4%
Average starting graduate salary:	£20,425	Average starting non-graduate salary:	£16,012

General Engineering

There is no change to the top three in the general engineering table, with Cambridge again extending its lead over Oxford and Durham. But there is a big surprise in fourth place, with Nottingham Trent entering the ranking above a clutch of well-established older universities. Entry standards might have dragged the university down, but there were not enough first-year students taking the subject to compile a reliable score, so the position is based on successes on the other three measures.

Cambridge has the highest entry standards and the most satisfied students, as well as the top grades in the 2008 Research Assessment Exercise, when 45 per cent of the university's work was classified as world-leading. Only on employment does any other university get a look in, Bristol leading convincingly on this measure. For the second year in a row every Bristol graduate was in graduate-level work or further study sixth months after completing a degree.

Wales has two universities in the top ten, with Cardiff leading Swansea. Aberdeen is the top university in Scotland. As in the specialist branches of engineering, there is an enormous spread of entry grades, from well over 500 points at Oxford and Cambridge to less than 200 at Birmingham City, Glamorgan and some of the universities which have too few students to publish a reliable score.

Applications were up by 14 per cent to more than 9,000 by the official deadline for entry in 2009. But there were only 3.5 applications per place in the previous year, making admissions the least competitive of any of the main branches of engineering.

Nationally, the subject is in the top 20 for employment, with almost 80 per cent of all those completing a degree going straight into graduate jobs or further study. Only one university in this year's ranking registered positive destinations for fewer than half of its general engineering graduates. The subject is also among the most rewarding financially. Average starting salaries close to £24,000 for graduate-level jobs place general engineering sixth on this measure.

- Engineering Council: **www.engc.org.uk**
- Engineering and Technology Board: **www.etechb.co.uk**
- Institution of Engineering and Technology: **www.theiet.org**

General Engineering

General Engineering	Research quality/7	Entry standards	Student satisfaction %	Graduate prospects %	Overall rating
1 Cambridge	4.6	564	85	94	100.0
2 Oxford	3.7	544	82	93	94.4
3 Durham	2.5	480	79	91	85.7
4 Nottingham Trent	2.7		82	87	85.3
5 Warwick	3.2	422	71	89	81.8
6 Cardiff	3.1	368	75	83	81.3
7 Exeter	2.5	335	82	77	80.1
8 Bristol		470	81	100	79.1
9 Leicester	2.4	283	81	77	78.3
10 Swansea	3.2	240	74		75.7
11 Aberdeen	2.8	365	70		74.9
12 West of England	2.4	338	75	67	74.3
13 Greenwich	1.0		75	81	70.3
14 Hertfordshire	2.4		73	58	69.4
15 Liverpool John Moores	2.9		70	54	68.5
16 Edinburgh Napier	1.6	277		72	68.4
17 Sheffield Hallam	1.7	206	72	78	68.2
18 Strathclyde	2.7		70	57	68.1
19 Central Lancashire	1.4		67	84	67.1
20 Glasgow Caledonian	1.1	293	77	56	66.8
=21 De Montfort	1.7	200	73	67	66.2
=21 Wolverhampton	1.5	204	75	65	66.2
=23 Coventry	1.0		75	65	65.3
=23 Bournemouth	1.7	207	76	52	65.3
25 Oxford Brookes	1.8	210	70		64.5
26 Queen Mary, London	2.1	234	62	75	64.3
27 Ulster		219	69	81	61.5
28 Birmingham City		199	77	56	59.9
=29 Glamorgan	2.4	189	62	51	59.4
=29 London South Bank	2.4		64	47	59.4

Employed in graduate job:	59%	Employed in non-graduate job and studying:	2%
Employed in graduate job and studying:	9%	Employed in non-graduate job:	15%
Studying:	10%	Unemployed:	5%
Average starting graduate salary:	£23,876	Average starting non-graduate salary:	£15,349

Geography and Environmental Sciences

Geography and environmental sciences have been benefiting from growing interest in "green" issues among potential students. Physical geography and environmental sciences are slightly more popular than human and social geography, but both had more than 14,000 applicants early in 2009. Both also had more than five applications to the place in 2008 and had little resort to Clearing.

Cambridge has maintained its lead over Oxford in this year's ranking, with the highest entry standards and one of the best research scores. The top four all had 30 per cent of their research rated as world-leading in the 2008 assessments. The grades helped Bristol move up to fourth place, just behind Durham.

The sixth-placed London School of Economics has by far the best employment score, seven points ahead of Newman, its nearest challenger for the percentage of graduates going straight into graduate-level employment or further study. Aberystwyth, in eighth place, University College Plymouth St Mark & St John (Marjon), which is 43rd, and Canterbury Christ Church (53rd) tie for the most satisfied students.

St Andrews and Glasgow are the only Scottish universities in the top 20, while Aberystwyth remains well ahead of the competition in Wales. Sheffield Hallam is the highest-placed new university, just outside the top 30.

Entry grades are not as high as they are in some other popular subjects. Although 11 universities average more than 400 points at entry, only Cambridge tops 500 and even some old universities have averages of less than 300. The subjects are also in the bottom half of the employment and salaries tables. In the latest survey, more than a third of graduates were in low-level jobs six months after completing their courses, although the unemployment rate was no worse than average for all subjects. There are some low scores for employment in the ranking for geography and environmental science – notably at Salford, where only a quarter of those completing a degree were in graduate-level jobs or continuing their studies six months after leaving.

- British Cartographic Society: **www.cartography.org.uk**
- Royal Geographical Society (with the Institute of British Geographers): **www.rgs.org**
- Royal Scottish Geographical Society: **www.geo.ed.ac.uk/rsgs**

Geography and Environmental Sciences	Research quality/7	Entry standards	Student satisfaction %	Graduate prospects %	Overall rating
1 Cambridge	3.6	505	87	81	100.0
2 Oxford	3.6	489	82	75	95.0
3 Durham	3.6	462	81	74	93.3
4 Bristol	3.6	455	77	82	92.8
5 St Andrews	3.0	457	83	73	91.6
6 London School of Economics	3.2	422	72	93	90.8
7 University College London	3.3	436	79	73	89.7
8 Aberystwyth	3.1	336	89	68	88.7
9 Southampton	3.0	402	80	73	88.5
10 Sheffield	3.2	415	81	67	87.7
11 Leeds	3.4	382	80	70	87.4
12 Exeter	3.0	378	83	68	87.3
=13 Reading	3.2	352	83	68	87.0
=13 East Anglia	3.3	392	81	66	87.0
15 Birmingham	2.7	379	83	69	86.5
16 Nottingham	3.0	425	77	69	86.4
17 Lancaster	3.0	389	83	64	86.2
18 Glasgow	2.2	389	87	61	85.5

Geography and Environmental Sciences cont.	Research quality/7	Entry standards	Student satisfaction %	Graduate prospects %	Overall rating
=19 Royal Holloway	3.1	320	85	64	85.1
=19 Edinburgh	2.8	427	74	73	85.1
21 Leicester	2.1	349	86	68	84.9
22 Loughborough	2.3	365	84	67	84.5
23 Dundee	2.8	347	80	67	83.7
24 King's College London	3.2	365	76	69	83.6
25 Cardiff	3.2	329	80	65	83.5
26 Manchester	2.9	397	79	59	83.2
27 Newcastle	2.4	382	74	73	82.4
28 Hull	2.6	300	83	65	81.9
29 Queen's, Belfast	2.4	316	83	65	81.6
30 Queen Mary, London	3.5	312	77	62	81.2
31 Sheffield Hallam	2.7	286	86	56	80.9
32 Strathclyde	1.2	369	80	73	80.6
33 Swansea	2.8	317	81	56	80.0
=34 Aberdeen	2.3	318	80	64	79.9
=34 York	2.6	359	76		79.9
36 Sussex	2.9	380	76	56	79.6
37 Liverpool	2.4	344	81	55	79.0
38 Newman		272		86	78.6
39 Keele		284	82	82	76.8
40 Bath Spa	0.8	282	88	61	76.5
41 Plymouth	2.2	280	83	51	76.0
42 Portsmouth	1.7	276	84	56	75.6
=43 Chester	0.8	273	86	61	75.0
=43 Marjon, Plymouth	0.9		89	51	75.0
=43 Bradford	2.7	231	72	69	75.0
46 Gloucestershire	0.9	259	80	70	74.7
47 Ulster	1.9	256	82	55	74.3
48 Bangor		294	78	78	74.1
49 Stirling	1.9	270		60	73.7
=50 West of England	1.1	265	86	51	73.1
=50 Brighton	1.7	267	80	53	73.1
52 Kingston	1.7	230	76	65	72.5
=53 Coventry	0.9	303	78	60	72.3
=53 Canterbury Christ Church		241	89	58	72.3
55 Manchester Metropolitan	1.8	249	80	50	71.5
56 Cumbria		287	79	66	70.9
57 Northampton	1.0	237	83	53	70.7
58 Northumbria		276	85	55	70.4
=59 Nottingham Trent	0.7	258	78	62	70.3
=59 Edge Hill	0.5	254	79	62	70.3
61 Hertfordshire		228	83	63	69.8

62 Worcester	0.8	205	77	62	67.8
63 Westminster	2.3		69	49	67.2
64 Staffordshire		222	79	61	67.0
=65 Oxford Brookes		278	77	56	66.8
=65 St Mary's College		222	78	63	66.8
67 Anglia Ruskin	1.3		75	50	66.6
68 Sunderland	0.8	264	69	55	64.7
=69 Liverpool John Moores		223	79	49	63.8
=69 Brunel	1.6		69	49	63.8
71 Greenwich		215	67	68	62.7
72 Edinburgh Napier		276		48	62.6
73 Southampton Solent		189	79	45	61.4
74 Bournemouth	2.1	236	59	48	60.5
75 Glamorgan		233	74	43	59.9
76 Leeds Metropolitan		211	69	50	58.3
77 Derby		204	68	52	58.0
78 Salford	1.6	235	63	25	54.5

Employed in graduate job:	35%	Employed in non-graduate job and studying:	3%
Employed in graduate job and studying:	6%	Employed in non-graduate job:	29%
Studying:	22%	Unemployed:	5%
Average starting graduate salary:	£19,591	Average starting non-graduate salary:	£14,886

Geology

Cambridge has stretched its lead over Oxford in geology, with the best performance in the 2008 Research Assessment Exercise to add to the highest entry standards in the table. St Andrews has by far the best employment score, a quality that has taken the university from last year's seventh place into the top three.

Glasgow and Leicester, which had the best score in the previous National Student Survey, tie for the most satisfied students. The only universities to come close to their satisfaction levels were Aberystwyth and Exeter, both in the bottom half of the table.

All but five of the 28 institutions in this year's rankings are pre-1992 universities. Plymouth is the highest-placed of the new universities, the others filling the bottom four places. Cardiff is the top university in Wales and two of the top seven in the UK are in Scotland.

Applications to study geology have fluctuated in recent years, but the subject was booming at the start of 2009, with an increase in applications of more than 15 per cent bringing the total to 6,600. The subject was already close to the average ratio of applications to places, with about 1,400 students beginning courses in 2008. Oxbridge apart, there is less contrast in entry standards than in many other subjects. The average is above 200 points at every university in the ranking, and only five average less than 300. Relatively few places are filled in Clearing.

Three quarters of geology students go on to graduate jobs or further study within six months of graduation, although the unemployment level is above the average for all subjects, at 7 per cent. Average salaries for graduate-level jobs were in the top 20 for all subjects, at more than £21,000, when the latest survey was compiled.

Geology cont.

Some of the leading universities expect candidates to have two, or even three, scientific or mathematical subjects at A level.

- Geological Society of London: **www.geolsoc.org.uk**

Geology	Research quality/7	Entry standards	Student satisfaction %	Graduate prospects %	Overall rating
1 Cambridge	4.4	559	86	85	100.0
2 Oxford	4.1	542	82	89	97.4
3 St Andrews	3.0	434	82	95	90.5
4 University College London	3.6	444	79	78	87.5
5 Imperial College	3.4	447	76	85	87.4
6 Southampton	3.2	381	88	74	87.0
7 Glasgow	2.2	373	92	84	86.9
8 Liverpool	3.1	383	87	77	86.8
9 Bristol	3.5	429	79	78	86.7
10 Leicester	2.7	379	92	71	85.5
11 East Anglia	3.4	372	83	76	85.3
12 Durham	3.0	413	83	76	85.0
13 Edinburgh	3.0	413	77	84	84.4
14 Aberdeen	2.6	347	82	86	83.4
15 Royal Holloway	3.2	313	81	78	82.4
16 Manchester	3.2	362	81	70	81.8
17 Exeter	1.6	341	90	81	81.7
18 Cardiff	3.0	333	82	71	80.7
19 Leeds	3.0	380	73	79	80.3
20 Birmingham	2.9	369	82	65	80.2
21 Bangor	2.5	284	79	71	75.9
22 Aberystwyth		359	90	73	72.9
23 Plymouth	2.2	229	81	65	72.1
24 Keele		306	87	76	70.6
25 Portsmouth	2.0	254	74	62	67.7
26 Brighton	1.7		73	60	65.3
27 Wolverhampton		210	73	46	53.5
28 Kingston		210	67	50	51.5

Employed in graduate job:	44%	Employed in non-graduate job and studying:		1%
Employed in graduate job and studying:	4%	Employed in non-graduate job:		18%
Studying:	27%	Unemployed:		7%
Average starting graduate salary:	£21,400	Average starting non-graduate salary:		£15,563

German

Six universities have disappeared from the German ranking since last year's *Guide*, when there had been another drop of ten institutions. This reflects a worldwide decline in the language that has been worrying the German government, as well as academic linguists.

Applications were down by more than 4 per cent at the start of 2009, albeit following the beginnings of a recovery earlier in the decade.

Cambridge makes it five years in a row as the leader in German, but again there is considerable movement further down the ranking. Oxford moves up two places to second, just ahead of St Andrews, which was outside the top ten in last year's *Guide* and not even in the top 20 the year before that.

Grades for German in the 2008 Research Assessment Exercise were lower than in many other subjects. Southampton, in tenth place, achieved the best results, with Oxford's the next best. The top two are only five points apart on average entry grades, with Cambridge in the lead.

Swansea and Warwick tie for the most satisfied students in a subject where satisfaction levels are generally high. The 2008 National Student Survey showed that only one of the 36 universities in the ranking satisfied less than 70 per cent of its undergraduates.

Hull, in 25th place, has the best employment record for the second successive year, with an impressive 92 per cent finding graduate jobs or continuing their studies within six months of finishing courses. Only St Andrews comes within five percentage points of this score. Just two new universities are left in the table, occupying the bottom two places.

Despite the drop in demand for degrees in German, there are still more than five applications for every place. Nine out of ten undergraduates enter with A levels or equivalent qualifications, and entry standards are relatively high, especially at the leading universities. At half of the universities in the table, entrants average more than 400 points.

As in other modern languages, career prospects are reasonable: almost 70 per cent of leavers go straight into graduate jobs or further study, and the unemployment rate is below average. The subject has dropped out of the top 20 for starting salaries, but the average was still almost £20,000 in graduate-level jobs at the time of the latest survey. Most universities in the table offer German *ab initio* as part of a languages package.

- Chartered Institute of Linguists: **www.iol.org.uk**
- Goethe-Institut: **www.goethe.de/enindex.htm**
- National Centre for Languages (CILT): **www.cilt.org.uk**

German	Research quality/7	Entry standards	Student satisfaction %	Graduate prospects %	Overall rating
1 Cambridge	3.0	534	88	81	100.0
2 Oxford	3.1	529	86	78	98.7
3 St Andrews	2.9	409	84	87	94.6
4 Durham	2.9	497	80	74	92.6
5 Warwick	2.3	431	90	69	91.1
6 Exeter	2.6	440	88	66	90.9
7 King's College London	3.0	423	79	79	90.8
8 Bath	2.2	440	85	77	90.4
9 Leeds	2.9	420	84	68	90.0
=10 Southampton	3.2	426	86	55	89.0
=10 Birmingham	2.7	369	87	70	89.0
12 Edinburgh	2.8	461	74	75	88.0
13 Swansea	2.3	302	90	73	87.3

	Research quality/7	Entry standards	Student satisfaction %	Graduate prospects %	Overall rating
14 Bristol	2.5	444	74	77	86.6
15 Royal Holloway	2.8	347	80	73	86.1
16 Heriot-Watt	1.7	391	88	69	85.9
17 Aston	1.3	359	85	85	85.7
18 Nottingham	2.1	400	83	69	85.3
19 Manchester	2.8	419	79	56	83.5
20 Glasgow	1.6	444	79	70	83.2
21 Lancaster	1.8	383	80	72	82.9
22 University College London	3.0	444	69	64	82.6
23 Sheffield	1.8	414	79	68	82.5
24 Aberdeen	1.3	346	85	72	82.0
25 Hull		281	89	92	81.2
26 Cardiff	2.3	380	79	57	80.5
27 Newcastle	2.6	446	72	50	78.7
28 Queen Mary, London	1.8	333	80	61	77.8
29 Reading	1.7	339	80		77.7
30 Queen's, Belfast	1.2	370	79		76.3
31 Liverpool	2.2	314	79	50	75.7
32 East Anglia		371	80	65	72.8
=33 Bangor		272	80	67	69.5
=33 Ulster	1.7		72	52	69.5
35 Manchester Metropolitan	1.1	266	75	57	68.9
36 Nottingham Trent		260	79	69	68.8

Employed in graduate job:	42%	Employed in non-graduate job and studying:	3%
Employed in graduate job and studying:	5%	Employed in non-graduate job:	24%
Studying:	22%	Unemployed:	4%
Average starting graduate salary:	£19,971	Average starting non-graduate salary:	£15,364

History

Success in the 2008 research assessments allowed Oxford to move on from the embarrassment of being outscored in the previous exercise by neighbouring Oxford Brookes, but it was not enough to overhaul Cambridge at the top of the history table. In fact, Imperial College London's work on the history of science won the top research grade this time, but history is not an undergraduate subject at Imperial so it does not appear in the table. Six universities tied for the top research score in this ranking: Cambridge, Oxford, University College London, Liverpool, Kent and Essex.

Average entry scores at Oxford and Cambridge are within a point of each other, at close to four As at A level with an additional AS level. But other leading universities' entry standards are closer to the top two than in many other subjects: all the top dozen – and another nine universities further down the ranking – average more than 400 points. That is because there are more than five applications for every place and, with the total up by over 7 per cent at the start of 2009, competition is likely to increase. History is always among the ten most popular degree choices.

Satisfaction levels are high at most of the 90 universities in the ranking, but the top scores are to be found outside the top 30. Teesside, Chichester and St Mary's College, Twickenham, all satisfied at least 90 per cent of their final-year undergraduates, but Portsmouth has the highest rate, at 93 per cent, for the second year in a row.

Employment scores are much more variable. The London School of Economics again has by far the best record, with 88 per cent of its historians finding graduate-level jobs or continuing to study within six months of graduation. No other university reaches the 80 per cent mark and eight are below 40 per cent – a worrying statistic since the figures were collected well before this year's slump in graduate employment.

History's currency in the jobs market has been a matter of debate. Surveys have shown a strong representation of historians among business leaders, celebrities and senior politicians, but more are in non-graduate jobs than those categorised as graduate occupations six months after completing courses.

St Andrews remains the top university in Scotland, while Cardiff does the same in Wales. Oxford Brookes is the highest-placed new university, just outside the top 30, with Portsmouth and Huddersfield close behind.

- Historical Association: **www.history.org.uk**
- Institute of Historical Research: **www.history.ac.uk**
- Royal Historical Society: **www.royalhistoricalsociety.org**

History	Research quality/7	Entry standards	Student satisfaction %	Graduate prospects %	Overall rating
1 Cambridge	3.8	515	89	77	100.0
2 Oxford	3.8	514	85	79	98.0
3 Durham	2.9	491	88	75	95.0
4 London School of Economics	3.6	472	77	88	94.2
5 King's College London	3.1	468	84	77	93.1
6 Warwick	3.7	467	80	76	92.6
7 York	3.1	474	84	70	91.5
8 University College London	3.8	447	78	76	91.0
9 St Andrews	3.0	468	85	67	90.4
10 Exeter	3.0	428	87	68	90.0
11 Sheffield	3.6	446	80	67	89.4
12 Southampton	3.6	405	83	62	88.0
13 Queen Mary, London	3.3	356	83	73	87.9
14 Leeds	2.9	436	83	67	87.7
=15 Liverpool	3.8	389	85	53	86.6
=15 East Anglia	2.9	383	89	57	86.6
=17 Glasgow	3.1	410	86	54	86.3
=17 Kent	3.8	332	83	62	86.3
19 Leicester	2.7	356	86	62	84.8
20 Royal Holloway	2.9	380	79	68	84.4

	Research quality/7	Entry standards	Student satisfaction %	Graduate prospects %	Overall rating
21 Aberdeen	3.4	341	84	56	84.2
22 Birmingham	2.9	400	81	61	83.9
=23 Edinburgh	3.1	455	73	66	83.5
=23 School of Oriental and African Studies	3.3	359	78	66	83.5
25 Hull	2.8	303	87	60	83.4
26 Essex	3.8	322	83	53	83.1
27 Lancaster	2.7	399	84	52	82.7
28 Bristol	2.6	444	68	79	82.0
29 Nottingham	2.6	420	77	63	81.9
30 Dundee	2.8	368	86	48	81.6
31 Oxford Brookes	3.2	307	80	57	80.4
=32 Portsmouth	2.3	273	93	48	80.3
=32 Huddersfield	2.0	289	87	62	80.3
34 Cardiff	2.2	413	82	51	79.6
35 Sussex	3.2	375	74	55	79.1
=36 Newcastle	2.3	406	73	65	78.7
=36 Keele	2.8	308	78	61	78.7
38 Manchester	3.2	418	70	55	78.3
=39 Reading	2.3	335	82	53	78.1
=39 Queen's, Belfast	2.8	338	77	57	78.1
41 Glamorgan	2.4	226	84	64	78.0
42 Hertfordshire	3.4	240	83	48	77.8
43 Teesside	2.2	264	90	45	77.4
44 Bath Spa	1.9	280	84	58	76.8
45 Stirling	2.5	273	83	52	76.5
=46 Bangor	2.5	277	81	54	76.1
=46 Aberystwyth	2.1	314	83	48	76.1
48 Swansea	2.5	303	82	46	75.5
49 St Mary's College		243	92	67	75.4
=50 Central Lancashire	1.9	251	82	59	75.0
=50 De Montfort	1.8	249	87	51	75.0
52 Strathclyde	1.9	369	78	51	74.8
53 Chichester	1.4	256	91	46	74.7
54 Nottingham Trent	1.6	259	82	61	74.5
55 Sunderland	2.2	231	84	50	74.3
56 Winchester	2.6	263	84	39	74.1
57 Chester	2.3	270	78	54	73.7
=58 West of England	1.9	285	83	45	73.5
=58 Lincoln	1.7	277	79	58	73.5
60 Goldsmiths College	1.8	325	76	56	73.1
61 Lampeter	1.8	271	75	63	72.4
62 Newman	0.9	214	86	60	72.3
63 Anglia Ruskin	2.9	242	78	43	71.9

64 Ulster	2.6	247	78	45	71.5
65 Plymouth	1.4	269	78	55	70.4
66 Kingston	1.6	247	77	55	70.2
=67 Northampton	1.9	193	87	39	70.1
=67 Greenwich	1.9	215	80	49	70.1
69 Wolverhampton	1.6	219	80	46	68.2
70 Northumbria	1.1	280	77	50	68.0
71 Sheffield Hallam	1.7	282	76	41	67.6
72 Brighton	3.6	266	68	31	67.2
73 Canterbury Christ Church	1.4	230	83	37	67.1
74 Roehampton	2.0	257	72	46	66.5
75 Bradford	1.5	249	77	41	66.3
76 Cumbria	1.3	304	69	53	66.2
77 Brunel		288	74	58	65.2
78 Gloucestershire	1.4	240	74	46	65.0
79 Edge Hill	1.5	225	72	50	64.9
80 Worcester	0.5	234	77	51	64.6
81 Manchester Metropolitan	1.1	283	74	39	63.8
82 Salford	1.5	231	71	45	63.2
83 Derby		230		53	63.0
84 Coventry		294		42	62.4
85 Westminster	1.2	261		36	62.2
86 Staffordshire		208	78	43	60.7
87 York St John		253	77	40	60.4
88 Liverpool John Moores	1.1	231	73	30	59.2
89 Newport	1.0		69	40	57.7
90 Leeds Metropolitan		240	74	32	56.8

Employed in graduate job:	28%	Employed in non-graduate job and studying:	4%
Employed in graduate job and studying:	4%	Employed in non-graduate job:	32%
Studying:	25%	Unemployed:	6%
Average starting graduate salary:	£19,197	Average starting non-graduate salary:	£14,651

History of Art, Architecture and Design

Cambridge's lead at the top of the table for history of art, architecture and design could hardly be slimmer. But it is Glasgow that is the challenger this year, rather than London's Courtauld Institute, the one-time leader. Glasgow has moved up from sixth place, largely thanks to the best grades in the 2008 Research Assessment Exercise, which classified 85 per cent of its work as world-leading or internationally excellent. But Cambridge has a predictably massive lead on entry standards and is one of the two universities with the most satisfied students. The other is third-placed East Anglia, which has made an even bigger leap up the table.

There were good scores in art history for most universities in the National Student Survey published in 2008. Only one of the 26 institutions in the ranking failed to satisfy at least 70 per cent of final-year undergraduates. But employment scores are low: the subject is in the bottom ten for "positive destinations". Only Sussex and Bristol saw more than

History of Art, Architecture and Design cont.

70 per cent of leavers go straight into graduate-level employment or further study and the proportion dropped below 40 per cent at two universities.

Neither Wales nor Northern Ireland is represented in this year's table. Only five new universities are left, all at the bottom of the table, with Kingston the highest-placed.

The specialised nature of the jobs market makes for uncertain prospects immediately after graduation. Starting salaries are in the bottom 20 for all subjects, averaging nearly £19,000 at the time of the last survey.

Fewer than 4,000 undergraduates take full-time degrees in the history of art, although another 1,000 are registered on part-time courses. The majority of students are female. Entry standards are high, with a third of the table averaging more than 400 points and only one university less than 250.

- Association of Art Historians: **www.aah.org.uk**
- Society of Architectural Historians of Great Britain: **www.sahgb.org.uk**

History of Art, Architecture and Design	Research quality/7	Entry standards	Student satisfaction %	Graduate prospects %	Overall rating
1 Cambridge	2.6	516	89	67	100.0
2 Glasgow	4.5	416	86	61	99.8
3 East Anglia	4.4	360	89	59	97.4
4 York	4.2	384	85	64	97.3
5 Courtauld	4.2	444	76	65	95.8
6 University College London	3.7	435	77	66	94.6
7 St Andrews	3.0	418	85	62	93.7
8 Sussex	4.2	386	72	71	93.4
9 Warwick	3.0	423	80	59	90.4
10 Birmingham	3.6	379	80	53	89.0
11 Edinburgh	2.8	455	73	63	88.9
12 Aberdeen	2.9	323	84	60	87.9
13 Reading	2.8	334	83	56	86.3
14 Nottingham	3.3	352	77	58	86.2
15 Leeds	2.8	373	82	52	86.1
=16 Leicester	2.1	372	85		85.7
=16 Bristol	2.4	416	69	70	85.7
18 Goldsmiths College	2.8	312	76	65	84.2
19 Southampton	2.5		83	48	83.3
20 School of Oriental and African Studies	3.1	315	78	54	83.1
21 Manchester	4.2	347	72	45	83.0
22 Kingston	2.3		77	48	78.1
23 Oxford Brookes	2.6	329	80	37	77.6
24 Brighton	3.6	272	71	47	77.5
25 Plymouth	2.3	288	76	37	72.5
26 Roehampton		232	72	47	61.6

Employed in graduate job:	30%	Employed in non-graduate job and studying:	4%
Employed in graduate job and studying:	4%	Employed in non-graduate job:	34%
Studying:	22%	Unemployed:	5%
Average starting graduate salary:	£18,975	Average starting non-graduate salary:	£15,749

Hospitality, Leisure, Recreation and Tourism

Sports courses have been removed from this still wide-ranging category in order to give a fast-growing set of courses a ranking of their own. With them have gone most of last year's top ten, since the leading sports courses had the highest entry scores and the best research grades in the wider grouping of subjects. But what remains is a much more coherent table that should be of more use in choosing a university.

The new table contains fewer than 50 institutions, compared with the previous 80. Most are new universities, although three of the top five are older foundations. Surrey, with its 40-year reputation in hotel and tourism management, dominates the ranking. It is one of only four universities with average entry grades of more than 300 points and it achieved the best results in the 2008 Research Assessment Exercise. The University of the Arts London has the highest entry standards, but does not reach the top 30 overall because of low employment and student satisfaction scores.

Bath Spa has the best employment score, achieving "positive destinations" for 80 per cent of its graduates in the latest survey. Nationally, the proportion in graduate-level jobs or further study six months after completing a degree is the lowest of any subject: more than half of all graduates were in lower-level work or unemployed at that point. The subjects fare somewhat better in terms of starting salaries: the average of £18,600 for graduate-level jobs is at least not in the bottom ten.

All but six of the institutions in the table are new universities, of which Central Lancashire is the highest-placed, in third, only a fraction behind Stirling. UWIC is the top university in Wales.

The category covers a variety of courses, most directed towards management in the leisure and tourism industries. The subjects are among the most popular degree choices, with more than 26,000 applications early in 2009, after an increase of nearly 17 per cent. Foundation degrees had seen even stronger growth.

- Association for Tourism in Higher Education: **www.athe.org.uk**
- Council for Hospitality Management Education: **www.chme.org.uk**
- Institute of Hospitality: **www.instituteofhospitality.org**
- Leisure Studies Association: **www.leisure-studies-association.info**

Hospitality, Leisure, Recreation and Tourism	Research quality/7	Entry standards	Student satisfaction %	Graduate prospects %	Overall rating
1 Surrey	2.3	336	80	67	100.0
2 Stirling	2.1	271	75	65	90.6
3 Central Lancashire	2.0	203	81	72	90.5
4 Southampton	1.9		75	66	88.8
5 Bournemouth	1.5	256	75	78	87.6

Hospitality, Leisure, Recreation and Tourism cont.	Research quality/7	Entry standards	Student satisfaction %	Graduate prospects %	Overall rating
6 Sheffield Hallam	1.9	238	79	57	86.3
7 Plymouth	1.6	222	85	47	83.6
8 Hertfordshire	1.7	227	72	66	83.5
9 Brighton	1.8	231	73	53	81.1
10 West of England	1.1	265	74	65	81.0
11 Manchester Metropolitan	1.7	249	72	51	80.9
12 Robert Gordon		285		79	80.7
13 UWIC, Cardiff	1.4	241	79	39	77.9
14 Bath Spa		228	85	80	77.7
15 Queen Margaret Edinburgh		307		62	75.9
16 Edinburgh Napier		271		70	75.6
17 Chester	1.4	227	68	54	75.1
18 Sunderland	1.5	166	76		74.9
=19 Oxford Brookes		270	79	67	74.2
=19 Strathclyde		322	81	50	74.2
21 Westminster		224	77	75	72.2
=22 Manchester		300	74	50	68.9
=22 Portsmouth		242	80	52	68.9
24 Hull		221	82	53	68.8
25 Glasgow Caledonian		299	73	50	68.6
26 Winchester		222	78	57	67.8
27 Gloucestershire		226	75	60	67.5
28 Lincoln		228	80	49	67.3
29 Salford		205	80	52	66.7
30 Glamorgan		247	79	44	66.6
31 Leeds Metropolitan		245	70	59	65.9
32 Derby		241	71	53	64.9
33 University of the Arts London		371	55	52	64.8
34 Coventry		236	74	48	64.6
35 Ulster		237	77	41	64.4
36 University College Birmingham		220	77	44	64.3
37 Huddersfield		231	76	40	63.3
38 Liverpool John Moores		158	72	65	63.0
39 Buckinghamshire New		246	65	53	62.1
40 London South Bank		157	76	50	61.1
41 Cumbria		221	72	42	60.9
42 Canterbury Christ Church		196	77	37	60.8
43 Southampton Solent		165	68	60	60.5
44 Greenwich		208	59	55	57.1
45 Thames Valley		125	69	56	56.8
46 Middlesex		151	71	44	56.4
47 Wolverhampton		164	67	46	55.7
48 Bedfordshire	1.2		61	20	54.7

Employed in graduate job:	38%	Employed in non-graduate job and studying:	3%
Employed in graduate job and studying:	3%	Employed in non-graduate job:	44%
Studying:	6%	Unemployed:	5%
Average starting graduate salary:	£18,621	Average starting non-graduate salary:	£15,236

Iberian Languages

There are big changes in the Iberian languages table this year, but not at the very top. Cambridge remains well ahead of the field, with the highest entry standards and equal top employment record. Nottingham moves up three places, sharing with Manchester the best results in the 2008 Research Assessment Exercise, but it is second-placed Durham and Southampton, one place behind, that have made the most progress. Swansea and Birmingham have gone in the opposite direction, dropping ten and 17 places respectively.

Leicester and Hull produced the best rating in the 2008 National Student Survey, which showed high levels of satisfaction in most universities. Only four universities failed to satisfy at least 70 per cent of the final-year undergraduates. All but six of the institutions in the ranking are pre-1992 universities. Portsmouth is the highest-placed of the new universities and, for the second year in a row, the only one in the top 30. Entry standards are high and still rising: twice as many universities as last year (17) average over 400 points and none slips below 200.

Spanish has been growing in popularity as an alternative to French in schools, and is a common choice as an element of a broader modern languages degree. There had been a small rise in applications at the start of 2009, although the total was still not far above 1,800. The table also includes Portuguese, which had only a dozen applications at degree level, although it is still offered at 18 universities, at least as part of a broader languages programme.

The languages are a little below halfway in the employment table, but do better in this year's salary league. At close to £20,500, the average starting salary is in the top 25 and ahead of the rate for other languages. Employment prospects appear to be more evenly spread than in many subjects: only one of the 43 universities in the table saw fewer than half of their leavers go into graduate jobs or further training in 2007.

- Association for Contemporary Iberian Studies: **www.iberianstudies.net**
- Association of Hispanists of Great Britain and Ireland: **www.dur.ac.uk/hispanists**
- Instituto Cervantes: **http://londres.cervantes.es/en/default.shtm**
- National Centre for Languages (CILT): **www.cilt.org.uk**

Iberian Languages	Research quality/7	Entry standards	Student satisfaction %	Graduate prospects %	Overall rating
1 Cambridge	3.5	534	88	81	100.0
2 Durham	3.0	497	80	74	91.1
3 Southampton	3.2	436	84	67	89.0
4 Oxford	2.7	519	80	68	88.9
5 Bath	2.2	423	87	78	88.8
6 St Andrews	2.6	443	83	72	88.2
7 Nottingham	3.7	382	73	77	86.8

Iberian Languages cont.

	Research quality/7	Entry standards	Student satisfaction %	Graduate prospects %	Overall rating
8 Sheffield	2.9	408	83	65	85.5
9 Leeds	2.9	421	77	68	84.4
=10 King's College London	3.2	405	68	75	83.4
=10 Heriot-Watt	1.7	391	88	69	83.4
12 Manchester	3.7	404	69	68	83.1
13 Edinburgh	2.5	481	63	81	82.8
14 Lancaster	1.8	362	80	79	82.6
15 Queen's, Belfast	2.6	379	76	72	82.4
16 Bristol	1.8	425	77	75	82.1
17 University College London	2.2	453	75	69	82.0
18 Swansea	2.2	316	83	73	81.7
19 Aberdeen	2.2	340	84	66	81.0
20 Leicester	2.0	341	89	59	79.8
21 Kent	1.5	335	81	76	79.7
22 Aston	1.3	388	85		79.5
23 Exeter	2.3	419	74	64	79.3
24 Birmingham	2.2	408	80	58	78.9
25 Portsmouth	2.3	230	88		78.8
26 Queen Mary, London	3.1	340	80	55	78.7
27 Liverpool	2.5	342	73	69	78.0
=28 Stirling	1.6	322		73	76.3
=28 Cardiff	2.3	399	74	57	76.3
30 Royal Holloway	2.3	350	80	53	75.4
31 Strathclyde	1.2	382	80	62	75.2
32 Sussex		387	81	70	73.9
33 Newcastle	2.6	450	72	43	73.6
34 Hull		278	89	68	72.5
35 Glasgow	1.4	410	62	71	72.1
36 East Anglia		359	80	65	70.6
37 Northumbria		281	73	76	68.0
38 Manchester Metropolitan	1.1	294	75	57	67.8
39 Nottingham Trent		260	79	69	67.5
40 Ulster	0.8	296	72	54	64.7
41 Roehampton	1.5	224	73	52	64.4
42 Salford		322	74	55	63.4
43 Liverpool John Moores		211	73	54	58.1

Employed in graduate job:	44%	Employed in non-graduate job and studying:	2%
Employed in graduate job and studying:	6%	Employed in non-graduate job:	25%
Studying:	18%	Unemployed:	5%
Average starting graduate salary:	£20,473	Average starting non-graduate salary:	£15,865

Italian

Cambridge continues to lead a group of 22 universities offering Italian – 12 fewer than three years ago. It has the top score on three of the four measures and is only one percentage point off on student satisfaction for a clean sweep. Leicester has the most satisfied students in a subject that produced almost universally high scores in the 2008 National Student Survey. No university failed to satisfy at least 70 per cent of undergraduates.

Cambridge's lead is considerable on the other three measures. Its average entry grades are almost 40 points higher than Durham's and the 80 per cent of research judged to be world-leading or internationally excellent in the latest assessments was a much higher proportion than at second-placed Oxford.

It is also the only university to see 80 per cent of leavers go straight into graduate-level jobs or postgraduate courses.

Leeds, which has the second-best research score, has jumped seven places to finish third this year, while Durham's rise to fifth is even bigger. Swansea, another improver, is the top university in Wales, while Edinburgh is the best-placed of three Scottish universities in the bottom third of the table. There are only two new universities left in the ranking, filling the bottom two places.

Fewer than 500 students are studying Italian as a separate subject at degree level, although others include the language in combined degree programmes. Only 80 started degrees in 2008 and there were less than 300 applications at the start of the following year. A high proportion – up to 15 per cent – secure places in Clearing. Most students have no previous knowledge of the language, but there is a high completion rate.

The low numbers can make for big swings in the annual statistics: two years ago, for example, starting salaries were in the bottom six, whereas in this year's guide they are in the top 30, averaging more than £20,000.

- Chartered Institute of Linguists: **www.iol.org.uk**
- National Centre for Languages (CILT): **www.cilt.org.uk**
- Society for Italian Studies: **www.sis.ac.uk**

Italian	Research quality/7	Entry standards	Student satisfaction %	Graduate prospects %	Overall rating
1 Cambridge	4.4	534	88	81	100.0
2 Oxford	3.2	494	86	65	90.3
3 Leeds	3.5	425	85	59	86.9
4 Bath	2.2	429	84	73	86.3
5 Durham	1.6	497	80	74	85.1
6 Swansea	1.6		81	78	84.6
7 Bristol	2.9	432	79	70	84.5
8 Birmingham	2.5		83	63	84.2
9 Warwick	3.4	430	82	55	84.1
10 Exeter	1.9	430	79	73	82.8
11 Leicester	1.6		89	54	81.6
12 Manchester	2.9	401	81	54	80.8
13 Reading	3.2	305	80	57	78.7

Italian cont.	Research quality/7	Entry standards	Student satisfaction %	Graduate prospects %	Overall rating
14 Cardiff	2.3	355	81	57	78.5
15 University College London	2.6	417	71	65	78.2
16 Edinburgh	1.1	457	70	79	77.8
17 Royal Holloway	1.7	324	80	61	75.9
18 Glasgow	1.5	401	79	52	75.0
19 Lancaster	1.8		80	50	74.5
20 Strathclyde	1.2		81	50	73.2
21 Nottingham Trent		260	79	69	70.6
22 Manchester Metropolitan	1.1	266	75	57	68.9

Employed in graduate job:	40%	Employed in non-graduate job and studying:	2%
Employed in graduate job and studying:	6%	Employed in non-graduate job:	31%
Studying:	16%	Unemployed:	5%
Average starting graduate salary:	£20,201	Average starting non-graduate salary:	£16,636

Land and Property Management

Another three institutions have dropped out of the Land and Property Management table, leaving only five universities, compared with 23 in 2005 edition of the *Guide*. The subject tends to have small intakes, making it impossible to compile reliable scores for some universities even though they are still offering courses. A total of 24 universities and one college advertised degrees in this field in 2009.

Cambridge maintains the lead, with entry standards that are 100 points higher than at second-placed Reading and nearly 200 points above Ulster's. Cambridge also has the best employment score and registered the best performance in the 2008 Research Assessment Exercise.

The response to the 2008 National Student Survey was too low to produce a score for Cambridge, but Ulster, in fourth place, had the highest levels of satisfaction elsewhere. Reading was close behind.

Land and Property Management has been enjoying considerable success in the graduate jobs market, finishing in the top ten for "positive destinations" both this year and last. The unemployment rate was below 3 per cent at the end of 2007, when 85 per cent of that summer's leavers had gone straight into graduate-level jobs or continued their studies. Graduates' prospects inevitably depend to some extent on the state of the property market, which was still buoyant when these statistics were collected. The ranking reflects this, with both Cambridge and Reading registering "positive destinations" for at least 90 per cent of their graduates.

Only about 2,000 students are taking the subject at degree or diploma level, although the subjects are often included in wider environmental programmes. Starting salaries in graduate-level jobs were close to £23,000 in 2007, placing them among the top 15 subjects.

- Chartered Institute of Housing: **www.cih.org**
- Institute of Residential Property Management: **www.irpm.org.uk**
- Royal Institution of Chartered Surveyors: **www.rics.org**

Land and Property Management	Research quality/7	Entry standards	Student satisfaction %	Graduate prospects %	Overall rating
1 Cambridge	3.7	511		94	100.0
2 Reading	3.1	405	78	90	93.2
3 Westminster	1.4	243	70	85	79.2
4 Ulster		321	79	76	78.9
5 Birmingham City	1.5	243	68		76.2

Employed in graduate job:	58%	Employed in non-graduate job and studying:	1%
Employed in graduate job and studying:	20%	Employed in non-graduate job:	11%
Studying:	7%	Unemployed:	3%
Average starting graduate salary:	£22,883	Average starting non-graduate salary:	*

Law

Law attracts more applications than any other single subject – more than 78,000 at the start of 2009, after a small rise in the demand for places. Entry standards reflect its popularity: nine subjects have higher average entry scores, but only in medicine do so many universities make such testing demands. Almost a third of the 91 universities have average entry scores of more than 400 points. However, it is still possible to secure a place at a handful of new universities with less than 200 points. Nationally, there were only just over five applications to the place in 2008.

The top three are unchanged, led by Cambridge with the highest entry standards and best employment score. Law is only just in the top 20 subjects for employment because of some low scores at the bottom of the ranking, but several universities saw more than 90 per cent of graduates go straight into graduate-level jobs or continue studying.

Aspiring solicitors go on to take the Legal Practice Course, while those aiming to be barristers take the Bar Vocational Course, so it is no surprise that law has by far the highest proportion engaged in postgraduate study. Many law graduates opt for careers in other areas, but the 3 per cent unemployment rate shows that they are still in demand.

Once more, the most satisfied students are not at the top universities. That distinction goes to Sunderland, in 44th place, followed by Derby, at 52nd. The two new universities have swapped positions, but also filled the leading positions on this measure last year. Scores in law were generally high in the 2008 National Student Survey. Only seven universities – and only two of the top 50 – failed to satisfy at least 70 per cent of the undergraduates.

The London School of Economics, in third place, achieved the best grades in the 2008 Research Assessment Exercise, when three quarters of its submission was rated world-leading or internationally excellent. Good results in the RAE have also helped Nottingham move six places up the table to fourth.

Aberdeen remains the top university in Scotland, while Cardiff is now well clear of the rest in Wales. Buckingham again holds the highest position outside the traditional universities, cementing its place in the top 40 despite not being eligible, as a private university, to enter the RAE. West of England is only a fraction behind, as the leading new university in the state system.

Law cont.

Average starting salaries are not as high as tales of riches in "magic circle" firms might suggest. At less than £20,000, the average for graduate-level jobs is in the bottom half of the earnings league.

- Law Society of England and Wales: **www.lawsociety.org.uk**
- Law Society of Northern Ireland: **www.lawsoc-ni.org**
- Law Society of Scotland: **www.lawscot.org.uk**

Law	Research quality/7	Entry standards	Student satisfaction %	Graduate prospects %	Overall rating
1 Cambridge	3.2	531	90	94	100.0
2 Oxford	3.8	528		87	98.7
3 London School of Economics	4.2	513	75	92	94.5
4 Nottingham	3.5	463	82	87	92.4
5 University College London	3.9	488	74	92	92.3
6 King's College London	2.5	467	86	84	90.7
7 Birmingham	2.7	432	86	83	89.6
8 Aberdeen	1.7	417	86	93	88.8
9 Queen Mary, London	2.9	407	85	80	88.3
10 Durham	3.5	488	73	85	88.2
11 Edinburgh	3.2	480	73	87	88.0
12 Bristol	2.6	467	77	88	87.8
13 Southampton	2.2	436	86	81	87.6
14 Glasgow	2.6	483	74	91	87.4
15 Dundee	2.2	419	82	86	86.5
=16 Strathclyde	2.9	454	74	86	85.9
=16 Kent	3.4	362	80	80	85.9
18 Cardiff	3.2	422	78	78	85.5
19 Newcastle	1.7	452	85	78	85.2
20 Exeter	2.1	417	83	80	85.1
21 Leicester	1.8	373	86	83	84.9
22 Warwick	2.2	462	78	79	84.2
=23 Reading	2.9	379	81	75	84.0
=23 Liverpool	2.3	412	77	85	84.0
=23 Sussex	2.3	376	82	80	84.0
26 Queen's, Belfast	3.2	407	72	84	83.6
27 Manchester	2.3	467	76	77	83.4
28 East Anglia	1.8	383	83	80	82.6
29 Hull	2.0	329	79	86	81.3
30 Sheffield	2.5	415	72	81	81.0
31 Lancaster	2.0	408	77	77	80.6
32 Keele	2.3	330	76	86	80.5
33 Leeds	2.6	442	71	77	80.4
34 Robert Gordon	0.7	348		92	78.9
35 School of Oriental and African Studies	2.0	403	71	82	78.8

36 Oxford Brookes	2.2	332	74	78	77.2
37 Aberystwyth	1.6	328	80	75	77.1
=38 Swansea	2.1	317	80	69	77.0
=38 Nottingham Trent	0.8	316	81	83	77.0
40 Buckingham		264	89	82	76.5
41 West of England	1.2	313	81	75	76.3
42 Loughborough		338	79	88	76.0
43 Essex	2.1	324	75	73	75.8
44 Sunderland	0.4	217	94	72	75.5
45 Northumbria		363	79	82	74.8
46 Portsmouth	1.6	300	76	75	74.6
47 Brunel	2.1	360	63	84	74.5
48 Surrey	1.6	366	66	85	74.4
49 Manchester Metropolitan	1.7	310	72	79	74.2
=50 Central Lancashire	0.8	276	79	81	74.1
=50 Edinburgh Napier	0.4	328		85	74.1
=52 Glamorgan	0.8	277	85	70	73.9
=52 Derby		248	92	69	73.9
=54 Stirling	1.7	313		70	73.7
=54 City	1.6	362	65	84	73.7
56 De Montfort	1.1	230	82	75	73.4
57 Glasgow Caledonian	0.8	373	74	73	72.9
58 Hertfordshire	1.7	255	77	72	72.8
59 Brighton	2.4	260		66	72.6
=60 Ulster	2.8	313	71	61	72.5
=60 Kingston	0.7	278	80	75	72.5
62 East London	1.7	202	79	74	72.3
63 Teesside		275	89	65	72.2
64 Bangor		305	82	73	71.6
65 Salford	1.0	330			71.1
66 Westminster	1.6	294	66	76	69.5
67 Lincoln	0.7	251	78	68	68.8
68 Staffordshire		258	80	71	68.7
69 Liverpool John Moores		255	81	68	68.0
70 Plymouth	1.7	260	76	55	67.9
=71 Gloucestershire		256	80	67	67.6
=71 Buckinghamshire New		173	82	74	67.6
73 Huddersfield		252	76	74	67.5
74 Sheffield Hallam	0.5	276	75	68	67.4
75 Greenwich	0.6	241	74	70	66.8
76 Abertay	1.2	326		56	66.7
77 Middlesex	0.8	200	70	79	66.5
78 Coventry	0.3	289	76	62	66.2
79 Bournemouth	0.3	297	74	65	66.0
=80 Birmingham City		274	74	70	65.9
=80 Southampton Solent	0.1	201	75	75	65.9
82 Bedfordshire		215	85	56	65.4

Law cont.

	Research quality/7	Entry standards	Student satisfaction %	Graduate prospects %	Overall rating
83 Wolverhampton	1.2	185	73	65	65.0
84 Bradford	2.4	241	74	42	64.6
85 Edge Hill		241	85	48	64.0
86 Northampton		242	78	50	61.1
87 Leeds Metropolitan		290	62	72	60.9
88 Anglia Ruskin		244	71	57	59.8
89 Thames Valley		199	69	63	59.1
90 London South Bank		194	69	58	57.4
91 Canterbury Christ Church		193	73	42	54.9

Employed in graduate job:	21%	Employed in non-graduate job and studying:	6%
Employed in graduate job and studying:	5%	Employed in non-graduate job:	18%
Studying:	47%	Unemployed:	3%
Average starting graduate salary:	£19,805	Average starting non-graduate salary:	£15,693

Librarianship and Information Management

The ranking for librarianship and information is the only one in this year's *Guide* that has no change in the top five places, which account for half of the table. Sheffield could have regained the lead from Loughborough since it has the best scores on three of the four measures, but was let down by a drop in student satisfaction.

Loughborough has the most satisfied students and is second on entry standards and employment prospects, so actually stretches its lead at the top of the table.

King's College London produced the top results in the 2008 Research Assessment Exercise but does not have undergraduate courses in this field. Sheffield was close behind, with two thirds of its work classed as world-leading or internationally excellent, followed by third-placed University College London.

Employment prospects, even among such a small group of universities, are extremely variable. While 80 per cent of Sheffield graduates found graduate-level work or further courses within six months of competing a degree, the rate at the bottom three universities was below 40 per cent. This contributes to an above-average unemployment rate of 8 per cent, but still leaves the subjects outside the bottom 20 overall.

Student numbers are low – almost half the universities in the table did not recruit enough undergraduates for entry grades to be published. Although there is one more university in the table than there was in last year's *Guide*, that is still four fewer than four years ago. There is no representative for Scotland and only Aberystwyth from Wales. Brighton is the highest-placed new university.

Librarianship and information management are not the poor payers that their reputation might suggest, however. Average starting salaries in graduate-level jobs are close to £20,000 – mid-way in the listing of subject areas.

- Association for Information Management: **www.aslib.com**
- Chartered Institute of Library and Information Professionals: **www.cilip.org.uk**

Librarianship and Information Management	Research quality/7	Entry standards	Student satisfaction %	Graduate prospects %	Overall rating
1 Loughborough	2.6	334	88	78	100.0
2 Sheffield	3.4	346	69	80	93.9
3 University College London	3.2		73	63	88.8
4 Aberystwyth	2.3		76	62	85.4
5 Brighton	2.0	290	70	53	79.3
6 Northumbria	1.1	242	76	65	78.6
7 Liverpool John Moores	1.3	242	74		74.5
8 London South Bank	0.8		80	36	73.0
9 Leeds Metropolitan	2.2		70	36	72.8
10 Manchester Metropolitan	1.1	184	65	38	62.4

Employed in graduate job:	56%	Employed in non-graduate job and studying:	2%
Employed in graduate job and studying:	4%	Employed in non-graduate job:	24%
Studying:	5%	Unemployed:	8%
Average starting graduate salary:	£19,958	Average starting non-graduate salary:	£15,904

Linguistics

There was a big drop in applications for linguistics – almost 15 per cent – at the start of 2009, when most subjects were seeing healthy increases. Following a decline in the previous year as well, this left barely 2,000 applications in a subject where the competition for places was already lower than average. However, entry standards remain comparatively high: this is one of the few tables in which no university's entrants average less than 250 points. A third of the universities in the ranking have an average of more than 400 points and eight out of ten students arrive with A levels or their equivalent.

Cambridge remains the clear leader, with the most satisfied students and high scores on the other measures. Second-placed Oxford has the highest entry standards, while the the School of Oriental and African Studies, in London has easily the best employment score. Oxford and Cambridge were the only other institutions to see three quarters of their linguists go straight into graduate-level work or further study. Although only the bottom two universities dropped below 50 per cent on this measure, the rate was below 60 per cent in more than half of the table.

Queen Mary, University of London, produced the best grades in the 2008 Research Assessment Exercise, moving up to third place as a result. Eighty per cent of its research was considered world-leading or internationally excellent.

Edinburgh is Scotland's only representative in the table, while Cardiff is well ahead of Bangor in Wales. Wolverhampton is the highest-placed new university, only just outside the top ten in a ranking that is dominated by the older foundations. Portsmouth and the West of England are the only other post-1992 universities in the top 20.

Linguistics is close to the bottom ten subjects for immediate employment prospects, although the unemployment rate is less than half last year's rate, at only 3 per cent. Average starting salaries for graduate jobs are in the bottom ten, at less than £18,000.

- British Association for Applied Linguistics: **www.baal.org.uk**
- Linguistics Association of Great Britain: **www.lagb.org.uk**

Linguistics	Research quality/7	Entry standards	Student satisfaction %	Graduate prospects %	Overall rating
1 Cambridge	2.7	504	90	86	100.0
2 Oxford	2.0	517	87	77	93.2
3 Queen Mary, London	3.6	326	85		90.1
4 University College London	2.7	412	84	71	89.1
5 Cardiff	3.5	403	80	60	88.2
6 Edinburgh	3.3	437	82	54	87.9
7 Sheffield	2.9	422	75	64	84.9
8 York	3.1	426	70	63	83.2
9 Lancaster	2.6	405	80	57	82.8
10 Essex	3.1	354	75	62	81.9
11 Wolverhampton	2.7		79	52	80.1
12 School of Oriental and African Studies	1.8	335	69	90	79.9
13 Leeds	2.0	392	80	54	78.4
14 Newcastle	2.2	424	72	56	78.1
15 Portsmouth	2.3	282	81		76.5
16 Manchester	2.4	390	68	55	75.7
=17 Reading	2.0		78	53	74.8
=17 Sussex	1.2	391	69	75	74.8
19 Salford	1.7	300	82		73.8
20 West of England	2.2	290	71	58	71.6
21 Hertfordshire	2.2	251	73	55	70.4
22 York St John		304	86	53	66.9
23 King's College London		374	72	59	65.4
24 Westminster	0.9		74	51	64.6
25 Bangor	1.7	250	71	44	63.7
26 Ulster	2.2	284	56	37	59.1

Employed in graduate job:	34%	Employed in non-graduate job and studying:	4%
Employed in graduate job and studying:	4%	Employed in non-graduate job:	33%
Studying:	21%	Unemployed:	3%
Average starting graduate salary:	£17,681	Average starting non-graduate salary:	£14,535

Materials Technology

More than 10,000 students applied for one of the many variations of materials technology in 2008, but there had been a drop of more than 15 per cent early in 2009. Courses in this category cover three distinct areas: materials science, mining and engineering; textiles technology and printing; and marine technology. The leading universities demand chemistry and sometimes also physics or maths at A level or its equivalent.

Cambridge retains the leadership it won from Oxford two years ago. Cambridge received outstanding grades in the 2008 Research Assessment Exercise. Only 5 per cent of the university's research was considered less than world-leading or internationally excellent.

Oxford has the highest entry standards, although there are no separate scores for Cambridge or fourth-placed Nottingham in this category. Imperial College London, in third place, is the only other university whose entrants average more than 400 points. Other entry scores are tightly bunched, with only one university averaging less than 250 points. Loughborough has the most satisfied students.

Imperial and Exeter, in eighth place, share the best graduate employment record. Swansea is the only Welsh university in the table and there is no representative from Scotland. Four new universities remain in the ranking, of which Sheffield Hallam has the best scores.

Employment prospects are slightly below average for all subjects: two thirds of those completing a degree go straight into graduate-level work or further study, but the unemployment rate was 7 per cent when the last statistics were compiled. Average starting salaries for those who find graduate jobs are also below average, at less than £19,000.

- Institute of Materials, Minerals and Mining: **www.iom3.org**
- UK Centre for Materials Education (materials science): **www.materials.ac.uk**

Materials Technology	Research quality/7	Entry standards	Student satisfaction %	Graduate prospects %	Overall rating
1 Cambridge	4.5		85	85	100.0
2 Oxford	3.6	509	82	81	98.3
3 Imperial College	2.9	432	80	86	92.2
4 Nottingham	3.5		84	77	90.4
5 Loughborough	3.2	288	88	77	86.7
6 Birmingham	3.1	314	77	84	85.3
7 Sheffield	2.9	309	79	83	84.8
8 Exeter	1.6	320	82	86	82.2
9 Leeds	3.4	358	71	68	81.5
10 Queen Mary, London	2.6	298	77	71	78.6
11 Manchester	3.4	362	65	63	77.5
12 Sheffield Hallam	1.7	282	83		75.8
13 Swansea	2.8	245	73	68	73.9
14 Manchester Metropolitan	1.3	282	61	70	65.4
15 De Montfort	1.7	283	60	44	59.1
16 University of the Arts London		263		55	56.9

Employed in graduate job:	51%	Employed in non-graduate job and studying:	1%
Employed in graduate job and studying:	5%	Employed in non-graduate job:	25%
Studying:	12%	Unemployed:	7%
Average starting graduate salary:	£18,871	Average starting non-graduate salary:	£14,764

Mathematics

Maths has been enjoying a renaissance as a degree subject since sixth-form numbers began to recover earlier in the decade. Another 10 per cent increase in applications at the start of 2009 brought the total back above 35,000 – over 10,000 more than there were five years ago.

Mathematics cont.

The number of places has grown as well – more than 6,400 started degrees in 2008 – but the ratio of applications to places is still well over 5 : 1.

This shows in the high entry grades. Eight universities had average entry grades of more than 500 points, a number exceeded only in medicine, while another 15 averaged more than 400 points. The totals are boosted by the fact that many candidates for the leading universities take two A levels in the subject, as well as two or three others.

Oxford has overtaken Cambridge to head the table this year, with the best overall research grades (first in statistics, first equal in applied maths and second in pure maths) Ninety per cent of its work in statistics and operational research was considered world-leading or internationally excellent. Warwick managed the next-best grades, including top place in pure maths, helping the university four places up the table, to third.

Cambridge still has the highest entry standards, but fifth-placed Leicester has the most satisfied students. Maths attracted high satisfaction levels in most universities in the 2008 National Student Survey, but Greenwich was the only other university to satisfy 90 per cent of its undergraduates. The top employment score was at Glamorgan, where more than nine out of ten of those completing degrees went straight into graduate-level jobs or continued their studies. Nowhere did the proportion of "positive destinations" fall below 50 per cent. Often cited as one of the subjects most likely to lead to a lucrative career, maths is among the top 20 subjects for employment. It does better still in the earnings league, with average starting salaries close to £23,000.

Fourth-placed St Andrews is the top university in Scotland, while Cardiff, in joint 35th place retained that position in Wales. Hertfordshire (at joint 24th) is the highest new university, joined in the top 30 by Portsmouth (at 28th) and Greenwich (at joint 29th).

- London Mathematical Society: **www.lms.ac.uk**
- Maths Careers: **www.mathscareers.org.uk**
- Royal Statistical Society: **www.rss.org.uk**

Mathematics	Research quality/7 Pure Mathematics	Research quality/7 Applied Mathematics	Research quality/7 Statistics	Entry standards	Student satisfaction %	Graduate prospects %	Overall rating
1 Oxford	3.9	3.7	4.4	552	85	87	100.0
2 Cambridge	3.7	3.7	3.7	566	83	86	97.9
3 Warwick	4.0	3.4	3.4	542	75	81	91.8
4 St Andrews	1.8	3.4	2.6	523	83	78	91.2
5 Leicester	2.4	2.1		367	91	84	90.9
6 Keele		2.8		351	83	89	89.7
=7 Durham	3.0	3.1	2.2	532	78	79	89.6
=7 Imperial College	4.3	3.1	3.5	508	75	79	89.6
9 Bath	3.2	3.2	3.0	492	75	85	89.5
10 Loughborough	2.5	2.3		384	86	81	88.4
11 Aberdeen	3.1			368		80	88.2
12 Glasgow	2.6	2.3	2.5	413	84	79	88.0
13 University College London	3.0	2.3	2.3	471	78	82	87.9

14 Bristol	3.6	3.4	3.4	501	72	78	87.6
=15 York	2.3	2.4		455	77	73	87.2
=15 Sheffield	2.7	2.3	2.5	410	83	78	87.2
17 Edinburgh	3.4	2.9	2.2	474	75	78	86.9
18 Birmingham	2.6	2.1		430	83	76	86.7
=19 Nottingham	2.6	3.1	3.2	465	79	73	86.5
=19 Southampton	2.1	3.0	2.9	449	75	83	86.5
=19 Surrey		3.0		382	79	80	86.5
22 Lancaster	2.3		2.8	421	83	73	86.1
23 London School of Economics	2.1		2.6	504	72	84	85.5
=24 Heriot-Watt	3.4	2.9	2.2	376	78	80	85.1
=24 Hertfordshire	2.6			221	83	87	85.1
26 Exeter	2.5	2.6		381	84	69	84.3
27 Newcastle	1.9	2.8	2.5	433	76	78	83.8
28 Portsmouth		3.1		274	82	74	83.7
=29 East Anglia	2.8	2.0		390	87	63	83.6
=29 Greenwich			1.6	214	90	83	83.6
31 King's College London	3.2	2.8		434	75	73	83.4
32 Kent	1.6	2.3	3.1	280	76	89	83.1
33 Strathclyde		2.4	2.1	377	78	76	82.2
34 Northumbria		2.1		265	83	81	82.1
=35 Sheffield Hallam	1.3	1.3	1.3	262	89	77	81.6
=35 Cardiff	1.9			431	78	74	81.6
37 Queen's Belfast	2.1			366	76	80	81.2
38 Aston	2.0	2.0	2.0	344		78	80.9
=39 Sussex		2.3		395	81	65	80.8
=39 Glamorgan		1.1		265	81	91	80.8
=41 Liverpool	2.2	2.8	1.6	391	80	62	79.8
=41 Manchester	3.0	3.2	2.8	444	75	59	79.8
=41 Leeds	2.5	2.7	3.3	423	72	70	79.8
44 West of England		0.8		297	84	81	79.5
45 Royal Holloway	1.1			368	78	79	79.1
46 Reading		1.9	1.8	333	80	68	77.9
47 Stirling		1.9		293		75	77.6
=48 Manchester Metropolitan	2.0			303	82	63	77.1
=48 Oxford Brookes		0.9		280		87	77.1
50 Dundee		2.2		327		65	76.3
51 Swansea	1.9			328	74	69	75.3
52 Nottingham Trent	1.6	1.6	1.6	267	70	82	74.6
53 Queen Mary, London	2.6	2.3	2.1	300	75	62	74.3
54 Plymouth		1.3	1.4	274	84	59	74.2
55 Chester		0.9		263	78	74	73.5
56 Aberystwyth	1.9			332	78	54	73.0
57 Coventry	1.0	1.3		293		72	72.7
58 Brunel		2.3	2.5	289	73	59	72.4
59 Brighton		0.9		263		76	72.3
60 Kingston				229	81	76	71.6

Mathematics cont.	Research quality/7 Pure Mathematics	Research quality/7 Applied Mathematics	Research quality/7 Statistics	Entry standards	Student satisfaction %	Graduate prospects %	Overall rating
61 City	1.5			307	73	65	71.3
62 Central Lancashire				316		73	71.0
63 Edge Hill				321		71	70.6
64 Cumbria				246	68	88	68.9
65 Wolverhampton				259		72	68.1
66 Essex				302	72	69	66.9
67 Liverpool John Moores				239		62	62.5

Employed in graduate job:	35%	Employed in non-graduate job and studying:	2%
Employed in graduate job and studying:	15%	Employed in non-graduate job:	18%
Studying:	25%	Unemployed:	5%
Average starting graduate salary:	£22,904	Average starting non-graduate salary:	£16,171

Mechanical Engineering

Cambridge's lead in mechanical engineering is the largest in any subject: second-placed Bristol is more than ten percentage points behind. Cambridge has by far the highest entry standards and the best research grades. Only Robert Gordon and Harper Adams have better employment records. Even on student satisfaction, only fourth placed Loughborough has a better score.

Elsewhere in the table, Imperial College London and Loughborough have moved up to third and fourth places respectively, while Bath has slipped down the top ten. Cardiff remains the top university in Wales and Strathclyde does the same in Scotland. Northumbria is the leading new university, just outside the top 20.

The open access policies pursued by many of the new universities are reflected in the fact that more than a third of their entrants are admitted without A levels or their equivalent. However, only three universities have average entry scores of below 200 points.

Mechanical engineering now attracts more applicants than any other branch of the wider discipline. Indeed, it was among the 20 most popular subjects at the start of 2009, following a rise in applications of almost 20 per cent. The number of places has also risen by more than 1,000 over a five-year period, so there were fewer than five applications per place in 2008. Most universities demand maths and another science subject (usually physics) at A level or its equivalent.

The subject is in the top 20 for employment, despite an above-average unemployment rate of 7 per cent in the latest survey. Almost 80 per cent of graduates go straight into graduate-level work or continue their studies. Mechanical engineering does even better in the earnings league: average starting salaries of more than £23,000 in graduate jobs put it in the top ten for all subjects.

- Engineering and Technology Board: www.etechb.co.uk
- Institution of Mechanical Engineers: www.imeche.org

Mechanical Engineering

	Research quality/7	Entry standards	Student satisfaction %	Graduate prospects %	Overall rating
1 Cambridge	4.6	564	85	94	100.0
2 Bristol	3.4	468	84	87	89.6
3 Imperial College	3.8	498	76	88	88.8
4 Loughborough	3.2	372	87	88	87.6
5 Southampton	2.8	439	80	91	85.7
6 Cardiff	3.1	399	82	83	84.4
7 Bath	2.5	451	82	84	83.7
8 Sheffield	3.7	390	75	84	83.5
9 Nottingham	3.5	380	78	79	82.5
10 Newcastle	2.9	360	78	88	81.8
11 Strathclyde	2.4	441	75	89	81.7
=12 Nottingham Trent	2.7		79	86	81.5
=12 Surrey	3.1	321	78	88	81.5
14 Queen's, Belfast	2.9	373	77	86	81.4
15 Liverpool	3.1	371	72	83	79.2
16 Edinburgh	2.7	415	71	84	78.6
17 Aberdeen	2.8	341	68	91	77.0
18 King's College London	2.2	348	82	73	76.8
19 Leeds	3.3	337	71	77	76.6
20 Sussex	2.6		75	80	76.3
21 Northumbria	2.1	257	80	85	75.7
22 Birmingham	3.1	358	68	75	75.0
23 Liverpool John Moores	2.9	241	71	88	74.9
24 Greenwich	3.6		68	73	74.6
25 Manchester	3.2	417	63	73	74.3
26 Lancaster	2.4	318	70	85	74.2
27 Brunel	2.3	361	69	79	73.4
28 Glasgow	2.2	384	72	72	73.1
=29 Heriot-Watt	2.5	351	68	79	73.0
=29 Robert Gordon		334		97	73.0
31 Aston	2.0	312	68	90	72.7
32 Hull	1.8	232	75	89	72.3
33 West of England	2.4	267	72	77	71.8
34 University College London	2.8	416	64	67	71.5
=35 Swansea	2.3	301	70	78	71.3
=35 Manchester Metropolitan	1.5	234	80	79	71.3
37 Portsmouth	2.0	231	75	82	71.0
38 Harper Adams		282	77	98	70.7
=39 Brighton	2.6		69	71	69.4
=39 Dundee		313	80	84	69.4
=41 Queen Mary, London	2.1	309	80	51	68.7
=41 Hertfordshire	2.4	237	70	73	68.7
43 Huddersfield	1.8	250	77	69	68.6

	Research quality/7	Entry standards	Student satisfaction %	Graduate prospects %	Overall rating
44 Coventry	1.0	288	75	77	67.9
45 Bradford	2.1	227	75	64	67.3
46 Bolton	1.7		81	52	66.1
47 City	2.2	215	68	70	65.3
48 Plymouth	1.3	251	79	59	65.2
49 Sheffield Hallam	1.7	186	70	75	64.6
50 Staffordshire	2.1	216	68	63	63.1
51 Oxford Brookes		270	72	72	60.9
52 Ulster		231	72	75	60.6
53 Kingston	1.4	225	68	61	60.0
54 Central Lancashire		215	77	62	59.1
55 London South Bank	2.4	208	56		58.3
56 Birmingham City		198	65	64	53.3
57 Sunderland	1.0	169		55	52.5

Employed in graduate job:	60%	Employed in non-graduate job and studying:	1%
Employed in graduate job and studying:	7%	Employed in non-graduate job:	14%
Studying:	12%	Unemployed:	7%
Average starting graduate salary:	£23,572	Average starting non-graduate salary:	£17,426

Medicine

There are two tables for medicine in this year's *Guide*: one with the same format as the rankings for other subjects, giving an overall guide to medical schools, and the other detailing the different branches of medicine graded in the 2008 Research Assessment Exercise (RAE). Those who know the area of medicine in which they want to specialise may want to take both into account in choosing a course.

The number of universities in the ranking is growing year by year, as graduates begin to emerge from the medical schools established earlier in the decade. There are three newcomers this year – Warwick, East Anglia, and Brighton and Sussex – but still just over four percentage points cover all the schools. No subject has such high entry standards – eight schools average more than 500 points – and hardly any graduate fails to move straight into graduate-level employment or further study.

Oxford takes over from Cambridge at the top of the table, with the highest levels of satisfaction and one of the many 100 per cent employment records. Second-placed Cambridge had the best results in the RAE, with at least 80 per cent of its research considered world-leading or internationally excellent in all but one of the eight specialisms.

Research and student satisfaction are the two measures which largely determine positions in the ranking. Edinburgh has moved up three places, with the best research grades outside Oxbridge, while a high level of student satisfaction helps Dundee to jump ten places.

Only dentistry has more applications for each place than the 8.6 in medicine. Even though candidates are restricted to four medical schools, the subject was once more among

Medicine

Medicine	Research quality/7	Entry standards	Student satisfaction %	Graduate prospects %	Overall rating
1 Oxford	3.8	540	88	100	100.0
2 Cambridge	4.1	555	..	99	99.6
3 Edinburgh	3.6	547	79	99	99.2
4 Aberdeen	3.1	490	83	100	98.9
=5 University College London	3.5	513	76	99	98.6
=5 Imperial College	3.4	515	73	100	98.6
=7 Glasgow	2.6	518	75	100	98.4
=7 Dundee	2.3	500	81	100	98.4
=7 Newcastle	2.6	494	80	100	98.4
10 St Andrews	2.2	506	86	99	98.1
11 Hull-York	2.9	473	79	..	98.0
12 Leeds	2.6	470	79	100	97.9
=13 King's College London	2.7	467	75	100	97.6
=13 Leicester	2.1	477	80	100	97.6
=15 Liverpool	2.5	481	67	100	97.5
=15 Birmingham	2.7	499	65	100	97.5
=15 Warwick	2.3	..	70	100	97.5
18 Queen's, Belfast	2.2	450	76	100	97.4
=19 Manchester	3.0	489	68	99	97.3
=19 Bristol	2.7	475	64	100	97.3
=19 Keele	1.6	458	79	100	97.3
=19 St George's	2.0	461	74	100	97.3
=19 Brighton & Sussex Medical School	1.7	486	80	..	97.3
24 Sheffield	2.3	481	67	100	97.1
25 Southampton	2.7	457	83	98	96.9
=26 Cardiff	2.3	475	60	100	96.8
=26 Queen Mary, London	3.2	433	71	99	96.8
28 Nottingham	1.8	485	68	99	96.6
29 Peninsula Medical School	2.3	431	75	99	96.0
30 East Anglia	2.0	422	82	98	95.9

Employed in graduate job:	88%	Employed in non-graduate job and studying:	0%
Employed in graduate job and studying:	7%	Employed in non-graduate job:	0%
Studying:	5%	Unemployed:	0%
Average starting graduate salary:	£28,900	Average starting non-graduate salary:	*

the top three in terms of total applications at the start of 2009. There had been a small rise in the demand for places after two years of decline.

The designation of new medical schools was expected to ease this pressure, but entry standards have risen again this year, with no medical school averaging less than 420 points. Most schools demand chemistry and either biology or physics, as well as evidence of commitment to the subject through work experience or voluntary work. Nearly all schools interview candidates and several use one of the two specialist aptitude tests (see chapter 1).

Undergraduates have to be prepared to work long hours, particularly towards the end of

Medicine cont.

the course. But medicine is top of the earnings league, with average starting salaries of almost £29,000 in 2007.

The table below shows only those institutions contained in the Medicine table on the previous page. It shows the areas in which each university submitted research for assessment. The Research Quality scores shown are those included in the calculation for Research Quality in the Medicine table.

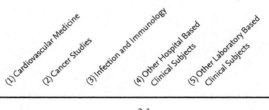

Medicine Research Quality Details	(1) Cardiovascular Medicine	(2) Cancer Studies	(3) Infection and Immunology	(4) Other Hospital Based Clinical Subjects	(5) Other Laboratory Based Clinical Subjects
Aberdeen				3.1	
Birmingham	2.0	3.2	2.3	3.3	
Brighton & Sussex Medical School				1.7	
Bristol	2.5		2.2	2.4	
Cambridge	4.1	4.0	4.0	4.0	4.5
Cardiff	1.8	2.7	2.4	1.4	
Dundee					2.4
East Anglia					
Edinburgh				4.2	
Glasgow	2.9	3.5	2.6	1.9	
Hull-York					
Imperial College	3.1	3.1	3.6	3.7	
Keele					0.9
King's College London	3.4	2.3	3.0	3.5	1.8
Leeds	2.1	3.2		1.7	
Leicester	2.5	2.3	1.8	1.7	
Liverpool		2.1	3.0	2.4	
Manchester	3.1	4.0		2.8	2.1
Newcastle		3.4		2.9	3.0
Nottingham			1.5	1.8	1.5
Oxford	4.5	3.5	4.5	3.8	4.1
Peninsula Medical School				2.4	
Queen Mary, London		3.3		3.2	
Queen's, Belfast		2.4		2.2	1.7
Sheffield	1.4	2.4	2.1	2.3	
Southampton		3.1		2.6	
St Andrews					2.2
St George's	2.1		2.0	1.6	
University College London		3.4	3.4	4.0	
Warwick				2.0	

- British Medical Association: **www.bma.org.uk**
- NHS Careers: **www.nhscareers.nhs.uk**
- Student BMJ: **http://student.bmj.com**

(6) Epidemiology and Public Health	(7) Health Services Research	(8) Primary Care and Other Community Based Clinical Subjects	(9) Psychiatry, Neuroscience and Clinical Psychology	(12) Allied Health Professions and Studies	(14) Biological Sciences	(15) Pre-clinical & Human Biological Sciences
2.6	3.6	3.2				
2.6	2.9	3.7	1.4			
3.8	3.4	3.4	2.4			2.6
4.3		3.1	4.2			
		2.5	3.4			
		2.0				
2.0	2.0					
			2.6			
2.5			1.3			
1.5	3.9			2.9		
4.0			2.5			
		2.3				
	2.3		2.7			
2.6	3.0				2.8	
2.6						
	2.4					
2.8		4.2	2.1			
1.7	2.4		1.9			
1.9		3.6	1.8			
3.9	3.1	4.5	2.7			
	2.2					
3.8	3.5		2.0			
1.9				2.7		
	2.8		2.1			
		3.7				
2.7			1.1			
3.2	1.5	2.2	3.0			
	2.7					

Middle Eastern and African Studies

Oxford had a big lead in Middle Eastern and African studies last year and registered the best performance in the 2008 Research Assessment Exercise. It retains its top position this year, but with a reduced margin.

Durham takes over at second place, even though it does not lead on any individual measure. Third-placed Exeter has the most satisfied students, while Edinburgh, in fourth place, leads on entry standards. The School of Oriental and African Studies, in London, has the best employment record, but no university saw three quarters of those completing a degree go straight into graduate-level work or continue their studies.

Edinburgh is the only university in the table from outside England. Westminster has re-entered the ranking this year to provide the only new university presence.

The small numbers make for big swings even in the national statistics. Middle Eastern and African studies had by far the highest unemployment rate in last year's employment table, at 13 per cent, but this year that figure is down to just 4 per cent. The subjects appear in the top ten of the earnings league this year, with average starting salaries close to £23,500, whereas 12 months ago the figure was less than £20,000 and they were outside the top 20.

Middle Eastern Studies is the larger of two small subjects, in terms of student numbers. There were fewer than 500 applications for Middle Eastern subjects at the official deadline for entry in 2009 and only 100 for African studies. The vast majority – all, in the case of African studies – come with A levels or their equivalent. Completion rates are good, and a high proportion graduate with a first or 2:1.

- African Studies Association of the UK: **www.asauk.net**
- British Society for Middle Eastern Studies: **www.dur.ac.uk/brismes**
- Egypt Exploration Society: **www.ees.ac.uk**
- Society for the Promotion of Byzantine Studies: **www.byzantium.ac.uk**

Middle Eastern and African Studies	Research quality/7	Entry standards	Student satisfaction %	Graduate prospects %	Overall rating
1 Oxford	3.9		81	68	100.0
2 Durham	3.0		78	73	95.3
3 Exeter	2.2	419	84	73	95.1
4 Edinburgh	3.4	500	66	69	93.5
5 School of Oriental and African Studies	3.1	346	65	74	87.0
6 Birmingham	2.9	358	79	45	82.8
7 Salford	1.5		79	60	80.3
8 Manchester	2.6	343	69	55	79.8
9 Leeds		337	75	68	75.1
10 Westminster		230	67	67	66.4

Employed in graduate job:	33%	Employed in non-graduate job and studying:	10%
Employed in graduate job and studying:	3%	Employed in non-graduate job:	25%
Studying:	25%	Unemployed:	4%
Average starting graduate salary:	£23,414	Average starting non-graduate salary:	£17,692

Music

Music has been growing in popularity as a degree subject. There were more than 20,000 applications at the start of 2009, including a growing number seeking places on Foundation degrees. Growth in the demand for places had resumed after a year's decline, with nearly 6 per cent more candidates at degree level and 17 per cent more opting for two-year courses. Nine out of ten degree applicants come with A levels.

There can be considerable variation in the character of courses, from the practical and vocational programmes in conservatoires to the more theoretical. But entry standards tend to be high throughout: ten of the 64 universities in this year's ranking average at least 400 points, while only two slip below 200. Most universities expect candidates to have music at A level, but may accept a distinction or merit in Grade 8 music exams.

Oxford maintains its lead in the music ranking with the highest entry standards and the most satisfied students. Royal Holloway, in 17th place, recorded the best grades in a high-scoring set of research assessments. No less than 90 per cent of its research was considered world-leading or internationally excellent.

Employment scores varied enormously, with the specialist institutions again leading the way. The Royal College of Music tops the pile with 97 per cent of graduates going straight into graduate-level work or continuing their studies. The Royal Academy of Music and the Royal Scottish Academy of Music also registered at least 90 per cent "positive destinations", whereas three universities fell below 50 per cent on this measure.

Birmingham City is the top new university, just ahead of Huddersfield, both of which make the top 30 this year. As in most subjects, the new universities suffer for their lower entry grades, although selection is as much a matter of musical ability as academic achievement.

The 5 per cent unemployment rate in the latest survey remains surprisingly low for a subject in which career prospects are notoriously uncertain. However, music has slipped out of the top half of the employment table, with 30 per cent of leavers in non-graduate jobs six months after graduation. Starting salaries were already well down the table and remain in the bottom four.

- Incorporated Society of Musicians: **www.ism.org**
- Royal Musical Association: **www.rma.ac.uk**

Music	Research quality/7	Entry standards	Student satisfaction %	Graduate prospects %	Overall rating
1 Oxford	4.5	466	89	81	100.0
2 Cambridge	4.5	462	81	79	94.9
3 King's College London	4.5	455	79	82	94.3
4 Manchester	4.7	423	80	79	93.2
5 Royal Academy of Music	3.4		81	93	93.1
6 York	4.5	427	78	77	91.2
7 Nottingham	3.7	439	82	74	91.1
8 Southampton	4.6	371	83	67	89.4
9 Bristol	3.1	384	82	81	89.1
10 Birmingham	4.7	437	77	67	89.0

Music cont.

	Research quality/7	Entry standards	Student satisfaction %	Graduate prospects %	Overall rating
11 Sheffield	4.4	355	82	69	88.0
12 Newcastle	4.0	358	80	74	87.3
13 Royal Scottish Academy of Music and Drama	2.3			90	86.6
14 Bangor	3.3	305	86	72	86.3
15 Queen's, Belfast	3.7	347	81	68	85.2
16 Cardiff	2.9	354	83	70	85.0
17 Royal Holloway	5.2	347	75	65	84.8
18 Edinburgh	3.0	435	77	67	84.2
19 Royal College of Music	2.5	312	72	97	83.4
20 School of Oriental and African Studies	3.9			67	83.3
21 Durham	3.3	412	70	77	83.2
22 Royal Northern College of Music	1.8		77	88	83.1
23 Keele	3.1	287	81	73	82.1
24 Leeds	3.1	357	78	66	81.8
25 Goldsmiths College	3.5	334	71	75	80.9
26 Glasgow	3.6	425	67	68	80.6
=27 Surrey	3.1	374	74	61	79.4
=27 Birmingham City	2.3	307	71	87	79.4
29 Sussex	3.1	357	75	61	79.0
30 Huddersfield	3.3	284	77	64	78.3
=31 City	3.5	280		66	78.0
=31 Bath Spa	1.8	310	81	65	78.0
33 Ulster	1.4	310	72	87	77.6
34 Hull	1.8	261	81	70	77.2
35 Liverpool	2.5	348	75	62	76.9
36 Lancaster	3.6	323	70	63	76.8
37 East Anglia	1.6	269	76	75	75.7
38 Brunel	2.4	334	68	73	75.2
39 De Montfort	2.6	198	77	67	73.7
40 Strathclyde		380	71	76	73.5
41 Glamorgan		292	73	82	72.6
42 Aberdeen	2.1	308		57	71.5
=43 Coventry	2.2	273	73	58	71.1
=43 Edinburgh Napier	0.4	344		67	71.1
45 Oxford Brookes	2.1	229	77	56	70.7
46 Canterbury Christ Church	1.8	243	73	58	68.9
47 Salford	1.3	212	76	61	68.4
48 Plymouth	2.3	162	77	52	67.4
49 Westminster	1.6	284	65	63	67.2
50 Falmouth		271	75	61	67.0
=51 Hertfordshire	1.1	258	74	50	66.4
=51 Middlesex		244	70	73	66.4
=51 Anglia Ruskin	1.3	235	71	59	66.4

54 Roehampton		240	67	73	64.6
55 Wolverhampton		211	73	63	64.5
56 Thames Valley	0.6	204	70	65	64.3
57 Chichester		234	76	53	64.0
58 Kingston	0.6	232	71	54	63.2
59 York St John		226	72	52	61.7
60 Brighton	3.6	239	61	33	60.8
61 Central Lancashire		215	67	60	60.3
=62 Essex		215	70	45	57.9
=62 Buckinghamshire New		264	66	45	57.9
64 Derby		226	61	50	55.2

Employed in graduate job:	35%	Employed in non-graduate job and studying:	4%
Employed in graduate job and studying:	6%	Employed in non-graduate job:	26%
Studying:	24%	Unemployed:	5%
Average starting graduate salary:	£17,157	Average starting non-graduate salary:	£14,204

Nursing

Nursing has been one of the main growth points of higher education since becoming a graduate profession, and a number of universities have taken in nursing and midwifery colleges. Indeed, 54,000 applications placed nursing among the five most popular subjects early in 2009. This represented an increase of almost 16 per cent, with even bigger growth in the demand for places on two-year Foundation degrees. Although there had been a decline in 2008, this followed three years of double-digit increases.

Having jumped from sixth place to first in last year's table, Edinburgh has maintained its position with much the highest entry grades and the most satisfied students. It also has one of several 100 per cent graduate employment records. The subject is in the top four for employment, with only 2 per cent of 2007 graduates unemployed at the end of the year. However, it is not in the top 20 for starting salaries, which average less than £21,000 in graduate-level jobs.

With Glasgow providing Edinburgh's strongest competition after a rise of eight places, there are two Scottish universities at the top of the table. Southampton is up to third, while fifth-placed Manchester produced the best performance in the 2008 Research Assessment Exercise, with 85 per cent of its submission considered world-leading or internationally excellent.

Glasgow Caledonian is the highest-placed new university in a ranking where less than a third of the institutions are pre-1992 foundations. Glamorgan and Central Lancashire join it in the top 20.

Entry standards are more closely bunched than in many tables. Only Edinburgh, Southampton and Nottingham average more than 350 points for A levels and Highers, while just four have averages below 200 points. Almost two thirds of the students arrive without A levels, but there are five applications per place. A quarter of those who join pre-registration programmes drop out, but the wastage rate is nearer 10 per cent thereafter.

- Just for Nurses: **www.justfornurses.co.uk**
- The Royal British Nurses' Association: **www.r-bna.com**
- Royal College of Nursing: **www.rcn.org.uk**

Nursing

	Research quality/7	Entry standards	Student satisfaction %	Graduate prospects %	Overall rating
1 Edinburgh	3.4	414	91	100	100.0
2 Glasgow	2.7	340	85	100	93.3
3 Southampton	4.5	363	76	96	93.2
4 York	3.8	293			92.9
5 Manchester	4.7	312	77	92	90.6
6 Sheffield	2.5		80	100	89.5
7 Queen's, Belfast	1.9	281	86	99	89.3
8 Nottingham	2.8	351	77	95	89.1
9 Ulster	4.2	256	72	98	87.9
10 East Anglia	1.9	284	86	96	87.8
=11 Cardiff	2.3	265	81	98	87.4
=11 Glasgow Caledonian	2.7	303	80	94	87.4
13 King's College London	2.3	297	75	98	86.1
=14 Surrey	0.7	321	80	100	86.0
=14 Stirling	2.7		74	98	86.0
16 Bradford	1.9	328	74	98	85.9
17 Liverpool	2.0	332	82	90	85.6
18 Glamorgan	1.9	263	81	97	85.5
19 Central Lancashire	2.3	298	77	95	85.4
20 Dundee	2.3	214	82	98	85.1
21 Queen Margaret Edinburgh		312		100	84.7
22 Thames Valley	2.0		76	97	84.4
23 Leeds	3.1	308	66	96	84.3
=24 Sheffield Hallam	1.7	260	76	99	84.1
=24 City	3.5	284	72	91	84.1
26 Swansea	1.8	275	71	100	83.6
27 Edinburgh Napier	1.8			97	83.4
28 De Montfort	1.7	334	73	93	83.3
29 Cumbria		287		100	83.2
30 Teesside		314	81	95	82.7
31 Kingston/St George's	2.1	244	76		82.1
32 West of England	1.8	248	71	97	80.8
33 Chester	0.9	260	72	99	80.7
34 Huddersfield		288	79	94	80.4
35 Brighton	0.9	284	69	99	80.3
=36 Oxford Brookes		278	76	96	79.9
=36 Robert Gordon		319		92	79.9
38 Glynd r	1.1	172	85	93	79.7
39 Salford	2.1	210	75	91	79.4
=40 London South Bank	1.7	209		95	79.3
=40 Greenwich	1.5	214	82	88	79.3
42 Worcester		219		100	79.1
=43 Hertfordshire	3.0	208	70	89	78.8

Rank	University					
=43	Canterbury Christ Church		243	75	98	78.8
45	Abertay		246		97	78.7
46	Middlesex	1.7		80	85	78.6
47	Manchester Metropolitan	1.2	167	73	100	78.5
48	Northumbria	2.5	314	80	72	78.4
=49	Birmingham		331	78	86	78.2
=49	Birmingham City		263		94	78.2
51	Anglia Ruskin		256	74	96	78.0
52	Hull		210	75	99	77.6
=53	Northampton		259		94	77.5
=53	Bournemouth	2.0	219	68	93	77.5
55	Edge Hill	1.5	214	82	84	77.4
56	Wolverhampton		334	70	90	77.2
57	Bangor		184	77	98	76.9
58	Plymouth	1.7	232	68	92	76.6
59	Coventry		219		95	76.2
60	Keele		227		94	75.7
61	Leeds Metropolitan		259	75	88	75.1
62	Bedfordshire		197	74	93	74.2
63	Liverpool John Moores	1.8	213	65	89	73.8
64	Staffordshire		202	64	93	70.8

Employed in graduate job:	86%	Employed in non-graduate job and studying:	0%
Employed in graduate job and studying:	8%	Employed in non-graduate job:	3%
Studying:	2%	Unemployed:	2%
Average starting graduate salary:	£20,967	Average starting non-graduate salary:	£15,434

Other Subjects Allied to Medicine

The "allied to medicine" category covers audiology, complementary therapies, counselling, health services management, health sciences, nutrition, occupational therapy, optometry, ophthalmology, orthoptics, osteopathy, physiotherapy, podiatry, radiography and speech therapy. Traditional universities dominate the top ten, but big names such as Bristol and Birmingham find themselves outside the top 30.

Aston has taken over from Cardiff at the top of the table, moving up from fourth place with the most satisfied students and a good employment record. Second-placed Leeds and Bangor, in 32nd place, both saw all their leavers go straight into graduate-level work or further study.

Cambridge, in fourth place, has a predictably huge lead on entry standards. But, like Bristol, Durham and Imperial College London, it did not enter the 2008 Research Assessment Exercise in this group of subjects. Leeds and University College London, which only just makes the top 30, share the top research grades.

Stiff competition for places in subjects such as optometry and physiotherapy has been pushing up entry grades, with six universities averaging more than 400 points on the UCAS tariff, although four dropped below 200 in the latest survey. The choice of specialism also affects graduate employment rates, which range from full employment in graduate-level jobs to less than half that rate at the bottom of the table.

Other Subjects Allied to Medicine cont.

The table is more mixed than most in terms of the performance of new and old universities. Glasgow Caledonian is the highest-placed new university, while Portsmouth and Robert Gordon both make the top 20.

Across the whole range of subjects, almost half of the students arrive without A levels. Applications were up by more than 7 per cent at the start of 2009, topping 26,000. The subjects are now in the top 20 most popular degree choices. Three quarters of leavers go straight into graduate jobs – also in the top 20 – but average starting salaries are well below average for all subjects, at less than £19,500.

- Association of Health Professions in Ophthalmology: **www.ahpo.org**
- British Association/College of Occupational Therapists: **www.cot.org.uk**
- British Society of Audiology: **www.thebsa.org.uk**
- Chartered Society of Physiotherapy: **www.csp.org.uk**
- General Chiropractic Council: **www.gcc-uk.org**
- General Osteopathic Council: **www.osteopathy.org.uk**
- General Optical Council: **www.optical.org**
- Health Professions Council: **www.hpc-uk.org**
- NHS Careers: **www.nhscareers.nhs.uk**
- Royal College of Radiologists: **www.rcr.ac.uk**
- Royal College of Speech and Language Therapists: **www.rcslt.org**
- Society of Chiropodists and Podiatrists: **www.feetforlife.org**
- Society of Radiographers: **www.sor.org**

Other Subjects Allied to Medicine	Research quality/7	Entry standards	Student satisfaction %	Graduate prospects %	Overall rating
1 Aston	2.5	386	89	96	100.0
2 Leeds	3.1	325	83	100	97.2
3 Cardiff	2.8	384	79	92	95.0
4 Cambridge		558	86	84	94.4
5 Newcastle	2.7	427	82	76	93.8
6 Lancaster	3.0	364	80	80	91.5
7 Manchester	2.7	403	72	93	91.3
8 Exeter	2.8	351	78	88	91.2
9 Glasgow Caledonian	2.7	377	78	80	90.4
10 Bradford	1.8	375	80	87	90.0
=11 Hull	2.9		75	81	88.7
=11 Strathclyde	2.7	396	72	83	88.7
13 Nottingham	2.0	351	81	83	88.6
14 Imperial College		474		82	88.4
15 Queen Mary, London	3.0		73	84	88.3
16 Sheffield	2.6	373	79	71	88.0
17 Portsmouth	2.6	279	77	92	87.9
18 Southampton	1.1	391	82	81	87.6
19 King's College London	2.6	381	75	76	87.3
20 Robert Gordon	1.3	379		87	87.1

21 West of England	2.8	287	78	79	86.6
=22 Ulster	2.7	340	71	85	85.9
=22 Kent	1.6	282	86	77	85.9
24 City	1.8	303	73	94	84.6
25 Liverpool	2.0	346	68	93	84.3
26 Durham		390	84	78	83.8
27 Anglia Ruskin	1.1	326	77	89	83.7
28 Oxford Brookes	1.7	337	77	76	83.5
29 University College London	3.1	372	69	69	83.4
30 Brighton	0.9	303	82	81	83.0
31 Hertfordshire	2.4	279	72	85	82.8
32 Bangor		346	75	100	82.6
33 Birmingham		423	79	76	82.1
34 Nottingham Trent	2.7	279	70	82	82.0
35 Reading		448		70	81.8
36 Northumbria	1.5	286	79	78	81.7
37 East Anglia	0.8	379	78	70	81.3
38 Sheffield Hallam	1.2	322	75	81	81.1
39 Salford	1.7	274	75	80	80.4
40 Teesside	1.0	282	81	74	80.1
41 Queen Margaret Edinburgh	0.5	357		81	79.9
42 Northampton	0.8	240	77	92	79.7
43 St George's		307	78	88	79.4
44 Swansea	2.8	329	72	57	79.0
45 UWIC, Cardiff	1.0	300	75	78	78.4
46 Cumbria	0.1	305		88	77.5
47 Central Lancashire	1.5	257	78	65	76.8
48 Coventry	0.9	303		76	76.6
49 Keele		318		79	76.5
50 Manchester Metropolitan	1.5	333	71	66	76.4
51 Bristol		316	75	80	76.1
52 East London	1.7	237	74	72	75.8
53 De Montfort	1.4	255	74	71	75.7
=54 Birmingham City		292		81	75.5
=54 York St John	0.3	292	78	70	75.5
56 Leeds Metropolitan	0.6	302	75	69	74.8
57 London South Bank		180	78	91	74.6
58 Middlesex	1.5	224	65	89	74.1
59 Bedfordshire		188	75	93	74.0
60 Brunel	1.4	337	63	74	73.9
61 Canterbury Christ Church	0.4	261	68	84	72.4
=62 Greenwich		234	83	60	71.9
=62 Westminster	1.9	207	68	71	71.9
64 Edinburgh Napier	0.9			68	71.7
65 Essex		235		80	71.5
66 Chester	0.8	261	76	57	71.1
67 Plymouth	0.5	308	65	76	71.0

	Research quality/7	Entry standards	Student satisfaction %	Graduate prospects %	Overall rating
68 Kingston	1.4		72	57	70.7
69 Glamorgan	0.1	329	57	93	70.6
70 Roehampton	1.0		74	56	70.3
71 Liverpool John Moores	1.4	226	75	51	69.8
72 Lincoln	0.5	231	74	63	69.3
73 Huddersfield		245	73	68	69.1
74 St Mary's College		268	78	52	68.8
75 Derby		256	64	76	66.6
=76 Wolverhampton	1.1	167	70	58	65.1
=76 University College Birmingham		199	73	62	65.1
78 Abertay	0.7	269		42	61.9
79 Worcester	0.6			48	58.7

Employed in graduate job:	66%	Employed in non-graduate job and studying:	1%
Employed in graduate job and studying:	8%	Employed in non-graduate job:	14%
Studying:	7%	Unemployed:	4%
Average starting graduate salary:	£19,418	Average starting non-graduate salary:	£14,750

Pharmacology and Pharmacy

Pharmacology and pharmacy have been among the big successes of higher education in recent years. The numbers of applications and places have grown by a third since 2003 and the subjects are still in the top six for "positive destinations". Only 2 per cent of graduates were unemployed at the end of 2007 and nine out of ten went straight into graduate-level jobs or continued their studies. As a result, there are six applications for every place, making it one of the most competitive subjects in the *Guide*.

Edinburgh retains the top place that it won for the first time last year. It has the most satisfied students and the top research score. Queen's, Belfast moves up to second, as one of seven universities with 100 per cent employment records. Queen's was the only university in last year's *Guide* to achieve this feat in pharmacology and pharmacy, but it has now been joined by Nottingham, East Anglia, Aston, Robert Gordon and the School of Pharmacy, in London. The subject is in the top six for employment prospects and only three universities saw fewer than 70 per cent of their graduates go on to "positive destinations".

Entry standards are high and rising throughout the table. In the absence of scores for Cambridge or Edinburgh, Leeds has the best-qualified entrants. It is one of ten universities (nearly a third of the total) to average more than 400 points, while none slips below 250.

Robert Gordon is the top new university and is joined by Portsmouth in the top 20. Cardiff is the only representative of Wales in a table that contains six more institutions than there were two years ago.

Departments in England are evenly split between those specialising in pharmacy and pharmacology. Only four cover both. Since 1997, pharmacy degrees have been converted to the four-year MPharm, whereas pharmacology is available either as a three-year BSc or as an extended course. Surprisingly, given graduates' success in the labour market, the subjects are not high in the earnings league: average starting salaries below £19,000 for graduate-level jobs place them 45th out of the 62 subjects.

- Association of Pharmacy Technicians UK: **www.aptuk.org**
- British Pharmacological Society: **www.bps.ac.uk**
- National Pharmacy Association: **http://npa.co.uk**
- Royal Pharmaceutical Society of Great Britain: **www.rpsgb.org.uk**

Pharmacology and Pharmacy	Research quality/7	Entry standards	Student satisfaction %	Graduate prospects %	Overall rating
1 Edinburgh	4.2		91	78	100.0
2 Queen's, Belfast	2.7	401	89	100	97.1
3 Nottingham	4.0	419	76	100	96.1
4 East Anglia	2.6	382	89	100	95.4
5 Manchester	3.6	412	79	96	95.2
6 Bath	2.9	446	79	97	94.9
7 Leeds	2.8	447	87	80	94.1
8 Cardiff	2.6	399	83	98	93.2
9 Cambridge	2.9		86	85	92.6
10 Strathclyde	2.6	444	79	93	92.5
11 School of Pharmacy	3.2	397	75	100	91.7
12 Aston	2.5	410	78	100	91.3
13 University College London	3.0	411	80	82	90.1
14 Glasgow	2.6	391	83	81	89.2
15 Bristol	2.6	397	78	85	87.7
16 Liverpool	2.7	353	83	78	86.7
17 King's College London	2.6	384	73	91	85.9
18 Robert Gordon		402		100	85.4
19 Portsmouth	2.6	298	78	95	84.5
20 Bradford	2.6	315	78	91	84.4
21 De Montfort	2.0	302	83	93	84.3
22 Sunderland	0.9	328	83	96	82.5
23 Liverpool John Moores	1.4	341	76	98	82.1
24 Brighton	1.9	361	66	100	80.6
25 Southampton	2.3	391	79	57	80.5
26 Reading	2.1	329			80.3
27 Dundee		403	82	81	79.9
28 Aberdeen		379	85	77	79.0
29 Hertfordshire	1.7	288	86	70	78.8
30 Newcastle		381	80	86	78.7
31 Greenwich	1.3	274	87	65	76.3
32 Nottingham Trent	2.7		69	62	74.0
33 Kingston	1.4	257	78	74	73.2

Pharmacology and Pharmacy cont.

Employed in graduate job:	65%	Employed in non-graduate job and studying:	1%
Employed in graduate job and studying:	16%	Employed in non-graduate job:	6%
Studying:	11%	Unemployed:	2%
Average starting graduate salary:	£18,944	Average starting non-graduate salary:	£14,422

Philosophy

Many expected philosophy to struggle in the era of top-up fees, with perceptions of employability dominating subject choices. But there were still approaching six applications to the place in 2008 – one of the highest ratios in the arts and social sciences – and the demand for places had grown by nearly 16 per cent early in 2009.

Entry standards are correspondingly high, with more than a third of the 50 universities in the ranking averaging more than 400 points on the UCAS tariff. Top-placed Cambridge and Oxford, in second place, both have averages that are the equivalent of four As at A level and another at AS level.

The top scores on other measures are spread around universities in the top ten. The best employment record is at the London School of Economics, in third place overall, where an impressive 96 per cent of philosophers found graduate-level jobs or postgraduate courses within six months of completing a degree. However, the success rate was below 50 per cent at nine universities in the ranking and below 30 per cent at one.

The best of a generally high set of scores in the 2008 National Student Survey came at Aberdeen, where more than nine out of ten undergraduates were satisfied with their course. Only two universities failed to satisfy at least 70 per cent of their students.

University College London produced the best results in the 2008 Research Assessment Exercise, when three quarters of its submission was rated world-leading or internationally excellent. St Andrews was close behind on research and remains the top university in Scotland and fourth in the UK. Cardiff remains top in Wales, while Central Lancashire just pips Brighton to the distinction of the highest finish among the new universities.

Philosophy is just outside the bottom ten in the employment table, with more than a third of leavers starting their working life in non-graduate jobs. However, the subject is in the top 20 for starting salaries, with an average of nearly £21,500 for graduate-level work.

Relatively few philosophy undergraduates studied the subject at A level – indeed, Bristol warns that even an A in the subject is "not necessarily evidence of aptitude for philosophy at university." Degrees can require more mathematical skills than many candidates expect, especially when there is an emphasis on logic in the syllabus.

- British Philosophical Association: **www.bpa.ac.uk**
- Philosophical Society of England:
  http://atschool.eduweb.co.uk/cite/staff/philosopher/philsocindex.htm
- Royal Institute of Philosophy: **www.royalinstitutephilosophy.org**

Philosophy

	Research quality/7	Entry standards	Student satisfaction %	Graduate prospects %	Overall rating
1 Cambridge	3.5	554	89	84	100.0
2 Oxford	3.7	539	86	80	97.3
3 London School of Economics	3.7	474	76	96	92.9
4 St Andrews	4.1	485	84	61	91.7
5 Durham	2.6	488	79	78	87.6
6 Sheffield	3.8	436	81	61	87.3
=7 University College London	4.3	465	72	68	86.1
=7 King's College London	3.9	440	78	62	86.1
9 Aberdeen	1.5	305	91	78	85.0
10 Bristol	3.5	455	75	66	84.4
11 Stirling	3.4	293	83	67	83.4
=12 Exeter	2.9	403	83	57	83.1
=12 York	2.7	449	77	67	83.1
14 Warwick	2.7	479	76	65	82.9
=15 Dundee	2.3	364	84	63	82.2
=15 Essex	3.3	309	87	50	82.2
17 Nottingham	3.2	400	75	66	81.4
18 Newcastle	2.5	366	75	76	80.5
19 Leeds	3.1	389	77	56	80.1
=20 Edinburgh	3.1	450	70	64	79.7
=20 Cardiff	1.7	374	86	54	79.7
22 Glasgow	2.3	410	81	49	79.1
23 Reading	3.7	349	77	48	78.7
24 Hull	1.7	311	81	64	77.2
=25 Southampton	2.0	384	77	57	76.8
=25 Birmingham	2.0	396	74	64	76.8
27 East Anglia	1.8	352	79	52	74.9
28 Kent	2.0	316	76	62	74.8
29 Bradford	2.4		77	50	74.3
30 Sussex	2.6	375	69	59	74.2
31 Manchester	2.3	428	69	56	74.0
32 Lancaster	2.2	376	78	41	73.8
33 Central Lancashire		266	82	75	73.6
34 Brighton	3.6	248	78	38	73.1
=35 Liverpool	1.4	397	74	53	72.6
=35 Greenwich		270	87	56	72.6
37 Staffordshire	1.2		78	53	71.6
38 Oxford Brookes	0.8	290	79	57	70.7
39 West of England	0.8	265	83	50	70.6
40 Middlesex	3.1	225	72		70.1
41 Queen's, Belfast	2.4	326	74	37	69.6
=42 Hertfordshire	1.6	233	78	50	69.4
=42 Heythrop College	0.7	308	75	60	69.4

	Research quality/7	Entry standards	Student satisfaction %	Graduate prospects %	Overall rating
44 Keele		323	75	60	67.8
45 Manchester Metropolitan	2.0	263	74	38	66.8
46 Lampeter	0.9	229	74		63.0
47 Anglia Ruskin		255	78	37	62.5
48 Roehampton		248	72	50	61.7
49 Wolverhampton		219	71	43	58.4
50 Newport		245	73	29	57.1

Employed in graduate job:	30%	Employed in non-graduate job and studying:		4%
Employed in graduate job and studying:	4%	Employed in non-graduate job:		31%
Studying:	23%	Unemployed:		6%
Average starting graduate salary:	£21,466	Average starting non-graduate salary:		£15,312

Physics and Astronomy

There has been constant concern about the state of physics in recent years, with sixth-form numbers dropping and university departments closing. Two more universities have dropped out of the ranking this year. But more undergraduates started courses in 2008 than was the case five years earlier and there were still five applications for every place. There had been a 6 per cent increase in applications early in 2009, with more than 17,000 candidates seeking places.

Cambridge has stretched its lead at the top of the table, but Glasgow has jumped five places to become the nearest challenger. Cambridge has the highest entry standards but, once again, the other top scores are spread around the leading universities.

Glasgow and third-placed Oxford share the best employment record in a subject where almost half of all graduates continue their studies, either full or part-time. Although physics is just outside the top 20 subjects for employment prospects, all but two of the universities in the ranking saw at least 70 per cent of those completing degrees go straight into graduate-level jobs or further study.

Physics has also produced consistently high scores in the National Student Survey, with every university satisfying at least 70 per cent of undergraduates in the 2008 results. Aberystwyth has the top score of 90 per cent, but the lowest research grades in the table keep the university out of the top 30. Physics was one of the lowest-scoring subjects in the 2008 Research Assessment Exercise, when only Lancaster had more than 20 per cent of its work rated world-leading.

Both physics and astronomy command high entry grades: four of the top five average at least 520 points for A levels and Highers. Just seven of the 42 universities in the table average less than 300 points, leaving the rest tightly bunched. Most universities demand both physics and maths at A level, as well as good grades overall.

Swansea is just ahead of Aberystwyth as the leading university in Wales. Only two new universities are left in the table, both in the bottom five, with Nottingham Trent the higher-placed.

The profile of undergraduates is among the most traditional: only one in five is female and a similar proportion arrive without A levels or their equivalent. About 5 per cent transfer to other courses or drop out, usually at the end of the first year, but over half of those who remain get firsts or 2:1s. The subjects are in the top 20 for starting salaries, averaging almost £22,500 in graduate-level jobs.

- British Astronomical Association: **http://britastro.org**
- Institute of Physics: **www.iop.org**

Physics and Astronomy	Research quality/7	Entry standards	Student satisfaction %	Graduate prospects %	Overall rating
1 Cambridge	3.3	559	86	85	100.0
2 Glasgow	3.0	403	85	86	94.9
3 Oxford	2.8	551	79	86	94.6
4 Durham	3.0	528	84	77	94.1
5 Imperial College	3.0	523	78	84	93.9
6 Sheffield	3.0	392	87	81	93.5
7 Birmingham	2.9	458	88	74	93.3
8 St Andrews	3.3	483	79	79	92.9
9 Southampton	2.7	452	85	80	92.1
10 Aberdeen	2.8	364	83	85	91.9
11 Lancaster	3.4	384	83	71	90.4
12 Manchester	2.8	479	82	73	90.0
13 Warwick	2.6	493	82	75	89.8
14 Nottingham	3.3	422	77	77	89.7
15 Exeter	2.8	386	88	70	89.2
16 Leeds	2.5	424	79	81	88.2
17 Sussex	2.8	403	81	74	87.5
18 York	2.6	399	84	71	87.3
19 Liverpool	2.8	371	80	76	87.2
=20 University College London	3.0	437	72	79	87.1
=20 Edinburgh	3.1	466	76	71	87.1
=22 Hull	2.2	251	86	84	86.9
=22 Royal Holloway	2.4	346	85	75	86.9
=24 Bristol	2.8	459	77	73	86.8
=24 Bath	3.2	400	77	72	86.8
26 Loughborough	2.5	356	84	72	85.8
27 Keele	1.8	309	82	82	84.3
28 Heriot-Watt	2.7	339	78	73	84.0
29 King's College London	2.4	418	77	74	83.9
30 Leicester	2.6	373	76	74	83.8
31 Surrey	2.4	367	77	74	83.6
32 Swansea	2.4	282	77	80	83.4
33 Aberystwyth	1.3	237	90	77	82.1
34 Kent	2.5	254	77	76	81.7
35 Strathclyde	1.9	330	81	73	81.2
=36 Cardiff	2.0	341	80	71	81.0
=36 Queen's, Belfast	2.3	390	74	71	81.0

Physics and Astronomy cont.	Research quality/7	Entry standards	Student satisfaction %	Graduate prospects %	Overall rating
38 Queen Mary, London	2.5	314	80	64	80.3
39 Nottingham Trent	2.7	238	73	74	79.6
40 Hertfordshire	2.6	230	82	58	78.2
41 Dundee		320	82	81	75.2
42 Salford		211		71	65.9

Employed in graduate job:	28%	Employed in non-graduate job and studying:	2%
Employed in graduate job and studying:	9%	Employed in non-graduate job:	17%
Studying:	38%	Unemployed:	7%
Average starting graduate salary:	£22,249	Average starting non-graduate salary:	£16,234

Politics

Politics has been enjoying a boom as a degree subject. After substantial increases early in the decade, applications topped 25,000 at the start of 2009 after a 17 per cent rise that was more than double the average for all subjects. With more than five applications for every place, entry scores have been rising. Nineteen universities, almost twice as many as two years ago, average over 400 points and only one (just) less than 200 points.

Oxford holds onto top place with the highest entry grades and good scores on the other measures. St Andrews moves up to second, with the smallest possible lead over Sheffield, one of the two universities with the best results in the 2008 Research Assessment Exercise. The other was Essex, which also had three quarters of its research rated world-leading or internationally excellent.

For the second year in a row, the most satisfied students are at Portsmouth, which has moved up to 17th place and is the only new university in top 40. Scores in politics were generally high in the 2008 National Student Survey: only five of the 69 universities failed to satisfy at least 70 per cent of undergraduates.

Employment scores are much more variable. The London School of Economics, in sixth place, saw 90 per cent of politics graduates go straight into graduate-level jobs or continue their studies, but there were a dozen universities where the success rate fell below 50 per cent.

The subject is in the bottom 20 for job prospects. Although the unemployment rate is only just above average, almost a third of graduates start their careers in lower-level employment. Politics is in the top half of the earnings league, however, with starting salaries close to £21,000 for those who do find graduate-level employment.

- Political Studies Association of the UK: **www.psa.ac.uk**
- Politics Association: **www.politicsassociation.com**

Politics	Research quality/7	Entry standards	Student satisfaction %	Graduate prospects %	Overall rating
1 Oxford	3.5	534	84	87	100.0
2 St Andrews	2.1	498	84	83	92.8

3 Sheffield	4.3	426	79	74	92.7
4 Cambridge	2.6	501	80	80	92.1
5 Essex	4.3	356	84	67	91.8
=6 University College London	3.0	476	75	84	90.1
=6 London School of Economics	3.3	451	72	90	90.1
8 Warwick	2.9	474	77	73	88.2
9 Exeter	2.8	418	82	69	87.9
10 Durham	2.4	463	76	79	87.2
11 King's College London	2.3	438	78	76	86.3
12 Hull	1.9	345	83	75	84.4
13 Aberystwyth	3.8	324	80	52	83.8
14 School of Oriental and African Studies	2.7	429	73	68	82.9
15 York	2.3	457	74	68	82.6
16 Nottingham	2.5	420	72	74	82.5
=17 Bath	2.2	437	73	75	82.4
=17 Portsmouth	2.3	259	89	57	82.4
19 Glasgow	2.3	416	78	60	81.9
20 Cardiff	2.3	412	76	65	81.4
=21 Birmingham	2.0	388	79	62	80.8
=21 Newcastle	2.2	396	74	71	80.8
23 Surrey	1.6	301	85		80.7
24 Sussex	2.7	363	75	65	80.6
25 East Anglia	1.7	346	84	57	80.3
26 Leicester	1.2	326	86	63	80.2
27 Edinburgh	2.3	446	70	66	79.9
28 Bristol	2.0	454	67	79	79.7
29 Loughborough	2.0	318	82	57	79.3
30 Queen Mary, London	2.0	359	72	75	79.0
31 Kent	1.5	289	82	69	78.8
32 Bradford	2.4	301	74	71	78.7
33 Dundee	1.7	343	86	43	78.2
34 Manchester	2.6	433	68	60	78.0
35 Aberdeen	1.5	344	82	55	77.7
36 Southampton	1.5	373	74	68	77.3
=37 Leeds	1.2	396	74	67	76.5
=37 Keele	1.8	307	77	63	76.5
39 Reading	1.8	318	76	63	76.2
=40 Strathclyde	1.4	368	78	53	75.3
=40 Aston	1.3	351	78	58	75.3
42 Lancaster	1.3	376	77	53	74.6
43 Queen's, Belfast	2.2	349	71	56	74.4
44 Goldsmiths College	1.8	299	73	63	73.9
45 Swansea	1.4	289	77	57	73.3
46 Royal Holloway	1.6	390	68	63	73.1
47 De Montfort	1.3	219	84	51	72.9
=48 Robert Gordon	1.2			62	72.8
=48 Northumbria	1.7	278	75	57	72.8

	Research quality/7	Entry standards	Student satisfaction %	Graduate prospects %	Overall rating
=50 Brunel	1.5	294	71	66	72.3
=50 Plymouth	2.0	261	78	46	72.3
52 Oxford Brookes	1.2	305	73	61	71.8
53 Stirling	1.1	269	77	56	71.1
54 Coventry	1.0	284	79	48	70.8
55 Ulster	1.8	248	76	50	70.7
56 Liverpool	1.0	360	69	60	70.4
57 Nottingham Trent		192	79	68	68.8
58 Salford	1.5	255	75	45	68.2
59 West of England	0.8	244	78	48	68.0
60 UWIC, Cardiff		279	77	55	67.2
61 Lincoln	1.1	257	71	56	67.1
62 Kingston	1.2	206	75	45	65.4
63 Birmingham City	1.5	246	74	34	64.9
64 Huddersfield	0.3	232	76	47	64.4
65 Manchester Metropolitan	1.1	237		42	62.9
=66 Liverpool John Moores		230	78	39	62.5
=66 Westminster	1.2	237	71	38	62.5
68 Greenwich	0.4	211	71	51	62.1
69 Leeds Metropolitan		251	69	37	57.9

Employed in graduate job:	36%	Employed in non-graduate job and studying:	3%
Employed in graduate job and studying:	4%	Employed in non-graduate job:	29%
Studying:	21%	Unemployed:	6%
Average starting graduate salary:	£20,877	Average starting non-graduate salary:	£15,364

Psychology

Only law attracts more applications for a single subject than psychology. At the start of 2009, another 4 per cent increase in the demand for places brought took the number of applications over 73,000. The subject's popularity has continued to rise in spite of its relatively poor record in the graduate employment market: it is in the bottom six for the proportion of graduates with "positive destinations" and only two places higher for average starting salaries in graduate-level jobs.

Most undergraduate programmes are accredited by the British Psychological Society, which ensures that key topics are covered, but the clinical and biological content of courses still varies considerably. Some universities require maths and/or biology A levels among an average of at least three Bs, but others are much less demanding. The contrast is obvious in the ranking, with 20 universities averaging more than 400 points at entry and four dipping below 200 points.

Cambridge still has a comfortable lead over Oxford at the top of the table, although the two tie for the highest entry scores. Cambridge has the best employment record and the top performance in the 2008 Research Assessment exercise, when 80 per cent of its work was considered world-leading or internationally excellent.

East Anglia has the most satisfied students, but remains in the lower reaches of the top 30 because of low research and employment scores. A majority of graduates at no fewer than 35 universities were in low-level employment or unemployed six months after completing their degrees in 2007. Psychology is one of the biggest tables in the *Guide*, but these poor employment figures still represented more than a third of the ranking.

Bath makes the most progress at the top of the table, jumping ten places to fifth, while Glasgow leapfrogs St Andrews to become the top university in Scotland and sixth in the UK. Cardiff is the top university in Wales, while Northumbria is the only new university in the top 30.

- British Psychological Society: **www.bps.org.uk**

Psychology	Research quality/7	Entry standards	Student satisfaction %	Graduate prospects %	Overall rating
1 Cambridge	4.1	501	86	85	100.0
2 Oxford	4.0	501	81	77	94.9
3 University College London	3.7	471	80	77	92.4
4 York	3.1	461	83	68	89.0
5 Bath	3.9	493	74	67	87.8
6 Glasgow	3.0	393	83	72	87.5
7 St Andrews	3.1	470	83	60	87.3
8 Loughborough	3.2	400	83	65	86.6
9 Exeter	2.6	421	82	65	85.3
10 Birmingham	3.6	411	78	60	84.4
11 Sheffield	2.8	415	78	69	84.0
12 Cardiff	3.4	433	77	57	82.8
13 Bristol	2.5	453	73	70	82.3
14 Kent	2.0	362	79	73	81.5
15 Durham	2.8	428	77	59	81.2
16 Royal Holloway	3.0	390	79	56	81.1
17 Hull	1.7	313	82	75	80.7
=18 Southampton	2.8	417	77	57	80.3
=18 Leeds	2.4	430	77	60	80.3
20 Aberdeen	2.1	344	81	63	79.7
21 Sussex	2.8	388	74	63	79.5
22 Aston	2.5	376	77	62	79.2
23 Lancaster	2.1	395	79	58	79.1
=24 Essex	2.5	326	77	64	78.2
=24 Warwick	2.5	418	70	66	78.2
26 Nottingham	2.6	433	73	56	77.9
27 East Anglia	0.9	349	88	55	77.3
28 Bangor	3.0	310	75	59	76.7
=29 Leicester	1.2	360	77	67	76.4
=29 Edinburgh	2.8	424	72	52	76.4

Psychology cont.

	Research quality/7	Entry standards	Student satisfaction %	Graduate prospects %	Overall rating
=29 Northumbria	1.4	315	81	63	76.4
=32 Portsmouth	1.3	313	80	65	75.9
=32 Brunel	1.8	323	79	60	75.9
34 Strathclyde	1.4	385	74	65	75.6
=35 Newcastle	2.1	421	69	62	75.4
=35 Liverpool	1.6	387	78	53	75.4
37 Reading	2.6	388	74	50	75.1
38 Swansea	1.7	361	77	54	74.3
39 Surrey	2.1	394	70	59	74.2
40 City	2.1	368	70	62	74.1
41 Bournemouth	1.8	266	81	54	73.3
42 Goldsmiths College	2.3	319	72	58	73.0
43 Dundee	1.8	374	76	48	72.9
44 Manchester	2.2	417	67	53	72.6
45 Central Lancashire	1.3	268	78	62	72.3
46 West of England	1.8	293	84	39	71.8
47 Queen's, Belfast	1.6	352	78	45	71.6
=48 Keele	1.2	316	72	63	70.9
=48 Staffordshire	1.2	253	78	59	70.9
50 Nottingham Trent	0.8	292	78	59	70.8
51 Oxford Brookes	1.3	333	78	48	70.7
52 Lincoln	1.4	292	80	47	70.5
53 Hertfordshire	1.7	257	74	54	68.8
54 Stirling	1.2	297	74	53	68.7
55 Bath Spa	0.8	284	80	47	68.6
56 Teesside		271	82	54	68.5
57 Plymouth	1.7	301	77	41	68.4
=58 Coventry	0.7	295	75	54	67.9
=58 Heriot-Watt	0.5	332	80	42	67.9
=60 East London	1.3	191	72	67	67.7
=60 Edinburgh Napier	0.5	309		58	67.7
=62 Bradford	2.4	228	76	43	67.6
=62 Chester	0.8	283	76	53	67.6
=64 Westminster	0.9	297	75	47	66.5
=64 Glasgow Caledonian	0.7	327	77	42	66.5
66 York St John	0.3	284	76	54	66.4
67 St Mary's College		240	82	48	65.7
68 Manchester Metropolitan	1.8	309	71	39	65.4
=69 Brighton	1.6	328	71	38	65.3
=69 Sheffield Hallam	0.7	308	75	44	65.3
71 Winchester		277	78	49	65.1
72 Greenwich	0.9	234	72	56	65.0
73 Glamorgan	0.6	255	77	47	64.9

74 Middlesex	0.6	193	70	66	64.5
75 Sunderland	0.5	240	80	41	64.4
=76 Salford	1.7	292	69	41	64.2
=76 Liverpool John Moores	1.4	273	72	42	64.2
78 Ulster	1.4	258	79	30	64.0
=79 Canterbury Christ Church		246	75	53	63.7
=79 Thames Valley	0.3	197	77	53	63.7
81 Worcester		251	74	54	63.6
=82 De Montfort		236	80	44	63.5
=82 Abertay	0.9	263		48	63.5
84 Anglia Ruskin	1.9	262	68	43	63.3
=85 Northampton		243	79	43	63.1
=85 Gloucestershire	0.6	257	75	43	63.1
87 UWIC, Cardiff	1.0	268	72	43	63.0
88 Edge Hill		285	76	40	61.9
89 Queen Margaret Edinburgh		334		39	61.6
90 Kingston	1.0	262	68	45	61.1
91 Bedfordshire		182	75	52	61.0
92 Roehampton	1.1	229	66	51	60.8
93 Derby	0.8	258	68	44	60.2
94 Southampton Solent		253	70	49	60.1
95 Huddersfield		274	75	34	59.8
96 Leeds Metropolitan		308	63	52	59.4
97 Wolverhampton		243	66	54	59.0
98 Newman		247	74	37	58.9
99 Buckinghamshire New		208	70	50	58.8
100 Bolton	0.5	241	69	42	58.6
101 London South Bank	1.1	207	65	45	57.9
102 Cumbria		296	54	50	53.3

Employed in graduate job:	31%	Employed in non-graduate job and studying:	5%
Employed in graduate job and studying:	6%	Employed in non-graduate job:	37%
Studying:	17%	Unemployed:	5%
Average starting graduate salary:	£18,110	Average starting non-graduate salary:	£13,995

Russian and Eastern European Languages

Oxford and Cambridge were locked together at the top of last year's ranking for Russian and Eastern European languages, but Cambridge has pulled ahead with higher entry standards and the best score in the 2008 National Student Survey. The two ancient rivals are still tied on the employment measure, with more than eight out of ten graduates finding graduate-level jobs or continuing with further studies.

Below the top two places, there has been considerable movement. Bath moves up five places to tie with Exeter for third place on Exeter's re-entry to the table. Birmingham moves in the opposite direction, swapping places with Bath, while Portsmouth drops out of the ranking, removing the last new university. St Andrews also drops out, leaving Edinburgh as the leading university in Scotland.

Russian and East European Languages cont.

Entry standards are high throughout the table. Although three of the 13 universities do not have enough undergraduates taking Russian to calculate reliable entry scores, only one of the remainder averages less than 350 points on the UCAS tariff. Although there were fewer than 500 applications in 2008, that still represented five for each place.

Satisfaction levels are high in Russian departments. Every university satisfied more than 70 per cent of the undergraduates in the 2008 results. While still a minority language, Russian has been growing in popularity in schools. The 421 applications received by February 2009 represented an increase of almost 10 per cent on the previous year. Most students learn the language *ab initio*, however.

The small numbers make for exaggerated swings in institutional and national statistics: Russian was close to the bottom 20 subjects for employment prospects in last year's *Guide*, but has now moved up to the middle of the table. Starting salaries for those in graduate-level jobs are in the top 20, at almost £22,000.

- British Association for Slavonic and East European Studies: **www.basees.org.uk**
- National Centre for Languages (CILT): **www.cilt.org.uk**

Russian and East European Languages	Research quality/7	Entry standards	Student satisfaction %	Graduate prospects %	Overall rating
1 Cambridge	3.1	534	88	81	100.0
2 Oxford	3.7	497	84	81	98.2
=3 Bath	2.2		85	67	88.1
=3 Exeter	2.4	430	82		88.1
5 University College London	2.2	471	75	79	87.6
6 Sheffield	3.3	384	82	67	87.5
7 Bristol	2.7	427	74	79	86.5
8 Birmingham	2.5		83	62	86.4
9 Manchester	3.8	355	78		85.8
10 Nottingham	2.9	346	74	63	79.3
11 Edinburgh	1.7	441	71		78.5
12 Leeds	1.1	367	78	56	75.6
13 Glasgow	0.4		79	57	74.1

Employed in graduate job:	40%	Employed in non-graduate job and studying:		2%
Employed in graduate job and studying:	5%	Employed in non-graduate job:		21%
Studying:	24%	Unemployed:		8%
Average starting graduate salary:	£21,835	Average starting non-graduate salary:		£17,202

Social Policy

The London School of Economics (LSE) has retained its accustomed position at the head of the social policy ranking, stretching its lead over Bristol with much the highest scores for research and entry qualifications, as well as the best of a generally mediocre set of employment statistics.

In the 2008 assessments, 80 per cent of the LSE's research in the wider category of social work and policy and administration was rated world-leading or internationally excellent. Its average entry grades are 60 points ahead of third-placed Loughborough's, while only Bristol approaches the LSE's record of nearly eight out of ten of those completing a degree going straight into graduate-level jobs or further study.

Of the remaining universities, only Edinburgh and Nottingham had less than a third of their leavers unemployed or in low-level work six months after graduation. Social policy is among the bottom five subjects on this measure, although it does better in the earnings league, with starting salaries averaging about £19,500 in graduate-level jobs.

Loughborough and fourth-placed Hull have the most satisfied students, but there were good scores for most social policy degrees in the 2008 National Student Survey. Only five universities (including the LSE) failed to satisfy at least 70 per cent of their undergraduates.

Glasgow is just ahead of Edinburgh as the top university in Scotland, while Cardiff leads Swansea in Wales. There are 14 new universities in the table, with Portsmouth breaking into the top 20 this year and Nottingham Trent, De Montfort and Central Lancashire appearing in the top 25.

Entry standards are comparatively low and there were little more than three applications for each place in 2008. Although two thirds of entrants come with A levels or their equivalent, some courses cater very largely for mature students. The proportion of students getting firsts or 2:1s is relatively low.

Demand for places in social policy has fluctuated in recent years. There was an 8 per cent increase in applications early in 2009, following a decline in the previous year. A significant proportion of the places have been filled in Clearing in recent years.

- National Institute of Economic and Social Research: **www.niesr.ac.uk**
- UK Social Policy Association: **www.social-policy.com**

Social Policy	Research quality/7	Entry standards	Student satisfaction %	Graduate prospects %	Overall rating
1 London School of Economics	4.6	425	69	79	100.0
2 Bristol	2.9	348	76	76	93.1
3 Loughborough	2.7	358	86	50	91.3
4 Hull	2.1	297	86	65	90.7
5 Leeds	3.7	283	76	66	90.6
=6 Sheffield	3.1	338	77	62	90.4
=6 Southampton	3.8		76	56	90.4
8 Glasgow	2.6		80	64	90.2
9 Kent	3.6	244	77	65	89.0
10 Edinburgh	3.4		71	67	88.8
11 York	3.3	318	75	59	88.2
12 Bolton	1.9		84	59	87.4
=13 Birmingham	2.8	286	79	60	87.1
=13 Keele	2.9	311	74	64	87.1
15 Bath	3.9	346	70	51	86.6
16 Portsmouth	2.3		83	50	86.2
17 Nottingham	2.3	329	72	67	85.1

Social Policy cont.	Research quality/7	Entry standards	Student satisfaction %	Graduate prospects %	Overall rating
18 Cardiff	3.0	349	69	52	83.1
19 Stirling	2.5		78	50	82.9
20 Swansea	2.5	273	77	53	82.6
21 Queen's, Belfast	2.8	268	75	52	81.9
22 Nottingham Trent	2.8		71	57	81.2
23 De Montfort	1.6		75	62	80.3
24 Central Lancashire	2.0	208	79		78.5
25 Bangor	1.7		72	62	77.4
=26 Lincoln	1.8		78	43	76.4
=26 Salford	2.1	185	76	52	76.4
28 Brighton	1.6	304	72	48	76.2
29 Manchester	2.5	357	62	49	75.9
30 London South Bank	2.8		72	39	75.4
31 Newcastle		341	70	66	74.7
32 Sheffield Hallam	2.7	268	70	36	74.4
33 Ulster	2.6	250	72	35	73.7
34 Anglia Ruskin	1.7	252	73	37	71.5
35 Plymouth	2.3		69	39	70.9
36 Wolverhampton		150	76	66	69.7
37 Northampton		182	77	40	64.9
38 Manchester Metropolitan	1.3	138	69		63.0

Employed in graduate job:	30%	Employed in non-graduate job and studying:	5%
Employed in graduate job and studying:	6%	Employed in non-graduate job:	38%
Studying:	15%	Unemployed:	6%
Average starting graduate salary:	£19,550	Average starting non-graduate salary:	£14,079

Social Work

For all the bad publicity endured by social work in recent years, the subject remains among the 20 most popular choices for higher education candidates. That may be partly because it is also in the top dozen for employment prospects and – even more surprisingly – in the top ten for starting salaries, which averaged more than £23,000 in 2007.

Social work used to be unusual for having more students taking certificate or diploma courses than degrees, but the diploma was withdrawn in the move to a graduate profession. Extra places at undergraduate level have brought another 18 universities into the table this year, following the addition of 24 last year. Although entry grades are still the lowest in the Guide, more than 55,000 applications meant that there were still more than five applications per place in 2008.

The ranking had a new top three last year and there is another in this edition of the Guide. Sheffield, which has not appeared in the table for several year, re-enters at the top, with the only 100 per cent employment record. Bath, a previous leader of the ranking, moves up six places to second with the best results in the 2008 Research Assessment

Exercise, when three quarters of its work was rated world-leading or internationally excellent. And Kent jumps eight places to third, with the best score in the National Student Survey.

York, last year's leader, drops to fourth place, and is followed, as it was last year, by Queen's, Belfast. Bristol, another previous leader, has the highest entry standards, but only just makes the top 20 because of one of the lowest satisfaction ratings in the table.

Edinburgh has overtaken Stirling to become the top university in Scotland, while Glamorgan is the leader in Wales. The majority of the institutions in the table are new universities, but only Middlesex appears in the top 20. Entry grades are largely responsible: most of the older universities in the table have average entry scores of more than 300 points, whereas only Glasgow Caledonian and Robert Gordon, of the post-1992 universities, reach that threshold. More than a dozen average less than 200 points.

- British Association of Social Workers: **www.basw.co.uk**
- General Social Care Council: **www.gscc.org.uk**
- Social Care Association: **http://socialcareassociation.co.uk**

Social Work	Research quality/7	Entry standards	Student satisfaction %	Graduate prospects %	Overall rating
1 Sheffield	3.1	371	80	100	100.0
2 Bath	3.9		79	94	99.0
3 Kent	3.6	268	88	90	97.1
4 York	3.3	365	76	90	96.3
5 Queen's, Belfast	2.8	369	77	95	95.8
6 Lancaster	3.0		79	93	92.9
7 Edinburgh	3.4		69	96	90.7
8 Leeds	3.7	325	78	62	89.6
=9 Stirling	2.5		77	94	88.8
=9 Dundee	1.8	323	78	95	88.8
11 East Anglia	2.4	241	83		87.9
12 Sussex	2.8		72	93	87.0
13 Keele	2.9	223	74	94	85.7
14 Birmingham	2.8	324	66	82	84.5
15 Southampton	1.7	329	73	88	84.2
16 Glamorgan	2.1	269	76		83.4
17 Reading	2.2	289	67	94	83.2
18 Hull	2.1	253	72	95	83.0
19 Middlesex	2.1		73	86	81.5
20 Bristol	2.9	373	57	70	81.3
=21 Huddersfield	2.2	247	76	76	80.1
=21 Northumbria	1.7	248	70	96	80.1
23 Strathclyde	1.9	334	67	75	79.8
24 Bradford	2.4	278	61	90	79.7
25 Ulster	2.6	277	67	74	79.5
26 Anglia Ruskin	1.7	251	76	81	79.4
27 Nottingham Trent	2.8	214	64	91	79.3

Social Work cont.	Research quality/7	Entry standards	Student satisfaction %	Graduate prospects %	Overall rating
=28 West of England	1.3	234	73	97	79.1
=28 Oxford Brookes		267	83	94	79.1
30 Robert Gordon		316		89	78.7
31 London South Bank	2.8		66	78	78.6
32 Coventry	1.6	245	73	84	77.8
33 Plymouth	2.3	245	66	83	77.6
34 Teesside		247	81	95	77.2
35 De Montfort	1.6	205	69	96	76.8
36 Chester	0.9		78	85	76.3
37 Goldsmiths College	1.9		67	85	75.8
38 Southampton Solent		261	80	87	75.6
39 Glasgow Caledonian		319	84	64	75.4
40 Lincoln	1.8	219	69	84	75.3
41 Bedfordshire	2.2	159	73	81	74.6
42 Salford	2.1	271	61	75	74.4
43 Central Lancashire	2.0	151	68	93	74.0
44 UWIC, Cardiff		201	81	92	73.7
45 Sheffield Hallam	1.7	226	64	85	73.6
46 Gloucestershire	0.7	202	78	85	73.4
47 Birmingham City	1.5	237	59	90	72.2
=48 Bangor	1.7	229	66		71.4
=48 Newport	1.9	188	78	56	71.4
50 Portsmouth		244	72	87	70.6
51 Manchester Metropolitan	1.3	193	69	80	70.4
52 Hertfordshire	1.0	194	61	94	68.9
=53 Glynd r	1.0		68	78	68.3
=53 Staffordshire		195	75	84	68.3
55 Bournemouth		247	64	91	68.2
56 East London	1.5	136	68	82	67.5
57 Wolverhampton		243	71	75	67.0
58 Kingston		200	70	77	64.5
59 Northampton		209	68	78	64.2
60 Chichester		211	77	59	64.1
61 Greenwich		234	63	79	63.5
62 Brunel	1.7		57	66	62.2
63 Cumbria		197	74	58	61.7
64 Worcester		155	78	60	61.6
65 Royal Holloway	2.2		45	77	61.4
66 Sunderland		176	74	62	61.2
=67 Edge Hill	0.8	193	78	33	60.6
=67 Leeds Metropolitan		236	70	51	60.6
69 Roehampton		196	76	49	60.3
70 Canterbury Christ Church		207	64	51	55.8

71 Liverpool John Moores	204	59	57	54.5
72 Derby	151	62	60	53.4

Employed in graduate job:	69%	Employed in non-graduate job and studying:	2%
Employed in graduate job and studying:	7%	Employed in non-graduate job:	12%
Studying:	5%	Unemployed:	5%
Average starting graduate salary:	£23,354	Average starting non-graduate salary:	£15,572

Sociology

The popular image of sociology may be stuck in the 1960s, but it remains one of the largest of the social sciences. Applications were up by 5 per cent early in 2009, following a series of increases earlier in the decade. Numbers have remained buoyant despite an employment record that is in the bottom two for all subjects.

The top five in the ranking remain unchanged from last year. Cambridge is well clear in first place, as the university with by far the highest entry grades and the only one where more than 75 per cent of the sociologists had found graduate-level work or postgraduate courses within six months of completing a degree.

Bath achieved the best results in the 2008 Research Assessment Exercise, with three quarters of the university's work judged to be world-leading or internationally excellent. Grades in sociology were not as high as in many subjects, but Southampton also did well, with 70 per cent of research in the top two categories.

Aberdeen has the UK's most satisfied students, while St Mary's University College, in Twickenham, holds that distinction for England. Satisfaction levels are generally high in sociology. Derby, just outside the bottom ten, was close to St Mary's score in the 2008 National Student Survey.

More than a third of the institutions in the table (33) saw a majority of graduates taking low-level work or remaining unemployed six months after completing a degree. Nearly half of all sociology graduates were in that position at the end of 2007.

Aberdeen has overtaken Edinburgh to resume its position as the leading university in Scotland, while Cardiff is best-placed in Wales. Bedfordshire is the only new university in the top 30, but Glasgow Caledonian, Northumbria and Teesside are all the top 40.

Other subjects such as criminology, urban studies, women's studies and some communication studies are included in the category of sociology and a large number of institutions teach the subject as part of a combined studies or modular programme.

- The British Sociological Association: **www.britsoc.co.uk**

Sociology	Research quality/7	Entry standards	Student satisfaction %	Graduate prospects %	Overall rating
1 Cambridge	2.8	501	80	80	100.0
2 Surrey	3.2	326	83	69	92.6
3 Warwick	3.2	411	79	62	91.7
4 Loughborough	2.7	359	83	60	90.0
5 Leeds	3.7	354	79	58	89.6
6 Durham	2.7	411	77	63	89.4

Sociology cont.

	Research quality/7	Entry standards	Student satisfaction %	Graduate prospects %	Overall rating
7 Bath	3.9	346	69	73	88.3
8 Aberdeen	2.6	335	87	51	88.1
9 Essex	3.5	300	80	57	87.2
10 Exeter	2.9	357	79	56	86.8
11 Edinburgh	3.2	435	73	50	86.1
12 Lancaster	3.5	356	76	52	85.8
13 Southampton	3.8	345	77	49	85.7
14 London School of Economics	2.5	400	68	71	85.2
15 Glasgow	2.0	423	75	58	84.8
=16 Sheffield	3.1	361	72	60	84.3
=16 Bristol	2.2	391	68	74	84.3
18 Stirling	2.5	283	78	63	83.6
19 Kent	3.6	280	77	52	83.3
20 Sussex	2.9	373	70	61	83.2
21 Portsmouth	2.3	283	83	51	83.1
=22 Brunel	2.3	283	82	54	83.0
=22 Leicester	1.8		77	67	83.0
24 Cardiff	3.0	356	72	55	82.9
25 Manchester	3.7	372	71	47	82.7
26 Birmingham	1.5	357	78	59	82.4
27 York	3.4	335	74	47	81.7
28 Goldsmiths College	3.5	273	71	61	81.4
29 Nottingham	2.3	323	73	60	80.9
=30 Bedfordshire	2.2	219	80	60	80.5
=30 Aston	1.3	330	79	56	80.5
32 Newcastle	2.5	353	70	58	80.1
33 Strathclyde	1.2	378	70	65	79.5
34 Queen's Belfast	2.8	327	72	50	79.4
35 Liverpool	1.5	337	77	51	78.8
36 Hull	2.1	244	81	50	78.7
37 Northumbria	1.7	264	77	56	78.0
38 Glasgow Caledonian	0.9	305	81	51	77.8
39 Salford	2.2	247	78	49	77.4
40 Teesside	1.4	236	79	55	76.7
41 Robert Gordon	0.7	297		62	76.4
42 Worcester		267	80	62	75.9
43 St Mary's College		215	85	56	75.3
44 Birmingham City	1.5	251	80	43	74.7
45 Oxford Brookes		309	80	50	74.5
46 Staffordshire	1.3	213	79	51	74.4
47 Brighton	1.7	293	76	40	74.0
48 Keele		310	72	64	73.7
49 Edinburgh Napier	0.7	296		55	73.6

50 East London	2.0		72	49	73.4
51 Chester	0.9	250	74	57	72.9
=52 Anglia Ruskin		246	75	65	72.7
=52 Nottingham Trent		251	75	62	72.7
54 East Anglia		301	78	49	72.6
55 City	2.3	272	65	54	72.4
56 Lincoln		260	78	51	71.9
57 Bath Spa		282	79	47	71.8
58 Central Lancashire		244	78	52	71.3
59 Huddersfield	1.0	225	76		70.1
60 Ulster		258	81	38	69.6
61 Bradford	2.4	189	69	45	68.9
62 West of England	0.9	246	77	35	68.5
63 Coventry		249	77	43	68.4
=64 Plymouth	1.7	257	69	39	68.3
=64 Kingston	1.2	221	70	49	68.3
66 Canterbury Christ Church		240	76	46	68.0
67 Bangor		268	71	51	67.9
68 Abertay		287		43	67.8
=69 London South Bank		177	75	57	67.6
=69 Manchester Metropolitan	1.7	248	68	40	67.6
71 Southampton Solent		228	80	35	67.2
72 Sheffield Hallam		248	75	42	67.1
73 Wolverhampton		193	74	54	67.0
74 Gloucestershire		241	79	34	66.9
75 Derby		238	84	22	66.6
76 Roehampton	1.6	233	67	43	66.5
77 Greenwich		202	76	43	65.6
78 Glamorgan		224	75	41	65.5
79 Northampton		238	74	40	65.3
80 Buckinghamshire New		211	71	48	64.5
81 UWIC, Cardiff		239	77	30	64.1
82 Westminster		229	71	40	63.1
83 Liverpool John Moores		220	74	35	62.9
84 Leeds Metropolitan		238	67	39	60.9
85 Middlesex		169	69	44	60.6
86 Sunderland		218	67	38	59.6

Employed in graduate job:	33%	Employed in non-graduate job and studying:	4%
Employed in graduate job and studying:	4%	Employed in non-graduate job:	40%
Studying:	13%	Unemployed:	5%
Average starting graduate salary:	£18,339	Average starting non-graduate salary:	£14,548

Sports Science

This is the first appearance of a separate table for the growing range of courses listed under the category of sports science. In previous editions of the *Guide*, they have appeared in the broader ranking that covers hospitality, leisure and tourism, but the popularity of sport as a degree subject demands more detailed scrutiny. The 41,000 applications by February 2009 – 5 per cent up on the previous year – almost took sports science into the top ten subjects.

The subject covers more than 40 specialisms at degree level, from sports therapy to equestrian sport studies and marine sport technology. Many contain more science and less physical activity than candidates may expect. Brunel, for example, requires at least an AS level in one of the sciences. Many universities now offer sports scholarships for elite performers, but most are not tied to a particular course and, officially at least, do not mean that the normal entry requirements are waived.

Loughborough, the most famous name in university sport, tops the inaugural ranking, as it did the broader category in previous years. It is one of only two universities (with Bath) where entrants average more than 400 points on the UCAS tariff and it shares with Birmingham the best record in the 2008 Research Assessment Exercise. Both had 60 per cent of their research rated world-leading or internationally excellent.

The most satisfied students are at second-placed Exeter, another university with an illustrious sporting pedigree, through the former St Luke's College. Aberystwyth was the only other university where more than 90 per cent of the students declared themselves satisfied in the 2008 National Student Survey, but several others were close to this mark.

Glasgow is the top university in Scotland, while Bangor is the leader in Wales. Portsmouth is the leading new university, with a place in the top ten. Brighton, Liverpool John Moores, Sheffield Hallam, Chichester and Northumbria are all in the top 20.

Entry standards are modest: 15 universities average less than 200 points and three are below 150, the equivalent of less than two Cs at A level. However, one of the three, the new university of Glyndŵr, in North Wales, is also one of only three institutions to see more than eight out of ten graduates go straight into graduate-level work or continue their studies. Newman University College, in Birmingham, has the top score, while Bournemouth completes the trio.

Although the unemployment rate among sports science graduates is low, at only 3 per cent, more than a third begin their working life in non-graduate jobs. The subject is just outside the bottom ten for starting salaries.

- British Association of Sport and Exercise Sciences: **www.bases.org.uk**
- English Institute of Sport: **www.eis2win.co.uk**
- London 2012: **www.london2012.com**
- Scottish Institute of Sport: **www.sisport.com**
- Welsh Institute of Sport: **www.welsh-institute-sport.co.uk**

Sports Science	Research quality/7	Entry standards	Student satisfaction %	Graduate prospects %	Overall rating
1 Loughborough	3.1	408	87	67	100.0
2 Exeter	1.9	380	94	68	96.1

3 Durham	2.7	379	82	71	95.3
4 Birmingham	3.1	373	82	62	94.0
5 Glasgow	2.9	372	82	65	93.6
6 Strathclyde	2.6	365	75	70	90.6
7 Bath	2.1	404	76	69	90.4
8 Bangor	1.9	248	88	75	88.7
9 Portsmouth	2.6	252	88	59	86.6
10 Essex	1.9	261	85	71	86.3
=11 Edinburgh	2.3	390	77	52	85.0
=11 Southampton	1.9	322	81	61	85.0
=11 Brighton	1.8	287	80	71	85.0
14 Brunel	2.1	322	76	64	84.1
15 Ulster	1.6	268	86	65	83.7
16 Leeds	1.8	359	77	57	83.2
17 Liverpool John Moores	2.9	237	78	60	83.1
18 Sheffield Hallam	1.9	307	78	58	81.6
19 Chichester	1.2	211	88	65	80.4
20 Northumbria	1.2	286	82	62	80.2
21 Aberdeen	1.5	303	82	54	79.7
22 Swansea	0.4	274	86	66	79.2
23 Kent	2.4	185	80	61	79.1
=24 Newman	0.4	183	82	84	78.7
=24 Aberystwyth	1.0	259	92	52	78.7
26 Chester	1.4	240	78	67	78.5
27 UWIC, Cardiff	1.4	280	78	60	78.3
28 Leeds Metropolitan	2.2	257	67	67	78.2
29 Bournemouth		252	78	81	77.9
30 Dundee		398	80	55	77.4
31 Hull	0.7	221	80	73	77.3
32 Nottingham Trent	0.6	261	82	65	77.0
33 Manchester Metropolitan	1.5	225	74	65	75.8
34 Heriot-Watt	1.5	339	80	38	75.4
35 Robert Gordon		319		58	74.6
36 Hertfordshire	1.7	299	72	49	74.0
37 Coventry	0.9	277	76	58	73.9
38 Edinburgh Napier		276		62	73.2
39 Glyndŵr		135	82	81	73.1
40 St Mary's College	0.6	230	78	63	72.8
41 Bedfordshire	1.2	217	71	66	72.7
42 Staffordshire	1.0	149	87	57	72.3
43 Teesside		253	83	59	72.1
44 Greenwich		178	78	75	71.8
45 Sunderland	1.5	166	79		71.7
46 Worcester		251	80	61	71.6
47 York St John	0.5	242	80	54	70.9
48 Central Lancashire		232	84	55	70.5
49 Winchester		247	78	60	70.1

Sports Science cont.	Research quality/7	Entry standards	Student satisfaction %	Graduate prospects %	Overall rating
50 Canterbury Christ Church	1.0	188	74	60	69.8
51 Salford	1.7	206	82	37	69.4
52 Glamorgan	1.1	233	76	45	68.1
53 Cumbria		223	60	79	67.2
54 Gloucestershire	0.6	225	75	49	66.6
55 Lincoln		210	80	51	65.8
56 London South Bank	1.4		69	48	65.3
57 Wolverhampton		179	76	58	65.2
58 Northampton		192	81	51	65.1
59 Edge Hill		232	76	49	64.6
60 Roehampton	0.3	187	70	59	64.4
61 Marjon, Plymouth	0.2	203	79	45	64.0
62 Middlesex		202	65	65	63.5
63 East London		165	68	67	63.3
64 Buckinghamshire New	0.7	187	68	54	62.9
65 Abertay		258		45	62.5
66 West of England		245	65	54	61.7
67 Newport		188	69	55	61.0
68 Kingston		202	67	51	59.7
69 Southampton Solent		148	69	55	58.9
70 Plymouth		263	69	36	58.4
71 Huddersfield		263	59	38	54.5
72 Derby		179	47	47	47.7

Employed in graduate job:	36%	Employed in non-graduate job and studying:		4%
Employed in graduate job and studying:	7%	Employed in non-graduate job:		32%
Studying:	18%	Unemployed:		3%
Average starting graduate salary:	£18,572	Average starting non-graduate salary:		£14,159

Theology and Religious Studies

Cambridge stretches its lead in theology and religious studies, registering by far the highest entry grades and sharing with Chichester the distinction of having the most satisfied students. Durham, which shares second place with Oxford, produced the best results in the 2008 Research Assessment Exercise, when two thirds of its work was considered world-leading or internationally excellent.

Lampeter has the best employment record and is one of only five universities where more than eight out of ten of those completing degrees went straight into graduate-level jobs or continued their studies. However, only 3 per cent of graduates nationally are unemployed after six months, a rate that helps the subjects stay in the top half of the employment table. By no means all graduates go into the church, but the vocation helps to maintain this record.

Four Scottish universities appear in the top ten, with Edinburgh the highest-placed in fourth. But it is Exeter, which shares fifth place with St Andrews, that has made the most progress, moving up seven places since last year. Cardiff is the top university in Wales, while St Mary's College, Twickenham, again records the highest finish outside the pre-1992 universities.

Entry qualifications are more tightly bunched than in many of the subject tables. Only seven of the 37 institutions average more than 400 points and just two slip below 250 points. Theology and religious studies have enjoyed substantial increases in popularity during this decade, although applications were down slightly in the early part of 2009.

Starting salaries in graduate-level jobs are surprisingly competitive. The average rate at the end of 2007 was more than £19,000, taking theology and religious studies out of the bottom 20.

- British Association for the Study of Religions: **http://basr.open.ac.uk**
- Society for the Study of Theology: **www.theologysociety.org.uk**

Theology and Religious Studies	Research quality/7	Entry standards	Student satisfaction %	Graduate prospects %	Overall rating
1 Cambridge	3.6	498	91	81	100.0
=2 Durham	3.9	425	87	82	96.5
=2 Oxford	3.5	480	83	85	96.5
4 Edinburgh	3.3	429	82	73	89.6
=5 Exeter	2.3	398	87	78	89.2
=5 St Andrews	2.8	459	80	75	89.2
7 Aberdeen	3.2	314	85	72	86.0
8 Nottingham	3.0	390	78	74	85.6
9 Sheffield	3.1	363	83	69	85.4
10 Glasgow	2.1	368	81	78	85.0
11 Cardiff	1.8	359	84	70	82.4
12 Manchester	3.3	373	80	58	81.9
13 Lancaster	2.6	373	81	63	81.7
14 St Mary's College	2.0	255	83	79	81.1
=15 Chichester	1.1	279	91		80.6
=15 Bristol	2.4	408	70	75	80.6
17 Kent	1.9	323	74	79	79.4
18 Lampeter	1.8	265	75	86	79.3
19 King's College London	2.7	414	71	64	79.2
20 Hull		354	82	79	79.0
21 School of Oriental and African Studies	2.8	336	73	69	78.6
22 Chester	1.5	272	81	74	77.7
=23 Bangor	1.6	293	80	71	77.3
=23 Leeds	2.5	358	79	55	77.3
25 Stirling	1.6		83	61	76.5
26 Newman		231	85	81	76.4
27 Heythrop College	0.7	326	85	62	75.8
28 Birmingham	2.7	357	70	61	75.5
29 Oxford Brookes		319	88	63	75.3
30 Gloucestershire	1.7	251	75	76	75.2

	Research quality/7	Entry standards	Student satisfaction %	Graduate prospects %	Overall rating
31 Queen's, Belfast		350	79	70	74.1
32 York St John	0.6	267	87	60	73.3
33 Winchester	0.8	268	80	62	71.2
34 Cumbria	1.1	279	72	69	70.9
35 Bath Spa	0.4	318	83	51	70.2
36 Roehampton	1.4	223	72	69	69.8
37 Canterbury Christ Church	0.9	270	73	57	66.7

Employed in graduate job:	29%	Employed in non-graduate job and studying:	4%
Employed in graduate job and studying:	6%	Employed in non-graduate job:	24%
Studying:	33%	Unemployed:	3%
Average starting graduate salary:	£19,115	Average starting non-graduate salary:	£14,461

Town and Country Planning and Landscape

Cambridge again extends its lead in the ranking for town and country planning and landscape studies, with the best research grades and entry standards that are more than 120 points higher than the nearest challengers. No other university averages 400 points at entry, let alone more than 500. Competition was much closer in the 2008 Research Assessment Exercise: Cambridge had the most work placed in the top two categories, but fourth-placed Sheffield had a higher proportion judged to be world-leading.

There are high employment scores throughout the table: second-placed Reading and Manchester Metropolitan, which is 20th out of the 26 universities, both saw all their graduates find graduate-level work or continue their studies within six months of completing a degree. Only the bottom two in the table recorded such "positive destinations" for less than 70 per cent of those graduating in 2007.

Loughborough, which has jumped nine places to third this year, has the most satisfied students. Cardiff, in fifth place, is the top university outside England, while Heriot-Watt is the leader in Scotland. Sheffield Hallam, in seventh place is by some way the leading new university, but Nottingham Trent is also close to the top ten.

There was a big fall (more than 18 per cent) in applications for planning courses at the start of 2009, although the much smaller area of landscape design saw an increase. About 12 per cent of places across the whole category tend to be filled through Clearing. The size of university departments varies from more than 500 students to less than 150, with about a third of the total being postgraduates.

Job prospects have been good in recent years. The subjects are in the top ten of the employment table, with an unemployment rate well below average, at 3 per cent. Average starting salaries in graduate-level jobs do not match that position but, at £20,300, are still in the top half of the earnings league.

- Royal Town Planning Institute: **www.rtpi.org.uk**
- Planning Officers Society: **www.planningofficers.org.uk**
- Landscape Institute: **www.landscapeinstitute.org**

Town and Country Planning and Landscape	Research quality/7	Entry standards	Student satisfaction %	Graduate prospects %	Overall rating
1 Cambridge	3.7	511	77	92	100.0
2 Reading	3.1	390	77	100	93.4
3 Loughborough	3.5	346	88	80	92.8
4 Sheffield	3.5	357	76	96	92.0
5 Cardiff	3.4	358	74	93	90.0
6 Newcastle	3.2	347	73	94	88.4
7 Sheffield Hallam	2.7	284	86	85	86.5
8 Manchester	2.9	312	76	88	85.1
9 Heriot-Watt	2.7	349	72	87	84.2
10 University College London	2.9	390	63	86	82.2
11 Nottingham Trent	1.3	288	81	94	81.5
12 Birmingham	2.2	357		79	81.3
13 Liverpool	2.3	338	67	90	80.1
=14 Oxford Brookes	1.8	320	76	81	79.6
=14 West of England	2.0	298	75	84	79.6
16 Queen's, Belfast	1.8	320	73	85	79.0
17 Aberdeen	2.9	358	59	85	78.7
18 Dundee	1.7	317	74	81	78.1
19 Gloucestershire	1.9	242	82	79	78.0
20 Manchester Metropolitan	1.7	293	66	100	77.5
21 Liverpool John Moores	1.3	231	68	85	70.1
22 Birmingham City	1.5	189	77	72	69.7
23 Kingston	0.6	233	64	89	66.7
24 Leeds Metropolitan		245	70	75	64.0
25 Westminster	1.4		65	52	60.2
26 Ulster		268	69	41	56.1

Employed in graduate job:	52%	Employed in non-graduate job and studying:		3%
Employed in graduate job and studying:	15%	Employed in non-graduate job:		9%
Studying:	19%	Unemployed:		3%
Average starting graduate salary:	£20,320	Average starting non-graduate salary:		£17,110

Veterinary Medicine

Only medicine itself compares with veterinary medicine for high entry standards. Although there was a small drop in the demand for places at the start of 2009, this followed two years of big increases and there were still more than 7,000 applications. The number of places has been rising, but there are still more than seven applications for every place.

This year's ranking has one more vet school than the traditional six, with the arrival of Nottingham, which opened in 2006. It is not the only change since third-placed Edinburgh is the only one of the top five to finish in the same position as last year. Nottingham enters in second place, with the best grades in the 2008 Research Assessment Exercise, although it does not have a full set of statistics because its first students are yet to graduate.

Veterinary Medicine cont.

Liverpool takes over from Cambridge at the top of the table, sharing the best employment record with the Royal Veterinary College. Cambridge still has the highest entry standards but, surprisingly is not in the top four for research. The most satisfied students are at fifth-placed Glasgow, although Liverpool's score in the 2008 National Student Survey was only one point lower.

Every vet school registered "positive destinations" for at least 97 per cent of graduates, an even higher rate than last year. The results ensure that the subject remains in the top three for employment, behind medicine and dentistry. Starting salaries are high, at over £24,750, but vets are also behind economists and chemical engineers on this measure.

Most courses demand high grades in chemistry and biology, with some accepting physics or maths as one alternative subject. Cambridge and the Royal Veterinary College also set applicants a specialist aptitude test also used by a number of medical schools. Few candidates win places without evidence of commitment to the subject through work experience, either in veterinary practices or laboratories.

Vets' final qualifications are not classified, but between 5 and 15 per cent are awarded a commendation. The five-year courses have to meet the requirements of the Royal College of Veterinary Surgeons, and they vary in size from 65 to 155 students.

- Royal College of Veterinary Surgeons: **www.rcvs.org.uk**

Veterinary Medicine	Research quality/7	Entry standards	Student satisfaction %	Graduate prospects %	Overall rating
1 Liverpool	2.0	477	75	99	100.0
2 Nottingham	2.8	451			99.7
3 Edinburgh	2.7	502	68	97	99.6
4 Cambridge	2.0	540		97	99.4
5 Glasgow	2.2	472	76	97	98.9
6 Royal Veterinary College	2.4	441	64	99	98.2
7 Bristol	1.7	455	72	97	96.6

Employed in graduate job:	91%	Employed in non-graduate job and studying:	0%
Employed in graduate job and studying:	4%	Employed in non-graduate job:	1%
Studying:	2%	Unemployed:	1%
Average starting graduate salary:	£24,762	Average starting non-graduate salary:	*

Making Your Application

Once the nerve-wracking business of choosing courses is over, you may feel you can sit back and concentrate on getting the right results. Don't be fooled – there is another vital stage to go through if you are to attract the right offers and win that coveted place in higher education. Too many people take their eye off the ball in actually making the application. Surprising numbers of applicants each year spell their own name wrongly, or enter an inaccurate date of birth, or the wrong course code. And that is to say nothing of the damage that can be done in the personal statement and teachers' references.

In an era when there are relatively few interviews and more candidates each year achieve high A-level grades, what goes on your UCAS form is becoming more and more important – too important, many would say. The art of conveying knowledge of and enthusiasm for your chosen subject – preferably with supporting evidence from your school or college – can make all the difference. And, while UCAS will decode misspelt names, other errors in grammar or spelling present admissions officers with an easy starting point in cutting applications down to a more manageable number.

The applications process has come under increased scrutiny in recent years, as the fairness of university admissions has become a political issue, as well as an educational one. There have been a number of significant changes, including reducing the number of choices per applicant and, most recently, the introduction of an "adjustment period" of a week in which those whose results are better than expected can seek an alternative course.

The application process

Most applications for full-time higher education courses go through UCAS, although specialist admissions bodies still handle applications to the music conservatoires (Conservatoires UK Admissions Service: **www.cukas.ac.uk**) and some postgraduate courses, including teacher training (Graduate Teacher Training Registry: **www.gttr.ac.uk**). The trend is towards the UCAS model even among specialist providers, however: recruitment to nursing and midwifery diploma and degree courses in Scotland will switch to the UCAS system in 2010 and the art and design courses that used to recruit using the separate "Route B" scheme will also revert to the main system for 2010.

Universities that have not filled all their places, even during Clearing, will accept direct applications up to and after the start of the academic year, but UCAS is both the official route and the only way into the most popular courses.

Since 2006, all UCAS applications have been made online. The Apply electronic system is accessed via the UCAS website and is straightforward to use. For those who do not have the internet at home and prefer not to use school or college computers, the UCAS website lists 900 libraries, all over the UK, where you can make your application. Apply is available 24 hours a day, and, when the time comes, information on the progress of your application may arrive at any time.

Registering with Apply

The first step in the process is to register. If you are at a school or college, you will need to obtain a "buzzword" from your tutor or careers adviser – it is used when you log on to register. It links your application to the school or college so that the application can be sent electronically to your referee (usually one of your teachers) for your reference to be attached. If you are no longer at a school or college, you do not need a "buzzword", but you will need details of your referee. More information is given on the UCAS website.

To register, go to the UCAS website and click on "Apply". The system will guide you through the business of providing your personal details and generating a username and password, as well as reminding you of basic points, such as amending your details in case of a change of address. You can register separate term-time and holiday addresses – a useful option for boarders, who could find offers and, particularly, the confirmation of a place, going to their school when they are miles away at home. Remember to keep a note of your username and password in a safe place.

Throughout the process, you will be in sole control of communications with UCAS and your chosen universities. Only if you nominate a representative and give them your unique nine-digit application number (sent automatically by UCAS when your application is submitted), can a parent or anyone else give or receive information on your behalf, perhaps because you are ill or out of the country.

Once you are registered, you can start to complete the Apply screens. The details required cover the following areas:

- Personal details and some addition non-educational details for UK applicants.
- Your university choices.
- Details of your education so far including examination results and examinations still to be taken.
- Details of any jobs you have done.
- Your personal statement.
- A reference from one of your teachers.
- A declaration that you confirm that the information is correct and that you will be bound by the UCAS rules.
- Payment details (applications cost £19, or £9 if you apply to just one course).

The sections that follow cover the most important sections.

Personal details
This information is taken from your initial registration, and you will be asked for additional information, for example, on ethnic origin and national identity, used to monitor equal opportunities in the application process.

What matters most?
UCAS and the environmental group, Friends for the Future asked 25,000 applicants in 2007–08 what had been "very important" to them in choosing a course:
- 54% said the quality of teaching
- 44% said the reputation of the course
- 44% said the reputation of the institution
- 35% said the teaching methods on the course
Only 8% gave the same priority to nightlife, while 22% considered the distance from home "very important".

Choices

Since 2007–08, you have been restricted to a maximum of five, rather than six, courses on your UCAS form. The switch met remarkably little resistance – perhaps because most applicants, having set their heart on one or two courses with genuine appeal, were going through the motions by the time it came to choosing a sixth. Applicants in medicine, dentistry and veterinary science were already restricted to four choices, so they now have the option of only one additional choice in another subject.

The other important restriction is for those seeking places at Oxford or Cambridge, who cannot apply to both. For both Oxford and Cambridge you may need to take a written test and submit examples of your work (depending on the course selected) and, in addition, for Cambridge, you will be asked to complete a Supplementary Application Questionnaire once Cambridge has received your application from UCAS. The deadline for Oxbridge applications – and for all medicine, dentistry and veterinary science courses – is 15 October. For all other applications the deadline is 15 January (or 24 March for some specified art and design courses).

Applicants do not have to use up all five choices, although obviously you may reduce your chances of success by narrowing your options. If you do choose fewer than five courses, you can still add another to your form up to June 30, as long as you have not accepted or declined any offers. Nor do you have to choose five different universities if more than one course at the same institution attracts you – perhaps because the institution itself is the real draw and one course has lower entrance requirements than the other. Universities are not allowed to see where else you have applied, or whether you have chosen the same subject elsewhere. But they will be aware of multiple applications within their own institution. It is, in any case, more difficult to write a convincing personal statement if it has to cover more than one subject.

For each course you select, you will need to put the UCAS code on the form – and you should check carefully that you have the correct code and understand any special requirements that may be detailed on the UCAS description of the course. You will also need to indicate whether you are applying for a deferred entry (for example, if you are taking a gap year – see page 184).

Education

In this section you will need to give details of the schools and colleges you have attended, and the qualifications you have obtained or are preparing for. The UCAS website gives plenty of advice on the ways in which you should enter this information, to ensure that all your relevant qualifications are included with their grades. While UCAS does not need to see qualification certificates, it can double-check results with the examination boards to ensure that no-one is tempted to modify their results,

Personal statements

As the competition for places on popular courses has become more intense, so the value attached to the personal statement has increased. Admissions officers look for a sign of potential beyond the high grades that growing numbers of applicants offer. Many (but not all) value success in extracurricular activities such as drama, sport or the Duke of Edinburgh award scheme. But your first priority should be to demonstrate an interest in and understanding of your chosen subject beyond the confines of the exam syllabus.

This is not easy in a relatively short statement that can readily sound trite or pretentious. You should resist any temptation to lie, particularly if there is any chance of an interview. A claim to have been inspired by a book that you have not read will backfire instantly under questioning and, even without an interview, experienced academics are likely to see through grandiose statements that appear at odds with a teacher's reference. Genuine experiences of after-hours clubs, lectures or visits – better still, work experience or actual reading around the syllabus – are much more likely to strike the right note. Take advice from teachers and, if there is still time before you make your application, look for some subject-related activities that will help fill out your statement.

Admissions officers are also looking for evidence of character that will make you a productive member of their university and, eventually, a successful graduate. Taking responsibility in any area of school or college life suggests this, while evidence of initiative and self-discipline is also valuable, since higher education involves much more independent study than sixth-formers are used to.

Your overall aim in writing your personal statement is to persuade the admissions officer to pick you out of the piles of applications on his or her desk. That means trying to stand out from an often rather dull and uniform set of statements based around the curriculum and the more predictable sixth-form activities. Everyone is going to say they love reading, for example; narrow your interest down to an area of (real) interest. Don't be afraid to include the unusual, but bear in mind that an academic's sense of humour may not be the same as yours.

Give particular thought to why you want to study your chosen subject – especially if it is not one you have taken at school or college. You need to show that your interests and skills are well-suited to the course and, if it is a vocational degree, that you know how you envisage using the qualification. Admissions officers want to feel that you will be committed to their subject for the length of the course, which could be three, four or even five years, and capable of achieving good results.

Your school or college should be the best source of advice, since they see personal statements every year, but there are others. The UCAS website has a useful checklist of themes that you may wish to address, while sites such as **www.studential.com** also provide tips. But do not fall into the trap of cutting and pasting from the model statements included on such sites – both UCAS and individual universities have software that will spot plagiarism immediately. No fewer than one in twenty applicants came to grief in this way last year, and one year more than 200 applicants claimed to trace a passion for science back to setting their pyjamas on fire when experimenting with a chemistry set that they received as a birthday present. Plagiarists of this type are unlikely to be disqualified, but they destroy the credibility of their application.

Try not to cram in more than the limited space will allow – admissions officers will have many statements to go through, and judicious editing may be rewarded. As long as you write clearly – preferably in paragraphs and possibly with sub-headings – it will be up to you what to include. It is a personal statement. But consider these points:

- What attracts you to this subject (or subjects, in the case of dual or combined honours)?
- Have you undertaken relevant work experience or voluntary activities, either through school or elsewhere?
- Have you taken part in other extra-curricular activities that demonstrate character – perhaps as a prefect, on the sports field or in the arts?
- Have you been involved in other academic pursuits, such as Gifted and Talented

programmes, widening participation schemes, or courses in other subjects?
- Which aspects of your current courses have you found particularly stimulating?
- Are you planning a gap year? If so, explain what you intend to do and how it will affect your studies. Some subjects – notably maths – actively discourage a break in studies.
- What other outside interests might you include that show that you are well rounded?

The Apply system allows 4,000 characters, or 47 lines for your statement. While there is no requirement to fill all the space, it should not look embarrassingly short. UCAS recommends using a word-processing package to compile the statement before pasting it into the application system. This is because Apply will time-out after 35 minutes of inactivity, so there is a danger of losing valuable material. Working offline also has the advantage of leaving you with a copy and making it easier to show it to others.

References

Hand in hand with your personal statement goes the reference from your school, college or, in the case of mature students, someone who knows you well but is not a friend or family member. The reference has to be independent – you are specifically forbidden to change any part of it if you send off your own application – but that does not mean you should not try to influence what it contains. Most schools and colleges conduct informal interviews before compiling a reference, but it does no harm to draw up a list of the achievements that you would like to see included. Referees cannot know every detail of a candidate's interests and most welcome an aide memoire.

Timetable for Applications

May onwards	Find out about courses and universities. Attend university open days.
September	Registration starts for UCAS *Apply*.
15 October	Final day for applications to Oxford and Cambridge and for all courses in medicine, dentistry and veterinary science.
15 January	Final day for all other applications from UK and EU students to ensure that your application is given equal consideration with all other applicants. For 2010 this will be the deadline for some art and design courses (specified in UCAS Course Search).
16 January – 30 June	New applications continue to be accepted by UCAS, but only considered by universities if the relevant courses have vacancies.
26 February	Start of applications through UCAS Extra.
24 March	Final day for applications for those art and design courses that specify this date.
31 March	Universities should have sent decisions on all applications received by 15 January.
5 May	Final day by which applicants have to decide on their choices if application submitted by 15 January (exact date for each applicant will be confirmed by UCAS).
1 July	Any application received from this date held until Clearing starts.
6 July	Final day for applications through UCAS Extra.
mid August	Clearing and Adjustment start after publication of exam results.

The UCAS guidelines skirt around the candidate's right to see his or her reference, but it does exist. Schools' practices vary, but most now show the applicant the completed reference. Where this is not the case, the candidate can pay UCAS £10 for a copy, although at this stage it is obviously too late to influence the contents. Better, if you can, to see it before it goes off, in case there are factual inaccuracies that can be corrected.

Timing

The general deadline for applications through UCAS is 15 January and even those received up to 30 June will be considered if the relevant courses still have vacancies. After that, you will be limited to Clearing, or an application for the following year. In theory – and usually in practice – all applications submitted by the January deadline are given equal consideration. But the best advice is to get your application in early: before Christmas, or earlier if possible. Applications are accepted from September onwards, so the autumn half-term is a sensible target date for completing the process.

While no offers are made before the deadline, many admissions officers look through applications as they come in and may make a mental note of promising candidates. If your form arrives with the deadline looming, you may appear less organised than those who submitted in good time; and your application may be one of a large batch that receives a more cursory first reading than the early arrivals. Under UCAS rules, last-minute applicants should not be at a disadvantage, but why take the risk?

Next steps

Once your application has been processed by UCAS, you will receive a welcome letter confirming your choices and summarising what will happen next. The letter will contain a reminder of your identification number and the username and password that you used to apply. These will also give you access to Track, the online system that allows you to follow the progress of your application. Check all the details carefully: you have 14 days to contact UCAS to correct any errors. From 2010 universities will be able to make direct contact with you through Track, including arranging interviews.

After that, it is just a matter of waiting for universities to make their decisions, which can take days, weeks or even months, depending on the university and the course. Some obviously see an advantage in being the first to make an offer – it is a memorable moment to be reassured that at least one of your chosen institutions wants you – and may send their response almost immediately. Others take much longer, perhaps because they have so many good applications to consider, or maybe because they are waiting to see which of their applicants withdraw when Oxford and Cambridge make their offers. Universities are asked to make all their decisions by the end of March, and most have done so long before that.

Interviews

Unless you are applying for a course in health or education that brings you into direct contact with the public, the chances are you will not have a selection interview. For prospective medics, vets, dentists or teachers, a face-to-face assessment of your suitability will be crucial to your chances of success. Likewise in the performing arts, the interview may be as important as your exam grades. Oxford and Cambridge still interview applicants in all subjects, and a few of the top universities see a significant proportion. But the expansion of higher education has made it impractical to interview everyone, and many admissions experts are sceptical about interviews anyway.

What has become more common, however, is the "sales" interview, where the university is really selling itself to the candidate. There may still be testing questions, but the admissions staff have already made their minds up and are actually trying to persuade you to accept an offer. Indeed, you will probably be given a clear indication at the end of the interview that one is on its way. The technique seems to work, perhaps because you have invested time and nervous energy in a sometimes lengthy trip, as well as acquiring a more detailed impression of both the department and the university.

The difficulty can come in spotting which type of interview is which. The "real" ones require lengthy preparation, revisiting your personal statement and reading beyond the exam syllabus. Dress smartly and make sure that you are on time. Impressions count for a lot at interviews, so have a question of your own ready, as well as being prepared to give answers.

While you would not want to appear ignorant at a "sales" interview, lengthy preparation might be a waste of valuable time during a period of revision. Naturally, you should err on the side of caution, but if your predicted grades are well above the standard offer and the subject is not one that normally requires an interview, it is likely that the invitation is a sales pitch. It is still worth going, unless you have changed your mind about the application.

Offers

When your chosen universities respond to your application, there will be one of three answers:

- Unconditional Offer (U): This is a possibility only if you applied after satisfying the entrance requirements – usually if you are applying as a mature student, while on a gap year, after resitting exams or, in Scotland, after completing Highers.
- Conditional Offer (C): The university offers a place subject to you achieving set grades or points on the UCAS tariff.
- Rejection (R): You do not have the right qualifications, or have lost out to stronger competition.

If you have chosen wisely, you should have more than one offer to choose from, so you will be required to pick your favourite as your firm acceptance – known as UF if it was an unconditional offer and CF if it was conditional. Candidates with conditional offers can also accept a second offer, with lower grades, as an Insurance choice (CI). You must then decline any other offers that you have.

You do not have to make an Insurance choice – indeed, you may decline all your offers if you have changed your mind about your career path or regret your course decisions. But most people prefer the security of a back-up route into higher education if their grades fall short. You must be sure that your firm acceptance is definitely your first choice because you will be allocated a place automatically if you meet the university's conditions. It is no good at this stage deciding that you prefer your Insurance choice because UCAS rules will not allow a switch.

The only way round those rules – if your personal circumstances have changed, or you do much better than expected and are determined to "trade up" to another university – is through direct contact with the universities concerned. Your firm acceptance institution has to be prepared to release you so that your new choice can award you a place in Clearing. Neither is under any obligation to do so but, in practice, it is rare for a university to insist that a student joins against his or her wishes. Admissions staff will do all they can to persuade you that your original choice was the right one – as it may well have been, if your research was thorough – but it will almost certainly be your decision in the end.

UCAS Extra

If things do go wrong and you receive five rejections, that need not be the end of your higher education ambitions. From the end of February until the end of June, you have another chance through UCAS Extra, a listing of courses that still have vacancies after the initial round of offers. You will be notified if you are eligible for Extra and can then select courses marked as available on the UCAS website. Applications are made, one at a time, through UCAS Track. If you do not receive an offer, or you choose to decline one, you can continue applying for other courses until you are successful. About half of those applying through Extra normally find a place.

Results Day

Rule Number One on results day is to be at home, or at least in communication. Places are filled extremely rapidly with the newest electronic admissions systems, and you cannot afford to be on some remote beach if there are complications. If you get the grades stipulated in your conditional offer, the process should work smoothly and you can begin celebrating. You don't need to do anything – Track will let you know as soon as your place is confirmed and the paperwork will arrive in a day or two. You can phone the university to make quite sure, but it should not be necessary and you will be joining a long queue of people doing the same thing.

If the results are not what you hoped – and particularly if you just miss your grades – you need to be on the phone and taking advice from your school or college. In a year when results are better than expected, some universities will stick to the letter of their offers, perhaps refusing to accept your AAC grades when they had demanded ABB. Others will forgive a dropped grade to take a candidate who is regarded as promising, rather than go into Clearing to recruit an unknown quantity. Admissions staff may be persuadable – particularly if there are extenuating personal circumstances, or the dropped grade is in a subject that is not relevant to your chosen course. Try to get a teacher to support your case, and be persistent if there is any prospect of flexibility.

One option, if your results are lower than predicted, is to ask for papers to be re-marked, as growing numbers do each year. The school may ask for a whole batch to be re-marked, and you should ensure that your chosen universities know this if it may make the difference to whether or not you satisfy your offer. If your grades improve, the university will review its decision, but if by then it has filled all its places, you may have to wait until next year to start the course.

Results Day is bound to be stressful, unless you are absolutely confident that you achieved the required grades – more of a possibility in an era of modular courses with marks along the way. But for thousands of students Track has removed the agony of opening the envelope or scanning a results noticeboard. From midnight on the eve of A-level results day, the system informs those who have already won a place on their chosen course. You will not learn your grades until later, but at least your immediate future is clear.

If you took Scottish Highers, you will have had your results for more than a week by the time the A-level grades are published. If you missed your grades, there is no need to wait for A levels before you begin approaching universities. Admissions staff at English universities may not wish to commit themselves before they see results from south of the border, but Scottish universities will be filling places immediately and all should be prepared to give you an idea of your prospects.

Clearing

If the worst comes to the worst and you do not have a place on Results Day, there will still be plenty of options through the UCAS Clearing scheme. Over 43,000 people – approaching 10 per cent of all applicants – found a place through this route in 2008. Although the most popular courses fill up quickly, many remain open up to and beyond the start of the academic year. And, at least at the start of the process, the range of courses with vacancies is much wider than in Extra. You will not find Oxford or Cambridge, but most universities will list some courses, and most subjects will be available somewhere.

Clearing runs from Results Day until late September, matching students without places to full-time courses with vacancies. As long as you are not holding any offers and you have not withdrawn your application, you are eligible automatically. Indeed, you will go straight into Clearing if you apply after 30 June. You will be sent a Clearing number via Track to quote to universities.

After that, it is just a matter of trawling through the lists on the UCAS website, and elsewhere, before making a direct approach to the university offering the course that appeals most, and where you have a realistic chance of a place. Tens of thousands of hopefuls will be doing the same thing, so do not waste time on courses where the standard offer is far above your grades. Universities run Clearing hotlines and have become adept at dealing with a large number of calls in a short period, but you can still spend a long time on the phone at a time when the most desirable places are beginning to disappear. If you can't get through – or even if you can – send an email setting out your grades and detailing the course that interests you.

The best advice is to plan ahead and not to wait for Results Day to draw up a list of possible Clearing targets. Many universities publish lists of courses that are likely to be in Clearing on their websites from the start of August. Think again about some of the courses that you considered when making your original application, or others at your chosen universities that had lower entrance requirements – perhaps dual honours, rather than single honours. But beware of switching to another subject simply because you have the right grades – you still have to sustain your interest and be capable of succeeding over three or more years. Many of the students who drop out of degrees are those who chose the wrong course in a rush during Clearing.

In short, you should start your search straight away if you do find yourself in Clearing, and act decisively, but do not panic. Apply the same criteria that you used in choosing courses initially: look at the syllabus and satisfy yourself that you will enjoy the course, that the university is one which you are happy to attend, and that the qualification will take you where you want to go in your career. You can make as many approaches as you like, until you are accepted on the course of your choice.

Most of the available vacancies will appear in Clearing lists, but some of the universities towards the top of the league tables may have a limited number of openings that they choose not to advertise – either for reasons of status or because they do not want the administrative burden of fielding large numbers of calls to fill a handful of courses. If there is a course that you find particularly attractive – especially if you have good grades and are applying late – it may be worth making a speculative call. Sometimes a number of candidates holding offers drop grades and you may be on the spot at the right moment.

What are the alternatives?

If your results are lower than expected and there is nothing you want in Clearing, there are several things you can do. The first is to resit one or more subjects. The modular nature of most courses means that you will have a clear idea of what you need to do to get better grades. You can go back to school or college, try a "crammer" or take a job and revise in the evenings. Although some colleges have a good success rate with re-takes, you have to be highly focused and realistic about the likely improvements. Some of the most competitive courses, such as medicine, may demand higher grades for a second application, so be sure you know the details before you commit yourself to a year's delay.

Other options are to get a job and study part-time, or to take a break from studying and return later in your career. The part-time route can be arduous – many young people find a job enough to handle without the extra burden of academic work. But others find it just the combination they need for a fulfilling life. It all depends on your job, your social life and your commitment to the subject you will study. It may be that a relatively short break is all that you need to rekindle your enthusiasm for studying. Many universities now have a majority of mature students, so you need not be out of place if this is your chosen route.

Taking a gap year

The other increasingly popular option – despite the recession – is to take a gap year. About 7 per cent of applicants now defer their entry until the following year while they travel, or do voluntary or paid work. A whole industry has grown up around tailor-made activities, many of them in Asia, Africa or Latin America. Some have been criticised for doing more for the organisers than the underprivileged communities that they purport to assist, but there are programmes that are useful and character-building, as well as safe. Most of the overseas programmes are not cheap, but raising the money can be part of the experience. The alternative is to stay closer to home and make your contribution through organisations like Community Service Volunteers (**www.csv.org.uk**) or to take a job that will make higher education more affordable when the time comes.

Many admissions staff are happy to facilitate gap years because they think it makes for more mature, rounded students than those who come straight from school. The right programme may even increase your chances of winning a place, if it is relevant to your course. But there are subjects – maths in particular – that discourage a break because it takes too long to pick up study skills where you left off. From the student's point of view, you should also bear in mind that a gap year postpones the moment at which you embark on a career. This may be important if your course is a long one, such as medicine or architecture.

If you are considering a gap year, it makes sense to apply for a deferred place, rather than waiting for your results before applying. The application form has a section for deferments. That allows you to sort out your immediate future before you start travelling or working, and leaves you the option of changing your mind if circumstances change. Dealing with universities from the other side of the world is not ideal.

Useful websites

The following websites will help you find out more about the topics discussed in this chapter. For specific information on universities, visit their websites and for general information, consult the websites listed at the end of chapter 1.

Applications

The essential website for making an application is, of course, that of UCAS:
www.ucas.com
Within the UCAS site, there is much practical advice on how to apply:
www.ucas.com/students/startapplication/apply
For applications to music conservatoires, visit Conservatoires UK Admission service:
www.cukas.ac.uk
For applications for graduate teacher training, visit the Graduate Teacher Training Registry: **www.gttr.ac.uk**
For advice on your personal statement, visit
www.ucas.com/students/startapplication/apply/personalstatement
www.studential.com

Gap years

To help you consider options and start planning, visit:
www.gapadvice.org
For links to volunteering opportunities in the UK, visit:
www.do-it.org.uk
For links to many not-for-profit gap year organisations:
www.yearoutgroup.org
For work placements relevant to university courses, visit Year in Industry:
www.yini.org.uk

Also worth consulting
Community Service Volunteers: **www.csv.org.uk**
v (formerly Millennium Volunteers): **www.vinspired.com**
Worldwide Volunteering: **http://wwv.org.uk**
Lattitude Global Volunteering: **www.lattitude.org.uk**
Volunteer Africa: **www.volunteerafrica.org**

5

Finding Somewhere to Live

Going to university has changed a lot in recent years – not least in the all-important area of where students live. More are basing themselves at home, while the rest choose from a much wider variety of accommodation options than their predecessors enjoyed. The pattern of applications for 2009–10 suggests that the trend towards studying from home is accelerating, and there is no reason to think that will change while the downturn continues. Indeed, it may be a permanent shift, given the rising cost of taking a degree and the willingness of many young people to live with their parents well into their twenties.

More than one in five students now live at home – a figure that is inflated by the large number of mature students, but still a sign of the times. Yet most of those who can afford it still see moving away to study as integral to the rite of passage that student life represents. Some have little option because, in spite of the expansion of higher education, the course they want is not available locally. Others are happy to travel to secure their ideal place and widen their experience.

For most of those who take the "away" option, going to university will be the first time that have given any thought to the practicalities of living away from home. This can make the decision about where to live – both in terms of location and the type of accommodation – doubly difficult, but vital to get right. It may even influence your choice of university, since there are big differences across the sector in the cost and standard of accommodation – and your choice can have a significant impact on the quality of your life as a student.

How much will it cost?

Students in the UK are estimated to spend a total of nearly £4 billion a year on rent – almost twice as much as their combined spending on food, going out, books and music. A recent survey suggested that the average student is paying a weekly rent of more than £70, with those living in London paying around £90 a week and those at the cheaper end of the spectrum in Belfast, Lancaster and Liverpool paying less than £60 a week. Generally speaking, the cost of student accommodation is highest in London and the

Average student weekly rents in the towns surveyed in the NatWest Student Living Index 2008

Lancaster	£57.09	Portsmouth	£66.88	Manchester	£75.65
Liverpool	£57.74	Birmingham	£67.10	Brighton	£76.27
Belfast	£58.27	Southampton	£67.69	Glasgow	£76.40
Swansea	£60.58	Cardiff	£68.01	Edinburgh	£76.83
Sheffield	£61.69	Plymouth	£69.05	Exeter	£79.88
Newcastle	£63.06	Leeds	£69.11	Cambridge	£86.55
Dundee	£63.63	Leicester	£69.20	London	£90.24
Nottingham	£65.22	Bristol	£70.44	Oxford	£91.80
York	£66.70	Aberdeen	£71.20		

southeast of England and lowest in the Midlands and North of England, Wales, Scotland and Northern Ireland. But the NatWest Student Living Index shows considerable variations within those regions.

It is important to remember that both your living costs and your potential earnings should be factored into your calculations when deciding where to live. While living costs in London are, unsurprisingly, the highest – an estimated average of £131 a week excluding rent – your earnings potential is nearly double what it might be in other parts of the country. Students in London were earning over £100 a week on average in 2008, according to the NatWest survey, compared with less than £60 in Southampton. Of course, those earnings figures may be significantly lower this year, whereas there have been no reports of student rents declining dramatically.

The choices you have

No longer are you faced with a straightforward choice between a university hall of residence and a poor quality rented house. A report from the National Union of Students puts accommodation into 16 categories, ranging from luxurious university halls to a bedsit in a shared house. The choices include:

- University hall of residence, with individual study bedrooms and a full catering service; many will have en-suite accommodation.
- University halls, flats or houses where you have to provide your own food.
- Private, purpose-built student accommodation.
- Rented houses or flats, shared with fellow students.
- Living at home.
- Living as a lodger in a private house.

This chapter will provide you with more information to help you decide where you would like to live and whether you can afford it.

NatWest Student Living Index 2008

The NatWest Student Living Index was calculated as follows: for each town listed, average local weekly student expenditure on living and accommodation costs was divided by average local weekly income for working students. This provided a value, by which the 26 university towns were ranked. At the top is Plymouth, where an average student spends £217 a week but earns £115 from part-time work during terms. At the bottom was Exeter, where an average student spends £294 a week but earns only £67 from part-time work during terms. The figures in brackets are for 2007; NE indicates a new entry.

1. Plymouth (NE)	10. Aberdeen (18)	19. York (21)
2. Cambridge (13)	11. Newcastle (10)	20. Leicester (6)
3. Dundee (3)	12. Sheffield (11)	21. Oxford (24)
4. Brighton (2)	13. Glasgow (8)	22. Birmingham (7)
5. Portsmouth (NE)	14. London (4)	23. Swansea (NE)
6. Bristol (9)	15. Nottingham (27)	24. Manchester (15)
7. Leeds (1)	16. Lancaster (25)	25. Southampton (26)
8. Liverpool (5)	17. Cardiff (16)	26. Exeter (NE)
9. Belfast (19)	18. Edinburgh (23)	

Making your choice

Financial considerations are not the only factor you should consider when deciding where to live. Feeling comfortable and happy in your student home is of crucial importance to your success at university and to the quality of your experience. It is therefore worth investing some time to find the right place, and to avoid the false economy of choosing somewhere cheap where you may end up feeling depressed and isolated. Most students who drop out of university do so in the first few months, when homesickness and loneliness can be felt most acutely. Being warm and well fed is likely to have a positive effect on your studies.

Perhaps for these reasons, most undergraduates in their first year plump for living in university halls, which offer a convenient, safe and reliable standard of accommodation, along with a supportive community environment. If meals are included, then this adds further peace of mind both for students and their parents.

Wherever you chose to live, there are some general points you will need to consider, such as how safe the neighbourhood seems to be, and how long it might take you to travel to and from the university – especially during rush hour. A recent survey of travel time between term-time accommodation and the university found that most students in London can expect a commute of at least 30 minutes and often over an hour, while those living in Wales are usually much less than 30 minutes away from their university. Be sure to make use of any local or national Student Travel Card and any university or students' union transport system that may be provided to help you get back to your accommodation cheaply and safely.

Information to help you

In the university profiles (which are in the second half of this book), we provide details of what accommodation each university offers. You will be able to find the following:

- The number of university-provided places. A quick check against the number of undergraduates will show you how well provided for the university is.
- The percentage of places that are catered.
- The percentage of places that are self-catered.
- The weekly cost of catered and self-catered accommodation.
- A summary of the offer of accommodation that can be made to first years.

Money paid weekly for accommodation

	Overall	Catered halls	Self-catered halls/flats houses	Rented flats/ houses off campus	Own flats/ houses off campus	Home/ parents off campus
£0	14%	5%	2%	1%	33%	75%
£1–£40	3%	0%	0%	2%	6%	10%
£41–£60	16%	2%	10%	27%	13%	5%
£61–£80	32%	16%	35%	46%	9%	5%
£81–£100	18%	34%	38%	11%	10%	3%
£101–£150	10%	38%	12%	6%	14%	1%
over £150	7%	7%	3%	7%	14%	1%

Adapted from *Sodexo University Lifestyle Survey 2008*

- A summary of the offer of accommodation that can be made to international students.
- The web address for details of the university's accommodation provision.

Continuing to live at home

The first decision must be whether to move at all. If the course you want is within reasonable travelling time and you are happy in the family home, you may decide to stay there – particularly if money is tight. You can always move out later, as many students do when they have met others with whom they want to share.

The number of students living at home has been rising for several years. A report published by the Sutton Trust in 2008 found that those choosing this option tended to be state school or college students, and usually not those with the highest grades. There was also a strong representation of Asian students in the sample. But it is reasonable to assume that, in future, more applicants of all backgrounds will be considering student life at home.

The potential financial benefits of this are obvious, and there may also be advantages in terms of academic work if the alternative involves shopping, cooking and cleaning, as well as the other distractions of a student flat. The obvious downside is that you may miss out on a lot of the student experience, especially the social scene and the opportunity to make new friends.

There is no evidence that students living at home do any worse academically. The quality of your home environment should influence your decision when weighing up whether or not to take this option. If it is stressful or not conducive to studying then you are

Most popular place for private study
It is important that wherever you live, it will be easy for you to work, as much of your private study will be done there.

Own accommodation	63%
Library	26%
Resource Centre	4%
Social space (coffee shop, etc.)	3%
Other	4%

Sodexo University Lifestyle Survey 2008

probably better off moving out, even if it means having to take a job to make ends meet. On the other hand, there is a lot to be said for making use of supportive and flexible home conditions where these exist. If you are studying at a "new" university, you are more likely to have fellow students who also live at home.

What universities offer

You might think that opting to live in university accommodation is the most straightforward choice, especially since first-year students are invariably given priority in the allocation of places in halls of residence. Certainly if you go for university residences you benefit from being able to make arrangements in advance and at a distance, rather than having to be in the right place at the right time, as is often the way when searching for private housing. However, you may still need to select from a range of options because some universities will have a variety of accommodation on offer. You will need to consider which best suits your pocket and your preferred lifestyle.

New university accommodation

At the top end of the market, partnerships between universities and private firms have recently begun to lead the way. Private organisations such as UNITE plc (**www.unite-**

students.com) and LibertyLiving (**www.libertyliving.co.uk**) have been paid by universities to build and manage some of the most luxurious student accommodation the UK sector has ever seen. Rooms in these complexes are typically en suite and include facilities such as your own phone line, satellite TV, and internet access. Shared kitchens are also top quality and fitted out with all the latest equipment. This kind of accommodation naturally comes at a higher price, but offers the advantages of flexibility both in living arrangements and through a range of payment options.

Halls of residence

Many new or recently refurbished university-owned halls offer a standard of accommodation that is not far short of the privately built residences. One of the reasons for this is that rooms in these halls can be offered to conference delegates during vacations. Even though these halls are also at the pricier end of the spectrum, you will probably find that they are in great demand, and you may have to get your name down for one quickly to secure one of the fancier rooms. That said, you can often get a guarantee of some kind of university accommodation if you give a firm acceptance of an offered place by a certain date in the summer. This may not be the case, however, if you have gained your place through Clearing – although rooms in private halls might still be on offer at this stage.

While a few halls are single-sex, most are mixed, and often house over 500 students. They are therefore great places for making friends and becoming part of the social scene. One possible downside is that they can also be noisy places where it can be difficult at times to get down to some work. The more successful students learn, before too many essay deadlines and exams start to loom, to get the balance right between all-night partying and escaping to the library for some undisturbed study time. On the upside, if you feel in need of either personal or study support, this is often at hand either through a counselling service or from fellow students.

University self-catering accommodation

An alternative to halls, offered particularly by some older universities, are smaller, self-catering properties fitted out with a shared kitchen and other living areas. Students looking for a more independent and flexible lifestyle may prefer this option. Remember that if you choose this kind of university housing, you will be responsible for feeding yourself, and you may also have heating and lighting bills to pay. University properties are often on campus or nearby, and so travel costs should not pose a problem.

Catering in university accommodation

Many universities have responded to a general increase in demand from students for a more independent lifestyle, by providing more flexible catering facilities. A range of eateries, from fast food outlets to more traditional refectories, can usually be found on campus. Students in university accommodation may now be offered pay-as-you-eat deals as an alternative to full-board packages.

What after the first year?

After your first year of living in university residences you may well wish to, and will probably be expected to, move out to other accommodation. The only exceptions are in collegiate universities – particularly Oxford and Cambridge – which may allow you to stay on in college halls for another year or two, and particularly for your final year. Students from outside the EU are also sometimes guaranteed accommodation.

Practical details

If you have decided to start out in university accommodation, then you will probably be expected to sign an agreement to cover rent. These contracts can be for around 40 weeks, which includes the Christmas and Easter holiday periods or for just the length of the three university terms. These term-time contracts are common when a university uses its rooms for conferences during vacations. You will be required to leave your room empty during vacations. It is therefore advisable to check whether the university has storage space for you to leave your belongings – otherwise you will have to make arrangements to take all your belongings home between terms. International students may be offered special arrangements, in which they can stay in halls during the short vacation periods. Organisations like **www.hostuk.org** can also arrange for overseas students to stay in a UK family home at holiday times such as the Christmas break.

Being a lodger or staying in a hostel

A small number of students live as a lodger in a family home, an option most frequently taken up by international students. The usual arrangement is for a study bedroom and some meals to be provided, while other facilities such as a washing machine are shared. Students with particular religious affiliations or those from certain countries may wish to consider living in one of a number of hostels run by charities catering for certain groups. Most of these can be found in London.

Renting from the private sector

Every university city or town is awash with privately owned accommodation available via agencies or direct from individual landlords. Indeed, there has been so much of it that so-called "student ghettoes", where local residents feel outnumbered, have become hot political issues. Into this traditional market in rented flats and houses have come the new sector private-sector complexes and residences, often created in partnership with universities, adding considerably to the private-sector options. Examples can be seen online through sites such as **www.accommodationforstudents.com**, which are listed at the end of this chapter.

While there are always exceptions, a much more professional attitude and approach to managing rented accommodation has emerged among smaller providers, thanks to a

---

Type of Accommodation by Year of Study

1st year		2nd year onwards	
Self-catered halls	27%	Privately let flats/houses	52%
University self-catered flats/houses	19%	At home with parents/family	12%
At home with parents/family	15%	Commercially let flats/houses	10%
Privately let flats/houses	14%	Own flat/house	9%
Catered halls	13%	University self-catered flats/houses	7%
Own flat/house	10%	Self-catered halls	7%
Commercially let flats/houses	3%	Catered halls	3%

Sodexo University Lifestyle Survey 2008

combination of greater regulation and increasing competition. Nevertheless, it is wise to take certain precautions when seeking out private residences.

How to start looking for rented property

Contact your university's accommodation service and ask for their list of approved rented properties. Some have a Student Accommodation Accreditation Scheme, run in collaboration with the local council. To get onto an approved list under such schemes, landlords must show they are adhering to basic standards of safety and security, such as having an up-to-date gas and electric safety certificate. University accommodation officers should also be able to advise you on any hidden charges. For instance, you may be asked to pay a booking or reservation fee to secure a place in a particular property, and fees for references or drawing up a tenancy agreement are also sometimes charged. The practice of charging a "joining fee", however, has been outlawed.

Making a choice

Once you have made an initial choice on the area you would like to live in and the size of property you are looking for, the next stage is to look at possible places. If you plan to share, it is important that you all have a look at the property. If you will be living by yourself, take a friend with you when you go to view a property, since he or she can help you assess what you see objectively, and avoid any irrational or rushed on-the-spot decisions. Don't let yourself be pushed into signing on the dotted line there and then. Take time to visit and consider a number of options. It is often helpful to spend some time in the area in which you may be living, to check out the local facilities, transport, and the general environment at various times of the day and different days of the week. If you can stay in the area for a few days, this will help you get a more accurate idea of what living in the district will be like.

If you are living in private rented accommodation, it is likely that at least some of your neighbours will not be students. Local people often welcome students, but resentment sometimes builds up, particularly in areas of towns and cities that are dominated by student housing. It is important to respect your neighbours' rights, and not to behave in an anti-social manner.

Preparing for sharing

The people you are planning to share a house with may not be as unsavoury as the characters in the TV comedy *The Young Ones*, but you can be sure they will have some habits that you find at least mildly irritating. How well you cope with some of the downsides of co-habiting will be partly down to the kind of person you are – where you are on the spectrum between laid back and highly strung – but it will help a lot if you are sharing with people whose outlook on day-to-day living is not too far out of line with your own. If you have not already selected your own group of friends, universities and landlords can help by taking personal preferences and lifestyle into account when grouping tenants together. You can make this task easier if you give full details about yourself when filling in accommodation applications forms.

Potential issues to consider when deciding whether to move into a shared house include whether any of the housemates smoke, own a loud musical instrument that they may decide to play at any time of the day or night, or have a habit of spending hours on the telephone. With most students owning a mobile phone, the latter should not be a problem unless someone decides to save on their mobile bills by using a landline phone in your shared house instead. If this is the case, then you should arrange for individual billing, provided by a number of phone companies such as The Phone Co-op (**www.thephone.coop**). It will also be important to sort out broadband arrangements that will work for everyone in the house, and that you will be able to arrange access to the university system. It may seem like a drag, but it is usually a good idea to agree from the outset a rota for everyone to share in the household cleaning chores. Otherwise it is almost certain that you will live in a state of permanent unhygienic squalor or that one or two individuals will be left to clear up everyone else's mess.

The practical details about renting

It is a good idea to ask whether your house is covered by an accreditation scheme or code of standards. Such codes provide a clear outline of what constitutes good practice and the responsibilities of both landlords and tenants. Adhering to schemes like the National Code of Standards for Larger Student Developments compiled by Accreditation Network UK (**www.anuk.org.uk**) may well become a requirement for larger properties, including those managed by universities, now that the Housing Act is in force.
At the very least, make sure that if you are renting from a private landlord, you have his or her telephone number and home address. Some can be remarkably difficult to contact when repairs are needed or deposits returned.

HMOs

If you are renting a private house it may be is subject to the rules and regulations of the 2004 Housing Act in England and Wales (similar legislation applies in Scotland and Northern Ireland). Licenses are compulsory for all private Houses in Multiple Occupation (HMOs) with three or more stories that house five or more unrelated residents. The provisions of the Act also allow local authorities to designate whole areas in which HMOs of all sizes must be licensed. The good news is that these regulations are likely to be applied in sections of university towns and cities where most students live. This means that a house must be licensed, well-managed and must meet various health and safety standards, and its owner subject to various financial regulations. The bad news is that this could lead to a reduction in the number and range of privately rented properties on the market, or an increase in rental prices.

Tenancy agreements

Whatever kind of accommodation you go for, you must be sure to have all the paperwork in order and be clear about what you are signing up to before you move in. If you are taking up residence in a shared house, flat or bedsit, the first document you will have to grapple with is a tenancy agreement or lease offering you an "assured shorthold tenancy". Since this is a binding legal document you should be prepared to go through every clause with a fine-tooth comb. Remember that it is much more difficult to make changes or overcome problems arising from unfair agreements once you are a tenant than before you become one.

You would be well advised to seek help, in the likely event of your not fully understanding some of the clauses. Your university accommodation office or students' union are a good place to start, since they should know all the ins and outs, and have model tenancy agreements to refer to. A Citizens Advice Bureau or Law Advice Centre should also be able to offer you free advice. Watch out in particular for clauses that may make you jointly responsible for the actions of others with whom you are sharing the property. If you name your parent as a guarantor to cover any costs not covered by you, then they may also be liable for charges levied on all tenants for any damage that might not be your fault. A rent review clause could allow your landlord to increase the rent at will, whereas without such a clause, they are restricted to one rent rise a year. Make sure you keep a copy of all documents, and get a receipt (and keep it somewhere safe) for anything you have to pay for.

Contracts tend to be longer than for university accommodation – they will frequently commit you to paying rent for 52 weeks of the year. There are probably more advantages than disadvantages to this kind of arrangement. It means you don't have to move out in vacation periods, which you might have to in university halls to make way for conference delegates. You can store your belongings in your room when you go away (but don't leave anything really valuable behind if you can help it). You may be able to negotiate a rent discount for those periods when you are not staying in the property. The other advantage, particularly important for cash-strapped students, is that you have a base from which to find work and hold down a job during the vacations.

Deposits

On top of the agreed rent, you will need to provide a deposit or bond to cover any possible breakages or damage. This will probably set you back the equivalent of another month's rent. The deposit should be returned, less any deductions, at the end of the contract. However, be warned that disputes over the return of deposits are quite common, with the question of what constitutes reasonable wear and tear often the subject of disagreements between landlords and tenants. To protect students from unscrupulous landlords who withhold deposits without good reason, the 2004 Housing Act has introduced a National Tenancy Deposit Scheme under which deposits are held by an independent body rather than by the landlord. This is designed to ensure that deposits are fairly returned, and that any disputes are resolved swiftly and cheaply.

Inventories and other paperwork

You should get an inventory and schedule of condition of everything in the property. This is another document that you should check very carefully – and make sure that everything listed is as described. Write on the document anything that is different. The National Union of Students even suggests taking photographs of rooms and equipment when you first move in (putting the date on the pictures if you are using a digital camera), to provide you with additional proof should any dispute arise when your contract ends and you want to get your deposit back. If you are not offered an inventory, then make one of your own. You should have someone else witness and sign this, send it to your landlord, and keep your own copy.

You should ask your landlord for a recent gas safety certificate issued by a qualified CORGI engineer, a fire safety certificate covering the furnishings, and a record of current gas and electricity meter readings. Take your own readings of meters when you move in to make sure these match up with what you have been given, or make your own records if the landlord doesn't supply this information. This also applied to water meters if you are expected to pay water rates (although this isn't usually the case). If you are sharing a house with other full-time students only, then you will not have to pay Council Tax. However, you may be liable to pay a proportion of the Council Tax bill if you are sharing with anyone who is not a full-time student. You may need to get a Council Tax exemption certificate from your university as evidence that you do not need to pay Council Tax or should pay only a proportion, depending on the circumstances.

Security in rented accommodation

As students living in private housing are twice as likely to be burgled as those in university halls, it is worth running through this security checklist provided by the NUS:

Do you feel safe?

	Male	Female
In my accommodation	96%	96%
Day-time travelling to and from university	96%	98%
Night-time travelling to and from university	84%	61%

Sodexo University Lifestyle Survey 2008

- Check that the front and back doors are fitted with five-lever mortise locks in addition to standard catch locks.
- Make sure the door to your room has a lock, and always lock up when you leave it – especially for long periods such as during vacations.
- Check the locks and catches on accessible windows, especially those at ground-floor level.
- Before you move in, try to talk to neighbours about how safe the area is and whether there have been many instances of burglary or car crime.
- Ask your landlord to ensure that all previous tenants and holders of keys no longer have copies.
- If you find a property that you are keen to rent, but you are unsure about some of the security aspects, speak to the letting agency or landlord to discuss your concerns. They may be able to make the necessary changes to make the property more secure before you move in.

Safety and security

Once you have arrived and settled in, remember to take care of your own safety and the security of your possessions. You are particularly vulnerable as a fresher, when you are still getting used to your new-found independence. This may help explain why a fifth of students are burgled or robbed in the first six weeks of the academic year. Take care with valuable portable items such as mobile phones, iPods and laptops, all of which are tempting for criminals. Ensure you don't use them or have them obviously on display when you are out and about. If your mobile phone is stolen, call your network or 08701 123 123 to immobilise it.

Students' unions, universities and the police will provide plenty of practical guidance when you arrive. Following their advice will reduce the chance of you becoming a victim of crime, and so able to enjoy living in the new surroundings of your chosen university town.

Insurance

It is a false economy not to have adequate insurance to cover you for the loss or theft of valuable items. Your students' union will probably be able to advise you on where to go for the best deals. It may be that your parents' insurance will cover you when you are a student, and you should certainly check this. You should also keep a record somewhere safe of the serial and model numbers of expensive electrical equipment. If you have to claim on your insurance for these items you will need these details. Remember that whether you say it out loud or subconsciously think it, courting the notion that "it won't happen to me" is one of the best ways to ensure that it probably will.

Useful websites

The following websites will help you find out more about the topics discussed in this chapter. In the university profiles later in this book, we give an indication of costs for university-provided accommodation and details of university accommodation websites.

For advice on a range of housing issues, visit:
www.nus.org.uk/en/Student-Life/Housing-Advice/

The Shelter website has separate sections covering different housing regulations in England, Wales, Scotland and Northern Ireland:
www.shelter.org.uk

Private accommodation

As examples of a provider of private hall accommodation, visit:
www.unite-students.com
www.libertyliving.co.uk

There are a number of sites that will help you find accommodation, among which are:
www.accommodationforstudents.com
www.homesforstudents.co.uk
www.studentaccommodation.org
www.studentpad.co.uk

For guidance on private accommodation:

Accreditation Network UK runs an accreditation scheme for larger schemes (with Unipol):
www.anuk.org.uk
www.unipol.org.uk/national

To find your nearest Citizen's Advice Bureau, visit:
www.nacab.org.uk

To find your nearest Law Centre, visit:
www.lawcentres.org.uk/lawcentres

For security advice, visit the NUS security checklist:
www.nus.org.uk/en/Student-Life/Housing-Advice/Protect-yourself-from-crime/

For telephone sharing, visit the Phone Co-op:
www.thephone.coop

For general advice on safety, this Home Office site gives practical advice:
www.homeoffice.gov.uk/crime-victims/how-you-can-prevent-crime/student-safety/

6

Finding Out About University Sport

Sport used to be low down most applicants' list of priorities when choosing a university – it was a minority pursuit, mainly for dedicated hearties playing in competitive teams. Not any more. A growing proportion of students want to keep fit, even if they don't play competitive sport, and universities have joined a race of their own to provide the best facilities. Sport may still be a secondary consideration for most applicants, but particularly good (or particularly poor) facilities can sometimes swing the balance.

Universities have recognised this and have been investing in new facilities on an unprecedented scale. Some of the biggest multi-sports developments in the UK have been on university campuses, where facilities nationally are said to be worth an astonishing £20 billion.

The scale of higher education's involvement in the 2012 Olympic Games shows how far universities have travelled down the sporting road. There has been a report to the Prime Minister, separate organisations formed to coordinate activity and £10 million set aside for collaborative projects. Half of all UK universities have been identified as pre-Games training centres and several expect to host teams in 2012. Universities are lobbying to run courses at the Olympic site, and a number will be involved in the cultural programme for the Games, as well as in planning the legacy.

Where universities have been able to attract Lottery funding or have made sport a priority in the portfolio of subjects, the standard of facilities can be breathtaking. Naturally, not all can aspire to those standards, but most now offer facilities to compare with the best available commercially – and usually at a fraction of the price. So many facilities are also available to local communities that a recent survey of usage found that more than 20 per cent of bookings were by non-students.

However, being a full-time student offers unrivalled opportunities to discover and play a vast range of sports. Many universities still encourage departments not to schedule lectures and seminars on Wednesday afternoons, to give students free time for sport. Even those who spend long hours in the laboratory have more time for leisure activities now than they will be able to spare later in life. There are student-run clubs for all the major sports and – particularly at the larger universities – a host of minor ones. Or you can content yourself with high-quality gyms, with staff on hand to devise personalised training regimes. The cost varies widely between universities, and membership fees can represent a large amount to lay out at the start of the year, but most provide good value if you are going to be a regular.

All universities are conscious of the need to provide for a spread of ability. Sports scholarships for elite performers are now commonplace, but there will be plenty of opportunities, too, for beginners. University teams demand a hefty commitment in terms of training and practice sessions – often several a week – and in many sports standards are high. University teams often compete in local and national leagues.

The University of London women's volleyball team has won the English Volleyball Championships, for example, and Bath University's "Team Bath" have tasted success in the FA Cup.

For those who don't aspire to such heights, or whose interests are primarily social, there are thriving internal, or intramural, leagues. These provide opportunities for teams from halls of residence or faculties, or even a group of friends, to form a team and participate on a regular basis. Nor is university sport a male preserve – student teams were among the pioneers in mixed sport and are still strong in areas such as women's cricket, football and rugby.

British university sport has not become big business, as it is in the United States, but competitive standards have been rising. British Universities and Colleges Sport (BUCS) runs competitions in almost 50 sports, and ranks participating institutions. There is also international competition in a number of sports, and numerous examples of students being selected for Olympic and professional teams. The World Student Games have become one of the biggest occasions in the international sporting calendar.

Formed in 2008, BUCS has brought together the administration of university sport and the job of lobbying for the best possible facilities. The new organisation has a student membership, but will also play a role in the wider sporting community, as well as negotiating with the Government and other national and international bodies to promote, develop and enable participation in sport and active recreation.

A few universities are known particularly for sport, and are benefiting from its increasing popularity as a degree subject, as well as an extra-curricular activity. Several of this elite group had a head start as former physical education colleges. Loughborough is probably the best-known of them, but Leeds Metropolitan and Brunel are others with a similar pedigree. Other universities with different traditions, such as Bath and the University of East Anglia, also have a variety of outstanding facilities, while the likes of Stirling and UWIC have the same in a narrower range of sports.

As in so much else, Oxford and Cambridge are in a category of their own. The Boat Race and the Varsity Match (in rugby union) are the only UK university sporting events with a regular popular following, and there is a high standard of competition in other sports, but there is an ambivalent attitude to them in many colleges. While star rowers and rugby players do turn up on postgraduate diploma courses, the days of special consideration for sporty undergraduates appear to be over, and there are few of the sports scholarships offered at other universities.

For most universities, it is in the area of "sport for all" that most attention has been focused. Beginners are welcomed and coaching provided in a range of sports, from ultimate Frisbee to tai-chi, that would be difficult to match outside the higher education system. Check on university websites to see whether your usual sport is available, but don't be surprised if you come across a new favourite when you have the opportunity to try out some new sports as a student. Many universities have programmes designed to encourage students to take up a new sport, with expert coaching provided.

You may even end up wanting to coach, umpire or referee – and this is another area in which higher education has much to offer. Many university clubs and sports unions provide subsidised courses for students to gain qualifications that may be of use to the individual in later life, as well as benefiting university teams in the short term. Or you might want to try your hand at some sports administration, with an eye to your career. In most universities there is a sports (or athletic) union, with autonomy from the main students' union, which organises matches and looks after the wider interests of those who play. There are plenty of opportunities for those seeking an apprenticeship in the art of running a club, or larger organisation.

University sports facilities

Even the smallest university should provide reasonable indoor and outdoor sports facilities – a sports hall, modern gym equipment and outdoor pitches (usually including an all-weather surface and floodlights). Most will also have a swimming pool and extras such as climbing walls, but the smaller universities tend to make arrangements for students to use local sports centres and clubs when it is not feasible to provide for minority sports. The same goes for the really expensive ones, like golf, which is usually the subject of an arrangement with one or more local clubs that give students a discount. Specialist facilities, like boat houses and climbing huts, obviously depend on location, but the most landlocked university is likely to have a sailing club that organises regular activities away from campus, and a skiing club that runs at least annual trips to the mountains.

Many of the larger universities have spent millions of pounds improving their sports facilities, sometimes in partnership with local authorities, national sporting bodies or the Lottery. University campuses are ideal locations for national coaching centres, and many have been established in recent years. While some of the facilities are naturally reserved for elite performers, opportunities always exist for ordinary students to make use of them at reasonable rates, as well as occasionally rubbing shoulders with star players.

It is estimated that about £400 million has been spent on new or upgraded sports facilities at UK universities over the past six years. Universities now boast a significant proportion of the UK's 50-metre pools, for example, and more are planned. Other innovative schemes include Leeds Metropolitan's development of the Headingley cricket and rugby league grounds, providing teaching space for students during the week and improved facilities for players and spectators on match days.

Both the scale of investment and the emphasis on sport can be expected to increase in the run-up to the 2012 Olympics. The legacy for students should be considerable, as it was at the Commonwealth Games in Manchester and the World Student Games in Sheffield.

Beyond scrutinising the prospectus for the extent of university facilities, there are two important questions to ask: where are they and how much do they cost? Neither is easy to track down on the average university website.

How much?

Students who are used to free (if inferior) facilities at school often get a nasty surprise when they find that they are expected to pay to join the Athletic Union and then pay again to use the gym or play football. Because most university sport is subsidised, the charges are reasonable compared to commercial facilities, but the best deal may require a considerable outlay at the start. Some campus gyms and swimming pools now charge more than £300 a year, for example, which is still considerably cheaper than paying per visit if you intend to use the facilities regularly (and provides an incentive to carry on doing so). Most universities offer a variety of peak and off-peak membership packages – some for the entire length of your course.

Outdoor sports are usually charged by the hour, although clubs will also charge a membership fee. You may be required to pay up to £25 for membership of the Athletic Union (although not all universities require this). Fees for intra-mural sport are seldom substantial; teams will usually pay a fee for the season, while courts for racket sports tend to be marginally cheaper per session than in other clubs.

How far away?

University prospectuses tend to major on the quality of the five-a-side pitches without being as forthcoming about the prices. The other common complaint by students is that the playing fields are too far from the campus – understandable in the case of city centre universities, but still aggravating if you are having to arrange your own transport. This is where campus universities have a clear advantage.

For the rest, there has to be some trade-off between the quality of outdoor facilities and the distance you have to travel to use them. But universities are beginning to realise that long journeys depress usage of important (and expensive) facilities, and some have tried to find suitable land closer to lectures and halls of residence. Indoor sports centres should all be within easy reach.

Sport as a degree subject

Sports science and other courses associated with sport have seen big increases in recent years – so much so that the subject is close to the top ten in terms of popularity, with more than 40,000 applications at the start of 2009. A separate ranking for the subject is published for the first time this year on page 168.

As those who have taken sports science at A level will know, an interest in sport is invaluable but far from sufficient. The same goes for sporting excellence. If you are hoping to be rewarded with an academic qualification for three years on the sports field, you will be disappointed because there is serious science involved.

However, sport is a growing employment field and one that demands qualifications like any other. Entrance requirements vary widely, with some of the top courses asking for 360 points on the UCAS tariff, while others ask half this number or less.

Other degrees in the sports area are more closely focused on management, with careers in the leisure industry in mind – golf course management, for example, has proved popular with students despite being a target of those who see anything beyond the traditional academic portfolio as "dumbing down". Such courses are usually no less rigorous than general management degrees. The question is not whether the courses are up to standard, but whether a less specialised one will offer more career flexibility if a decline in popularity for the particular sport limits future opportunities. The chance to combine work and play for three years holds obvious attractions, but there will be opportunities to pursue your chosen sport at university in any case.

Sports scholarships

The number and range of sports scholarships have expanded just as rapidly as courses in the subject, but the two are usually not connected. Sports scholarships are for elite performers, regardless of what they are studying – indeed, they exist at universities with barely any degrees in the field. Imported from the United States, scholarships now exist in an array of sports. At Birmingham University, for example, there are specialist golf awards (as there are at ten other universities) and a scholarship for triathletes, as well as others open to any sport.

The value of scholarships varies considerably – sometimes according to individual prowess. The Royal and Ancient scholarships for golfers, for example, range from £500 for promising handicap golfers to £10,000 for full internationals. All of them demand that you meet the normal entrance requirements for your course and maintain the necessary academic standards, as well as progressing in your sport. In practice, most departments will be flexible about attendance and deadlines, as long as you make your requests well in advance.

Many sports scholarships offer benefits in-kind, in the form of coaching, equipment or access to facilities. The Government-funded Talented Athletes Scholarship Scheme, which is restricted to students at English universities who have achieved national recognition at under-18 level and are eligible to represent England, is one such example. The scholarships are worth £3,500 a year and can be put towards costs such as competition and training costs, equipment or mentoring. Further details are available at www.tass.gov.uk.

Part-time work
University sports centres are an excellent source of term-time (and out-of-term) employment. They beat other campus jobs, such as bar work, in terms of enjoyment and healthiness. Depending on your qualifications, you could earn up to £17 an hour for coaching, or more like £7 an hour as a receptionist or for other forms of assistance. You may also be trained in first aid, fire safety, customer care and risk assessment – all useful skills for future employment. The experience will help you secure employment in commercial or local authority facilities – and even for jobs such as stewarding at football grounds and music venues.

Administrative work within the Athletic Union of university sports organisation, is more likely to be unpaid, but may still provide useful experience that will add to your CV. So, indeed, does a position of responsibility in a club, or even captaining a team. Many employers value sport as an indication of self-confidence and team-working qualities. Most universities also have a sabbatical post in the Athletic Union or similar body, a paid position with responsibility for organising university sport and representing the sporting community within the university.

Useful websites
The following websites will help you find out more about the topics discussed in this chapter.

BUCS (British Universities and Colleges Sports)
www.bucs.org.uk
UK Sport
www.uksport.gov.uk
London 2012
www.london2012.com
Talented Athlete Scholarship Scheme
www.tass.gov.uk

Table of university sporting facilities

The following six pages outline the sporting facilities available at each of the universities covered in this book. The information has been compiled from a survey undertaken by University and College Sport in 2007 (with updated BUCS rankings and websites). The information only covers the facilities that universities provide centrally for all their students, and ignores any facilities there may be in halls of residence or colleges. At Oxford and Cambridge, for example, many colleges have facilities that are not reflected in the tables.

The table provides the following information:

- British Universities and Colleges Sports (BUCS) League Rankings 2007–08, based on all sports. Teams get points each year for their success in inter-university competitions and BUCS uses them to compile an annual league table. The universities with the highest rankings (eg, Loughborough, Bath and Birmingham) are therefore overall the most successful competitively. A number of institutions with teams in BUCS are not universities and so do not appear in the following table. The BUCS rankings are based on all teams in the leagues.
- An indication of whether the university has (Y for "yes") or does not have (N for "no") the following facilities:
  Sports hall
  Swimming pool
  Squash courts
  Climbing wall
  Indoor tennis courts
  Fitness facilities
  Winter grass pitches (eg, for football, rugby, etc.)
  Cricket pitches
  Artificial turf pitches
- The number of different sports with student clubs.
- The number of indoor sports with intramural competitions.
- The number of outdoor sports with intramural competitions.
- Whether instruction classes are available to encourage new participants (Y = yes; N = no).
- Whether sports scholarships or bursaries are available. Full details will need to be checked on university websites.
- Details of university websites devoted to sports. Students' unions websites usually have sports information as well. Where the main university website is given, visit that site and search for sports. The full web address is too long to give in this table.

Grey boxes show where information is not available.

University Sporting Facilities

Universities	BUCS ranking 2007–08	Sports hall?	Swimming pool?	Squash courts?	Climbing wall?	Indoor tennis court(s)?	Fitness facilities?
Aberdeen	28	Y	Y	Y	N	N	Y
Abertay	86	N	N	N	N	N	Y
Aberystwyth	66	Y	Y	Y	Y	Y	Y
Anglia Ruskin	95	Y	Y	Y	Y	Y	Y
Aston	89	Y	Y	Y	Y	N	Y
Bangor	73	Y	N	Y	Y	N	Y
Bath	2	Y	Y	Y	Y	Y	Y
Bath Spa	143	No further information reported					
Bedfordshire	106	Y	Y	N	Y	Y	Y
Birmingham	3	Y	Y	Y	Y	N	Y
Birmingham City	=112	N	N	N	N	N	N
Bolton	125	Y	N	N	Y	N	Y
Bournemouth	36	Y	Y	Y	Y	N	Y
Bradford	99	Y	Y	Y	Y	Y	Y
Brighton	48	Y	N	N	Y	N	Y
Bristol	12	Y	Y	Y	N	Y	Y
Brunel	21	Y	N	Y	Y	N	Y
Buckinghamshire New	105	No further information reported					
Cambridge	14	N	Y	Y	N	N	Y
Canterbury Christ Church	102	Y	N	N	N	N	Y
Cardiff	17	Y	N	Y	N	N	Y
Cardiff, University of Wales Institute	15	Y	Y	Y	N	Y	Y
Central Lancashire	45	Y	N	N	N	Y	Y
Chester	74	Y	Y	Y	N	N	Y
Chichester	67	Y	N	N	Y	Y	Y
City	115	Y	N	Y	N	N	Y
Coventry	70	Y	N	N	N	N	Y
Cumbria	85	Y	N	N	N	N	Y
De Montfort	94	Y	N	Y	N	N	Y
Derby	109	No further information reported					
Dundee	43	Y	Y	Y	N	Y	Y
Durham	4	Y	N	Y	Y	N	Y
East Anglia	62	Y	Y	Y	Y	N	Y
East London	133	No further information reported					
Edge Hill	110	Y	Y	Y	N	N	Y
Edinburgh	5	Y	Y	Y	Y	N	Y
Edinburgh Napier	65	No further information reported					
Essex	49	Y	N	Y	Y	N	Y
Exeter	11	Y	Y	Y	Y	Y	Y
Glamorgan	63	Y	N	Y	Y	N	Y

Winter grass pitch(es)?	Cricket pitch(es)?	Artificial turf pitch(es)?	Number of different sports with student clubs	Number of indoor sports with intra-mural competitions	Number of outdoor sports with intra-mural competitions	Instruction classes available?	Sports scholarships or bursaries available?	Sport website
Y	Y	Y	53	0	2	Y	Y	www.abdn.ac.uk/sportandrec
N	N	N	16	3	3	Y	Y	http://sport.abertay.ac.uk
Y	Y	Y	50	0	1	Y	N	www.aber.ac.uk/en/sportscentre
Y	N	N	60	5	5	Y	Y	www.anglia.ac.uk
Y	Y	Y	37	0	0	Y	Y	www.aston.ac.uk/sport
Y	N	Y	39	3	3	Y	Y	www.maesglas.co.uk
Y	Y	Y	47	8	6	Y	Y	www.teambath.com
								www.bathspa.ac.uk/bath
Y	Y	N	11	4	2	Y	Y	www.beds.ac.uk/studentlife/town
Y	Y	Y	43	3	4	Y	Y	www.sport.bham.ac.uk
Y	N	Y	20	1	1	Y	N	www.birminghamcitysu.com
N	N	N	9	3	0	Y	N	www.bolton.ac.uk/sport
Y	Y	N	15	7	3	Y	Y	www.bournemouth.ac.uk/sports
Y	Y	Y	34	13	14	Y	N	www.brad.ac.uk/sports
Y	Y	N	24	0	4	Y	Y	www.brighton.ac.uk/sport
Y	Y	Y	56	7	4	Y	Y	www.bris.ac.uk/sport
Y	N	Y	39	3	2	Y	Y	www.brunel.ac.uk/sport
								www.bucks.ac.uk
Y	Y	Y	53	12	7	Y	Y	www.sport.cam.ac.uk
Y	N	N	15	0	4	Y	Y	www.canterbury.ac.uk/sport
Y	Y	Y	59	0	3	Y	Y	www.cardiff.ac.uk/sport
Y	Y	Y	19	0	0	Y	Y	www3.uwic.ac.uk/English/sport
Y	Y	Y	35	0	1	Y	Y	www.uclan.ac.uk/sport
Y	N	Y	33	3	3	Y	Y	www.chester.ac.uk/sportandrecreation
Y	N	Y	17	0	1	Y	Y	www.chi.ac.uk/SportAtChichester.cfm
N	N	N	16	5	0	Y	N	www.city.ac.uk/studentcentre/saddlers
Y	Y	Y	34	4	2	Y	Y	www.coventry.ac.uk/cu/sport
N	N	N	12	8	2	Y	Y	www.cumbria.ac.uk
N	N	N	26	0	0	Y	N	www.dmu.ac.uk
								www.derby.ac.uk/sports
Y	Y	N	44	5	3	Y	Y	www.dundee.ac.uk/ise
Y	Y	Y	51	8	9	Y	Y	www.teamdurham.com
Y	Y	Y	46	18	8	Y	Y	www.sportspark.co.uk
								www.uel.ac.uk
Y	N	Y	12	0	0	Y	Y	www.edgehill.ac.uk/sportingedge
Y	Y	Y	59	3	5	Y	Y	www.sport.ed.ac.uk
								www.napier.ac.uk/napierlife
Y	Y	Y	45	15	7	Y	Y	www.essex.ac.uk/sport
Y	Y	Y	47	6	6	Y	Y	www.sport.ex.ac.uk
Y	N	Y	25	6	1	Y	Y	http://sport.glam.ac.uk

Universities	BUCS ranking 2007–08	Sports hall?	Swimming pool?	Squash courts?	Climbing wall?	Indoor tennis court(s)?	Fitness facilities?
Glasgow	29	Y	Y	Y	N	N	Y
Glasgow Caledonian	81	Y	N	N	N	N	Y
Gloucestershire	40	No further information reported					
Glyndŵr	132	No further information reported					
Goldsmiths College	131	Y	N	N	N	N	Y
Greenwich	104	Y	N	N	N	Y	Y
Heriot-Watt	46	Y	N	Y	Y	N	Y
Hertfordshire	52	Y	Y	Y	Y	N	Y
Huddersfield	100	Y	N	Y	N	N	Y
Hull	64	Y	N	Y	Y	N	Y
Imperial College	22	Y	Y	Y	Y	N	Y
Keele	69	Y	Y	Y	Y	N	Y
Kent	39	Y	N	Y	Y	Y	Y
King's College	54	N	N	Y	N	N	Y
Kingston	75	N	N	N	N	N	Y
Lampeter	143	No further information reported					
Lancaster	47	Y	Y	Y	Y	N	Y
Leeds	13	Y	N	Y	Y	N	Y
Leeds Metropolitan	7	Y	Y	Y	Y	Y	Y
Leicester	76	Y	N	Y	N	Y	Y
Lincoln	61	Y	N	Y	N	N	Y
Liverpool	32	Y	Y	Y	Y	N	Y
Liverpool Hope	96	No further information reported					
Liverpool John Moores	50	Y	Y	N	Y	N	Y
London Metropolitan	25	No further information reported					
London School of Economics	53	No further information reported					
London South Bank	90	Y	N	N	N	N	Y
Loughborough	1	Y	Y	Y	Y	Y	Y
Manchester	8	Y	Y	Y	N	N	Y
Manchester Metropolitan	71	Y	N	Y	N	N	Y
Middlesex	78	Y	N	N	N	N	Y
Newcastle	10	Y	N	Y	N	N	Y
Northampton	93	Y	N	N	N	N	Y
Northumbria	16	Y	N	Y	N	N	Y
Nottingham	6	Y	Y	Y	Y	Y	Y
Nottingham Trent	27	Y	N	Y	Y	N	Y
Oxford	9	Y	Y	Y	Y	N	Y
Oxford Brookes	41	Y	N	Y	Y	N	Y
Plymouth	42	N	N	Y	N	N	Y

Winter grass pitch(es)?	Cricket pitch(es)?	Artificial turf pitch(es)?	Number of different sports with student clubs	Number of indoor sports with intra-mural competitions	Number of outdoor sports with intra-mural competitions	Instruction classes available?	Sports scholarships or bursaries available?	Sport website
Y	Y	Y	46	2	2	Y	Y	www.ugsport.co.uk/home.asp
N	N	N	24	0	0	Y	Y	www.gcal.ac.uk/arc
								www.yourstudentsunion.com
								www.glyndwr.ac.uk
Y	Y	N	17	1	1	Y	N	www.gold.ac.uk/sports
Y	N	N	7	0	0	N	Y	www.gre.ac.uk/about/sports
Y	N	Y	32	3	2	Y	Y	www.hw.ac.uk/sports
Y	N	Y	24	1	2	Y	Y	www.student.hertssportsvillage.co.uk
N	N	N	28	0	0	Y	N	www2.hud.ac.uk/estates/sports
Y	Y	Y	38	1	1	Y	N	www.hullstudent.com/au
Y	Y	Y	73	5	4	Y	Y	www.imperial.ac.uk/sports
Y	Y	Y	32	2	1	Y	N	www.keelefm.co.uk
Y	Y	Y	40	5	4	Y	Y	www.kent.ac.uk/sports
Y	Y	N	51	0	0	Y	N	www.kclsu.org/clubs.php
Y	Y	N	27	0	1	Y	Y	www.kingston.ac.uk/sport
								www.lamp.ac.uk
Y	Y	Y	30	7	7	Y	N	www.sportscentrelancaster.co.uk
Y	Y	Y	63	9	6	Y	Y	www.leeds.ac.uk/sport
Y	N	Y	40	1	2	Y	Y	www.leedsmet.ac.uk/sport
Y	Y	Y	32	8	4	Y	Y	www.le.ac.uk/sports
Y	N	Y	40	2	1	Y	Y	www.lincoln.ac.uk
Y	Y	Y	43	3	3	Y	Y	www.liv.ac.uk/sports
								www.hope.ac.uk/hopeparksports
Y	N	Y	30	0	3	Y	Y	www.ljmu.ac.uk/sport
								www.londonmet.ac.uk/sports
								www.lsesu.com
Y	Y	N	13	1	0	Y	Y	www.lsbu.ac.uk/sports
Y	Y	Y	53	28	14	Y	Y	http://sdc.lboro.ac.uk
Y	Y	Y	44	5	7	Y	Y	www.manchester.ac.uk/sport
N	N	N	35	2	2	Y	N	www.mmu.ac.uk/sport
Y	Y	N	12	2	2	Y	Y	www.mdx.ac.uk/sport
Y	Y	Y	65	2	4	Y	Y	www.ncl.ac.uk/cprs
Y	N	N	15	0	1	Y	Y	www.northamptonunion.com
Y	Y	Y	27	4	2	Y	Y	www.teamnorthumbria.com
Y	Y	Y	73	4	6	Y	Y	www.nottingham.ac.uk/sport
Y	Y	Y	38	3	1	Y	Y	www.ntu.ac.uk/sport
Y	Y	Y	81	28	18	Y	Y	www.sport.ox.ac.uk
Y	Y	Y	30	1	1	Y	Y	www.brookes.ac.uk/sport
N	N	N	57	2	3	Y	Y	www.plymouth.ac.uk/recreation

University Sporting Facilities cont.

Universities	BUCS ranking 2007–08	Sports hall?	Swimming pool?	Squash courts?	Climbing wall?	Indoor tennis court(s)?	Fitness facilities?
Portsmouth	37	Y	N	Y	N	N	Y
Queen Margaret, Edinburgh	117	Y	N	N	N	N	Y
Queen Mary, London	82	Y	N	Y	N	N	Y
Queen's, Belfast	97	Y	Y	Y	Y	N	Y
Reading	26	Y	N	Y	N	N	Y
Robert Gordon	77	Y	Y	Y	Y	Y	Y
Roehampton	91	Y	N	N	N	N	Y
Royal Holloway	57	Y	Y	Y	N	N	Y
Salford	98	No further information reported					
Sheffield	23	Y	Y	Y	Y	N	Y
Sheffield Hallam	20	Y	N	N	N	N	Y
SOAS	138	No further information reported					
Southampton	18	Y	Y	Y	Y	N	Y
Southampton Solent	59	Y	N	N	N	N	Y
St Andrews	30	Y	N	Y	Y	N	Y
Staffordshire	87	Y	N	N	Y	Y	Y
Stirling	24	Y	Y	Y	N	Y	Y
Strathclyde	44	Y	Y	Y	N	N	Y
Sunderland	92	Y	Y	N	N	N	Y
Surrey	80	Y	N	Y	Y	N	Y
Sussex	51	Y	N	Y	N	N	Y
Swansea	31	Y	Y	Y	Y	N	Y
Swansea Metropolitan	139	No further information reported					
Teesside	72	Y	N	Y	Y	N	Y
Thames Valley	134	No further information reported					
Ulster	101	Y	N	Y	N	Y	Y
University of the Arts London	129	N	N	N	N	N	N
University College London	34	Y	N	Y	N	N	Y
UWE, Bristol	35	Y	N	N	N	N	N
Wales, Newport	121	Y	N	N	N	N	N
Warwick	19	Y	Y	Y	Y	Y	Y
Westminster	118	No further information reported					
West of Scotland	–	No further information reported					
Winchester	=112	Y	N	Y	N	N	Y
Wolverhampton	83	Y	N	Y	N	N	Y
Worcester	55	Y	Y	N	N	N	Y
York	48	Y	N	Y	N	N	Y
York St John	79	Y	N	N	Y	N	Y

A number of institutions with teams in the British Universities and Colleges Sports League are not universities and so do not appear in the above table. The BUCS rankings above are based on all teams in the leagues.

Winter grass pitch(es)?	Cricket pitch(es)?	Artificial turf pitch(es)?	Number of different sports with student clubs	Number of indoor sports with intra-mural competitions	Number of outdoor sports with intra-mural competitions	Instruction classes available?	Sports scholarships or bursaries available?	Sport website
Y	N	Y	49	6	3	Y	Y	www.port.ac.uk/sport
N	N	Y	12	0	0	Y	N	www.qmu.ac.uk/sports
N	N	N	30	4	7	Y	N	www.qmsu.org
Y	Y	Y	53	6	5	Y	Y	www.qub.ac.uk/sport
Y	Y	Y	50	5	2	Y	Y	www.sport.reading.ac.uk
N	N	N	30	0	0	Y	Y	www.rgu.ac.uk/rgusport
Y	N	N	20	0	3	Y	N	www.roehampton.ac.uk
Y	Y	N	36	0	0	Y	Y	www.rhul.ac.uk/sports
								www.salfordstudents.com
Y	Y	Y	48	4	4	Y	Y	www.usport.co.uk
Y	Y	Y	38	3	2	Y	Y	www.shu.ac.uk/sporthallam
								www.soasunion.org/pages/activities
Y	Y	Y	70	7	9	Y	Y	www.sportrec.soton.ac.uk
Y	Y	N	27	16	5	Y	Y	www.solent.ac.uk/sport
Y	Y	Y	46	7	7	Y	Y	www.st-andrews.ac.uk/sport
Y	N	Y	35	0	0	Y	N	www.staffs.ac.uk
Y	Y	Y	38	0	7	Y	Y	www.stir.ac.uk/sport
Y	Y	Y	36	3	0	Y	Y	www.strath.ac.uk/sport
N	N	N	33	3	0	Y	N	www.unisportsunderland.com
Y	Y	Y	35	7	1	Y	Y	www.unisport.co.uk
Y	Y	Y	20	5	1	Y	Y	http://www.sussex.ac.uk/sport
Y	Y	Y	50	6	1	Y	Y	www.swan.ac.uk/sport
								www.metsu.org
Y	N	Y	40	0	1	Y	Y	www.tees.ac.uk/sections/sport
								www.tvu.ac.uk/students
Y	Y	Y	42	2	0	Y	Y	www.uusport.com
N	N	N	17	0	0	N	N	www.suarts.org
Y	Y	N	33	3	0	Y	Y	www.uclunion.org/leisure-fitness
Y	Y	N	40	2	0	Y	Y	www.uwe.ac.uk/sport
N	N	N	0	2	1	Y	N	www.newport.ac.uk
Y	Y	Y	75	2	5	Y	Y	http://warwicksport.warwick.ac.uk
								www.wmin.ac.uk/page-5188
								www.sauws.org.uk/Sportsandsocieties
Y	Y	N	27	3	2	Y	N	www.winchesterstudents.co.uk
N	N	N	28	7	0	Y	Y	www.wlv.ac.uk/sport
Y	Y	Y	42	0	0	Y	Y	www.worc.ac.uk/student/sports
Y	Y	Y	58	5	9	Y	N	www.york.ac.uk/univ/sports
Y	N	Y	23	1	0	Y	Y	www.yorksj.ac.uk

7

The Cost of Studying

There is no point in jumping through all the hoops necessary to win a place at university if you are not going to be able to afford it when you get there. Studying for a degree today is a major financial undertaking that requires careful planning, not just on the part of the would-be student, but in most cases their family, too.

No one knows what the long-term effect of the recession will be, but most independent research continues to show that it is worth investing in a degree – as long as you pick the right course and work hard enough to ensure that you at least gain your qualification. The extra amount you earn during a lifetime, over and above what you would have got without a degree, should far outstrip the cost of your higher education in most subjects at most universities.

Funding help

Fortunately, there are still enough sources of funding to enable most students to meet the costs of higher education and live reasonably – albeit building up considerable debts in the process. But, once again, it takes perseverance to put together the best possible package. Depending on your family income and where you live in the UK, you may be entitled to a range of grants, bursaries or scholarships. And then there are further calculations to do on fee levels, the length of courses and the cost of living at different universities. With many families feeling the pinch, it has never been more important to get it right.

Expected Debt of UK Students on Graduation	
£0	12%
£1–£2,500	4%
£2,501–£5,000	4%
£5,001–£7,500	3%
£7,501–£10,000	12%
£10,001–£12,500	10%
£12,501–£15,000	13%
£15,001–£17,500	5%
£17,501–£20,000	20%
over £20,000	18%

Sodexo University Lifestyle Survey 2008

Getting into debt is now a fact of life for almost all students – the total owed to the Student Loans Company is now a staggering £22 billion and rising. Two thirds of those taking part in last year's Sodexo/*Times Higher Education University Lifestyle Survey* expected to owe at least £10,000 on graduation, some double that. Most research now puts average graduate debt at around £20,000 by 2010. The good news is that most of it is in the form of student loans, which are pegged to inflation and repayable only when a graduate is earning at least £15,000 a year – although many students also have bank overdrafts and owe money on credit cards.

Forewarned is forearmed, and a little bit of careful financial planning and research into help that is available can go a long way to helping you emerge from your university education with a level of debt that is not going to become a millstone for life. As well as student loans, which are still provided at generous rates and under very favourable terms and conditions, you can shop around for university bursaries and scholarships and other sponsorship packages, and seek out any supplementary support to which you may be entitled. The latter may include a maintenance grant: despite recent changes in eligibility, these are available to a much larger slice of the population than was the case in the early years of tuition fees.

However, even with a grant, you will need to gather together all the resources you can to survive. Analysis by the National Union of Students (NUS) suggests that it is not possible to get by on student loans and grants alone. Savings, earnings, and help from family and friends generally have to be added to the pot. The information provided below should at least help you understand how big your pot needs to be, and what you can expect to be added and taken away from it.

University tuition fees

A new student funding system was introduced in England and Northern Ireland in 2006 that also had a major impact on the systems in Scotland and Wales. The sands are still shifting: since the last edition of this *Guide*, "free" higher education has been restored for Scottish students attending Scottish universities, with the abolition of the graduate endowment (see below).

A review of top-up fees in England is due to start before the end of 2009, which will also consider the position of part-time students. And, as the *Guide* went to press, top-up fees were back on the agenda in Wales, where Welsh students have been spared the full impact of the English system (see below). Student finance has become a recurring problem for governments, as well as for the students themselves.

With changes, large or small, becoming almost an annual occurrence, it is essential to consult the latest information provided by Government agencies. It is worth checking the following websites for the latest information:

- England: **www.direct.gov.uk/studentfinance**
- Wales: **www.studentfinancewales.co.uk**
- Scotland: **www.saas.gov.uk**
- Northern Ireland: **www.studentfinanceni.co.uk**

What follows is a summary of the position for British students as at March 2009.

While there are substantial differences across the four countries of the UK, there is one important piece of common ground. Up-front payment of fees is no longer compulsory, as students can take out a fee loan (see below) to cover them. This is repayable in instalments after graduation, when your earnings reach the threshold set by the Government.

Fees in England and Northern Ireland

In England and Northern Ireland the maximum tuition fee for full-time undergraduates will be £3,225 in 2009–10, rising again in line with inflation in 2010–11. The review of tuition fees that is due to start in 2009 might allow universities to charge significantly more, but any rise above inflation is unlikely to come before 2012 and almost certainly would not apply to students beginning courses in 2010. Such a decision will be a political hot potato – particularly during an economic downturn – and the outcome of the review is far from certain.

Individual universities can, theoretically, charge less than the maximum, including setting different fees for different subjects. Some do charge less for foundation degrees and Higher National Diplomas, two-year courses that can be a cost-effective stepping stone to a full degree. But so far almost every university has been charging the top rate for full-time degree courses, and has been trying instead to lure students with a range of bursaries, scholarships and other offers, such as free laptops. Only two universities, Leeds Metropolitan University (£2,000) and the University of Greenwich (£2,900), are charging less than the maximum tuition fee for 2009–10, and some that used to charge less have now increased their fees to the maximum allowable and are offering scholarships or bursaries to compensate.

Fees in Scotland

In Scotland, the fee in 2009–10 is £1,820 (£2,895 for medical students), but only students coming to study in Scotland from other UK countries have to pay it. These students can also avoid having to pay up front by applying for a student loan administered by their funding agency. Students whose home is in Scotland and are studying at a Scottish university apply to the Student Awards Agency for Scotland (SAAS) to have their fees paid for them. Scottish students no longer have to contribute to a graduate endowment to cover this cost, following a decision by the Scottish Parliament to abolish graduate endowments.

Fees in Wales

The Welsh Assembly Government has agreed a similar fee policy to England, with universities allowed to charge variable fees of up to £3,225 in 2009–10. However, students who normally live in Wales and choose to study in Wales may be eligible for a tuition fee grant of up to £1,890 a year to offset this cost. Welsh students are also subsidised for some courses in universities outside the Principality, such as veterinary science, which are not available in Wales.

Student loans

Around 80 per cent of students take out a student loan, and it is not difficult to work out why. First of all, as noted earlier, it is very difficult to get by financially without one. If you don't take out a loan to cover your fees, then you will have to pay for them up front, and with living costs estimated to average more than £9,000 a year (over £11,000 in London), most students find it impossible to cover everything on savings and earnings alone. The only reasons to consider paying your fees up front might be if your parents are offering to meet the costs, or if a university is offering a discount if you do so. The University of Gloucestershire, for instance, has been offering a 10 per cent discount to those who pay the full fee in advance. There are two types of student loan – one to cover the cost of tuition fees and another to help you cover the cost of living.

Tuition fees in the UK by country

Country	Level
England	£3,225
Northern Ireland	£3,225
Wales	£3,225 (with grants up to £1,890 to students whose homes are in Wales)
Scotland	£1,820 (no fees paid by students whose homes are in Scotland)
Scotland (medicine)	£2,895 (no fees paid by students whose homes are in Scotland)

- Universities in England, Northern Ireland and Wales can charge reduced fees.
- The Scottish fees are fixed.

Tuition fees loan

In the case of fees loans, everyone can borrow up to the full amount needed to cover the cost of their tuition fees. For Welsh students studying in Wales this can mean only having to borrow £1,255 a year, as the rest can be covered by a non-repayable fee grant. Scots studying in Scotland are even better off, as there are no tuition fees to pay and so no need to take out a fees loan.

Maintenance loan

The second type of student loan, a maintenance loan, is means-tested. The amount you can borrow therefore depends on a number of factors, including your family income, where you intend to study, and whether you expect to be living at home. Final-year students also receive less than those in earlier years. The maximum maintenance loan available in 2009–09 is £4,950 (£6,928 in London) for a full academic year. Three quarters of the maintenance loan is available to you regardless of your family circumstances, while the remaining quarter is means-tested. If your parents are separated, divorced or widowed, then only the parent with whom you normally live will be assessed. However, if that parent has married again, entered into a civil partnership, or has a partner of the opposite sex, then both their incomes will be taken into account.

Maintenance loans in Scotland

In Scotland, the rules and regulations for maintenance loans are different. The loans available are lower than the rest of the UK, particularly in the case of students going to study in London, and the proportion that is means-tested is higher. In 2009–10 the maximum loan available is £5,710. All the latest details can be found at **www.saas.gov.uk**. A new review of student loans has been commissioned in Scotland that may affect entrants in 2010.

Maintenance Grant and Loan Amounts for a New First-year English Student 2009

Household income	Maintenance grant	Maintenance loan living away from home but not in London	Maintenance loan living away from home in London	Maintenance loan living at parents' home
£25,000	£2,906	£3,497	£5,475	£2,385
£30,000	£1,906	£3,997	£5,975	£2,885
£40,000	£711	£4,595	£6,573	£3,483
£50,000	£50	£4,925	£6,903	£3,813
£50,778	£0	£4,950	£6,928	£3,838

Source: Department for Innovation, Universities and Skills

- No maintenance grants are paid when the household income exceed £50,020.
- The size of the maintenance loan is reduced by £1 for every £5 of the total income over £50,778, until the loan is 72 per cent of the value of the full loan. Every eligible student, regardless of household income, is eligible to a loan equivalent to 72 per cent of the full loan.
- Total funding available is the maintenance grant plus the relevant maintenance loan.
- Schemes are different in Northern Ireland, Wales and Scotland and the relevant funding organisations should be consulted.

Loans for mature students

Mature students (those who are over the age of 25, married, or have supported themselves for at least three years before entering university) are assessed for loan and grant entitlements on their own income plus that of their spouse or partner. Grants are also available for those with children, for single parents, and for students with adult dependents. Further support is available for students with children through the Parents' Learning Allowance and Child Tax Credit system.

Payment of loans

Maintenance loans are usually paid in three instalments into your bank or building society account. English students should apply for grants and loans through Student Finance England, Welsh students through Student Finance Wales, Scottish students through the Student Awards Agency for Scotland, and those in Northern Ireland through Student Finance NI or their Education and Library Board. You should make your application as soon as you have received an offer of a place at university. European Union students from outside the UK will usually be sent an application form by the university that has offered them a place.

Repaying loans

Any money you borrow via the Student Loans Company that administers the scheme, is lent at a "nominal" interest rate. This fell in 2008–09 to 3.8 per cent, which was still very attractive compared with any loans available from high-street banks or credit card companies. Some students try to make their loan money for living costs go further by putting it into a high interest bank account or an ISA. Whatever you do with it, you won't have to start making repayments until you graduate and begin earning at least £15,000 a year. Even then, under new rules from 2008–09, you will be able to take a "repayment holiday" of up to five years after graduation, so you don't have to repay a penny in that time.

Remember, however, that interest on your loan continues to accrue from the time you take it out to until you have paid it off. The good news is that the amount you repay each month is linked to your income, rather than the amount you owe. Repayments are deducted through the tax system at a rate of 9 per cent on anything you are earning above £15,000 a year: for example monthly repayments for a graduate earning £20,000 a year would work out at £37.50 per month. If your income falls below the £15,000 threshold, then your repayments stop until you start earning more again.

Grants

In the good old days, most students didn't have to pay fees and many received relatively generous maintenance grants to help them cover day-to-day costs. After a brief disappearance, these non-repayable grants have made a comeback, and are particularly significant if you come from a low-income family. The size and type of grants available, and the rules and regulations governing their distribution, are different for each country of the UK. To receive a grant, students whose home is in England must apply through Student Finance England, in Wales to Student Finance Wales, those from Scotland must apply to the Student Awards Agency for Scotland, and those from Northern Ireland to Student Finance NI or their Education and Library Board. In addition, there are various types of bursaries and scholarships you can apply for, and other types of grants or support in each country to help students in particular circumstances, such as those that have a disability. What follows is a description of the maintenance grant arrangements country-by-country.

England

Students from England can apply for a maintenance grant from the Government and a bursary from their university. Maintenance grants in England are worth up to £2,906 in 2009–10, but the amount you actually get (paid in three instalments) depends on your family or "household residual" income. If you come from a household with an income of £25,000 a year or less, then you can get a full grant. A partial grant is available for all of those from households earning between £25,000 and £50,020 a year. The actual amount you will get in this case is subject to a fairly complicated calculation to work out how much your family should theoretically contribute to your upkeep. There is no obligation on your family to provide their share, but you will certainly receive some kind of grant from the state. However, those whose family income is calculated to be higher than £50,020 will not receive a grant. Another important rule is that for every £1 you receive in maintenance grant, the amount you can borrow in student loans falls by £1. Thus, it is not possible to have both a full grant and a maximum student loan.

The almost bewildering array of bursaries and scholarships on offer from universities is discussed in a separate section below.

Funding Timetable

It is vital that you sort out your funding arrangements before you start at university. Note that each funding agency has its own arrangements, and it is very important that you find out the exact details from them. The dates below give general indications of key dates.

March/April

- Online and paper application forms become available from funding agencies.
- You must contact the appropriate funding agency to make an application. For admission from 2009 onwards in England contact www.direct.gov.uk/studentfinance rather than your LEA.
- Complete application form as soon as possible. At this stage select the university offer that will be your first choice.
- Check details of bursaries and scholarships available from your selected universities.

May/June

- Funding agencies will give you details of the financial support they can offer.
- Last date for making an application to ensure funding is ready for you at the start of term (exact date varies significantly between agencies).

August

- Tell your funding agency if the university or course you have been accepted for is different from that originally given them.

September

- Take letter confirming funding to your university for registration.
- After registration, the first part of funds will be released to you.

Northern Ireland

Arrangements for applying for and receiving means-tested maintenance grants and university bursaries and scholarships are very similar in Northern Ireland to those in England. The main difference is that there is a more generous upper limit (£3,406 for 2009–10) on grants in Northern Ireland. There is also a Special Support Grant of the same value for full-time students who may be eligible to receive benefits such as Income Support or Housing Benefit while they are studying. However, you cannot receive both the maintenance grant and the Special Support Grant.

Wales

Students from Wales can apply for a means-tested Assembly Learning Grant of up to £2,906 in 2009–10. In addition, every full-time higher education student, regardless of where they come from in the UK, will be considered for a means-tested Welsh Bursary worth a maximum of £310 a year. This comes on top of whatever scholarships and bursaries Welsh institutions may offer.

Scotland

In Scotland, the maintenance grant is known as a Young Student's Bursary, and is also means-tested and does not have to be repaid. For 2009–10, the maximum bursary is £2,640 if you come from a family with an annual income of £19,310 or less. If your family income is between this amount and £34,195 you will be entitled to a partial bursary, but if it is higher than £34,195 you will receive nothing. You can get an additional student loan if your family income is £21,760 or less.

Bursaries and scholarships

Bursaries and scholarships offered by universities and colleges are an important part of the student financial support system ushered in by the Government to try to ensure people could still afford to go to university. All English universities and colleges charging more than £2,835 a year for a course are required to provide a non-repayable bursary or scholarship to students on these courses from low-income families who are receiving the full maintenance grant. What this means is that students who receive a full grant and are being charged the maximum tuition fee of £3,225 are entitled to a bursary or scholarship of at least £322. However, most universities are offering far more than this – and have also extended the principle to cover students in receipt of a partial grant. Some have been offering bursaries of £1,000 a year, or more, on the basis of household income, examination results and/or a home in the region.

Finding out about bursaries

There is now such a variety of bursaries and scholarships on offer that while, on the one hand, it is worth shopping around to see what you can get, on the other, you could well feel bewildered by the experience of doing so. The Universities and Colleges Admissions Service (UCAS) has done its best to help by getting institutions to provide information about what's on offer to students applying for particular courses on its course search pages at **www.ucas.com**. Another handy tool for students considering studying in England is an online "bursary map" where you can explore what is available from each English institution (**http://bursarymap.direct.gov**). The websites of individual institutions also carry details of scholarships, bursaries and other financial support available. Details are given in the table at the end of this chapter.

The whole system of bursaries and scholarships is overseen for England and Wales by the Office for Fair Access. It requires all universities to submit what are called "Access Agreements" that contain details of what fees they intend to charge and what scholarships and bursaries they are offering. Access Agreements also describe other kinds of financial support, such as "hardship funds". Some awards are guaranteed depending on your personal circumstances, while others are available through open competition. St Mary's University College, Twickenham, for instance, has been offering 75 "entry scholarships" worth up to £1,000 each for students who can demonstrate a high level of commitment and ability in sport, creativity or work for the community. Copies of access agreements can be found at **www.offa.org.uk**.

Applying for bursaries

Do take note of the application procedures for scholarships and bursaries, as these vary from institution to institution, and even from course to course within individual institutions. There may be a particular deadline you have to meet to apply for an award, or in some cases the university will work out for you whether you are entitled to an award by referring to your funding agency's financial assessment. Remember, too, that if your personal circumstances change part way through a course then your entitlement to a scholarship or bursary may be reviewed.

If you feel you still need more help or advice on scholarships or bursaries, you can get this in most cases by referring to a university's website or prospectus. Some institutions also maintain a helpline. Some questions you will need answered include whether the bursary or scholarship is automatic or conditional and, if the latter, when you will find out whether your application has been successful. For some awards, you won't know whether you have qualified until you get your exam results.

Another obvious question is how the scholarship or bursary on offer compares with awards made by another university you might consider applying to. Watch out for institutions that list entitlements that others don't mention but you would get anyway. Some institutions offer "fee remission" (a lower tuition fee) rather than scholarships or bursaries, which means you may have less cash in hand during your course, but will owe less after you have graduated.

Living in one country, studying in another

As each of the countries of the UK develop their own distinctive systems of student finance, they have been keen to address the question of how students leaving home in one country to go and study in another are affected. For instance, both the Scottish Parliament and the Welsh Assembly have put arrangements in place to try to ensure that Scottish and Welsh students accepting places at English universities are not financially disadvantaged.

UK students who cross borders to study pay the tuition fees of their chosen university and are eligible for a fees loan to cover these. They are also entitled to apply for the scholarships or bursaries on offer from that institution. Any maintenance loan or grant will still come from the awarding bodies of their home country.

The fees loan for Scottish students going to study in Northern Ireland, England or Wales is not dependent on family income, but students from low-income families can get relief from a means-tested non-repayable Students Outside Scotland Bursary. The income thresholds used to decide who qualifies for this are the same as those for the Young Students' Bursary (for Scottish students studying in Scotland, see above) but the maximum award is lower, at £2,150 (cf. £2,640) for 2009–10.

For students studying in Wales from September 2008, every eligible full-time higher education student, regardless of where they come from in the UK, was considered for a means-tested Welsh Bursary of a maximum of £310 a year.

European Union laws stipulate that EU students from outside the UK must be charged the same tuition fees as those paid by UK students who are studying in their home country, rather than the higher fees paid by students from outside the EU. They can also apply for a fee loan and may be considered for some of the scholarships and bursaries offered by individual institutions. Only students who have been living and studying in the UK for at least three years can apply for a maintenance loan or grant.

If you haven't, then you will need to apply for such assistance from the authorities in your own country. Tuition fee rules for non UK European Union students are the same in Scotland as for Scottish students – that is, you do not have to pay a tuition fee. There are also no fees to pay for exchange students coming to the UK, including those on the Socrates Programme.

Further sources of income

If you are feeling daunted by the potential costs, you can take some comfort from this section outlining just some of the ways you can raise additional money to help you cover your expenses.

Where the Money Comes From

Percentage of UK students receiving the following types of funding:

Student loans	79%
Parents	50%
Bank overdrafts	37%
Part-time job in term time	34%
Savings	32%
Student grants	29%
Part-time holiday work	26%
University bursaries	26%
Full-time holiday work	23%
Relatives (other than parents)	8%
Credit cards	8%
Bank loans	5%
Sponsorship	3%
Full-time job in term time	2%

Sodexo University Lifestyle Survey 2008

Taking a gap year

You can begin the process of earning money to help pay for your higher education even before you enter university, by taking a gap year. Many students are attracted to the idea of taking a year out because it offers them a chance to travel, gain new experiences, grow up a little – and maybe earn some money. Indeed, necessity seems to have recently shifted the reasons for taking a gap year from an emphasis on personal development to one more focused on boosting the bank balance in preparation for beginning life as a student. Of course, there is still potentially much more to taking a gap year than financial gain, and while short-term considerations may be focusing your mind in that direction, the longer-term benefits of taking part in cultural exchanges and courses, expeditions, volunteering or structured work placements are considerable for most people. Such benefits include gaining a place at university and embarking on a worthwhile career after graduation. Both university admissions officers and employers look for evidence in candidates that they have more about them than academic ability. The experience you gain on a gap year can help you develop many of the attributes they are looking for, such as interpersonal, organisational and teamwork skills, leadership, creativity, experience of new cultures or work environments, and enterprise.

Various organisations can help you find voluntary work, if this is the way you prefer to spend at least some of your year out. Some examples include v (**www.vinspired.com**), Lattitude Global Volunteering (**www.lattitude.org.uk**) and Volunteer Africa (**www.volunteerafrica.org**).

Work placements can be structured or casual. An example of the structured variety is the Year in Industry Scheme (**www.yini.org.uk**). Sponsorship is available mainly to those wishing to study engineering or business. To find out more, visit **www.everythingyouwantedtoknow.com**.

Further Government support

There are various types of support available from Government sources for students in particular circumstances, other than the main loans, grants and bursaries.

- Undergraduates in financial difficulties can apply for help from the Access to Learning Fund (Financial Contingency Fund in Wales, Hardship Fund in Scotland, Support Funds in Northern Ireland). These are allocated by universities to provide support for anything from day-to-day study and living costs to unexpected or exceptional expense. The university decides which students need help and how much money to award them. These funds are often targeted at older or disadvantaged students and finalists.
- Students with children can apply for a childcare grant, worth up to £225 a week if you have two or more children; and a parents' learning allowance, for help with course-related costs, of between £50 and £1,470.
- Students with disabilities can apply for a disabled students' allowance, worth up to £20,000 for full-time students.
- Any students with a partner, or another adult such as a family member who is financially dependent on them, can apply for an adult dependants' grant of up to £2,575.

If you do not qualify for any of this kind of financial support you may still be able to apply for a Career Development Loan available from Barclays, the Cooperative Bank and the Royal Bank of Scotland, in partnership with the Learning and Skills Council. Students on a wide range of vocational courses can borrow from £300 to £8,000 at a fixed rate of interest to fund up to two years of learning.

Part-time work

The need to hold down a part-time job during term time is now a fact of life for more than half of students. Unsurprisingly, students from a working-class background are more likely to need to earn while they learn. A report by UNITE showed that 51 per cent of students from low-income families worked during term time, compared with just over a third of those from higher-income families. If you need or want to earn during term time, it is important to try to ensure that you do not work so many hours that it starts to affect your studies. A survey by the NUS found that 59 per cent of students who worked felt it had an impact on their studies, with 38 per cent missing lectures and over a fifth failing to submit coursework because of their part-time jobs.

Student employment agencies, which can now be found on many university campuses, can help you get the balance right. These introduce employers with work to students seeking work, sometimes even offering jobs within the university itself. But they also abide by codes of practice that regulate both minimum wages and the maximum number of hours worked in term time (typically 15 hours a week).

According to the Halifax bank, the average working student puts in about 18 hours a week, and makes around £6,000 a year out of this. Some firms, such as the big supermarkets, offer continuing part-time employment to their school part-time employees when they go to university. Some students show some enterprise by making use of their expertise in areas like web design to earn some extra money. But most take on casual work in retail stores, restaurants, bars and call centres.

Most students, including those who don't work during term time, get a job during vacations. A Government survey found that 86 per cent of students in their second year of study or above worked during their summer vacation. Most of this kind of work is casual, but some is formalised in a scheme like the Shell Technology Enterprise Programme (**www.shell.org.uk**) or may be part of a sponsorship programme. Many vacation jobs are fairly mundane, but with a bit of imagination and get-up-and-go, it is possible to find more interesting work. Some students broaden their experience by working abroad, others work as film extras earning up to £140 a day, or do a variety of jobs at big events such as the Farnborough Air Show. It is also a good idea to try to use the summer holidays to get some work experience in a field that has some relevance to your career aspirations. Even if you don't get paid, this can significantly enhance your chances of finding employment after graduation.

Banks

You can be certain that once you become a student you will be inundated with special offers from banks, all keen to win you as a customer in the hope that you will remain so after graduation and well into your life as a highly paid professional. Make sure you shop around and try to think beyond the introductory offers of cash, discounted driving lessons, railcards, etc., and consider which account has the best long-term benefits. Banks are more sympathetic to your financial situation as a student than they have been for other customers in the recession, and will generally be ready to offer modest free overdraft facilities.

What you will need to spend money on

Living costs

The NUS estimated that in 2007–08 the average student living outside London would spend £9,176 a year on regular living costs, including rent, food, personal items, travel and leisure. For those living in the capital, the estimated average expenditure was £11,142. Little surprise, then, that a growing number of students are choosing to live at home and study at a local university. However, even this option is not necessarily low cost, once travel to and from the university is taken into account.

Certain costs are unavoidable. You have to have a roof over your head, eat enough, clothe yourself, and probably do a certain amount of travelling. But the cost of even these essential items can be cut down significantly through a mixture of shopping around and careful budgeting. If you set aside a certain amount of money a week for food, you will find it goes much further if you keep takeaways and ready-meals to a minimum, and stick to a shopping list when you go to a supermarket (shop at one of the cheaper supermarkets if possible). Some catering outlets at your university or in the students' union may well offer good value meals. If so, making use of these facilities can be a good way to ensure you eat reasonably healthily without blowing your budget. But probably the most economical way to eat is to cook and share meals with fellow students with whom you may be living in a shared house. Charity shops and markets are good places to hunt out bargain clothes, especially basic items such as jeans and tee shirts. Make sure you make full use of student travel cards and other offers and facilities available locally to help you cut the cost of travel. In certain locations, a bicycle is a very worthwhile investment (though not buying a lock for it may well prove a false economy).

If you can keep your essential costs down without starving yourself, then this will leave more money for what you would probably prefer to spend your money on – going out and personal items. Most students spend a good proportion of their budget on socialising, and this is certainly an important part of the university experience. You can have plenty of fun and keep your leisure costs down by making the most of the facilities, clubs and events provided by your students' union.

Studying costs

An NUS survey in 2008 estimated that the average student spends £471 a year on costs associated with course work and studying, but the amount you spend will be determined largely by the nature of your course and what you study. For some, the costs could amount to significantly more than £471. Additional financial support may be available for certain expenditure, but this is unlikely to cover you fully for spending on books, stationery, equipment, fieldwork or electives. A long reading list could prove very expensive if you tried to buy all of the required books brand new. Find out as soon as possible which books are available either in your university library or local libraries (you may need to be quick off the mark to get your hands on any books that are the first ones to be covered on your course). Another standard approach is to buy books second hand from students who no longer need them. Your students' union or your university may run second-hand book sales or offer a service helping students to buy and sell books. Another possible tactic is to share books with a fellow student: the only drawback being that you may both need to be working from a particular book at the same time!

Other costs

The first thing to say about any other costs you may incur is that you should do everything you can to keep them as low as possible. This may sound trite, but it is easy to let "other costs" get out of hand to the extent that they start to eat into your budget for day-to-day living. Mobile phone bills are a case in point. Look at your previous bills, or think carefully about your usage, and then shop around for the best deal to cover this. Remember that extras like downloading games or music, or sending pictures, can add significantly to your bill. Most of all, try to avoid getting tied up with an expensive and inflexible contract.

Overdrafts and credit cards

Another cost it is best to avoid is the cost of debt. Many banks offer free overdraft facilities for students, but if you go over that limit without prior arrangement, you can end up paying over the odds for your borrowing. Credits cards can be useful if managed properly. The best deals offer zero per cent interest on both balance transfers and purchases for a limited period – but if you don't pay off your debt before the offer period expires, you will start to incur hefty interest charges. Aside from these offers, the best way to manage a credit card is to set up a direct debit to pay off your balance in full every month, which means you will avoid paying any interest. One of the worst ways is just paying the minimum charge each month, which can cost you a small fortune over a long period. If you are the kind of person that spends impulsively and doesn't keep track of that spending, then you are probably better off without a credit card.

Insurance

One kind of additional spending that can actually end up saving you money is getting insurance cover for your possessions. Most students arrive at university with a number of items, such as digital cameras, mobile phones, laptops, CD players, MP3 players, and portable TVs, that are tempting and offer all-too-easy pickings for petty thieves. It is estimated that around a third of students fall victim to crime at some point during their time at university. If you shop around, you should be able to get a reasonable amount of cover for these kinds of items without it costing you an arm and a leg. It may be possible to add cover cheaply to your parents' policy.

What is the Money Spent on Every Week?

Rent	£77.30
Supermarket food	£18.40
Alcohol	£15.40
Utility Bills	£14.30
Cigarettes	£13.90
Transport	£12.30
Eating Out	£11.60
Buying Clothes	£11.10
Going Out	£10.60
Telephone Bills	£9.00
Books	£8.20

Information from the 2007 NatWest Money Matters survey, based on 8 months of term time. Survey information from 1,364 graduates and 1,104 students in May 2007, undertaken by Virtual Surveys Limited.

Planning your budget

University websites and many other sites offer guidance on preparing a budget, usually with the basic headings provided for you to complete. First, list out your likely income (grants, bursaries, loans, part-time work, savings, parental support) and then see how this compares with what you will spend. Try to be realistic and not too optimistic about both sides of the equation. Hopefully, you will end up either only slightly in the red, or preferably far enough in the black for you to be able to afford things you would really like to spend your money on.

Above all, remember to keep track of your finances so that your university experience isn't ruined by money worries or finding you can't go to the ball because the cash machine has eaten your card.

Useful websites

The following websites will help you find out more about the topics discussed in this chapter.

As a starting point, the Student Finance section within the direct.gov website covers the basics: **www.direct.gov.uk/studentfinance**. There is a useful Student Finance Calculator that you can reach from a link on the Student Finance home page.

UCAS also provides helpful advice: **www.ucas.com/students/studentfinance**
For England, visit Student Finance England: **www.studentfinanceengland.co.uk**
Office for Fair Access: **www.offa.org.uk**
For Wales, visit Student Finance Wales: **www.studentfinancewales.co.uk**
For Scotland, visit the Student Awards Agency for Scotland: **www.saas.gov.uk**

For Northern Ireland, visit the Department for Employment and Learning:
www.delni.gov.uk/index.cfm/area/information/page/StudentFinance
Online applications are made through Student Finance Northern Ireland:
www.studentfinanceni.co.uk
All UK student loans are administered by the Student Loan Company:
www.slc.co.uk

Bursaries
Each university in England, Wales and Northern Ireland has its own bursary scheme.
Website details are given in the University Profiles in this book (chapter 11). You can also
find out about bursaries using this online map: **http://bursarymap.direct.gov.uk**

Scholarships
Each university in the United Kingdom has its own selection of scholarships. Consult
university websites. Course-related scholarships are included on the UCAS site in the
description of a course.

Further help can be obtained from the following sites
Career Development Loans (CDL): **www.lifelonglearning.co.uk/cdl**
Educational Grants Advisory Service (EGAS):
www.direct.gov.uk/en/Dl1/Directories/DG_10011032
HM Revenue and Customs: **www.hmrc.gov.uk/students**
Need 2 Know, a student advice site: **www.need2know.co.uk/money/students**
NHS Student Bursaries for students on pre-registration health professional training
courses: **www.nhsstudentgrants.co.uk**
Support 4 Learning: **www.support4learning.org.uk/money**

Fees and bursaries at universities in England, Northern Ireland, Scotland and Wales
The table on the next eight pages provides information on the fees charged to UK, EU and
other international (non-EU) students. It also gives information on the bursary schemes
offered by each university to UK students.
- Wherever possible the information relates to 2009–10.
- In the headings, "those on full grant" refers to those receiving a full maintenance grant
  from their funding body; "those on partial grant" refers to those receiving any grant other
  than a full grant.
- HI refers to "Household Income". For young students this is usually the income of their
  parents. In England in 2009–10, a household income of £25,000 or less qualifies a student
  for a full grant. See page 213 for further details.
- Note that Scotland has no bursary system and Wales has its own system of fees and
  bursaries.

ENGLAND	Undergraduate fees UK / EU students	Undergraduate fees International students	University bursary for those on full grant. HI (Household Income) up to £25,000	University bursary for those on partial grant. HI (Household Income) above £25,000
Anglia Ruskin	£3,225	£9,300–£10,925	£319	n/a
Aston	£3,225	£10,200–£12,300	£800	HI up to £39,333: sliding scale £800–£160
Bath	£3,225	£10,600–£13,500	£1,200	HI up to £50K: sliding scale £900–£300
Bath Spa	£3,225	£9,000–£9,580	£1,200	HI up to £39K: sliding scale £1,200–£100
Bedfordshire	£3,225	£8,500	HI up to £18.8K: £842 then £632	HI up to £40.3K: sliding scale £632–£472 Above £40.3K, fixed bursary of £319
Birmingham	£3,225	£9,880–£12,800 £23,350 (medicine)	£860	HI up to £35,460: £860
Birmingham City	£3,225	£8,950–£13,500	£525	HI up to £50K: sliding scale £525–£325
Bolton	£3,225	£7,900	£350	HI up to £60K: sliding scale £350–£120
Bournemouth	£3,225	£8,000–£10,000	£319	n/a
Bradford	£3,225	£8,600–£10,900	Year 1 £500 Year 2 £700 Year 3 £900	HI up to £40K: Year 1 £500 Year 2 £700 Year 3 £900 HI up to £60K: Year 1 £400 Year 2 £500 Year 3 £600
Brighton	£3,225		£1,080	HI up to £40.3K: sliding scale £860–£540
Bristol	£3,225	£11,450–£14,750 £26,600 (medicine)	£1,200 + £1,075 (local students)	HI up to £40K: £770 HI up to £50K: £310 All plus £1,075 (local students)
Brunel	£3,225	£9,200–£11,100	£1,000	HI up to £33K: £500
Buckingham	£8,040[2]	£13,950[2]	n/a	(subject and academic scholarships available)

Institution				
Buckinghamshire New	£3,225		£500	£500
Cambridge	£3,225[3]	£9,747–£12,768[4] £23,631 (medicine)[4]	£3,250	HI up to £50K: sliding scale £2,000–£50
Canterbury Christ Church	£3,225	£7,650–£8,375	£860	HI up to £50K: partial award on a sliding scale
Central Lancashire (UCLan)	£3,225	£8,950–£9,450	£500 (£310 from Year 2)	HI up to £60K: £500 (£310 from Year 2)
Chester	£3,225	£7,182–£8,388[1]	£1,000	n/a
Chichester	£3,225	£8,300–£9,500	£1,077	HI up to £50K: sliding scale £1,026–£256
City	£3,225	£8,600–£9,500	£770	HI up to £30K: £360
Coventry	£3,225	£8,300	£320	HI up to £60K: £320
Cumbria	£3,225	£8,150	£1,290	HI up to £60K: sliding scale £1,290–£215
De Montfort	£3,225	£8,500–£9,000	£500	HI up to £50K: £500
Derby	£3,225	£7,800–£8,415	£830 + £300 (local address) or £830 + £400 (partner school)	HI £25K–£35K: £520 / HI £35K–£51K: £210 / All + £300 or £400 local bursary
Durham	£3,225	£10,560–£13,770	£1,300	n/a
East Anglia	£3,225	£9,850–£12,350 £19,260 (clinical medicine)	£600	HI up to £50K: £300
East London	£3,225	£9,510–£13,140	£310	n/a
Edge Hill	£3,225	£8,200	£500 + £200 learning support bursary	£200 learning support bursary
Essex	£3,225	£9,750–£11,990	£319	£25.5K: £419; increasing to max. £2,119 at £34K; decreasing to £50 at £50K
Exeter	£3,225	£10,000–£12,550 £13,000–£20,500[1] (medicine)	£1,500	HI up to £35K: £750
Gloucestershire	£3,225	£8,405	£319	n/a
Goldsmiths	£3,225	£9,870–£13,270	HI up to £19K: £1,000 then £500	HI up to £40K: up to £500
Greenwich	£2,900	£8,750	n/a	n/a
Hertfordshire	£3,225	£8,000	£1,000	n/a

ENGLAND	Undergraduate fees UK/EU students	Undergraduate fees International students	University bursary for those on full grant, HI (Household Income) up to £25,000	University bursary for those on partial grant, HI (Household Income) above £25,000
Huddersfield	£3,225	£8,250–£9,250	£500	n/a
Hull	£3,225	£9,500–£11,500 £21,600 (medicine)	£1,000	HI up to £40K: £500
Imperial	£3,225	£18,000–£20,400 £25,000–£37,300 (medicine)	£3,000	HI up to £50K sliding scale £2,000–£300
Keele	£3,225	£9,350–£11,800 £18,000–£22,000 (medicine)	£800	n/a (various schemes for HI up to £40K)
Kent	£3,225	£9,870–£11,990	£1,000	HI up to £40K sliding scale: £750–£250
King's College London	£3,225	£12,020–£15,080 £27,980 (medicine)	£1,350	HI up to £50K: sliding scale: £1,350–£100
Kingston	£3,225	up to £10,350	HI up to £1K: £1,000 then £600[1]	HI up to £39.3K: £310[1]
Lancaster	£3,225	£9,200–£11,100	HI up to £18,360: £1,315 then £500	HI up to £27.8K: £500
Leeds	£3,225	£10,300–£13,300 £24,500 (medicine)	£1,540	HI up to £36.6K: sliding scale £1,540–£335
Leeds Metropolitan	£2,000	£7,000–£7,500	n/a	n/a
Leicester	£3,225	£9,450–£12,650 £22,900 (medicine)	HI up to £20K: £1,319 HI up to £25K: £1,019	HI up to £40K: sliding scale £400–£100
Lincoln	£3,225	£8,524–£9,038	£600	HI up to £50K: sliding scale £370–£20
Liverpool	£3,225	£9,400–£12,000 £18,600 (medicine)	£1,400	n/a
Liverpool Hope	£3,225	£6,800	HI up to £17.5K: £800[1] HI up to £25K: £600[1]	HI £25K–£38K: £400[1]

University				
Liverpool John Moores	£3,225	£9,790–£10,450	£1,075	HI £25–£50K: £430
London Metropolitan	£3,225	£8,200[1]	HI up to £18K: £1,000 then sliding scale £975–£775[1]	HI £25.2K–£40K: sliding scale £750–£3101
London School of Economics	£3,225	£12,840	HI up to £25K: sliding scale £2,500–£1,044	HI up to £60K: sliding scale £966–£50
London South Bank	£3,225	£8,360–£8,600	Year 1 £500 Year 2 £750 Year 3 £750 (+ £250 graduation bonus for Hons graduates)[1]	Year 1 £500 Year 2 £750 Year 3 £750 (+ £250 graduation bonus for Hons graduates)[1]
Loughborough	£3,225	£10,400–£13,500	HI up to £24.1K: sliding scale £1,390 to £860 (doubled for mature students)	HI up to £35.4K: sliding scale £650–£220 (doubled for mature students)
Manchester	£3,225	£10,800–£13,400 £24,450 (medicine)	£1,250	n/a
Manchester Metropolitan	£3,225	£8,180–£13,400	HI up to £21K: £1,025 HI up to £25K: £475	HI £25K–£40K: £475
Middlesex	£3,225	£9,400	£319	n/a
Newcastle	£3,225	£10,215–£13,360 £24,735 (medicine)	£1,280	HI £25K–£32.2K: £640
Northampton	£3,225	£7,950–£8,450	£1,000	HI up to £30K: £700 HI up to £40K: £500
Northumbria	£3,225	£8,600–£9,050	£319	n/a
Nottingham	£3,225	£10,610–£13,910 £18,980 (veterinary medicine) £14,660–£25,480 (medicine)	£1,080	HI up to £34.5K: sliding scale £1,080 HI up to £44.5K: sliding scale £810–£270
Nottingham Trent	£3,225	£8,450–£9,600	£1,075	HI up to £40K: sliding scale £665–£360
Oxford	£3,225[3]	£11,750–£13,450[4] £24,500 (medicine)[4]	£3,225	HI up to £50K: sliding scale £3,225–£200

ENGLAND	Undergraduate fees UK / EU students	Undergraduate fees International students	University bursary for those on full grant. HI = (Household Income) up to £25,000	University bursary for those on partial grant. HI = (Household Income) above £25,000
Oxford Brookes	£3,225	£9,780–£11,284	HI £0–£5K: £1,800 HI £5K–£21K: £1,560 HI £21K–£25K: £1,050	HI up to £36K: sliding scale £1,050–£150
Plymouth	£3,225	£8,750 £13,000–£20,500[1] (medicine)	£1,010	HI £25K–£40K: £300
Portsmouth	£3,225	£8,750–£10,150	£900	HI up to £32K: £600
Queen Mary	£3,225	£9,500–£11,500 £15,350–£24,350 (medicine)	£1,078	HI up to £34.6K: £861
Reading	£3,225	£9,630–£11,610	£1,350	HI up to £35K: £900 HI up to £45K: £450
Roehampton	£3,225	£9,360	£500	n/a
Royal Holloway	£3,225	£11,555–£13,120	£750	HI up to £39.3K: £750
Salford	£3,225	£8,600–£10,700	£320	(subject and academic bursaries available)
Sheffield	£3,225	£10,420–£13,700 £24,760 (medicine)	HI up to £17.2K: £700 HI up to £25K: £430	HI up to £35.5K: £430
Sheffield Hallam	£3,225	£8,700–£10,300	£700	(subject and academic bursaries available)
SOAS	£3,225	£12,000	£860	HI £25K–£39.3K: £420
Southampton	£3,225	£9,660–£12,360 £22,240 (medicine)	£1,000	HI up to £35K: £500
Southampton Solent	£3,225	£6,475–£8,400	HI up to £18.3K: £1,075 HI up to £23K: £750 HI up to £28K: £500	HI up to £39.3K: £250
Staffordshire	£3,225	£9,385	HI up to £20.8K: £1,000 HI up to £25.5K: £850	HI up to £30.8K: £500

Institution				
Sunderland	£3,225	£8,300	£525	HI up to £39.3K: £525
Surrey	£3,225	£8,600–£11,000	HI up to £10K: £2,000 HI up to £25K: sliding scale[1]	HI up to £35K: sliding scale to £0.[1]
Sussex	£3,225	£9,975–£12,750 £23,678 (medicine)	£1,000	(subject and academic bursaries available)
Teesside	£3,225	£8,500	£1,025	n/a
Thames Valley	£3,225	£7,600–£8,900[1]	£1,060	HI £25K–£40K: £530
University of the Arts London	£3,225	£11,900	£319	Considered for £1,000 University Access Bursary
University College London	£3,225	£12,280–£16,080 £23,980 (medicine)	HI up to £11.9K: £2,775 HI up to £14.1K: £2,220 HI up to £16.2K: £1,650 then at least 50% of maintenance grant	At least 50% of maintenance grant
University for the Creative Arts	£3,225	£7,406–£9,507	£319	n/a
Warwick	£3,225	£10,900–£13,950	£1,800	HI up to £36K: £1,800
West of England	£3,225	£8,250–£8,700	£1,000	n/a
Westminster	£3,225	£9,830	£319	£319
Winchester	£3,225	£7,890	£820	HI up to £39.3K: £410
Wolverhampton	£3,225	£8,850	£500	HI up to £35K: £300
Worcester	£3,225	£8,400	£750	£625; if not eligible for maintenance grant: £500
York	£3,225	£10,271–£13,811 £21,600 (medicine)	£1,436	HI up to £35.9K: £718; HI up to £41K: £360
York St John	£3,225	£8,100–£11,100	HI up to £18,360: £1,610 HI up to £20,970: £1,075 HI up to £25K: £540	n/a

1 Figures for 2008–09
2 Duration of degree course is two years
3 UK & EU students eligible for tuition fee support not liable for College fees (Oxford)
4 Plus College fees (£5,212, Oxford; £4,000–£5,000, Cambridge)

NORTHERN IRELAND	Undergraduate fees UK / EU students	Undergraduate fees International students	University bursary for those on full grant (HI = Household Income)	University bursary for those on partial grant (HI = Household Income)
Queen's, Belfast	£3,225	£9,418–£11,539 / £12,757–£24,066 (medicine)	HI up to £18,360: £1,050[1] / HI up to £23.3K: £530[1]	n/a
Ulster	£3,325	£8,760	HI up to £18.2: £1,070 / HI up to £21.5K: £640	HI up to £40.2K: £320
SCOTLAND	Fees for Scottish students and eligible non-UK EU students		Fees for students from elsewhere in the UK	International fees
Aberdeen	Tuition fee paid by SAAS		£1,820 / £2,895 (medicine)	£9,250–£11,500 / £22,500 (medicine)
Abertay	Tuition fee paid by SAAS		£1,820	£8,150
Dundee	Tuition fee paid by SAAS		£1,820 / £2,895 (medicine)	£8,500–10,500 / £14,150–£22,000 (medicine)
Edinburgh	Tuition fee paid by SAAS		£1,820 / £2,895 (medicine)	£11,050–£14,500 / £17,950–£30,400 (medicine)
Edinburgh Napier	Tuition fee paid by SAAS		£1,820	£8,950–£10,390
Glasgow	Tuition fee paid by SAAS		£1,820 / £2,895 (medicine)	£9,800–12,950 / £18,750 (veterinary medicine) / £23,450 (dentistry) / £22,600 (medicine)
Glasgow Caledonian	Tuition fee paid by SAAS		£1,820	£9,000–£10,000
Heriot-Watt	Tuition fee paid by SAAS		£1,820	£9,360–£11,800
Queen Margaret	Tuition fee paid by SAAS		£1,820	£8,800–£9,700[1]
Robert Gordon	Tuition fee paid by SAAS		£1,820	£8,400–£10,800
St Andrews	Tuition fee paid by SAAS		£1,820	£11,750

	Undergraduate fees for UK and EU	Undergraduate fees International students	£2,895 (medicine)	£17,950 (medical science)
Stirling	Tuition fee paid by SAAS		£1,820	£9,400–£11,550
Strathclyde	Tuition fee paid by SAAS		£1,820	£9,500–£12,200
West of Scotland	Tuition fee paid by SAAS		£1,820	£9,300–£10,050
WALES	Undergraduate fees for UK and EU students. Welsh students eligible for fee grant up to £1,940.	Undergraduate fees International students	University bursary for those on full grant with HI up to £18,370. All UK nationals eligible for Welsh National Bursary of £319 which is included in the figures below.	University bursary for those on partial grant with HI over £18,370. Not eligible for Welsh National Bursary
Aberystwyth	£3,225	£8,695–£11,030	£1,000	HI from £18.3K to £39.3K: sliding scale £800–£200
Bangor	£3,225	£8,800–£9,900	£1,000	HI up to £38.3K: either £500 or £1,000
Cardiff	£3,225	£9,600–£12,300 £22,500 (medicine)	£1,050	HI up to £25K: £1,050 HI up to £39.3K: £500
Cardiff (UWIC)	£3,225	£7,800–£9,000 £11,000 (podiatry)	HI up to £18.3K: £500	HI up to £39.3K: £300
Glamorgan	£3,225	£9,250	£319 plus £500 residential allowance for non-local UK & EU students	£500 residential allowance for non-local UK & EU students
Glyndŵr	£3,225	£6,950	£1,000	HI up to £22K: £750 HI up to £95K: £500
Lampeter	£3,225	£8,988[1]	£319	n/a
Newport	£3,225	£7,750–£8,750	£319 plus £1,000 (limited)	HI up to £30K: £600 (limited) HI up to £40K: £300 (limited
Swansea	£3,225	£9,300–£11,900	£319	n/a
Swansea Metropolitan	£3,225	£7,500	£319 plus £500 if living more than 45 miles from University	£500 if living more than 45 miles from University (UK & EU students)

8

What Parents Should Do

This chapter looks at where to draw the line between constructive involvement and unwelcome interference. Nearly all students are adults, and university offers an environment where they can begin to make their own decisions and develop as individuals. A good starting point is to offer advice only when it is sought, and to leave direct contact with university administrators and academics to the student.

It should go without saying that, throughout the *Guide*, all references to parents apply equally to guardians and step-parents.

Student finance and parental involvement

No matter how independent students are meant to be, most parents still feel obliged to do what they can to help their children through university. In these straitened times, however, many families will find that is rather less than they would have hoped. The system is designed to enable undergraduates to pay their own way through a degree course – albeit building up considerable debts along the way – and it will simply have to work that way for more students than was the case in the prosperous years.

One interesting side-effect of this change might be to reduce the involvement of parents in other aspects of their children's higher education – something that has been growing noticeably in recent years. Many parents took responsibility for the original £1,000 fees introduced when Labour came to power because they had to be paid up-front. But the more costly "top-up" fees are met through loans that are only repayable after graduation, when the graduate's salary reaches £15,000. Parents will not even know when repayments begin, let alone be required to make a contribution.

"Helicopter parents"

However, universities have found that, in the controversy over the scale of top-up fees, the fact that mum and dad are no longer involved has passed many parents by. Anxious mothers and fathers are more inclined than ever to question what their children are getting for their £3,225 a year. There have been stories of parents challenging not just the amount and quality of tuition, but even the marking of essays and exams. The phenomenon, first reported in the United States, has given rise to the phrase "helicopter parents" – so called because they hover over their children's education when they should be letting go.

No one wants to think of themselves in that category, but it is not surprising – or reprehensible – that parents are taking more of an interest. Many more of today's parents have been to university themselves, so have the knowledge and confidence to offer advice, both in choosing where and what to study, and in the decisions facing students at university. One of the reasons that some then overstep the mark is that they are shocked that the amount of teaching and size of seminar groups are not what they recall from their own "free" higher education.

An associated reason is that family relationships have changed. Many teenage applicants are happy to accept a lift to an open day to get a second opinion on a university and their prospective course.

The family budget

Undoubtedly the main spur for heightened parental interest, however, is that, regardless of who pays the fees, higher education has been taking a bigger share of family budgets. Hundreds of thousands of students – particularly mature students – pay their own way through university. But every survey shows that families play an important (and, until now, growing) role where students move straight from school to higher education. Even at today's rates, fees remain a much less significant burden than living costs.

Laying the ground

The first thing any parent can do to smooth the path to university is to be encouraging about the value of higher education. Ideally, this should have started long before the application process, but it is especially important at this point. Particularly now that student debt has become a frequent media topic, it is only natural for sixth-formers and others thinking of higher education to have second thoughts.

The lure of a regular wage packet will be tempting, and there are plenty of young people who are not suited to full-time higher education – even after the years of rapid university expansion, most people still do not go to university. But those who are capable of going generally do not regret the decision. Many people look back on their student days as the best period of their life, as well as the one that shaped their personality and their career.

Three or four years as a student should still pay off for the individual in terms of lifetime earnings, as well as personal development. A little reassurance at this stage may make all the difference.

Making the choice

Any parent wants to help a son or daughter through the difficult business of choosing where and what to study. How big a role you play will depend on a number of factors, not the least of which is the extent to which your advice is wanted. In the end, it is the student's decision, and you can do no more than offer relevant information.

One important factor is the quality of advice available at school or college. If this is good, parental involvement should be marginal. But sometimes that is not the case, and you may have to call on other resources, including your own research.

A second factor is your own level of expertise: you may have opinions about particular universities or subjects, but are they up-to-date and based on evidence? Try not to give advice that is coloured by memories of your own student days. That was probably a quarter of a century ago, and higher education has changed out of all recognition in the intervening years.

- Overall 24 per cent of students said that one reason for going to university was because their parents expected it (31 per cent for those at traditional universities and 17 per cent for those at new universities).
- Only 2 per cent said that the most important reason for going to university was that their parents expected it.
- Only 11 per cent of students said that parental advice was one of the factors in choosing a particular university.
- 51 per cent of students rely on financial contributions from parents.

Sodexo University Lifestyle Survey 2008

Avoid second-hand opinions gleaned through the media or dinner party gossip. You may think that some subjects are a sure-fire route to lucrative employment, while others are shunned by employers, but are you right? And do you really know the strengths and weaknesses of more than 100 universities? The tables in chapter 1 offer a reality check, but even they cannot take account of institutional differences. The subject tables in chapter 3 show that the best graduate employment rates are often not at the obvious universities.

Above all, do not try to rewind your own career decisions through your children.

The fact that you enjoyed – or hated – a subject or a university does not mean that they will. You may have always regretted missing out on the chance to go to Oxbridge, or to become a brain surgeon, but they have their own lives to lead. Students who switch courses or drop out of university frequently complain that they were pressured into their original choice by their parents.

Check that choices are being made for sensible reasons, not on the basis of questionable gossip or trivial criteria. But beyond that, you should stay in the background unless there is a very good reason to play a more substantive role. Make a point of looking for important aspects of university life that the applicant might miss. Security, for example, usually does not feature near the top of a teenager's list of priorities, and likewise other practical issues, such as the proximity of student accommodation to lectures, the library and the students' union.

Many universities now publish guides specifically for parents and put on programmes for them at Open Days. The latter may be a way of separating prospective applicants from their more demanding "minders", but the programmes themselves can be interesting and informative. Do not worry that you will be an embarrassment by attending Open Days – thousands of parents do so, and you may add a critical edge to the proceedings. Like prospectuses, Open Days are part of the sales process, and it is easy for a sixth former to be carried away by the excitement surrounding a lively university. You are much more likely to spot the defects – even if they are ignored in the final decision.

Finding a place

Once the choices have been made, get to know the UCAS system and quietly ensure that deadlines are being met. The school should be doing this, but there is no harm in providing a little back-up, especially on parts of the process that take time and thought, such as writing the personal statement.

There is little a parent can do as the offers and/or rejections come rolling in, other than to be supportive. If the worst happens and there are five rejections, you may have to start the advice process all over again for a new round of applications through UCAS Extra. If so, a cool head is even more necessary, but the same principles apply.

Results day

Then, before you know it, results day is upon you. Make sure you are at home, rather than in some isolated holiday retreat. Your son or daughter needs to have access to instant advice at school or college, and to be able to contact universities straight away if Clearing or Adjustment is required. And your moral support will be much more effective face to face, rather than down a telephone line.

Whatever happens, try not to transmit the anxiety that you will inevitably be feeling to your son or daughter, especially if the results are not what was wanted. It is easy to make rash decisions about re-sitting exams or rejecting an insurance offer in the heat of the moment. Try to slow the process down and encourage clear and realistic thinking.

As at other stages in the application, make sure you know in advance what might be required, such as where to access Clearing lists. After that, if it is Clearing or Adjustment, you will need to be on hand to offer advice and again provide a taxi service for visits to possible universities. Clearing or Adjustment is all but over in a week, so the agony should be short-lived.

Before they go

Little more than a month after the tension of results day, everything should be ready for the start of term. Unless your son or daughter is one of the growing band choosing to stay at home to study, there will be forms to fill in to secure university accommodation, as well as student loans to sort out and registration to complete. You can perform useful services, like supplying recipe books if the first year is to be spent in self-catering accommodation, but now is the time for independence to become reality. Make sure that important details like insurance are not forgotten, but otherwise stand clear.

The one thing parents must do before the fledgling student flies the nest, however, is to agree a budget – and make clear that it is a real one. How large that budget is will depend on family circumstances and your attitude to independent living. Some parents want to ensure that their children leave university debt-free; others could never afford to do that, while yet others believe that paying your own way is part of the learning experience. The important thing is that student and parents know where they stand.

After they've left

Any new student is going to be nervous if they are leaving home for the first time and having to settle into a strange environment. But in most cases it isn't going to last long because everyone is in the same boat and freshers' weeks hardly leave time for homesickness. In any case, they won't want to let their apprehension show. The people who are likely to be emotional are the parents – especially if they are left with an empty nest for the first time. It can take a while to get used to an orderly, quiet house after all those years of mayhem.

Resist any temptation to decorate their bedroom and turn it into an office – it is more common than you might think, and psychologists say it can do lasting damage to family relationships. Keep in touch by phone, text or email, but try not to pry. You're not going to be told everything anyway – which is probably just as well. They will be back soon enough: many more students go home at weekends than used to be the case and, just as you were getting used to having the place to yourself, the Christmas vacation will remind you of how things used to be.

Lastly, do not become a helicopter parent. Your son or daughter may well seek your advice if they are dissatisfied with the course, their accommodation or some other aspect of university life. By all means, give advice, but leave them to sort the problem out. Universities will cite the Data Protection Act, or some other piece of legislation, as a reason that they can only deal with students, not their parents. What they really mean is that students are adults and should look after themselves.

Useful websites

Many universities now have special sections on their websites for parents of prospective students.

UCAS has a Parents section on its website:
www.ucas.com/parents
To find out more about open days, visit:
www.opendays.com

International Students

9

Nearly all UK universities are cosmopolitan places that welcome international students in large numbers. Britain is the world's second most popular study destination, and recent surveys suggest that, in the eyes of international students, it is almost as attractive as the market leader, the United States. More than 340,000 international students were taking higher education courses in the UK in 2007–08, a rise of 4.8 per cent on the previous year. They now make up over 15 per cent of all students at UK universities and colleges – and almost a third of all postgraduates, the fastest-growing group.

Large numbers of students continue to come from China, India, Malaysia, Nigeria, Pakistan, the USA, France, Germany and Greece. There has also recently been a significant influx of students from many of the new European Union (EU) member states, particularly Cyprus, Poland and Lithuania. In many UK universities you can expect to have fellow students from over 100 countries from around the world.

The results of a studies by the International Graduate Insight Group (i-graduate) suggest that international students are attracted to the UK chiefly because of the worldwide reputation of its universities and qualifications, high standards of teaching and research, and a perception that it is a safe place to live.

International students have been benefiting from the decline in the value of the pound, but the cost of studying and living in the UK remains relatively high and is naturally a concern for many. The i-graduate *International Student Barometer* asked international students for their views on UK universities.

Most satisfied		**Most dissatisfied**	
1	Teaching standards	1	Accommodation costs
2	Faith provision	2	Other living costs
3	Clubs and societies	3	Opportunites to earn money
4	International office	4	Financial support
5	Students' union	5	Work experience

This chapter alone cannot provide all the answers, but it is a good place to start, pointing you in the direction of other useful sources of information. You should certainly find out as much as you can about what living in Britain will be like. Further advice and information is available through the British Council at its offices worldwide, at more than 60 university exhibitions that it holds around the world every year, or at its Education UK website (**www.educationuk.org**). Another useful website for international students is provided by the UK Council for International Student Affairs (UKCISA) at **www.ukcisa.org.uk**. We recommend some further websites at the end of the chapter.

Where to study in the UK

The UK is made up of three countries: England, Scotland and Wales – which collectively may be referred to as Great Britain – plus the province of Northern Ireland. The vast majority of the UK's universities and other higher education institutions are in England. Of the 118 universities covered in *The Times Good University Guide*, 92 are in England,

14 in Scotland, ten in Wales and two in Northern Ireland. It is now over a decade since Scotland gained its own parliament and Wales formed a National Assembly Government. Each has devolved powers and sets fee limits for higher education, which in some cases has brought benefits for EU students. For example, EU students from outside the UK are able to receive a tuition fee grant of £1,940 a year plus a tuition fee loan of £1,285 when studying at a university in Wales. Latest applications figures show that Wales is currently enjoying the greatest growth in popularity among other EU applicants, while Scottish universities are seeing the fastest increase in applications among students from the rest of the world. All undergraduates from other EU countries are charged the same fees as those from the part of the UK where their chosen university is located, so the rate was £3,225 in England in 2009.

The origins of UK universities can be traced back to the ancient seats of learning at Oxford (1096) and Cambridge (1209) – known collectively as "Oxbridge" – and St Andrews

The Top Countries for Sending International Students to the UK

EU Countries		%	Non-EU Countries (Top 25)		%
Ireland	6,577	11.9	China	17,147	21.1
France	6,331	11.5	Malaysia	7,815	9.6
Germany	6,216	11.3	Hong Kong	6,591	8.1
Poland	5,156	9.3	India	4,310	5.3
Cyprus	4,863	8.8	Nigeria	3,647	4.5
Greece	4,533	8.2	United States	3,229	4.0
Spain	2,339	4.2	Pakistan	2,686	3.3
Sweden	1,997	3.6	Singapore	1,904	2.3
Italy	1,781	3.2	South Korea	1,747	2.1
Cyprus	1,683	3.1	Japan	1,654	2.0
Belgium	1,532	2.8	Sri Lanka	1,632	2.0
Lithuania	1,510	2.7	Norway	1,613	2.0
Portugal	1,247	2.3	Canada	1,504	1.9
Netherlands	1,114	2.0	Kenya	1,350	1.7
Finland	1,076	2.0	Russia	1,160	1.4
Latvia	855	1.5	United Arab Emirates	1,089	1.3
Slovakia	754	1.4	Brunei	1,082	1.3
Bulgaria	700	1.3	Bangladesh	1,063	1.3
Czech Republic	699	1.3	Saudi Arabia	1,059	1.3
Austria	660	1.2	Mauritius	997	1.2
Luxembourg	596	1.1	Vietnam	879	1.1
Hungary	577	1.0	Zimbabwe	873	1.1
Denmark	557	1.0	Switzerland	857	1.1
Romania	541	1.0	Iran	843	1.0
Estonia	483	0.9	Thailand	755	0.9
Malta	205	0.4	**All non-EU students**	**81,262**	
Slovenia	92	0.2			
All EU Students	**55,179**				

(1411) in Scotland. Although many people from outside Britain associate British universities with the Oxbridge image, in reality most higher education institutions in the UK are nothing like this. Some universities do still maintain a traditional culture, but most are modern institutions that place at least as much emphasis on teaching as research and offer many vocational programmes, often with close links with business, industry and the professions. The table below shows the universities that are most popular with international students.

UK universities have a worldwide reputation for high quality teaching and research. They maintain this position by investing heavily in the best academic staff, buildings and equipment, and by taking part in rigorous quality assurance monitoring. The main regulatory bodies include the Quality Assurance Agency for higher education (QAA), higher education funding councils for each country of the UK, and the Office for Standards in Education. Professional bodies also play an important role, and there is an Independent Adjudicator for Higher Education that handles student complaints that have not been resolved by universities' own internal complaints procedures.

The Universities Most Favoured by EU and Non-EU Students

Institution (Top 25)	EU Students	Institution (Top 25)	Non-EU Students
Napier	1,250	Manchester	3,004
University of the Arts London	1,110	Nottingham	2,477
Ulster	1,106	University of the Arts London	2,318
Bedfordshire	1,072	Imperial College	2,187
Westminster	1,056	University College London	1,893
Manchester	1,017	Northumbria	1,836
Coventry	978	Warwick	1,685
Kingston	960	London School of Economics	1,536
Wolverhampton	919	Greenwich	1,350
University College London	909	Hertfordshire	1,284
Brighton	904	Edinburgh	1,279
Aberdeen	899	Middlesex	1,266
Middlesex	884	Cardiff	1,206
Edinburgh	882	Bath	1,181
Kent	861	Manchester Metropolitan	1,153
Manchester Metropolitan	785	Sheffield	1,142
Anglia Ruskin	782	Birmingham	1,127
Nottingham	780	Leeds	1,113
King's College London	777	Cambridge	1,058
Imperial College	773	Kingston	1,030
Robert Gordon	746	King's College London	1,029
Warwick	728	City	1,019
Surrey	725	Oxford Brookes	1,006
Portsmouth	707	Bradford	992
Heriot-Watt	705	Queen Mary, London	985

What subjects to study?

You will find that strongly vocational courses are favoured by international students. Many of these in professional areas such as architecture, dentistry or medicine take one or two years longer to complete than most other degree courses. Traditional first degrees are mostly awarded at Bachelor level (BA, BEng, BSc, etc.) and last three to four years. There are also some "enhanced" first degrees (MEng, MChem, etc.) that take four years to complete. The relatively new Foundation degree programmes are mostly vocational and take two years to complete, with an option to study for a further year to gain a full degree.

The tables at the end of this chapter select the 24 most popular subjects and show which universities for each subject have the greatest numbers of students. Remember, though, that you need also to consider the details of any course that you wish to study and to look at the overall ranking of that university as given in our main League Table in chapter 2 and in the subject tables in chapter 3.

English language proficiency

The universities maintain high standards by generally setting high entry requirements, including proficiency in English. For international students, this usually includes a score of 6 or 7 in the International English Language Testing System (IELTS), which assesses English language ability through listening, speaking, reading and writing tests.

The Most Popular Subjects for International Students

Subject Group	EU	Non-EU	Total	%
Business and administrative studies	12,417	22,932	35,349	26%
Engineering and technology	5,836	13,382	19,218	14%
Social studies	5,266	7,203	12,470	9%
Creative arts and design	4,645	4,928	9,573	7%
Law	2,745	5,516	8,261	6%
Subjects allied to medicine*	3,707	4,263	7,970	6%
Biological sciences	4,244	3,379	7,623	6%
Computer science	2,675	4,156	6,832	5%
Languages	3,779	1,956	5,735	4%
Medicine and dentistry	967	3,020	3,987	3%
Architecture, building and planning	1,799	1,994	3,794	3%
Physical sciences	1,637	1,914	3,551	3%
Mathematical sciences	949	2,586	3,535	3%
Mass communications and documentation	1,689	1,488	3,177	2%
Historical and philosophical studies	1,387	1,235	2,622	2%
Education	548	434	982	1%
Agriculture and related subjects	279	339	618	0%
Combined	236	257	493	0%
Veterinary science	91	396	487	0%
Total	**54,897**	**81,379**	**136,276**	**100%**

*Subjects allied to medicine include Pharmacy and Nursing.

There are many private and publicly funded colleges throughout the UK that run courses designed to bring the English language skills of prospective higher education students up to the required standard. However, not all of these are Government approved. The web address for the list of Tier–4 Government approved education and training centres in the UK is given at the end of this chapter. Some private organisations such as INTO (**www.into.uk.com**) have joined with universities to create centres running programmes preparing international students for degree-level study. The British Council also runs English language courses at its centres around the world.

How to apply

You should read the information below in conjunction with that provided in chapter 4, which deals with the application process in some detail.

Some international students apply directly to a UK university for a place on a course, and others make their applications via an agent in their home country. But most applying for a full-time first degree course do so through the Universities and Colleges Admissions Service (UCAS). If you take this route, you will need to fill in an online UCAS application form at home, at school or perhaps at your nearest British Council office. There is lots of advice on the UCAS website about the process of finding a course and the details of the application system (**www.ucas.ac.uk/students/nonukstudents**).

Whichever way you apply, the deadlines for getting your application in are the same. For those applying from within an EU country, application forms must be received at UCAS by 15 January for most courses. Note that applications for Oxford and Cambridge and for all courses in medicine, dentistry and veterinary science have to be received at UCAS by 15 October. Some art and design courses also have a later deadline of 24 March (see chapter 4 for more details).

If you are applying from a non-EU country, you can submit your application to UCAS at any time between 1 September and 30 June preceding the academic year in which you plan to begin your studies. Most people apply well before the 30 June deadline to make sure that places are still available and to allow plenty of time for immigration regulations, and to make arrangements for travel and accommodation.

Entry and employment regulations

Since various high profile terrorist attacks in the UK and USA, visa regulations have been tightened. However, the main countries that welcome international students – including the UK, the USA, Australia and Canada – have made serious efforts to streamline visa processes and entry requirements to make them appear more welcoming. Students in some countries can also study for a degree qualification provided by a British university by enrolling at a university in their home country.

A global drive to promote the UK's universities was introduced in June 1999 and was later expanded, setting the target of recruiting an additional 100,000 international students to the UK's universities by 2011. Streamlining visa and entry procedures has been a key part of the initiative. However, many of the new rules and regulations are very new, and so it remains to be seen how effective they will prove to be. The British Government has been criticised for increasing visa fees, doubling fees for visa extensions, and ending the right to appeal against refusal of a visa. The most recent development is the introduction of a points system for entry – known as Tier 4, which came into effect in March 2009. Under this scheme, prospective students will be able to check whether they are eligible for entry against published criteria, and so assess their points score. Universities are also required to provide a Certificate of Acceptance for Study to their international student entrants. Prospective students have to demonstrate that, as well as the necessary qualifications, they have enough money for the first year of their specified course.

Since September 2007, all students wishing to enter the UK to study have been required to obtain entry clearance before arrival. The only exceptions are British nationals living overseas, British overseas territories citizens, British Protected persons, British subjects, and non-visa national short-term students who may enter under a new Student Visitor route. You can find more about all the latest rules and regulations for entry and visa requirements at **www.bia.homeoffice.gov.uk/studyingintheuk**.

Changes are also being made to make it easier for international student to work in the UK during and after their studies. The rules and regulations governing permission to work vary according to your country of origin. If you are from a European Economic Area (EEA) country (the EU plus Iceland, Liechtenstein and Norway), you don't need permission to work in the UK, although you will need to be ready to show an employer your passport or identity card to prove you are a national of an EEA country. Students from outside the EEA are allowed to work part-time for up to 20 hours a week during term time and to work full-time during vacations. From August 2008, a new International Graduate Scheme was introduced in England, Wales and Northern Ireland that allows all international graduates to work for up to two years after completing their course. In many ways this is similar to the Fresh Talent initiative in Scotland, set up to attract inward migration to counter a declining population. Under the scheme, international students can apply for an initial two-year extension to stay on after graduation, to live and work in Scotland. So far over 8,000 graduates have taken up this chance, and the scheme will continue to run under the new UK-wide points based migration system.

Bringing your family

In the UK, most universities can help to arrange facilities and accommodation for families as well as for single students. The family members you are allowed to bring with you are your husband or wife, civil partner (a same-sex relationship that has been formally registered in the UK or your home country) and dependent children.

If you are a national of any country from outside the EEA, your family will be subject to immigration policy. You will need to show that you can support them financially, that you can arrange appropriate accommodation, and that they will leave the UK when you have finished your studies. Your family members will usually be able to study (children under 16 are required to attend full-time education), and any over the age of 16 should be able to work as long as you have permission to stay for over 12 months. You can find out more about getting entry clearance for your family at **www.ukcisa.org.uk/student/info_sheets/your_family.php**.

Support from British universities

Support for international students is more comprehensive than in many countries, and begins long before you arrive in the UK. Many universities have advisers – and sometimes offices or even whole campuses – in other countries. Some will arrange to put you in touch with current students or graduates who can give you a first-hand account of what life is like at a particular university. Pre-departure receptions for students and their families, as well as meet-and-greet arrangements for newly arrived students, are common. You can also expect an orientation and induction programme in your first week, and many universities now have "buddying" systems where current students are assigned to new arrivals to help them find their way around, adjust to their new surroundings, and make new friends. Each university also has a students' union that organises social, cultural and sporting events and clubs, including many specifically for international students. Both the university and the students' union are likely to have full-time staff whose job it is to look after the welfare of students from overseas.

International students also benefit from free medical and subsidised dental and optical care and treatment under the UK National Health Service, plus access to a professional counselling service and a university careers service.

At university, you will naturally encounter people from a wide range of cultures and walks of life. Getting involved in student societies, sport, voluntary work, and any of the wide range of social activities on offer will help you gain first-hand experience of British culture, and, if you need it, will help improve your command of the English language.

Useful websites

For information about studying in Britain, visit:
The British Council, with its dedicated Education UK site
www.educationuk.org
Within the Education UK site, you can download a copy of their guide *Studying and Living in the United Kingdom.*

The UK Council for International Student Affairs (UKCISA). UKISA produce a wide range of factsheets on all aspects of studying in the UK:
www.ukcisa.org.uk

UCAS, for full details of courses available and an explanation of the application process:
www.ucas.com/students/nonukstudents

For the latest information on entry and visa requirements, visit:
www.bia.homeoffice.gov.uk/studyingintheuk

List of approved Tier–4 educational establishments:
**www.bia.homeoffice.gov.uk/sitecontent/documents/employersandsponsors/
pointsbasedsystem/registerofsponsorseducation**

UK Student Life, a guide designed to explain British daily life and culture to international students:
www.ukstudentlife.com

For a general guide to Britain, available in many languages:
www.visitbritain.com

The Most Popular Subjects and Universities for International Students

Business Studies

	EU	Non-EU
Middlesex	216	488
Northumbria	245	406
Westminster	345	302
Aston	134	510
Bedfordshire	315	323
Royal Holloway	166	420
Anglia Ruskin	426	124
Hull	176	368
Manchester	130	363
Hertfordshire	143	346
All overseas students	9,286	13,871

Computer Science

	EU	Non-EU
Greenwich	34	238
East London	31	230
Middlesex	48	193
Portsmouth	57	147
Northumbria	27	170
Coventry	65	116
Imperial College	83	93
Bradford	99	75
Bedfordshire	108	60
Manchester	54	113
All overseas students	2,673	4,106

Law

	EU	Non-EU
Northumbria	21	582
King's College London	166	170
Kent	132	183
Leicester	166	137
London School of Economics	41	233
Warwick	54	194
West of England	44	182
Buckingham	11	215
Manchester	34	190
Cardiff	12	211
All overseas students	2,742	5,517

Economics

	EU	Non-EU
London School of Economics	87	363
University College London	72	343
Warwick	78	288
Manchester	59	240
Royal Holloway	81	187
Essex	91	171
Bath	42	149
York	36	152
Nottingham	80	105
Cambridge	39	134
All overseas students	1,801	4,360

Accounting and Finance

	EU	Non-EU
Manchester	78	372
City	108	309
London School of Economics	38	372
Essex	58	283
Warwick	55	218
Lancaster	65	205
West of England	14	217
London South Bank	51	176
Kent	25	189
Durham	10	194
All overseas students	1,445	6,733

Art and Design

	EU	Non-EU
University of the Arts London	650	1,672
University for Creative Arts	190	127
Nottingham Trent	39	259
Birmingham City	62	152
Middlesex	106	80
Kingston	64	103
Wolverhampton	113	34
Goldsmiths College	59	76
Coventry	42	69
Brighton	57	53
All overseas students	2,476	3,504

Electrical and Electronic Engineering

	EU	Non-EU
Imperial College	84	295
Birmingham City	21	209
Northumbria	13	182
Manchester	32	161
Birmingham	12	175
Sheffield	11	173
Bradford	41	127
Nottingham	11	138
Southampton	29	119
Strathclyde	13	112
All overseas students	**1,078**	**4,281**

Medicine

	EU	Non-EU
King's College London	109	165
Manchester	52	206
Leicester	29	155
Nottingham	29	151
Imperial College	44	121
Edinburgh	33	131
University College London	52	110
Southampton	24	132
Glasgow	34	116
St George's	28	120
All overseas students	**894**	**2,758**

Biological Sciences

	EU	Non-EU
Imperial College	73	202
Edinburgh	187	72
University College London	70	88
Manchester	45	93
Wolverhampton	56	60
Cambridge	48	64
Nottingham	35	76
Aberdeen	68	37
Oxford	41	54
Glasgow	57	31
All overseas students	**1,915**	**2,090**

Hospitality, Leisure, Recreation, and Tourism

	EU	Non-EU
Thames Valley	146	327
University College Birmingham	115	240
University of the Arts London	32	191
Brighton	120	49
Surrey	60	87
Edinburgh Napier	45	95
Leeds Metropolitan	76	62
Oxford Brookes	70	68
Bournemouth	51	75
Bedfordshire	110	9
All overseas students	**1,579**	**2,013**

Mechanical Engineering

	EU	Non-EU
Imperial College	77	208
Nottingham	21	192
Bradford	47	114
Coventry	44	89
Bath	40	92
Hertfordshire	14	112
Sheffield	11	107
Southampton	39	73
University College London	38	71
King's College London	29	77
All overseas students	**1,028**	**2,848**

Mathematics

	EU	Non-EU
Imperial College	85	243
University College London	52	241
Warwick	49	190
Oxford	40	181
Manchester	62	139
London School of Economics	35	164
Cambridge	60	103
Bath	52	85
Southampton	16	91
Heriot-Watt	28	77
All overseas students	**957**	**2,595**

Politics

	EU	Non-EU
St Andrews	93	185
London School of Economics	72	197
Kent	205	52
Warwick	64	81
Sussex	81	41
Aberdeen	93	27
Edinburgh	27	82
Aberystwyth	75	32
Royal Holloway	58	36
Nottingham	60	28
All overseas students	1,938	1,547

Other Subjects Allied to Medicine

	EU	Non-EU
Bournemouth	125	144
Dundee	19	231
Queen Margaret Edinburgh	95	62
Imperial College	44	112
Cardiff	20	102
Greenwich	55	63
Cambridge	48	66
Manchester Metropolitan	49	37
Robert Gordon	75	2
Salford	45	27
All overseas students	1,574	1,533

Civil Engineering

	EU	Non-EU
Edinburgh Napier	273	7
Bradford	121	65
Imperial College	37	132
Nottingham	28	110
East London	46	91
Queen's, Belfast	30	99
Liverpool	46	64
Leeds	30	80
Portsmouth	64	37
University College London	27	70
All overseas students	1,607	1,800

Communication and Media Studies

	EU	Non-EU
Westminster	102	74
Goldsmiths College	65	108
University of the Arts London	71	92
Liverpool John Moores	19	105
Middlesex	73	42
Thames Valley	60	44
Wolverhampton	81	15
Oxford Brookes	28	50
Bournemouth	38	37
London South Bank	46	18
All overseas students	1,554	1,263

Psychology

	EU	Non-EU
University College London	30	84
Aberdeen	84	26
Nottingham	24	78
York	9	87
Middlesex	51	41
Ulster	86	1
Royal Holloway	47	39
East London	48	38
Glasgow	63	15
St Andrews	38	32
All overseas students	1,869	1,225

Pharmacology and Pharmacy

	EU	Non-EU
Sunderland	118	169
Brighton	193	59
Robert Gordon	225	26
Nottingham	9	172
Liverpool John Moores	47	120
Manchester	24	134
Bath	18	133
Strathclyde	5	134
Bradford	36	75
School of Pharmacy	12	98
All overseas students	954	1,705

Architecture

	EU	Non-EU
Nottingham	40	176
Robert Gordon	81	72
Greenwich	84	34
Manchester Metropolitan	44	67
East London	64	39
Oxford Brookes	46	52
Plymouth	70	18
Bath	41	44
University College London	18	67
Westminster	57	26
All overseas students	**1,226**	**1,145**

General Engineering

	EU	Non-EU
Coventry	336	33
Cambridge	59	197
Oxford	18	107
Edinburgh Napier	59	45
Manchester	18	73
Wolverhampton	12	59
Warwick	18	48
Ulster	58	1
Nottingham	7	40
Southampton	19	20
All overseas students	**780**	**921**

English

	EU	Non-EU
Portsmouth	92	143
Wolverhampton	82	19
St Andrews	13	70
Edinburgh	18	60
Bedfordshire	63	7
Canterbury Christ Church	47	22
Cardiff	0	67
Salford	46	19
Anglia Ruskin	37	21
Aberdeen	42	9
All overseas students	**1,196**	**937**

Aeronautical and Manufacturing Engineering

	EU	Non-EU
Imperial College	41	83
Kingston	21	90
Nottingham	9	87
Glyndŵr	85	9
Glamorgan	11	78
Sheffield Hallam	0	85
Sheffield	10	72
Bath	23	44
Southampton	25	37
City	10	51
All overseas students	**488**	**1,178**

Drama, Dance and Cinematics

	EU	Non-EU
University of the Arts London	161	226
Bedfordshire	66	58
University for the Creative Arts	84	30
Kingston	42	25
Wolverhampton	54	13
Royal Holloway	23	32
Thames Valley	29	16
Aberystwyth	38	6
Kent	29	14
Middlesex	25	15
All overseas students	**1,174**	**760**

Chemical Engineering

	EU	Non-EU
Imperial College	32	230
Manchester	16	193
Nottingham	8	131
University College London	36	101
Birmingham	11	97
Cambridge	16	65
Loughborough	5	71
Sheffield	7	54
Bath	7	53
London South Bank	4	36
All overseas students	**194**	**1,243**

10 Oxbridge

Oxbridge (as Oxford and Cambridge are called collectively) has different admissions arrangements to the rest of the university system. Although part of the UCAS network, the two universities have different deadlines from the rest of the system, you can only apply to one or the other, and selection is in the hands of the colleges rather than the university centrally. Most candidates apply to a specific college, although you can make an open application if you are happy to go anywhere.

There have been reforms to the admissions system at both universities in recent years, in order to make the process more user-friendly to those who do not have school or family experience to draw upon. In particular, the business of choosing a college has been intimidating for many prospective applicants. Candidates are now distributed around colleges more efficiently, regardless of the choices they make initially.

There is little to choose between the two universities in terms of entrance requirements, and a formidable number of successful applicants have the maximum possible grades. However, that does not mean that the talented student should be shy about applying: both have fewer applicants per place than many less prestigious universities, and admissions tutors are always looking to extend the range of schools and colleges from which they recruit. For those with a realistic chance of success, there is little to lose except the possibility of a wasted space on the UCAS application.

Overall, there are about four applicants to every place at Oxford and Cambridge, but there are big differences between subjects and colleges. As the tables in this chapter show, competition is particularly fierce in subjects such as medicine and English, but those qualified to read metallurgy or classics have a much better chance of success. The pattern is similar to that in other universities, although the high degree of selection (and self-selection) that precedes an Oxbridge application means that even in the less popular subjects the field of candidates is certain to be strong.

These two universities' power to intimidate prospective applicants is based partly on myth. Both have done their best to live down the "Brideshead Revisited" image, but many sixth-formers still fear that they would be out of their depth there, academically and socially. In fact, the state sector produces about half the entrants to Oxford and Cambridge, and the dropout rate is lower than at many other universities. The "champagne set" is still present and its activities are well publicised, but most students are hard-working high achievers with the same concerns as their counterparts on other campuses. A joint poll by the two universities' student newspapers showed that undergraduates were spending much of their time in the library or worrying about their employment prospects, and relatively little time on the river or even in the college bar.

State school applicants

Both universities and their student organisations have put a great deal of effort into trying to encourage applications from state schools, and some colleges have launched their own campaigns. Such has been the determination to convince state school pupils that they will get a fair crack of the whip that a new concern has grown up of possible bias against independent school pupils. In reality, however, the dispersed nature of

Oxbridge admissions discounts any conspiracy. Some colleges set relatively low standard offers to encourage applicants from the state sector, who may reveal their potential at interview. Some admissions tutors may give the edge to candidates from comprehensive schools over those from highly academic independent schools because they consider theirs the greater achievement in the circumstances. Others stick with tried and trusted sources of good students. The independent sector still enjoys a degree of success out of proportion to its share of the school population.

Choosing the right college

Simply in terms of winning a place at Oxford or Cambridge, choosing the right college is not quite as important as it used to be. Both universities have got better at assessing candidates' strengths and finding a suitable college for those who either make an open application or are not taken by their first-choice college.

At Oxford, subject tutors from around the university put candidates into bands at the start of the selection process, using the results of admissions tests as well as exam results and references. Applicants are spread around the colleges for interview and may not be seen by their preferred college if the tutors think their chances of a place are better elsewhere. Almost a quarter of last year's successful candidates were offered places by a college other than the one they applied to.

Cambridge relies on the "pool", which gives the most promising candidates a second chance if they were not offered a place at the college to which they applied. Those placed in the pool are invited back for a second round of interviews early in the new year. The system lowers the stakes for those who apply to the most selective colleges – nearly 3,000 applications were pooled in 2007 and 752 received offers of places. Cambridge still interviews 90 per cent of applicants, whereas the new system at Oxford has resulted in more immediate rejections in some subjects. In medicine, fewer than half of Oxford's applicants were interviewed in 2007, while in biochemistry almost all were.

Cambridge: The Tompkins Table 2008

College	2008	2007	College	2008	2007
Selwyn	1	4	Robinson	17	20
Emmanuel	2	1	Peterhouse	18	25
Trinity	3	6	King's	19	18
Gonville and Caius	4	10	St John's	20	19
Magdalene	5	13	Fitzwilliam	21	14
Churchill	6	15	Girton	22	21
Jesus	7	9	Murray Edwards	23	23
Christ's	8	2	Newnham	24	22
Corpus Christi	9	8	Homerton	25	26
Pembroke	10	7	Hughes Hall	26	29
St Catharine's	11	5	Wolfson	27	27
Downing	12	3	Lucy Cavendish	28	24
Clare	13	17	Sidney Sussex	29	12
Trinity Hall	15	16	St Edmund's	29	28
Queens'	16	11			

However, most Oxbridge applicants still apply direct to a particular college, not only to maximise their chances of getting in, but because that is where they will be living and socialising, as well as learning. Most colleges may look the same to the uninitiated, but there are important differences. Famously sporty colleges, for example, can be trying for those in search of peace and quiet.

Thorough research is needed to find the right place. Even within colleges, different admissions tutors may have different approaches, so personal contact is essential. The tables in this chapter give an idea of the relative academic strengths of the colleges, as well as the varying levels of competition for a place in different subjects. But only individual research will suggest where you will feel most at home. For example, women may favour one of the few remaining single-sex colleges (Murray Edwards, Newnham and Lucy Cavendish at Cambridge). Men have no such option.

The findings in the Tompkins Table (see page 249) are not officially endorsed by Cambridge University itself. However, since 2007 we have been able to publish the "official" Norrington Table from Oxford. Sanctioned or not, both tables give an indication of where the academic powerhouses lie – information which can be as useful to those trying to avoid them as to those seeking the ultimate challenge. Although there can be a great deal of movement year by year, both tables tend to be dominated by the rich, old foundations. Both tables are compiled from the degree results of final-year undergraduates. A first is worth five points; a 2:1, four; a 2:2, three; a third, one point. The total is divided by the number of candidates to produce each college's average.

In both universities, teaching for most students is based in the colleges. In practice, however, this arrangement holds good in the sciences only for the first year. One-to-one tutorials, which are Oxbridge's traditional strength for undergraduates, are by no means universal. However, teaching groups remain much smaller than in most universities, and the tutor remains an inspiration for many students. Both Oxford and Cambridge give

Oxford: The Norrington Table 2008

College	2008	2007	College	2008	2007
Merton	1	1	Wadham	16	18
St John's	2	6	University	17	12
Balliol	3	4	Hertford	18	9
Magdalen	4	2	St Edmund Hall	19	=13
Christ Church	5	3	Exeter	20	25
New College	6	5	St Peter's	21	19
Queen's	7	16	Brasenose	22	21
Jesus	8	=13	Mansfield	23	28
Lincoln	9	8	St Catherine's	24	23
St Hugh's	10	26	Harris Manchester	25	30
Corpus Christi	11	24	Pembroke	26	10
Trinity	12	7	Worcester	27	11
St Anne's	13	15	Somerville	28	20
Keble	14	17	St Hilda's	29	27
Oriel	15	29	Lady Margaret Hall	30	22

Cambridge Applications and Acceptances by Course

Arts	Applications		Acceptances		Acceptances to Applications %	
	2008	2007	2008	2007	2008	2007
Anglo-Saxon, Norse and Celtic	51	66	19	27	37.3	40.9
Archaeology and Anthropology	164	144	81	54	49.4	37.5
Architecture	392	429	40	51	10.2	11.9
Asian and Middle Eastern Studies	185	n/a	59	n/a	31.9	n/a
Classics	158	158	81	81	51.3	51.3
Classics (4 years)	37	37	13	8	35.1	21.6
English	880	895	204	208	23.2	23.2
Geography	356	312	120	97	33.7	31.1
History	758	744	220	201	29.0	27
History of Art	110	119	30	28	27.3	23.5
Modern and Medieval Languages	564	603	188	197	33.3	32.7
Music	165	176	66	76	40.0	43.2
Oriental Studies	n/a	171	n/a	38	n/a	22.2
Philosophy	240	258	47	54	19.6	20.9
Theology and Religious Studies	155	134	55	53	35.5	39.6
Total Arts	*4,215*	*4,246*	*1,223*	*1,173*	*29.0*	*27.6*
Social Science	**2008**	**2007**	**2008**	**2007**	**2008**	**2007**
Economics	1,264	1,160	185	177	14.6	15.3
Land Economy	262	235	60	57	22.9	24.3
Law	1,075	1,123	220	206	20.5	18.3
Social and Political Sciences	638	673	112	113	17.6	16.8
Total Social Sciences	*3,239*	*3,191*	*577*	*553*	*17.8*	*17.3*
Science and Technology	**2008**	**2007**	**2008**	**2007**	**2008**	**2007**
Computer Science	231	227	73	71	31.6	31.3
Engineering	1,364	1,224	332	297	24.3	24.3
Mathematics	1,174	1,116	257	231	21.9	20.7
Medical Sciences	1680	1,395	310	268	18.5	19.2
Natural Sciences	2111	2,013	640	641	30.3	31.8
Veterinary Medicine	375	351	76	66	20.3	18.8
Total Science and Technology	*6935*	*6,326*	*1,688*	*1,574*	*24.3*	*24.9*
Education	109	130	43	62	39.4	47.7
Total	**14,498**	**13,763**	**3,531**	**3,300**	**24.4**	**23.9**

Note: the dates refer to the year in which the acceptances were made.
Mathematics includes those applying for mathematics, mathematics with computer science, and mathematics with physics.
The Tripos course at Cambridge in chemical engineering, linguistics, management studies and manufacturing engineering can only be taken after Part 1 of another Tripos. The entries for these courses are recorded under the first-year subjects taken by the student involved.

Oxford Applications and Acceptances by Course

Arts	Applications 2008	Applications 2007	Acceptances 2008	Acceptances 2007	Acceptances to Applications % 2008	Acceptances to Applications % 2007
Ancient and Modern History	79	82	20	16	25.3	19.5
Archaeology and Anthropology	78	72	21	21	26.9	29.2
Classical Archaeology and Ancient History	78	91	22	21	28.2	23.1
Classics	259	255	122	118	47.1	46.3
Classics and English	33	39	6	9	18.2	23.1
Classics and Modern Languages	36	31	10	9	27.8	29.0
Economics and Management	939	843	73	96	7.8	11.4
English	1,090	1,171	227	239	20.8	20.4
English and Modern Languages	145	143	26	23	17.9	16.1
European and Middle Eastern Languages	47	39	7	13	14.9	33.3
Fine Art	175	160	19	21	10.9	13.1
Geography	272	299	78	85	28.7	28.4
Modern History	780	780	233	236	29.9	30.3
Modern History and Economics	57	39	8	12	14.0	30.8
Modern History and English	80	84	9	9	11.3	10.7
Modern History and Modern Languages	78	102	17	19	21.8	18.6
Modern History and Politics	240	237	48	44	20.0	18.6
History of Art	69	73	12	9	17.4	12.3
Law	935	959	179	186	19.1	19.4
Law with Law Studies in Europe	254	277	27	29	10.6	10.5
Mathematics and Philosophy	87	81	21	19	24.1	23.5
Modern Languages	553	506	178	171	32.2	33.8
Modern Languages and Linguistics	71	76	23	20	32.4	26.3
Music	165	188	70	54	42.4	28.7
Oriental Studies	150	156	42	40	28.0	25.6
Philosophy and Modern Languages	78	55	20	13	25.6	23.6
Philosophy and Theology	103	102	29	19	28.2	18.6
Physics and Philosophy	100	86	18	13	18.0	15.1
PPE	1,192	1,291	232	238	19.5	18.4
Theology	115	114	39	50	33.9	43.9
Total Arts	**8,338**	**8,431**	**1,836**	**1,852**	**22.0**	**22.0**

applicants the option of leaving the choice of college to the university. For those with no ready source of advice on the colleges, this would seem an attractive solution to an intractable problem, but it is also a risky one: a slightly lower proportion succeeds in this way than by applying to a particular college and, inevitably, you may end up somewhere that you hate.

The applications procedure
Both universities have set a UCAS deadline of 15 October 2009 for entry in 2010. For

Oxford Applications and Acceptances by Course cont

Sciences	Applications		Acceptances		Acceptances to Applications %	
	2008	2007	2008	2007	2008	2007
Biochemistry	200	238	86	99	43.0	41.6
Biological Sciences	315	280	111	105	35.2	37.5
Chemistry	478	507	193	190	40.4	37.5
Computer Science	109	82	22	24	20.2	29.3
Earth Sciences (Geology)	74	67	34	32	45.9	47.8
Engineering Science	534	462	166	136	31.1	29.4
Engineering, Economics and Management	91	120	9	15	9.9	12.5
Experimental Psychology	190	242	48	51	25.3	21.1
Human Sciences	78	100	29	31	37.2	31.0
Materials Science; Materials, Economics and Management	66	59	30	28	45.5	47.5
Mathematics	836	828	169	173	20.2	20.9
Mathematics and Computer Science	68	52	28	16	41.2	30.8
Mathematics and Statistics	145	143	26	29	17.9	20.3
Medicine	975	1,085	151	149	15.5	13.7
Physics	662	695	173	170	26.1	24.5
Physiological Sciences	61	61	23	24	37.7	39.3
PPP	168	187	36	36	21.4	19.3
Engineering and Computer Science	n/a	n/a	n/a	n/a	n/a	n/a
Total Sciences	**5,050**	**5,208**	**1334**	**1,308**	**26.4**	**25.1**
Total Arts and Sciences	**13,388**	**13,639**	**3,170**	**3,160**	**23.7**	**23.0**

Note: the dates refer to the year in which the acceptances were made.

both Oxford and Cambridge you may need to take a written test and submit examples of your work – the exact requirements vary depending on the course you select, so check this carefully. See page 20 for details of application tests. In addition, once Cambridge receives your UCAS form, you will be asked to complete a Supplementary Application Questionnaire. You may apply only to either Oxford or Cambridge in the same admissions year, unless you are seeking an Organ award at both universities. Interviews take place in September for those who have left school or applied early, but in December for the majority. By the end of October, the first group can expect an offer, a rejection or deferral of a decision until January. The main group of applicants to Oxford will receive either a conditional offer or a rejection by Christmas, while in Cambridge the news arrives early in the new year.

For more information about the application process and preparation for interviews, visit **www.cam.ac.uk/admissions** and **www.ox.ac.uk/admissions**.

Oxford College Profiles

Balliol

Balliol College, Oxford OX1 3BJ
01865 277777   undergrad.admissions@balliol.ox.ac.uk   www.balliol.ox.ac.uk
Undergraduates: 398   Postgraduates: 287

Famous as the *alma mater* of many prominent post-war politicians, including Harold Macmillan, Denis Healey and Roy Jenkins, the university's last Chancellor, Balliol has maintained a strong presence in university life and is usually well represented in the Union and most other societies. Academic standards are formidably high, as might be expected in the college of Wycliffe and Adam Smith, notably in the classics and social sciences. PPE is notoriously oversubscribed. Library facilities are good and include the Tylor law library. Balliol began admitting overseas students in the 19th century and has cultivated an attractively cosmopolitan atmosphere. It is one of only two colleges to have an entirely student-run bar, the focal point for evening socialising. Most undergraduates are offered accommodation in college for three years, with second year accommodation off-site. There has been a trend in recent years for second-year students to live out, mainly in east Oxford. Graduate students are usually lodged in the Graduate Centre at Holywell Manor. Centrally located, with a JCR pantry that is open all day, Balliol is convenient as well as prestigious.

Brasenose

Brasenose College, Oxford OX1 4AJ
01865 277510 (admissions)   admissions@bnc.ox.ac.uk   www.bnc.ox.ac.uk
Undergraduates: 372   Postgraduates: 179

Brasenose may not be the most famous Oxford college, but it makes up for its discreet image with an advantageous city-centre position. The *alma mater* of David Cameron, Brasenose was one of the first colleges to admit women in the 1970s, and now usually has a 45:55 split within each year, so that, for example, the major undergraduate office, President of the JCR, has been filled as often by a woman as a man. But BNC, as the college is often known, still has the image of a rugby haven, and has the lowest proportions of students from state schools in the university. Named after the door knocker on the 13th-century Brasenose Hall, the college has a pleasant, intimate ambience which most find conducive to study. Law, PPE, medicine and modern history are traditional strengths, and competition for places in these subjects is intense. However, the college has been a consistently poor performer in the Norrington Table. Its library is open 24 hours a day and there is a separate law library. All undergraduate rooms have internet connections. Sporting standards are as high as at many much larger colleges and the college's rowing club is one of the oldest in the university. Two annexes, the St Cross Building and Frewin Court, mean nearly all undergraduates can live in.

Christ Church

Christ Church, Oxford OX1 1DP

01865 276181 (admissions)   admissions@chch.ox.ac.uk   www.chch.ox.ac.uk

Undergraduates: 427   Postgraduates: 216

The college founded by Cardinal Wolsey in 1525 and affectionately known as The House has come a long way since Evelyn Waugh mythologised its aristocratic excesses in *Brideshead Revisited*, although it is still heavily dominated by students from private schools. Academic pressure is reasonably relaxed, although natural high-achievers prosper and the college's history and law teaching is highly regarded. The college is now fifth in the Norrington Table. The magnificent 18th-century library is one of the best in Oxford. It is supplemented by a separate law library. Christ Church has its own art gallery, which holds over 2,000 works of mainly Italian Renaissance art. Sport, especially rugby, is an important part of college life. The river is close by for the aspiring oarsman, and the college has good squash courts. Accommodation for all three years is rated by Christ Church undergraduates as excellent and includes flats off Iffley Road as well as a number of beautifully panelled shared sets (double rooms) in college. The modern bar adds to the lustre of a college justly famous for its imposing architecture. Its chapel is also the cathedral of the Diocese of Oxford – England's smallest medieval cathedral.

Corpus Christi

Corpus Christi College, Oxford OX1 4JF

01865 276693 (admissions tutor)   admissions.office@ccc.ox.ac.uk   www.ccc.ox.ac.uk

Undergraduates: 239   Postgraduates: 108

Corpus, one of Oxford's smallest colleges, is naturally overshadowed by its Goliath-like neighbour, Christ Church, but makes the most of its intimate, friendly atmosphere and exquisite beauty. Like The House, it has an exceptional view across the Meadows. Although the college has only around 340 students including postgraduates, it has an admirable library open 24 hours a day. Academic expectations are high and English, Classics, PPE and medicine are especially well-established. Perhaps unsurprising, then, that Corpus stormed to a headline grabbing victory in this years' *University Challenge* final, although the team were subsequently disqualified and stripped of their title. Corpus is able to offer accommodation to all its undergraduates, one of its many attractions to those seeking a smaller community in Oxford. The college is also one of the most generous with bursaries, giving travel, book and vacation grants at an almost unparalleled level across the university. Scholars are particularly well rewarded.

Exeter

Exeter College, Oxford OX1 3DP

01865 279648 (academic secretary)   admissions@exeter.ox.ac.uk   www.exeter.ox.ac.uk

Undergraduates: 347   Postgraduates: 193

Exeter is the fourth oldest college in the university and was founded in 1314 by Walter de Stapeldon, Bishop of Exeter. Nestling between the High Street and Broad Street, site of most of the city's bookshops, it could hardly be more central. The college boasts handsome buildings, the exceptional Fellows' garden and attractive accommodation for most undergraduates for all three years of their university careers, with plans afoot to refurbish the college's accommodation in the east of the city, although many second year students currently live out. Exeter does have academic pedigree, but has slipped down the Norrington Table in recent times. It is, however, often accused of being rather dull. Given its glittering roll-call of alumni, which includes Martin Amis, J.R.R. Tolkien, Alan Bennett, Richard Burton, Imogen Stubbs and Tariq Ali, this seems an accusation that, on the face of it at least, is hard to sustain. The arrival of Frances Cairncross, the former managing editor of *The Economist*, in 2004 has created a new dynamic at the college, with regular, high-profile, speaker events and the incorporation of a college careers service. The college has recently announced that it will take over the buildings of Ruskin College in Walton Street, although complete occupation is not expected until 2014.

Harris Manchester

Harris Manchester College, Oxford OX1 3TF
01865 271009 (admissions)   enquiries@hmc.ox.ac.uk   www.hmc.ox.ac.uk
Undergraduates: 83   Postgraduates: 103

Founded in Manchester in 1786 to provide education for non-Anglican students, Harris Manchester finally settled in Oxford in 1889 after spells in both York and London. A full university college since 1996, the newest and smallest college, its central location with fine buildings and grounds in Holywell Street is very convenient for the Bodleian, although the college itself does have an excellent library. Harris Manchester admits only mature students of mostly 25 years and above to read for both undergraduate and graduate degrees, predominantly in the arts. All students must be 21 or older. There are also groups of visiting students from American universities and some men and women training for the ministry. Most of its members live in and all meals are provided, indeed the college encourages its members to dine regularly in hall. The college has few sporting facilities (a croquet lawn and a college punt), but members can use two central Oxford gyms without charge and can play football, cricket, swimming and chess as well as playing on other college or university teams. Other outlets include the college Drama Society and also the chapel, a focal point to many there.

Hertford

Hertford College, Oxford OX1 3BW
01865 279404 (admissions)   admissions@hertford.ox.ac.uk   www.hertford.ox.ac.uk
Undergraduates: 385   Postgraduates: 162

Though tracing its roots to the 12th century, Hertford is determinedly modern. It was one of the first colleges to admit women (in 1976). Hertford also helped set the trend towards offers of places conditional on A-levels, which paved the way for the abolition of the entrance examination. It is still popular with state school applicants, and is one of the least stuffy colleges, with a reputation for attracting students from a broad range of backgrounds. The college lacks the grandeur of Magdalen, of which it was once an annex, but has its own architectural trademark in the Bridge of Sighs. It is also close to the History Faculty library (Hertford's neighbour), the Bodleian and the King's Arms, perhaps Oxford's most popular pub. Academic pressure at Hertford is relaxed, but the quality of teaching, especially in English, is generally thought admirable. Accommodation has improved, thanks in part to the Abingdon House and Warnock House complex close to the Thames near Folly Bridge, and the college can now lodge all of its undergraduates at any one time, albeit in disparate parts of the city. The bar, offering some notorious cocktails, serves as a central social hub, and is popular with students across the university. Like most congenial colleges, Hertford is often accused of being claustrophobic and inward-looking – a charge most Hertfordians would ascribe simply to jealousy.

Jesus

Jesus College, Oxford OX1 3DW
01865 279721 (admissions)   admissions.officer@jesus.ox.ac.uk   www.jesus.ox.ac.uk
Undergraduates: 343   Postgraduates: 148

Jesus, the only Oxford college to be founded in the reign of Elizabeth I, suffers from something of an unfair reputation for insularity. Its students, whose predecessors include T.E. Lawrence and Harold Wilson, describe it as "friendly but gossipy" and shrug off the legend that all its undergraduates are Welsh. Close to most of Oxford's main facilities, Jesus has three compact quads, the second of which is especially enticing in the summer. The college's JCR is well-equipped, with a pool table, large projector screen television, and a hatch serving tea and toast throughout the day. Academic standards are high and most subjects are taught in college. Physics, chemistry and engineering are especially strong. Rugby and rowing also tend to be taken seriously. Accommodation is almost universally regarded as excellent and relatively inexpensive. Self-catering flats in north and east Oxford have enabled every graduate to live in throughout his or her Oxford career. The range of accommodation available to undergraduates is similarly good and is available for the full length of any course. The college's Cowley Road development, also the site of the college's sports ground, has been described by the students' union as "some of the plushest student housing in Oxford".

Keble

Keble College, Oxford OX1 3PG
01865 272711 (admissions)   college.office@keble.ox.ac.uk   www.keble.ox.ac.uk
Undergraduates: 425   Postgraduates: 196

Keble, named after John Keble, the leader of the Oxford Movement, was founded in 1870 with the intention of making Oxford education more accessible, and the college remains proud of "the legacy of a social conscience". With around 400 undergraduates, Keble is one of the biggest colleges in Oxford, while its uncompromising Victorian Gothic architecture also makes it one of the most distinctive. Once famous for the special privileges it extended to rowers, the college's academic performance varies from year to year. It is strong in the sciences, where it benefits from easy access to the Science Area, the Radcliffe Science Library and the Mathematical Institute. The college's sporting record remains exemplary, with the rugby team regularly dominating university competitions, although some students find the overflow of the sporting ethos into the college's social life overbearing. Undergraduates are guaranteed accommodation in their first two years and the college can also accommodate most undergraduates in their final year. Its library is open 24 hours a day and all rooms have internet connections. The college hall, where students wishing to dine must wear gowns six nights a week, has recently been intensively cleaned to restore it to its former glory and is one of the most impressive in the university. The refurbished "spaceship" and Café Keble are particular attractions. The college also has a well-equipped gym and a modern theatre, the acoustics of which are rated the best in the university.

Lady Margaret Hall

Lady Margaret Hall, Oxford OX2 6QA
01865 274311 (admissions)   admissions@lmh.ox.ac.uk   www.lmh.ox.ac.uk
Undergraduates: 394   Postgraduates: 179

Lady Margaret Hall, Oxford's first college for women, has been co-educational since 1978 and now enjoys an equal gender balance. For many students, LMH's comparative isolation – the college is three quarters of a mile north of the city centre – is a real advantage, ensuring a clear distinction between college life and university activities, and a refuge from tourists. For others it means a long journey to central library facilities. Although the neo-Georgian architecture is not to everyone's taste, the college's beautiful gardens back onto the Cherwell river, allowing LMH to have its own punt house and 12 acres of land. The students' union describes life at the college as "relaxed". It generally hovers around the bottom of the Norrington Table, although English is strong, producing a high proportion of firsts each year. Accommodation is guaranteed for first and third years, and for the great majority of second years. The college's two recent accommodation buildings have the remarkable attraction of private bathrooms in all their rooms. On-going extensive building works on site will provide further housing for graduate students and radically improve JCR facilities. LMH shares most of its sports facilities with Trinity College, though it has squash and tennis courts on site and has become a leading rowing college. The library is open 24 hours and is well-stocked for English and Classics, with a separate law library. It has long been one of Oxford's dramatic centres, and has recently attained a strong presence in student journalism and the Oxford Union.

Lincoln

Lincoln College, Oxford OX1 3DR
01865 279836 (admissions)   info@lincoln.ox.ac.uk   www.lincoln.ox.ac.uk
Undergraduates: 305   Postgraduates: 282

Small, central Lincoln cultivates a lower profile than many other colleges with comparable assets. The college's 15th-century buildings and beautiful library – a converted Queen Anne church – combine to produce a delightful environment in which to spend three years. Academic standards are high, particularly in arts subjects, although the college's relaxed atmosphere is justly celebrated. Accommodation is provided by the college for all undergraduates throughout their careers and includes rooms above the Mitre, a medieval inn. Students parade around Oxford in sub fusc (formal wear) on Ascension Day while choristers from the University Church beat the parish bounds. The college has a healthy rivalry with neighbouring Brasenose. Historically, Lincoln students must invite their Brasenose counterparts into the bar for free drinks every Ascension Day, in recognition of a time when a Lincoln man was saved from a town mob by the college's neighbours. Graduate students have their own centre a few minutes' walk away in Bear Lane and at the EPA Science Centre close to the university science area. Finalists live in a recently refurbished complex on Museum Road, by Keble and the University Parks. Lincoln's small size and self-sufficiency have led to the college being accused of insularity. Lincoln's food is outstanding, among the best in the university. Sporting achievement is impressive for a college of this size, in part a reflection of its good facilities.

Magdalen

Magdalen College, Oxford OX1 4AU
01865 276063 (admissions)   admissions@magd.ox.ac.uk   www.magd.ox.ac.uk
Undergraduates: 417   Postgraduates: 169

Perhaps the most beautiful college in Oxford or Cambridge, Magdalen is known around the world for its tower, its deer park and its May morning celebrations – when students threw themselves off Magdalen Bridge into the river Cherwell. This practice has now been banned after shallow water resulted in a large number of injuries. The college has shaken off its public school image to become a truly cosmopolitan place, with a large intake from overseas and an increasing proportion of state school pupils. Magdalen's record in English, history and law is second to none, while its science park at Sandford is bound to bolster its reputation in the sciences. The college is academically very strong and is now fourth in the Norrington Table. Library facilities are excellent, especially in history and law. First-year students are accommodated in the Waynflete Building and are allocated rooms in subsequent years by ballot. Undergraduates can be housed in college for the full length of their course. Rents are not cheap compared to other colleges, but there is always financial help on offer. Sets in cloisters and in the palatial New Buildings are particularly sought after. Magdalen is also conveniently placed for the plethora of pubs and places to eat in east Oxford. The college bar is one of the best in Oxford and the college is a pluralistic place, proud of its drama society and choir. In recent years the college has become particularly strong at rowing. Elsewhere, enthusiasm on the sports field makes up for a traditional lack of athletic prowess.

Mansfield

Mansfield College, Oxford OX1 3TF
01865 270920 (admissions)   admissions@mansfield.ox.ac.uk   www.mansfield.ox.ac.uk
Undergraduates: 218   Postgraduates: 67

Mansfield's graduation to full Oxford college status in 1995 marked the culmination of a long history of development since 1886. Its spacious, attractive site is fairly central, close to the libraries, the shops, the University Parks and the river Cherwell. With just over 200 undergraduates, the community is close-knit, although this can verge on the claustrophobic. Recent moves to increase intake numbers may change that. The less intimidating atmosphere of Mansfield is, perhaps, helped by its strong representation of state-school students. First and third years live in college accommodation. The library is open 24 hours. Mansfield students share Merton's excellent sports ground and have numerous college teams. The college has recently become a hotbed of student journalism, providing numerous editors of university publications over the past few years. Despite its former theological background, students are not admitted on the basis of religion and can read a wide variety of subjects. Mansfield is home to the Oxford Centre for the Environment, Ethics and Society (OCEES) and the American Studies Institute backs onto its gardens, evidence of the strong links between Mansfield and the United States, which is reflected by some 35 visiting students annually. It also spearheads the Oxford FE Initiative, which encourages applications to the university from further education colleges.

Merton

Merton College, Oxford OX1 4JD
01865 276299 (admissions)   admissions@admin.merton.ox.ac.uk   www.merton.ox.ac.uk
Undergraduates: 314   Postgraduates: 260

Founded in 1264 by Walter de Merton, Bishop of Rochester and Chancellor of England, Merton is one of Oxford's oldest colleges and one of its most prestigious. Quiet and beautiful, with the oldest quad in the university, Merton has high academic expectations of its undergraduates, consistently reflected in a position at the top of the Norrington Table, where it is currently placed. History, English, physics, PPE and chemistry all enjoy a formidable track record. The medieval library is the envy of many other colleges. Accommodation is some of the cheapest in the university, of a good standard and offered to students for all three years. Merton's food is well-priced and among the best in the university; formal Hall is served six times a week. Kitchens are provided for the first and third years who live in college. Merton's many diversions include the Merton Floats, its dramatic society, the Neave (Politics) Society, an excellent Christmas Ball and the peculiar Time Ceremony, which celebrates the return of GMT. Sports facilities are excellent, although participation tends to be more important than the final score.

New College

New College, Oxford OX1 3BN
01865 279512 (admissions)   admissions@new.ox.ac.uk   www.new.ox.ac.uk
Undergraduates: 423   Postgraduates: 222

New College is large, old (founded in 1379 by William of Wykeham) and much more relaxed than most expect when first confronting its daunting facade. It is a bustling place, as proud of its excellent music and its bar as of its strength in law, history and PPE. In the past two years the college has moved into the top five of the Norrington Table. Traditionally in the bottom third of colleges for attracting state school students, the college has been making particular efforts to increase this proportion, inviting applications from schools that have never sent candidates to Oxford. The Target Schools Scheme, designed to increase applications from state schools, is well established. Almost all undergraduates will be able to have college accommodation for three years. The college's library facilities are impressive, especially in law, classics and PPE. The sports ground is nearby and includes good tennis courts. Women's sport is particularly strong, especially on the river. A sports complex, named after Brian Johnston, opened in 1997, at St Cross Road. The sheer beauty of New College remains one of its principal assets and the college gardens are a memorable sight in the summer. In spite of these traditional charms, the college has strong claims to be considered admirably innovative. Music is a feature of college life, and the college has some of the best practice facilities in the university. The Commemoration Ball, held every three years, is a highlight of Oxford's social calendar.

Oriel

Oriel College, Oxford OX1 4EW
01865 276522 (admissions)   admissions@oriel.ox.ac.uk   www.oriel.ox.ac.uk
Undergraduates: 307   Postgraduates: 136

In spite of its reputation as a bastion of muscular privilege, Oriel is a friendly college with a strong sense of identity. In recent years the college has succeeded in ridding itself of its image of being home to the archetypal "Tory boy" characters. The college is sometimes described as having "a strong crew spirit" reflecting its traditions on the river. Academic pressure is relaxed by Oxford standards, although the college has recently risen to the middle of the Norrington Table. The well-stocked library is open 24 hours a day. Oriel's sporting reputation is certainly deserved and its rowing eight is rarely far from the head of the river. Other sports are well catered for, even if their facilities are considerably farther away than the boathouse, which is only a short jog away. Accommodation is of variable quality, but Oriel can provide rooms for all three years for those students who require them. Scholars and Exhibitioners chasing firsts in their final year are given priority in the ballot for college rooms. Extensive new accommodation has been completed one mile away off the Cowley Road and at the Island Site on Oriel Street. Oriel also offers a lively drama society, a Shakespearian production taking place each summer in the front quad. College meals are cheap, with students charged little more than £5 for three meals a day in hall.

Pembroke

Pembroke College, Oxford OX1 1DW
01865 276412 (admissions)   admissions@pmb.ox.ac.uk   www.pmb.ox.ac.uk
Undergraduates: 383   Postgraduates: 110

Although its alumni include such extrovert characters as Dr Johnson and Michael Heseltine, Pembroke is one of Oxford's least dynamic colleges. The college is historically poor financially, but academic results are solid, and have improved significantly in recent years. The college has Fellows and lecturers in almost all the major university subjects. Pembroke expects to accommodate all first years and most final-year undergraduates. The building of a new annexe means that all students will be housed by 2011 (at an estimate). The Sir Geoffrey Arthur building on the river, ten minutes' walk from the college, offers excellent facilities; in addition to 100 student rooms there is a concert room, computer room and a multigym. College food is reasonable, though some find formal Hall every evening rather too rich a diet. Rugby and rowing are strong, with Pembroke usually behind only Oriel and Magdalen on the river, and squash and tennis courts are available at the nearby sports ground. Over the past few years Pembroke's intake has had among the lowest proportion of state-school students in the university.

Queen's

Queen's College, Oxford OX1 4AW
01865 279161   admissions@queens.ox.ac.uk   www.queens.ox.ac.uk
Undergraduates: 333   Postgraduates: 126

One of the most striking sights of the High Street, Queen's has now shed its exclusive "northern" image to become one of Oxford's liveliest and most attractive colleges. The college's academic record is average, although results have improved recently and it is now placed seventh in the Norrington Table. Modern languages, chemistry and mathematics are reckoned among the strongest subjects. Queen's does not normally admit undergraduates for the honours school of English language and literature, theology, computer science or geography, and is seen as strong in history and politics. The library is as beautiful as it is well stocked. All students are offered accommodation, first years being housed in modernist annexes in east Oxford, and the college is in the process of converting all rooms into en-suite facilities. Queen's can be insular and is largely apolitical, but has a strong college enthusiasm for sport, particularly rugby and netball. The college's beer cellar is one of the most popular in the university and the JCR facilities are also better than average. An annual dinner commemorates a student who is said to have fended off a bear by thrusting a volume of Aristotle into its mouth. Postgraduates are accommodated in St Aldate's House, a modern building close to the centre of town.

St Anne's

St Anne's College, Oxford OX2 6HS
01865 274840 (admissions)   enquiries@st-annes.ox.ac.uk   www.st-annes.ox.ac.uk
Undergraduates: 446   Postgraduates: 213

Architecturally uninspiring (a Victorian row with concrete "stack-a-studies" dropped into their back gardens), St Anne's makes up in community spirit what it lacks in awesome grandeur. One of the largest colleges, it has a relatively high proportion of state-school students. A women's college until 1979, its academic standing has fluctuated, having been in last place in the Norrington Table in the middle of the last decade, but now scoring around mid-table. PPE is particularly strong. The library is very well-stocked and is rich in law, Chinese and medieval history texts. It is now open 24 hours. Accommodation is guaranteed to all undergraduates, and the college also operates an equalisation scheme which gives up to £800 to students wishing to live out. It is situated to the north of the city centre, although not as far out as St Hugh's. Three new accommodation blocks contain 150 student rooms, including four for disabled students, while the older rooms have been refurbished. Half of all rooms are en suite.

St Catherine's

St Catherine's College, Oxford OX1 3UJ
01865 271703 (admissions)   admissions@stcatz.ox.ac.uk   www.stcatz.ox.ac.uk
Undergraduates: 489   Postgraduates: 183

Arne Jacobsen's modernist design for "Catz", one of Oxford's youngest and largest under-graduate colleges, has attracted much attention as the most striking contrast in the university to the lofty spires of Magdalen and New College. Close to the Law, English and Social Science faculties, the university science area and the pleasantly rural Holywell Great Meadow, St Catherine's is nevertheless only a few minutes' walk from the city centre. Academic standards are especially high in mathematics and physics though the college has recently plumbed the depths of the Norrington Table. The well-liked Wolfson library is open till midnight on most days. Rooms are small but tend to be warmer than in other, more venerable colleges, and are now available on site for first, second and third years. There is an excellent theatre, as well as an on-site punt house, gym and squash courts. The college is host to the Cameron Mackintosh Chair of Contemporary Theatre, currently held by Kevin Spacey. Recent incumbents have included Sir Ian McKellen, Alan Ayckbourn and Lord Attenborough. St Catherine's has one of the best JCR facilities in Oxford.

St Edmund Hall

St Edmund Hall College, Oxford OX1 4AR
01865 279011 (admissions)   admissions@seh.ox.ac.uk   www.seh.ox.ac.uk
Undergraduates: 390   Postgraduates: 149

St Edmund Hall – "Teddy Hall" – has one of Oxford's smallest college sites but also one of its most populous. The college offers students the chance to live in its medieval quads right in the heart of the city. With the male/female ratio nearly equal, the college is shedding its image as a home for "hearties", and the authorities have gone out of their way to tone down younger members' rowdier excesses. Nonetheless, the sporting culture is still vigorous and the college usually does well in rugby, football and hockey. The college is also known across the university for its "bops" – the name given to student discos. Academically, the college has put recent poor performances behind it and is now found in the middle of the Norrington Table, and has some impressive names among its fellowship as well as a marvellous library, originally a Norman church. College accommodation is reasonable and can be offered for three years, either on the main site or in North or East Oxford. The college has three annexes, one near the University Parks, and two on Iffley Road, where many of the rooms have private bathrooms. Hall food is better than average.

St Hilda's

St Hilda's College, Oxford OX4 1DY

01865 286620 (admissions)   college.office@st-hildas.ox.ac.uk   www.st-hildas.ox.ac.uk

Undergraduates: 398   Postgraduates: 123

Last October marked a milestone for St Hilda's and the university as a whole, as the college welcomed its first mixed sex intake. Although the college, founded in 1893, lasted more than 100 years as an all-female institution, the governing body voted in 2006 to admit men. Male students now make up nearly half of the first year. The college has long languished at the bottom end of the Norrington Table, but is a distinctive part of the Oxford landscape and is usually well represented in university life. The 65,000-volume library is growing fast and accommodation for readers was extended in 2005. St Hilda's also boasts one of the largest ratios of state school to independent undergraduates in Oxford. Accommodation is guaranteed to first years and finalists. The JCR has its own punts, which are available free for college members and their guests. Many of the rooms offer some of the best river views in Oxford. Social facilities are limited, but this is expected to change with the influx of men. The standard of food is high.

St Hugh's

St Hugh's College, Oxford OX2 6LE

01865 274910 (admissions)   admissions@st-hughs.ox.ac.uk   www.st-hughs.ox.ac.uk

Undergraduates: 404   Postgraduates: 186

One of the lesser-known colleges, St Hugh's was criticised by students in 1987 when it began admitting men. There is now an equal male/female ratio, a better balance than at most Oxford colleges. Like Lady Margaret Hall, St Hugh's picturesque setting is a bicycle ride from the city centre. It is an ideal college for those seeking a place to live and study away from the madding crowd, and is well liked for its pleasantly bohemian atmosphere and beautiful gardens. Academic pressure remains comparatively low. This year the college jumped to tenth place from its usual position in the lower regions of the Norrington Table. History is particularly strong. St Hugh's guarantees accommodation to undergraduates for all three years, although the standard of rooms is variable. Sport, particularly football, is taken quite seriously. As the college enjoys extensive grounds compared to most colleges, there is space for a croquet lawn and tennis courts.

St John's

St John's College, Oxford OX1 3JP

01865 277317 (admissions)   admissions@sjc.ox.ac.uk   www.sjc.ox.ac.uk

Undergraduates: 396   Postgraduates: 216

St John's is one of Oxford's powerhouses, excelling in almost every field and boasting arguably the most beautiful gardens in the university. Founded in 1555 by a London merchant, it is richly endowed and makes the most of its resources to provide undergraduates with an agreeable and challenging three years. The work ethic is very much part of the St John's ethos, and academic standards are high, with English, chemistry and history among the traditional strengths, though all students benefit from the impressive library. The college is second only to Merton in the Norrington Table and has one of the highest proportions of state-school students in Oxford. As might be expected of a wealthy college, the accommodation is excellent and guaranteed for three or four years. The college's riches allow it to subsidise accommodation costs to a large degree, as well as providing generous book grants. St John's has a strong sporting tradition and offers good facilities, but the social scene is limited. As befits such an all-round strong college, entry is fiercely competitive. The college is very close to two of Oxford's landmark pubs: the Eagle and Child and the Lamb and Flag.

St Peter's

St Peter's College, Oxford OX1 2DL
01865 278863 (admissions)   admissions@spc.ox.ac.uk   www.spc.ox.ac.uk
Undergraduates: 354   Postgraduates: 99

Opened as St Peter's Hall in 1929, St Peter's has been an Oxford college since 1961. Its medieval, Georgian and 19th-century buildings are in the city centre and close to most of Oxford's main facilities. Though still young, St Peter's is well represented in university life and has pockets of academic excellence, rising to tenth in the Norrington Table in 2004, although it has since fallen far back into the bottom half. History tutoring is particularly good. There are no Fellows in classics at the college. Accommodation is offered to students for first and third years and about 60 per cent of second years. Although previously prohibited from cooking on the main site, students now have a kitchenette with limited facilities. Student rooms vary from traditional rooms in college to new purpose-built rooms a few minutes' walk away. The college's facilities are impressive, including one of the university's best JCRs. The college has a proud sporting heritage, being particularly strong at rugby and rowing. St Peter's is known as one of Oxford's most vibrant colleges socially. It is strong in acting and journalism, and has a recently refurbished bar. It has recently suffered from a severe shortage in funding, and made its chaplain redundant.

Somerville

Somerville College, Oxford OX2 6HD
01865 270619 (admissions)   secretariat@some.ox.ac.uk   www.some.ox.ac.uk
Undergraduates: 391   Postgraduates: 74

The announcement, early in 1992, that Somerville was to go co-educational sparked an unusually acrimonious and persistent dispute within this most tranquil of colleges. Protests were doomed to failure, however; the first male undergraduates arrived in 1994 and now account for half the students. Lady Thatcher was one of those who flocked to their old college's defence, illustrating the fierce loyalty Somerville inspires. The college's atmosphere appears to have survived the momentous change, although the culture of protest reappeared when a number of students refused to pay the Government's tuition fees in 1998. The college has relatively strong state-school representation. Accommo-dation, including 30 small flats for students, is of a reasonable standard, and is guaranteed for first years and students sitting university examinations, as well as roughly a third of all other students. The JCR operates a rent equalisation scheme for those who live out in their second year. There are kitchens in all college buildings, but hall food is towards the cheaper end of the university. Sport is strong at Somerville and the women's rowing eight usually finishes near the head of the river. The college's hockey pitches and tennis courts are nearby. The 100,000-volume library is open 24 hours a day and is one of the most beautiful in Oxford. Students at the college have a strong track record of involvement in the university's student union.

Trinity

Trinity College, Oxford OX1 3BH
01865 279860 (admissions)   admissions@trinity.ox.ac.uk   www.trinity.ox.ac.uk
Undergraduates: 313   Postgraduates: 95

Architecturally impressive and boasting beautiful lawns (which you can walk on), Trinity is one of Oxford's least populous colleges, admitting some eighty undergraduates each year. It is ideally located, beside the Bodleian, Blackwell's bookshop and the White Horse pub. Cardinal Newman, an alumnus of Trinity, is said to have regarded Trinity's motto as "Drink, drink, drink". Academic pressure varies, but the college has recently made impressive steps up the ranks of the Norrington Table of academic performance and the college produces its fair share of Firsts, especially in arts subjects. Trinity has shaken off its reputation for apathy, and whilst members are active in all walks of university life, the college has its own debating and drama societies, as well as sharing a fierce rivalry with neighbouring Balliol. The proportion of state-school entrants has been rising, but is still poor. Accommodation is of a reasonable standard and undergraduates can live in for three years. Students rate the food highly. All undergraduates are given a room on the main site in their first and second year, with the great majority of third and fourth-year students living in a purpose built block 1.5 miles north of the college. However, this year some second years have had to be housed in blocks of flats in the town centre due to lack of space on site.

University

University College, Oxford OX1 4BH
01865 276959 (admissions)   admissions@univ.ox.ac.uk   www.univ.ox.ac.uk
Undergraduates: 369   Postgraduates: 191

University is the first Oxford college to be able to boast a former student in the Oval Office. Indeed, the college seems certain to benefit from its unique links with former President Clinton, a Rhodes Scholar at University in the late 1960s. The college is probably Oxford's oldest, though highly unlikely to have been founded by King Alfred, as legend claims. Academic expectations are high and the college prospers in most subjects, although it maintains a relatively modest standing in the Norrington Table. Physics, PPE and maths are particularly strong. That said, University has fewer claims to be thought a powerhouse in the manner of St John's, arguably its greatest rival. Students who are accepted to read courses with a mathematical element are invited to a free week-long maths course just before the beginning of their first term, providing a head-start in their studies. Accommodation is guaranteed to undergraduates for all three years, with third years lodged in an annexe in north Oxford about a mile and a half from the college site on the High Street, although the vast majority of third years choose to live out in rented accommodation. Sport is strong and University has been well represented and successful on the rugby field in the last few years, but the college has a reputation for being quiet socially. Students from the state sector are poorly represented, with the college having one of the lowest proportions of places to state-school students. This is despite a generous bursary scheme.

Wadham

Wadham College, Oxford OX1 3PN
01865 277545 (admissions)   admissions@wadh.ox.ac.uk   www.wadh.ox.ac.uk
Undergraduates: 450   Postgraduates: 136

Founded by Dorothy Wadham in 1609, Wadham is known in about equal measure for its academic track record – the college generally ranks in the top third in examination performance – and its leftist politics. The JCR – or student union as it has rebranded itself – is famously dynamic and politically active, although the breadth of political opinion is greater than its left-wing stereotype suggests. Wadham students are notoriously trendy, although some in the university find the atmosphere at the college slightly forced. That said, the college is very strong in admitting students from state schools. And for somewhere supposedly unconcerned with such fripperies, its gardens are surprisingly beautiful. The somewhat rough-hewn chapel is similarly memorable. The college has a good 24-hour library. Accommodation is guaranteed for at least two years and there are many large, shared rooms on offer. Journalism and drama play an important part. Highlights in the social calendar are Queerbop, a celebration of all things gay, and Wadstock, the college's open-air music festival. Tickets to both are always sold out.

Worcester

Worcester College, Oxford OX1 2HB
01865 278391 (admissions)   admissions@worc.ox.ac.uk   www.worc.ox.ac.uk
Undergraduates: 418   Postgraduates: 159

Worcester is to the west of Oxford what Magdalen is to the east: an open, rural contrast to the urban rush of the city centre. The college's rather mediocre exterior conceals a delightful environment, including some characteristically muscular Baroque Hawskmoor architecture, a garden and a lake. The college has been rising up the Norrington Table and was only just outside the top ten in 2007 – its best result of the decade, although it is now back in the bottom five. The 24-hour library is strongest in the arts. Accommodation, guaranteed for two years and provided for the majority of third years, varies in quality from ordinary to conference standard in the Canal Building. More en-suite accommodation, next to the new gym, is now available. Sport plays an important part in college life, as befits the only college with playing fields on site. Worcester has had recent successes in football, hockey and cricket. Formal halls are available six nights a week and a bargain at less than £2. Like Magdalen and New, it is home to the Commemoration Ball once every three years, a highlight of the Oxford social calendar. More than half of the 2008 intake was from the state system, but the average over the last three years (which the university considers more representative) is still just over 50 per cent.

Cambridge College Profiles

Christ's

Christ's College, Cambridge CB2 3BU
01223 334953 (admissions)   admissions@christs.cam.ac.uk   www.christs.cam.ac.uk
Undergraduates: 395   Postgraduates: 95

Christ's prides itself on its academic strength, but offers one third of places on "easy offers", anything as low as two E grades at A levels. The college is confident of its ability to identify potential high-flyers at interview and, in effect, prepared to circumvent A-levels as the principal criteria for entry to ease the pressure on good applicants and allow them to read around their subject. However, to receive an "easy offer", applicants need to have a strong academic record and "be making outstanding progress in their current studies." The college has a 49:51 state-to-independent ratio, although the College is keen to increase the number of state school applicants, and have been active in outreach and access work this year. Women make up about 40 per cent of the students. Christ's has a reputation for being dominated by hard-working medics, natural scientists and mathematicians, although it is also strong in history and English. Students have described the atmosphere at the college as intimate and cosy, but some complain of short bar opening hours and a poor relationship between undergraduates and Fellows. Accommodation is guaranteed to all undergraduates in college for the duration of the course. Rooms on offer vary from the gothic splendour of some of the old buildings on site to the more modern New Court "Typewriter", which has been recently refurbished, offering students en-suite accommodation and private balconies. The college has a visuals arts centre where the college's artist in residence – who this year is giving student life drawing classes – works, and a newly refurbished performance space, the Yusuf Hamied Theatre. Christ's Films – widely considered to be one of the best film societies in the university – and the Christ's Amateur Dramatics Society are active student groups. College sport has flourished in recent years with teams competing to a good standard, particularly in rowing and football. The playing fields, shared with St Catharine's, are situated on Barton Road, about two miles away. Notable alumni include Charles Darwin and the poet John Milton.

Churchill

Churchill College, Cambridge CB3 0DS
01223 336202 (admissions)   admissions@chu.cam.ac.uk   www.chu.cam.ac.uk
Undergraduates: 440   Postgraduates: 210

Students at Churchill claim they are the most unpretentious of Cambridge colleges – and proud of the fact the college allows its students to walk on the grass. This informality stems from the youth of the college, as well as its relatively high state-school intake, 56 per cent. Founded in 1958 to help meet "the national need for scientists and engineers and to forge links with industry", Churchill has seen a recent rise up the Tompkins Table, finishing in the top 10 last year. The college has a noticeably high proportion of scientists and men: only one in three students are female. Compared to the breathtaking architecture of other Cambridge colleges, Churchill's modern and functional architecture strikes many as ugly, with some students saying the "1960s brutalism is something you get used to." Another perceived flaw is its distance from the city centre. Others argue that the distance offers much-needed breathing space. One undeniable advantage is Churchill's ability to provide every undergraduate with a room in college for all three years. Also, the college's weekly "pav" dances have become popular amongst Cambridge students in recent years. There are extensive on-site playing fields, and the college does well in rugby, hockey and rowing. The university's only student radio station (broadcasting to Churchill and New Hall) is based here, and they have recently developed new state of the art music facilities. The College Archive Centre houses the papers of both the college's namesake, Winston Churchill, and the former prime minister Margaret Thatcher.

Clare

Clare College, Cambridge CB2 1TL
01223 333246 (admissions)   admissions@clare.cam.ac.uk   www.clare.cam.ac.uk
Undergraduates: 490   Postgraduates: 300

One of the most beautiful Cambridge Colleges, Clare occupies a quiet yet central position behind Caius and looking onto the "backs". It is also one of the oldest of the colleges, founded in 1326. Despite these accomplishments, Clare is known among students as one of the friendliest and welcoming places to study, with an active bar and frequent live music. Accommodation is guaranteed for all three years, either in college – where life centres around the 17th-century Old Court – or nearby hostels. The college has recently finished the Gillespie Centre, which will house undergraduates and provide conference facilities. The 49:51 ratio of male to female students is better than many colleges, while systematic attempts to raise the proportion of state-educated students has left those from independent schools in a minority (39 per cent). Clare's extracurricular life is a big attraction. Music thrives, and the choir records and tours regularly. Clare Cellars (comprising the bar and JCR) has fast become one of the best run student venues in the university – providing everything from jazz to hip hop to comedy. One of the few gripes amongst students is that its playing fields, which are shared with Peterhouse and Clare Hall, are well away from its location in the centre of the city.

Corpus Christi

Corpus Christi College, Cambridge CB2 1RH
01223 338056 (admissions)   admissions@corpus.cam.ac.uk   www.corpus.cam.ac.uk
Undergraduates: 250   Postgraduates: 150

Corpus Christi's small size inevitably makes it one of the more intimate colleges in Cambridge, with the fewest undergraduates in the university. Some argue that allows for a cohesive community, others feel it can become a goldfish bowl. Although small, it is traditionally broad-based academically. The college was founded in 1352, making it one of the oldest colleges in Cambridge. Mixed with the old architecture, however, is a state-of-the-art undergraduate library – which has improved study facilities in the college – and a new student centre, both of which opened recently. The college's formal halls have a good reputation – voted sixth best by one student magazine. The kitchen fixed charge is above average but the college is known for a good formal hall. Almost all undergraduates are allocated a room in college or neighbouring hostels. The library is open 24 hours a day. There is a fairly even social balance: the independent-to-state ratio is about 40:60. The college bar has an enviable atmosphere. The sporting facilities, at Leckhampton (just over a mile away), are among the best in the university and include an outdoor swimming pool. The size of the college means that its sporting reputation owes more to enthusiasm than success, however. Drama is also well catered for, and the college owns The Playroom, the university's best small theatre.

Downing

Downing College, Cambridge CB2 1DQ
01223 334826 (admissions)   admissions@dow.cam.ac.uk   www.dow.cam.ac.uk
Undergraduates: 412   Postgraduates: 280

Hidden away behind the bustle of Regents Street, close to the city centre yet off the tourist trail, lies Downing College. As a result, its neo-Classical quadrangle and beautiful architecture is easily missed by anyone not looking for it. Founded in 1800 for the study of law, medicine and natural sciences, these are still thought to be the college's strong subjects. Indeed Downing is often called "the law college". A reputation for hard-playing, hard-drinking rugby players and oarsmen is proving hard to shake off. The college has many successful sports teams – with its own on-site tennis, netball and squash courts, a gym and plenty of open space (The Paddock). The college is one of the best on the river, but lost its men's title to Trinity College this year. Downing currently guarantees a place in college accommodation for three years; the completion of a new accommodation block in 2000 allowed students to be housed throughout a first degree. The library, opened in 1993, has won an award for its architecture. There is a good mix between students with state and independent school backgrounds (57:43). The student-run bar/party room has improved college social life, particularly after the three candlelit formal dinners a week, and a new student theatre is opening on site in the summer of 2009.

Emmanuel

Emmanuel College, Cambridge CB2 3AP
01223 334290 (admissions)   admissions@emma.cam.ac.uk   www.emma.cam.ac.uk
Undergraduates: 491   Postgraduates: 224

Despite being one of the most academically successful colleges, Emmanuel, more commonly known as "Emma", is keen to present itself as the "friendly" Cambridge college. The college is proud of students' achievements in sport and music, as well as their academic success. Emmanuel topped the unofficial Tompkins Table of Cambridge colleges for academic achievement for a number of years, but was beaten last year into second place. Despite this achievement, and being one of the wealthiest of the colleges, Emma has an unpretentious atmosphere: students and fellows share an open-air pool in the Fellows garden, the college bar is stylish and strikingly modern. For the last few years Emma has consistently kept the state to independent student ratio at about 60:40, and around half of all undergraduates are women. All students are guaranteed accommodation for the duration of their course. Second years are housed in college hostels. With self-catering facilities limited, most students eat in Hall. The college offers expedition grants to undergraduates every year, and has a large hardship fund. In the summer, the college gardens, with tennis courts and a duck pond, offer a welcome haven from exam pressures. The sports grounds are excellent, if some distance away, and the women's rowing team came head of the river last year.

Fitzwilliam

Fitzwilliam College, Cambridge CB3 0DG
01223 332030 (admissions)   admissions@fitz.cam.ac.uk   www.fitz.cam.ac.uk
Undergraduates: 475   Postgraduates: 220

Based in the city centre until 1963, Fitzwilliam now occupies a large, modern site on the Huntingdon Road. What it may lack in architectural splendour, "Fitz" makes up in friendly informality. The college was established in 1869, with the aim of widening access to the university. They are proud of this tradition, and now 58 per cent of its undergraduates come from the state sector. The college is notably "unstuffy", with a good college bar, popular ENTS events and a strong sporting reputation. In recent years the college sports teams have been among the best in the university. The football and rugby teams have enjoyed great success, and there are extensive and well-kept sports facilities close by, including gym, football, rugby, cricket, hockey and tennis grounds – as well as squash courts on site. Music also thrives at the college: Fitz is the only college in Cambridge to have access to a professional string quartet. The college has a 250-seater auditorium for performances, and is currently developing (to open in 2010) a new library and IT centre, designed by the award-winning architect Edward Cullinan. Under-graduates are guaranteed college accommodation for three or four years, either on site or in nearby housing.

Girton

Girton College, Cambridge CB3 0JG
01223 338972 (admissions)   admissions@girton.cam.ac.uk   www.girton.cam.ac.uk
Undergraduates: 490   Postgraduates: 207

As students at Girton readily admit, "you've probably never heard of Girton, half of Cambridge students haven't". Its anonymity is due to its distance from the city centre. Admittedly, the centre is only a 15-minute bike ride away, but in Cambridge terms that is as long a commute as you can get. However, its comparative isolation inevitably encourages a strong community spirit, and students get to enjoy its beautiful grounds away from the tourists and the relative bustle of the city. Girton stands on a 50-acre site – complete with woods and orchards – so there is no question of overcrowding: rooms are available for the entire course. The majority of second-year students live in Wolfson Court (near the University Library, closer to town). Some find that the long corridors remind them of boarding school. Since becoming coeducational in 1977, the college has maintained a balanced admissions policy. Around half of the undergraduates admitted are from state schools. Girton also has one of the highest proportion of women Fellows in any mixed college. The on-site sporting facilities, which include an indoor swimming pool, are excellent. The college is active in most sports and particularly strong in football. The formal Hall, though excellent and popular, is held only once a week.

Gonville and Caius

Gonville and Caius College, Cambridge CB2 1TA

01223 332440 (admissions)　　　admissions@cai.cam.ac.uk　　　www.cai.cam.ac.uk

Undergraduates: 475　　　Postgraduates: 230

Gonville and Caius College – to confuse the outsider, the college is usually known as Caius (pronounced "keys") – is among the most beautiful of Cambridge's colleges, as well as one of the most central. It has an excellent academic reputation, especially in medicine and history, although maths and law are also highly rated. Caius also has one of the largest and most architecturally impressive student libraries in Cambridge, housed in the Cockerell Building next door to the college. Accommodation, though guaranteed for three years, varies in quality depending on how lucky you are. Most first years are housed in Harvey Court, a five-minute walk away across the river. Adjacent to Harvey Court is the £13-million Stephen Hawking Building, named after the college's most famous fellow, which opened in October 2006. Providing en-suite accommodation for 75 students and eight fellows, the building boasts some of the highest-standard student accommodation in Cambridge. Third years live in the idyllic surroundings of the old courts. Those unlucky in the room ballot though, especially second years, live in college hostels over a mile away. An ongoing gripe is that undergraduates are obliged to eat in Hall at least 45 times a term, whilst self-catering facilities can be poor. Some argue that enforced Halls ensure that students meet regularly though – and they tend to be louder and more informal than at other colleges. The college is working to diminish its public school reputation – whereas not long ago only 42 per cent of students came from state schools, most recently that figure has risen to 57 per cent. Caius has one of the best and most competitive boat clubs in the university, but most sports are fairly relaxed. A lively social scene is helped by the fortnightly "bops".

Homerton

Homerton College, Cambridge CB2 8PH

01223 747252 (admissions)　　　admissions@homerton.cam.ac.uk　　www.homerton.cam.ac.uk

Undergraduates: 600　　　Postgraduates: 640 PGCE and other graduate courses

Homerton's origins were in 18th-century London, and it moved to Cambridge in 1894. For the last 30 years Homerton has been an Approved Society within the University, even though students have been university members throughout that time. In February 2009, however, the University Council approved a proposal to give Homerton full College status, which Homerton hopes will be completed by the end of the year. Known primarily as a teaching college, Homerton has recently started accepting students onto a wide range of courses. The college will continue to specialise in education, including teacher training – through the BA degree and the postgraduate certificate in education (PGCE) courses offered by the Faculty of Education – but now offers places for many of the other courses offered by the university at both undergraduate and postgraduate level. All first years have rooms in college in new accommodation blocks. In the second year, accommodation may be in college or in private rented houses, but final-year students can live in if they wish. Due to its history as an institution for Education Studies, the student body is predominantly female and from a state-school background. The college's position, a mile from the city centre in its own large grounds, means that the onus is on Homerton students to take the initiative and get involved in university activities. Many do. Homerton is like the other undergraduate colleges in what it offers, and students can take advantage of Formal Hall, sport (there are on-site playing fields), music and drama.

Hughes Hall

Hughes Hall, Wollaston Road, Cambridge CB1 2EW
01223 334897 (admissions)   ugadmissions@hughes.cam.ac.uk   www.hughes.cam.ac.uk
Undergraduates: 70   Postgraduates: 430

Hughes Hall admits mature undergraduates over the age of 21 and affiliated students (who already have a good honours degree from another university). The college is the oldest graduate college in the University, founded in 1885 for the training of graduate women teachers. Since then it has become a lively and cosmopolitan community of 500 mature undergraduate and graduate students studying for nearly all the degrees offered by the University. It has a large international community, and supports the application of overseas students. Accommodation within the college is available for all single undergraduates and affiliated students throughout their course. The college is centrally located, with a new accommodation block and attractive gardens. Students must be happy – they say the worst thing about the college is that no one knows where it is.

Jesus

Jesus College, Cambridge CB5 8BL
01223 339455 (admissions)   undergraduate-admissions@jesus.cam.ac.uk   www.jesus.cam.ac.uk
Undergraduates: 489   Postgraduates: 270

For those of a sporting inclination Jesus is perhaps the ideal college. Within its spacious grounds there are football, rugby and cricket pitches, as well as three squash courts and no less than ten tennis courts, while the Cam, and the university boat houses, are just a few hundred yards away. With these facilities, it is hardly surprising that sports, in particular rowing, rugby and hockey, rate high on many students' agendas. That said, sporting prowess is far from the whole story. The music society thrives, and has extensive practice facilities. Although Jesus lacks a theatre of its own, the college is active in university drama. On the academic front, the Fellows-to-undergraduates ratio is generous. There is an excellent and stylish new library which, unlike many college libraries, is open 24 hours. Accommodation is another plus. Rooms in college are guaranteed for all first and half of third-year students. All other students live in attractive college houses directly opposite the college. Regardless of where you are placed though, you are likely to have good lodgings, though first years have complained that their cooking facilities are poor. Over half the undergraduates are state educated and the college is keen to encourage more applications from the state sector. The college grounds – particularly The Chimney walkway to the porter's lodge – are attractive.

King's

King's College, Cambridge CB2 1ST

01223 331255 (admissions) undergraduate.admissions@kings.cam.ac.uk www.kings.cam.ac.uk

Undergraduates: 400   Postgraduates: 280

King's "right-on" reputation has become something of an in-joke. Despite its grand surroundings, it has done away with many Cambridge traditions. Gone are gowns, a Fellows' "High Table" at dinner, and superior rooms to reward good results. Formal Halls are banned, and May Balls replaced by June Events. The college was one of the first of the all-male colleges to admit women, and is actively involved in an initiative to increase the number of candidates from socially and educationally disadvantaged backgrounds. The college has a 70:30 state-to-independent ratio. The students' union is active politically. The famous King's Bar is painted a socialist red, with some students insisting on painting on a yellow hammer and sickle for the full effect. The college has fewer undergraduates than the grandeur of its buildings might suggest, one result being that accommodation is guaranteed, either in college or in hostels. With the highest ratio of Fellows to undergraduates in Cambridge, it is not surprising that King's has been one of the most academically successful colleges. Sport at King's is anything but competitive. The world-famous chapel and choir form the heart of an outstanding music scene.

Lucy Cavendish

Lucy Cavendish College, Cambridge CB3 0BU

01223 330280 (admissions)   lcc-admissions@lists.cam.ac.uk   www.lucy-cav.cam.ac.uk

Undergraduates: 127 (women only)   Postgraduates: 115

Lucy Cavendish pitches itself as the college for "smart, inspirational women". Since its creation in 1965, Lucy Cavendish has given hundreds of women over the age of 21 the opportunity to read for Tripos subjects. A number of its students had already started careers and/or families when they decided to enter higher education. The college seeks to offer financial support to those with family responsibilities, though as yet it has no childcare facilities. The college has particularly strong provision for the teaching of medicine and veterinary medicine. Accommodation is provided for all who request it, either in the college's three Victorian houses or in its three modern residential blocks. The college's small size enables all students to get to know one another, within an intimate and informal atmosphere. All the Fellows are women. For subjects not covered by the Fellowship, there is a well-established network of university teachers. One concern amongst students is the lack of a vibrant social atmosphere, meaning students have to venture elsewhere for fun, though the college does have close ties with other mature colleges.

Magdalene

Magdalene College, Cambridge CB3 0AG

01223 332135 (admissions)   admissions@magd.cam.ac.uk   www.magd.cam.ac.uk

Undergraduates: 345   Postgraduates: 239

As the last college to admit women (1988), Magdalene has still to throw off a lingering image as home to hordes of public school hearties. However, the college now takes just under half of its undergraduates come from the independent sector, and about half of those undergraduates are now women. That said, the sporty emphasis, on rugby and rowing in particular, is undeniable. The nearby playing fields are shared with St John's and the college has its own Eton fives court. Magdalene's academic standing has improved of late – it finished fifth in last year's Tompkins table, with 25 per cent of its undergraduates achieving a First. Students are heavily involved in university-wide activities from drama to journalism, as well as sport. Accommodation is provided for all undergraduates, either in college or in one of 21 houses and hostels, "mostly on our doorstep". Magdalene is proud of its river frontage, the longest in the university, which is especially memorable in the summer. One attractive prospect for undergraduates is that they may also be eligible for travel grants from the college, ranging from £50 to £2,000.

Murray Edwards

Murray Edwards College, Huntingdon Road, Cambridge CB3 0DF
01223 762229 (admissions) admissions@murrayedwards.cam.ac.uk www.murrayedwards.cam.ac.uk
Undergraduates: 360 (women only)   Postgraduates: 99

Murray Edwards College was until last year known as New Hall. The college was established in 1954 to allow more young women to study in Cambridge, but was never awarded a name. It became known as "New Hall", and remained unnamed for more than 50 years. Last year however, Ros Smith, a New Hall graduate, and her husband, Steve Edwards, gave the college a £30-million endowment, and, at last, a new name. One of three remaining all-women colleges, Murray Edwards enjoys a largely erroneous reputation for feminism and academic underachievement, not helped by a much-publicised whitewash on *University Challenge*. The college occupies a modern grey-brick site next door to Fitzwilliam. The college has a large state-school intake: this winter, the state-to-independent ratio was 65:35. The college lays claim to certain paradoxes. While a rent strike early in the 1990s is still remembered, tradition is far from rejected. The following year saw New Hall's first-ever May Ball, an event hosted jointly with Sidney Sussex. Its results regularly place the college near the bottom of the academic league. The college is known for its unusual split-level bar, but many students choose to socialise elsewhere. Accommodation has improved in recent years, with new rooms, many en suite, now on offer. Sport is a good mixture of high-fliers and enthusiasts, with grounds, shared with Fitzwilliam, half a mile away. The college is particularly proud of its collection of contemporary women's art – the second largest in the world.

Newnham

Newnham College, Cambridge CB3 9DF
01223 335783 (admissions)   adm@newn.cam.ac.uk   www.newn.cam.ac.uk
Undergraduates: 380 (women only)   Postgraduates: 170

Newnham has long had to battle with a blue-stocking image. Its entry in the university prospectus used to insist that it "is not a nunnery" and that the atmosphere in this all-women college is no stricter than elsewhere. It even has a "Newnham Nuns" drinking club to make the point. With about a 55:45 state–independent ratio, the college has also cast off a reputation for public-school dominance. Newnham is in the perfect location for humanities students, with the lecture halls and libraries of the Sidgwick Site just across the road. The college still has all-women Fellows. Around 95 per cent of students live in for all three years. This is not to say that ventures into the social, sporting and artistic life of the university are the exception rather than the rule. Newnham students are anything but insular. As well as being blessed with the largest and most beautiful lawns in Cambridge, Newnham has its playing fields and tennis courts on site. The boat club has been notably successful, while the college competes to a high standard in tennis, cricket and a number of minority sports.

Pembroke

Pembroke College, Cambridge CB2 1RF
01223 338154 (admissions)   adm@pem.cam.ac.uk   www.pem.cam.ac.uk
Undergraduates: 400   Postgraduates: 294

Another college with a reputation for public school dominance, Pembroke's image is changing: today, 54 per cent of its intake come from state schools. Rowing and rugby still feature prominently, but with women undergraduates recently outnumbering men for the first time, its traditional reputation is giving way to a more relaxed atmosphere. Around two thirds of all undergraduates live in college, including all first years. The rest are housed in fairly central college hostels, though the standards of these are variable. That said, the college has recently completed a new student accommodation block that contains a gym, music rooms, and a new art room. Academically, Pembroke is towards the top of the Tompkins Table, and has been steadily improving over the last ten years. Engineering and natural sciences are thought to have the largest number of undergraduates. The bar is inevitably the social focal point, but a restriction on advertising means that Pembroke "bops" attract few students from other colleges. The Pembroke Players generally stage one play a term in the Old Reader, which also doubles as the college cinema, and many Pembroke students are involved in university dramatics. The Old Library is a popular venue for classical concerts. Indeed music is a Pembroke strength. Nestled in one of the quads is the college chapel, built by Sir Christopher Wren. In a city of memorable college gardens, Pembroke's are among the best.

Peterhouse

Peterhouse, Cambridge CB2 1RD
01223 338223 (admissions)   admissions@pet.cam.ac.uk   www.pet.cam.ac.uk
Undergraduates: 251   Postgraduates: 156

The oldest and amongst the smallest of the colleges, Peterhouse has also had to contend with an image problem. But while by no means as reactionary as its critics would have it, Peterhouse is certainly not overly progressive, and 60 per cent of its students are male. However the state–independent ratio is around 54:46, about average among the colleges. The college's diminutive size inevitably makes for an intimate atmosphere, but this does not mean that its undergraduates never venture beyond the college bar. Peterhouse is known above all as "the history college", and while history is indeed seen as a traditional strength, there are thought to be no more historians than physicists or engineers. Academically, the college is generally a mid-table performer, but last year rose from 25th to 18th in the Tompkins Table. Relations between students and Fellows broke down after the cancellation in November 2007 of the 2008 May Ball. Student protests and boycotts of Hall and the college bar followed. The 13th-century candle-lit dining hall provides what by common consent is the best food in the university. The student newspaper *Varsity* reported this year that the college's rents are the lowest in Cambridge, and undergraduates live in for at least two years, the remainder choosing rooms in college hostels, most within ten minutes' walk. The sports grounds are shared with Clare and are about a mile away. The college teams have a less than glittering reputation, not surprisingly, given its size.

Queens'

Queens' College, Cambridge CB3 9ET

01223 335540 (admissions)   admissions@queens.cam.ac.uk   www.queens.cam.ac.uk

Undergraduates: 490   Postgraduates: 350

There is a strong case for claiming that Queens' is the most tightly knit college in the university. With all undergraduates housed in college for the full three years, a large and popular bar (open all day) and outstanding facilities, including Cambridge's first college nursery, it is easy to see why. Queens' also has the distinction of attracting an above-average number of applicants. The state–independent ratio for new undergraduates is 54:46, but only 42 per cent of students are female. Though not to all tastes, the mix of architectural styles, ranging from the medieval Old Court to the 1980s Cripps Complex, is as great as any in the university. In addition to three excellent squash courts, the Cripps Complex is also home to Fitzpatrick Hall, a multipurpose venue containing Cambridge's best-equipped college theatre and the hub of Queens' renowned social scene. Friday and Saturday night "bops" are extremely popular. The college has an excellent academic record. Apart from squash, Queens' is not especially sporty, although there is a gym and squash courts on site. The playing fields (one mile away) are shared with Robinson.

Robinson

Robinson College, Cambridge CB3 9AN

01223 339143 (admissions)   apply@robinson.cam.ac.uk   www.robinson.cam.ac.uk

Undergraduates: 383   Postgraduates: 174

Robinson is the youngest college in Cambridge and admitted its first students in 1979. Its unspectacular architecture has earned it the nickname "the car park". On the other hand, having been built with one eye on the conference trade, rooms are more comfortable than most, and the majority have their own bathrooms and online links to the university computer network. Almost all students live in college or in houses in the attractive gardens. The college is one of the few with rooms adapted for disabled students. Robinson has sometimes been close to the bottom of the academic tables. After a brief surge up the academic tables a couple of years ago, it has fallen back to middle of the Tompkins league once more. One in four Fellows are women, one of the highest proportions in any mixed college. Its youth and admissions policy (64 per cent are from state schools) ensure that Robinson has one of the more unpretentious atmospheres. The auditorium is the largest of any college and is a popular venue for films, plays and concerts. The college fields (shared with Queens') are home to excellent rugby and hockey sides, and the boat club is also successful. The college has optional twice-weekly formal halls where students describe the atmosphere as "very down to earth". The college has two newly built graduate buildings providing state-of-the-art facilities as well as 48 new graduate rooms.

St Catharine's

St Catharine's College, Cambridge CB2 1RL
01223 338319 (admissions)   undergraduate.admissions@caths.cam.ac.uk   www.caths.cam.ac.uk
Undergraduates: 436   Postgraduates: 200

Known to everyone as "Catz", this is a medium-sized, 17th-century college standing opposite Corpus Christi on King's Parade. The principal college site, with its distinctive three-sided main court, though small, provides accommodation for all its first and third years. The majority of second years live in flats at St Chad's Court, a ten-minute walk away. Catz was once not considered one of the leading colleges academically. However, its status is much changed. Having been top of the Tompkins Table in 2005, the college has hovered around top ten ever since. It has a reputation as a friendly place. About half of the students are women, and the split between independent and state school undergraduates accepted to the college is 43:57. A new library and JCR have improved the facilities considerably, and there is a strong musical tradition. College social life centres on the large bar, which has been likened, among other things, to a ski chalet or sauna. St Catharine's recently proudly announced that it was the first college to be awarded Fair Trade status. With a reputation for being sporting rather than sporty, Catz is one of the few colleges that regularly puts out three rugby XVs, and also has a good record in football and hockey. The playing fields are a ten-minute walk away and the college boasts its own Astroturf pitch.

St Edmund's College

St Edmund's College, Mount Pleasant, Cambridge CB3 0BN
01223 336086 (admissions)   admissions@st-edmunds.cam.ac.uk   www.st-edmunds.cam.ac.uk
Undergraduates: 100   Postgraduates: 230

St Edmund's is primarily a graduate college, with over half its students coming from overseas. Of 330 members, there are 100 mature undergraduates (at least 21 years of age) including affiliated students, who have a prior degree from another university. The college is set in quiet grounds and is conveniently placed to the northwest of the city centre. The college buildings currently house 218 single students, and some of the accommodation has been constructed specifically for students with physical disabilities. In addition there are six maisonettes that are suitable for students with children, and eight flats for married couples. A new building with an additional 70 student rooms opened in October 2006. The college has recently invested in a new library, teaching rooms, a gym and music practice rooms. In recent times, St Edmund's students have become regulars in the university sports team, earning an impressive number of "blues" (awarded for competing in a varsity match against Oxford), whilst a number also represent their own countries as well. The college's lively student executive organise regular social events in the bar and pool room.

St John's

St John's College, Cambridge CB2 1TP

01223 338703 (admissions)   admissions@joh.cam.ac.uk   www.joh.cam.ac.uk

Undergraduates: 580   Postgraduates: 390

Second only to Trinity in size and wealth, St John's has an enviable reputation in most fields and is sometimes resented for it. The wealth translates into excellent accommodation in college for almost all undergraduates throughout their three years, as well as book grants and a new 24-hour library. St John's riches ensure the best possible facilities, both academic and social. Its May Ball, a biennial end-of-year party was voted the "seventh-best party in the world". St John's has a formidable academic record, and English and natural sciences have been recent strengths. A reputation for heartiness persists and the female intake is below average at around 40 per cent. St John's receives relatively few applications from state-school students, and the latest figures saw the intake of state students fall to 38 per cent, joint-lowest among the college's with Trinity. The boat club has a powerful reputation, but rugby, hockey and cricket are all traditionally strong. In such a large community, however, all should be able to find their own level. Extensive playing fields shared with Magdalene are a few hundred yards away, and the boathouse is extremely good. The college film society organises popular screenings in the Fisher Building, which also contains an art studio and drawing office for architecture and engineering students. Music is dominated by the world-famous choir. Excellent as the facilities are, some students find that the sheer size of St John's can be daunting, and this makes it hard to settle into. Others argue that such a large college provides a diverse atmosphere where "everybody can find their niche".

Selwyn

Selwyn College, Cambridge CB3 9DQ

01223 335896 (admissions)   admissions@sel.cam.ac.uk   www.sel.cam.ac.uk

Undergraduates: 377   Postgraduates: 150

Despite its reputation as one of the more relaxed and down-to-earth colleges, Selwyn made an appearancein 2008 at the top of the Tompkins Table. Nearly a third of all its undergraduates received a first class degree that year, cementing its reputation as a heavyweight academic college. Before then, the college had made a slow creep up the table, finishing fourth in 2007 from midway down the table the year before. Nonetheless, one undergraduate described the college as "the least overtly intellectual college". Selwyn has a relatively unpressured atmosphere behind "the Backs", and near the Sidgwick site where most humanities are taught, making it an ideal position for arts and humanities students, though engineering is also a perceived strength. One of the first colleges to go mixed (1976), now approaching half of Selwyn's undergraduates are female. Its state–independent ratio stands at about 55:45. A major new development means the college can now provide undergraduate accommodation to all students on site for the whole time they are at Selwyn. Students also claim that the food at hall has improved dramatically following a joint effort with the head chef. The college was a leader in IT provision, being one of the first to provide all college rooms with online connections, and there are two well-stocked computer rooms. As well as the usual college groups, the music society is especially well supported. The bar is popular if a little "hotel-like".

Selwyn bucks the trend for a summer ball or June event, and hosts the popular snow ball each December. In sport, the novice boat crews have done well in recent years, as have the hockey and badminton sides, but the emphasis is as much on enjoyment as achievement. The grounds are shared with King's and are three quarters of a mile away.

Sidney Sussex

Sidney Sussex College, Cambridge CB2 3HU
01223 338872 (admissions)   admissions@sid.cam.ac.uk   www.sid.cam.ac.uk
Undergraduates: 370   Postgraduate: 190

Students at this small, central college are forever the butt of jokes about Sidney being mistaken for the branch of Sainsbury's over the road. Despite its location in the heart of the city, the college's large private gardens award the college an unexpectedly tranquil environment behind the redbrick walls. All students are housed either in college or one of 11 nearby hostels. The college's unpretentious atmosphere is cultivated by the students, 62 per cent of whom are from state schools, and half of whom are women. Despite its size, Sidney has an active social life, boasting one of the few student-run bars in the university and maintaining fortnightly "bop" dances like many of the larger colleges. The college choir has made some critically acclaimed recordings, and tours regularly in the UK and overseas. Sports are taken less seriously, with enthusiasm and enjoyment the focus of the students' sporting endeavours. Exam results at the college improved steadily for a number of years, although the last two years have seen a slight decline: the college fell from 9th, its best score in the Tompkins table in 2006, to 14th this year. Sports grounds are shared with Christ's and are a 10-minute cycle ride away. Sidney's size means that the college is a tight-knit community, although some students find such insularity suffocating rather than supportive.

Trinity

Trinity College, Cambridge CB2 1TQ
01223 338422 (admissions)   admissions@trin.cam.ac.uk   www.trin.cam.ac.uk
Undergraduates: 655   Postgraduates: 357

The legend that you can walk from Oxford to Cambridge without ever leaving Trinity land typifies Cambridge undergraduates' views about the college, even if it is not true. Indeed, the college is almost synonymous with size and wealth – it is the largest and wealthiest of all Cambridge colleges. Founded by Henry VIII, its endowment is almost as big as the other colleges' put together. There was a view that every Trinity student was an arrogant public schoolboy. Though less true than it was, only about 38 per cent of undergraduates came from state schools, and only 35 per cent of undergraduates are women, among the lowest proportions in any college. Being rich, Trinity offers book grants to every student as well as generous travel grants and spacious, reasonably priced rooms in college for all first and third-year students as well as many second years. The rooms are amongst the cheapest at the university as they are subsidised by the college. The college generally features in the top ten academically, coming third last year. Trinity has a well-established reputation as a centre of excellence for sciences and maths, but is also strong in a number of arts subjects. Christopher Wren designed the college's iconic library, which backs onto the river. Trinity rarely fails to do well in most sports, with cricket in the forefront. The playing fields are half a mile away.

Trinity Hall

Trinity Hall, Cambridge CB2 1TJ
01223 332535 (admissions)   admissions@trinhall.cam.ac.uk   www.trinhall.cam.ac.uk
Undergraduates: 369   Postgraduates: 241

Trinity Hall or "Tit Hall" is one of the oldest and smallest colleges in Cambridge, resulting in a remarkably close community of students. The outstanding performance of its oarsmen has ensured the prevailing view of Trinity Hall as a "boaty" college, but it is also known for its drama, music and bar. The Preston Society is one of the better college drama groups, and stages regular productions. Weekly recitals keep the music society busy. The small bar is invariably packed. Not surprisingly, many undergraduates rarely feel the need to go elsewhere for their entertainment, although there has been considerable involvement in the students' union recently. The college is strong academically, despite an unusually low position in the recent tables, with equal numbers of students studying arts and sciences. Almost half of the undergraduates are women, and in recent years the college has dramatically increased the number of state-school students at the college, who now make up 64 per cent of new intakes. All first years and approximately half the third years live in college, which is situated on the Backs behind Caius. The remainder take rooms either in two large hostels close to the sports ground, or in college accommodation about five minutes' walk away. The college offers a number of travel bursaries and hardship funds for current students.

Wolfson

Wolfson College, Barton Road, Cambridge CB3 9BB
01223 335918   ug-admissions@wolfson.cam.ac.uk   www.wolfson.cam.ac.uk
Undergraduates: 90   Postgraduates: 510

Wolfson, although primarily a graduate college, has about 90 mature or affiliated undergraduates. Wolfson is one of three colleges that admit students for the graduate course in medicine. Its life is enriched by the high proportion (about 50 per cent) of overseas students. The relationship between senior and junior members is informal; common rooms, facilities and social activities are equally open to both. The college has a relaxed atmosphere – the average age is 27, about 50 per cent of students come from state schools, and the college regularly hosts senior academic visitors, journalists and specialists. The college is situated in west Cambridge, close to the University Library and the arts faculties – or as the students say, nearer to the M11 than the Cam. The main buildings of Wolfson College were built in the 1970s around attractive garden courts. The college has accommodation for most students who want to live in college. There is also some accommodation for couples.

University Profiles

The following profiles contain valuable information about each university. Each profile includes some standard information, which is described below:

- the postal address.
- the telephone number for admission enquiries.
- the e-mail or web address for admissions and prospectus enquiries.
- the address of the main university website.
- the address of the students' union website.

The Times **rankings** These figures are taken from the main League Table. See chapter 2, *The Top Universities*, for this table and the sources of the data. The headings, which follow those in the main League Table, are fully explained in Chapter 2.

Undergraduates The first figure is for full-time undergraduates. The second figure (in brackets) gives the number of part-time undergraduates. The figures are for 2007–08, and are the most recent provided by HESA.

Postgraduates The first figure is for full-time postgraduates. The second figure (in brackets) gives the number of part-time postgraduates. The figures are for 2007–08, and are the most recent provided by HESA.

Mature students The percentage of first degree entrants who were 21 or over at the start of their studies. The figures are from 2006–07, and are from HESA.

Overseas students The number of undergraduate overseas students (both EU and non-EU) as a percentage of full-time undergraduates. The figures relate to 2007–08, and are based on HESA data.

Applications per place The number of applicants per place for 2008 as calculated by UCAS.

From state-school sector The number of young full-time undergraduate entrants from state schools or colleges in 2006–07 as a percentage of total young entrants. The figures are published by HESA.

From working-class homes The number of young full-time undergraduate entrants in 2006–07 whose parental occupations are skilled, manual, semi-skilled or unskilled (Social Classes IIIM–V) as a percentage of total young entrants. The figures are published by HESA.

Accommodation The information was obtained through a survey made of all university accommodation services, and their help is gratefully acknowledged.

Undergraduate fees and bursaries A summary of the fees and bursaries being offered in 2009 unless otherwise indicated. This is not comprehensive, so check the details with the individual universities and see chapter 7, *The Cost of Studying*. The information was obtained with the assistance of the individual universities and their help is gratefully acknowledged. Bursary schemes can change every year and must be checked with universities. Universities also have many scholarship schemes, for example, to encourage applicants for particular subjects or from particular areas. Again, it is essential to check university websites. Wherever possible, a specific website address is given.

Comments on campus facilities apply to the universities' own sites only. New universities, in particular, operate "franchised" courses at further education colleges, which are likely to have lower levels of provision. Prospective applicants should check out the library and social facilities before accepting a place away from the parent institution.

Some famous names are missing from our university listings: the Open University, the separate business and medical schools, Birkbeck College and Cranfield University among them. Their omission is no reflection on their quality, simply a function of their particular roles. The *Guide* is based on provision for full-time undergraduates and the factors judged to influence this. The Open University (**www.open.ac.uk**), though Britain's biggest university, with 178,000 students, is not included because most of the measures used in our listing do not apply to it. As a non-residential, largely part-time institution, Birkbeck College, London (**www.bbk.ac.uk**), could also not be compared in many key areas. Cranfield (**www.cranfield.ac.uk**) no longer offers undergraduate degrees while Manchester Business School (**www.mbs.ac.uk**) and London Business School (**www.lbs.ac.uk**) are also entirely postgraduate. Specialist institutions such as the Royal College of Art (**www.rca.ac.uk**) and St George's Hospital Medical School (**sgul.ac.uk**) could not fairly be compared with generalist universities. A number of colleges with degree-awarding powers also do not appear because they have yet to be granted university status. However, at the end of the book, we list higher education colleges with their addresses and websites.

The University of London is a federal university composed of a number of institutions. In this profile section, the pages on the University of London (pages 420–1) outline the colleges of the university that are not listed separately in this guide. There are separate entries on the leading undergraduate colleges. Founded in 1893, the University of Wales remained a federal university until 2007, becoming the degree-awarding authority to accredited higher education institutions in Wales. In addition it plays an active role in promoting Welsh language and culture. See **www.wales.ac.uk**. The leading Welsh higher education institutions have their own entries. During 2009 Lampeter and Trinity University College Carmarthen merge to form Trinity Saint David.

University of Aberdeen

Aberdeen has been marking the early years of its sixth century with a series of ambitious projects. Aided by one the most successful fundraising schemes at any UK university, it has been recruiting high-calibre academics and has transformed the student services. Next on the list is a £28-million sports centre, due to open in the autumn of 2009, and a futuristic new library costing £57 million, planned for 2011.

The university built on a sharply improved performance in the 2001 Research Assessment Exercise and had some good results in 2008, when more than half of the work submitted was judged to be world-leading or inter-nationally excellent. Health services research and theology, divinity and religious studies produced the best results in the UK, while computer science and informatics, anthropology, English and history also did particularly well.

Research income grew by more than a third over five years, cementing Aberdeen's ambitions to be recognised among the top 100 universities in the world.

Teaching audits carried out in the early years of the decade followed the successful pattern established in the original round of inspections. The 7.5 per cent growth in applications at the start of 2009 was among the biggest in Scotland, following two years of decline.

Female students now outnumber the men, but Aberdeen still considers itself a "balanced" university because roughly half of its students study medicine, science or engineering, and half the arts or social sciences. Most are not even admitted to a particular department, allowing them to try out three or four subjects before committing themselves at the end of their first or even second year. The modular system, covering almost 600 first-degree programmes, is so flexible that the majority of students change their intended degree before graduation.

Medicine, law and divinity head Aberdeen's traditional strengths – the university established the English-speaking world's first chair in medicine and has produced its share of advances since. The Institute of Medical Sciences, which has brought together all Aberdeen's work in this area, boasts state-of-the-art laboratory facilities. Another £16.5 million has been invested on the same site in a new teaching and learning centre for anatomy and clinical skills.

Biological sciences have developed considerably in recent years, becoming second only to the social sciences in terms of size. Biomedicine is particularly strong, and the university's links with the oil industry show in geology's high reputation.

King's College
Aberdeen AB24 3FX
01224 272090/91 (admissions)
sras@abdn.ac.uk
www.abdn.ac.uk
www.ausa.org.uk

The Times Rankings
Overall Ranking: =33

Student satisfaction:	=8	(81%)
Research quality:	=30	(1.9)
Entry standards:	33	(363)
Student–staff ratio:	39	(15.1)
Services & facilities/student:	43	(£1,194)
Expected completion rate:	89	(77.3%)
Good honours:	35	(67.6%)
Graduate prospects:	31	(74.4%)

The university is also the main centre for agriculture in Scotland and part of a new European network for the subject.

Today's university is a fusion of two ancient institutions which came together in 1860. With King's College dating back to 1495 and Marischal College following almost a century later, Aberdeen likes to boast that for 250 years it had as many universities as the whole of England. The original King's College buildings are the focal point of an appealing campus, complete with cobbled main street and some sturdily handsome Georgian buildings, about a mile from the city centre. Medicine is at Foresterhill, a 20-minute walk away, adjoining the Aberdeen Royal Infirmary. Buses link the two sites with the Hillhead residential complex, and there is a free late-night service. The Aberdeen arm of Northern College has now joined the fold and moved to the main campus, restoring the university's original involvement in teacher training, and forming its fifth faculty.

More than a third of all students come from the north of Scotland, but taking one in ten from outside Britain ensures a cosmopolitan atmosphere. Students from England and the 120 nationalities from further afield are generally prepared for Aberdeen's remote location and, although the winters are long, the climate is warmer than the uninitiated might expect. As the

energy capital of Europe, transport links are good. Students find the city lively and welcoming but expensive, although its prosperity does provide a good selection of part-time jobs from the JobLink service.

Student facilities are good: there an NHS medical practice on campus and The Hub brings together dining and retail outlets with support services, including the Accommodation Office and Students' Association. There is also a city centre bar and first-class sports facilities, which will be improved still further with the opening of the new sports centre, part-funded by Aberdeen City Council and Sports Scotland. The ICT network has over 1,000 computers for student use. The university's residential stock has been growing and all new undergraduates are guaranteed a place.

Undergraduate Fees and Bursaries

- Scottish-domiciled and EU students: no fees payable.
- Non-Scottish UK-domiciled student fees: £1,820 a year (£2,895 medicine).
- International student fees: £9,250–£11,500; £22,500 (medicine).
- Scholarships based on circumstances or by competition.
- For full details see the university's website: www.abdn.ac.uk/sras/undergraduate/ bursaries_scholarships.shtml

---

Students

Undergraduates:	9,020	(1,375)
Postgraduates:	2,395	(1,345)
Mature students:	16.6%	
Overseas students:	14.4%	
Applications per place:	4.7	
From state-sector schools:	81.8%	
From working-class homes:	25.3%	

For detailed information about fees, grants and bursaries and how they work, see chapter 7.

Accommodation

Number of places and costs refer to 2009–10

University-provided places: about 2,504

Percentage catered: 29%

Catered costs: £124–£145 a week (38 weeks).

Self-catered costs: £72–£116 a week (38–40 weeks).

First-year students are guaranteed accommodation.

International students: as above.

Contact: studentaccomm@abdn.ac.uk

University of Abertay

Abertay doubled in size during the 1990s and has grown further since up-front tuition fees were abolished for Scottish students. There are now more than 5,000 students, mainly in Dundee, but with several hundred in locations as far afield as Malaysia, Singapore and India. The former central institution has enjoyed a series of good teaching scores and has improved a projected dropout rate that had crept up above one in five of all those starting degrees. Almost a quarter of the undergraduates come from socially deprived areas and practically all attended state schools. More than a third come from working-class homes.

The former Dundee Institute of Technology had already established its academic credentials when university status arrived in 1994, with teaching in economics rated more highly than in some of Scotland's elite universities. Subsequent assessments were solid, without living up to that early promise, but economics, engineering and environmental sciences were given the highest possible rating in later inspections. More recently, two of the first four degree accreditations awarded by Skillset, the Government-sponsored training council for the creative industries, went to Abertay courses. The university has since been accredited as the first Interactive Media Academy in the UK, working with industrial partners from across the broadcast, interactive and wider digital media sectors.

Research is not being ignored. Abertay is proud of its record in establishing a series of specialist centres, in areas as diverse as wood technology, urban water systems, bioinformatics, earth systems and environmental sciences. The university opened Europe's first research centre dedicated to computer games and digital entertainment and a major environmental science centre. Earth systems and environmental sciences and general engineering, mineral and mining engineering produced the best scores in the latest research assessments. Environmental sciences also had the best rating in Scotland in the 2001 RAE.

Abertay plays to its strengths with a limited range of courses, and is not shy about its achievements. Among them is a high-tech approach that permeates all four of the university's schools, while spending on libraries and computers is among the highest per student in Britain, providing one computer for every four students.

Based mainly in the centre of Dundee, all the university's buildings are within 15 minutes' walk of each other. The imposing Dudhope Castle is a conference and events venue, but the other buildings are more

---

Bell Street
Dundee DD1 1HG
01382 308080
sro@abertay.ac.uk
www.abertay.ac.uk
www.abertaystudents.com

The Times Rankings
Overall Ranking: 95

Student satisfaction:	–	(–)
Research quality:	=71	(0.4)
Entry standards:	63	(279)
Student–staff ratio:	=89	(19.8)
Services & facilities/student:	11	(£1,603)
Expected completion rate:	=108	(70.1%)
Good honours:	104	(48.3%)
Graduate prospects:	112	(53.3%)

modern and functional. New facilities have been added gradually, from the £6-million student centre, which opened in 2005, to the innovative White Space facility, the university's flagship creative learning and working environment, where students work alongside industry professionals who are working on real commercial or broadcast projects. A 500-bed student village is next on the list, due to open at the start of the academic year in 2010.

Entrance requirements have been rising, although for most courses other than high-demand areas such as computer games, they are still modest. Well-qualified A-level students are eligible for direct entry into second year. Degrees are predominantly vocational, with more subjects being added every year. Forensic science, mental nursing, visual communications and media design, computer arts and sports coaching and development have been followed recently by the likes of food and consumer sciences, creative sound production, and ethical hacking and countermeasures. All courses can be taken on a part-time basis, and the aim is for new programmes to offer students the chance to spend at least 30 per cent of their time in industry.

The university's revamped modular degree scheme means that undergraduates take a maximum of eight modules a year. First-year students are assessed by coursework alone in the first semester, with examinations at the end of the year. Students can complete a Certificate of Higher Education after one year, a diploma after two, an ordinary degree after three, or honours in four years. Abertay is piloting a new problem-based learning approach among first-year students focusing on real-world issues and learning by doing rather than sitting in lectures.

Dundee has a large student population and is improving as a youth centre where the cost of living is modest. More than 30 per cent of the undergraduates are over 21 on entry, many living locally. This lifts the pressure on university-owned beds sufficiently to allow all first years to be guaranteed accommodation.

Undergraduate Fees and Bursaries

Scottish-domiciled and EU students: no fees payable.
- Non-Scottish UK-domiciled student fees: £1,820 a year.
- International student fees: £8,150
- Scholarships based on circumstances or by competition.
- For full details see the university's website: www.abertay.ac.uk

Students		
Undergraduates:	3,250	(305)
Postgraduates:	375	(210)
Mature students:	35.3%	
Overseas students:	18.2%	
Applications per place:	3.9	
From state-sector schools:	96.5%	
From working-class homes:	37.0%	

For detailed information about fees, grants and bursaries and how they work, see chapter 7.

Accommodation

Number of places and costs refer to 2009–10
University-provided places: 500
Percentage catered: 0%
Self-catered costs: £58.00–£98.50 a week (37 or 38 weeks).
New first years are given priority provided conditions are met. Some residential restrictions.
International students: prioritised by distance from Dundee.
Contact: accommo@abertay.ac.uk

Aberystwyth University

The oldest of the Welsh universities, Aberystwyth has changed its title from the University of Wales, Aberystwyth, to emphasise its independence and is now awarding its own degrees. Aber has long prided itself on a modern outlook: the modular degree system has been running since 1993, covering academic and vocational courses, and the principle of flexibility was established long before that. Uniquely in the UK, every student is offered the opportunity of a year's work experience in commerce, industry or the public sector, either at home or abroad. Students who have taken advantage of the scheme have achieved better than average degrees and enhanced their employment prospects. The mix served Aberystwyth well in the National Student Survey, winning it a place in the top 10 per cent of UK universities and making it the clear leader for student satisfaction in Wales. Geography and environmental science, sport and exercise science, Welsh and physics all produced outstanding results.

Aber is always heavily oversubscribed even though the number of places has increased. Over a third of the students are from Wales. An agreement to collaborate with Bangor University in a range of subjects, from business to science, emphasises teaching in Welsh. An attractive seaside location does the university no harm when the applications season comes around. The demand for places was up by more than any other university in Wales in 2008 and a 12 per cent increase at the start of 2009 underlined its popularity.

The university has expanded significantly in recent years, with a new School of Management and Business as well as a department of Sports and Exercise Science among the additions. A £3.6-million centre for theatre, film and television studies, and a purpose-built sports and exercise science centre are among the latest developments on the Penglais campus, which overlooks the town. A new building for the highly rated International Politics Department opened in 2006 and a £10-million Visualisation Centre followed in 2007, providing virtual reality facilities for academic and industrial partnerships.

More than 90 per cent of the undergraduates come from state schools or colleges – a far higher proportion than the mix of subjects would imply – but less than 30 per cent come from working-class homes and only about half that number hail from areas that send few students to higher education. However, the dropout rate of around 10 per cent is one of the lowest in Wales.

In 2008 Aberystwyth established the new Institute of Biological, Environmental and Rural Sciences (IBERS) following a merger

Old College
King Street,
Aberystwyth, Ceredigion SY23 2AX
01970 622021 (admissions)
ug-admissions@
  aber.ac.uk
www.aber.ac.uk
www.aberguild.co.uk

The Times Rankings
Overall Ranking: 46

Student satisfaction:	=8	(81%)
Research quality:	=37	(1.7)
Entry standards:	50	(310)
Student–staff ratio:	62	(17.6)
Services & facilities/student:	72	(£1,047)
Expected completion rate:	36	(87.5%)
Good honours:	58	(61.1%)
Graduate prospects:	113	(53.0%)

with the Institute of Grassland and Environmental Research. With over 300 staff and an annual budget in excess of £25 million, IBERS is one of the largest groups of scientists and support staff working in this field in Europe, and caters for more than 1,000 undergraduate and research students. Its remit is to look for creative solutions to some of the major challenges faced by the world today in the areas of sustainable land use, climate change, renewable energy and the security of food and water supplies. The institute gives Aber the widest range of land-related courses in the UK.

Over the next five years, £55 million will be invested in new teaching and research facilities and academic appointments. International politics produced the best results in the 2008 research assessments, with 40 per cent of work rated world-leading. Computer science, geography and earth sciences, Welsh, and theatre, film and television also did well.

Entrance scholarships and bursaries are available in a range of subjects, even though Welsh students have been spared the full impact of top-up fees. Aber boasts one of higher education's most informative websites and also publishes a 12-page guide for parents. There is 24-hour access to the computer network, and the four university libraries are complemented by the National Library of Wales.

The town of Aberystwyth is compact, and travel to other parts of the UK slow, so applicants should be sure that they will be happy to spend three years or more in a tight-knit community. The students' guild is the largest entertainment venue in the region and the arts centre has been extended at a cost of £3.5 million. The alternative prospectus, produced by students, has stopped describing the seaside town of 25,000 people as the "Welsh California", but a recent survey rated it students' favourite university town in the UK. There is plenty of out-of-season accommodation to supplement the university's 3,700 places, all of which are now online. Sports facilities are good for the size of institution, with 50 acres of pitches, a newly refurbished swimming pool, a climbing wall and specialist outdoor facilities for water sports.

Undergraduate Fees and Bursaries

- Fees for UK/EU students: £3,225 (grant of up to £1,940 for Welsh students).
- International student fees: £8,695–£11,030
- Bursary of £1,000 (household income up to £18,370), then sliding scale to £200.
- Scholarships based on circumstances or by competition.
- For full details see the university's website: www.aber.ac.uk/en/scholarships/

Students		
Undergraduates:	6,085	(2,045)
Postgraduates:	710	(1,025)
Mature students:	11.2%	
Overseas students:	9.2%	
Applications per place:	3.2	
From state-sector schools:	94.9%	
From working-class homes:	28.7%	

For detailed information about fees, grants and bursaries and how they work, see chapter 7.

Accommodation

Number of places and costs refer to 2009–10
University-provided places: more than 3,500
Percentage catered: 19%
Catered costs: £87.85–£100.80 a week (30–36 weeks).
Self-catered costs: £67.90–£94.90 a week (30–36 weeks).
First years are guaranteed accommodation.
International students: as above.
Contact: www.aber.ac.uk/residential
accommodation@aber.ac.uk

Anglia Ruskin University

The last university to retain the polytechnic title discarded it in 2005 to avoid confusion among employers and overseas applicants. The former APU took the name of John Ruskin, who founded the Cambridge School of Art, which evolved into the university. Campus developments have continued apace since the change. A new student centre on the larger of the university's two main sites, in Chelmsford, houses support services as well as the normal union facilities, while the music and arts faculty building in Cambridge has new and enhanced teaching and practice facilities.

The university has also acquired the former Homerton College School of Health Studies in Cambridge, after a long period of partnership. A new health and social care building was added in Chelmsford in 2007, with bespoke counselling rooms, simulated hospital wards, operating theatres, and a complementary medicine suite. A £15-million faculty building, which includes a mock courtroom for law students, followed in September 2008. The 22-acre Rivermead campus also boasts an impressive business school and a sports hall.

The region's first polytechnic was an amalgamation of two well-established higher education colleges, but the twin bases in Chelmsford and Cambridge remain distinct. The two very different locations are far enough apart to limit contact, although electronic networking and a central administration mean that key academic facilities are available throughout the university.

The university has more than 24,000 full- and part-time students who are taught primarily on the two main campuses, but also through a growing network of 16 regional partners. Anglia Ruskin has signed up to deliver higher-education courses in Peterborough, Harlow and King's Lynn in partnership with local further education colleges.

East Anglia has always lagged behind other parts of England for participation in higher education and, although the university has continued to grow, it has sometimes struggled to fill its places. Applications showed a spectacular 23 per cent increase in 2007 and have remained healthy since. Nearly all the students attended state schools or colleges and more than a third are from working-class homes.

There were good reports, under the new healthcare assessments, for nursing and midwifery and allied health professions. But only one university had lower satisfaction levels in the National Student Survey published in 2008 – Anglia's scores have fallen consistently since the survey was introduced. Drama produced by far the best results, while the score for teacher

---

Rivermead Campus: Bishop Hall Lane, Chelmsford, Essex CM1 1SQ
Cambridge Campus: East Road, Cambridge CB1 1PT
0845 271 3333 (enquiries)
answers@anglia.ac.uk
www.anglia.ac.uk
www.angliastudent.com

The Times Rankings
Overall Ranking: 103

Student satisfaction:	=106	(68%
Research quality:	=95	(0.2)
Entry standards:	=80	(257)
Student–staff ratio:	=86	(19.7)
Services & facilities/student:	108	(£773)
Expected completion rate:	100	(74.3%)
Good honours:	72	(55.5%)
Graduate prospects:	65	(66.2%)

training was one of the lowest in any subject.

Only 71 academics were entered for the Research Assessment Exercise in 2008, but almost a third of their work was considered world-leading or internationally excellent. All but one of the nine subject areas had some top-rated research, with history, English and psychology producing the best grades.

Each undergraduate has an adviser to help compile a degree package which looks at the chosen subject from different points of view to maximise future job prospects. There is also an Employer Mentoring Scheme for second-year undergraduates planning for the transition from study to work. Each student is carefully matched with a mentor from their chosen career field who volunteers time to provide skills-building, support and encouragement.

Employers play a part in planning courses which are integrated into a modular system which extends from degree level to professional programmes, including a modest selection of vocational two-year Foundation degrees. The Business School, for example, has developed a work-based course with Barclays Bank, where the students are sponsored and salaried for all three years. The programme is now being offered to other businesses in order to aid retention and staff development.

The social scene varies between the two campuses. There is limited collaboration with Cambridge University, for example on the new Cambridge Centre for Cricketing Excellence, and a base for Anglia Ruskin's Rowing Club. Some students find Chelmsford dull, but the social scene is said to be improving. Neither base is far from London by train.

Undergraduate Fees and Bursaries
- Fees for UK/EU students: £3,225
- International student fees: £9,300–£10,925
- Bursary on full grant: £319
- The university does not award bursaries for students on partial maintenance grants.
- Scholarships based on circumstances or by competition.
- For full details see the university's website: www.anglia.ac.uk/ruskin/en/home/student_essentials/student_finance.html

Students

Undergraduates:	9,415	(7,285)
Postgraduates:	715	(1,595)
Mature students:	48.0%	
Overseas students:	8.5%	
Applications per place:	4.1	
From state-sector schools:	98.2%	
From working-class homes:	37.1%	

For detailed information about fees, grants and bursaries and how they work, see chapter 7.

Accommodation
Number of places and costs refer to 2009–10
University-provided places: Cambridge, 831 plus 182 referral rooms; Chelmsford, 511
Percentage catered: 0%
Self-catered costs: Cambridge: £63.65–£120.00 a week; Chelmsford: £83.73–£88.98 a week.
Most first years are accommodated (35-mile radius restriction at Cambridge campus only).
International students: conditions apply.
Contact: cambaccom@anglia.ac.uk
essexaccom@anglia.ac.uk

Aston University

Aston has always gloried in its role as a tight-knit, vocational, urban university, which has swum against the tide of British higher education over the past decade. Small and lively, set in the heart of Birmingham, it has remained resolutely specialist in science and technology, business and languages, concentrating on the sandwich degrees which have served its graduates so well in the employment market. But its strategy up to 2012 is for "sustainable growth in key areas" to provide financial security and the size necessary to boost research performance and become a top ten university.

Aston did break into the top 20 in *The Times* table, although it has slipped back in the past two years, mainly due to less favourable staffing levels and lower spending on student facilities. Despite some modest growth recently, the university still has little more than 7,000 undergraduates. But, with healthy funding from industry and commerce, Aston has been investing in its future, boosting staffing in business, engineering and languages, and developing the campus.

Applications have been steady in recent years, the start of 2009 seeing a small rise that was well below the national average. However, the general trend has been upwards for most of the decade, despite consistent increases in entry grades.

Business and management led the way in the 2008 Research Assessment Exercise, with health subjects also producing good grades from a smaller submission. While 45 per cent of the work submitted in the four subject areas was judged to be world-leading or internationally excellent, the results placed Aston near the bottom of the first tables of traditional universities.

As befits a one-time college of advanced technology, Aston is strong in the sciences, although the highly rated business school accounts for almost half of the students. A £20-million extension to the business school has seen an increase in staff from 80 to over 120.

There is a wide range of combined honours programmes for those who prefer not to specialise. Nearly four out of five Aston graduates go straight into jobs, often returning to the scene of work placements, which have become the norm for 70 per cent of Aston's undergraduates. At the forefront of employer-led degrees, Aston was awarded £1.6 million to set up a Foundation Degree Centre to establish new courses and explore other ways of delivering qualifications. The Foundation degree in electrical power engineering has attracted several large companies, while others include hearing aid technology and pharmaceutical technology.

The university's dropout rate has been

Aston Triangle
Birmingham B4 7ET
0121 204 4444 (general
  admissions)
ugenquiries@aston.ac.uk
www.aston.ac.uk
www.astonguild.org.uk

The Times Rankings
Overall Ranking: 25

Student satisfaction:	13	(80%)
Research quality:	=48	(1.2)
Entry standards:	=31	(365)
Student–staff ratio:	=49	(16.5)
Services & facilities/student:	20	(£1,507)
Expected completion rate:	28	(91.0%)
Good honours:	49	(63.6%)
Graduate prospects:	=17	(78.1%)

improving and another sharp drop took it under 8 per cent in the latest statistics – well below national average for Aston's subjects. Socially, the intake is diverse, with more than a third of the under-graduates coming from working-class homes. Nearly a quarter of the students are from Birmingham and more than four in ten come from the West Midlands more broadly.

The 40-acre campus, a ten-minute walk from the centre of Birmingham, is barely recognisable from the university's early days. Recent building programmes have brought all Aston's residential and academic accommodation onto one carefully landscaped site. Almost half of the undergraduates live on campus, with places guaranteed for first years. A new phase of construction for residential accommodation began in 2008, with a £200-million project adding 2,400 en-suite rooms by 2014. The first block should be open in 2010. Recent developments in sporting facilities have included the addition of a new gymnasium, while an £8-million Academy of Life Sciences merges research with private practice in eye care and brain imaging. Another £4 million has been spent upgrading the IT and computing network.

Aston was among the pioneers of "smart cards", giving students access to university facilities and enabling them to make purchases on campus, once they have money in their accounts. There is plenty of opportunity to use them in a buzzing social scene, which most students find to their taste. The guild of students has always been very active, both socially and politically.

Undergraduate Fees and Bursaries
- Fees for UK/EU students: £3,225
- International student fees: £10,200–£12,300
- Bursary on full grant: £800
- Bursaries on partial grant: household income up to £39K: sliding scale £800–£160.
- Scholarships based on circumstances or by competition.
- For full details see the university's website: www.aston.ac.uk/fees

Students		
Undergraduates:	6,825	(330)
Postgraduates:	1,610	(800)
Mature students:	10.7%	
Overseas students:	16.1%	
Applications per place:	6.7	
From state-sector schools:	91.6%	
From working-class homes:	36.2%	

For detailed information about fees, grants and bursaries and how they work, see chapter 7.

Accommodation
Number of places and costs refer to 2009–10
University-provided places: 2,117
Percentage catered: 0%
Self-catered accommodation: £65.57 (standard) – £106.66 (en suite) a week.
First years are guaranteed accommodation if they fulfil requirements and apply by the deadline.
International fee-paying students: as above.
Contact: accom@aston.ac.uk;
www.aston.ac.uk/accommodation

Bangor University

Bangor, like Aberystwyth and Swansea, is another part of the University of Wales to assert its independence, taking the title of Bangor University while continuing to award degrees through the University of Wales. It has recorded strong performances in the first four National Student Surveys. While Bangor slipped slightly in 2007, it improved in 2008, finishing only just outside the top 30. Students in environmental science, geography, history, law and finance and accounting were the most satisfied. The "small and friendly" nature of the university and the city no doubt helped. Bangor's community focus dates back to a 19th-century campaign which saw local quarrymen putting part of their weekly wages towards the establishment of a college. The College of Education and Lifelong Learning continues the tradition with courses across North Wales, but the university has also built a worldwide reputation in areas such as environmental studies and ocean sciences.

The 2008 research assessments identified world-leading work in all Bangor's 19 subject areas. The university claimed the grades for accounting and finance to be the best in the UK, with electronic engineering second and both sports science and Welsh in the top ten in their respective subjects. Teaching assessments were impressive, with half of the subjects rated as excellent. There is a high proportion of small-group teaching and tutorials, as well as one of Britain's largest peer guiding schemes, which sees senior students mentoring new arrivals.

Bangor merged with a nearby teacher training college, Colleg Normal, in 1996, and that site is now part of the university. All schools are within walking distance of each other, apart from ocean sciences, which is two miles away in Menai Bridge. The university estate is being redeveloped, with the addition of a £5-million environmental sciences building, while a £3.5-million Cancer Research Institute is attracting specialists of international repute.

An academic reorganisation has grouped the 26 academic schools into six colleges: arts and humanities; business, social sciences and law; education and lifelong learning; natural sciences; health and behavioural sciences; and physical and applied sciences. A combination of private funds and a £5-million European grant has been used to establish a new Management Development Centre on a waterfront site. A new School of Creative Studies and Media has been established, offering a variety of new courses including new media, film studies, creative studies with law and creative technologies. Other developments include new courses in music technology,

Bangor
Gwynedd LL57 2DG
01248 382017
admissions@bangor.ac.uk
www.bangor.ac.uk
www.undeb.bangor.ac.uk

The Times Rankings
Overall Ranking: 55

Student satisfaction:	=28	(77%)
Research quality:	=43	(1.5)
Entry standards:	61	(283)
Student–staff ratio:	77	(18.9)
Services & facilities/student:	76	(£998)
Expected completion rate:	=58	(83.9%)
Good honours:	=69	(55.7%)
Graduate prospects:	61	(67.8%)

cancer biology, electronics, information and communications technology, law with media studies, English with songwriting, and 4-year Masters degrees in marine science and environmental science.

Based little more than a stone's throw from Snowdonia with its attractions for sports enthusiasts, Bangor is an expanding centre for Welsh-medium teaching. Although a majority of students come from outside Wales – there is a strong link with Ireland, for example – more than 10 per cent of the students speak the language and one of the seven halls of residence is Welsh-speaking. The university also has a flourishing international exchange programme, with some unusual partner institutions: Poland and Italy are favourite destinations for linguistics students; biologists tend to head for Sweden or Norway.

Bangor does better than most traditional universities when judged against access benchmarks. More than nine out of ten students come from state schools or colleges, and one in three come from working-class homes. Over £2.5 million has gone into a new bursary scheme, offering students from low-income families up to £1,000 a year on some courses, as well as 40 merit scholarships of £3,000 for high-fliers and new excellence scholarships worth up to £5,000 each in a range of subject areas. The university's Talent Opportunities Programme, which operates in 11 schools across North Wales, targets potential applicants from lower socio-economic families, who have little or no history of going on to university.

Applications have increased annually, with the exception of 2008, when all the Welsh universities suffered. There had been another 9 per cent rise at the start of 2009.

There is a strong focus on student support – the pioneering dyslexia unit, for example, offering individual and group support throughout students' courses. New investment in residential accommodation means that all first-year students can be offered places. Bangor is also one of the most cost-effective places in which to study – one survey made it the second-cheapest university in the UK.

Undergraduate Fees and Bursaries

- Fees for UK/EU students: £3,225 (grant of up to £1,940 for Welsh students).
- International student fees: £8,800–£9,900
- Bursary of £1,000 (household income up to £18,370).
- Bursaries on partial grant: household income up to £38.3K: either £500 or £1,000.
- Scholarships based on circumstances or by competition.
- For full details see the university's website: www.bangor.ac.uk/studentfinance/

Students		
Undergraduates:	6,630	(1,835)
Postgraduates:	1,395	(665)
Mature students:	23.7%	
Overseas students:	9.1%	
Applications per place:	3.9	
From state-sector schools:	95.5%	
From working-class homes:	32.9%	

For detailed information about fees, grants and bursaries and how they work, see chapter 7.

Accommodation

Number of places and costs refer to 2009–10

University-provided places: approx 2,400

Percentage catered: 8%

Catered costs: £98.50 (31-week contract) a week.

Self-catered costs: £66.50 – £103.50 (40-week contract) a week.

All first-year students are guaranteed places. International students: as above.

Contact: halls@bangor.ac.uk

University of Bath

Bath is in the throes of a £70-million "campus enhancement plan" and the next few years will see the addition of further facilities for science, extra student accommodation and more teaching space. But, for the moment, it remains a relatively small university with 9,000 undergraduates. The additional places will cater to some degree for the burgeoning demand at an institution that enjoys both an attractive location and a high academic reputation. Although applications have slipped in the past two years, this followed a succession of increases during a period of rising entrance requirements. Bath's healthy showing in league tables may be one reason for its popularity – it has never been out of the top 20 in *The Times* League Table.

Students like the "small and friendly" image the university projects, and one of the lowest dropout rates in Britain suggests that they are well supported. The library is open 24 hours a day, seven days a week. Few can fail to be impressed by the magnificence of the city's architecture. The modern campus on the edge of Bath, with some undistinguished buildings dating from its origins as a technological university in the 1960s, offers an unfortunate contrast. But the 200-acre site has pleasant grounds and is functional, with academic, recreational and residential facilities in close proximity. New teaching facilities for chemistry were added in 2003, followed by a £2.8-million physics facility, and 468 new study bedrooms have also been added recently. More lecture theatres and computer laboratories have eased the pressure on teaching space.

The university has abandoned plans for a campus in Swindon and has withdrawn from a small site there, which catered for 300 full and part-time students, bringing higher education to one of the few remaining counties without a university.

Research is Bath's greatest strength: 60 per cent of the work submitted for the 2008 Research Assessment Exercise was judged to be world-leading or internationally excellent. Social work and social policy, business and management, and computer science and informatics did particularly well, but there were good results in a number of areas.

Bath was also close to the top 20 universities in the 2008 National Student Survey. Pharmacology, toxicology and pharmacy; aerospace engineering; architecture; biosciences; and European languages produced the best results.

The latest academic developments have seen the establishment of a School for Health and an Institute for Contemporary Interdisciplinary Arts, both engaged in teaching as well as research. Most courses

---

Claverton Down
Bath BA2 7AY
01225 386959 (admissions)
admissions@bath.ac.uk
www.bath.ac.uk
www.bathstudent.com

The Times Rankings
Overall Ranking: 13

Student satisfaction:	=20	(78%)
Research quality:	=24	(2.0)
Entry standards:	11	(440)
Student–staff ratio:	=37	(15.0)
Services & facilities/student:	32	(£1,358)
Expected completion rate:	=8	(95.7%)
Good honours:	13	(75.1%)
Graduate prospects:	9	(81.9%)

throughout the university have a practical element, and assessors have praised the university for the work placements it offers. The majority of students take sandwich courses or include a period of study abroad, which helps to produce consistently outstanding graduate employment figures.

The university's other great claim to fame lies in its sports facilities, which were already among the best in Britain before the addition of a £30-million training village, funded with Lottery money. The campus acquired a 50-metre swimming pool by this route, to which it has added an indoor running track, a new multipurpose sports hall, eight indoor tennis courts, an indoor jumps and throws hall, air pistol and fencing sale, a judo dojo and even a simulated bobsleigh and skeleton start area. There is a strong tradition in competitive sports: the university pioneered sports scholarships more than 20 years ago, and they are now worth up to £12,000 a year for performers of international calibre. There are also courses to do the facilities justice, as recognised in a near-perfect score for teaching quality in sport and leisure. Bath claims that its students have access to more free sports facilities than any other university in Britain, from the swimming pools to badminton, squash and tennis courts to grass and astroturf pitches.

Students – nearly a quarter of whom were educated at independent schools – may find the campus quiet at weekends and struggle to afford some of Bath's attractions, but they value its location. When they tire of the beauty of Bath, the nightlife of Bristol is only a few minutes away. The two cities have a combined student population of more than 50,000. The students' union is active and the university has been upgrading its student support services, for example through the introduction of a new virtual learning environment and the provision of laptops adapted for use by students with disabilities. More than nine out of ten students surveyed say they would recommend the university to family and friends.

Undergraduate Fees and Bursaries

- Fees for UK/EU students: £3,225
- International student fees: £10,600–£13,500
- Bursary on full grant: £1,200
- Bursaries on partial grant: household income up to £50K: sliding scale £900–£300.
- Scholarships based on circumstances or by competition.
- For full details see the university's website: www.bath.ac.uk/students/ scholarships

---

Students

Undergraduates:	8,745	(330)
Postgraduates:	1,515	(2,375)
Mature students:	10.7%	
Overseas students:	21.0%	
Applications per place:	7.0	
From state-sector schools:	77.2%	
From working-class homes:	19.1%	

For detailed information about fees, grants and bursaries and how they work, see chapter 7.

Accommodation

Number of places and costs refer to 2009–10
University-provided places: 3,264
Percentage catered: 0%
Self-catered cost: £80–£125 a week.
First years guaranteed accommodation if conditions are met, and applications received by 3 September.
International students: as above. Exchange students are housed on a reciprocal basis.
Contact:
www.bath.ac.uk/accommodation/enquiry/

Bath Spa University

Bath Spa is one of the growing number of new "teaching-led" universities created under Government reforms. But it is far from new in other respects and not without research strengths. Its Newton Park headquarters, four miles outside the World Heritage city of Bath, is in grounds landscaped by Capability Brown in the eighteenth century, with a handsome Georgian manor house, owned by the Prince of Wales, as its centrepiece. A second campus, housing the Bath School of Art and Design, is undergoing a £6-million redevelopment and boasts facilities that are among the most modern in the country. The history of the predecessor colleges goes back 150 years, with some famous alumni, including Body Shop founder Anita Roddick and Turner Prize winner Sir Howard Hodgkin.

In recent years, the new university has undertaken its biggest-ever building programme to cater for growing student numbers. However, applications were down in 2008 and a 3 per cent increase at the start of 2009 was well below that national average. With around 7,000 students, it is still comparatively small, but the range of courses has been growing steadily. At Newton Park, the base for all students except those taking art and design subjects, the students' union has practically doubled in size, a library extension has added about 120 workstations and £4.8 million has been spent on an impressive university theatre with a 200-seat auditorium. A new creative writing centre is housed in the 14th-century gatehouse, bringing it into student use for the first time.

Bath Spa has been awarding its own degrees since 1992 – much longer than some of the other new arrivals on the university scene. Subjects assessed for teaching quality averaged 22 points out of 24 and results in all the National Student Surveys have been good, especially for teaching quality. The university has been designated a national centre for excellence in teaching and learning in the creative industries, bringing significant investment in the Schools of Music and Performing Arts, English and Creative Studies, and Art and Design. Half of the subjects in which the university entered the 2008 Research Assessment Exercise (art and design, communication, cultural and media studies, English, history and music) were judged to have some world-leading work. About a third of the students are postgraduates, including a large cohort training to be teachers. The university now has the power to award its own research degrees.

Despite a setting that would seem to be a magnet for applicants from independent

Newton Park
Newton St Loe
Bath BA2 9BN
01225 875875
enquiries@bathspa.ac.uk
www.bathspa.ac.uk
www.bathspasu.co.uk

The Times Rankings
Overall Ranking: =74

Student satisfaction:	=28	(77%
Research quality:	=71	(0.4)
Entry standards:	59	(287)
Student–staff ratio:	=106	(21.6)
Services & facilities/student:	113	(£615)
Expected completion rate:	=39	(87.0%)
Good honours:	=33	(67.7%)
Graduate prospects:	=98	(59.0%)

schools, 95 per cent of the home intake is state-educated and over a quarter are from working-class homes. Two thirds of the students are female, reflecting the arts and social science bias in the curriculum, and 25 per cent are over 25. The latest projected dropout rate, of 10 per cent, is significantly better than the national average for the university's courses and entry grades. There are about 500 overseas students from a variety of countries.

The university has a number of partner further education colleges in the region, where a range of two-year Foundation degrees are delivered, the latest of which include musical theatre, professional musicianship, contemporary circus and physical performance, and further education management. Many students then progress to the university campuses to complete an honours degree. About 85 per cent of first years attending Bath Spa itself are offered hall places. Students like the "small and friendly" atmosphere, which the university is anxious to retain in spite of the temptation to go for more substantial growth. Sports facilities are not extensive, but a new gym is being built and the countryside – on and off campus – is a major draw.

Undergraduate Fees and Bursaries
- Fees for UK/EU students: £3,225
- International student fees: £9,000–£9,580
- Bursary on full grant: £1,200
- Bursaries on partial grant: household income up to £39K: sliding scale £1,200–£100.
- Scholarships based on circumstances or by competition.
- For full details see the university's website: www.bathspa.ac.uk/prospectus/money-matters/getting-money/scholarships.asp

Students

Undergraduates:	4,360	(525)
Postgraduates:	655	(1,935)
Mature students:	28.1%	
Overseas students:	2.8%	
Applications per place:	5.7	
From state-sector schools:	95.1%	
From working-class homes:	31.3%	

For detailed information about fees, grants and bursaries and how they work, see chapter 7.

Accommodation

Number of places and costs refer to 2009–10
University provided places: 971
Percentage catered: 0%
Self catered: £68–78 a week (48 weeks) plus bills and internet
First years are housed in university-managed or accredited accommodation provided requirements are met. Residential restrictions apply.
International students: as above.
Contact: accommodation@bathspa.ac.uk

University of Bedfordshire

The former Luton University has never looked back since taking over De Montfort University's Bedford campus and establishing the University of Bedfordshire in 2006. The move made the new university the main provider of higher education in a relatively prosperous county and allowed it to shed a name that – however unfairly – had become a liability. In fact, Luton's teaching ratings were described by no less an authority than Charles Clarke, as Education Secretary, as "bloody brilliant", but there was no escaping the unglamorous image.

Applications for courses beginning in 2009 were 22 per cent up at the beginning of the year, following equally impressive rises in the two previous years. With two quite different sites to its name, the new university is expanding and developing. It has already spent £60 million on the two main campuses, adding a well-equipped media arts centre and an impressive learning resources centre in Luton. The Bedford redevelopment is now complete, with a new campus centre comprising a 280-seat auditorium and a students' union, as well as an accommodation block for 500 students. Two new gyms and a series of sports science laboratories opened in 2006. A free shuttle bus service operates between the two sites.

The next stage will cost £70 million and should be completed during the 2010–11 academic year. There will be a new student centre at the heart of the Luton campus and extensive new residential accommodation.

The Bedford campus, once a teacher training college, is a 20-minute walk from the town centre in a "self-contained leafy setting". It houses the Faculty of Education and Sport, with 3,000 students and plans for more. Although there are partner colleges in Bedford, Dunstable and Milton Keynes, the bulk of the students remain in Luton. The centrepiece of the campus, in the midst of the shopping area, is the striking atrium which leads into the learning resources centre.

There is also an attractive management centre and conference venue at Putteridge Bury, a neo-Elizabethan mansion three miles outside Luton. Nursing and midwifery students in the growing Faculty of Health and Social Sciences are based at the Butterfield Park campus, near Luton, which opened in 2008, or at the even newer Oxford House development, in Aylesbury, Buckinghamshire. There are additional teaching facilities at Stoke Mandeville and Wycombe General hospitals. A postgraduate medical school is run in partnership with Hertfordshire and Cranfield universities, as part of the Government's £1-billion investment in

Park Square
Luton
Bedfordshire LU1 3JU
01582 489286
enquiries via website
www.beds.ac.uk
www.ubsu.co.uk

The Times Rankings

Overall Ranking: =71

Student satisfaction:	=54	(75%)
Research quality:	=95	(0.2)
Entry standards:	104	(215)
Student–staff ratio:	=42	(15.6)
Services & facilities/student:	24	(£1,431)
Expected completion rate:	98	(75.1%)
Good honours:	105	(47.8%)
Graduate prospects:	64	(66.7%)

healthcare across Bedfordshire and Hertfordshire.

Courses in the new university maintain the vocational character that Luton pursued after dropping a number of traditional academic subjects. The portfolio of two-year Foundation degrees, for example, is among the largest in the country, stretching from football studies and specialist make-up design to sustainable construction and animation for industry. The university pioneered electronic assessment, with more than 10,000 students in disciplines from accountancy to biology tested by computer. Bedfordshire students also benefit from a national centre of excellence in personal development planning and employability, awarded to Luton in 2005.

Almost all of Bedfordshire's entrants are from state schools and over 40 per cent come from working-class backgrounds. Around a half are mature students, many taking access courses to bring them up to degree or diploma standard. About a third of the school-leavers arrive through Clearing and nearly as many students take part-time courses. Surprisingly high numbers – nearly a quarter – are from outside the EU, many of them taking postgraduate courses.

The university celebrated much-improved results in the 2008 Research Assessment Exercise, registering at least some world-leading work in earth systems and environmental science; social work, social policy and administration; sport, tourism and leisure; English language and literature; and communications, cultural and media studies.

Neither Luton nor Bedford is particularly famous for its social scene, but both have their share of pubs, clubs and restaurants. London is only half an hour away by train for those seeking something livelier. There is enough accommodation to guarantee a place for all first years, and the sports facilities are improving, albeit from a low base in Luton.

Undergraduate Fees and Bursaries

- Fees for UK/EU students: £3,225
- International student fees: £8,500
- Bursary on full grant: household income up to £18.8K: £842 then £632.
- Bursaries on partial grant: household income up to £40.3K: sliding scale £632–£472; household income above £40.3K, fixed bursary of £319.
- Scholarships based on circumstances or by competition.
- For full details see the university's website: www.beds.ac.uk/howtoapply/money/fees/ug

Students

Undergraduates:	8,085	(4,115)
Postgraduates:	1,005	(990)
Mature students:	50.0%	
Overseas students:	18.6%	
Applications per place:	3.5	
From state-sector schools:	99.0%	
From working-class homes:	42.5%	

For detailed information about fees, grants and bursaries and how they work, see chapter 7.

Accommodation

Number of places and costs refer to 2008–09
University-provided places: about 1,617
Percentage catered: 0%
Self-catered costs: £71.50–£100.00 a week.
Policy for first-year students: all first years are guaranteed a place provided conditions are met.
International students: as above.
Contact:
www.beds.ac.uk/studentlife/accommodation
studentservices.bedford@beds.ac.uk
accommodation@beds.ac.uk

University of Birmingham

Birmingham set itself the target of becoming the "Oxbridge of the Midlands", which may have been ambitious, but its position in *The Times* ranking is a fair starting point. A consultants' report in 2004 found the university had a boring image, but that is being addressed. The university has recruited Professor David Eastwood, chief executive of the Higher Education Funding Council for England, to maximise its undoubted potential.

Students come to Birmingham from more than 150 countries, but the university enjoys particularly high prestige in its own region. Since 2008 it has been made up of five colleges. Entry standards are high, averaging the equivalent of more than ABB at A level. With over six applicants for each place, they are likely to remain so, but aspiring students still flock to the largest open days in Britain each June. There is also an additional open day for upper sixth-formers in September. Applications were up by slightly more than the national average at the start of 2009, at more than 8 per cent.

The university's enduring reputation is based on its research, with 16 per cent of the work submitted for the 2008 Research Assessment Exercise regarded as world-leading. Music, physics, computer science, mechanical engineering, European studies and law did particularly well.

Many of the teaching scores were impressive, too, with mathematics, biological sciences, physiotherapy, sociology, and electrical and electronic engineering all recording maximum points. Birmingham also did well in the 2008 National Student Survey, finishing ahead of most of the big city universities. Law, physics, economics and maths produced the best results.

In recent years, Birmingham has added an £11.8-million student facilities building at the Medical School, a new £16.4-million home for Sport and Exercise Sciences and a £10-million learning centre, and spent £47.5 million on refurbishing student accommodation as part of an investment programme in staff, buildings and equipment that is costing a total of £225 million. Engineering was reorganised, following a year-long review, to promote an interdisciplinary approach, responding to employers' wish for more flexibility. Students can enter either a BA or BSc degree programme, combining technology with subjects ranging from Latin or modern Greek to the management of floods and other natural disasters.

The 230-acre campus in leafy Edgbaston is dominated by a 300-foot clocktower, which is one of the city's best-known landmarks, and boasts its own station. Dentistry is located in the city,

---

Edgbaston
Birmingham B15 2TT
0121 415 8900 (admissions)
admissions@bham.ac.uk
www.bham.ac.uk
www.guildofstudents.com

The Times Rankings
Overall Ranking: 22

Student satisfaction:	=20	(78%)
Research quality:	=19	(2.1)
Entry standards:	20	(403)
Student–staff ratio:	=34	(14.9)
Services & facilities/student:	16	(£1,552)
Expected completion rate:	14	(93.6%)
Good honours:	25	(70.9%)
Graduate prospects:	39	(72.7%)

while part of the School of Education is in Selly Oak, a mile from the Edgbaston campus. Drama is also located there, along with the BBC Drama Village, which is part of a strategic alliance between the university and the corporation.

Most of the halls and university flats are conveniently located in an attractive parkland setting near the main campus. There are almost 5,000 university-owned beds, following a ten-year programme of expansion, and accommodation in the private sector is also plentiful.

The campus is less than three miles from the centre of Birmingham, but the area has plenty of shops, pubs and restaurants of its own. With its own nightclub among the facilities on campus, some students do not even stray that far, but the city is acquiring a growing reputation among the young, which is helping to make the university even more popular. Some 40 per cent of Birmingham graduates choose to make the city their home.

Student facilities are on a par with the best in the country, with many restaurants and bars, a live music venue, an art gallery, a medical practice on campus, and an outdoor pursuits centre on Coniston Water, in the Lake District. Birmingham has always been concerned with the body as well as the mind; compulsory exercise was only abandoned in 1968. The Active Lifestyles Programme, the voluntary modern-day equivalent, attracts 4,000 students to 150 different courses. Tutors with national qualifications run classes from beginner to advanced level. In addition, Birmingham has ranked in the top three in British Universities competitions for the past 15 years.

Undergraduate Fees and Bursaries
- Fees for UK/EU students: £3,225
- International student fees: £9,880–£12,800 (£22,350 medicine)
- Bursary on full grant: £860
- Bursaries on partial grant: household income up to £35.4K: £860.
- Scholarships based on circumstances or by competition.
- For full details see the university's website: www.as.bham.ac.uk/study/support/finance/

Students

Undergraduates:	16,055	(1,975)
Postgraduates:	5,475	(4,735)
Mature students:	8.8%	
Overseas students:	9.1%	
Applications per place:	6.5	
From state-sector schools:	78.2%	
From working-class homes:	22.1%	

For detailed information about fees, grants and bursaries and how they work, see chapter 7.

Accommodation

Number of places and costs refer to 2009–10
University-provided places: 4,262
Percentage catered: 42%
Catered costs: £109.50–£156.78 a week
Self-catered costs: £78.45–£125.71 a week
All first years are guaranteed housing (subject to conditions).
International students: as above
Contact: ugradaccomm@bham.ac.uk
www.birminghamstudentpad.co.uk

Birmingham City University

The former UCE Birmingham (in turn originally the University of Central England) was renamed Birmingham City University (BCU) in 2007 to emphasise its location, reinforce its close links with the city and give the university a stronger identity. It must wish it had made the change years ago, having seen applications soar by more than 35 per cent – one of the biggest increases ever at any university – at the start of 2009. The switch was part of the Vice-Chancellor's strategy to build on the university's traditionally close links with business and the professions. An emphasis on employability is underlined by a £300,000 project to create "future-proof" graduates with training and education resources to help develop skills and knowledge for the workplace.

The annual satisfaction survey goes to half of the student body, in a model that helped inform the new national equivalent. The results are taken seriously: a recent exercise led to the introduction of internet tutorials in engineering and new help with research for undergraduates in law and social science. The long-standing initiative is just one of the activities of the influential Centre for Research into Quality, headed by one of the university's most senior academics.

The university has a proud record of extending access to higher education: nearly 46 per cent of its students come from working-class homes and 98 per cent attended state schools or colleges. The drop-out rate had crept up in the latest figures to almost 20 per cent, although this was still close to the national average for the university's courses and entry grades. About half of the full-time students come from the West Midlands, many from ethnic minorities. BCU also has one of the largest programmes of part-time courses in Britain, making it the biggest provider of higher education in the region. Students can enter through the network of associated further education colleges, which run foundation and access programmes.

Eight campuses straggle across the city, but about half of students are concentrated on the modern City North campus at Perry Barr, three miles from the city centre. A new city-centre campus in the Eastside district, near Millennium Point, has been given planning permission and will form the centrepiece of a £250-million investment in new and improved facilities. It will cater for about 10,000 students in creative and performing arts, media, technology and design. The relocation of engineering and computing to Millennium Point in 2001 provided a new focus for the university. Facilities in the £114-million Lottery-funded centre are open to the public. The

---

Perry Barr
Birmingham B42 2SU
0121 331 5595 (enquiries)
choices@bcu.ac.uk
www.bcu.ac.uk
www.birminghamcitysu.com

The Times Rankings
Overall Ranking: 77

Student satisfaction:	=90	(72%)
Research quality:	=95	(0.2)
Entry standards:	79	(258)
Student–staff ratio:	=49	(16.5)
Services & facilities/student:	40	(£1,217)
Expected completion rate:	96	(75.5%)
Good honours:	65	(57.3%)
Graduate prospects:	=67	(65.7%)

Birmingham School of Acting also moved into £4-million purpose-built facilities at Millennium Point in 2007.

The Edgbaston campus has been refurbished for the Faculty of Health, with a prize-winning library, IT suites, teaching facilities and recreational space. The Birmingham Institute of Art and Design (BIAD) spreads over four campuses from Gosta Green and the impressive listed Venetian Gothic Fine Art campus at Margaret Street, both in the city centre, to Bournville. This facility was refurbished at a cost of £20 million and occupies part of the Cadbury village. The largest institute of its kind outside London, it also includes the world famous and newly refurbished School of Jewellery in the city's famous Jewellery Quarter.

One of the university's best-known features is its Conservatoire, housed in part of Birmingham's smart convention centre. Courses from opera to world music have given it a reputation for innovation, which was recognised in an excellent rating for teaching. Most other teaching ratings were mediocre, although art and design, education and health subjects scored well and the teacher education courses consistently produce among the best scores in Ofsted inspections. The university was awarded a national centre for excellence in teaching and learning for health and social care.

The university has been increasing its portfolio of high-tech degree courses like electronic commerce, communications and network engineering, and electronic systems. Its research funding will double after successful assessments in 2008, which registered some world-leading work in all seven areas covered by the university's submission. In art and design, 30 per cent were given the top grade, placing BCU in the top ten for the subject.

University-owned accommodation is guaranteed for most first years, and there is a relatively cheap and plentiful private housing sector. The Pavilion, adjacent to the City North Campus, has added £4.5 million of conference and sports facilities, comprising 43 acres. Further new sports facilities are planned for City North Campus by 2009–10. The city's youth scene is highly rated.

Undergraduate Fees and Bursaries

- Fees for UK/EU students: £3,225
- International student fees: £8,950–£13,500
- Bursary on full grant: £525
- Bursaries on partial grant: household income up to £50K: sliding scale £525–£325.
- Scholarships based on circumstances or by competition.
- For full details see the university's website: www.bcu.ac.uk/prospective/finance

Students

Undergraduates:	13,695	(6,065)
Postgraduates:	1,320	(2,165)
Mature students:	39.5%	
Overseas students:	5.1%	
Applications per place:	3.5	
From state-sector schools:	97.7%	
From working-class homes:	45.9%	

For detailed information about fees, grants and bursaries and how they work, see chapter 7.

Accommodation

Number of places and costs refer to 2008–09
University-provided places: 2,146
Percentage catered: 0%
Self-catered costs: £64–£98 a week (40 weeks).
Accommodation guaranteed for first years if conditions are met.
International students are guaranteed accommodation.
Contact:www.bcu.ac.uk/accommodation
accommodation@uce.ac.uk

University of Bolton

The largest town in England finally got a university in 2005, and now the institution has a single campus in the centre of Bolton. The rationalisation of sites has provided additional and enhanced teaching space, facilities to interact with industry and a new students' union. University status had an instant impact: Bolton recorded the biggest increases in applications in the UK for two successive years. Although applications were down by nearly 8 per cent the start of 2009, following another substantial drop in the previous year, the demand for places remains well above pre-university days.

The university traces its roots back as far as 1824 to one of the country's first three mechanics institutes. There are now more than 11,000 students but there are no plans for further dramatic growth. The university sees itself as a regional institution, with three quarters of the students coming from the North West, many through partner colleges. But there is also an international dimension, with long-established links in Malaysia and a regular contingent of overseas students from 70 different countries. In September 2008 the university opened a new site in the United Arab Emirates offering a range of undergraduate and postgraduate courses identical to those taught at Bolton.

The £1-million university campus near Dubai has 150 students and is intended to take 700 within five years, giving those at Bolton the opportunity to study in the UAE for part of their degree course.

Bolton has set itself the ambitious target of climbing into the top half of the university system within 15 years. Judged on our criteria, it has some way to go, but it is not unusual for brand-new universities to make their debut near the foot of the table. Even in its days as an institute of higher education, it was competitive in categories such as spending per student on the library and other facilities, but it is dragged down by other indicators. Student satisfaction is not one of these: the university almost made the top ten in rankings of the first National Student Survey and, although ratings slipped a little in 2007, Bolton remains in the top half of our table for student satisfaction.

The university is not research-driven, but engineering, architecture and the built environment, social work and social policy all contained some world-leading research in the 2008 assessments. A centre for research and innovation in materials which opened in 2003 is to be the first of a series of "knowledge exchange zones". Bolton is not one of the new breed of "teaching-only" universities; it has been accredited for research degrees for more

---

Deane Road
Bolton BL3 5AB
01204 903903 (general enquiries)
contact via website
www.bolton.ac.uk
www.bisu.co.uk

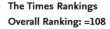

The Times Rankings
Overall Ranking: =108

Student satisfaction:	=54	(75%)
Research quality:	=85	(0.3)
Entry standards:	105	(213)
Student–staff ratio:	=78	(19.0)
Services & facilities/student:	111	(£697)
Expected completion rate:	114	(56.0%)
Good honours:	79	(53.5%)
Graduate prospects:	97	(59.1%)

than ten years and acquired its new status under the old rules. About 1,700 of the students are postgraduates, taking qualifications up to and including PhDs.

The £11.3-million building programme at the Deane campus has included a design studio and three floors of teaching and learning space where students work on actual briefs for companies seeking design solutions; an Innovation Factory housing, among others, special effects laboratories and a product design studio. Also included within this development is a new social learning zone which includes a students' union bar and social facilities, a computer access room and new students' union offices and advice centre. Now completed, this combined student services are will cover floor space equivalent to the size of a football pitch. A swimming pool and sports complex will be next. The 700 reasonably priced residential places go a long way in an institution with a high proportion of home-based students. More than half of the students are over 20 at entry.

The university exceeds all the access measures designed to widen participation in higher education: nearly all the students are state-educated, over four in ten are from working-class homes and the proportion from areas without a tradition of higher education is almost twice the national average for Bolton's subjects and entry qualifications. The downside – and an important one – is that over four in ten students are projected to leave without a qualification, by far the highest proportion in England. The university has an action plan to bring the rate down to the national average for its courses and qualifications by 2012.

Undergraduate Fees and Bursaries
- Fees for UK/EU students: £3,225
- International student fees: £7,900
- Bursary on full grant: £350
- Bursaries on partial grant: household income up to £60K: sliding scale £350–£120 .
- Scholarships based on circumstances or by competition.
- For full details see the university's website: www.bolton.ac.uk/ProspectiveStudents/ Undergraduate/Finance/UgFtFinance/ Home.aspx

Students,		
Undergraduates:	3,735	(2,645)
Postgraduates:	640	(825)
Mature students:	53.8%	
Overseas students:	7.8%	
Applications per place:	6.7	
From state-sector schools:	99.0%	
From working-class homes:	46.4%	

For detailed information about fees, grants and bursaries and how they work, see chapter 7.

Accommodation
Number of places and costs refer to 2009–10
University-provided places: 700
Percentage catered: 0%
Self-catered costs: £2,665 annually (41 weeks); £65 a week. Fuel bills are included in the cost.
All first years are generally accommodated.
International students: accommodation is secured for these students.
Contact: accomm@bolton.ac.uk

Bournemouth University

Once a university that gloried in the absence of traditional academic disciplines, Bournemouth has been subtly changing its image. Its latest corporate plan speaks of a university "geared to the professions with passionate commitment to academic excellence". Research moved up the agenda with a £1-million investment in 80 PhD studentships, and the aim is to increase undergraduates' entry qualifications year on year.

Bournemouth's forte has always been in identifying gaps in the higher education market and then filling them with innovative programmes. Degrees in public relations, retail management, scriptwriting and tax law are among the examples. The university also boasts the National Centre of Computer Animation. The mix has been popular with students: there was an impressive 12 per cent rise in applications at the start of 2009, the latest in a series of increases.

The university claims a number of firsts in its growing portfolio of courses, notably in the area of tourism, media-related programmes and conservation. It was no surprise to find Bournemouth among the pioneers of two-year Foundation degrees. Now much expanded, the courses are being delivered in further education colleges from Somerset to Wiltshire, supporting the needs of business in the creative arts, media and tourism.

Many of Bournemouth's courses have an international focus and all students are encouraged to improve their linguistic ability. A majority of undergraduates take sandwich courses, and 70 per cent do work placements. The result is an employment rate which is the university's proudest achievement: nearly four out of five graduates go straight into jobs. The Retail Management degree notched up eight successive years of full employment and is still running at over 90 per cent. Students are offered personal development planning, both online and with trained staff, while 1,400 first-years also take advantage of peer-assisted learning, receiving advice from more experienced undergraduates.

Journalism, accounting, archaeology, marketing and tourism, transport and travel produced the highest satisfaction levels in the National Student Survey published in 2008. Media courses are a particular strength, with entry requirements well above the university's modest average. State-of-the-art equipment includes a motion capture facility for real-time animation, which is used in teaching and available for use by outside companies. The university has been designated as England's only centre

---

Fern Barrow
Talbot Campus
Poole
Dorset BH12 5BB
01202 524111
enquiries@
  bournemouth.ac.uk
www.bournemouth.
  ac.uk
www.subu.org.uk

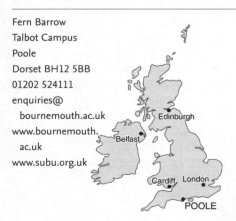

The Times Rankings
Overall Ranking: 58

Student satisfaction:	=67	(74%)
Research quality:	=71	(0.4)
Entry standards:	56	(289)
Student–staff ratio:	102	(20.8)
Services & facilities/student:	70	(£1,059)
Expected completion rate:	50	(85.2%)
Good honours:	62	(58.9%)
Graduate prospects:	29	(75.5%)

for excellence in media practice.

Computer animation was the star performer in the 2001 research assessments, which saw much-needed improvement on the previous exercise. In 2008, eight of the ten subject areas contained at least some world-leading research, with art and design and communication, cultural and media studies producing the best grades. The results will triple Bournemouth's research grant.

Among the new developments planned is the world's first fully commercial teaching hotel, a four-star establishment with public- and private-sector backing, which is due to open in 2009. New teaching and residential accommodation has been added in recent years, with more to come. A multimillion-pound library opened in 2003. There are now two campuses – the original Talbot site in Poole and a dedicated campus in Bournemouth town centre – with partner colleges in Bridgwater, Yeovil, Bournemouth and Poole, Dorchester, Salisbury and Weymouth.

The southern seaside location and the subject mix attract more middle-class students than most new universities, although over 90 per cent attended state schools and colleges. Students are discouraged from bringing cars (which are banned within a mile of the town-centre campus), but many still do. The area has plenty to offer students during the summer season. Although it naturally becomes less lively in the winter months, Bournemouth no longer shuts up when the tourists go home. The students' union's Old Fire Station bar is the favourite among many nightlife options. Bournemouth offers a wide range of accommodation, from around 2,300 places in university halls to bed-and-breakfast lets and shared houses.

Undergraduate Fees and Bursaries

- Fees for UK/EU students: £3,225
- International student fees: £8,000–£10,000
- Bursary on full grant: £319
- The university does not award bursaries for students on partial maintenance grants.
- Scholarships based on circumstances or by competition.
- For full details see the university's website: www.bournemouth.ac.uk/futurestudents/ undergraduate/funding/index.html

Students

Undergraduates:	11,260	(4,335)
Postgraduates:	1,395	(885)
Mature students:	29.6%	
Overseas students:	6.0%	
Applications per place:	4.8	
From state-sector schools:	94.7%	
From working-class homes:	29.7%	

For detailed information about fees, grants and bursaries and how they work, see chapter 7.

Accommodation

Number of places and costs refer to 2009–10

University-provided places: about 2,890 (2,310 in halls; 580 head tenancy).

Percentage catered: 0%

Self-catered costs: £75–£92 a week.

The university expects to offer all first years a place to live. Residential restrictions apply.

International students: guaranteed if conditions are met.

Contact: accommodation@bournemouth.ac.uk

University of Bradford

Bradford has declared itself an "ecoversity", addressing issues of sustainable development in all its practices, including the curriculum. The most visible sign will be the opening of a sustainable student village in 2010, which will cater mainly for first-year and international students. The development is part of a £70-million modernisation plan that includes a £7-million investment in new and upgraded teaching facilities. Another project produced a distinctive four-storey Atrium, which has brought together all student support services in a single, open plan social space.

Still a relatively small university of 13,000 students, Bradford has carved out a niche for itself with mature students, who now make up over a quarter of all undergraduates. They relish the vocational slant and the accent on work experience and placement courses, which regularly place Bradford towards the top of the graduate employment tables. Demand for places recovered after a difficult period, although applications were down by more than the national average this year and last. Admission requirements have been rising, although they are modest compared with many old universities.

Nearly one in five of the university's students are from overseas, many of them taught in partner institutions in locations as diverse as Poland, India, Malaysia and Hong Kong. Nearer home, there are alliances with a number of further education colleges to help boost participation in a region where it is well below the national average. The colleges offer ten Foundation degrees in areas such as public sector administration, community justice, engineering technology and enterprise in IT. Perhaps the best known is in health and social care, where the university was already expanding opportunities locally, bringing about a fourfold increase in enrolments by young women from South Asian families.

The relatively small, lively campus is close to the city centre. Health students have their own building a few minutes' walk away, while a shuttle bus service runs to the highly rated management school is two miles away in a 14-acre parkland setting. The eventual aim is to develop a health and science quarter, with the School of Health Studies housed in its own building on campus. Other projects will enhance the academic facilities and create more social space for students, beginning with improved laboratories for chemical and forensic science, more teaching accommodation and new sports facilities including a gym and climbing wall and an improved sports hall

Nursing, pharmacy and other health studies all did well in teaching quality

---

Bradford
West Yorkshire BD7 1DP
0800 073 1225 (freephone)
course-enquiries@
  bradford.ac.uk
www.bradford.ac.uk
www.ubuonline.co.uk

assessments, while politics and the interdisciplinary human studies programme, which combines psychology, literature and sociology with the study of philosophy, was awarded full marks. The university also did well in the first national student satisfaction survey, although it was in the bottom half of the table in 2008.

Some 80 per cent of the work submitted for the 2008 Research Assessment Exercise was placed in the top two categories, although more than a third of the academics were not entered. Social work and social policy, politics, civil engineering and pharmacy produced the best results. Politics includes the university's best-known offering of peace studies, which has acquired an international reputation. Recent attempts to raise Bradford's research profile have included the £6-million Institute of Pharmaceutical Innovation opened in 2003 and an Institute of Cancer Therapeutics in 2005.

The university has launched suites of ICT and media studies courses to add to those in e-commerce and internet computing, computer animation and special effects, interactive systems and video games design. Computer-assisted learning is increasing in many subjects, making use of unusually extensive IT provision and a new wireless network. Some courses feature online assessment and the use of laptops in lectures.

More southerners are being attracted to Bradford's status as Britain's cheapest student city. The 1,000 places in self-catering halls are reasonably priced and all have internet connections. There is particularly good provision for disabled students, who account for 6 per cent of the university population. The university's senior management group includes a Director of Student Engagement to ensure that the student voice is heard in future developments. The students' union operates a free late-night "safety bus" for those living within two miles of the campus.

Undergraduate Fees and Bursaries
- Fees for UK/EU students: £3,225
- International student fees: £8,600–£10,900
- Bursary of £900–£500 for those on a full grant, depending on year in course.
- Bursaries for those on partial grant based on household income up to £40K, depending on year in course £900–£500; up to £60K, £600–£400.
- Scholarships based on circumstances or by competition.
- For full details see the university's website: www.bradford.ac.uk/external/tuitionfees/support/bursaries09.php

---

Students

Undergraduates:	8,045	(1,290)
Postgraduates:	1,430	(1,610)
Mature students:	31.1%	
Overseas students:	18.9%	
Applications per place:	3.8	
From state-sector schools:	93.9%	
From working-class homes:	49.0%	

For detailed information about fees, grants and bursaries and how they work, see chapter 7.

Accommodation

Number of places and costs refer to 2009–10
University-provided places: 1,000
Percentage catered: 0%
Self-catered costs: £53.00–£91.50 (deluxe en-suite) a week (42-week contracts)
All first-year undergraduate and postgraduate students are guaranteed accommodation (terms and conditions apply).
Contact: halls-of-residence@bradford.ac.uk
www.brad.ac.uk/accommodation

University of Brighton

Brighton came of age as one of the first new universities to be awarded a medical school, but is equally well known for imaginative initiatives in its region. It has set up a centre in Hastings and runs a number of schemes, both to draw people from the region into higher education and to help them with practical problems. The £28.5-million medical school, run jointly with neighbouring Sussex University, is training 128 doctors a year and has proved popular with applicants (www.bsms.ac.uk). Brighton was already heavily engaged in other health subjects, such as nursing and midwifery. The medical school's headquarters, on Brighton's Falmer campus, has also provided a new base for applied social sciences, such as criminology and applied psychology, which are among the university's most sought-after degrees.

The two universities have been collaborating since Brighton was a polytechnic. There is a joint research building for science policy and management studies, and a joint accord guarantees the offer of a place to all suitably qualified applicants from the Channel Island of Jersey. Brighton does the same for applicants from Sussex and leads a Learning Network for the county. Almost a third of undergraduates now come through these accords.

Brighton was again one of the top new universities in the 2008 Research Assessment Exercise. Art and design produced the best results, with two thirds of the work submitted considered world-leading or internationally excellent. Business management, sports studies and mechanical and aeronautical engineering also did well. Teacher training, physiotherapy and architecture, building and planning achieved the best scores in the latest National Student Survey. The plaudits have not gone unnoticed: applications were up by almost 10 per cent at the start of 2009, the latest in a series of impressive figures.

Brighton's strengths in art and design – recognised in the award of national teaching centres in design and creativity – have been at the forefront of the university's rise. But the university also has a growing reputation in areas such as sport and hospitality, as well as scoring well in teacher education rankings. It was the first university to achieve an "outstanding" rating from the Office for Standards in Education for management and quality assurance across the full range of primary, secondary and post-compulsory teacher education courses.

The Design Council's national archive is lodged on campus, and the four-year fashion textiles degree offers work placements in the United States, France and Italy, as well as Britain.

Mithras House
Lewes Road
Brighton BN2 4AT
01273 600900
enquiries@brighton.
  ac.uk
www.brighton.ac.uk
www.ubsu.net

Four sites house the five faculties. Art and Design has the prime location opposite the Royal Pavilion, with sports science, service management and the health professions at Eastbourne and the other subjects on the outskirts of Brighton, at Falmer and Moulsecoomb, the university's headquarters, where work has started on a new building for education, languages, literature and communication.

Over £100 million has been spent on new facilities and refurbishment since university status arrived in 1992 and another £100 million has been committed for the next three years, half of it on student accommodation and learning facilities. Existing facilities include a flight simulator, a fully functional news room for the university's sports journalists, modern clinical skills laboratories for pharmacy, and a custom-designed culinary arts studio. At Eastbourne there is a new library and extensive sports and leisure facilities, including a sports centre with three gymnasia and a dance studio, a refurbished swimming pool and fitness facilities. Sport-science laboratories and 354 en-suite residential places have been added and improvements made to the learning resources centre, lecture theatres and refectory. The extensive modernisation of the Falmer campus continues, with a £23-million building for biosciences due to open in 2010.

The university has a cosmopolitan air, with more overseas students and a more middle-class UK intake than most of the former polytechnics. Around a third of the full-time undergraduates are over 21 on entry, often attracted by strongly vocational courses and the prospect of three years at "London by the sea". Most students have a personal tutor to advise on combinations within the modular degree scheme.

Students have taken to the "managed learning environment", known as Studentcentral, an interactive service providing online access to teaching materials and other information. Most also like Brighton, although the cost of living is high for those not in hall. There is a lively social scene and part-time work is plentiful. Eastbourne is also surprisingly popular, and both towns offer plentiful accommodation to supplement the university's stock.

Undergraduate Fees and Bursaries

- Fees for UK/EU students: £3,225
- International student fees: £9,240–£10,740
  £23,678 (medicine)
- Bursary on full grant: £1,080
- Bursaries on partial grant: household income up to £40.3K: sliding scale £860–£540.
- Scholarships based on circumstances or by competition.
- For full details see the university's website: www.brighton.ac.uk/studentlife/money/

Students

Undergraduates:	12,995	(4,120)
Postgraduates:	1,505	(2,600)
Mature students:	34.8%	
Overseas students:	10.1%	
Applications per place:	5.2	
From state-sector schools:	93.0%	
From working-class homes:	29.4%	

For detailed information about fees, grants and bursaries and how they work, see chapter 7.

Accommodation

Number of places and costs refer to 2008–09
University-provided places: 2,000; 270 in private sector university-managed houses or flats.
Percentage catered: 43%
Catered costs: £110–£127 a week.
Self-catered costs: £66–£100 a week.
First years have priority if conditions are met.
International students: guaranteed accommodation if conditions are met.
Contact: accommodation@brighton.ac.uk
a.eastbourne@brighton.ac.uk

University of Bristol

Bristol is the most popular multi-faculty university in Britain, judged in terms of applications per place – 11 hopefuls vie for every degree slot. It has long been a natural alternative to Oxbridge, favoured particularly by independent schools, whose pupils take more than a third of the places. In order to broaden the intake, departments are encouraged to make slightly lower offers to the most promising applicants from schools and colleges with poor records at A level. Applications were down at the start of 2009, when most universities registered healthy increases, but competition remained intense.

The university's academic credentials are not in doubt – it broke into the top 40 in the *Times Higher Education*/QS world rankings for 2008. But it has found it difficult to attract working-class teenagers, who fear that they would be out of place socially, if not academically. In 2006–07 only about one in seven came from a working-class home – the lowest proportion outside Oxbridge. Tiny numbers are recruited from the schools in the bottom half of the A-level league tables and few come from Scotland or the north of England, but £1 million a year is being spent on efforts to recruit more widely.

Overall entry standards remain among the highest at any university. A modular course system is now well established, although the majority of students still take single or dual honours degrees. Bristol has no intention of aping the growth plans of some of its rivals, but there has been modest expansion to 12,000 full-time undergraduates and the university has continued to live up to expectations in assessments of teaching and research. Almost two thirds of the work submitted for the 2008 Research Assessment Exercise was rated in the top two categories, with epidemiology and public health, health services research, chemistry, mathematics, drama, mechanical engineering and economics producing the best results.

There are 31 Fellows of the Royal Society and similar numbers in other learned societies.

Bristol was given the best rating among the small group of universities seeking to demonstrate their creditworthiness to the money markets. The university celebrated its centenary in 2009 and launched a new fundraising campaign with a target of £100 million by 2014. The previous campaign helped the university to create new chairs and embark on a number of building projects. The highly rated chemistry department, for example, moved into a well-appointed new centre in 2000, allowing new medical science laboratories to be constructed in the department's former premises. Both chemistry and

Senate House
Tyndall Avenue
Bristol BS8 1TH
0117 928 9000 (admissions)
ug-admissions@
bristol.ac.uk
www.bristol.ac.uk
www.ubu.org.uk

The Times Rankings
Overall Ranking: 10

Student satisfaction:	=67	(74%)
Research quality:	7	(2.6)
Entry standards:	=9	(447)
Student–staff ratio:	=12	(13.1)
Services & facilities/student:	9	(£1,657)
Expected completion rate:	10	(95.6%)
Good honours:	5	(81.5%)
Graduate prospects:	8	(82.0%)

medical sciences now have national teaching and learning centres, and the university has also been chosen to host four centres to train doctoral scientists and engineers.

An impressive sports centre at the heart of the university precinct opened in 2004 and there are plans for a new boathouse and a health and fitness centre. Neurology and dynamics engineering opened new buildings in 2004 and a new students' union is among the projects included in investment plans totalling £300 million over the next six years. Life sciences, nanoscience, physics and mathematics are all scheduled to benefit from well-equipped new buildings between 2007 and 2010. The £11-million Centre for Nanoscience and Quantum Information, which opened in 2008, contains some of the "quietest" labs in the world, with extremely low levels of vibrational and acoustic noise, and tight controls on temperature and air movement. The first stage of a programme of refurbishment for the university's library facilities was completed in 2009.

The city is one of the most attractive in Britain, as well as possessing a vibrant youth culture. An academic think tank named it European City of the Year in 2009. It is also relatively prosperous, offering job opportunities to students and graduates alike. The university merges into the centre, its famous Gothic tower dominating the skyline from the junction of two of the main shopping streets. Departments dot the hillside close to the picturesque harbour area.

The current students' union is less of a social centre than in some universities, partly because of the intense competition from nightclubs. Most students enjoy life in Bristol, although some find the high cost of living a serious drawback, while parts of the city suffer from the same security concerns as any big urban conurbation. The dropout rate is among the lowest in Britain.

Undergraduate Fees and Bursaries
- Fees for UK/EU students: £3,225
- International student fees: £11,450–£14,750 (£26,600 medicine)
- Bursary on full grant: £1,200 + £1,075 (local students)
- Bursaries on partial grant: household income up to £40K: £770; up to £50K: £310. All plus £1,050 (local students).
- Scholarships based on circumstances or by competition.
- For full details see the university's website: www.bris.ac.uk/studentfunding

---

Students		
Undergraduates:	12,135	(835)
Postgraduates:	3,085	(1,755)
Mature students:	6.4%	
Overseas students:	10.8%	
Applications per place:	11.4	
From state-sector schools:	63.1%	
From working-class homes:	14.3%	

For detailed information about fees, grants and bursaries and how they work, see chapter 7.

Accommodation
Number of places and costs refer to 2008–09
University-provided places: about 4,000
Percentage catered: 45%
Catered costs: £98–£152 a week.
Self-catered costs: £52–£125 a week.
First years are guaranteed one offer of accommodation provided conditions are met.
International students: accommodation is guaranteed provided conditions are met.
Contact: accom-office@bris.ac.uk
www.bristol.ac.uk/accommodation/

Brunel University

Still less than 50 years old, Brunel has recently completed a £250-million programme to upgrade and centralise its teaching, research and sporting facilities. For the first time since its early years, the whole university is located on the main Uxbridge campus. The building programme has added a £6.5-million outdoor sports complex and a £7-million indoor athletics and netball centre, making a fitting home for the former Borough Road College and its illustrious sporting traditions. There is also a hugely extended university library, increased residential accommodation, more catering and social amenities and enhanced teaching and research facilities. An accommodation complex comprising 1,228 en-suite rooms and 112 studio flats opened in 2008.

There is still plenty of scope for development. The university has quadrupled in size, with more than 13,000 students sharing a spacious, but hitherto uninspiring, main campus that had an isolated feel despite affording easy access to central London.

In recent years, Brunel has introduced more variety into a portfolio of degrees that was once given over almost entirely to sandwich courses. About a third of all undergraduates still take four-year degrees that incorporate work placements, but new developments have tended to be conventional three-year arts, social science or sports programmes. There has also been significant growth in courses specialising in new technologies, such as multimedia design and broadcast media. Other innovations include creative writing, journalism, sonic arts, aviation engineering and pilot studies, motorsport engineering, screenwriting and games design.

Work placements and the inclusion of skills modules, such as oral and written communication, business and computer literacy, in degree courses have helped maintain a consistently good record in the graduate employment market. Many courses are validated by professional institutions.

Substantial investment in research centres and academic recruitment produced significant improvements in the latest Research Assessment Exercise, when Brunel registered one of the biggest increases in the numbers of staff entered. Almost nine out of ten academics were assessed, compared with barely more than six out of ten in 2001. Income for research has grown by 70 per cent in four years, while consultancy earnings are also up by 21 per cent.

A recent review of all aspects of learning in NHS-funded health

---

Uxbridge
Middlesex UB8 3PH
01895 265265 (admissions)
admissions@brunel.ac.uk
www.brunel.ac.uk
www.brunelstudents.com

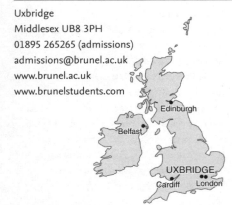

The Times Rankings
Overall Ranking: 47

Student satisfaction:	=90	(72%)
Research quality:	=41	(1.6)
Entry standards:	=45	(319)
Student–staff ratio:	=63	(17.8)
Services & facilities/student:	14	(£1,576)
Expected completion rate:	42	(86.4%)
Good honours:	45	(64.9%)
Graduate prospects:	60	(67.9%)

programmes produced a "commendable" rating and Brunel also scored well in an institutional audit. Sporting excellence is also being maintained, with four graduates winning Olympic medals in 2008 and several students competing in the games – notably Montell Douglas, who broke the British 100 metres record on the day before she graduated. Brunel has also been selected as a pre-training site for the 2012 Olympics and is likely to be a training base for international teams in the run-up to the London Games.

More than a third of the undergraduates are from working-class homes – significantly more than the national average for the subjects on offer – and more than half come from ethnic minorities. The level of applications to the university has been rising, despite increased entry scores, which now average 320 points, although the 2 per cent increase at the start of 2009 was below the national average. The projected total of 13 per cent leaving without a qualification is better than the UK average for Brunel's subjects and entry grades.

Student union facilities are good and students like Brunel's intimacy, although the university has not done well in National Student Surveys. However, it moved up 20 places in the 2008 survey, with English and design registering the second most satisfied students in the country. The residential stock has been increased in recent years and new undergraduates will be guaranteed accommodation on campus in 2010. The university won an award for its provision for disabled students.

Undergraduate Fees and Bursaries
- Fees for UK/EU students: £3,225
- International student fees: £9,200–£11,100
- Bursary on full grant: £1,000
- Bursaries on partial grant: household income up to £33K: £500.
- Scholarships based on circumstances or by competition.
- For full details see the university's website: www.brunel.ac.uk/ugfunding

Students

Undergraduates:	9,740	(665)
Postgraduates:	2,320	(1,540)
Mature students:	18.5%	
Overseas students:	10.5%	
Applications per place:	6.3	
From state-sector schools:	92.5%	
From working-class homes:	37.7%	

For detailed information about fees, grants and bursaries and how they work, see chapter 7.

Accommodation
Number of places and costs refer to 2008–09
University-provided places: 3,229
Percentage catered: 0%
Self-catered costs: £81.41–£99.96 a week (36 weeks).
All new full-time first-year students are eligible for on-campus accommodation.
International students: as above.
Contact: www.brunel.ac.uk/life/accommodation
accom-uxb@brunel.ac.uk

University of Buckingham

Britain's only private university describes itself as the country's smallest and friendliest – a claim borne out by the National Student Survey published in 2008, in which Buckingham students emerged as the most satisfied in England. Its business and economics degrees were among the only courses in the UK to register 100 per cent satisfaction.

Even before the advent of top-up fees elsewhere, Buckingham claimed to be no more expensive than other universities because its intensive two-year degrees cut maintenance costs and accelerate entry into employment. Fees for UK undergraduates taking the two-year degree are now £16,000, and there are further discounts for payment in advance. Foreign students pay £27,900 and there is a range of scholarships for both home and overseas candidates.

The university, which celebrated its 30th anniversary in 2006, has no ambitions to follow its peers into the mass higher education market: it values the personal approach that comes with having fewer than 10 students to each member of staff, when the UK average is 17. One-to-one tutorials, which have all but disappeared outside Oxbridge and are by no means universal there, are common at Buckingham. The average teaching group contains about six students.

A Conservative-backed experiment of the 1970s, Buckingham had to wait almost ten years for its royal charter, but is now an accepted part of the university system. Although in 1992 it installed Baroness Thatcher as Chancellor, the university has no party political ties. Dr Terence Kealey, a biochemist from Cambridge University, became the latest Vice-Chancellor in April 2001, declaring an ambition for Buckingham to "one day" challenge the cream of American higher education. He has recruited a number of high-profile libertarians, including Chris Woodhead, the former Chief Inspector of Schools.

Buckingham's private status excludes it from the funding council's assessment of teaching and research, making it impossible to place in our league table. However, the university commissioned its own audit of teaching standards from the Quality Assurance Agency, which gave it a clean bill of health in 2004. The university's degrees carry full currency in the academic world and teaching standards are high. Education courses now have accreditation from the Teacher Training Agency, and law and business remain popular, but the start of 2009 saw an 8 per cent drop in applications to follow an even steeper decline in the previous year.

The university runs on calendar years, rather than the traditional academic variety, although some courses give the option of

Hunter Street
Buckingham MK18 1EG
01280 81400
info@buckingham.ac.uk
www.buckingham.ac.uk
student.union@
  buckingham.ac.uk

Edinburgh
Belfast
BUCKINGHAM
Cardiff
London

The Times Rankings
not applicable

entering in July or September. Most degree courses run for two 40-week years, minimising disruptive career breaks for the many mature students. About three quarters of the students are from overseas, but the proportion from Britain has been growing. Students have the option of a three-year degree in the humanities, and the university is still hoping to open the UK's first private medical school, despite the withdrawal of Brunel University from the scheme.

Even before the QAA audit, the two-year degree had been fully assessed by Professor John Clarke, a founder member of the university staff. Although hardly neutral, he concluded that the individual tuition given to Buckingham students, made possible by unusually generous staffing levels, allowed the system to succeed. He acknowledged that "undercapitalisation" has prevented the university achieving as much as it hoped, although only four universities spend as much per student on information technology.

Recent additions to the subjects on offer include multimedia journalism and media communications, both paired with English. A BSc has been added in business enterprise, complementing a new business advice hub for the locality. The most striking development, however, is the postgraduate medical school launched in 2008 with a two-year MD in clinical medicine. The course is expected to attract overseas medical graduates who find it difficult to secure junior doctor posts as a result of recent Government restrictions.

Campus facilities have improved considerably in recent years, although they cannot compare with those available at traditional universities. Buckingham operates on three sites, all within easy walking distance of each other. An academic centre containing computer suites, lecture theatres and student facilities provides a focal point that was missing previously.

The social scene is predictably quiet, given the size of the university and the workload, especially at weekends. There is a university cinema and the town is pretty with a good selection of pubs and restaurants. Milton Keynes or Oxford are near, except that Buckingham has no rail station, although a good bus service operates throughout the week with extra buses at weekends.

Undergraduate Fees and Bursaries

- Fees for UK/EU students: £8,040*
- International student fees: £13,950*
- Bursary on full grant: n/a
- Bursaries on partial grant: n/a

* Duration of degree course is two years.

Students

Undergraduates:	675	(45)
Postgraduates:	235	(25)
Mature students:	45.0	
Overseas students:	63.2%	
Applications per place:	11.0	
From state-sector schools:	79.5	
From working-class homes:	n/a	

For detailed information about fees, grants and bursaries and how they work, see chapter 7.

Accommodation

Number of places and costs refer to 2008–09
University-provided places: 457
Percentage catered: 0%
Self-catered accommodation: £890–£1,520 a term.
Most first years are accommodated.
International students: same as above.
Contact: accommodation@buckingham.ac.uk

Buckinghamshire New University

Having waited a couple of years longer for university status than the group of higher education colleges promoted in 2005, Buckinghamshire New University has been making up for lost time. The first phase of a £200-million campus redevelopment was due to be completed for the academic year beginning in 2009 and students have been responding enthusiastically to a portfolio of innovative courses and an attractive package of financial support and extra-curricular benefits for students. The 33 per cent rise in applications at the start of 2009 was one of the biggest ever recorded by a UK university.

The redevelopment will allow most students to be based at the main campus in High Wycombe – the exception being those taking nursing, who are to move into a new building in nearby Uxbridge. The new Gateway Building at High Wycombe will transform the town-centre campus with improved teaching, social and administrative space. The complex will include a new sports hall, gym, treatment rooms and sports laboratory, which will be available to the public as well as to students. At the same time, collaboration with two of the world's biggest IT companies is developing one of the most advanced student networks in UK higher education. An outdoor sports village is in the next phase of the university's ten-year development plan.

Sport is an important part of life at the new university, which sponsors the London Wasps rugby union team in a partnership which trades coaching for Bucks students for courses for Wasps players. But the university's main aim is contribute to the social and economic life of the region, embracing workplace learning and close ties with local businesses. Employees of the bed company, Dreams, which is based in High Wycombe, will take a new Foundation degree in retail management while at work, for example. Bucks has also won awards for its training of commercial pilots and its courses for music industry management. Other Foundation degrees include one for the motorsport industry and another in "protective security management".

There are more than 9,000 full and part-time students, 90 per cent of whom are taking first degrees and a third of whom are over 25. Nearly 60 per cent of the students are female. Academic departments are divided into three faculties: Creativity and Culture, Society and Health, and Enterprise and Innovation. Only 26 staff were entered for the 2008 Research Assessment Exercise –

Queen Alexandra Road
High Wycombe
Buckinghamshire HP11 2JZ
0800 0565 660 (enquiries)
advice@bucks.ac.uk
www.bucks.ac.uk
www.bucksstudent.com

The Times Rankings
Overall Ranking: 112

Student satisfaction:	=106	(68%)
Research quality:	=108	(0.1)
Entry standards:	109	(210)
Student–staff ratio:	99	(20.3)
Services & facilities/student:	59	(£1,110)
Expected completion rate:	78	(79.8%)
Good honours:	108	(46.3%)
Graduate prospects:	114	(50.9%)

half of them in art and design, which registered the only world-leading research. However, an institutional audit expressed "broad confidence" in academic standards.

The projected dropout rate for undergraduates entering in 2006 had risen to 14 per cent, but this was still lower than at most comparable institutions and more than three percentage points better than the national average for its subjects and entry qualifications. Nor was this achieved by neglecting the Government's widening participation agenda: almost all the entrants are from state schools or colleges, and more than a third are from working-class homes.

The university has a particular focus on student support, devoting more than a third of its fee income to bursaries – one of the biggest proportions in England. In 2009–10, all full-time UK undergraduates (apart from nursing students, who are eligible for Government bursaries) received an annual, non means-tested £500 cash award. In addition, the Big Deal scheme offers free entry to all entertainment events, free use of all sports facilities and a programme of extra-curricular activities such as lessons in cookery and motor mechanics. The university also pays student representatives.

One disappointment has been consistently low scores in the National Student Survey, which has left Bucks in the bottom five for the last two years. The extensive building work on the main campus may have been a factor. Its own annual survey, carried out by independent academics, has been more complimentary. Beyond the campus, High Wycombe has the usual range of pubs and clubs for a medium-sized town, but will not be a magnet for students. The university has opened an art gallery in the main shopping centre to showcase students' work, as part of its efforts to maintain a strong relationship with the town.

Undergraduate Fees and Bursaries
- Fees for UK/EU students: £3,225
- International student fees: £7,800–£8,500
- Bursary on full grant: £500
- Bursaries on partial grant: £500
- Scholarships based on circumstances or by competition.
- For full details see the university's website: www.bucks.ac.uk/courses/undergraduate/fees_bursaries.aspx

Students		
Undergraduates:	4,970	(3,690)
Postgraduates:	170	(435)
Mature students:	36.8%	
Overseas students:	11.8%	
Applications per place:	3.0	
From state-sector schools:	97.0%	
From working-class homes:	36.8%	

For detailed information about fees, grants and bursaries and how they work, see chapter 7.

Accommodation
Number of places and costs refer to 2008–09
University-provided places: 1,100
Percentage catered: 0%
Self-catered costs: a week: £68.60–£87.85 a week (44 weeks)
First-year students are guaranteed accommodation. Residential restrictions apply. International students: same as above.
Contact: accom@bucks.ac.uk

University of Cambridge

Cambridge put the cat among the pigeons by becoming the first university to announce that it would demand at least one A* at A level when the new grade is introduced in 2010. It already had clearly the highest entry standards in the UK, with additional tests, such as its own STEP papers, in some subjects.

Until 2001, Cambridge had also enjoyed an unbroken run at the top of *The Times* League Table, and even now it is practically inseparable from first-placed Oxford. The university produced the best results in the 2008 Research Assessment Exercise and the university still tops far more of our subject tables than any of its rivals. Nearly a third of its research was considered world-leading and over 70 per cent was rated in the top two categories.

Traditionally supreme in the sciences, where it is ranked second only to Harvard in the *Times Higher Education*/QS World University Rankings, Cambridge has also strengthened the arts and social sciences. Cambridge has been in the top three overall every year that the rankings have been published.

At first, Cambridge students did not respond in sufficient numbers for the university to be included in the National Student Survey. But the 2008 results put Cambridge in the top three, with undergraduates in theology and religious studies, history and archaeology particularly satisfied. The Tripos system was a forerunner of the currently fashionable modular degree, allowing students to change subjects (within limits) midway through their courses. Students receive a classification for each of the two parts of their degree.

More students now come from state schools than the independent sector – a trend the university is keen to continue – but the proportion of working-class undergraduates remains low, at less than 12 per cent. Summer schools, student visits and, in some colleges, sympathetic selection procedures, are helping to attract more applications from comprehensive schools and further education colleges.

The application system was simplified slightly for the 2009 entry, with candidates no longer required to complete an initial Cambridge form, as well as their UCAS form. However, they are still sent the Supplementary Application Questionnaire, covering the applicant's academic experience in more detail.

A lively alternative prospectus, available from the students' union, used to say there was no such thing as Cambridge University, just a collection of colleges. Where applications are concerned, this is still true, as it is to some extent socially. Making the right choice of college is crucial, both to

---

Kellet Lodge
Tennis Court Road
Cambridge CB2 1QJ
01223 333308
admissions@cam.ac.uk
www.cam.ac.uk
www.cusu.cam.ac.uk

The Times Rankings
Overall Ranking: 2

Student satisfaction:	1	86%
Research quality:	1	(3.7)
Entry standards:	1	(539)
Student–staff ratio:	6	(11.6)
Services & facilities/student:	3	(£2,385)
Expected completion rate:	1	(99.0%)
Good honours:	2	(87.0%)
Graduate prospects:	3	(85.5%)

maximise the chances of winning a place and to ensure an enjoyable three years if you are successful. Applicants can take pot luck with an open application if they prefer not to opt for a particular college. But, though the statistics show that this route is equally successful, only a minority take it. Most teaching is now university-based, especially in the sciences, and a shift of emphasis towards the centre has been taking place more generally. The trend may accelerate if a £1-billion funding appeal to mark the university's 800th anniversary, in 2009, is successful. It had passed the £800-million mark in July 2008.

Cambridge boasts numerous successful partnerships with the private sector, several of which benefit undergraduates as well as researchers. The university was also chosen for a Government-sponsored partnership with the Massachusetts Institute of Technology to promote entrepreneurship and, more recently, was selected to host one of five Academic Health Science Centres to lead biomedical innovation.

Such is the scale of development that almost £500-million worth of building is either planned or under construction. The university is looking to the outskirts of the city to expand. The West Cambridge site will take a mixture of teaching and research buildings, and there are plans for more on green-belt land further north. In the long term, up to three new colleges could be built, but there will be few extra places for undergraduates in the foreseeable future.

With around four applicants for each place – fewer still if you choose your subject carefully – the competition for places appears less intense than at the popular civic universities, but the real difference is that nine out of ten entrants have at least three A grades at A level. The pressure does not end there: the amount of high-quality work to be crammed into eight-week terms can prove a strain, although the projected dropout rate of less than 1 per cent is the lowest at any university offering conventional degrees.

Undergraduate Fees and Bursaries

- Fees for UK/EU students: £3,225*
- International student fees: £9,747–£12,768†
  (£23,631 medicine)†
- Bursary on full grant: £3,250
- Bursaries on partial grant: household income up to £50K: sliding scale £2,000–£50.
- Scholarships based on circumstances or by competition.
- For full details see the university's website: www.cam.ac.uk/admissions/undergraduate/finance/support.html

* UK & EU students eligible for tuition fee support not liable for College fees.
† Plus College fees (£4,000–£5,000)

Students		
Undergraduates:	11,760	(3,925)
Postgraduates:	5,695	(1,365)
Mature students:	6.3%	
Overseas students:	12.1%	
Applications per place:	4.2	
From state-sector schools:	57.7%	
From working-class homes:	11.5%	

For detailed information about fees, grants and bursaries and how they work, see chapter 7.

Accommodation

See chapter 10 for information about individual colleges.

Canterbury Christ Church University

This former Church of England college started branching out well before university status arrived in 2005. There is a network of campuses right across Kent, the most populous county in England but, until recently, one of the most sparsely provided with higher education. At the purpose-built campus at Broadstairs, for example, the university offers subjects as diverse as commercial music, digital media, business, police studies, photography and child and youth studies. There is also an imposing country house and one-time convalescent home outside Tunbridge Wells, mainly for postgraduates, as well as a newly expanded Medway site at Chatham, operated in conjunction with Greenwich and Kent universities, and a new University Centre at Folkestone, offering performing and visual arts, also developed in partnership with Greenwich. The Medway campus hosts health programmes in nursing, radiography, occupational therapy and operating department practice, and education programmes in childhood and early years studies.

The majority of the 15,000 students, however, are at the university's Canterbury headquarters. The main campus, which dates from 1962, is a few minutes' walk from the city centre, but the university has several buildings in other parts of Canterbury. One is being developed as a £30-million library, learning and student services centre, with specialist teaching and IT facilities, to open in 2009. It will have a café, two garden terraces, an atrium and multipurpose floor space for public events, conferences, exams, teaching and exhibitions. A new sport centre, a short walk from the main campus, is also due to be ready in 2009 and planning permission has been given for a purpose-built music venue to open in 2011.

The Church of England link was underlined with the installation of the Archbishop of Canterbury as the university's Chancellor in 2005. Religious studies is available as a single-honours degree or as part of the modular scheme, which covers the arts and humanities, business and management, social and applied sciences, education, and health and social care. The large health and teacher training programmes make the university the largest provider of higher education to the public services in Kent. Canterbury is one of the few Grade 1 providers of teacher training offering the full range of courses from early years to primary, secondary, further and higher education. Policing studies and a new law degree are other big recruiters.

North Holmes Road
Canterbury CT1 1QU
01227 782900 (prospectus)
admissions
  @canterbury.ac.uk
www.canterbury.ac.uk
www.ccsu.co.uk

The Times Rankings
Overall Ranking: 98

Student satisfaction:	=78	(73%)
Research quality:	=95	(0.2)
Entry standards:	95	(238)
Student–staff ratio:	=68	(18.3)
Services & facilities/student:	112	(£633)
Expected completion rate:	77	(80.2%)
Good honours:	99	(49.7%)
Graduate prospects:	=98	(59.0%)

Religious studies registered the best teaching quality grades, but all the assessments were good, as have been the results from successive national student satisfaction surveys. Canterbury Christ Church was one of the new "teaching-led" universities, but still entered staff in seven areas in the 2008 Research Assessment Exercise. The best grades came in education and music, both of which had 10 per cent of their work assessed as world-leading.

Nearly 97 per cent of the under-graduates are state-educated and more than a third come from working-class homes. The dropout rate of around 15 per cent is around the national average for the university's courses and entry qualifications. The university's applications were up by more than 10 per cent at the start of 2009, the third successive year of big increases.

All the campuses are connected by a microwave link, which provides fast access to teaching and learning materials, as well as email. The new Drill Hall Library at Medway provides 147,000 items, 370 computers and 250 study spaces for Canterbury, Greenwich and Kent students.

Social and sports facilities naturally vary between the campuses, although the students' union is present on all of them. Residential accommodation is not plentiful, but first years are given priority.

The pressure is eased to some extent because two thirds of the students come from Kent, many of them among the 7,000 taking part-time courses.

Undergraduate Fees and Bursaries

- Fees for UK/EU students: £3,225
- International student fees: £7,650–£8,375
- Bursary on full grant: £860
- Bursaries on partial grant: household income up to £50K: partial award on a sliding scale.
- Scholarships based on circumstances or by competition.
- For full details see the university's website: www.canterbury.ac.uk/support/student-support-services/students/finance/finance-index.asp

---

Students

Undergraduates:	7,330	(4,505)
Postgraduates:	1,250	(2,460)
Mature students:	36.2%	
Overseas students:	6.6%	
Applications per place:	4.0	
From state-sector schools:	96.9%	
From working-class homes:	34.6%	

For detailed information about fees, grants and bursaries and how they work, see chapter 7.

Accommodation

Number of places and costs refer to 2009–10
University-provided places: 1,435
Percentage catered: 12%
Catered costs: £112.40–£117.40 a week. Food is purchased on Smart card basis.
Self-catered costs: £80–£96 a week.
Accommodation guaranteed for first years if conditions are met.
International students: as above.
Contact: accommodation@canterbury.ac.uk
www.canterbury.ac.uk/support/accommodation

Cardiff University

Cardiff has established itself as the front-runner in Welsh higher education and a leading player in the UK and beyond. It is a member of the Russell Group of 20 research-led universities and has two Nobel Laureates on its staff. No longer a member of the University of Wales, Cardiff now has more than 25,000 students and 5,500 staff, making it a match for most of its peers in teaching and research. A third of the students come from Wales, but the 3,000 from overseas testify to Cardiff's international reputation.

The 2008 Research Assessment Exercise rated almost 60 per cent of the work submitted in the top two categories, with 33 of the 34 subject areas containing some world-leading research. Journalism, media and cultural studies; English; city and regional planning; and business produced the best results.

Teaching quality is also highly rated. An audit by the Quality Assurance Agency complimented the university on its "powerful academic vision and well-developed and effectively articulated mission to achieve excellence in teaching and research". Student support services, including counselling facilities and the help offered to dyslexics, were among the features singled out for praise.

Cardiff has done well in the first four National Student Surveys. In 2008, students were particularly satisfied with the learning resources and academic support available to them. Cardiff is the first university in Wales to be awarded the Frank Buttle Trust Quality Mark which recognises support for looked after children in higher education.

Many full-time degrees share a common first year, and the modular system of courses makes undergraduate study flexible thereafter. New courses include electronic and communication engineering, medical pharmacology, marine geoscience, and politics and international relations.

The university enjoys a central location in Wales' capital, occupying a significant part of the civic complex around Cathays Park. In recent years, there has been major investment in new buildings and equipment, and extensive refurbishment. Recent projects include almost £30 million invested in brain and body imaging facilities at the former University of Wales College of Medicine, which became part of the university with the backing of £60 million from the Welsh Assembly and other sources. Library services are being transformed in order to boost access to resources and improve the environment for the study of rare collections. The School of Optometry and Vision Sciences moved into a £21-million building in 2007 and a new Medical School building opened in 2008, making room for more students. The

---

P.O. Box 921
Cardiff CF10 3XQ
029 2087 9999 (admissions)
admissions@cardiff.ac.uk
www.cardiff.ac.uk
www.cardiffstudents.com

Edinburgh
Belfast
London
CARDIFF

The Times Rankings
Overall Ranking: 26

Student satisfaction:	=28	(77%)
Research quality:	=32	(1.8)
Entry standards:	=21	(394)
Student–staff ratio:	=30	(14.7)
Services & facilities/student:	47	(£1,177)
Expected completion rate:	18	(92.4%)
Good honours:	36	(66.8%)
Graduate prospects:	20	(77.6%)

school is a mile away from the main campus at Heath Park, where the five healthcare schools share a 53-acre site with the University Hospital of Wales.

A new IT working environment gives students online access to information about their studies and social life, including reading lists and timetables to social events and networking groups. Other recent developments include the establishment of the Cardiff International Academy of Voice, providing individual training for opera stars of the future, while the School of Earth, Ocean and Planetary Sciences has invested in its own research vessel for a programme of research and teaching voyages.

With more than 5,100 rooms, the university can accommodate all first years and a considerable number of returning students. Rents are among the lowest in the UK, according to a National Union of Students survey.

Entry requirements have been rising, despite recent expansion, and the graduate employment record is good. Only eight universities had more applications than Cardiff at the start of 2009. The university has been bucking the national trend with increases in applications in science, technology, engineering and maths. One undergraduate in seven comes from an independent school, but still more than one in five have a working-class back-

ground. The projected dropout rate had been creeping up, but was back down to 6.5 per cent – by far the lowest in Wales – in the latest survey.

The city of Cardiff is popular with students. The main residential site at Talybont boasts a "sports village", and there is also a city-centre fitness suite and a sports ground available to students. The university is continuing to update its sports facilities across the three sites, one being an upgrade of the floodlit grass training pitch to a new 3G rubber crumb synthetic pitch.

Undergraduate Fees and Bursaries

- Fees for UK/EU students: £3,225 (grant of up to £1,940 for Welsh students).
- International student fees: £9,600–£12,300; £22,500 (medicine)
- Bursary of £1,050 (household income up to £25,000).
- Bursary of £500 (household income up to £39,300).
- Scholarships based on circumstances or by competition.
- For full details see the university's website: www.cardiff.ac.uk/for/prospective/ug/scholarships/index.html

Students

Undergraduates:	16,050	(3,770)
Postgraduates:	3,430	(3,335)
Mature students:	14.4%	
Overseas students:	8.4%	
Applications per place:	6.0	
From state-sector schools:	85.8%	
From working-class homes:	21.8%	

For detailed information about fees, grants and bursaries and how they work, see chapter 7.

Accommodation

Number of places and costs refer to 2008–09

University-provided places: 5,164

Percentage catered: 5.2%

Catered costs: £70–£80 a week.

Self-catered costs: £56–£84 a week.

All first years are guaranteed accommodation if conditions are met.

Policy for international students: as above

Contact: residences@cardiff.ac.uk

Cardiff, University of Wales Institute (UWIC)

The University of Wales Institute in Cardiff has an international reputation for sport, but other areas are also benefiting from a £50-million programme of new facilities. The £20-million Cardiff School of Management should be open on the Llandaff campus for the start of the 2010–11 academic year. A Food Industry Centre opened in 2009 and the Cyncoed campus has a new student centre with a nightclub and all the normal catering and leisure facilities.

UWIC was the most improved university in Wales and had one of the biggest rises in the UK in the 2008 National Student Survey. Initial teacher training, media studies and tourism, transport and travel produced the best results. But applications were still down by 5 per cent at the start of 2009, when most universities were posting healthy increases.

Two thirds of UWIC's 10,000 students are Welsh, half of them from Cardiff or the Vale of Glamorgan. More than 90 per cent attended state schools and, although little more than three out of ten come from working-class homes, the 10 per cent who come from areas sending few students to higher education is close to

the benchmark set according to the mix of courses. The dropout rate is lower than the average for new universities.

UWIC is one of Britain's leading centres for university sport, with team performances to match some excellent facilities. In recent years, the Institute has had British university champions in gymnastics, trampolining, athletics, rugby union, rugby league, boxing, squash, archery, weightlifting and judo. More than 300 past or present students are internationals in 30 sports, world and Olympic champions among them. The £7-million National Indoor Athletics Centre is UWIC's pride and joy, but other facilities are also of high quality.

Academically, the large School of Art and Design is the star performer, with 70 per cent of the work submitted to the 2008 Research Assessment Exercise rated either world-leading or internationally excellent. Sport also registered some world-leading research and all six teacher training courses are rated as excellent by Estyn, the school inspectorate. UWIC also did well in the Higher Education Academy's satisfaction survey of postgraduate research students.

Entrance requirements are generally modest, but the menu of largely vocational courses means that many students come with qualifications other than A levels. About a quarter are mature students and

---

Cardiff Institute
Western Avenue
Cardiff CF5 2YB
029 2041 6044 (enquiries)
uwicinfo@uwic.ac.uk
www.uwic.ac.uk
www.uwicsu.co.uk

The Times Rankings
Overall Ranking: 76

Student satisfaction:	=67	(74%)
Research quality:	=71	(0.4)
Entry standards:	=77	(261)
Student–staff ratio:	92	(19.9)
Services & facilities/student:	41	(£1,205)
Expected completion rate:	62	(83.2%)
Good honours:	89	(51.8%)
Graduate prospects:	87	(61.5%)

there are 850 international students from 125 different countries. Many are among the 23 per cent postgraduates – the largest proportion in Wales. UWIC courses are also taught at partner colleges in Kuala Lumpur, Singapore and Dhaka.

The four Cardiff sites are all within three miles of the city centre. The Cyncoed campus, which houses education and sport, is the centre of activity, particularly for first-year students. The athletics centre is there, together with a multitude of outdoor facilities and also the Welsh Sports Centre for the Disabled. Student facilities, including the Institute's largest bar, have been upgraded recently. A £2-million learning centre opened in 2005; the IT suite has 250 computers available 24 hours a day.

Howard Gardens is the home of fine art, while the Llandaff campus hosts design, engineering, food science and health courses. A £3-million student centre at Llandaff, which opened in 2003, includes a dyslexia support unit among a number of advice and representation services, and a learning centre with more than 300 computers. Business, hospitality and tourism are taught at the Colchester Avenue campus.

Students tend to like Cardiff as a city, and UWIC's enterprising union does its best to make their time there as lively as possible. It owns a nightclub and bar in the city centre to add to the campus choices. Before the recent expansion, it was possible to guarantee accommodation to all first years, and 90 per cent still live in halls. UWIC is the only university to have been awarded the Government's Charter Mark four times, the judges commenting particularly on the level of satisfaction among students.

Undergraduate Fees and Bursaries

- Fees for UK/EU students: £3,225 (grant of up to £1,940 for Welsh students).
- International student fees: £7,800–£9,000; £11,000 (podiatry).
- Bursary of £500 (household income up to £18,370).
- Bursary of £300 (household income up to £39,300).
- Scholarships based on circumstances or by competition.
- For full details see the university's website: www3.uwic.ac.uk/english/studyatuwic/finance/bursaries/pages/home.aspx

Students

Undergraduates:	6,645	(820)
Postgraduates:	1,225	(1,210)
Mature students:	25.8%	
Overseas students:	8.0%	
Applications per place:	3.8	
From state-sector schools:	94.5%	
From working-class homes:	30.6%	

For detailed information about fees, grants and bursaries and how they work, see chapter 7.

Accommodation

Number of places and costs refer to 2009–10
University-provided places: 928
Percentage catered: 34%
Catered cost: £108.50–£117.50 a week.
Self-catered costs: £74.50–£93.00 a week.
First-year students have no guarantee, terms and conditions apply.
International students: accommodation is reserved, subject to availability and if conditions are met.
Contact: accomm@uwic.ac.uk

University of Central Lancashire (UCLan)

A big university at the heart of England's newest city, only eight English institutions have a bigger teaching budget than UClan. Its students account for a sixth of the population of Preston during term time. A total of £60 million has been spent on the modern, town-centre campus, as the university has doubled in size – and still the building continues. The new £5-million dental school was one of the first to open in over a century, while the £15-million Media Factory, with its facilities for music, theatre, dance, film, photography and media studies, has prompted a surge in applications for arts and fashion courses.

An extended and refurbished students' union boasts one of the largest student venues in the country, and well-equipped new buildings have opened recently for science, health and business subjects. A new Futures Centre brings together advice on careers and work placements, employability and enterprise course electives, business start-up and self-employment services. All students are encouraged to develop their CVs, engage in course-related employment during vacations and to draw on the experience of local employers and alumni.

Amid the expansion, the university has revamped its pioneering credit accumu-lation and transfer system, allowing undergraduates to mix and match from a menu of more than 3,000 courses. Electives are used to broaden the curriculum, so that up to 11 per cent of students' time is spent on subjects outside their normal range. The university has also launched two unusual scholarships: the Gilbertson Award, which offers free postgraduate study to every UCLan undergraduate who achieves a first-class degree; and the International Bursary, which gives students the opportunity to study or work abroad.

The former polytechnic has acquired a high reputation in some apparently unlikely fields. Astrophysics, which benefits from two observatories in Britain and a share in the Southern African Large Telescope, saw applications increase by a third in 2008. Following dentistry, the UK's first new architecture degree for ten years was launched in 2009. Linguistics and journalism produced the best results in the 2008 Research Assessment Exercise, but nursing, history and social work also did well. The university has since invested £10 million in ten research centres in areas as diverse as philosophy and nuclear science. The Confucius Institute promotes and supports the development of Chinese language and culture throughout the North West region.

UCLan is opening a £10-million campus in Burnley in 2009, in partnership with

---

Preston PR1 2HE
01772 201201
uadmissions@uclan.ac.uk
www.uclan.ac.uk
www.yourunion.co.uk

The Times Rankings
Overall Ranking: 78

Student satisfaction:	=40	(76%)
Research quality:	=71	(0.4)
Entry standards:	=85	(252)
Student–staff ratio:	98	(20.2)
Services & facilities/student:	65	(£1,083)
Expected completion rate:	102	(72.9%)
Good honours:	=100	(49.3%)
Graduate prospects:	49	(70.1%)

Burnley College, which already offers a number of the university's degree and Foundation degree courses. A new Centre for Outdoor Education has been developed at Llangollen, in north Wales, enabling the university to launch a degree in the subject. UCLan is one of only two universities to be awarded the Carbon Trust Standard and now runs modules in sustainability.

Scores in the National Student Survey have been steady, with sports science and tourism, transport and travel doing particularly well in 2008. More than a third of Central Lancashire's students come from working-class homes. A high proportion are local people in their twenties or thirties, many of whom come through the well-established lifelong learning networks run in colleges throughout the North West. No fewer than 14 per cent of the university's students are taught in colleges but, unlike some institutions involved in "franchising", Central Lancashire has won official praise for the quality of its external programmes. Applications were up by an impressive 15 per cent at the start of 2009, following a year in which UCLan increased its share of north-west England's total applications.

The social scene in Preston may not compare with Manchester or Liverpool, but neither do the security risks, and the cost of living is low. Both cities are within easy reach, and the student union's "Feel" club nights have won national recognition.

Although still not the most fashionable university, UCLan commands great loyalty among its students.

Rents for the nearly 2,000 places in university accommodation are among the lowest in Britain and the 60-acre Preston Sports Arena is one of the best in higher education. Three miles from the main campus, the centre is available to clubs throughout the region but there are reserved periods for students, who can also book at peak times. It has been chosen as a pre-Olympic training base.

Undergraduate Fees and Bursaries
- Fees for UK/EU students: £3,225
- International student fees: £8,950–£9,450
- Bursary on full grant: £500 (£310 from Year 2)
- Bursaries on partial grant: household income up to £60K: £500 (£310 from Year 2).
- Scholarships based on circumstances or by competition.
- For full details see the university's website: www.uclan.ac.uk/information/ prospective_students/fees_and_finance/index. php

---

Students
Undergraduates:	n/a	(n/a)
Postgraduates:	n/a	(n/a)
Mature students:	32.8%	
Overseas students:	7.8%	
Applications per place:	3.3	
From state-sector schools:	97.2%	
From working-class homes:	38.1%	

For detailed information about fees, grants and bursaries and how they work, see chapter 7.

Accommodation
Number of places and costs refer to 2008–09
University-provided places: around 2,000
Percentage catered: 0%
Self-cateredcosts: £69.93–£81.00 a week.
The Student Accommodation Service will assist all first years find suitable accommodation either in University owned/leased halls of residence, private sector registered halls, or shared houses.
International students: as above.
Contact: saccommodation@uclan.ac.uk

Chester University

The picturesque Roman city of Chester is one of those places that outsiders probably always expected to have its own university. Indeed, William Gladstone was among the founders of the first Church of England teacher training college there in 1839. Although it took until 2005 for that college to achieve university status, it had been building up a solid reputation in a number of subjects beyond education. Applications were up by much less than the national average at the start of 2009, but the demand for places remains more buoyant than in pre-university days.

The main campus is only a short walk from the centre of Chester, a 32-acre site boasting manicured gardens and a number of new developments. A new students' union is just one of a stream of improvements, the latest of which include a new building for health and social care. The university has also converted a former school into a base for the Faculty of Arts and Media.

The Warrington campus, which has seven halls of residence, focuses on media courses and has seen the addition of state-of-the-art production facilities in collaboration with Granada Television and a new students' union. The university has also signed a partnership agreement with the BBC, which is intended to open up new employment opportunities in the media industry and develop new talent ahead of the transfer of parts of the corporation to Salford in 2011. The library has been extended to three times its original size and a business centre opened for students and local firms. The campus is expected to be the focus of future development to accommodate modest increases in student numbers.

Chester was among the top ten universities in the first National Student Survey. Although it has slipped out of the top 50 since then, geography and development studies has twice achieved the rare feat of registering 100 per cent satisfaction, while English and maths also produced good scores. Chester was the first of the universities created in 2005 to be granted the power to award research degrees. Four of the ten subject areas entered for the 2008 Research Assessment Exercise contained at least some world-leading work. History was the most successful, with nearly half of its submission placed in the top two categories.

With 13,500 students, including part-timers, Chester is among the biggest of the new universities established that year. Over a quarter of undergraduates are mature students and three quarters are female. Nearly all are state-educated, and more than a third have working-class

---

Parkgate Road
Chester CH1 4BJ
01244 511000 (admissions)
enquiries@chester.ac.uk
www.chester.ac.uk
www.chestersu.com

roots. The projected dropout rate of 15 per cent was back to the national average for the university's courses and entry standards in the latest statistics. About a third of the undergraduates take combined honours degrees and many courses of all types include a period of extended work experience. There is also a limited range of Foundation degrees, mainly in health subjects but now including courses in business or leadership and management for RAF personnel. The Foundation degree in Muslim youth work is the first of its kind, as is one in mortuary science. Among the more traditional subjects are new degrees in English language, politics, and accountancy and finance.

A student contract of the type that is likely to become commonplace elsewhere in the higher education sector sets out clear conditions on the offer of a place, as well as detailing the university's responsibilities. Students promise to "study diligently, and to attend promptly and participate appropriately at lectures, courses, classes, seminars, tutorials, work placements and other activities which form part of the programme." The university undertakes to deliver the student's programme, but leaves itself considerable leeway beyond that.

However, Chester offers considerable support and facilities for its students. It was the first UK university to receive the maximum five-star rating from the British Quality Foundation for its student support and guidance and its careers and employability departments. There are libraries on both sites and extensive sports facilities, especially on the main campus, catering partly for the large physical education programme. Most first years are offered one of the growing number of hall places, although there is not yet enough university accommodation to make this a guarantee. Student union facilities form the basis of the social scene on both campuses, but Chester has more to offer for those looking further afield.

Undergraduate Fees and Bursaries

- Fees for UK/EU students: £3,225
- International student fees: £7,182–£8,388*
- Bursary on full grant: £1,000
- Bursaries on partial grant: n/a
- Scholarships based on circumstances or by competition.
- For full details see the university's website: www.chester.ac.uk/undergraduate/moneymatters.html

* Figures for 2008–09

Students		
Undergraduates:	7,565	(2,975)
Postgraduates:	580	(2,400)
Mature students:	27.4%	
Overseas students:	1.9%	
Applications per place:	5.9	
From state-sector schools:	96.7%	
From working-class homes:	36.7%	

For detailed information about fees, grants and bursaries and how they work, see chapter 7.

Accommodation

Number of places and costs refer to 2009–10
University-provided places: 1000
Percentage catered: 46%
Catered costs: £63.00–£128.45 a week.
Self-catered costs: £52.85–£87.15 a week.
First years cannot be guaranteed accommodation.
International students: guaranteed accommodation if they apply by advertised date.
Contact: www.chester.ac.uk/accommodation

University of Chichester

Chichester is the smallest of the nine universities created in 2005, formed from an amalgamation of two former teacher training colleges. But it features consistently among the leading modern universities in league tables. It was outscored by only one of its peers in the National Student Survey published in 2008, when biology, business, history, philosophy and sports science all showed very high levels of satisfaction. These achievements were reflected in a 17 per cent rise in applications for courses beginning in 2009 – the second big increase in three years.

The university traces its history back to 1839, when the college that subsequently bore his name was founded in memory of William Otter, the education-minded Bishop of Chichester. It became a teacher training college for women, who still account for two thirds of the places. Two further stages preceded university status – twenty years as the West Sussex Institute of Higher Education, following an amalgamation with the nearby Bognor Regis College of Education, and then seven as University College Chichester. The Chichester campus – now the larger of two – continues to carry the Bishop Otter name, signifying a continuing link with the Church of England.

The two faculties operate on both sites, one covering business, arts and the humanities; the other sport, social sciences and education. The portfolio of some 50 courses ranges from adventure education to humanistic counselling, fine art and theology. The PE teacher training course is the largest in the country – the university now trains one in five PE teachers in England – and is highly rated by Ofsted. Sport was the only area in which the university registered any world-leading work in the 2008 Research Assessment Exercise, but history and drama, dance and performing arts also produced good results.

The Mathematics Centre, at Bognor, has an international reputation, working with over 30 countries as well as teaching the university's own students. It has become a focal point for curriculum development in Britain and elsewhere.

About 30 per cent of the 5,000 students are over 21 on entry. Almost all are state educated and, despite the comfortable south coast location, the proportions from working-class homes and areas of low participation in higher education are both slightly above the national average for the university's courses and entry grades. The projected dropout rate, at less than 8 per cent, is half the benchmark figure. The university runs summer taster sessions and has a series of partnerships with

---

Bishop Otter Campus
College Lane
Chichester
W. Sussex PO19 6PE
01243 816000
admissions@chi.ac.uk
www.chi.ac.uk
www.chisu.org

schools in the Channel Islands and Sussex to encourage a broader intake. Courses are also run in collaboration with Isle of Wight College, where fees are pegged at £1,200, and with the Academy of Play and Child Psychotherapy, in Uckfield, East Sussex.

Both of the university's campuses are within ten minutes' walk of the sea and the 647 residential places are roughly equally divided between them. There is a university bus service linking the two and student union bars at each. Sports facilities are good and competitive teams surprisingly successful for such a small university. The university has been chosen to provide training facilities for competitors in athletics, boxing, road cycling and table tennis before the 2012 Olympic Games. The bid was based on Chichester's expertise in sports science, as well as its facilities.

The small cathedral city of Chichester is best known as a yachting venue and, while Bognor's days as a leading holiday resort are well in the past, it is said to have the longest stretch of coastline in the south where all types of watersports are available. Both locations offer a good supply of private housing and some student-oriented bars. Much of the surrounding countryside has been designated an area of outstanding natural beauty.

Undergraduate Fees and Bursaries

- Fees for UK/EU students: £3,225
- International student fees: £8,300–£9,500
- Bursary on full grant: £1,077
- Bursaries on partial grant: household income up to £50K: sliding scale £1,026–£256.
- Scholarships based on circumstances or by competition.
- For full details see the university's website: www.chi.ac.uk/studentfinance

Students

Undergraduates:	3,075	(720)
Postgraduates:	280	(725)
Mature students:	30.9%	
Overseas students:	3.4%	
Applications per place:	4.5	
From state-sector schools:	96.4%	
From working-class homes:	35.7%	

For detailed information about fees, grants and bursaries and how they work, see chapter 7.

Accommodation

Number of places and costs refer to 2008–09
University-provided places: 647
Percentage catered: 66.5%
Catered costs: £94.45 (shared) – £126.30 (en suite) a week.
Self-catered costs: £73.50 (shared) – £104.30 (en suite) a week.
First years are accommodated on a first come, first served basis.
International students: as above.
Contact: accommodation@chi.ac.uk

City University London

Having marketed itself for some time as the "international university in the heart of London", City has now added the name of the capital to its title to cash in on its greatest asset. Students come from more than 150 different countries to study on the borders of the financial district. Once a college of advanced technology, a third of City students now study business, a third health subjects and the remaining third law, computing, engineering, journalism, and the arts.

The university has maintained its links with business, industry and the professions, reaping the benefits with consistently good graduate employment figures. The university's graduates play their part, with more than 4,000 of them offering practical help to current students through an online careers network. Courses have a practical edge, and many of the staff hold professional, as well as academic, qualifications.

Steady growth in the last five years has seen student numbers reach almost 22,000, including large contingents of postgraduates and part-timers. Numbers doubled during the 1990s, partly due to the incorporation of a nursing and midwifery college at nearby St Bartholomew's Hospital and the Charterhouse College of Radiography. Applications have been increasing, although the 3.6 per cent increase at the start of 2009 was half the national average. It was always going to be hard to match an exceptional rise in the previous year.

Development is continuing at the university's headquarters in fashionable Islington. The most ambitious project has been the £42-million home for the business school, which opened in 2002. Another £20 million went into an impressive new building for the School of Social Sciences. Now the students' union is being refurbished and £12 million is being raised for a new School of Arts.

The Cass Business School is one of City's great strengths. It was the first Western university to forge links with the Bank of China, running an Executive MBA programme in Shanghai as the first step to a wider role in business education throughout east and southeast Asia. City has links with 50 European universities and many more further afield, and many students spend a year of their course abroad.

The university had already boosted its legal provision by incorporating the Inns of Court School of Law in 2001. The City Law School, which includes the university's original department, offers London's only "one-stop shop" for legal training, from undergraduate to professional courses.

City is also working with Queen Mary, University of London, in a range of

Northampton Square
London EC1V 0HB
020 7040 5060
ugadmissions@city.ac.uk
www.city.ac.uk
www.citysu.com

The Times Rankings
Overall Ranking: 49

Student satisfaction:	=90	(72%)
Research quality:	=48	(1.2)
Entry standards:	49	(316)
Student–staff ratio:	=63	(17.8)
Services & facilities/student:	80	(£993)
Expected completion rate:	=55	(84.3%)
Good honours:	37	(66.6%)
Graduate prospects:	10	(81.4%)

subjects, starting with medicine and other health subjects, journalism and engineering. The two universities jointly host a national centre for teaching and learning in nursing and midwifery.

City has a particularly high reputation in music, where it is associated with the Guildhall School of Music and Drama. Together with nursing and midwifery, music achieved the university's best results in the 2008 Research Assessment Exercise. Social work and social policy also produced good results.

Like other universities in London, City has struggled to make an impression in the National Student Survey, although 80 per cent of undergraduates were satisfied overall. Civil engineering, finance and accounting did particularly well in the 2008 survey.

Journalism is highly regarded and the university has launched the UK's first graduate school of journalism in new £12-million facilities. There is also a flourishing sub-degree programme for adults, which ranges from sitcom writing to e-business. The changes have maintained City's position among the most popular universities in London, with nearly eight applications for each undergraduate place.

Official performance indicators for higher education have brought mixed news: the dropout rate has been falling but almost 15 per cent is still high for a traditional university. City has a good record among its peers for widening participation in higher education, with four out of ten undergraduates coming from working-class homes. Students tend to be more concerned about their inability to afford the attractions of a trendy part of London. Most fall back on the extended students' union, but this is usually shut at weekends for lack of demand. Sports facilities are poor by current university standards, although the indoor sports centre is conveniently located.

Undergraduate Fees and Bursaries

- Fees for UK/EU students: £3,225
- International student fees: £8,600–£9,500
- Bursary on full grant: sliding scale to £770.
- Bursaries on partial grant: household income up to £30K: £360.
- Scholarships based on circumstances or by competition.
- For full details see the university's website: www.city.ac.uk/study/money/undergraduate/index.html

---

Students

Undergraduates:	7,835	(6,695)
Postgraduates:	4,460	(2,420)
Mature students:	38.4%	
Overseas students:	15.8%	
Applications per place:	7.6	
From state-sector schools:	88.8%	
From working-class homes:	40.0%	

For detailed information about fees, grants and bursaries and how they work, see chapter 7.

Accommodation

Number of places and costs refer to 2009–10
University-provided places: 1,344
Percentage catered: 0%
Self-catered costs: £100–£190 a week.
Accommodation is guaranteed for first years if conditions are met. Residential restrictions apply.
International students: preference is given to new overseas students.
Contact: accomm@city.ac.uk
www.city.ac.uk/studentcentre/housing

Coventry University

Coventry is investing £160 million over ten years in its 33-acre campus close to the city centre, much of it going on student facilities. The showpiece turreted library cost £20 million and is almost entirely naturally ventilated and lit. The £5-million student centre, opened in 2006, contains everything from the accommodation and careers services to the Finance and Academic Registry, as well as lounge space. Next on the list are a student enterprise centre, containing a new students' union and featuring a roof garden among its many facilities, and a new home for the Faculty of Engineering and Computing.

The university has already added other facilities, including more residential accommodation, a £7-million arts centre and a sports centre, during a decade in which student numbers doubled to more than 20,000.

Coventry traces its origins back to 1843 with the foundation of the College of Design and its links with the motor industry of the Midlands were reflected in its earlier title of Lanchester Polytechnic, named after a leading engineering figure. It has adopted an innovative approach to computer-assisted learning, supported by an expanded computer network. The university was chosen to house national centres of excellence in teaching for e-learning in health and social care, as well as in maths, and transport and product design.

The university has a focus on employment, which is reflected in a predominantly vocational curriculum. The Start-Up Café encourages business networking and local employers are engaging with the programme of work-based learning. The Add+vantage Scheme is designed to help full time undergraduate students improve their employability whilst studying. Its modules cover a wide range of skills and help students gain work-related knowledge and prepare for a career.

The majority of students exercise their right to take "free-choice modules" that cover the full range of university provision, with IT skills and languages particularly popular. Coventry has been building up its portfolio of courses, introducing eye-catching degrees in subjects such as ethical hacking and network security, disaster management, forensic chemistry, criminology and boat design.

Languages and economics produced the best scores in an otherwise mediocre set of results in the National Student Survey published in 2008. Research grades improved in the 2008 assessment exercise, when small amounts of world-leading work were recognised in seven of the

---

Priory Street
Coventry CV1 5FB
024 7615 2222 (admissions)
studentenquiries
@coventry.ac.uk
www.coventry.ac.uk
www.cusu.org

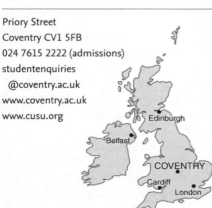

The Times Rankings
Overall Ranking: =71

Student satisfaction:	=54	(75%)
Research quality:	=85	(0.3)
Entry standards:	62	(280)
Student–staff ratio:	=80	(19.1)
Services & facilities/student:	=56	(£1,122)
Expected completion rate:	97	(75.2%)
Good honours:	=59	(61.0%)
Graduate prospects:	62	(67.5%)

16 areas in which the university made submissions. Art and design and electrical and electronic engineering produced the best results. Design benefits from a revolutionary £1.6-million digital modelling workshop, sponsored by the Bugatti Trust, which provides full-scale vehicle modelling facilities for undergraduates as well as researchers.

Among the initiatives to improve the student experience has been the introduction of tangible rewards for excellent teaching and further development of electronic learning. The Centre for Academic Writing offers advice on essays and theses, with group sessions and one-to-one appointments, while the Maths Support Centre includes a statistics advisory service and specialist support service for students with dyslexia.

Almost 40 per cent of the undergraduates have working-class backgrounds, many from areas of low participation in higher education. Applications have been healthy and were up by more than the national average at the start of 2009, following a good year in 2008. The projected dropout rate had improved in the latest survey, but still stands at 20 per cent.

More than most universities, Coventry is a creature of its city, and the civic-minded approach of the university has created many town–gown links. The main buildings open out from the ruins of the bombed cathedral, as university and public facilities mingle in the city. Student residences are within easy walking distance of the campus and city centre. Students welcome the relatively low cost of living in Coventry, and, as at most modern universities, the student body encompasses a wide range of ages.

Undergraduate Fees and Bursaries

- Fees for UK/EU students: £3,225
- International student fees: £8,300
- Bursary on full grant: £320
- Bursaries on partial grant: household income up to £60K: £320.
- Scholarships based on circumstances or by competition.
- For full details see the university's website: www.coventry.ac.uk/cu/studentfunding

Students

Undergraduates:	11,560	(5,275)
Postgraduates:	1,880	(1,660)
Mature students:	27.9%	
Overseas students:	11.6%	
Applications per place:	4.0	
From state-sector schools:	96.6%	
From working-class homes:	39.4%	

For detailed information about fees, grants and bursaries and how they work, see chapter 7.

Accommodation

Number of places and costs refer to 2009–10
University-provided places: 2,460
Percentage catered: 24.4%
Catered costs: £99 a week (10 meals).
Self-catered costs: £84–£134 (40–50 weeks).
First-year students are guaranteed housing provided conditions are met.
International students: given priority.
Contact: accomm.ss@coventry.ac.uk;
www.coventry.ac.uk/undergraduate-study/accommodation

Cumbria University

One of the largest counties without a university of its own has put that right through the amalgamation of a former teacher training college and an arts institute, with the addition of the two Cumbrian campuses of the University of Central Lancashire. The new Cumbria University is divided between Carlisle, Penrith, Ambleside and Lancaster, as well as running a specialist teacher education centre in east London. There are also partnerships with the four further education colleges in the county to provide higher education locally.

The new university, which has more than 12,000 students, was finally established in 2007, after a series of false starts. It is the largest provider of higher education in Cumbria by a considerable margin. There are four faculties: arts, design and media; business, social sciences and sport; health, medical science and social care; and science and natural resources.

The biggest of the component parts is the former St Martin's College, which was founded in Lancaster by the Church of England in 1964 to train teachers. It took in a nursing college and another teacher training college, in Ambleside, during the 1990s. The main base remains in Lancaster, a ten-minute walk from the

town centre, with a modern library and excellent sports facilities, including a £2.5-million sports complex, gymnastics centre and fitness centre. The Ambleside campus has an outdoor studies centre and a new learning resources centre. There are plans for more residences and improved sports facilities. The nearest railway station is a 20-minute drive away at Windermere.

There are two main sites in Carlisle, the larger of which is in a parkland setting close to the River Eden. The second campus, closer to the city centre, boasts a new Learning Gateway, an innovative multimedia learning resource centre, and a sports centre with a four-court sports hall and well-equipped fitness room. The former Cumbria Institute of the Arts can trace its history in Carlisle back to 1822, eventually becoming the only specialist institute of the arts in north-west England and one of only a small number of such institutions in the country. The creative arts are one of the main areas for development in the university's initial planning.

The main Cumbrian campus acquired from the University of Central Lancashire is a mile outside Penrith, in landscaped gardens overlooking the fells, and caters mainly for agriculture and forestry. A former agricultural college, it has broadened into related areas such as

---

Fusehill Street
Carlisle
Cumbria CA1 2HH
01228 616234
contact via website
www.cumbria.ac.uk
www.thestudentsunion.
org

The Times Rankings
Overall Ranking: 83

Student satisfaction:	=101	(70%)
Research quality:	=108	(0.1)
Entry standards:	83	(256)
Student–staff ratio:	=34	(14.9)
Services & facilities/student:	110	(£741)
Expected completion rate:	57	(84.2%)
Good honours:	102	(48.8%)
Graduate prospects:	44	(71.4%)

environmental management and other subjects not directly related to land-based industries. Courses include outdoor education and leadership, geography, business, tourism, sport and computing. Library and learning resource facilities have been improved and residential accommodation expanded. There are also two farms, one adjacent to the campus and a working hill farm 15 miles away within the national park.

In the longer term, the university is planning a £160-million transformation of its estate, almost half of which will go on a new campus in Carlisle. The proposals include plans for further development at all the existing centres to maintain a "Cumbria-wide presence".

Cumbria made its debut in the lower reaches of *The Times* league table and made some progress, now being out of the bottom 20. Some of the statistics used still relate to the combined scores of St Martin's College and the Cumbria Institute. However, the university was bottom of the initial rankings from the 2008 Research Assessment Exercise, recording only a small amount of world-leading research in theology, divinity and religious studies. There was some improvement in the National Student Survey results published in 2008, but the university remained close to the bottom 20, with geography and environmental science producing the most satisfied students.

The early focus of the university is on attracting more students from a region of low participation in higher education, as well as on serving the social and economic needs of the county. Applications were up by 12 per cent at the start of 2009, following a substantial increase the previous year when there was a decline at most universities.

Undergraduate Fees and Bursaries

- Fees for UK/EU students: £3,225
- International student fees: £8,150
- Bursary on full grant: £1,290
- Bursaries on partial grant: household income up to £60K: sliding scale £1,290–£215.
- Scholarships based on circumstances or by competition.
- For full details see the university's website: www.cumbria.ac.uk/FutureStudents/ FeesFinance/MoneyMatters.aspx

---

Students

Undergraduates:	5,360	(4,515)
Postgraduates:	1,090	(1,075)
Mature students:	23.1%	
Overseas students:	2.4%	
Applications per place:	3.5	
From state-sector schools:	98.6%	
From working-class homes:	32.1%	

For detailed information about fees, grants and bursaries and how they work, see chapter 7.

Accommodation

Number of places and costs refer to 2009–10
University-provided places: 821
Percentage catered: 65%
Catered costs: £90.95–£103.95 (41 weeks).
Self-catered costs: £50–£82 a week.
First years are guaranteed halls accommodation if Cumbria is first choice.
International students: guaranteed halls accommodation if conditions are met.
Contact: www.cumbria.ac.uk/FutureStudents/ Accommodation/

De Montfort University

An emphasis on research paid off spectacularly for De Montfort in the 2008 official assessments, when the university achieved the best results of any post-1992 university. Some 43 per cent of the work submitted was rated world-leading or internationally excellent. Almost all the subject areas contained some world-leading research and in the case of English language and literature the proportion reached an outstanding 40 per cent. Communication and media studies and drama, dance and performing arts also produced excellent results.

Accolades in the previous Research Assessment Exercise helped to bring in annual research income of about £10 million a year in external research grants and contracts. The university has 1,500 staff engaged in research and 450 research degree students. Much of the successful work took place in the Institute of Creative Technologies, which acts as a catalyst for research that defies the traditional boundaries of computer science, the digital arts and humanities, and is already exciting the interest of the business world.

Another £3.7 million was spent on creative technology studios, which feature video, audio and radio production suites, recording studios and laboratories with the latest broadcast and audio analysis technology. A Performance Arts Centre for Excellence (PACE) had already opened, allowing the university to deliver innovative teaching for students of dance, drama and music technology.

Once spread over a network of campuses in a 50-mile radius, De Montfort is concentrating its efforts on its original base in Leicester. The university is putting more than £100 million into consolidating a more manageable estate, some of it provided by the city council and local businesses. Having departed Milton Keynes, Lincoln and Bedford, there are now only two campuses, both in Leicester itself, following the relocation of health and life sciences to the university's headquarters. Another 11 colleges are associates, linked into the university's network and offering its courses. A formal agreement commits the colleges, which stretch from north Oxfordshire to Liverpool, to work with each other as well as with De Montfort.

Campus developments include the diversion of part of the ring road to allow the university to open up the 15th-century Magazine Gateway building, which will become the focal point of a university quarter with public open spaces and new links to the city centre. A £35-million building for business and law, due to open in September 2009, will be at its heart. The

---

The Gateway
Leicester LE1 9BH
08459 454647 (enquiries)
enquiry@dmu.ac.uk
www.dmu.ac.uk
www.
demontforstudents.com

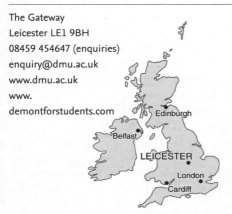

The Times Rankings
Overall Ranking: =66

Student satisfaction:	=28	(77%)
Research quality:	=60	(0.6)
Entry standards:	=89	(248)
Student–staff ratio:	=54	(17.0)
Services & facilities/student:	93	(£882)
Expected completion rate:	=71	(81.5%)
Good honours:	92	(51.1%)
Graduate prospects:	=67	(65.7%)

24-hour library has been remodelled with wireless networks and rooms equipped with audio visual and IT facilities for preparing presentations.

The professional accounting courses were awarded "premier" status in a worldwide accreditation scheme, and the university houses a national teaching centre for drama, dance and theatre studies. Recent results in the National Student Survey have seen a big improvement on the first two rounds, with English, history, music, politics and business producing the highest levels of satisfaction.

De Montfort's range of programmes has been expanding and applications were up by more than 14 per cent at the start of 2009. Among the recent additions is a BSc in Green Energy Technology and another in Public and Community health, tackling issues such as increases in sexually transmitted infections and obesity.

The dropout rate has improved considerably: at less than 15 per cent, it is now below the national average for the university's courses and entry grades. The university has abandoned semesters and gone back to a three-term year, partly because it believed the prospect of imminent assessment encouraged some students to give up at Christmas in their first year. De Montfort has a proud record for widening access to higher education with almost 43 per cent of students coming from working-class homes. It was one of the first to set up an employment agency to help students find part-time work during their course of study as well as find careers upon graduation. Strong links with local business and industry manifest themselves in courses such as the BSc in media production, run in conjunction with the BBC, and in the provision of facilities such as the telematics laboratory sponsored by Orange, the mobile telephone company.

Accommodation difficulties have been addressed, with the addition of new halls within walking distance of lectures. All first years, apart from locals, are now guaranteed a place in halls and rents in the private sector are among the lowest in England.

Undergraduate Fees and Bursaries

- Fees for UK/EU students: £3,225
- International student fees: £8,500–£9,000
- Bursary on full grant: £500
- Bursaries on partial grant: household income up to £50K: £500
- Scholarships based on circumstances or by competition.
- For full details see the university's website: www.dmu.ac.uk/funding

Students

Undergraduates:	14,080	(3,040)
Postgraduates:	830	(2,440)
Mature students:	27.2%	
Overseas students:	4.8%	
Applications per place:	3.9	
From state-sector schools:	97.1%	
From working-class homes:	42.8%	

For detailed information about fees, grants and bursaries and how they work, see chapter 7.

Accommodation

Number of places and costs refer to 2009–10
University-provided places: 2,399
Percentage catered: 0%
Self-catered costs: £74–£90 a week.
First years are guaranteed accommodation.
Residential restrictions apply.
International students: guaranteed accommodation.
Contact: housing@dmu.ac.uk

University of Derby

Derby sees itself as a prototype for the modern university, providing courses at all levels from the age of 16 into retirement. Although not as extensive as the original plans for spanning further and higher education in the same institution, a merger with High Peak College and the subsequent creation of the University of Derby Buxton have stayed true to the model. While accepting that Derby will never scale the heights in league tables such as ours, the university set itself the target of becoming the pre-eminent university of its type by 2020. Its yardsticks are student satisfaction, employability and cost-effectiveness.

The university takes pride in its record for widening access, although higher entry grades have coincided with the recruitment of more students from affluent families. Derby still has among the highest proportions of state-educated undergraduates in England, nearly four in ten are from working-class homes and two in ten are from areas of low participation in higher education – all well above the national average for the courses and entry qualifications. But the latest projected dropout rate was more than 23 per cent, still slightly above the benchmark figure for the university.

Campus developments are continuing, with a £21-million art and design campus bringing together courses previously spread around three different sites. The new site forms one part of a £55-million estates strategy that is creating a University Quarter for Derby. The college already has a new home in the centre of Buxton, where the purchase of the Devonshire Royal Hospital for a nominal fee has provided an ideal centre for courses in tourism and hospitality management, as well as further education programmes. The landmark building, which has a bigger dome than St Paul's Cathedral, houses two training restaurants and a health spa that also provides training, in addition to academic facilities.

There are three main sites in and around Derby. The Kedleston Road campus, two miles north of the city centre, is the largest, catering for most of the main subjects as well as the students' union headquarters and multi-faith centre. The £1.5-million Clinical Skills Suite was built to NHS "Red Book" standards, featuring hospital wards, counselling rooms and diagnostic radiography facilities. The site's three tower blocks are being refurbished and made greener in a £13.5-million project to be completed by 2010, which will make them more energy efficient with the installation of photovoltaic panels to generate some of their own electricity. A new all-weather sports pitch was added in 2009.

Kedleston Road
Derby DE22 1GB
08701 202330 (enquiries)
askadmissions@
  derby.ac.uk
www.derby.ac.uk
www.udsu.co.uk

Edinburgh
Belfast
DERBY
London
Cardiff

The Times Rankings
Overall Ranking: 104

Student satisfaction:	=90	(72%)
Research quality:	=108	(0.1)
Entry standards:	101	(231)
Student–staff ratio:	=89	(19.8)
Services & facilities/student:	64	(£1,091)
Expected completion rate:	91	(76.5%)
Good honours:	107	(46.6%)
Graduate prospects:	110	(54.9%)

The Mickleover campus, which specialises in education and health, is also in a suburban location. In addition, the university has opened a new £400,000 centre in Chesterfield to teach nursing.

Courses are modular and a foundation programme allows students to begin work at a partner college before transferring to the university. Derby has also awarded more work-based qualifications than any other UK university. Distance learning is a growth area, either online or through Derby's nine regional centres. Prospective students can even sample a virtual open evening. Business and management is by far the biggest academic area, but work placements are encouraged in all subjects. The accent on employability continues with an eight-week course on key skills, such as CV preparation and interview technique. Derby has also been in the forefront of the adoption of new teaching methods, pioneering the use of interactive video for a national scheme. A variety of courses, from Foundation degrees to postgraduate qualifications, are available online. The School of Flexible and Partnership Learning, which spans the entire university, won an award for the imaginative use of distance learning.

The university has spent £30 million in five years to maintain its guarantee of accommodation for all first years. Students seem to appreciate the university's efforts because Derby comes out well in its own satisfaction surveys, although this was not reflected in the latest national equivalent. Law fared particularly well in the last three national surveys, with some of the most satisfied students in the country. Education also did well in the survey published in 2008, but most of the other results were disappointing. Applications were up by more than 5 per cent at the start of 2009, following a good year in 2008.

Undergraduate Fees and Bursaries

- Fees for UK/EU students: £3,225
- International student fees: £7,800–£8,415
- Bursary on full grant: £800 + £300 (local address) or £830 +£400 (partner school).
- Bursaries on partial grant: household income £25K–£35K: £520; £35K–£51K: £210; All + £300 or £400 local bursary.
- Scholarships based on circumstances or by competition.
- For full details see the university's website: www.derby.ac.uk/fees

---

Students		
Undergraduates:	9,330	(3,685)
Postgraduates:	590	(2,545)
Mature students:	40.1%	
Overseas students:	7.5%	
Applications per place:	4.8	
From state-sector schools:	98.3%	
From working-class homes:	38.6%	

For detailed information about fees, grants and bursaries and how they work, see chapter 7.

Accommodation

Number of places and costs refer to 2009–10
University-provided places: 2,300
Percentage catered: 0%
Self-catered costs: £73.00–£91.25.
First-year students are guaranteed accommodation if they apply before 31 August.
Policy for international students: as above.
Contact: www.derby.ac.uk/accommodation
Student Living – tel: 01332 594180
(126 Nuns St, Derby, DE1 3LQ)

University of Dundee

Dundee describes itself as "Scotland's most enterprising university" and, while there would be other claimants to that title, it has certainly been among the liveliest in recent years. A long series of good quality ratings and the acquisition of education, nursing and art colleges, which doubled its size and greatly increased its scope, have been complemented by high-profile research successes, especially in medicine and the life sciences. The message appears to be getting through to prospective students: applications shot up by 88 per cent in five years, and the 16 per cent increase at the start of 2008 was comfortably the highest in Scotland.

The university now has about 17,000 students, of whom two thirds are under-graduates, including a healthy number from overseas. It has been looking outwards to achieve the "critical mass" which experts regard as essential to break into the higher education elite, appointing professors at the rate of one a month for four years.

A £200-million campus redevelopment designed by the leading architect, Sir Terry Farrell, is now complete. Almost £40 million of this was spent on wireless-networked student residences. A new teaching block houses education and social work, which moved onto the main campus in 2008, and there have been extensions to the library and the sports centre. Best-known for the life sciences, where research into cancer and diabetes is recognised as world-class, the university had already opened new buildings for interdisciplinary research, applied computing and clinical research.

Set in 20 acres of parkland, the medical school is the one of the few components of the university outside the compact city-centre campus – some of the nursing and midwifery students are 35 miles away in Kirkcaldy, while education and social work are waiting to move from the former Northern College campus, two miles outside the centre.

Biochemistry is the flagship department, housed in the £13-million Wellcome Trust Building. Its academics were the first in Britain to be invited to take part in Japan's Human Frontier science programme and are now the most-quoted researchers in their field. Indeed, three out of 20 of the UK's most cited scientists – Professor Sir David Lane (cancer), Professor Sir Philip Cohen (diabetes and cell signalling) and Professor Peter Downes (cell signalling) – are based at the university.

More than half the work submitted for the 2008 Research Assessment Exercise was rated world-leading or internationally excellent. Dundee recorded the best

---

Nethergate
Dundee DD1 4HN
01382 384160 (enquiries)
srs@dundee.ac.uk
www.dundee.ac.uk
www.dusa.co.uk

DUNDEE
Edinburgh
Belfast
London
Cardiff

The Times Rankings
Overall Ranking: 41

Student satisfaction:	=20	(78%)
Research quality:	=43	(1.5)
Entry standards:	29	(371)
Student–staff ratio:	23	(14.0)
Services & facilities/student:	55	(£1,124)
Expected completion rate:	107	(71.4%)
Good honours:	40	(65.8%)
Graduate prospects:	28	(75.6%)

results in Scotland for art and design, civil engineering, biological and laboratory-based clinical sciences. Undergraduates in English and politics were almost 100 per cent satisfied in the National Student Survey published in 2008. Medicine and architecture, building and planning also recorded extremely high levels of satisfaction.

Vocational degrees predominate, helping to produce the university's consistently good graduate employment record. The university sends more graduates into the professions than any other institution in Scotland and only Oxbridge graduates came out ahead of Dundee's in a national survey of starting salaries. All degrees include a career planning module and an internship option, and students are now provided with their own personal development website. Among the new courses introduced recently are forensic anthropology, sports biomedicine and innovative product design. The highly rated design courses are taught at the former Duncan of Jordanstone College of Art.

There has been an emphasis on opportunities for women ever since Dundee's separation from St Andrews University in 1967, and the addition of teacher training has increased the female majority. Two thirds of Dundee's students are from Scotland and nearly one in ten from Northern Ireland. One in five come from areas with little tradition of higher education and more than a quarter are from working-class homes. They enjoy a welcoming atmosphere and a cost of living which is lower than in most university cities. Private accommodation is plentiful for those who are not housed by the university. New students even have their own website. The city is profiting from recent regeneration programmes and becoming more fashionable. Spectacular mountain and coastal scenery are close at hand, but social life tends to be concentrated on the students' union, which is one of the largest and most active in Scotland.

Undergraduate Fees and Bursaries
- Scottish-domiciled and EU students: no fees payable.
- Non-Scottish UK-domiciled student fees: £1,820 a year (£2,895 medicine).
- International student fees: £8,500–10,500; £14,150–£22,000 (medicine).
- Scholarships based on circumstances or by competition.
- For full details see the university's website: www.dundee.ac.uk/undergraduate/fees_funding

Students		
Undergraduates:	8,555	(2,510)
Postgraduates:	1,325	(4,325)
Mature students:	26.1%	
Overseas students:	9.3%	
Applications per place:	5.1	
From state-sector schools:	88.6%	
From working-class homes:	25.5%	

For detailed information about fees, grants and bursaries and how they work, see chapter 7.

Accommodation
Number of places and costs refer to 2009–10
University-provided places: 1,809
Percentage catered: 0%
Self-catered costs: £71.54–£110.18 a week.
Entrant students guaranteed accommodation if conditions are met. No residential restrictions. International students are guaranteed accommodation if conditions are met.
Contact: residences@dundee.ac.uk
www.dundee.ac.uk/residences

Durham University

Long established as a leading alternative to Oxford and Cambridge, Durham has a collegiate structure and picturesque setting that attracts a largely middle-class student body. However, although more than a third of undergraduates come from independent schools, the university is attracting more applicants from non-traditional backgrounds. All those who receive an offer are invited to a special open day to see if Durham is the university for them. Since around 80 per cent come from outside the northeast of England, most are seeing the small cathedral city for the first time.

Applications are made to one of the 15 colleges, all of which have been mixed since 2004. The newest, Josephine Butler College – a self-catering college with around 400 bedrooms – accepted its first intake of students in 2006. Colleges range in size from 300 to 1,100 students and are the focal point of social life, although all teaching is done in central departments. There are significant differences in atmosphere and student profile, ranging from the historic University College, in Durham Castle, to modern buildings on the city's outskirts.

Durham has been among the top 20 universities for student satisfaction for the last three years. Theology and religion, classics and linguistics, other languages, education, and subjects allied to medicine produced particularly good results in 2008. Winning a place is far from easy – entrance requirements are among the highest in Britain – but the dropout rate of less than 3 per cent is also among the lowest in any university.

More than 60 per cent of the work submitted for the 2008 Research Assessment Exercise was rated world-leading or internationally excellent. Applied maths, archaeology and theology and religion achieved among the best results in the UK. Music, English and geography and environmental science also did well. A £3-million grant to establish a centre for fundamental physics should place Durham at the forefront of world research on the structure of the universe. The Calman Learning Centre, on the Science Site, incorporates lecture theatres, seminar and conference facilities and a "techno café". The site will also see the construction of a landmark "Gateway" development, containing a new law school and student services centre. The project has been brought forward by a year as part of the Government's attempts to stimulate the local economy, but will still not be completed until 2012.

Durham is generally quite traditional. Wherever possible, teaching takes place in small groups and most assessment is by

University Office
Old Elvet, Durham DH1 3HP
0191 334 6128 (admissions office)
admissions@durham.ac.uk
www.durham.ac.uk
www.dsu.org.uk

The Times Rankings
Overall Ranking: 8

Student satisfaction:	=14	(79%)
Research quality:	=8	(2.5)
Entry standards:	7	(459)
Student–staff ratio:	33	(14.8)
Services & facilities/student:	13	(£1,578)
Expected completion rate:	4	(96.7%)
Good honours:	10	(77.5%)
Graduate prospects:	=15	(78.3%)

written examination. However, the establishment of the Queen's Campus, in Stockton-on-Tees, broke the mould of tradition. Initially a joint venture with Teesside University, Stockton is now Durham's own venture into community education. Entry standards are lower than in the main university, and subjects such as business, primary education and psychology have helped broaden the university's intake. Some £750,000 has been spent improving social facilities for the 2,000 students there and more than £3 million has been earmarked for improved sporting facilities, relocating some of the university's elite sports activities as part of a strategy to increase integration between Durham and Stockton.

The Stockton campus has also seen the fulfilment of Durham's long-held ambition to restore the medical education it lost when Newcastle University went its own way almost 45 years ago. In another joint project, this time with Newcastle, 95 students do the first two years of their training on Teesside, concentrating on community medicine, before transferring to Newcastle to complete their training. Medicine has added to the 200-plus undergraduate study programmes. Undergraduates are also offered a variety of generalist "free elective" modules, such as environmental economics and personal language learning. The aim is to make Durham graduates even more employable.

The university dominates the city of Durham to an extent which sometimes causes resentment, but adds considerably to the local economy. For those looking for nightlife, or just a change of scene, Newcastle is a short train journey away. Sports facilities are excellent, and Durham is among the premier universities in national competitions: it came fourth in national student championships in 2008. Among the alumni are the current and former England cricket captains, Andrew Strauss and Nasser Hussain, and rugby World Cup winner, Will Greenwood. The university runs Centres of Excellence in cricket and fencing, and has plans to build on its existing strengths in rowing, rugby and hockey.

Undergraduate Fees and Bursaries

- Fees for UK/EU students: £3,225
- International student fees: £10,560–£13,770
- Bursary on full grant: £1,300
- The university does not award bursaries for students on partial maintenance grants.
- Scholarships based on circumstances or by competition.
- For full details see the university's website: www.dur.ac.uk/undergraduate/finance/dgs

Students

Undergraduates:	11,275	(365)
Postgraduates:	3,115	(1,520)
Mature students:	6.4%	
Overseas students:	8.3%	
Applications per place:	6.7	
From state-sector schools:	61.9%	
From working-class homes:	15.0%	

For detailed information about fees, grants and bursaries and how they work, see chapter 7.

Accommodation

Number of places and costs refer to 2009–10
University-provided places: 5,758
Percentage catered: 67%
Catered costs: £4,689 (3 terms, Durham)
Self-catered costs: £4,173 (3 terms, Durham)
£4,125 (38-week contract, Stockton campus)
All full-time students become members of one of the university's colleges or societies.
International students: all first years are guaranteed accommodation.
Contact: admissions@durham.ac.uk

University of East Anglia

UEA has been one of the big winners in the National Student Survey, finishing in the top ten every year. The results published in 2008 were the university's best ever, with 92 per cent of final-year undergraduates declaring themselves satisfied with their overall experience. Pharmacy registered 100 per cent satisfaction, while physical sciences, history and archaeology also produced high scores. Students appear to like the scale of this relatively small campus university, as well as the quality of its courses, but the news is only beginning to get through to sixth-formers. Applications were up by 11 per cent at the start of 2009, following a good year in 2008.

The university has been engaged in an ambitious building and refurbishment programme on the 320-acre site on the outskirts of Norwich. It has included 560 more en-suite student bedrooms, a new health centre, the extension and refurbishment of the central library, catering facilities and students' union, as well as a new building for the schools of Nursing and Midwifery and Medicine, and the construction of an INTO English language centre for overseas students. Next will be a £3.9-million extension to the Sportspark, a new lecture theatre and seminar building, a Biomass generator facility that should reduce the university's carbon emissions by 34 per cent in two years, and the regeneration of The Square, UEA's social centre.

Health studies have been among UEA's fastest-developing areas. The university was awarded one of the first new medical schools for 20 years, graduating its first doctors in 2007, and has since added pharmacy and speech and language therapy degree courses.

Some of the broad subject combinations that the university pioneered from its origins in the 1960s – such as development studies and environmental sciences – are highly regarded in the academic world. With successive 5* ratings for research followed by a good result in the 2008 Research Assessment Exercise, environmental sciences is the flagship school. The Climatic Research Unit and the Government-funded Tyndall Centre for Climate Change Research are among the leaders in the investigation of climate change – UEA contributed more than any other university in the world to the 2007 Nobel Prize-winning Intergovernmental Panel on Climate Change. History of art and culture and media did even better in the latest RAE, with half of their research considered world-leading.

Art history has the benefit of the Sainsbury Centre for the Visual Arts,

Norwich NR4 7TJ
01603 591515 (admissions office)
admissions@uea.ac.uk
www.uea.ac.uk
www.ueastudent.com

The Times Rankings
Overall Ranking: =28

Student satisfaction:	7	(83%)
Research quality:	=32	(1.8)
Entry standards:	34	(361)
Student–staff ratio:	=56	(17.1)
Services & facilities/student:	39	(£1,231)
Expected completion rate:	48	(85.4%)
Good honours:	28	(70.1%)
Graduate prospects:	41	(71.9%)

perhaps the greatest resource of its type on any British campus. The centre, which has been refurbished and extended, houses a priceless collection of modern and tribal art, in a building designed by Lord (Norman) Foster. Creative writing is another star-studded area, with authors Michèle Roberts and Andrew Cowan taking up where Andrew Motion, the Poet Laureate, and the late Malcolm Bradbury left off.

Almost nine out of ten undergraduates come from state schools or colleges, but less than a quarter have a working-class background. Since 1999, most have had the opportunity of work experience as part of their course. An academic adviser guides all students on their options under the modular course system and monitors their progress right through to graduation.

Dropout rates have fluctuated, but the latest projected figure of 13 per cent was a substantial increase on the previous year. Most students come from outside the region, although there is an unusually large contingent of mature students for a traditional university, who tend to be more local. The university also runs a programme of over 200 evening and day courses across Norfolk and Suffolk.

The number of university-owned beds has increased considerably, ensuring that first years can be guaranteed accommodation unless they live locally. The

excellent sporting facilities are based around the £17.5-million Sportspark, which boasts an Olympic-sized swimming pool, fitness and aerobics centres, athletics track, climbing wall, courts and pitches. Student membership was only £17.50 a year in 2008–09, with discounted rates for all facilities. The university was chosen as the base for the English Institute of Sport in the East, developing a sports science network for the region.

The university is situated in parkland, with easy access to the medieval city of Norwich, which can boast a pub for every day of the year and was voted one of the best small cities in the world in the 2007 Liveable Communities awards. Rail links to London now take less than two hours, while Norwich airport offers flights through Amsterdam and Paris worldwide.

Undergraduate Fees and Bursaries

- Fees for UK/EU students: £3,225
- International student fees: £9,850–£12,350
  £19,260 (clinical medicine)
- Bursary on full grant: £600
- Bursaries on partial grant: household income up to £50K: £300
- Scholarships based on circumstances or by competition.
- For full details see the university's website: www.uea.ac.uk/mac/aao/courses/UG/Fees

Students		
Undergraduates:	9,790	(3,055)
Postgraduates:	2,135	(715)
Mature students:	31.6%	
Overseas students:	9.0%	
Applications per place:	4.3	
From state-sector schools:	87.9%	
From working-class homes:	24.3%	

For detailed information about fees, grants and bursaries and how they work, see chapter 7.

Accommodation

Number of places and costs refer to 2009–10
University-provided places: 3,400
Percentage catered: 0%
Self-catered costs: £1,915.20–£3,630.90 (38 weeks)
First years guaranteed accommodation if conditions are met. Distance restrictions apply. International students (non EU) are guaranteed accommodation if conditions are met.
Contact: accom@uea.ac.uk
www.uea.ac.uk/accommodation

University of East London

The University of East London (UEL) has spent more than £190 million on its Docklands campus, within sight of London City Airport, and is now unrecognisable from its early days as a pioneering polytechnic. Student residences and recreational facilities sit side by side with academic buildings in a prize-winning waterside development for more than 7,000 students. The final pieces in the jigsaw were the business school and Knowledge Dock, a support centre for local companies, which opened in 2006, and a £40-million student village on the Royal Albert Dock, which added another 800 beds in 2007. The campus has helped to attract substantial growth in applications to UEL, although there had been a decline at the start of 2009, when most universities experienced healthy increases. Student numbers have shot up from 12,000 to 20,000 since 2001.

The capital's first new campus for 50 years gave the university a new focal point, with its modern version of traditional university features like cloisters and squares. Students of fashion, fine art, graphic design, product design, media and cultural studies were first into new premises, followed by UEL's highly rated School of Architecture and the Visual Arts and electrical and manufacturing engineering in 2005. Business, computing and technology have now completed the academic set.

The university's original campus in Stratford is also being redeveloped, with a new library and learning centre, student residences and facilities for part-time and evening courses. The Centre for Clinical Education in Podiatry, Physiotherapy and Sports Sciences, incorporating the new London Foot Hospital, opened there in 2006. The Great Hall in University House now incorporates a high-tech, 230-seat fully retractable lecture theatre, while the health and bioscience laboratories have been refurbished and refitted. New buildings for education and law are next on the development plan.

All but one of the nine subject areas in which UEL entered the 2008 Research Assessment Exercise contained at least some world-leading research. In communication, culture and media studies, the proportion was 20 per cent, with another 60 per cent of work rated internationally excellent. Sociology and art and design also produced good results.

Teacher training courses have been given good marks by the Office for Standards in Education. Finance and accounting achieved the best results in an otherwise poor set of scores in the National Student Survey published in 2008, which left UEL among the bottom

University House
Romford Road
London E15 4LZ
020 8223 3333 (admissions)
admiss@uel.ac.uk
www.uel.ac.uk
www.uelsu.net

The Times Rankings
Overall Ranking: =108

Student satisfaction:	=101	(70%)
Research quality:	=71	(0.4)
Entry standards:	113	(191)
Student–staff ratio:	=106	(21.6)
Services & facilities/student:	37	(£1,257)
Expected completion rate:	106	(71.5%)
Good honours:	114	(44.4%)
Graduate prospects:	=82	(62.7%)

ten universities.

UEL's focus is more concerned with extending access to higher education than competing with the elite universities. Barely more than half of the new first year intake now arrive with A levels and a majority are over 21 on entry – many choosing to start courses in February. Many degrees are vocational and employers are closely involved in course planning. The university has pioneered a work-based learning initiative, offering accredited placements with local employers.

Almost half of UEL's students come from working-class homes, many from the area's large ethnic minority population. A successful mentoring scheme for black and Asian students has become a model for other institutions. A guidance unit advises local people who are considering returning to education. The university is also strong on provision for disabled students and houses the new Rix Centre for Innovation and Learning Disability. The projected dropout rate has been improving considerably – the latest figure of less than 20 per cent is better than the national average for UEL's courses and entry qualifications. Graduate employment rates have also been improving, with the university operating mentoring and placement programmes that involve almost 1,000 businesses, including many in the City or Canary Wharf.

University-owned accommodation is still not plentiful for the number of students, although there are now more than 1,100 flats and studios on the Docklands campus and the rents are good value for London. Because many choose to live at home, all first years who request accommodation are housed. The social mix means that UEL has not been the place to look for the archetypal partying student lifestyle, although the Docklands campus is beginning to change this. New students' union premises have been added on both the Stratford and Docklands campuses, each of which also has some sports facilities.

Undergraduate Fees and Bursaries

- Fees for UK/EU students: £3,225
- International student fees: £9,510–£13,140
- Bursary on full grant: £310
- The university does not award bursaries for students on partial maintenance grants.
- Scholarships based on circumstances or by competition.
- For full details see the university's website: www.uel.ac.uk/students/being_student/money.htm

Students

Undergraduates:	11,005	(3,415)
Postgraduates:	2,640	(2,365)
Mature students:	55.4%	
Overseas students:	11.6%	
Applications per place:	3.2	
From state-sector schools:	98.5%	
From working-class homes:	45.9%	

For detailed information about fees, grants and bursaries and how they work, see chapter 7.

Accommodation

Number of places and costs refer to 2008–09
University-provided places: 1,100
Percentage catered: 0%
Self-catered costs: £92–£124 a week (39 weeks)
First-year students are guaranteed accommodation if conditions are met.
International students: same as above.
Docklands Campus 020 8223 5093/4
www.uel.ac.uk/studentlife/accommodation/index.htm
dlres@uel.ac.uk

Edge Hill University

Based at Ormskirk, near Liverpool, Edge Hill is one of the fastest growing universities in the UK, as well as one of the newest. It has almost doubled its complement of students since the millennium to reach the 20,000 mark. Applications increased three-fold in that time, culminating in a 13 per cent rise in 2008, although growth had stalled when the official deadline passed for courses beginning in 2009.

There are plans for significant expansion with the purchase of land adjoining the existing site, but the next generation of students will have to make do with improvements to the current campus. Over £100 million has been spent on it already and more is on the way. A £14-million home to house the Faculty of Health, the SOLSTICE e-learning centre and a 900-seat theatre were completed in 2007. A new £8-million Business School opened early in 2009 and additional student residences will be ready for the new academic year.

Although university status arrived only in 2005, Edge Hill has been training teachers since the 19th century. Having moved to its 75-acre landscaped campus in the 1930s, it has long since expanded into other subjects, but it remains the largest provider of secondary teacher training and courses for classroom assistants. It has also won the lion's share of funding to deliver further training for qualified secondary school teachers.

Other big recruiters are health, business, sport and media courses. A £5-million expansion of resources for the performing arts opened in 2005 and there are industry-standard facilities for animation, TV and other media areas. Nursing, midwifery and other health care programmes were commended by inspectors in 2005 and the university's primary and secondary teacher training courses were rated as outstanding by Ofsted in 2007–08.

Courses are determinedly job-related – three quarters of graduates leave with professional accreditation. Among the latest additions is Chinese studies, which is available as a joint honours programme with English or business.

All students have a personal tutor, as well as access to counsellors and financial advice. Satisfaction levels have been above average in the National Student Survey, with good scores for students' personal development, as well as for assessment and feedback – the main bone of contention for undergraduates at most universities. Law and criminology produced by far the best results, with 100 per cent overall satisfaction among final-year undergraduates.

St Helens Road
Ormskirk
Lancashire L39 4QP
01695 575171
enquiries@edgehill.ac.uk
www.edgehill.ac.uk
www.edgehillsu.com

The Times Rankings
Overall Ranking: 88

Student satisfaction:	=20	(78%)
Research quality:	=108	(0.1)
Entry standards:	=89	(248)
Student–staff ratio:	=89	(19.8)
Services & facilities/student:	66	(£1,082)
Expected completion rate:	80	(79.2%)
Good honours:	109	(46.1%)
Graduate prospects:	=105	(56.8%)

Beyond Ormskirk, there are seven satellite campuses in Liverpool, Manchester and other parts of the North West to facilitate local learning. The largest is based in the grounds of University Hospital Aintree, where students in the Faculty of Health can see at first-hand how a busy hospital runs. In addition, a range of further education colleges in the North West teach the university's Foundation degrees.

Four in ten undergraduates have a working-class background and almost a quarter come from areas without a tradition of higher education. Almost two thirds of the university's fee income goes on bursaries and outreach activities. Edge Hill won an award for a student finance support package that rewards achievement, as well as encouraging students to complete their studies, rather than simply offering incentives for enrolling. The dropout rate has been falling: the latest projection of 18 per cent is only slightly above the national average for the university's courses and entry qualifications.

There are almost 700 hall places on the Ormskirk campus, with a further 144 due to be completed for the 2009–10 academic year, and 25 acres of sporting facilities. The £3.9-million Sporting Edge complex, which was part funded by a Lottery grant, is open to staff, students and the local community. The university has been chosen as a pre-Olympic training centre for athletics, road cycling and archery.

Undergraduate Fees and Bursaries
- Fees for UK/EU students £3,225
- International student fees £8,200
- Bursary on full grant: £500 + £200 learning support bursary.
- Bursaries on partial grant: £200 learning support bursary.
- Scholarships based on circumstances or by competition.
- For full details see the university's website: www.edgehill.ac.uk/study/fees

Students			
Undergraduates:	6,410	(6,395)	
Postgraduates:	720	(6,610)	
Mature students:	34.4%		
Overseas students:	0.9%		
Applications per place:	3.9		
From state-sector schools:	98.3%		
From working-class homes:	39.8%		

For detailed information about fees, grants and bursaries and how they work, see chapter 7.

Accommodation
Number of places and costs refer to 2008–09
University provided places: 678
Percentage catered: 45%
Catered costs: £82.00 a week (38–40 weeks)
Self-catered costs: £51–£63 a week (40 weeks)
First years cannot be guaranteed housing.
Residential restrictions apply.
International students: guaranteed accommodation if conditions are met.
Contact: www.edgehill.ac.uk/study/accommodation

University of Edinburgh

Edinburgh retains a special status in Scotland, where the university is regarded as the nearest thing to Oxbridge north of the border. Despite having to play second fiddle to St Andrews in our League Table recently, it is seldom far from the top ten in the UK and was in the top 25 universities in the world in the last *Times Higher Education*/QS global rankings.

Like Oxbridge, Edinburgh has been trying to widen its intake, especially since the arrival of Sir Tim O'Shea as Principal – the first non-Scot to hold the ancient office in modern times. More than £10 million has been raised for access bursaries of £1,000 a year, with the university steadily increasing number of awards, which now stand at 180. Other measures include an eight-week summer school for teenagers from local schools and support for students in the transition to higher education and later in their courses. The university has always attracted a high proportion of middle-class candidates – many from England – and is a favourite in independent schools, whose students take about a third of the places. Selection guidelines aim to look more broadly at candidates' potential, reducing minimum entry requirements and placing more weight on references and personal statements.

The measures appeared to have an instant impact, with a succession of big increases in applications continuing while several Scottish universities were experiencing declines. The 4.5 per cent rise at the start of 2009 was more modest, but demand for places has held up in generally problematic areas such as engineering and modern languages. There are plans for further increases in overseas students, who already number more than 6,000, testifying to Edinburgh's worldwide reputation.

The university, which is a member of the Russell Group of 20 UK research universities, has stepped up its fund-raising activities. They have already contributed to a new informatics building, as well as to the development of a "BioQuarter", a groundbreaking collaboration between the university, Scottish Enterprise, NHS Lothian, and the city council that is intended to consolidate Scotland's reputation as a world leader in biomedical science. A 100-acre site for biomedical research is located alongside the medical school, and the new Royal Infirmary at Little France. A new building for the Scottish Centre for Regenerative Medicine, housing researchers from a range of disciplines including those from the university's renowned Institute for Stem Cell Research, will open in 2010.

Almost two thirds of the work submitted for the 2008 Research Assessment Exercise was rated as world-leading or internation-

---

Old College
South Bridge
Edinburgh EH8 9YL
0131 650 4360
sra.enquiries@ed.ac.uk
www.ed.ac.uk
www.eusa.ed.ac.uk

The Times Rankings

Overall Ranking: 14

Student satisfaction:	=67	(74%)
Research quality:	=3	(2.8)
Entry standards:	=9	(447)
Student–staff ratio:	=8	(12.4)
Services & facilities/student:	19	(£1,511)
Expected completion rate:	29	(90.4%)
Good honours:	6	(80.6%)
Graduate prospects:	22	(76.9%)

ally excellent, the highest proportion in Scotland. The university's entry was among the largest in the UK and produced strong results across the board. The College of Medicine and Veterinary Medicine was the star performer, with all of the work in hospital-based clinical subjects rated at the international level and 40 per cent at the highest grade. Informatics, linguistics and English literature also produced outstanding results.

The incorporation of Moray House, whose Holyrood site houses education, made Edinburgh the largest university in Scotland, now with nearly 24,000 students. Yet, despite the new approach to selection, entry standards for the 600 undergraduate degree programmes remain high, whether in A levels or Highers. Nine candidates compete for every place. The university's buildings are scattered around the city, but most border the historic Old Town. The science and engineering campus is two miles to the south.

Departments organise visiting days in October for those thinking of applying and in the spring for those holding offers. There is also an annual open day in June and regular student-led guided tours. New students join one of three Colleges, which are divided into 21 Schools, and generally take three subjects in both their first and second years. Every student has a Director of Studies to help them narrow down the selection of a final degree and give personal advice when necessary.

Considerable sums have been spent making the university more accessible to the 1,600 disabled students, who can also call on the services of a disability office. All students are issued with a smart card for access to university facilities. The students' union operates on several sites and sports facilities are excellent.

The city is a treasure-trove of cultural and recreational opportunities. Most students thrive on Edinburgh life, even though the cost of living can make it difficult to do it justice. Some scientists complain of isolation, although there is a regular bus link with the main university area around George Square. The plentiful stock of residential accommodation was increased recently.

Undergraduate Fees and Bursaries

- Scottish-domiciled and EU students: no fees payable.
- Non-Scottish UK-domiciled student fees: £1,820 a year (£2,895 medicine).
- International student fees: £11,050–£14,500, £17,950–£30,400 (medicine)
- Scholarships based on circumstances or by competition.
- For full details see the university's website: www.scholarships.ed.ac.uk www.scholarships.ed.ac.uk/bursaries

Students

Undergraduates:	16,060	(725)
Postgraduates:	4,985	(1,790)
Mature students:	10.9%	
Overseas students:	12.9%	
Applications per place:	9.1	
From state-sector schools:	68.0%	
From working-class homes:	15.7%	

For detailed information about fees, grants and bursaries and how they work, see chapter 7.

Accommodation

Number of places and costs refer to 2009–10
University-provided places: about 6,300
Percentage catered: about 30%
Catered costs: £148–£184 a week
Self-catered costs: £81–£106 a week.
First years are guaranteed an offer of accommodation providing they fulfil requirements. Residential restrictions apply.
International students: accommodation guaranteed if conditions are met.
Contact: www.accom.ed.ac.uk

Edinburgh Napier University

Napier was Scotland's first and largest polytechnic, and also appointed the first woman to lead a university north of the border. Professor Joan Stringer moved from neighbouring Queen Margaret University College (as it then was) with the declared aim of making Napier "one of the leading modern universities in the United Kingdom". It is now in the midst of a £100-million redevelopment programme to help achieve that ambition.

Now an institution of more than 13,000 students, with 3,500 part-timers, it has continued to grow, largely thanks to increased recruitment from the Continent and further afield. Around 20 per cent of full-time undergraduates are from overseas. An International College, launched in 2007, offers them a dedicated service, with pastoral and recruitment activities, as well as support for Napier's many programmes in China, Hong Kong and Malaysia. The demand for places has remained buoyant at a time when it has faltered elsewhere in Scotland. Growth in applications of almost 14 per cent at the start of 2009 was the latest in a series of healthy increases.

Two new libraries, a purpose-built music centre and refurbishment of the science laboratories underlined Napier's ambitions, with a £5-million computing centre completing the first phase of the university's development plan at the university's headquarters in Merchiston, the student district of Edinburgh. This was followed by the £30-million transformation of the university's Craiglockhart campus, a one-time military hospital, where Scotland's biggest business school has been built. It features a glass atrium housing a cyber café and two spherical lecture theatres with a total of 600 seats, and a new fitness suite was added in 2007.

Next on the list is the Sighthill campus, in the west of Edinburgh, which will be closed throughout 2009–10 while construction work takes place. Sighthill will become home to the Faculty of Health, Life and Social Sciences, bringing the faculty under one roof for the first time in a sustainable and well-equipped building for teaching and learning. New sports facilities are among the other improvements planned for the campus, complementing council proposals for an athletics arena nearby.

The university is named after John Napier, the inventor of logarithms. The tower where he was born still sits among the concrete blocks of the Merchiston campus. There are several smaller sites, mainly in the leafy south of Edinburgh, but the eventual aim is to have one campus for each of the three faculties.

Craiglockhart Campus
Edinburgh EH14 1DJ
08452 606040
contact via website
www.napier.ac.uk
www.napierstudents.
 com

EDINBURGH

Belfast

London
Cardiff

The Times Rankings
Overall Ranking: 65

Student satisfaction:	–	(–)
Research quality:	=71	(0.4)
Entry standards:	=54	(291)
Student–staff ratio:	67	(18.2)
Services & facilities/student:	91	(£895)
Expected completion rate:	104	(72.6%)
Good honours:	52	(62.4%)
Graduate prospects:	38	(72.9%)

Napier has been held up as a model to other universities trying to reduce wastage rates. The university uses its own students to mentor newcomers, runs bridging programmes and offers pre-term introductions to staff and information on facilities, as well as running summer top-up courses in a variety of subjects. The Confident Futures programme helps students make the transition to higher education and teaches employability skills and personal development. However, the latest projected dropout rate of more than 16 per cent is still more than the UK average for the subjects on offer.

Library and information management achieved by far the best results in the 2008 Research Assessment Exercise, when just over a fifth of the university's submission was considered world-leading or internationally excellent. A new Skillset Screen Academy, run in partnership with Edinburgh College of Art, reflects the university's strong reputation in film education.

Most of the avowedly vocational courses include a work placement, and the close relationship with industry and commerce helps to produce consistently good graduate employment figures. The modular course system allows movement between courses at all levels and has allowed students the option of starting courses in February, rather than September. Links with a network of partner colleges encourage progression from further to higher education.

The dispersed nature of the university does nothing for the social scene, although Edinburgh is hardly dull. Some students find life too quiet in the evenings and at weekends, although the students' association, in partnership with local clubs, organises regular party nights in the city centre.

Undergraduate Fees and Bursaries

- Scottish-domiciled and EU students: no fees payable.
- Non-Scottish UK-domiciled student fees: £1,820 a year.
- International student fees: £8,950–£10,390
- Scholarships based on circumstances or by competition.
- For full details see the university's website: www.napier.ac.uk/napierlife/money/Pages/default.aspx/

Students		
Undergraduates:	8,470	(2,220)
Postgraduates:	1,070	(1,230)
Mature students:	46.2%	
Overseas students:	19.9%	
Applications per place:	2.7	
From state-sector schools:	96.1%	
From working-class homes:	33.0%	

For detailed information about fees, grants and bursaries and how they work, see chapter 7.

Accommodation

Number of places and costs refer to 2009–10
University-provided places: 900
Percentage catered: 0%
Self-catered costs: £86 average cost a week.
First years are guaranteed a place provided requirements are met. Residential restrictions apply.
International students are guaranteed a place as long as requirements are met.
Contact: accommodation@napier.ac.uk

University of Essex

Essex has long since moved out of the shadow of its radical past, acquiring a reputation for high-quality research, especially in the social sciences. The social science departments led a strong set of results in the 2008 Research Assessment Exercise (RAE) and Essex also broke into the top 20 in the National Student Survey, after the biggest of three successive increases in satisfaction levels. The university began to reap the rewards with a 13 per cent rise in applications at the start of 2009.

There are still fewer than 9,000 full-time students, a quarter of whom are postgraduates. The student population is unusually diverse for a traditional university, with high proportions of mature and overseas students. Nearly a third of the undergraduates are from working-class homes and over 95 per cent went to state schools or colleges – a significantly higher proportion than the subject mix would suggest.

Economics (with 95 per cent of its submission rated in the top two categories) and politics (where 45 per cent was judged to be world-leading) led the way in the latest RAE. But almost two thirds of the work submitted by the university was found to be world-leading or internationally excellent. Both politics and sociology produced the best results in the country, while the newly-formed Essex Business School ranked second in the UK for accounting and finance. History and philosophy boasted the most satisfied students in the 2008 National Student Survey, which showed that 88 per cent of Essex's final-year undergraduates were generally satisfied with their course.

The university has been building up its science departments – the biological sciences department is one of its largest. Computer science is also strong and a BSc in computer games and internet technology shows Essex keeping pace with changing demands in graduate employment. But improvements in the university's academic performance could not disguise the fact that the glass and concrete campus, set in 200 acres of parkland on the outskirts of Colchester, was showing distinct signs of a quarter of a century's wear and tear. The university has been carrying out a programme of refurbishment at the same time as expanding student facilities. Teaching and administration blocks, which cluster around a network of squares, are gradually being transformed and extra catering and residential facilities added.

Recent building includes a Networks Centre for computer science and electronic systems engineering, featuring a powered floor system for robotics and an iDorm laboratory. Another £6 million was spent on two prize-winning 500-seat lecture theatres which can be combined for exhibitions,

---

Wivenhoe Park
Colchester
Essex CO4 3SQ
01206 873666 (enquiries)
admit@essex.ac.uk
www.essex.ac.uk
www.essexstudent.com

The Times Rankings
Overall Ranking: 43

Student satisfaction:	=40	(76%
Research quality:	=32	(1.8)
Entry standards:	52	(302)
Student–staff ratio:	=18	(13.7)
Services & facilities/student:	28	(£1,385)
Expected completion rate:	37	(87.4%)
Good honours:	=59	(61.0%)
Graduate prospects:	=82	(62.7%)

conferences or graduation ceremonies, and work has started on a new social sciences building. Sustainable energy and technology are being used whenever possible, with recent projects featuring ground source heat pumps, solar panels, rainwater harvesting and a wind turbine.

Essex champions academic breadth, and in each of the four faculties, students follow a common first year before specialising. They may take four or five different subjects before committing themselves to a particular degree. Social and sporting facilities are good, the more so following an extension of the Sports Centre and the refurbishment of the students' union bars. There are now four bars, an enlarged and refurbished nightclub and numerous cafés on campus. Some 40 acres of land are devoted to sports facilities, used extensively by individual students and over 40 university sports clubs.

First years new to Colchester and all overseas students are guaranteed university accommodation, all of which is now networked to the university IT system and equipped with telephones giving free access to the internal phone system. Some ground-floor flats on campus have been adapted for disabled students. The library has been extended to provide 1,100 reader spaces and is open for over 84 hours a week, with the Large Reading Room open 24 hours a day, Monday to Thursday.

The incorporation of the East 15 acting school, in Loughton, has enhanced the university's provision in theatre studies, and was the university's first venture beyond Colchester. A third campus opened in Southend in 2007, offering courses in business, health education and the arts. It also includes health and dental facilities, the latter staffed by senior dental students from Barts and the London School of Medicine and Dentistry. Another regional project sees Essex collaborating with the University of East Anglia on University Campus Suffolk, which offers courses in Ipswich and at smaller centres across the county. Essex degrees are also taught at Writtle College, near Chelmsford, the Colchester Institute and South East Essex College, in Southend.

Undergraduate Fees and Bursaries

- Fees for UK/EU students: £3,225
- International student fees: £9,750–£11,990
- Bursary on full grant: £319
- Bursaries on partial grant: household income up to £25.5K: £419; increasing to max. £2,119 at £34K; decreasing to £50 at £50K.
- Scholarships based on circumstances or by competition.
- For full details see the university's website: www.essex.ac.uk/studentfinance/ug/ university_support/bursary.aspx

Students

Undergraduates:	7,455	(1,360)
Postgraduates:	1,765	(935)
Mature students:	24.3%	
Overseas students:	20.7%	
Applications per place:	4.2	
From state-sector schools:	95.5%	
From working-class homes:	32.6%	

For detailed information about fees, grants and bursaries and how they work, see chapter 7.

Accommodation

Number of places and costs refer to 2008–09
University-provided places: 3,605
Percentage catered: 0%
Self-catered costs: £61.46–£95.13 a week.
New first years living outside the borough of Colchester are guaranteed accommodation if conditions are met.
International students: new students are guaranteed accommodation if conditions are met; priority given to students in final year.
Contact: admit@essex.ac.uk

University of Exeter

Exeter is one of Britain's most popular universities in terms of first-choice applications, not only in its traditional strong suit of the arts and social sciences, but increasingly also in the sciences, which are to benefit from an £80-million investment. Applications were up by an impressive 19 per cent at the start of 2009, following good results in the National Student Survey (NSS) and the Research Assessment Exercise (RAE).

English literature, drama, law, history and psychology are among the most heavily subscribed courses in their fields, and successful applicants appear not to be disappointed. Exeter has been among the top ten universities in every year that the NSS has been published, with accounting and finance, management and drama boasting the most satisfied students in their fields in 2008.

The latest RAE saw Exeter move up the pecking order of research universities, with most of its work judged to be world-leading or internationally excellent despite a much larger submission (involving 95 per cent of academics) than most of its peers. English, classics, archaeology, and accounting and finance did particularly well. The successes will produce one of the biggest grant increases at any university in England. Exeter is also leading a £14-million

partnership of southwest universities, including Bristol and Bath, to boost research in areas of economic importance.

The university boasts one of the most attractive settings of any university, and now plans to invest £450 million on its main campus. This includes £150 million for student residences, substantial investment in the Business School, new facilities for biosciences and a £48-million centrepiece for the campus. The Forum Project, will feature an extended library, student services and main university reception area.

More than a quarter of the undergraduates come from independent schools – a much higher proportion than the national average for the subjects Exeter offers, although this figure has been dropping. Professor Steve Smith, the Vice-Chancellor, has put broadening the social mix at the top of his agenda, particularly targeting schools and colleges in the rural South West. Location is partly responsible for the relatively rarefied social mix. There is no large centre of population and despite sophisticated shopping and a lively entertainment scene, South West cathedral cities are not what every teenager is looking for.

A £100-million campus near Falmouth, in Cornwall, has helped boost applications. New degrees in law, history and politics and a range of combined honours degrees not available in Exeter have proved extremely popular. The Camborne School of Mines,

---

Northcote House
The Queen's Drive
Exeter, Devon EX4 4QJ
01392 263855 (admissions)
ug-ad@exeter.ac.uk
www.exeter.ac.uk
www.exeterguild.org/
www.fxu.org.uk/

which has been a department of the university since 1993, is also based on the Cornwall campus, on a site shared with University College Falmouth.

The other big development of recent years was the opening of Peninsula Medical School (www.pms.ac.uk), in association with Plymouth University, in 2002. Recruitment has been strong and Peninsula was the only successful bidder for a new dental school in 2006. The four-year Bachelor of Dental Surgery has an annual intake of 64 science graduates or health service professionals. Applications more than doubled in its second year when the increase was 10 per cent nationally.

Arabic and Islamic studies have benefited from support from the Middle East and Exeter has an office in Dubai. A longstanding focus is exemplified by the growing range of four-year programmes "with international study" and its 180 partner universities worldwide. All students are offered tuition in foreign languages and even some three-year degrees include the option of a year abroad.

Career management skills are built into degree programmes and students can gain work experience through the university's employability and business project programmes. The Careers and Employment Service has been expanded to increase the work experience and placement opportunities available to students, 7,000 of whom undertook employability training in 2007.

The main Streatham Campus is close to the centre of Exeter and has a lively social scene. The highly rated schools of education, sport and health sciences are a mile away in the former St Luke's College. Some £8 million has been invested in sports facilities, which are among the best in the country. Exeter is one of only nine UK universities to have indoor tennis facilities to national competition standards and a new £2-million cricket centre opened in March 2009. Exeter is one of the UK's top sporting universities and was placed eleventh in the 2007–08 national rankings. The university's students devote around 100,000 volunteering hours a year – the most in Britain.

Undergraduate Bursaries and Scholarships

- Fees for UK/EU students: £3,225
- International student fees: £10,000–£12,550 £13,000–£20,500 (medicine)*
- Bursary on full grant: £1,500
- Bursaries on partial grant: household income up to £35K: £750.
  Scholarships based on circumstances or by competition.
- For full details see the university's website: www.admin.exeter.ac.uk/academic/ scholarships/
* Figures for 2008–09

Students

Undergraduates:	10,010	(640)
Postgraduates:	2,770	(1,285)
Mature students:	11.2%	
Overseas students:	6.4%	
Applications per place:	6.0	
From state-sector schools:	72.8%	
From working-class homes:	16.7%	

For detailed information about fees, grants and bursaries and how they work, see chapter 7.

Accommodation

Number of places and costs refer to 2009–10
University-provided places: 4,224
Percentage catered: 37%
Catered costs: £108.01–£171.50 a week (31 weeks)
Self-catered costs: £69.86–£119.00 a week (40, 44 or 51 weeks).
Unaccompanied first years are guaranteed accommodation provided conditions are met.
International students: as above.
Contact: accommodation@exeter.ac.

University of Glamorgan

Glamorgan attracted by far the biggest rise in applications, at some 18 per cent, of any university in Wales at the start of 2009. The opening of a striking new £35-million campus in the centre of Cardiff in 2007 has made all the difference, increasing the demand for courses based there by more than 60 per cent. The university's Cardiff School of Creative and Cultural Industries offers an "eclectic mix of teaching and research in the theory and practice of media, design and the arts". Students work in an ultra-modern new building, known as the ATRiuM, and have access to 1,350 rooms in privately run halls of residence.

The new development followed a merger with the Royal Welsh College of Music and Drama, with its conservatoire courses. However, most of Glamorgan's 21,000 students will remain on the Treforest campus, 20 minutes by train from Cardiff, overlooking the market town of Pontypridd. Others take Glamorgan courses in five overseas centres or in a growing number of further education colleges across Wales. Four have become accredited colleges, guaranteeing places on degree courses if students meet set conditions, while Merthyr Tydfil College has become the university's Faculty of Further Education.

The university produced good results in the 2008 Research Assessment Exercise, albeit from a low entry in most subjects. Almost a third of the work submitted was judged to be world-leading or internationally excellent, with English and nursing and midwifery doing especially well.

Originally based in a large country house, Glamorgan now has a large, modern campus. The Law School moved to new premises on the main campus in 2008 with upgraded facilities including a moot courtroom, while accommodation for mathematics and computing has had a £5-million refurbishment. The Faculty of Health Sport and Science are on the Glyntaff site, a short walk from the main campus. They are housed in new buildings and restored tramsheds, a reminder of the industrial past of the area. The popular Institute of Chiropractic is one of only two university-based centre for training chiropractors in the UK.

The business school is the largest in Wales, and the university was among the first providers of the Foundation degree. The range of two-year courses has since expanded rapidly, covering subjects as diverse as football and rugby coaching, surveying and costume construction. The vocational approach pays dividends for graduate employment, which is consistently good, although the projected dropout rate is easily the highest in Wales and among the worst in the UK, at 29 per cent.

Llantwit Road
Treforest
Pontypridd
Mid Glamorgan CF37 1DL
0800 716925 (enquiries)
enquiries@glam.ac.uk
www.glam.ac.uk
www.glamsu.com

The Times Rankings
Overall Ranking: 94

Student satisfaction:	=67	(74%)
Research quality:	=71	(0.4)
Entry standards:	76	(263)
Student–staff ratio:	=68	(18.3)
Services & facilities/student:	60	(£1,103)
Expected completion rate:	111	(69.1%)
Good honours:	=85	(52.4%)
Graduate prospects:	=90	(60.4%)

The intake is more socially diverse than elsewhere in the Principality. Over 40 per cent of undergraduates come from working-class homes and 15 per cent are from areas with no tradition of higher education.

Glamorgan did well in the early rounds of the National Student Survey, but scores have dipped in the last two years. Business students were the only ones to register more than 90 per cent satisfaction, while fewer than half of those on some technology courses declared themselves satisfied overall. However, the Faculty of Advanced Technology has been designated a centre of excellence for Wales, while three National Partnership awards testify to high standards in course design and delivery. Degrees in computer forensics, computer games development, lighting and design technology and aerospace courses are all designed with employers' needs in mind.

Many of the 9,000 full-time undergraduates live around Pontypridd, while others choose Cardiff, which is both livelier and a better source of accommodation. However, the Pontypridd campus has been developing, with an extension to the students' union, which is the focus of social life. There is also a modern a recreation centre.

The sports facilities are good enough for Glamorgan to have been awarded the 2001 British University Games and to become one of six centres of excellence in cricket. The university's playing fields have been used for training purposes by leading football and rugby teams. Glamorgan is successful in student competitions, especially in rugby, and offers a number of sports bursaries for students with international potential. But there is also a wide range of health and fitness classes for those with lower aspirations.

Undergraduate Fees and Bursaries

- Fees for UK/EU students: £3,225 (grant of up to £1,940 for Welsh students).
- International student fees: £9,250.
- Bursary of £319 (household income up to £18,370) plus £500 residential allowance for non-local UK and EU students.
- £500 residential allowance for non-local UK and EU students.
- Scholarships based on circumstances or by competition.
- For full details see the university's website: www.glam.ac.uk/money

Students		
Undergraduates:	11,235	(7,825)
Postgraduates:	1,580	(2,070)
Mature students:	41.8%	
Overseas students:	13.3%	
Applications per place:	3.7	
From state-sector schools:	98.5%	
From working-class homes:	42.2%	

For detailed information about fees, grants and bursaries and how they work, see chapter 7.

Accommodation

Number of places and costs refer to 2008–09
University-provided places: 1,108
Percentage catered: 0%
Self-catered costs: £64 (standard) – £78 (en suite) a week (39 weeks).
First-year students are offered accommodation.
Local restrictions apply.
International students are guaranteed housing.
Contact: accom@glam.ac.uk

University of Glasgow

More distinctively Scottish than its rivals in Edinburgh or St Andrews, almost half of Glasgow's students come from within 30 miles of the city and three quarters are from north of the border. There was a high proportion of home-based students long before the city became fashionable, but the university also attracts students from some 120 countries. They seem to enjoy the experience, voting Glasgow second in the UK in the independent International Student Barometer. British students are also pretty satisfied – Glasgow was in the top 30 in the National Student Survey published in 2008, with geology and biology registering 100 per cent satisfaction levels and computer science only a whisker away.

Glasgow enjoys the rare distinction of having been established by Papal Bull, and began its existence in the Chapter House of Glasgow Cathedral in 1451. Since 1871 it has been based next to Kelvingrove Park in the city's fashionable west end on the Gilmorehill campus, with its 104 listed buildings – more than any other British university. A major addition, opened in 2002, houses the prestigious medical school, while a £15-million cancer research centre followed in late 2006.

Education occupies a separate campus nearby, while the Vet School and outdoor sports facilities are located at Garscube, four miles away. The innovative Crichton College campus in Dumfries is taking higher education to southwest Scotland with liberal arts and teacher education degrees. A new student centre opened on the Gilmorehill site in 2008, with student services and catering facilities, while an £18-million small animal hospital for the Vet School is opening in 2009. The environmental research building has won awards as one of the "greenest" in Scotland.

Glasgow has adopted an increasingly outward-looking style in recent years, marked by the launch of the Common-wealth Scholarship scheme in 2008, which celebrates the city's success as host of the 2014 Commonwealth Games by offering 53 students from developing countries the chance to study at the university. A "synergy" agreement with neighbouring Strathclyde University involves teaching and research partnerships, the latest establishing a joint department of naval architecture and marine engineering.

Not that Glasgow is a stranger to innovation: it was the first university in Britain to have a school of engineering, for example, and the first in Scotland to have a computer. Today it is a member of the Russell Group of 20 leading research universities. More than half of the work submitted for the 2008 Research

---

University Avenue
Glasgow G12 8QQ
0141 330 4440 (prospectus hotline)
prospectus@gla.ac.uk
www.gla.ac.uk
www.theguu.com
www.qmu.org.uk

The Times Rankings
Overall Ranking: 19

Student satisfaction:	=14	(79%)
Research quality:	=17	(2.2)
Entry standards:	=14	(412)
Student–staff ratio:	15	(13.2)
Services & facilities/student:	30	(£1,377)
Expected completion rate:	41	(86.6%)
Good honours:	24	(71.3%)
Graduate prospects:	30	75.4%)

Assessment Exercise was considered world-leading or internationally excellent. Art history was the most highly-rated in the UK and the Vet School joint top in its field, with 14 subjects showing the best results in Scotland.

Almost half of the university's applications are for Arts or Sciences degrees, reflecting the popularity of a flexible system of study where students can delay choosing which subject within Arts or Science to specialise in until the end of their second year. Total applications were up by more than 14 per cent at the start of 2009, the biggest increase in Scotland.

Overseas recruitment has remained strong, as Glasgow has moved into the top 75 in the *Times Higher Education*/QS world university rankings. But the home market has not been overlooked. The Club 21 programme, which provides students with paid work experience placements, involves more than 100 employers from Abbey to T-Mobile, some of whom sponsor undergraduates at £1,000 a year, as part of an arrangement to forge closer links with local business.

Over a fifth of the students are from working-class homes. The university operates a number of access initiatives, including the Top Up programme, which has been working with schools in the West of Scotland since 1999, and the Talent Awards, 50 annual awards of £1,000 a year for academically able entrants who could face financial difficulties in taking up a place at Glasgow.

Most students like the combination of campus and city life, with the relatively low cost of living an added attraction – the city has been rated among the most cost-effective in which to study. But the dropout rate of more than 13 per cent is above the average for the subjects on offer and entry qualifications. Undergraduates have the choice of two students' unions, with more than 100 clubs and societies, plus a sports union supporting 46 different clubs and activities.

Undergraduate Fees and Bursaries

- Scottish-domiciled and EU students: no fees payable.
- Non-Scottish UK-domiciled student fees: £1,820 a year (£2,895 medicine).
- International student fees:£9,800–12,950; £18,750 (veterinary medicine); £22,600 (medicine); £23,450 (dentistry)
- Scholarships based on circumstances or by competition.
- For full details see the university's website: www.gla.ac.uk/bursaries www.gla.ac.uk/scholarships

---

Students

Undergraduates:	14,720	(3,915)
Postgraduates:	2,990	(2,105)
Mature students:	13.2%	
Overseas students:	7.0%	
Applications per place:	5.4	
From state-sector schools:	86.6%	
From working-class homes:	21.9%	

For detailed information about fees, grants and bursaries and how they work, see chapter 7.

Accommodation

Number of places and costs refer to 2009–10
University-provided places: 3,521
Percentage catered: 6.7%
Catered costs: £112.84–£125.16 a week.
Self-catered costs: £69.37–£104.93 a week.
First years are guaranteed accommodation if conditions are met. Deadline applies.
International students: first years are guaranteed accommodation if conditions are met. 20% of returners are also housed.
Contact: accom@gla.ac.uk

Glasgow Caledonian University

Glasgow Caledonian has spent more than £70 million transforming previously mediocre facilities into a single campus that does justice to a modern university of more than 16,000 students. Only four universities are bigger north of the border. Over 80 per cent of the buildings are new or have been upgraded, and improvements are still being made. The health building brings together teaching and research facilities and includes a virtual hospital, where students can hone their clinical and interpersonal skills. The Saltire Centre, which has brought all library and student services together for the first time, opened in 2006 with study spaces for 1,800 students.

With the accent firmly on widening participation in higher education, the university will always struggle in league tables such as ours, but it is well-regarded by employers, and applications have generally been healthy. They showed a 3 per cent increase at the start of 2009. Caledonian is among the top UK universities for attracting students from areas without a tradition of higher education, and more than a third of its undergraduates come from working-class homes. The university has argued forcefully that extending access should be rewarded more generously if such students are to receive the support they need to make a success of higher education.

The projected dropout rate has been coming down, but it is still close to one in five – considerably more than the UK average for Caledonian's courses and entry qualifications. The university has introduced a series of measures designed to improve retention. Telltale signs are monitored, such as non-attendance at lectures, and better academic, social and financial support offered to those at risk of dropping out.

Consolidated on its city-centre campus, Caledonian's original two sites have now been reduced to one with the sale of the Park Campus, in the west end of the city, to Glasgow University. Leisure facilities have been improved with a new building for the health faculty, opened by Thabo Mbeki, who named it in honour of his father. Physiotherapy was the only subject since chemistry's success in 1993 to be rated Excellent for teaching, and Caledonian now boasts among the most extensive health programmes in Britain.

A string of other subjects (mainly on the science side) were considered Highly Satisfactory. Business is the other big area, the Caledonian Business School boasting more undergraduates than any other institution in Scotland, with over 1,000 in each year group. The university pioneered

---

70 Cowcaddens Road
Glasgow G4 0BA
0141 331 8681 (enquiries)
info@caledonianchoice.com
www.gcal.ac.uk
www.caledonianstudent.
 com

The Times Rankings
Overall Ranking: 60

Student satisfaction:	=54	(75%)
Research quality:	=85	(0.3)
Entry standards:	=42	(328)
Student–staff ratio:	103	(21.0)
Services & facilities/student:	88	(£933)
Expected completion rate:	90	(76.8%)
Good honours:	38	(66.5%)
Graduate prospects:	57	(68.8%)

subjects such as entrepreneurial studies and risk management – the only university in the country to do so – and offers highly specialist degrees, such as tourism management, fashion marketing, leisure management and consumer protection.

Half of the 14 subject areas in which the university entered the 2008 Research Assessment Exercise contained at least some world-leading work. Health subjects produced the best results and entered the largest numbers for assessment.

Degrees in all areas are strongly vocational, and are complemented by a wide portfolio of professional courses. A high proportion of students choose sandwich courses, and the university operates on a modular system. The REAL@Caledonian online student facility combines enhanced learning technology with a informal cyber-café atmosphere.

The legacy of Queen's College, which catered mainly for women, has ensured that the proportion of female students is the highest of any university in Britain. Sports and social facilities have been among the priorities in the building programme. Some students find that the high proportion of their peers living at home detracts from the social scene, but Glasgow is a very lively city with a large student population.

Undergraduate Fees and Bursaries
- Scottish-domiciled and EU students: no fees payable.
- Non-Scottish UK-domiciled student fees: £1,820 a year.
- International student fees: £9,000–£10,000
- Scholarships based on circumstances or by competition.
- For full details see the university's website: www.gcal.ac.uk/student/money/index.html

Students		
Undergraduates:	10,290	(3,790)
Postgraduates:	1,335	(1,350)
Mature students:	37.4%	
Overseas students:	4.2%	
Applications per place:	4.4	
From state-sector schools:	96.6%	
From working-class homes:	34.6%	

For detailed information about fees, grants and bursaries and how they work, see chapter 7.

Accommodation
Number of places and costs refer to 2009–10
University-provided places: 660
Percentage catered: 0%
Self-catered costs: £74.80–£86.20 a week.
Students under 19 living outside the Glasgow area have priority for accommodation.
International students: non-EU students given priority if conditions are met.
Contact: accommodation@gcal.ac.uk; www.caledonian.ac.uk/study/studentlife/accommodation/index.html

University of Gloucestershire

With a main campus on the site of a former botanical garden, it was natural for Gloucestershire to focus on green issues. The university has placed sustainability at the head of its priorities, topping the Green League of Universities in 2008 for its all-round environmental performance. There are allotments for students, a free bus service and bike loan schemes, as well as diplomas in environmentalism and an International Research Institute in Sustainability. The approach may be one factor in the growing popularity of the university: an increase in applications of almost 20 per cent at the start of 2009 was one of the biggest in the UK.

One of the more recent additions to the list of universities, Gloucestershire is also the first for more than a century to have formal links with the Church of England. Although its religious origins have been played down in recent years and students of all faiths are welcomed, the university includes church appointees on its governing body and Lord Carey, the former Archbishop of Canterbury, is its first Chancellor. This did not prevent the university dropping theology at degree level as part of a curriculum review, although the subject will be back in the prospectus for 2010–11.

Before university status in 2001, Cheltenham and Gloucester College of Higher Education had been the product of a merger between a church college and the higher education wing of a college of arts and technology. After considerable expansion during the 1990s, there are now about 8,500 students, including 2,500 part-timers, and 1,000 academic and support staff. The main subject areas are law and IT, business management, the arts, media and design, humanities, the environment, teacher education, leisure and tourism, social sciences and sport. The university prides itself on a good range of work placements, which include Microsoft and Disneyworld.

The main campus is on the attractive site of the former College of St Paul and St Mary, a mile outside Cheltenham. There has also been considerable development of the Gloucester campus, on the site of a former domestic science college which became part of the university in 2002. Although middle-class Cheltenham is a world away from more working-class Gloucester socially, the two centres are only seven miles apart and students are not as isolated as they are in some split-site institutions. There are also two smaller sites in Cheltenham: Pittville for art and design, and Francis Close Hall for a range of subjects, including education. The latter also houses a national centre of excellence in the teaching of geography,

---

The Park Campus
The Park
Cheltenham GL50 2RH
0844 011100 (prospectus)
admissions@glos.ac.uk
www.glos.ac.uk
www.yourstudentsunion
.com

The Times Rankings
Overall Ranking: 68

Student satisfaction:	=67	(74%)
Research quality:	=85	(0.3)
Entry standards:	94	(239)
Student–staff ratio:	=49	(16.5)
Services & facilities/student:	45	(£1,190)
Expected completion rate:	=68	(82.1%)
Good honours:	68	(56.2%)
Graduate prospects:	=75	(64.2%)

environment and related disciplines. The free bus service links all four sites and also serves Cheltenham railway station. In addition, the former Urban Learning Foundation, in London, became part of the university in 2003, providing a very different setting for teacher training courses.

Gloucestershire did not quite repeat the success it enjoyed in the previous research assessments when the exercise was repeated in 2008. Some world-leading research was found in five of the 12 areas in which the university submitted work, with the small education entry producing the best results. But less than 20 per cent of all work reached the top two categories. Results in the National Student Survey have been variable, with only law, English and geography recording satisfaction levels of more than 90 per cent in 2008.

The university's intake is as diverse as its locations, with 95 per cent of undergraduates from state schools and nearly a third from working-class homes. The projected dropout rate has improved dramatically, the latest projection of 10 per cent falling to well below the national average for the subjects offered and the students' entry qualifications. The new and well-equipped sport-oriented Oxstalls campus, in Gloucester, where participation in higher education has always been low, will focus particularly on access initiatives.

The university's sports facilities include a sports hall and tennis courts, but are not extensive for a university of 8,500 students, in spite of the addition of a gym at the Oxstalls campus. Likewise accommodation, with around 1,300 beds, although the university assures its students that it has access to enough private sector places to meet all their needs. First years are given preference in the allocation of hall places and "enhancement of the student experience" is one of the priorities in the university's strategic plan. Cheltenham is the livelier of the two bases in terms of nightlife, but neither is dull and facilities are improving.

Undergraduate Fees and Bursaries
- Fees for UK/EU students: £3,225
- International student fees: £8,405
- Bursary on full grant: £319
- The university does not award bursaries for students on partial maintenance grants.
- Scholarships based on circumstances or by competition.
- For full details see the university's website: www.glos.ac.uk/money/Pages/default.aspx

---

Students

Undergraduates:	5,580	(1,120)
Postgraduates:	530	(1,290)
Mature students:	21.3%	
Overseas students:	5.5%	
Applications per place:	3.6	
From state-sector schools:	95.0%	
From working-class homes:	32.2%	

For detailed information about fees, grants and bursaries and how they work, see chapter 7.

Accommodation
Number of places and costs refer to 2008–09
University-provided places: about 1,350
Percentage catered: 0%
Self-catered costs: £69–£102 a week.
First-year undergraduates have priority for halls.
International students: first-year undergraduates are guaranteed accommodation if conditions are met.
Contact: accommodation@glos.ac.uk

Glyndŵr University

The former North East Wales Institute of Higher Education took the name of the medieval Welsh prince Owain Glyndŵr, who championed the establishment of universities throughout Wales in the early 15th century, when it was awarded university status in 2008. Based on two campuses in Wrexham, the limit of the new university's current territorial ambitions is a site in Northop, Flintshire, operated in partnership with the Welsh College of Horticulture.

There are fewer than 3,000 full-time students and another 4,500 part-timers, whose qualifications will continue to be awarded by the University of Wales. Nearly a third are from overseas, many from other EU countries, India or China. As NEWI, there were only two applications per place – a lower ratio than at any UK university. But at the start of 2009, Glyndŵr was enjoying the customary boost that accompanies a change of status, with applications rising by 23 per cent.

Sports science produced by far the most satisfied students in the National Student Survey published in 2008. No other area managed more than 85 per cent satisfaction, although over half of the subjects had too few responses for scores to be compiled. The results were an improvement on the previous year, but not enough to escape the bottom 20.

Fewer than half of the undergraduates are school-leavers and nearly all of them are state-educated. The 45 per cent from working-class homes represent the biggest proportion in Wales and one of the biggest in the UK. Glyndŵr also has the largest proportion of disabled students in Wales and was nominated for an award for its provision for them. There is a dedicated centre for students with disabilities that assesses students' needs before they embark on a course.

Among a raft of new courses for 2009 are a Foundation degree in floristry and floral design and degrees in mobile computing and therapeutic childcare. The university has even launched a degree in equestrian psychology, examining the way in which horses learn and investigating their bond with humans. Bursaries of up to £1,000 a year are available for all UK students, dependant on family income, and entrants to full-time courses with more than 300 UCAS points are eligible for one-off scholarships of another £1,000.

Glyndŵr entered only 27 academics for the 2008 Research Assessment Exercise, but almost a quarter of their work was judged to be world-leading or internationally excellent. Computer science and materials both reached the top grade for a small proportion of their work, and the university's research funding will

Mold Road
Wrexham
N. Wales LL11 2AW
01978 290666
sid@glyndwr.ac.uk
www.glyndwr.ac.uk
www.glyndwr.ac.uk/en/
Studentsupport/
StudentsGuild/

The Times Rankings
Overall Ranking: 97

Student satisfaction:	=90	(72%)
Research quality:	=95	(0.2)
Entry standards:	=106	(212)
Student–staff ratio:	=86	(19.7)
Services & facilities/student:	78	(£996)
Expected completion rate:	=108	(70.1%)
Good honours:	95	(50.6%)
Graduate prospects:	53	(69.3%)

more than double as a result.

The two campuses in Wrexham are within five minutes' walk of each other. Most courses are taught at the larger Plas Coch site, next to the Wrexham FC ground. The North Wales School of Art and Design is based at the Regent Street campus, nearer the town centre. The Flintshire campus is in a rural setting, not far from Wrexham, and offers land-based courses. A new media and design centre is due to open on the Flintshire campus in 2011.

The modern sports centre, in Wrexham, is one of the features of the university. There are two floodlit artificial pitches with different surfaces, a human performance laboratory and indoor facilities that include a sports hall with a 1,000 square-metre sprung floor. The centre has hosted a number of big sporting events, as well as conferences.

Two thirds of the students are from the local area, many living at home, which inevitably affects the social scene. But Wrexham is not without nightlife and both Manchester and Liverpool are within reach for those in search of more sophisticated shopping or clubbing.

Undergraduate Bursaries and Scholarships

- Fees for UK/EU students: £3,225 (grant of up to £1,940 for Welsh students).
- International student fees: £6,950
- Bursary of £1,000 (household income up to £18,370).
- Bursary of £750 (household income up to £22,000).
- Bursary of £500 (household income up to £95,000).
- Scholarships based on circumstances or by competition.
- For full details see the university's website: www.glyndwr.ac.uk/en/Coursesfees/ Feesscholarshipsbursaries/

Students

Undergraduates:	2,505	(4,120)
Postgraduates:	255	(385)
Mature students:	57.0%	
Overseas students:	28.7%	
Applications per place:	2.0	
From state-sector schools:	98.8%	
From working-class homes:	45.6%	

For detailed information about fees, grants and bursaries and how they work, see chapter 7.

Accommodation

Number of places and costs refer to 2008–09

University-provided places: 414

Percentage catered: 0%

Self-catered costs: £50–£77 a week (based on 37-week contract).

First-year undergraduates are guaranteed accommodation.

International students: guaranteed housing.

Contact: www.glyndwr.ac.uk/ Studentsupportservices/en/Accommodation/ accommodation@glyndwr.ac.uk

Goldsmiths, University of London

Dubbed the "campus of cool", Goldsmiths is best known for excellence in the arts, but it stresses that it brings the same creative approach to a wider range of subjects, spanning humanities, social sciences and teacher training. The nickname, which does no harm in recruiting students, came from the inclusion of Goldsmiths alongside MTV, Apple and the Tate among 50 "cool brandleaders" identified by the Brand Council. Alumni include Mary Quant and Damien Hirst among many other famous names, such as Malcolm McLaren and Linton Kwesi Johnson. Graduates of the college have won the Turner Prize no fewer than six times.

There is another side to Goldsmiths, however, in its tradition of community-based courses, which predates membership of the University of London. Evening and other part-time classes are still as popular as conventional degree courses and many subjects can be studied from basic to postgraduate levels. A history of providing educational opportunities for women is reflected in one of the largest proportions of female students in the British university system – nearly two thirds at the last count.

Determinedly integrated into its southeast London locality, the campus has a cosmopolitan atmosphere. A third of all undergraduates are over 21 on entry (a large proportion of these over 30), many coming from the area's ethnic minorities, and there is a growing proportion of overseas students. The age profile helped Goldsmiths to a rise in applications of more than 10 per cent at the start of 2009.

The older premises have been likened to a grammar school, with their long corridors of classrooms. But the Rutherford Building, containing library and IT services, won an award from the Royal Institute of British Architects, and a Grade II listed former baths building has been converted to provide more space for research and art studios. The new Ben Pimlott Building, which features a dramatic metal "scribble" by the acclaimed architect Will Alsop, contains state-of-the-art studio facilities and two multi-disciplinary centres for interaction between the arts and social sciences.

Although dominated by the arts, Goldsmiths' portfolio of subjects stretches through the humanities and social sciences as far as computing and psychology. More than half of the work submitted for the 2008 Research Assessment Exercise was considered world-leading or internationally excellent. Communication, cultural and media

Lewisham Way
New Cross
London SE14 6NW
020 7919 7766 (admissions)
admissions@gold.ac.uk
www.gold.ac.uk
www.gcsu.org.uk

The Times Rankings
Overall Ranking: 45

Student satisfaction:	=90	(72%)
Research quality:	=19	(2.1)
Entry standards:	47	(318)
Student–staff ratio:	10	(12.7)
Services & facilities/student:	104	(£806)
Expected completion rate:	45	(85.7%)
Good honours:	43	(65.2%)
Graduate prospects:	=55	(69.0%)

studies led the way, but there were good results, too, in music, sociology and art and design.

Undergraduates have shown themselves generally been satisfied in the National Student Survey although, in common with other London universities, really high scores have been hard to come by. Media studies and psychology produced the best results in 2008.

Employment prospects are good, especially for an institution with such a high proportion of students taking performing arts subjects, where a period of unemployment after graduation is commonplace. Indeed, on postgraduate courses, recent success rates have been among the best in Britain.

Student politics has survived at Goldsmiths to an extent not seen at many universities – the union building was given the name Tiananmen – while a college in which Alex James and Graham Coxon, from Blur, are just two of a number of successful rock alumni cannot fail to have a thriving music scene. The union has a strong tradition in volunteering and an award-winning newspaper, and recently won a gold Sound Impact Award recognising work on ethical and environmental issues.

The surrounding area enjoyed a mini-boom before the recession as a prime location for loft apartments. Although sky-high prices put them way beyond the reach of the student housing market, there are plenty of more reasonably priced options in the vicinity. Most first years are allocated one of the 971 residential places within walking distance of the campus and overseas students can be housed throughout their course. Sports enthusiasts have been less well provided for, although there is a well-equipped and affordable gym on campus. There is also a swimming pool and indoor complex in Deptford, but the main pitches are eight miles away.

Undergraduate Fees and Bursaries

- Fees for UK/EU students: £3,225
- International student fees: £9,870–£13,270
- Bursary on full grant: household income up to £19K: £1,000 then £500.
- Bursaries on partial grant: household income up to £40K: up to £500.
- Scholarships based on circumstances or by competition.
- For full details see the university's website: www.gold.ac.uk/ug/costs/

Students			Accommodation
Undergraduates:	4,520	(765)	Number of places and costs refer to 2008–09
Postgraduates:	1,430	(785)	University-provided places: 971 (college halls)
Mature students:	33.6%		Percentage catered: 0%
Overseas students:	12.8%		Self-catered costs: £85–£114 a week.
Applications per place:	4.8		Priority is given to new full-time students.
From state-sector schools:	91.6%		International students will be given priority for
From working-class homes:	30.2%		accommodation throughout their degree
			programme. See website for further details.
			Contact: accommodation@gold.ac.uk
For detailed information about fees, grants and			www.goldsmiths.ac.uk/accommodation
bursaries and how they work, see chapter 7.			020 7919 7130

University of Greenwich

Becoming one of three universities charging British and EU undergraduates less than £3,000 a year was a gamble that appeared not to pay off in the first year of top-up fees. Applications dropped in any case, but they have since been recovering. The university was enjoying an above-average increase of 8.5 per cent when the official deadline passed for courses beginning in 2009, when fees for degree courses will reach £2,900 (other than in pharmacy, where the full £3,225 will be charged). The aim is to strike a balance between affordability for the maximum number of students and the need to invest in the university.

The university's move, completed in 2002, into the former Royal Naval College buildings designed by Sir Christopher Wren provided a campus worthy of one of the most desirable titles in the higher education world. Its name has always conjured up images of history and science in equal measure, and the main campus is now part of a World Heritage site.

Wren's baroque masterpiece is being used, with the former Dreadnought Hospital, to teach over half the university's students in humanities, business, law, maths, computing and maritime studies. Four halls provide more than 1,300 places.

Under the leadership of Baroness Blackstone, the former Higher Education Minister, Greenwich has dropped the soubriquet of "regional university" but still draws primarily from southeast London and Kent, a populous county that until recently had only a single university. The prize-winning Medway campus, centred on the former naval base at Chatham, has been developed in partnership with Kent and Canterbury Christ Church universities. New student accommodation for an additional 140 students opened there in 2008, together with an improved café for Greenwich students in the main Pembroke building. Some £20 million has gone into one of the first new schools of pharmacy for 20 years, as well as the schools of science and engineering, the Natural Resources Institute, nursing and some business courses. A joint learning resources centre serves Chatham Maritime and the University of Kent's neighbouring premises. Another shared facility has improved teaching facilities and expanded student services, the campus having already exceeded the original target of 6,000 students.

Other schools are situated at Avery Hill, a Victorian mansion on the outskirts of southeast London, where a £14-million sports and teaching centre opened in 2006, with a new gym and refurbished café following in 2008. As well as a sports hall and 220-seat lecture theatre, there are

Old Royal Naval College
Park Row,
Greenwich
London SE10 9LS
0800 005 006 (course
 enquiries)
courseinfo@greenwich.
 ac.uk
www.gre.ac.uk
www.suug.co.uk

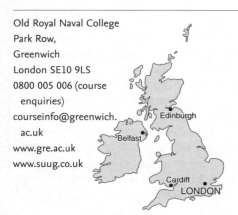

The Times Rankings
Overall Ranking: 106

Student satisfaction:	=78	(73%)
Research quality:	=85	(0.3)
Entry standards:	=106	(212)
Student–staff ratio:	109	(22.9)
Services & facilities/student:	=100	(£829)
Expected completion rate:	94	(75.8%)
Good honours:	112	(44.9%)
Graduate prospects:	94	(59.6%)

laboratories for health courses that replicate NHS wards. A neighbouring building is now the main base for the School of Health and Social Care. The campus also contains a student village of 1,300 rooms, as well as teaching accommodation for the social sciences, architecture, landscape and construction, and the large education faculty, which is one of the few to offer both primary and secondary teacher training courses. The Avery Hill TV studio has also been refurbished to meet current industrial standards.

Results in the National Student Survey have improved dramatically in the last two years, with accounting, history, pharmacy and philosophy demonstrating particularly high levels of satisfaction in 2008. The university achieved mixed results from a large entry to the 2008 Research Assessment Exercise, which showed a quarter of the work reaching world-leading or internationally excellent levels. The small mechanical engineering group produced by far the best results, but architecture and history also did well. A fifth of the university's income is from research and consultancy – the largest proportion at any former polytechnic.

Eleven associated colleges in Kent and London teach the university's courses, while strong links with institutions in Europe and further afield provide a steady flow of overseas students, as well as exchange opportunities for those at Greenwich. The university is the UK's top recruiter of students from India, and also takes large numbers from Mauritius and Nigeria.

A commitment to extending access to higher education has led to low entrance requirements in many subjects and a relatively high proportion of mature students. More than 97 per cent of undergraduates are state-educated, almost half coming from working-class homes. Both figures are significantly higher than the national average for Greenwich's courses and entrance qualifications. The downside is a projected dropout rate of more than 20 per cent, although even this figure is better than the university's benchmark.

Undergraduate Fees and Bursaries

- Fees for UK/EU students £2,900
  £3,225 (pharmacy)
- International student fees £8,750
- The university does not award bursaries for students on full maintenance grants.
- The university does not award bursaries for students on partial maintenance grants.
- Scholarships based on circumstances or by competition.
- For full details see the university's website: www.gre.ac.uk/students/finance

---

Students

Undergraduates:	13,025	(6,080)
Postgraduates:	2,030	(3,370)
Mature students:	48.1%	
Overseas students:	12.9%	
Applications per place:	5.6	
From state-sector schools:	97.9%	
From working-class homes:	46.1%	

For detailed information about fees, grants and bursaries and how they work, see chapter 7.

Accommodation

Number of places and costs refer to 2009–10
University-provided places: 2,400
Percentage catered: 0%
Self-catered costs: £81.20–£151.41 a week.
First years are guaranteed a place.
International students: new students get priority.
Contact: www.gre.ac.uk/about/accommodation; accommodation-AH@gre.ac.uk (Avery Hill) accommodation-GM@gre.ac.uk (Greenwich) accommodation-ME@gre.ac.uk (Medway)

Heriot-Watt University

Heriot-Watt is investing £10 million to increase its academic staff by 50 per cent, boosting teaching and research in business and technology in order to become a world-leading university within ten years. The first phase will cost £2 million and bring 25 new appointments. The university is already Scotland's most international institution, with a campus in Dubai and a total of 12,000 students in approved learning centres overseas or taking distance learning courses.

Heriot-Watt also produces more graduates than any of its rivals north of the border in the physical sciences, mathematics, engineering and in the built environment. Concentration on these areas is fitting for a university which commemorates James Watt, the pioneer of steam power, and George Heriot, financier to King James VI. It has fostered interdisciplinary teaching and research, with a battery of employment-related degrees.

Heriot-Watt is also one of the most commercially diversified universities in Britain, with the share of private research funding consistently among the highest in the UK per member of academic staff. About half of the university's income, around £60 million, comes from research, training and commercial services.

More than half of the work in a larger-than-average submission for the 2008 Research Assessment Exercise was rated world-leading or internationally excellent. Maths produced by far the best results, but there were good grades, too, in petroleum engineering, physics, general engineering, the built environment, and art and design. The last institutional review of the university's quality, in 2006, produced the top grade of "broad confidence". Heriot-Watt has also done well in the latest National Student Survey, with languages and chemistry producing the highest levels of satisfaction in 2008.

The main campus, close to Edinburgh Airport and 20 minutes drive from the city centre, still has a modern feel more than 40 years after it opened. The university remains small in terms of full-time students – there are about 7,000 on the Riccarton campus, with another 1,000 in Dubai taking business, engineering, science, or technology courses. Overseas students also fill a fifth of the places at Riccarton. Heriot-Watt won the Scottish Council of Development and Industry's 2007 award for Outstanding International Achievement in Scotland's Universities, partly for its support for international students.

Science, engineering, management and languages are located on the Edinburgh campus. There is a postgraduate campus in Orkney, specialising in renewable

---

Riccarton
Edinburgh EH14 4AS
0131 449 5111
enquiries@hw.ac.uk
www.hw.ac.uk
www.hwusa.org

The Times Rankings
Overall Ranking: 40

Student satisfaction:	=54	(75%)
Research quality:	=37	(1.7)
Entry standards:	38	(350)
Student–staff ratio:	=42	(15.6)
Services & facilities/student:	46	(£1,183)
Expected completion rate:	=75	(80.3%)
Good honours:	41	(65.5%)
Graduate prospects:	=25	(76.2%)

energy, and a Scottish Borders Campus in Galashiels, 35 miles south of Edinburgh, which specialises in textiles, fashion, textiles design and management. Heriot-Watt and Borders College have signed a partnership agreement for a long-term collaboration to deliver higher and further education in the historically under-provided region. Both institutions will share the site from 2009.

The subject mix serves graduates well: Heriot-Watt is seldom far from the top of the employment league tables. The latest projected dropout rate of less than 12 per cent is an improvement on previous figures, bringing the rate below the UK average for the university's subjects and entrance qualifications. More than half of the undergraduates are from Scotland, and 15 per cent from other parts of Britain, over 90 per cent of them from state schools and colleges.

The Edinburgh campus has an attractive parkland setting, with the students' union at its heart and halls of residence conveniently placed. Students have complained that the six-mile journey to the city centre leaves them isolated, but there are now frequent bus services. Sports enthusiasts are well provided for, and representative teams do well. Hearts, one of Edinburgh's two Scottish Premier League football clubs, have their sports academy on campus, which is used by students and local people as well as the young professionals. Music also thrives: there is a professional musician-in-residence and a number of scholarships, as well as a varied programme of events.

Undergraduate Fees and Bursaries
- Scottish-domiciled and EU students: no fees payable.
- Non-Scottish UK-domiciled student fees: £1,820 a year.
- International student fees: £9,360–£11,800
- Scholarships based on circumstances or by competition.
- For full details see the university's website: www.undergraduate.hw.ac.uk/scholarships/

Students		
Undergraduates:	5,065	(330)
Postgraduates:	1,530	(3,140)
Mature students:	14.4%	
Overseas students:	21.5%	
Applications per place:	3.9	
From state-sector schools:	91.8%	
From working-class homes:	27.6%	

For detailed information about fees, grants and bursaries and how they work, see chapter 7.

Accommodation
Number of places and costs refer to 2009–10
University places provided: 1,619
Percentage catered: 19%
Catered costs: £108.30–£118.20 a week.
Self-catered costs: £75–£90 a week.
All new first years are guaranteed accommodation provided conditions are met and applications in place by 22 August.
International students: as above.
Contact : SWS@hw.ac.uk

University of Hertfordshire

Hertfordshire has become a model for the "business-facing" university, serving the needs of local employers and improving the job prospects of its students in the process. The university even runs the local bus service and plays an important role in steering the local economy. A purpose-built £120-million campus, close to the existing Hatfield headquarters, opened in 2003, bringing the university together for the first time and providing outstanding facilities. The de Havilland campus, named after the aircraft manufacturer which once occupied the site, houses business, education and the humanities. It has a 24-hour resources centre, £15-million sports complex and 1,600 networked, en-suite residential places. The two sites are linked by cycleways, footpaths and shuttle buses.

As Hatfield Polytechnic, the university's reputation was built on engineering and computer science, but health subjects now account for by far the largest share of places. An innovative degree in paramedic science was Britain's first, its students using the UK's largest medical simulation centre to train to treat patients in emergency situations. The university is still hoping for a medical school, although its last bid was not successful. A new School of Pharmacy and a postgraduate medical school have strengthened its position. Increased research activity resulted in the establishment of the Health and Human Sciences Institute.

Art and design is also growing, particularly the multimedia courses. In 2005, the university launched a new School of Film, Music and New Media and in 2007 built a new £10-million media centre, with the latest technology for the teaching of music, animation, film, television and multimedia, based on the College Lane campus. The includes the largest art gallery in the eastern region, which mounts regular public exhibitions, while a 460-seat auditorium enhances the cultural programme. An Automotive Centre has upgraded teaching facilities for that branch of engineering, as well as boosting interaction with industry.

Professor Tim Wilson, the Vice-Chancellor, has been trying to widen the university's base through collaboration with local further education colleges. The intake is more diverse than might be expected, given the location and subject mix: 98 per cent of undergraduates are state-educated and 40 per cent come from working-class homes. The projected dropout rate has improved and, at less than 16 per cent, is back below the national average for the subject mix and entry grades.

At the start of 2009, applications were up by almost 16 per cent. Many students

College Lane
Hatfield
Herts AL10 9AB
01707 284800 (admissions)
admissions@herts.ac.uk
www.herts.ac.uk
www.uhsu.herts.co.uk

Edinburgh
Belfast
Cardiff
HATFIELD
London

The Times Rankings
Overall Ranking: =66

Student satisfaction:	=78	(73%)
Research quality:	=85	(0.3)
Entry standards:	=92	(244)
Student–staff ratio:	27	(14.4)
Services & facilities/student:	12	(£1,593)
Expected completion rate:	=66	(82.3%)
Good honours:	106	(47.3%)
Graduate prospects:	=69	(65.3%)

include work placements in their degrees, the close links with employers sometimes bringing in valuable research and consultancy contracts, and contributing to a consistently good graduate employment record. However, Hertfordshire's record in the National Student Survey has been disappointing. The most satisfied students were in health subjects in the survey published in 2008.

Hertfordshire produced some of the best results of any post-1992 university in the 2008 Research Assessment Exercise, with approaching half of its submission judged to be world-leading or internationally excellent. History, nursing and midwifery, engineering and computing collecting the highest grades.

The award-winning library and resource centre on the main campus is Britain's biggest, offering 24-hour access to hundreds of computer workstations. A second centre on the de Havilland campus provides another 1,100 workstations. The StudyNet information system has been a leader in its field, giving all staff and students their own storage space. Students can use it for study, revision or communication, as well as to access university information.

In September 2009, the university will open the doors to the Forum – a new student venue on the College Lane campus. It will include an auditorium for live gigs and club nights, a nursery, a convenience store and a multi-storey car park, as well as quiet areas.

A £15-million sports complex, the Hertfordshire Sports Village, boasts some of the best university-based facilities in Britain. Although principally for student use, it is also open to local residents.

Undergraduate Fees and Bursaries

- Fees for UK/EU students: £3,225
- International student fees: £8,000
- Bursary on full grant: £1,000
- The university does not award bursaries for students on partial maintenance grants.
- Scholarships based on circumstances or by competition.
- For full details see the university's website: www.herts.ac.uk/courses/bursaries-and-scholarships/home.cfm

Students		
Undergraduates:	15,685	(3,100)
Postgraduates:	2,025	(2,025)
Mature students:	26.9%	
Overseas students:	11.3%	
Applications per place:	3.7	
From state-sector schools:	97.9%	
From working-class homes:	39.9%	

For detailed information about fees, grants and bursaries and how they work, see chapter 7.

Accommodation

Number of places and costs refer to 2009–10
University-provided places: 3,300
Percentage catered: 0%
Self-catered costs: £65–£103 a week.
First years are guaranteed accommodation if conditions are met.
International students: as above.
Contact: Accommodation@herts.ac.uk

University of Huddersfield

Official performance indicators for higher education have shown Huddersfield living up to its mission to help produce a more diverse student population, and it has opened satellite centres in Barnsley and Oldham to widen participation further. More than four out of ten full-time students are from working-class homes – far in excess than the national average for the university's courses and entry qualifications – and the numbers coming from areas without a tradition of higher education are among the highest in the country. The dropout rate has also been improving, and the latest projection of 15 per cent is also better than the benchmark set for the university.

Imaginative conversions and new buildings have finally allowed the university to come together on one town-centre campus. The university capitalised on Huddersfield's industrial past to ease the strain on facilities that were struggling to cope with expansion which reached 13 per cent a year at its peak. There are now more than 20,000 students. Canalside, a refurbished mill complex, has provided extra space for mathematics and computing, and education occupies another mill site – this time a £4-million recreation of the original. The university is even creating "pocket parks" and a landscaped area along the reopened Narrow Canal to provide additional green space. Human and health sciences have also acquired new premises, and an additional £4 million has been spent on a new students' union, allowing drama courses to take over the existing union complex. The new union, opened by Huddersfield's Chancellor, *Star Trek* actor Patrick Stewart, includes alcohol-free social areas to encourage participation by those overseas students and ethnic minorities who would otherwise avoid the facilities.

A tradition of vocational education dates back to 1841, and the university has a long-established reputation in areas such as textile design and engineering. But there are less obvious gems such as music and social work, as well as teacher training, for which Huddersfield was awarded a national centre of excellence. Scores in the National Student Survey dropped sharply after an encouraging start in the initial round, however. History, physiotherapy and teacher training produced by far the most satisfied students in the 2008 survey. The university's own satisfaction surveys suggest that students value the friendliness and helpfulness of staff.

Most of the areas in which Huddersfield entered the 2008 Research Assessment Exercise contained at least

---

Queensgate
Huddersfield
West Yorkshire HD1 3DH
0870 901 5555 (prospectus)
admissions@hud.ac.uk
www.hud.ac.uk
www.huddersfield
  student.com

Edinburgh
Belfast
HUDDERSFIELD
London
Cardiff

The Times Rankings
Overall Ranking: 87

Student satisfaction:	=67	(74%)
Research quality:	=95	(0.2)
Entry standards:	75	(265)
Student–staff ratio:	=46	(16.1)
Services & facilities/student:	90	(£897)
Expected completion rate:	74	(81.2%)
Good honours:	88	(51.9%)
Graduate prospects:	104	(56.9%)

some world-leading work. A third of the university's submission was placed in the top two categories, with music producing by far the best results and social work also doing well. A flourishing relationship with industry produces more private income than is achieved in many larger institutions, as well as influencing courses.

The most popular courses are in human and health sciences. Many arts and social science courses have a vocational slant. Politics, for example, includes a six-week work placement, which often takes students to the House of Commons. A third of the students in all subjects take sandwich courses, one of the highest proportions in Britain, and more than 4,000 have some element of work experience. The approach has been paying off with graduate employment figures and applications.

Most residential accommodation is now concentrated in the Storthes Hall Park student village, but additional accommodation is available at Ashenhurst, just over a mile from the campus. Recent developments mean the 1,712 residential places are enough to guarantee accommodation to first years, and private housing is cheap and plentiful in Huddersfield. Students are also encouraged to follow a structured fitness programme at the upgraded campus sports centre. Town–gown relations are good and the cost of living low. Most students like the town's friendly atmosphere, although they tend to base their social life on the students' union. It is not far to Leeds for those in search of serious clubbing.

Undergraduate Fees and Bursaries

- Fees for UK/EU students: £3,225
- International student fees: £8,250–£9,250
- Bursary on full grant: £500
- The university does not award bursaries for students on partial maintenance grants.
- Scholarships based on circumstances or by competition.
- For full details see the university's website: www.hud.ac.uk/student_finance/

Students

Undergraduates:	11,595	(5,185)
Postgraduates:	1,060	(2,590)
Mature students:	36.8%	
Overseas students:	5.5%	
Applications per place:	4.3	
From state-sector schools:	97.6%	
From working-class homes:	42.9%	

For detailed information about fees, grants and bursaries and how they work, see chapter 7.

Accommodation

Number of places and costs refer to 2009–10
University-provided places: 1,711 in privately-owned halls
Percentage catered: 0%
Self-catered costs: £65.95–£82.95 a week (43 weeks).
First years are guaranteed accommodation provided conditions are met.
International students: as above.
Contact: info@campusdigs.com;
www.campusdigs.com

University of Hull

Hull recorded one of the biggest rises in applications of any university at the start of 2009. Its 25 per cent increase followed a big drop in the previous year, but growth on this scale is almost unprecedented for a traditional university. The success came after the latest in a string of excellent performances in the National Student Survey. The university has been in or around the top ten for overall student satisfaction in every round of the survey, with American studies, history, history and archaeology, philosophy, and theology and religious studies producing the best of a consistently good set of results published in 2008.

The university and the city have always commanded loyalty among students, who appreciate the modest cost of living and ready availability of accommodation, as well as the quality of courses. Research plaudits have been more elusive, however. No subject was rated internationally outstanding in the 2001 assessments and Hull had the lowest proportion of world-leading research among England's older universities the 2008 exercise. Health subjects, geography and environmental science, and drama, dance and performance achieved the best grades. An Institute for Learning encourages academics to put research findings into practice, developing training courses and developing the university's interest in lifelong learning.

A longstanding focus on Europe shows in the wide range of languages available at degree level, with the purpose-built Language Institute heavily used by students of all subjects. Strength in politics – confirmed by one of three grade 5 assessments for research, as well as the teaching quality success – is reflected in a steady flow of graduates into the House of Commons. The Westminster Hull Internship Programme (WHIP) offers a year-long placement and month-long internships for British politics and legislative studies students.

However, the university was criticised for deciding to close mathematics following poor recruitment to the honours degree.

After years of relative stability, Hull expanded rapidly, both on its spacious home campus and through mergers. First it added nursing to its portfolio of courses with the acquisition of the former Humberside College of Health, then it took in University College Scarborough and finally the university bought the adjacent campus of the former Humberside (now Lincoln) University. There are now nearly 20,000 under-graduates, including part-timers. The main academic development has been the

---

Cottingham Road
Hull HU6 7RX
01482 466100 (admissions)
admissions@hull.ac.uk
www.hull.ac.uk
www.hullstudent.com

The Times Rankings
Overall Ranking: 44

Student satisfaction:	=8	(81%)
Research quality:	51	(1.1)
Entry standards:	60	(285)
Student–staff ratio:	=75	(18.7)
Services & facilities/student:	62	(£1,096)
Expected completion rate:	=39	(87.0%)
Good honours:	64	(57.7%)
Graduate prospects:	35	(73.2%)

establishment of a medical school in conjunction with York University, which takes 150 students a year (www.hyms.ac.uk). Hull's patient development, in collaboration with the local health authority, of a postgraduate medical school was rewarded with the award of a traditional school housed in a landmark building on the former Humberside (West) campus. The West Campus also contains a Business Quarter, incorporating the Business School and a new Enterprise Centre to support local business.

The original 94-acre main campus has also seen considerable development, with improvements to social facilities, new buildings for languages and chemistry, a Graduate Research Institute and a state-of-the-art sport, health and exercise science laboratory. The campus, with its art gallery and highly automated library, is less than three miles from the centre of Hull.

The Scarborough campus has also seen investment, with new laboratories for music technology and digital arts, and a renovated café bar. Hull has always maintained a roughly equal balance between science and technology and the arts and social sciences, but the Scarborough campus has tipped the scales towards the arts.

More than 90 per cent of the undergraduates are state-educated – one of the highest proportions at any pre-1992 university – while three in ten are from working-class homes. The projected dropout rate had improved in the latest survey: at 10 per cent, it was below average for the university's courses and entry qualifications.

Student leisure facilities, which were always good but becoming crowded, have been upgraded as part of the campus building programme. The students' union, which was rated the second best in Britain in a new awards scheme in 2008, has been refurbished and features the popular "Asylum" nightclub. New football pitches have been added recently on campus and the Sports and Fitness Centre has been attracting praise.

Undergraduate Fees and Bursaries

- Fees for UK/EU students: £3,225
- International student fees: £9,500–£11,500 £21,600 (medicine)
- Bursary on full grant: £1,000
- Bursaries on partial grant: household income up to £40K: £500.
- Scholarships based on circumstances or by competition.
- For full details see the university's website: www.hull.ac.uk/money

Students

Undergraduates:	11,015	(7,300)
Postgraduates:	1,620	(1,070)
Mature students:	25.5%	
Overseas students:	8.3%	
Applications per place:	2.9	
From state-sector schools:	92.6%	
From working-class homes:	30.9%	

For detailed information about fees, grants and bursaries and how they work, see chapter 7.

Accommodation

Number of places and costs refer to 2009–10
University-provided places: 2,601 (owned stock); 150 (leased/associated stock)
Percentage catered: 49%
Catered costs: £80.00–£122.92 (31 weeks).
Self-catered costs: £84.00–£98.70 a week (31–50 weeks).
Unaccompanied first years are guaranteed accommodation if conditions are met.
International students: as above.
Contact: rooms@hull.ac.uk

Imperial College of Science, Technology and Medicine

Regularly in the top three in *The Times* League Table, London's specialist college of science, engineering and medicine is also in the top six in the world rankings published by the *Times Higher Education/QS*. Over 6,000 academic staff include Nobel prizewinners, 66 Fellows of the Royal Society and 74 Fellows of the Royal Academy of Engineering. Imperial's submission for the 2008 Research Assessment Exercise contained a higher proportion of world-leading or inter-nationally excellent work (73 per cent) than any other university's submission. Pure maths, civil engineering and history of science produced the best results.

Imperial is not recommended for academic slouches, but tough entrance requirements ensure that they are a rare breed in any case. The projected dropout rate of less than 3 per cent is among the lowest in the country. Such is the level of competition that applications were dropping, but there had been a modest increase when the official deadline passed for courses beginning in 2009. There are about 14,000 applications for 2,400 places and, even in subjects that struggle for candidates elsewhere, entrants average better than an A and two Bs at A level. The average points score on the UCAS tariff of entrants in 2008 was 355. Nearly 40 per cent of the undergraduates are from independent schools – one of the highest proportions at any university and considerably more than the national average for Imperial's courses.

Engineering degrees last four years and lead to an MEng. The college has been expanding its range of European exchanges, with a variety of prestigious technological institutions available for courses such as the MSc in physics.

Medicine has been the main area of development: mergers with the St Mary's, Charing Cross and Westminster, and Royal Postgraduate teaching hospitals producing one of the biggest faculties of medicine in the UK. In 2007, Imperial formed the UK's first Academic Health Science Centre in partnership with Imperial College Healthcare NHS Trust in order to translate research advances into patient care. The partnership was named as one of the UK's five Academic Health Science Centres in 2009, denoting international excellence in biomedical research, education and patient care.

Imperial celebrated its centenary in 2007 and has left the University of London to trade on its global reputation. It has been redeveloping and expanding facilities on its main campus, in the heart of South Kensington's museum district, most

Exhibition Road
South Kensington
London SW7 2AZ
020 7594 8014
registry@imperial.ac.uk
www.imperial.ac.uk
www.imperialcollege
 union.org

The Times Rankings
Overall Ranking: 3

Student satisfaction:	=54	(75%)
Research quality:	=5	(2.7)
Entry standards:	3	(489)
Student–staff ratio:	2	(10.3)
Services & facilities/student:	1	(£3,518)
Expected completion rate:	3	(97.1%)
Good honours:	32	(68.5%)
Graduate prospects:	2	(88.4%)

recently with the construction of a new sports centre and halls of residence complex. The growing business school is Imperial's main concession to the academic world beyond science, technology and medicine.

The Undergraduate Research Opportunities Programme provides opportunities for "hands-on" experience of the research activities of college staff and postgraduates. A voluntary scheme open to all undergraduates, it is especially popular in the summer vacation, when students can be paid bursaries and international undergraduates can participate without needing a work permit. There is also a vacation placement scheme during the summer for undergraduates to acquire work experience.

Imperial's specialisms have the effect of making it one of the most male-dominated university institutions in Britain, although the number of female students doubled during the 1990s and now stands at more than a third. The imbalance shows in a social scene which many students find limited, despite the largest selection of clubs and societies in the country. Outdoor sports facilities are remote, but Wednesday afternoons are left free to encourage students to make the effort to exercise.

Student satisfaction levels have been above the national average and good for London, where many universities have struggled in the National Student Survey. Biological subjects, computer science and chemical, process and energy engineering produced the best results in the survey published in 2008.

Undergraduate Fees and Bursaries
- Fees for UK/EU students: £3,145
- International student fees: £18,000–£20,400
                              £25,000–£37,300 (medicine)
- Bursary on full grant: £3,000
- Bursaries on partial grant: household income up to £50K sliding scale £2,000–£300.
- Scholarships based on circumstances or by competition.
- For full details see the university's website: www3.imperial.ac.uk/ugprospectus/money

Students		
Undergraduates:	8,535	(0)
Postgraduates:	4,125	(1,185)
Mature students:	5.5%	
Overseas students:	34.7%	
Applications per place:	5.7	
From state-sector schools:	62.0%	
From working-class homes:	18.3%	

For detailed information about fees, grants and bursaries and how they work, see chapter 7.

Accommodation
Number of places and costs refer to 2009–10
University-provided places: 2,837
Percentage catered: 0%
Self-catered costs: £55.00–£188.65 a week.
First years are guaranteed accommodation provided all conditions are met.
International students: as above.
Contact: accommodation@imperial.ac.uk

University of Keele

Keele has set itself the goal of becoming the "ultimate 21st-century campus university" and is investing more than £70 million to provide the necessary facilities. The broad Foundation course and four-year degree that made the university's name is a fading memory, but it remains committed to breadth of study in order also to be the leading interdisciplinary institution in Britain.

The majority of the degree courses are two-subject dual honours degrees, with single honours degrees in health, law and other professional subjects. Popular combinations include criminology and psychology, geology and physical geography, history and politics, and biology and forensic science. More unusual pairings include geology and music, and mathematics and sociology. Students have a choice of over 500 degree courses in all. Most provide the opportunity of a semester abroad – an option open to students on almost all subject combinations.

An emphasis on research since an improved set of results in the 2001 assessments brought limited success in the 2008 exercise. A total of 45 per cent of the work submitted was judged to be world-leading or internationally excellent, but Keele was still towards the bottom of the traditional universities on this measure. The most successful subjects were history and music.

Green issues have been rising up the university's agenda as it achieved the Carbon Trust Standard. A degree in environment and sustainability is being introduced in 2009 entry and an innovative research hub for the study and development of sustainable forms of energy is planned.

However, health subjects have been the main focus of development. First degrees in physiotherapy and nursing and midwifery have been added to the well-established postgraduate medical school. Keele has also been teaching a five-year undergraduate medical course. Some 130 students each year are taught in new facilities on the Keele campus, three miles away at the University Hospital of North Staffordshire NHS Trust and at the Associate Teaching Hospital at the Shrewsbury and Telford Hospitals NHS Trust in Shropshire. Students now take the new Keele undergraduate degree programme (MBChB), which is in the process of validation by the GMC. A part-time BSc in osteopathy has been introduced in collaboration with the College of Osteopaths and a well-equipped School of Pharmacy opened in 2006, building on a long-established track record in the subject at postgraduate level.

Keele
Staffordshire ST5 5BG
01782 584005 (admissions)
undergraduate@
  keele.ac.uk
www.keele.ac.uk
www.kusu.net

The Times Rankings
Overall Ranking: 42

Student satisfaction:	=28	(77%)
Research quality:	=48	(1.2)
Entry standards:	=45	(319)
Student–staff ratio:	26	(14.3)
Services & facilities/student:	=51	(£1,148)
Expected completion rate:	32	(89.1%)
Good honours:	46	(64.4%)
Graduate prospects:	=47	(70.4%)

All Keele's courses are modular, with the academic year divided into two 15-week semesters, with breaks at Christmas and Easter. The university remains small by modern standards – around 7,600 full-time students – despite 75 per cent growth during the 1990s. The proportion of postgraduates has also been growing, with a quarter of the students now taking higher degrees. The demand for undergraduate places bounced back spectacularly at the start of 2009 after two disappointing years. An 18 per cent increase was more than double the national average.

Keele has a good record in the National Student Survey, with 88 per cent of final-year undergraduates satisfied overall. There was total satisfaction in anatomy, physiology and pathology and in medical science and pharmacy. The university has recovered from a blip in last year's statistics to record a projected dropout rate of less than 9 per cent – well above the benchmark set according to the university's subjects and entry qualifications. Nine out of ten undergraduates are state-educated, a figure exceeded by only two traditional universities in England, and more than a quarter come from working-class homes. Keele has been proactive in trying to broaden its intake, targeting 12 and 13-year-olds with a special website, as well as running masterclasses in local schools and hosting a summer school at the university.

The attractive 617-acre campus outside Stoke-on-Trent is the largest in England. Nearly 70 per cent of all undergraduates live on campus, which inevitably dominates the social scene as well as providing part-time employment for hundreds of students. The students' union offers entertainment on campus every night of the week and houses five bars and two purpose-built entertainment venues. The university's sports facilities have benefited from investment in a new all-weather pitch, and the leisure centre has recently refurbished its fitness suite. Keele has an active athletic union with over 30 different sports clubs. The cost of living is also relatively low in the Potteries and the surrounding area.

Undergraduate Fees and Bursaries

- Fees for UK/EU students: £3,225
- International student fees: £9,350–£11,800
  £18,000–£22,000 (medicine)
- Bursary on full grant: £800
- Bursaries on partial grant: household income up to £40K: various schemes available.
- Scholarships based on circumstances or by competition.
- For full details see the university's website: www.keele.ac.uk/undergraduate/bursaries/Bursaries2009booklet.pdf

Students

Undergraduates:	6,325	(2,710)
Postgraduates:	810	(1,570)
Mature students:	18.2%	
Overseas students:	6.5%	
Applications per place:	4.7	
From state-sector schools:	90.8%	
From working-class homes:	26.7%	

For detailed information about fees, grants and bursaries and how they work, see chapter 7.

Accommodation

Number of places and costs refer to 2009–10
University-provided places: 3,200
Percentage catered: 0% (optional meal plan available)
Self-catered costs: £64–£105 a week.
First years are guaranteed accommodation on campus if conditions are met.
International students: guaranteed accommodation for the duration of their course.
Contact: sas@keele.ac.uk

University of Kent

Kent has capitalised sensibly on its position near the Channel ports, specialising in international programmes, as well as the flexible degree structures that have been the hallmark of most 1960s universities. Styling itself "the UK's European university", Kent now has a postgraduate site in Brussels, as well as giving many undergraduates the option of a year spent elsewhere in Europe or in the United States. This process should accelerate with the establishment of the Transmanche University with four counterparts in northern France, which took its first students in 2006. The project, backed by both Governments, involves joint courses at a variety of levels and research collaboration and is only one of a number of collaborations in France.

The university is broadening its horizons at home as well, however, assuming a regional role. Access courses throughout the county allow students to upgrade their qualifications to university standard, but the main focus is on the Medway towns, where Kent is involved in ambitious projects with Greenwich and Canterbury Christ Church universities and Mid-Kent College. The Medway campus, based in the old dockyard has already exceeded its target of 6,000 students by 2010, with a new School of Pharmacy among the main features of a £50-million development. The first intake of pharmacists was 50 per cent larger than planned and the school is eventually expected to take 430 students.

The original low-rise campus, set in 300 acres of parkland overlooking Canterbury, is tidy rather than architecturally distinguished. The student centre has a nightclub big enough to attract big-name bands, as well as a theatre, cinema and bars. A university centre serves 3,000 part-time students across Kent and a series of associate colleges offer university courses. Entry grades are variable, with offers pitched according to the UCAS points tariff, although those taking A levels are expected to pass at least three subjects (one of which may be general studies).

Applications have been increasing, partly thanks to the Medway development, and early 2009 saw a spectacular rise of almost 20 per cent rise in the demand for places. Medway's applications had risen by 27 per cent in the previous year. Kent is strongest in the social sciences, although biosciences, philosophy and drama, dance and theatre studies took pride of place in the teaching assessments, each registering a maximum score. The university takes teaching standards seriously, encouraging all academics to take a Postgraduate Certificate in Higher Education. Kent academics have been awarded National

Canterbury
Kent CT2 7NZ
0800 975 3777 (all enquiries)
information@kent.ac.uk
www.kent.ac.uk
www.kentunion.co.uk

The Times Rankings
Overall Ranking: 39

Student satisfaction:	=8	(81%)
Research quality:	46	(1.4)
Entry standards:	48	(317)
Student–staff ratio:	=56	(17.1)
Services & facilities/student:	=51	(£1,148)
Expected completion rate:	35	(87.8%)
Good honours:	53	(61.7%)
Graduate prospects:	42	(71.8%)

Teaching Fellowships in each of the last three years.

The university was also much more successful in the 2008 research assessments than in previous exercises, with more than half of its submission placed in the top two categories. Thirty per cent of research in social policy was considered world-leading.

Kent has been building up its science departments, among which computing is particularly well regarded, but still a majority of the students take arts or social sciences. Graduates of all disciplines fare well in the employment market – the university regularly features among the top 20 for graduate starting salaries. It is also in the top ten for student satisfaction, with particularly high levels in health subjects, anthropology and finance.

The university has a more mixed intake than many in the south of England: nine out of ten undergraduates are from state schools and a quarter come from working-class homes. Significant numbers of American and European students give the university a cosmopolitan feel and campus security is good, but some complain that Canterbury itself is expensive and limited socially.

Students on the main campus are attached to one of four colleges, although they do not select it themselves. There is a separate college for postgraduates. The colleges act as the focus of social life, and include academic as well as residential facilities. They provide accommodation for all first years. Among £100 million of completed or planned capital developments has been an expansion of sports facilities and residential accommodation at the Parkwood student village, bringing the total number of residential places to 4,274. Developments in 2008 included 540 new study bedrooms, a 480-seat lecture theatre and more seminar rooms on the main campus, and further development of the Medway campus, including the addition of 400 bedrooms at Victory Pier to be ready in September 2009.

Undergraduate Fees and Bursaries

- Fees for UK/EU students: £3,225
- International student fees: £9,870–£11,990
- Bursary on full grant: £1,000
- Bursaries on partial grant: household income up to 40K sliding scale £750–£250.
- Scholarships based on circumstances or by competition.
- For full details see the university's website: www.kent.ac.uk/studying/funding/

Students

Undergraduates:	11,390	(3,770)
Postgraduates:	1,355	(1,295)
Mature students:	18.9%	
Overseas students:	13.1%	
Applications per place:	4.2	
From state-sector schools:	92.0%	
From working-class homes:	24.9%	

For detailed information about fees, grants and bursaries and how they work, see chapter 7.

Accommodation

Number of places and costs refer to 2008–09
University-provided places: 4,300
Percentage catered: 18%
Catered costs: £102–£115 a week.
Self-catered costs: £83–£122 a week.
First years are guaranteed accommodation provided applications received before 31 July.
International students: as above
Contact: hospitality-enquiry@kent.ac.uk
www.kent.ac.uk/hospitality

King's College London

One of the oldest and largest of London University's colleges, King's has been cementing its reputation among the elite of British higher education. Sixty per cent of the work submitted to the 2008 Research Assessment Exercise was judged to be world-leading or internationally excellent, with cardiovascular medicine, dentistry, nutritional sciences, philosophy, languages and the Centre for Computing in the Humanities among the leaders in their fields. The results followed another rise in the world rankings published by *Times Higher Education*/QS, leaving the college just outside the top 20.

King's is now concentrated on four main campuses close to the Thames. Most departments are within walking distance of each other, on the original Strand site or the Waterloo campus, with medicine, dentistry and biomedical and health sciences based not far away at Guy's Hospital, near London Bridge, and in the St Thomas' Hospital campus, across the river from the Houses of Parliament. A fifth site, at Denmark Hill, in south London, houses the Institute of Psychiatry and more medicine and dentistry.

Students seem to like the outcome: King's did well in the National Student Survey published in 2008 and was in the leading group of institutions in London.

The most satisfied students were in classics, law and music. An institutional audit by the Quality Assurance Agency gave King's the highest mark, stressing the excellence of the student support services. Applications have been steady, with 5 per cent growth at the start of 2009. There are now 14,000 undergraduates and 7,000 graduate students in nine schools of study.

Medical subjects have been the main growth point, with King's boasting five Medical Research Council centres – more than any other university. Among the medical courses are successful programmes catering for mature students and school-leavers who have attended London comprehensives with generally poor A-level results.

A £500-million transformation of the college estate is still in progress. Biomedical and health sciences students occupy the largest university building in London, near Waterloo Station, and share purpose-built facilities on the Guy's Campus with medicine and dentistry. There is to be further development of the St Thomas' site for medical education and hospital use following the opening of the new and ground-breaking Evelina Children's Hospital.

Another property deal has created the largest new university library in Britain since World War II at the former Public Record Office in Chancery Lane. A

Strand
London WC2R 2LS
020 7836 5454
thecompass@kcl.ac.uk
www.kcl.ac.uk
www.kclsu.org

The Times Rankings
Overall Ranking: 12

Student satisfaction:	=40	(76%)
Research quality:	=24	(2.0)
Entry standards:	13	(415)
Student–staff ratio:	5	(11.4)
Services & facilities/student:	6	(£1,821)
Expected completion rate:	19	(92.3%)
Good honours:	21	(72.8%)
Graduate prospects:	5	(83.2%)

donation of £4 million by a graduate has underwritten the spectacular Maughan Library with 1,400 networked reader places. A £40-million redevelopment of the Grade I listed King's Building has provided new teaching facilities, wireless internet access, social and catering facilities.

Once known primarily for science, King's now excels in a wide range of subjects in nine schools of study, including such unusual features as Britain's only department devoted entirely to Portuguese – one of four language departments rated internationally outstanding in the latest research assessments. War studies is another unusual and well-regarded department.

Clinical psychology, nursing, midwifery, health visiting and physiotherapy did well in a major review in 2005. A new clinical research facility at St Thomas' Hospital allows researchers at King's and clinical staff at the hospital to undertake multidisciplinary research focusing on nutrition, obesity and cardiovascular health.

King's was one of the two founding colleges of London University, and the full extent of the college's ambitions is clear from its mission statement, which includes having all its departments rated as excellent for both teaching and research. King's is also a solid bet for a good degree for those who satisfy its demanding entry requirements, with over 70 per cent reaching the First or 2:1 classification. More than a quarter of the undergraduates come from independent schools. Every student is allocated a personal tutor, and much of the teaching is in small groups. Student facilities on the Strand and Guy's campuses have been upgraded recently. There are 2,654 residential places, and the college also has access to 511 places in the intercollegiate halls of London University. Some of the outdoor sports facilities are a long way from the college, but are accessible by train.

Undergraduate Fees and Bursaries

- Fees for UK/EU students: £3,225
- International student fees: £12,020–£15,080 £27,980 (medicine)
- Bursary on full grant: £1,350
- Bursaries on partial grant: household income up to £50K sliding scale £1,350–£100.
- Scholarships based on circumstances or by competition.
- For full details see the university's website: www.kcl.ac.uk/funding

Students

Students		
Undergraduates:	11,635	(2,475)
Postgraduates:	4,100	(2,900)
Mature students:	25.2%	
Overseas students:	13.3%	
Applications per place:	8.1	
From state-sector schools:	72.4%	
From working-class homes:	21.8%	

For detailed information about fees, grants and bursaries and how they work, see chapter 7.

Accommodation

Number of places and costs refer to 2008–09
University-provided places: 2,654; 666 intercollegiate; 125 Liberty Living
Percentage catered: 17.7%; 100% intercollegiate
Catered costs: £112.70–£180.60 a week.
Self-catered costs: £68.95–£127.20 (40 weeks).
New full-time students are guaranteed one year in accommodation if conditions are met.
International students: priority for those who have not previously lived or studied in the UK.
Contact: 020 7848 2759; www.kcl.ac.uk/accomm

Kingston University

Having established itself as one of the fastest-growing new universities, with over 22,000 students, Kingston is developing a learning environment to match. The university has revitalised its four sites, spending more than £65 million in a decade on capital projects. Three new buildings opened in 2007 alone. One provides six floors of teaching and study space and a new central courtyard on the main Penrhyn Road campus; another is a three-storey teaching extension at the Faculty of Engineering's Roehampton Vale site; while the Kingston Hill campus has acquired more computer study space in the learning resources centre and a Learning Café with computer facilities.

Applications have been buoyant, bucking the trend among former polytechnics and enabling the university to reduce the numbers recruited through Clearing. Results in the National Student Survey have improved, after disruptive building work depressed initial satisfaction levels and contributed to a fall in *The Times* league table. The new facilities have won plaudits from staff and students alike. Journalism, languages and pharmacy students were the most satisfied.

The university markets itself as in "lively, leafy London", making a virtue of its suburban location as well as its proximity to the bright lights. It has four campuses in the southwest of the capital: two, close to Kingston town centre; another, two miles away at Kingston Hill, and the fourth in Roehampton Vale, where a site once used as an aerospace factory now contains a new technology block. A flight simulator and the university's own Learjet continue the tradition and a Foundation degree in aeronautical engineering is ministers' favourite example of the two-year course. Kingston boasts the third largest engineering faculty in London, behind Imperial College and Brunel.

The four campuses are linked by an extensive network of 2,000 computers. Among the facilities in the new buildings are multiple projection systems, video conferencing, interactive displays and built-in voting systems. Students can take advantage of 24-hour opening in some of the main learning resources centres and a high-tech self-issue system for borrowing books and other resources.

Approaching a third of the university's submission to the 2008 Research Assessment Exercise was rated world-leading or internationally excellent. The best results were in nursing, where 15 per cent of the work reached the top level, and in business and management studies, where the proportion was 10 per cent, making Kingston the highest-rated new university in the field. The star performance was in

---

River House
53–57 High Street
Kingston upon Thames
Surrey KT1 1LQ
08700 841347
admissions-info@
 kingston.ac.uk
www.kingston.ac.uk
www.kusu.co.uk

history of art, architecture and design, where half of the submission was at least internationally excellent.

Nursing is part of the Faculty of Health and Social Care Sciences, a collaboration with St George's Hospital Medical School, which recently added pharmacy to its portfolio of courses. Radiotherapy students are among the first in the country to hone their clinical skills in a simulated cancer treatment room. The Centre for Paramedic Science serves as a hub for course delivery and a raft of revolutionary research projects and positions the two institutions at the forefront of paramedic education.

Well over a quarter of Kingston's places go to mature students and more than a third to those from working-class families – both groups with low completion rates nationally. The latest projected dropout rate is 16 per cent, a second successive improvement and less than the national average for the subjects on offer. Students get extra support in their first, most difficult, year. The university's attempts to widen access to higher education have been particularly successful among ethnic minorities, who account for more than half of the undergraduates.

To make the university more responsive to its students, it provides a "one-stop shop", which deals with student issues ranging from careers and accommodation to complaints and financial advice. The university's responsiveness and the accessibility of staff were singled out for praise in a quality audit. Over £20 million has been spent on halls of residence, most recently with extensions and refurbishment of the two largest halls, which now have 2,360 rooms. Students like the location, on the fringe of London, although complaints about the high cost of living are common.

Undergraduate Fees and Bursaries

- Fees for UK/EU students: £3,225
- International student fees: up to £10,350
- Bursary on full grant: household income up to £1K: £1,000 then £600.*
- Bursaries on partial grant: household income up to £39.3K: £310.*
- Scholarships based on circumstances or by competition.
- For full details see the university's website: www.kingston.ac.uk/undergraduate/money-matters/

* Figures for 2008–09

Students			Accommodation
Undergraduates:	16,760	(2,150)	Number of places and costs refer to 2009–10
Postgraduates:	2,110	(2,965)	University-provided places: 2,360
Mature students:	34.4%		Percentage catered: 0%
Overseas students:	12.5%		Self-catered costs: £90.50–£113.50 a week.
Applications per place:	4.7		The university is able to offer accommodation to
From state-sector schools:	95.8%		most first-years (conditions apply).
From working-class homes:	37.2%		International students: offered places if application is made in good time and subject to availability.

For detailed information about fees, grants and bursaries and how they work, see chapter 7.

Contact: accommodation@kingston.ac.uk
www.kingston.ac.uk/accommodation/

Lampeter, University of Wales

In the whole of England and Wales, only Oxford and Cambridge were awarding degrees before Lampeter. Yet only Buckingham University is smaller today. In fact, Lampeter claims to be the smallest publicly funded university in Europe, making a virtue of its size by stressing its friendly atmosphere and intimate teaching style. That size will increase considerably in 2010, following a merger with Trinity University College, 23 miles away in Carmarthen, but Lampeter will remain a quiet, rural outpost.

The new **University of Wales, Trinity Saint David** will constitute a more substantial academic unit, with greater financial security, to serve West Wales. The title echoes Lampeter's original name of St David's College. But, although the merger will have taken place before the new academic year begins in 2010, applications for that year will be handled by the two existing institutions.

As the University of Wales, Lampeter, applications were down by more than a quarter, to less than 700, in 2008, following a 15 per cent decline in the previous year. But the available places were still filled and the start of 2009 saw a small rise demand. Those who go are enthusiastic about Lampeter: it has recorded high levels of satisfaction in every year of the National Student Survey.

Based on an ancient castle and modelled on an Oxbridge college, St David's College was established to train young men for the Anglican ministry. That title receded into the small print, as the University of Wales allowed its member institutions to drop their college titles. But the original quadrangle remains and the chapel is in daily use. There have been significant changes in the last few years – notably a big expansion in distance learning and the introduction of such subjects as Chinese studies, anthropology, IT, management, and film and media studies. There are now 300 course combinations available in the joint honours programme. A degree in Voluntary Sector Studies, which won a Queen's Anniversary Prize, is offered part-time and by distance learning so that students can combine study with volunteering and personal commitments.

Lampeter remains arts-dominated: even IT leads to a BA, and the Bachelor of Divinity is the only other undergraduate degree. Lampeter is best known for theology, but archaeology produced the best results by far in the 2008 Research Assessment Exercise. The small campus includes a mosque for the growing number of Muslim students attracted by a well-endowed programme of Islamic studies. But students are opting increasingly for broad courses such as medieval studies,

College Street
Lampeter
Ceredigion SA48 7ED
01570 422351
admissions@
  lamp.ac.uk
www.lamp.ac.uk
www.lamp.ac.uk/su

The Times Rankings
Overall Ranking: 79

Student satisfaction:	=67	(74%)
Research quality:	=52	(1.0)
Entry standards:	=85	(252)
Student–staff ratio:	29	(14.6)
Services & facilities/student:	114	(£482)
Expected completion rate:	64	(82.7%)
Good honours:	84	(52.8%)
Graduate prospects:	86	(61.8%)

which includes archaeology, classics and theology, as well as history, English and Welsh. Media studies, which benefits from a well-equipped media centre for film and television students, is also growing in popularity. A new research centre opened in 2008, housing the Founders' Library collections and the historical archives, and bringing the university's library resources together on one site for the first time since 1966.

Courses are modular, but degrees are still divided into two parts, with the first year designed to ensure breadth of study. Most courses now include the option of a January start and undergraduates can try a new language, such as Arabic, Greek or Welsh. Part two normally takes a further two years, although philosophy takes three.

Lampeter is deep in Welsh-speaking rural West Wales, and both the university and the students' union have strong bilingual policies. The university is also taking Welsh to a wider audience, with the only university course teaching the language over the internet.

Although only four hours from London and two from Cardiff, Lampeter's geographical position could be a problem for the unprepared. The town has only 4,000 inhabitants, with among the lowest crime rates in Britain, and the nearest station is more than 20 miles away at Carmarthen. A high proportion of the students run cars. The students' union is the centre of social life – not surprising when the university's guide to the town lists its attractions as "cafés, pubs, a curry house and a French patisserie". Most students have made a deliberate choice to avoid the bright lights, and many would like to remain in the area after graduation, although jobs are scarce.

The location helps to produce a relatively high proportion of students from areas with little tradition of higher education and almost 40 per cent from working-class homes. The college's size can make for big fluctuations in the various published indicators. The projected dropout rate, for example, has dipped below 10 per cent and hovered around 20 per cent at different times. The current 16 per cent projection is below the UK average for the subjects and entry qualifications.

Undergraduate Fees and Bursaries

- Fees for UK/EU students: £3,225 (grant of up to £1,940 for Welsh students).
- International student fees: £8,988*
- Welsh National Bursary of £319 for all UK students (household income up to £18,370).
- No other bursaries available.
- Scholarships based on circumstances or by competition.
- For full details see the university's website: www.lamp.ac.uk/scholarships

* Figures for 2008–09

Students		
Undergraduates:	1,100	(5,790)
Postgraduates:	375	(620)
Mature students:	42.3%	
Overseas students:	11.5%	
Applications per place:	2.9	
From state-sector schools:	92.5%	
From working-class homes:	38.9%	

For detailed information about fees, grants and bursaries and how they work, see chapter 7.

Accommodation

Number of places and costs refer to 2008–09

University-provided places: around 500

Percentage catered: 0%

Self-catered costs: £58.69–£74.76 a week (30, 33 or 36 weeks).

First years can normally be placed in university accommodation.

International students: guaranteed housing for first year.

Contact: www.lamp.ac.uk/accommodation/index.htm

Lancaster University

Having celebrated its 40th birthday, Lancaster has almost completed a £300-million makeover for its campus to give it a more modern feel and increase its capacity by up to 50 per cent. Still a relatively small institution, the aim is to establish itself in the leading group of research universities and help improve the local economy. A member of the N8 Group of northern research universities, Lancaster is invariably the highest-placed institution in the northwest in league tables. It has done well in all four National Student Surveys, finishing just outside the top ten in the results published in 2008. The best results came in French, geography and maths.

Lancaster did not quite repeat the scale of success achieved in the 2001 Research Assessment Exercise in 2008, but still more than 60 per cent of its work was rated as world-leading or internationally excellent. Physics was the star performer, with the best results in the country, but there were good results in health studies, computer science, management, sociology and art and design. The university has also won nine National Teaching Fellowships since the scheme was launched in 2000.

A new 24-hour student learning space at the centre of the campus will provide students with flexible learning environments and social space with up-to-date technology. Infolab 21, the £15-million centre of excellence in information communication technology, acts as a technology transfer and incubation facility and houses a training facility for high-tech businesses. Other recent developments include a leadership centre for the highly rated Management School, while the Lancaster Institute for the Contemporary Arts has brought together art, music and theatre studies with the university's public art gallery, concerts and theatre.

Lancaster is another of the campus universities of the 1960s which has always traded on its flexible degree structure. Most undergraduates can broaden their first-year studies by taking a second or third subject. The final choice of degree comes only at the end of that year. Combined degree programmes, with 200 courses to choose from, are especially popular. The degree portfolio now includes medicine, with students taking a five-year course following the Liverpool University curriculum. The first students will graduate in 2009 and new developments include a research centre specialising in bipolar disorder and a new Centre for Organisational Health and Wellbeing.

The projected dropout rate of less than 7 per cent is lower than the average for the subjects on offer. Lancaster also exceeds

Bailrigg
Lancaster LA1 4YW
01524 592028 (admissions)
ugadmissions@
    lancaster.ac.uk
www.lancaster.ac.uk
www.lusu.co.uk

The Times Rankings
Overall Ranking: 23

Student satisfaction:	=14	(79%)
Research quality:	=12	(2.4)
Entry standards:	25	(388)
Student–staff ratio:	=18	(13.7)
Services & facilities/student:	26	(£1,407)
Expected completion rate:	15	(93.3%)
Good honours:	29	(69.6%)
Graduate prospects:	74	(64.3%)

expectations for the recruitment of state-school students, but the proportion from working-class homes is marginally below the benchmark for the university's courses.

The previously uninspiring campus has benefited from recent developments, which have included refurbished lecture theatres, sports facilities and residences. The university is a ten-minute bus ride from Lancaster, three miles away. Students join one of nine residential colleges, which become the centre of most students' social life. Most house between 800 and 900 students in self-catering accommodation. Some 3,400 new and updated residential places came on stream in 2005 and the pioneering 800-room Eco Residence, which opened in 2008, has won an environmental award. Students can live in town houses with shared facilities and monitor their bills. As part of the developments, Cartmel and Lonsdale colleges have transferred to the New Alexandra Park area of the campus with enhanced social facilities.

The campus has a reputation for being one of the safest in the UK. Sports facilities are good and conveniently placed. Work on a £20-million sports centre with climbing wall (built to Chancellor Chris Bonington's specifications) will start in 2009. For the outdoor life, the Lake District is within easy reach. Road and rail communications are good but, while Manchester and Liverpool are within easy reach, Lancaster is inevitably more limited than larger university centres in terms of off-campus life.

Undergraduate Fees and Bursaries
- Fees for UK/EU students: £3,225
- International student fees: £9,200–£11,100
- Bursary on full grant: household income up to £18,360: £1,315 then £500.
- Bursaries on partial grant: household income up to £27.8K: £500.
- Scholarships based on circumstances or by competition.
- For full details see the university's website: www.lancaster.ac.uk/ugfinance

Students

Undergraduates:	7,790	(2,440)
Postgraduates:	1,985	(1,505)
Mature students:	5.5%	
Overseas students:	12.0%	
Applications per place:	4.9	
From state-sector schools:	90.3%	
From working-class homes:	22.0%	

For detailed information about fees, grants and bursaries and how they work, see chapter 7.

Accommodation

Number of places and costs refer to 2008–09
University-provided places: 6,700 (plus 600 places in university-managed houses)
Percentage catered: 0%
Self-catered costs: £66.50–£107.30 a week.
All first years are normally accommodated but there is no formal guarantee for Insurance, Clearing and late applicants.
International students are guaranteed accommodation throughout their studies.
Contact: CRO@lancaster.ac.uk

University of Leeds

The rise of Leeds as a shopping and clubbing centre has added to the attractions of a university which has long been one of the giants of the higher education system. It is second only to Manchester University in terms of applications received, although the demand for places was down at the start of 2009 when most universities were enjoying healthy increases. The university is in the midst of a £360-million campus development plan designed to propel it into the top 50 universities in the world. It is currently just outside the top 100 in the world rankings published by *Times Higher Education*/QS.

An unusually wide range of degrees gives applicants more than 650 undergraduate programmes to choose from, with over 2,000 academic staff teaching 32,000 students, including more than 8,000 postgraduates.

The university occupies a 98-acre site within walking distance of the city centre. The buildings are a mixture of Victorian and modern, the latest of which are Leeds' newest theatre and a £16-million building to house student services. Other improvements include a new swimming pool and fitness centre which is under construction, and new buildings for the schools of earth and environment and law.

Nine other colleges in various parts of the county offer Leeds courses, but handle their own admissions. Further afield, Leeds is also part of the Worldwide Universities Network, which brings together 16 research-led universities to collaborate on research, postgraduate degree programmes and continuing professional development. There is a thriving study abroad programme and the university has links with over 250 universities around the world. A free-standing language unit caters for casual learners as well as specialists.

Leeds operates modular courses, enabling its students to take elective modules or combine complementary subjects. Almost a quarter now take dual honours or interdisciplinary combinations such as nanotechnology, women's studies or international studies. The university was chosen to house a national centre of excellence in interdisciplinary teaching and another in assessment and learning in medical practice settings.

The 2008 Research Assessment Exercise scores showed improvement since 2001, with over 60 per cent of the university's submission rated as world-leading or internationally excellent. Electrical and electronic engineering produced the best results in the country, with social work and social policy, English, Italian, geography and nursing also highly rated.

Leeds
West Yorkshire LS2 9JT
0113 343 2336
ask@leeds.ac.uk
www.leeds.ac.uk
www.luuonline.com

Edinburgh
Belfast
LEEDS
London
Cardiff

The Times Rankings
Overall Ranking: 27

Student satisfaction:	=40	(76%)
Research quality:	=24	(2.0)
Entry standards:	24	(392)
Student–staff ratio:	=21	(13.9)
Services & facilities/student:	54	(£1,143)
Expected completion rate:	23	(91.9%)
Good honours:	19	(73.4%)
Graduate prospects:	45	(71.1%)

The Quality Assurance Agency gave Leeds the best possible verdict on its academic processes in 2008. The National Student Survey published in the same year showed that improved satisfaction levels had been maintained, with dentists and zoologists 100 per cent satisfied and geographers not far behind. The verdict on learning resources was especially positive, thanks to one of the largest libraries at any UK universities and an extensive IT network. Sports and social facilities are also first rate.

Leeds teams regularly excel in competition and the university hosts one of five centres of cricketing excellence.

More than a quarter of the undergraduates come from independent schools, and there is a low proportion of working-class students – less the one in five. But the projected dropout rate has improved and, at less than 8 per cent, matches the national average for the university's courses and entry grades. The already large students' union, famous for its long bar and big-name rock concerts, has been extended to cope with the latest phase in the university's expansion. A £4.5-million upgrade has provided a new venue, more shops and catering facilities. Town–gown relations are generally good.

Undergraduate Fees and Bursaries
- Fees for UK/EU students: £3,225
- International student fees: £10,300–£13,300
                                      £24,500 (medicine)
- Bursary on full grant: £1,540
- Bursaries on partial grant: household income up to £36.6K sliding scale £1,540–£335.
- Scholarships based on circumstances or by competition.
- For full details see the university's website: www.leeds.ac.uk/students/fees/index.htm

Students

Undergraduates:	21,895	(1,950)
Postgraduates:	5,800	(2,605)
Mature students:	8.9%	
Overseas students:	6.6%	
Applications per place:	6.9	
From state-sector schools:	73.9%	
From working-class homes:	19.7%	

For detailed information about fees, grants and bursaries and how they work, see chapter 7.

Accommodation

Number of places and costs refer to 2008–09
University-provided places: 7,650
Percentage catered: 17%
Catered costs: £90–£140 a week.
Self-catered costs: £70–£124 a week.
Single first years are guaranteed a place provided conditions are met.
International students: guaranteed to full fee-paying undergraduates if conditions are met.
Contact: accom@leeds.ac.uk
www.leeds.ac.uk/accommodation/overview.htm

Leeds Metropolitan University

Leeds Met took the bold step of becoming the first university to set fees below the £3,000-a-year maximum allowed in 2006 and, having resisted the temptation to go above £2,000 subsequently, has been by far the cheapest in England at which to take a full-time degree. Fees are likely to rise for 2010–11, following the departure of Professor Simon Lee, the Vice-Chancellor, who championed the pricing policy. Both applications and enrolments hit record levels initially and further increases followed, but the university's finances felt the strain. The rate also limited the scope for bursaries for students from poor backgrounds, but there had been another 10 per cent rise in the demand for places at the start of 2009.

Leeds Met already had a reputation for widening participation in higher education: it is one of the largest providers of Foundation degrees and has more than 27,000 students (17,000 of whom are full-time undergraduates). Four out of ten students come from the Yorkshire and Humberside region, and around a quarter are over 21 on entry. More than nine out of ten are state-educated and almost a third come from working-class homes. Partnerships with 23 colleges from Belfast to Nottinghamshire are designed to produce the equivalent of an American state university system, enabling students to take Leeds Met courses locally.

Some 2,500 students come from 90 countries outside the UK. Only just over half are taking conventional full-time degrees, such is the popularity of sandwich and part-time courses. The projected dropout rate of nearly 16 per cent is just below the official benchmark based on the university's courses and entry qualifications. As part of its efforts to widen access, Leeds Met runs a course for sixth-formers from the region, awarding UCAS points for those who complete successfully. There is also a wide range of summer schools, including one for Asian women and one for Afro-Caribbean boys.

There are two bases in Leeds: the Civic Quarter Campus, close to the city centre, and the Headingley Campus, three miles away in the 100 acres of park and woodland of Beckett Park. The latter boasts outstanding sports facilities, including the £2-million Carnegie Regional Tennis Centre, as well as teaching accommodation for education, informatics, law and business. Over 7,000 students take part in some form of sporting activity, and there is a range of £2,000 sports scholarships. The university has been named a UK Centre for Coaching Excellence.

The Civic Quarter campus is the subject of a £100-million development

---

Civic Quarter
Leeds
West Yorkshire LS1 3HE
0113 812 3113 (enquiries)
http://prospectus.
  leedsmet.ac.uk/main/
  enquiry.htm
www.lmu.ac.uk
www.leedsmetsu
  .org.uk

The Times Rankings
Overall Ranking: 101

Student satisfaction:	=106	(68%)
Research quality:	=95	(0.2)
Entry standards:	=80	(257)
Student–staff ratio:	104	(21.1)
Services & facilities/student:	83	(£975)
Expected completion rate:	=68	(82.1%)
Good honours:	=81	(53.0%)
Graduate prospects:	92	(59.9%)

programme, which began with the opening in 2005 of a new film school. A futuristic lecture theatre complex next to Leeds Civic Hall now houses the business school. The former BBC building has reopened as Old Broadcasting House, where new facilities are being developed for the Faculty of Arts and Society. And, in the first development of its kind, a new stand has been built at the Headingley rugby ground, with classrooms, coaching facilities and social space for use by the university and the two professional clubs. A media centre along similar lines is planned for the neighbouring Test and county cricket ground.

Relatively few academics were entered for the 2008 Research Assessment Exercise, but nearly a third of their work was judged to be world-leading or internationally excellent. Communication, cultural and media studies, sport and library and information management produced the best results. Students are included on the committees that design and manage courses, although the impact has not been obvious in the National Student Survey. Leeds Met was again among the bottom group of universities in the 2008 results.

There is a growing emphasis on educational technology, which was enhanced by a £20-million learning resources centre. More than 400 computers, audiovisual presentation studios and study areas are available all hours. Contacts with small and medium-sized businesses have been carefully fostered as part of the university's successful attempts to maintain a good record in graduate employment. Like its older neighbour, Leeds Met is benefiting from the city's growing reputation for nightlife, but it is making its own contribution with a famously lively entertainments scene. With 4,500 bed spaces, those who accept places before Clearing are guaranteed university accommodation.

Undergraduate Fees and Bursaries
- Fees for UK/EU students: £2,000
- International student fees: £7,000–£7,500
- The university does not award bursaries for students on full maintenance grants.
- The university does not award bursaries for students on partial maintenance grants.
- Scholarships based on circumstances or by competition.
- For full details see the university's website: www.leedsmet.ac.uk/visiting/index_finance.htm

---

Students,

Undergraduates:	17,115	(6,195)
Postgraduates:	1,420	(2,485)
Mature students:	24.3%	
Overseas students:	4.4%	
Applications per place:	4.5	
From state-sector schools:	92.6%	
From working-class homes:	32.5%	

For detailed information about fees, grants and bursaries and how they work, see chapter 7.

Accommodation
Number of places and costs refer to 2008–09
University-provided places: 4,500
Percentage catered: 0%
Self-catered costs: £72.25–£129.50 a week.
First years with Conditional Firm or Unconditional Firm offers guaranteed accommodation.
International students: guaranteed accommodation if conditions are met.
Contact: accommodation@leedsmet.ac.uk
www.leedsmet.ac.uk/accomm

University of Leicester

Leicester has been enjoying a period of unprecedented success, after many years living in the shadow of the big city universities. Consistently in the top five in the National Student Survey (NSS) and named as the *Times Higher Education* University of the Year in 2008, it has shown the scale of its ambitions with a £1-billion development plan. The Queen opened the university's new £32-million library in 2008 and another £12 million is being spent on a new students' union. The university's qualities are being recognised by applicants: an impressive 16 per cent rise at the start of 2009 continued a run of increases. The NSS showed 100 per cent satisfaction in geology and in electronic and electrical engineering, with 92 per cent of final-year undergraduates across the university declaring themselves satisfied overall with their course.

Although Leicester will celebrate its 90th anniversary in 2011, it only approaches the size of other big city universities by dint of rapid growth in postgraduate and distance learning programmes. The 8,000 full-time undergraduates based on the main campus represent much less than half of the student population. Professor Robert Burgess, the Vice-Chancellor, has focused on strengthening research, although the results of official assessments in 2008 showed little improvement on 2001. Leicester entered a much larger proportion of its academics than many of its peers, but the outcome was that less than half of the university's submission was considered world-leading or internationally excellent. The star performer was the small department of museum studies, which produced the highest proportion of world-leading research in any subject at any UK university, with almost two thirds of its work placed in that top category.

The university has scaled down an initial enthusiasm for two-year Foundation degrees. But efforts continue to broaden Leicester's intake, for example through a summer school for local teenagers. Nine out of ten undergraduates come from state schools and more than a quarter come from working-class homes, making Leicester the only university in our top 20 to meet both benchmarks. The 7 per cent projected dropout rate is also below the national average for the university's courses and entry grades.

Leicester hosts national centres of excellence for teaching and learning in geography, genetics and physics. The university also has a long-established reputation in space science, with Europe's largest university-based space research facility, including the £52-million National Space Centre.

University Road
Leicester LE1 7RH
0116 252 5281 (admissions)
admissions@le.ac.uk
www.le.ac.uk
www.leicesterstudent.org

The Times Rankings
Overall Ranking: 15

Student satisfaction:	=5	(84%)
Research quality:	=30	(1.9)
Entry standards:	35	(360)
Student–staff ratio:	=30	(14.7)
Services & facilities/student:	=22	(£1,489)
Expected completion rate:	16	(93.0%)
Good honours:	23	(71.6%)
Graduate prospects:	=25	(76.2%)

The medical school, which allows graduates in the health and life sciences to qualify in four years, has among the most modern facilities in Britain. The siting of a medically based interdisciplinary research centre at the university was another indication of strength. The genetics department, where DNA genetic finger-printing was discovered, has helped make Leicester's academics among the most cited in Britain, according to Thomson Scientific, which monitors research.

Other than clinical medicine which is taught at the city's three hospitals, all teaching and much residential accommodation is concentrated in a leafy suburb a mile from the city centre. Its location, adjacent to one of Leicester's main parks, is popular with students. The new library has doubled the available space and brought the total number of workspaces to 1,500.

The students' union runs one of the most popular university nightclubs, the Venue. Extensive residential accommodation includes a £21-million 600-bed en-suite development. First years are guaranteed a residential place and many second- and third-year students also live in hall, although the majority choose to live in the reasonably priced private accommodation available nearby. The main sports facilities are conveniently located; in 2008–09, students paid £50 a year to use them.

Undergraduate Fees and Bursaries

- Fees for UK/EU students: £3,225
- International student fees: £9,450–£12,650
                                 £22,900 (medicine)
- Bursary on full grant: household income up to £21K: £1,319; household income up to £25K: £1,019.
- Bursaries on partial grant: household income up to £40K: sliding scale £400–£100.
- Scholarships based on circumstances or by competition.
- For full details see the university's website: www.le.ac.uk/fees

Students		
Undergraduates:	8,000	(1,595)
Postgraduates:	2,380	(3,380)
Mature students:	13.9%	
Overseas students:	12.2%	
Applications per place:	5.2	
From state-sector schools:	89.5%	
From working-class homes:	26.0%	

For detailed information about fees, grants and bursaries and how they work, see chapter 7.

Accommodation

Number of places and costs refer to 2009–10
University-provided places: 4,168
Percentage catered: 34%
Catered costs: £100.10–£149.80 a week (30 weeks).
Self-catered costs: £72.80–£145.60 (42 weeks).
First-year students are guaranteed accommodation if conditions are met.
International students: as above, with priority to those returning.
Contact: www.le.ac.uk/accommodation

University of Lincoln

The opening of an impressive purpose-built campus alongside a marina in the centre of Lincoln brought about the most dramatic transformation of any university in recent times. Humberside University, as it had been, even gave its new location pride of place in its title. Five years later it went a step further, selling the previous headquarters campus in Hull and becoming the University of Lincoln. While not moving out of Hull entirely, the university is concentrating its activities there on a much smaller city-centre site.

The switch has paid undoubted dividends, helping to attract high-quality academics. The number of professors grew from eight to 87 in four years. Student applications increased for five years in a row before the introduction of top-up fees, despite rising admission requirements, and the upward trend resumed with a 14 per cent rise at the start of 2007 and a further 9 per cent in 2009.

New science laboratories, sports facilities, an architecture school, a library in a converted warehouse and a students' union and entertainment venue in a former railway engine shed have taken the cost of the development in Lincoln to over £100 million, and another £30 million has been committed to complete the main campus. The latest developments are a £6-million performing arts centre, including a 450-seat theatre and three large studio spaces, and the Human Performance Centre – a regional facility for excellence in sport, coaching and exercise science.

The various projects have won two regeneration awards. The campus now has around 1,000 beds, while purpose-built private developments in close proximity to the university now provide well over 2,000 further residential places. Only the School of Health and Social Care remains in Hull, following the transfer of art and design degree provision in the city to Hull College.

Lincoln initially concentrated on social sciences, but the university now has a wider range of courses. Following the acquisition of former art and design and agriculture colleges from De Montfort University in 2001, the university now has more than 8,000 students in and around Lincoln. The School of Architecture has over 400 students. Art and design is based in the city centre, while animal, biological and equine studies are at Riseholme Park, a 1,000-acre site ten minutes outside Lincoln. Riseholme has been chosen as one of the training centres for equine events ahead of the 2012 Olympic Games.

The university was determined to achieve a high-profile return in the Research Assessment Exercise in 2008 to

---

Brayford Pool
Lincoln LN6 7TS
01522 882000 (enquiries)
www.lincoln.ac.uk/home/
  enquiries/index.htm
www.lincoln.ac.uk
www.lincolnsu.com

The Times Rankings
Overall Ranking: 86

Student satisfaction:	=54	(75%)
Research quality:	=63	(0.5)
Entry standards:	=73	(266)
Student–staff ratio:	111	(23.7)
Services & facilities/student:	96	(£865)
Expected completion rate:	=51	(85.0%)
Good honours:	67	(57.1%)
Graduate prospects:	=90	(60.4%)

match a sharp rise in its research income over recent years. Lincoln entered more of its academics for assessment than many institutions in its peer group and improved on previous results, with 28 per cent of its submission judged to be world-leading or internationally excellent. The result will be a £2-million boost in research grants. Communication, cultural and media studies and computer science and informatics produced the highest grades.

All students take the Effective Learning Programme, which uses computer packages backed up by weekly seminars to develop necessary study skills, and produce a detailed portfolio of all their work. Some degrees can be taken as work-based programmes, with credit awarded for relevant aspects of the jobs.

Lincoln was the first university to win a Charter Mark for exceptional service. Results in the National Student Survey have improved, with finance and accounting, media studies, marketing, psychology and biology boasting the most satisfied undergraduates in 2008. More than a third of the undergraduates come from working-class homes and the projected dropout rate of 14 per cent is both an improvement on previous years and better than the average for the subjects on offer, given the entry standards. Only three universities devote as much of their tuition fee income to bursaries and scholarships as Lincoln. The city is adapting to its new student population with new bars and clubs, although the social scene there is not the prime draw for students.

Undergraduate Fees and Bursaries
- Fees for UK/EU students: £3,225
- International student fees: £8,524–£9,038
- Bursary on full grant: £600
- Bursaries on partial grant: household incomes up to £50K: sliding scale £370–£20.
- Scholarships based on circumstances or by competition.
- For full details see the university's website: www.lincoln.ac.uk/fees

---

Students

Undergraduates:	8,280	(2,245)
Postgraduates:	440	(675)
Mature students:	21.4%	
Overseas students:	6.5%	
Applications per place:	3.5	
From state-sector schools:	97.5%	
From working-class homes:	36.3%	

For detailed information about fees, grants and bursaries and how they work, see chapter 7.

Accommodation

Number of places and costs refer to 2008–09
University-provided places: Hull, 200; Lincoln, 1,037; Riseholme Park, 180
Percentage catered: 13% (Riseholme Park only)
Catered costs: £91–£129 a week (half-board)
Self-catered costs: £85–£95 a week.
Student accommodation prioritised by distance. International students are given detailed information and assistance.
Contact: accommodation@lincoln.ac.uk
www.lincoln.ac.uk/accommodation

University of Liverpool

Liverpool has invested £200 million to improve its 100-acre precinct for a student population that has reached over 19,000. The dozen projects included a £17-million library scheme, a £36-million restructuring of the Faculty of Engineering, and the transformation of the redbrick Victoria Building into a public gallery and museum during Liverpool's year as the Capital of Culture, in 2008. A new headquarters building houses a one-stop shop for student services, and sports facilities have been renovated and extended. A new small animal teaching hospital opened in 2007, bringing all veterinary science clinical teaching onto one site. Current projects include a new look for the campus, replacing street furniture, signage and lighting. The guild of students is about to undergo a £4-million refurbishment and new teaching laboratories for science subjects should be ready in 2011.

The university is continuing to modernise its portfolio of courses while preserving a well-established reputation for research. Liverpool is among the top 15 recipients of research funds, with outside income increasing dramatically in recent years. And there has been substantial investment in new educational technology, helping to cope with the demands of extra undergraduates. The main library is now open 24 hours and the medical school has also been expanded. The university has been awarded a national centre of excellence to develop professionalism in medical students. Full-time numbers throughout the university are almost exactly balanced between the sexes. Geography and environmental science, pharmacology, toxicology and pharmacy, history and English had the most satisfied undergraduates in the 2008 National Student Survey.

A £50-million fundraising drive aims to establish world-class centres of excellence in management, law, medicine, engineering, veterinary science and architecture. More than half of the work submitted for the 2008 Research Assessment Exercise was judged to be world-leading or internationally excellent. Computer science, materials, architecture, English and history produced particularly good results. But the RAE results have also resulted in closure proposals for five departments, including politics and philosophy, where relatively low grades left financial question marks for the future.

Liverpool prides itself on strength across the board and opened a new university in Suzhou, China, in partnership with Xi'an Jiaotong University, in 2006. Chinese students can complete the latter part of their studies in Liverpool,

Liverpool L69 3BX
0151 794 5927 (enquiries)
ugrecruitment@liv.ac.uk
www.liv.ac.uk
www.lgos.org.uk

The Times Rankings
Overall Ranking: =28

Student satisfaction:	=40	(76%)
Research quality:	=32	(1.8)
Entry standards:	26	(387)
Student–staff ratio:	7	(12.2)
Services & facilities/student:	36	(£1,273)
Expected completion rate:	27	(91.2%)
Good honours:	31	(68.8%)
Graduate prospects:	40	(72.5%)

while Liverpool-based students are offered work experience at Suzhou Industrial Park, which is home to 53 "Fortune 500" companies. Liverpool is popular with international students, 88 per cent of whom expressed satisfaction with their experience in 2008.

Applications from home and overseas were up by more than 5 per cent at the start of 2009. New courses for 2009–10 included avionic systems with pilot studies and mechatronics and robotic systems, both with a year in industry. Physics with nuclear science is planned for 2010–11. One of Europe's largest facilities for training dentists opened in 2007, marking the start of a £6-million investment programme following the award of another 125 dental places from 2009.

Liverpool was among the first traditional universities to run access courses for adults without traditional academic qualifications. The projected dropout rate of 8 per cent is below the national average for the courses and entry grades. Even before the introduction of top-up fees, the university was awarding record numbers of scholarships and bursaries to widen opportunities further. They include 30 in memory of John Lennon, mainly for Merseyside residents. Other access initiatives include a purpose-built children's centre to help mature students and staff, with 68 subsidised places. The proportion of state-educated students is higher than at the other civic universities and nearly a quarter of the undergraduates are from working-class homes.

The 3,357 places in halls of residence, self-catering flats and houses are more than enough to guarantee accommodation to all first years. The suburban setting of the main halls complex and the focus of social life on the guild of students means that there is less integration than at some other civic universities, but there is no shortage of nightlife.

Undergraduate Fees and Bursaries
- Fees for UK/EU students: £3,225
- International student fees: £9,400–£12,000
  £18,600 (medicine)
- Bursary on full grant: £1,400
- The university does not award bursaries for students on partial maintenance grants.
- Scholarships based on circumstances or by competition.
- For full details see the university's website: www.liv.ac.uk/study/undergraduate/money/

Students		
Undergraduates:	13,265	(3,145)
Postgraduates:	1,980	(985)
Mature students:	12.6%	
Overseas students:	7.9%	
Applications per place:	6.2	
From state-sector schools:	84.8%	
From working-class homes:	24.7%	

For detailed information about fees, grants and bursaries and how they work, see chapter 7.

Accommodation
Number of places and costs refer to 2009–10
University-provided places: 3,357
Percentage catered: 59%
Catered costs: £106.05–£120.40 a week.
Self-catered costs: £80.15–£90.86 a week.
First-year students are guaranteed accommodation if requirements are met.
International students: as above.
Contact: accommodation@liverpool.ac.uk
www.liv.ac.uk/accommodation

Liverpool Hope University

Liverpool Hope continues to opt out of league tables after finishing at the bottom of our table on its only appearance in *The Times Good University Guide*. It has improved some scores since then, but the university believes that the criteria used in league tables do not reflect its emphasis on widening participation in higher education. Hope even hides its application rates from public view, but only four universities in England have a higher projected dropout rate.

Hope is a unique ecumenical institution formed from the merger of two Catholic and one Church of England teacher training colleges in 1980. The two churches' leading figures on Merseyside described the union as a "sign of hope", unintentionally providing the title for one of the nine new universities created in 2005. It describes itself as "teaching led, research informed and mission focused" and includes "taking faith seriously" among its five key values.

Student satisfaction rates have levelled off at close to the UK average after variable results in the first three years of the National Student Survey. Historical and philosophical studies produced by far the best results published in 2008.

Theology was again the top scorer for research, although a small amount of world-leading work was found in applied social sciences. Overall, only 12 per cent of the university's submission reached the top two grades – placing it among the bottom five on this measure.

University status provided a bigger boost in demand for places than at any of the 2005 newcomers, but it is not clear whether this has continued since Hope has now also become the only institution to suppress the publication of its applications figures. Most students opt for combined subject degrees, choosing after the first year whether to give them equal weight or to go for a major/minor arrangement. Gaming technology and Irish studies is one of the more unusual combinations suggested; environmental management and dance another. Subjects are grouped into four "deaneries": arts and humanities; education; business and computing; sciences and social sciences.

Nearly 30 per cent of the undergraduates are over 20 on entry and female students outnumber their male counterparts by more than two to one. Hope comfortably exceeds all of the official benchmarks for widening participation in higher education. Almost all the undergraduates attended state schools or colleges, over four out of ten are from working-class families and almost a quarter are from areas with little tradition of higher education – the fifth-highest proportion in England. This is

Hope Park
Liverpool L16 9JD
0151 291 3295 (admissions)
admission@hope.ac.uk
www.hope.ac.uk
www.hopesu.co.uk

The Times Rankings
Liverpool Hope blocked the release of data from the Higher Education Statistics Agency and so we cannot give any ranking information.

partly the result of the Network of Hope, which brings university courses to sixth-form colleges across the northwest of England, in areas where there is limited higher education. Combined honours, Foundation degrees and postgraduate teacher training courses are taught in Bury, Wigan and Blackburn. The downside of the university's access agenda is a projected dropout rate of almost 26 per cent, significantly more than the national average for the courses and entry qualifications.

The university's own premises are now concentrated on two sites in Liverpool, with a residential outdoor education centre set in 20 acres of woodland in the heart of Snowdonia, North Wales. The main campus is three miles from the city centre in the suburb of Childwall, while the performing arts are based at the more central Everton campus, which also boasts a £15-million headquarters for community education activities. The £5-million main library, on the Hope campus, has 250,000 items and 700 study spaces, with electronic access from other sites.

Sports facilities have been improving and there are student union bars on both campuses. The university has a range of residential accommodation, some of it provided by a private firm, and is able to guarantee places for first years and all overseas students.

Undergraduate Fees and Bursaries

- Fees for UK/EU students: £3,225
- International student fees: £6,800
- Bursary on full grant: household income up to £17.5K: £800; household incomes up to £25K: £600.*
- Bursaries on partial grant: household income from £25K–£38K: £400.*
- Scholarships based on circumstances or by competition.
- For full details see the university's website: www.hope.ac.uk/general-information/student-funds.html

* Figures for 2008–09

Students

From state-sector schools: 98.2%
From working-class homes: 41.9%

For detailed information about fees, grants and bursaries and how they work, see chapter 7.

Accommodation

Number of places and costs refer to 2009–10
University-provided places: 1,012
Percentage catered: 24% (optional catering package)
Optional Catered costs: £86.66 a week.
Self-catered costs: £66.66–£93.05 a week.
First years are guaranteed accommodation if Liverpool Hope is their first choice.
International students: housing is subject to availability, but all needs are catered for.
Contact: accommodation@hope.ac.uk

Liverpool John Moores University (LJMU)

Naming itself after a football pools millionaire was just the start for one of the most innovative of the new universities. Always keen to portray itself as "forward-thinking", LJMU is focusing on giving its graduates the skills to succeed in an increasingly competitive employment market. Work-related learning is included in every degree and all undergraduates are encouraged to become expert in up to eight transferable skills, applicable to a wide range of professions and careers. They can have their abilities verified through an employer-validated skills statement. The initiative to give degrees the WoW (world of work) factor won a coveted business award.

Earlier innovation included Britain's first student charter, which became a template for others. LJMU also launched the first distance learning degree in astronomy and the first degree in criminal justice. It has been investing £100 million to transform its three campuses by 2012. An Art and Design Academy opened in 2009 and a £22-million life sciences building, with a 70-metre indoor track and laboratories for testing cardiovascular ability, motor skills and biomechanics functions, is set to follow.

The two learning resource centres serving different academic areas and a state-of-the-art media centre are open all hours. Many lectures have been replaced by computer-based teaching, freeing academic staff for face-to-face tutorials. Student numbers increased substantially in the early years of the decade and applications were up again by almost 10 per cent at the start of 2009.

Mainly concentrated in an area between Liverpool's two cathedrals, the university is now one of Britain's biggest with 24,000 students in the city and another 4,500 taking LJMU courses overseas. Arts and science courses occupy separate sites within easy reach of the city centre, with the IM Marsh campus three miles away for education and community studies. Nearly half of the students are drawn from the Merseyside area. A "learning federation" embracing four further education colleges in St Helens, Southport and Liverpool itself adds to the regional flavour.

A growing research reputation is a source of particular pride: LJMU was one of only two new universities to have a subject (sports science) rated internationally outstanding in the 2001 Research Assessment Exercise. There is now a national centre of excellence in teaching and learning in PE, dance, sport and exercise sciences. A third of the research assessed in 2008 was rated as world-

---

Roscoe Court
4 Rodney Street
Liverpool L1 2TZ
0151 231 5090
recruitment@livjm.ac.uk
www.livjm.ac.uk
www.l-s-u.com

The Times Rankings
Overall Ranking: 99

Student satisfaction:	=78	(73%)
Research quality:	=71	(0.4)
Entry standards:	=92	(244)
Student–staff ratio:	85	(19.6)
Services & facilities/student:	82	(£979)
Expected completion rate:	93	(76.1%)
Good honours:	=110	(45.7%)
Graduate prospects:	=100	(58.8%)

leading or internationally excellent, with 12 of the 17 subject areas having some work in the top category. Architecture, electrical and electronic engineering, general engineering and sports science produced the best results.

The International Centre for Digital Content, a partnership with Mersey Television, has been developing a range of new courses, including masters programmes in computer games design and e-commerce. A £1.6-million maritime centre features the UK's most advanced 360-degree shiphandling simulator.

The university's efforts to extend access to higher education are successful: there are significantly more state-educated undergraduates than average for the subjects offered and four in ten are from working-class homes. Two thirds of undergraduates qualify for bursaries and there is a range of scholarships, including six worth £10,000 a year. LJMU has also been addressing concerns about its dropout rate but, after initial improvements, the projected rate remains above 20 per cent – higher than the official benchmark for the university.

Student facilities have been improving. The conversion of a city-centre hotel was one of a number of residential projects which have allowed the university to guarantee a place for young entrants, including those who enter through Clearing. The university now claims to have more accommodation than students requiring it.

Undergraduate Fees and Bursaries
- Fees for UK/EU students: £3,225
- International student fees: £9,790–£10,450
- Bursary on full grant: £1,075
- Bursaries on partial grant: household income £25–£50K: £430.
- Scholarships based on circumstances or by competition.
- For full details see the university's website: www.ljmu.ac.uk/StudyLJMU/Fees/

Students

Undergraduates:	15,115	(4,865)
Postgraduates:	1,795	(2,670)
Mature students:	22.4%	
Overseas students:	8.0%	
Applications per place:	4.1	
From state-sector schools:	96.3%	
From working-class homes:	40.8%	

For detailed information about fees, grants and bursaries and how they work, see chapter 7.

Accommodation
Number of places and costs refer to 2009–10
University-provided places: 3,300 plus 15,000 through Liverpool Student Homes.
Percentage catered: 0%
Self-catered costs: £64–£104 a week.
All new students are guaranteed a place in university accommodation.
International students: as above.
Contact: accommodation@ljmu.ac.uk
www.ljmu.ac.uk/accommodation
(0151) 231 4166

University of London

The federal university is Britain's biggest by far, despite the loss of Imperial College in 2007. Some other prestigious members have considered going their own way and applied for their own degree-awarding powers to hold in reserve, but they are bound together by the London degree, which enjoys a high reputation worldwide. Reforms to the university's governance have given the colleges more autonomy and look to have staved off further departures for now.

London students do have access to some joint residential accommodation, sporting facilities and the University of London Union. But most identify with their college.

The following colleges – some of which have dropped the word "college" from their title to underline their university status – have separate entries, and each also appears within the main university League Table.

Goldsmiths, University of London
King's College London
London School of Economics and Political
  Science
Queen Mary
Royal Holloway
School of Oriental and African Studies
University College London

Many of London's teaching hospitals have now merged with colleges of the university:

King's College now incorporates Guys and St Thomas's (the United Medical and Dental Schools of Guys and St Thomas's).

Queen Mary now incorporates St Bartholomew's and the Royal London School of Medicine and Dentistry.

University College now incorporates the Royal Free Hospital Medical School and the Eastman Dental Hospital.

In addition, the School of Slavonic and Eastern European Studies is now part of University College.

Eleven colleges do not have separate entries in the *Guide*. These are listed below and opposite, with useful postal, telephone, and electronic contacts.

Birkbeck College
Malet Street, London WC1E 7HX
0845 601 0174 (course enquiries)
info@bbk.ac.uk
www.bbk.ac.uk
14,150 undergraduates, mainly part-time.
Apply direct, not through UCAS.

Senate House
Malet Street
London WC1E 7HU
020 7862 8360/61/62
enquiries@london.ac.uk
www.london.ac.uk
www.ulu.co.uk

Edinburgh
Belfast
Cardiff
LONDON

Enquiries: to individual colleges, institutes or schools.

Central School of Speech and Drama
Embassy Theatre, Eton Avenue,
London NW3 3HY
020 7722 8183
enquiries@cssd.ac.uk
www.cssd.ac.uk
570 undergraduates. Acting and theatre
practice.

Courtauld Institute of Art
Somerset House,
London WC2R 0RN
020 7848 2645
ugadmissions@courtauld.ac.uk
www.courtauld.ac.uk
160 undergraduates. History of art degree.

Heythrop College
Kensington Square,
London W8 5HQ
020 7795 4202 (admissions enquiries)
enquiries@heythrop.ac.uk
www.heythrop.ac.uk
380 undergraduates. Degrees in theology
and philosophy.

Institute of Education
20 Bedford Way,
London WC1H 0AL
020 7612 6000
info@ioe.ac.uk
www.ioe.ac.uk
310 undergraduates; mainly postgraduate
education courses.

London Business School
Regent's Park.
London NW1 4SA
020 7000 7000
webenquiries@london.edu
www.london.edu
Postgraduate MBA and other courses.

**London School of Hygiene and Tropical
Medicine**
Keppel Street,
London WC1E 7HT
020 7299 4646 (enquiries)
registry@lshtm.ac.uk
www.lshtm.ac.uk
Postgraduate medical courses.

Royal Academy of Music
Marylebone Road,
London NW1 5HT
020 7873 7373 (general office)
registry@ram.ac.uk
www.ram.ac.uk
320 undergraduates. Degrees in music.

Royal Veterinary College
Royal College Street,
London NW1 0TU
020 7468 5149 (undergraduate admissions)
registry@rvc.ac.uk
www.rvc.ac.uk
1,,430 undergraduates. Degrees in
veterinary medicine.

St George's, University of London
Cranmer Terrace,
London SW17 0RE
020 8672 9944 (general enquiries)
www.sgul.ac.uk
3,705 undergraduates. Degrees in
medicine.

School of Pharmacy
29–39 Brunswick Square,
London WC1N 1AX
020 7753 5831 (enquiries)
registry@pharmacy.ac.uk
www.pharmacy.ac.uk
705 undergraduates. Degrees in pharmacy.

London Metropolitan University

London Met has boycotted league tables since making its debut in our *Guide* five years ago, perilously close to the bottom of *The Times* ranking. It continues to block the release of data from the Higher Education Statistics Agency, but those figures that are available paint a mixed picture. Student satisfaction levels have increased, for example, but the university remained close to the bottom five in the National Student Survey published in 2008.

The immediate difficulty facing the university is a cut of at least £15 million in its grant over the misreporting of student numbers. Hundreds of staff posts will be lost and the Vice-Chancellor, Professor Brian Roper, has resigned. The last reported dropout rate was 21.6 per cent – just below the national average for the university's courses and entry qualifications.

London Met specialises in extending higher education boundaries to bring in groups who are under-represented at traditional universities. Since its establishment from the merger of London Guildhall and North London universities, it has developed hundreds of new degree courses, described as both intellectual and vocational, and which allow students to study citizenship, ethics or enterprise alongside their main subject. Many prepare students for professional qualifications and gain credit for work experience or volunteering.

Recent developments have seen four "business-related" departments join together to form the London Metropolitan Business School which, with 10,000 students and more than 100 courses, will be one of Europe's largest. An "international medical degree" was launched in September 2008, through the University of Health Studies, in Antigua. The five-year programme will be based in London and graduates will complete the United States Medical Licensing Examination, enabling them to practise in America.

With over 28,000 students, 7,000 of whom are from other countries, it has become the biggest single institution in the capital. However, applications have been uneven: although the demand for places had risen by nearly 5 per cent at the start of 2009, this followed a 17.5 per cent decline in the previous year. Fortunately, overseas recruitment has remained healthy. London Met has more undergraduates from other EU countries than any university.

The university's sites are centred on the City of London and north London's Holloway Road. A new graduate school, designed by Daniel Libeskind, opened soon after the merger, and an impressive

31 Jewry Street
London EC3N 2EY
020 7133 4200 (enquiries)
admissions@londonmet.
 ac.uk
www.londonmet.ac.uk
www.londonmet
 su.org.uk

The Times Rankings
London Metropolitan blocked the release of data from the Higher Education Statistics Agency and so we cannot give any ranking information.

£30-million science centre followed in 2006. This features a "superlab" of 280 workstations that is Europe's largest, as well as a multipurpose gym and sports therapy facilities.

Among a variety of craft subjects, the silversmithing and jewellery courses are the largest in Britain, with facilities to match, while those in furniture restoration and conservation were the first of their kind in Europe.

Courses are also directed at the local community. More than a third of the students are Afro-Caribbean and the proportion of mature students is among the highest in England. One of London Met's first objectives was to improve student retention: student support services, from admission to careers advice, have been remodelled and there is a particular emphasis on academic and pastoral counselling on entry and at other key points of courses.

London Met entered more academics than most former polytechnics in the 2008 Research Assessment Exercise, when almost a quarter of the work submitted was placed in the top two categories. About half of the 21 subject areas contained some world-leading research, with architecture, media studies, education and social studies producing the best results. Education, maths and statistics and sociology had the most satisfied undergraduates.

Residential accommodation is limited, but many of London Met's students live at home. Sports facilities are still not extensive, although competitive teams are successful. However, the social scene is lively, particularly in north London.

Undergraduate Fees and Bursaries
- Fees for UK/EU students: £3,225
- International student fees: £8,200*
- Bursary on full grant: household income up to £18K: £1,000 then sliding scale £975–£775.*
- Bursaries on partial grant: household income £25.2K–£40K: sliding scale £750–£310.*
- Scholarships based on circumstances or by competition.
- For full details see the university's website: www.londonmet.ac.uk/student-services/saifs

* Figures for 2008–09

Students
From state-sector schools: 97.3%
From working-class homes: 43.8%

For detailed information about fees, grants and bursaries and how they work, see chapter 7.

Accommodation
Number of places and costs refer to 2008–09
University-provided places: Students have access to accommodation in a wide range of halls of residences provided by specialist student accommodation providers.
Percentage catered: 0%
Self-catered costs: £98–£260 a week.
The university cannot guarantee a place in halls.
International students: first years given priority.
Contact: accommodation@londonmet.ac.uk

London School of Economics and Political Science

Always one of the big names of British higher education, the LSE is in the top four social science institutions in the world, according to the *Times Higher Education*/QS global rankings. With more than 14 applications for every place, this is reflected in more competition for admission than at any UK university. Only Oxford, Cambridge and Imperial College London have higher average entry grades.

The school has added 1,000 places in recent years – mostly on postgraduate courses – having seized the chance to tackle a longstanding shortage of teaching space by acquiring former Government buildings near the school's Aldwych headquarters.

Sir Howard Davies, the Director, has built on the progress made by his predecessor, Professor Anthony Giddens, the academic face of Tony Blair's Third Way, who brought in a number of big names from other top universities.

The school has a cosmopolitan feel that derives from the highest proportion of overseas students at any publicly funded university. Due to national funding restrictions, only a relatively small proportion of the extra places have been for UK undergraduates.

The LSE has produced 29 heads of state and 13 Nobel prizewinners in economics, literature and peace – including George Bernard Shaw, Bertrand Russell, Friedrich von Hayek and Amartya Sen. The nationals of more than 150 countries take up half of the places. At the undergraduate level, only the much larger Manchester University has more applications from overseas. Its international character not only gives the LSE global prestige but also an unusual degree of financial independence. Less than a fifth of its income is from the Higher Education Funding Council.

More than a third of British undergraduates are from independent schools – one of the highest ratios in the country and much higher than the funding council's benchmark figure. Efforts are being made to attract a broader intake with Saturday classes and summer schools. The projected dropout rate of 3 per cent is among the lowest at any university and applications have been steady – there had been a 3 per cent increase at the official deadline for courses beginning in 2009. However, average scores in the National Student Survey published in 2008 were the lowest of any pre-1992 university. Only in law and accounting were 80 per cent of final-year undergraduates satisfied overall with their courses.

Areas of study range more broadly than the name suggests: law, management and

Houghton Street
London WC2A 2AE
020 7955 7125
stu.rec@lse.ac.uk
(pre-application)
ug-admissions@lse.ac.uk
(post-application)
www.lse.ac.uk
www.lsesu.com

The Times Rankings
Overall Ranking: 7

Student satisfaction:	=78	(73%)
Research quality:	=3	(2.8)
Entry standards:	4	(483)
Student–staff ratio:	16	(13.3)
Services & facilities/student:	8	(£1,699)
Expected completion rate:	5	(96.5%)
Good honours:	11	(76.0%)
Graduate prospects:	1	(90.6%)

history are all on the curriculum and there is even a small contingent of scientists. Only Cambridge recorded higher average scores than the LSE in the 2008 research assessments, which saw almost 70 per cent of the work submitted rated world-leading or internationally excellent. Ninety-five per cent of the economics submission, 80 per cent in social policy and 75 per cent in law reached the top two categories.

The LSE does not hide its light under a bushel: it describes itself as "the world's leading social science institution for teaching and research". A pan-European survey also showed the school's students to be more active in student associations, more entrepreneurial and more open to opportunities to work abroad than those at other leading universities. The students' union claims to be the only one in Britain to hold weekly general meetings at which every student may attend and vote, while the 120 student societies cover an unusually wide range of interests.

Improvements were being made to the campus long before the opportunity arose to expand. A £30-million Norman Foster-designed redevelopment of the Lionel Robbins Building now houses a much-improved library. The move was a welcome one since the number of books borrowed by LSE students is more than four times the national average, according to a recent survey. Routes between most of the buildings have been pedestrianised and a new student services centre has opened.

Partying is not the prime attraction of the LSE for most applicants, who tend to be serious about their subject, but London's top nightspots are on the doorstep for those who can afford them. The 3,650 residential places for 8,500 full-time students offer a good chance of avoiding central London's notoriously high private sector rents.

Undergraduate Bursaries and Scholarships
- Fees for UK/EU students: £3,225
- International student fees: £12,840
- Bursary on full grant: sliding scale to £25K: £2,500–£1,044.
- Bursaries on partial grant: household income up to £60K: sliding scale £966–£50.
- Scholarships based on circumstances or by competition.
- For full details see the university's website: www.lse.ac.uk/financialSupportOffice/

Students
Undergraduates:	3,860	(60)
Postgraduates:	4,690	(495)
Mature students:	3.4%	
Overseas students:	49.5%	
Applications per place:	14.7	
From state-sector schools:	65.9%	
From working-class homes:	18.2%	

For detailed information about fees, grants and bursaries and how they work, see chapter 7.

Accommodation
Number of places and costs refer to 2009–10
University-provided places: 3,650
Percentage catered: about 36%
Catered costs: from £67–£160 a week.
Self-catered costs: £73–£199 a week.
First years are guaranteed an offer of accommodation.
Policy for international students: same as above.
Contact: accommodation@lse.ac.uk
to apply online: www.lse.ac.uk/accommodation

London South Bank University

Once marketed as "the university without ivory towers", London South Bank University's mission statement underlines the point with an emphasis on wealth creation and the labour market. The university was in the top ten in the last survey of graduate starting salaries. A 2007 study by PricewaterhouseCoopers found that a LSBU degree increased lifetime earnings by more than £185,000, which was nearly £26,000 more than the national average.

Over 70 per cent of students are from the capital, most of them from south London and especially from the area's wide range of ethnic minorities. Of nearly 17,000 undergraduates, over a third are part-time and half are on sandwich courses. Fewer than half enter with traditional academic qualifications. Applications were buoyant throughout the period following the introduction of top-up fees and the start of 2009 saw another big increase, of nearly 12 per cent.

The proportion of mature entrants is among the highest in Britain, encouraged by initiatives such as the summer school for local people to upgrade their qualifications. The Fast Track to Higher Education programme has been expanded to include English, IT and science, as well as the original mathematics. The courses, some of which are tailored to the needs of mature students and some for younger students, start at the end of June and are limited to 15 hours a week so as not to affect students' benefit entitlement.

Diploma and degree courses run in parallel so that students can move up or down if they are better suited to another level of study. The university offers a wide range of Foundation and pre-degree courses in business and accounting, law, tourism and hospitality, design and engineering, and science and technology for international students

Specialist facilities, such as the Centre for Explosion and Fire Research, show that the vocational theme carries through into research. Although the university entered only 87 academics for the 2008 Research Assessment Exercise, their average grades were among the best of the new universities. More than 40 per cent of the submission was rated as world-leading or internationally excellent, with social policy, engineering and communication, culture and media studies leading the way.

LSBU is in the midst of a 15-year programme to develop its campus in Southwark, near the Elephant and Castle, and not far from the South Bank arts complex. The nine-storey Keyworth Centre upgraded much of the teaching accommodation and provided a new focal point for the university. The flagship

103 Borough Road
London SE1 0AA
020 7815 7815
course.enquiry@lsbu.ac.uk
www.lsbu.ac.uk
www.lsbsu.org

The Times Rankings
Overall Ranking: 113

Student satisfaction:	=99	(71%)
Research quality:	=85	(0.3)
Entry standards:	114	(179)
Student–staff ratio:	113	(25.2)
Services & facilities/student:	=100	(£829)
Expected completion rate:	110	(69.4%)
Good honours:	=77	(53.7%)
Graduate prospects:	81	(63.2%)

building "Keyworth II" is due to open in 2009, housing the Faculty of Health and Social Care, and providing facilities for the Department of Education and for Sports and Exercise Science.

Some health students are based on the other side of London, in hospitals in Romford and Leytonstone, where there are limited learning resources, supplementing those in Southwark. The university now trains 40 per cent of London's nurses.

The capital's attractions are on the doorstep of the main campus but, with nearly 45 per cent of the students coming from working-class homes, many cannot afford them. The official projected dropout rate is more than 27 per cent, a proportion exceeded by only two UK universities. But LSBU insists that the true rate is less than half that figure because most students do complete their courses eventually; they just take longer than the standard course length.

A new hall of residence means that the university now has residential places within ten minutes' walk of the main campus. There are not enough rooms to guarantee places for all first years, but the 2,000 overseas students are all given places if they want them. Sports facilities improved considerably with the extension of the campus sports centre and the launch of the Academy of Sport. Representative teams have been quite successful in recent years – especially in basketball – and sports bursaries of £3,000 are available for elite performers.

Undergraduate Fees and Bursaries
- Fees for UK/EU students   £3,225
- International student fees   £8,300–£8,600
- Bursary on full grant: Year 1 £500; Year 2 £750; Year 3 £750 (+ £250 graduation bonus for Hons graduates).*
- Bursaries on partial grant: Year 1 £500; Year 2 £750; Year 3 £750 (+ £250 graduation bonus for Hons graduates).*
- Scholarships based on circumstances or by competition.
- For full details see the university's website: www.lsbu.ac.uk/fees

* Figures for 2008–09

Students

Undergraduates:	10,085	(6,625)
Postgraduates:	1,440	(4,190)
Mature students:	58.9%	
Overseas students:	10.5%	
Applications per place:	4.2	
From state-sector schools:	98.5%	
From working-class homes:	44.8%	

For detailed information about fees, grants and bursaries and how they work, see chapter 7.

Accommodation

Number of places and costs refer to 2009–10
University-provided places: 1,400
Percentage catered: 0%
Self-catered costs: £91.00 (standard) – £111.50 (en suite) a week.
First-year UK students are not guaranteed accommodation, but high priority is given to those who live outside Greater London area.
International students: first years are guaranteed accommodation if conditions met.
Contact: accommodation@lsbu.ac.uk

Loughborough University

Loughborough has been in the top ten universities for student satisfaction every year since the National Student Survey was launched. In 2008, six of the university's subjects were ranked top in the UK – chemical engineering, information science, physics, building, materials and ergonomics – and more than nine out of ten undergraduates declared themselves satisfied overall. Loughborough has also won the first three *Times Higher Education* awards for best student experience, after separate national polls of undergraduates. The message is getting through to sixth-formers with 19 per cent growth in applications at the start of 2009, following healthy increases in the previous two years.

Still best known for its successes on the sports field, Loughborough has enhanced its academic reputation recently, consistently finishing well up *The Times* rankings and improving its performance in the 2008 Research Assessment Exercise. Although the results were patchy, more than half of the research in art and design was considered world-leading, and there were particularly good results in architecture and sport. The Office for Standards in Education also rates Loughborough in its top category for teacher training in physical education, design and science.

The university remains a major centre of engineering with more than 2,800 students in a £20-million integrated engineering complex. Aeronautical, automotive and civil engineering are particularly strong, although art and design, business and sports science now all have more students than any single branch of the discipline.

The original 216-acre campus has benefited from a sustained construction programme which included a large student union extension and a new business school, as well as the gradual refurbishment of residential accommodation. The first phase of a £68-million on-campus accommodation development opened in 2008 and more than 5,000 rooms now all have telephone and internet connections. The development will eventually provide another 1,300 new bedrooms in four new halls.

The size of the campus has been increased by 75 per cent following the purchase of the adjacent Holywell Park site. This will become the focus for research and collaboration with industry, including a £59-million BAE-sponsored Systems Engineering Innovation Centre. The university prides itself on a close relationship with industry, which accounts for its record haul of six Queen's Anniversary Prizes. Arts facilities are improving with the upgrading of the Cope Auditorium to serve the campus and local community.

Ashby Road
Loughborough
Leicestershire LE11 3TU
01509 263171 (switchboard)
www.lboro.ac.uk/
   prospectus/
contact via website
www.lboro.ac.uk
www.lufbra.net

The Times Rankings
Overall Ranking: 17

Student satisfaction:	=2	(85%)
Research quality:	=19	(2.1)
Entry standards:	30	(368)
Student–staff ratio:	=54	(17.0)
Services & facilities/student:	34	(£1,340)
Expected completion rate:	26	(91.3%)
Good honours:	=33	(67.7%)
Graduate prospects:	27	(75.7%)

The business school is being extended and a £12.7-million building for Health, Exercise and Biological Sciences is under construction.

Most subjects are available either as three-year full-time or four-to-five-year sandwich courses, which includes a year in industry. This has helped to give graduates an outstanding employment record, as well a dropout rate of less than 5 per cent, which is particularly low for the subjects Loughborough offers. The university is a leader in the use of computer-assisted assessment, offering students the chance to gauge their own progress online.

Loughborough remains pre-eminent in British university sport, both in terms of facilities and performance. More than 50 past and present students took part in the 2008 Beijing Olympic and Paralympic Games, bringing home three Olympic medals and reaching nineteen finals. Representative teams have a record second to none and the programme of sports scholarships is the largest in the university system.

The heavily oversubscribed School of Sport and Exercise Science moved into new premises in 2002, and in recent years the campus has acquired a 50-metre swimming pool, national academies for cricket and tennis, a gymnastics centre and a high-performance training centre for athletics. The university also opened the UK's only centre for disability sport in 2005 and was shortlisted as a possible training camp for the British team ahead of the 2012 Olympics in London. Joining the Olympic effort will be the new £15-million Sports Technology Institute, as well as enhanced research, innovation and enterprise in sport and leisure in the longer term.

Social activity is concentrated on the students' union. The relatively small town of Loughborough, a mile away, is never going to be a clubber's paradise, but both Leicester and Nottingham are within easy reach.

Undergraduate Fees and Bursaries

- Fees for UK/EU students: £3,225
- International student fees: £10,400–£13,500
- Bursary on full grant: household income up to £24.1K: sliding scale £1,390 to £860 (doubled for mature students).
- Bursaries on partial grant: household income up to £35.4K: sliding scale £650–£220 (doubled for mature students).
- Scholarships based on circumstances or by competition.
- For full details see the university's website: www.lboro.ac.uk/admin/ar/funding/index.htm

---

Students

Undergraduates:	11,170	(295)
Postgraduates:	3,505	(1,680)
Mature students:	3.5%	
Overseas students:	9.8%	
Applications per place:	5.0	
From state-sector schools:	81.7%	
From working-class homes:	21.7%	

For detailed information about fees, grants and bursaries and how they work, see chapter 7.

Accommodation

Number of places and costs refer to 2009–10
University-provided places: 5,625
Percentage catered: 43%
Catered costs: £3,974.60–£5,746.10
Self-catered costs: £2,644.20–£5,495.10
First-year first-choice students are guaranteed accommodation.
International students: guaranteed housing in same residence for two years.
Contact: SAC@lboro.ac.uk
http://accommodation.lboro.ac.uk

University of Manchester

Always among the giants of British higher education, with 23 Nobel prizewinners to its credit, Manchester became larger and more powerful in 2004 through a merger with neighbouring UMIST. The largest conventional university in Britain kept its familiar name, but is now headed by a Vice-Chancellor from the other side of the world. Professor Alan Gilbert arrived from the University of Melbourne shortly before the new institution was formed.

Some departments were already administered jointly with UMIST and the two institutions only separated fully in 1993, so the new institution has been able to avoid some of the problems associated with other university mergers. A £400-million building and refurbishment programme, the largest ever in UK higher education, will be complete by the end of 2009 and another £250 million of investment is planned by 2015. At the same time, a raft of new professors has been appointed. The aim is not only to break into higher education's "golden triangle" of Oxford, Cambridge and London, but to make Manchester one of the top 25 universities in the world by 2015. By then, the aim is to have at least five Nobel laureates on the staff. The first joined in 2006 and there have been other high-profile appointments, such the novelist

Martin Amis as Professor of Creative Writing.

Manchester was among the top ten universities in the 2008 Research Assessment Exercise, with almost two thirds of its submission considered world-leading or internationally excellent. The university's claim to have "smashed the golden triangle" may have been wishful thinking, but there were particularly strong performances in cancer studies, nursing, biology, dentistry, engineering, sociology, development studies, Spanish and music and drama.

The university has produced consistently good scores in the National Student Survey, with 100 per cent satisfaction in classics in 2008 and high scores in biology, dentistry, and anatomy, physiology and pathology.

Manchester has reclaimed its place as the university with the largest number of applicants since the merger. The demand for places had been growing, but applications were down slightly at the start of 2009, when most universities saw substantial increases. One of the priorities in the new institution's founding strategy is to broaden the undergraduate intake, with a particular focus on increasing recruitment from the city and its surrounding area. However, in addition to the normal bursary package for British students, Manchester is aiming eventually

Oxford Road
Manchester M13 9PL
0161 275 2077 (admissions)
ug-admissions@
  manchester.ac.uk
www.manchester.ac.uk
www.umsu.
  manchester.ac.uk

The Times Rankings
Overall Ranking: 24

Student satisfaction:	=78	(73%)
Research quality:	=12	(2.4)
Entry standards:	=14	(412)
Student–staff ratio:	17	(13.6)
Services & facilities/student:	=22	(£1,489)
Expected completion rate:	25	(91.6%)
Good honours:	26	(70.4%)
Graduate prospects:	33	(73.8%)

to have 750 awards for students from educationally deprived backgrounds in developing countries.

UMIST's legacy was a strong reputation among academics and employers alike in its specialist areas of engineering, science and management. Surveys of employers frequently placed UMIST among their favourite recruiting grounds, helping to produce an unrivalled network of industrial sponsorship. Employers have rated Manchester's careers service the best at any university. The merger also produced the largest engineering school in the UK, with a £20-million budget and 1,200 students.

A £14-million extension to the School of Chemistry, the second-largest in Britain, opened in 2007. There already was a federal business school, which is among the strengths of the merged institution, as is the medical school, which was rewarded for impressive teaching ratings with extra places in collaboration with Keele University. A new teaching block caters for the additional 230 places a year.

The city's famed youth culture and the university's position at the heart of a huge student precinct already help to ensure keen competition for places – and hence high entry standards in most subjects. Sports facilities, which were already first rate, have improved still further since the city hosted the Commonwealth Games.

Students get discount rates at the aquatics centre opened for the games on campus, for example. The city's reputation for violent crime has subsided, but the students' union (which has the largest premises in the country) runs late-night minibuses, self-defence classes, and regular safety campaigns. Students tend to be fiercely loyal both to the university and their adopted city.

Undergraduate Fees and Bursaries

- Fees for UK/EU students: £3,225
- International student fees: £10,800–£13,400 £24,450 (medicine)
- Bursary on full grant: £1,250
- The university does not award bursaries for students on partial maintenance grants.
- Scholarships based on circumstances or by competition.
- For full details see the university's website: www.manchester.ac.uk/undergraduate/funding/

Students

Undergraduates:	24,930	(1,920)
Postgraduates:	6,940	(3,575)
Mature students:	12.5%	
Overseas students:	15.1%	
Applications per place:	6.0	
From state-sector schools:	77.2%	
From working-class homes:	21.3%	

For detailed information about fees, grants and bursaries and how they work, see chapter 7.

Accommodation

Number of places and costs refer to 2009–10
University-owned/managed places: 9,200
Percentage catered: (approx) 30%
Catered costs: £4,300–£4,900 (40 weeks)
Self-catered costs: £3,000–£4,300 (40 weeks); £3,000–£4,000 (37 weeks).
All first years are guaranteed accommodation provided conditions are met.
International students paying overseas fees are guaranteed accommodation if conditions met.
Contact: accommodation@manchester.ac.uk

Manchester Metropolitan University

With over 33,000 students, including more than 6,000 part-timers, Manchester Metropolitan is neck and neck with its recently merged neighbour for the title of the largest conventional higher education institution in Britain. But the giant institution boasts quality as well as quantity: more than a third of the work entered for the 2008 Research Assessment Exercise was rated as world-leading or internationally excellent. Education, English and art and design produced the best results.

Although the former polytechnic has not been able to sustain the lead it held briefly over Manchester University in applications, still only a handful of institutions are more popular. The demand for places has grown throughout most of the decade and there had been another 12 per cent increase in applications at the start of 2009. Longstanding commitments to extending access are being continued: even among the full-time undergraduates, a fifth are over 25 and more than a third come from working-class homes.

Almost 1,000 courses cover more than 70 subjects, with the menu of programmes including a growing range of two-year Foundation degrees. The university takes teaching seriously: small groups are used whenever possible and staff are encouraged to take a three-year MA in teaching. Many courses also involve work placements. MMU has more professionally accredited courses than any other university.

Education courses have also fared well in the Teacher Training Agency's performance indicators, especially for primary training. The university trains more teachers than any other and has launched a Centre for Urban Education to develop its expertise further. Some 800 trainees and other students taking contemporary arts and sports science are at the former Crewe and Alsager College campuses, 40 miles south of Manchester and now rebranded as MMU Cheshire. The remaining education students are based at Didsbury, five miles out of the centre of Manchester, with those taking community studies. A single Institute of Education covers both centres.

The Crewe and Alsager campuses are six miles apart, but free transport is provided between the two. Although the rural location inevitably makes for a quieter life than in Manchester, Alsager has an arts centre with two theatres, a dance studio and an art gallery, as well as extensive sports facilities. The Crewe campus, which has seen a district of the

---

All Saints Building
Oxford Road
Manchester M15 6BH
0161 247 6969 (admissions)
admissions@mmu.ac.uk
www.mmu.ac.uk
www.mmunion.co.uk

The Times Rankings
Overall Ranking: 90

Student satisfaction:	=90	(72%)
Research quality:	=63	(0.5)
Entry standards:	=73	(266)
Student–staff ratio:	=86	(19.7)
Services & facilities/student:	84	(£972)
Expected completion rate:	81	(79.0%)
Good honours:	66	(57.2%)
Graduate prospects:	79	(63.8%)

town rebranded as the University Quadrant, has its own nightclub. The university has begun to develop Crewe as its Cheshire base, adding sports facilities and residential accommodation, as well as more lecture theatres. The opening of a £30-million student village is the first piece of a rebuilding programme at Crewe, which will be home to academics and students in business and management, the arts, exercise and sport science, humanities and social studies, education and teacher training.

The five sites in Manchester will eventually be reduced to two linked campuses. The university will move from leafy Didsbury in the southern suburbs and create a £70-million "campus for the professions" in the city centre that will be one of the most environmentally sustainable in the UK, uniting provision for teachers, nurses, health and youth workers. The new site is close to the existing All Saints campus, on the university's border with Hulme and Moss Side.

New science and engineering buildings at All Saints cost £42 million – part of a £300-million building programme for the university as a whole. The large business school will benefit from a new £65-million building next to the Mancunian Way. Overseas links have expanded rapidly in recent years, offering exchange opportunities in Europe and farther afield,

as well as establishing teaching bases abroad.

However, more than half of the students come from the Manchester area, easing the pressure on accommodation in a city of nearly 70,000 students. Some 85 per cent of hall places are reserved for first years, with priority going to the disabled and those who live furthest from the university. The city's attractions do no harm to recruitment levels, but much depends on where the course is based; students at Crewe and Alsager can feel isolated. Some potential applicants are daunted by the sheer size of the university, but individual courses and sites usually provide a social circle.

Undergraduate Fees and Bursaries

- Fees for UK/EU students: £3,225
- International student fees: £8,180–£13,400
- Bursary on full grant: household income up to £21K: £1,025; household income up to £25K: £475.
- Bursaries on partial grant: household income £25K–£40K: £475.
- Scholarships based on circumstances or by competition.
- For full details see the university's website: www.mmu.ac.uk/studentfinance/index.php

---

Students

Undergraduates:	24,090	(3,545)
Postgraduates:	2,370	(2,960)
Mature students:	19.3%	
Overseas students:	7.4%	
Applications per place:	4.7	
From state-sector schools:	94.6%	
From working-class homes:	35.9%	

For detailed information about fees, grants and bursaries and how they work, see chapter 7.

Accommodation

Number of places and costs refer to 2008–09
University-provided places: 5,100
Percentage catered: 6%
Catered costs: Manchester: £87 a week; Cheshire: £88.50 a week.
 Self-catered costs: Manchester: £70–£100 a week; Cheshire: £63– £80 a week.
All new full-time students will be housed if requirements are met. Local restrictions apply.
International students: as above.
Contact: www.mmu.ac.uk/accommodation/

Middlesex University

Middlesex has been changing the character of its intake, reorganising its courses and becoming more international, and now physical changes are on the way. A £100-million building programme will concentrate the university on three sites in north London. The new package seems to be encouraging a revival in recruitment among home students, which has been patchy in recent years. An 8.5 per cent increase in applications at the start of 2009 was better than the national average. Overseas recruitment has been Middlesex's salvation in lean years: international students make up 15 per cent of its intake. A longstanding commitment to Europe sees more than 1,000 students arriving from the Continent and even more come from further afield. There is a network of 11 regional offices, producing a student population drawn from 130 countries. Its successes in the overseas market won a Queen's Award for Enterprise and the university has now opened its own campus in Dubai offering business degrees and short courses in a variety of subjects.

Now almost 22,000 strong, including part-timers, the university aims to carry on growing. Partner colleges at home and abroad participate in exchanges and/or offer Middlesex qualifications. The university has reorganised its schools to focus on its strengths in business, computing and the arts. Media students benefit from a new Skillset Academy, in partnership with Top TV and the SAE Institute.

The highly flexible course system allows students to start many courses in January if they prefer not to wait until autumn, and offers the option of an extra five-week session in July and August to try out new subjects or add to their credits. Nine out of ten students take vocational courses, many at postgraduate or sub-degree level. The business school is the biggest subject area, but almost half of the undergraduates are on multidisciplinary programmes.

Almost 40 per cent are over 21 on entry and half of the full-timers come from London. Nearly all the British students are from state schools and only three universities have a higher proportion from working-class homes. The downside of the access policy is that more than a third of undergraduates are not expected to complete their courses in the expected time. The official projection has been rising alarmingly and is now the second-highest in the UK. Even before the introduction of top-up fees, Middlesex was attempting to attract better-qualified students by offering scholarships worth £1,000 a year for UK entrants with good

---

North London Business Park
The Burroughs
London NW4 4BT
020 8411 5555 (enquiries)
enquiries@mdx.ac.uk
www.mdx.ac.uk
www.musu.mdx.ac.uk

The Times Rankings
Overall Ranking: 105

Student satisfaction:	=101	(70%)
Research quality:	=63	(0.5)
Entry standards:	112	(194)
Student–staff ratio:	110	(23.4)
Services & facilities/student:	10	(£1,645)
Expected completion rate:	112	(64.7%)
Good honours:	94	(50.8%)
Graduate prospects:	73	(64.4%)

grades. There are also two scholarships of £30,000 on offer for potential Olympic champions at the 2012 Games.

For some time, the university has been reducing the number of campuses dotted around London's North Circular Road. The latest to close was Enfield in 2008, its courses transferring to Hendon, where £50 million has been invested in a library, learning resources centre and roofing in the main quadrangle to provide meeting space. Other new student facilities at Hendon include a fitness suite, expanded nursery and refectory. The campus, which boasts one of the country's few Real Tennis courts, already housed the business school and has added sport and health subjects. The other locations include a picturesque country estate at Trent Park and an art and design campus at Cat Hill.

Nurses and other health students are based in four London teaching hospitals and on a campus at Archway which is shared with the University College and Royal Free Hospital medical schools. There is also a joint degree in veterinary nursing run with the Royal Veterinary College.

Results in the National Student Survey have been disappointing, only accounting, finance and law reaching satisfaction levels of 85 per cent in 2008. The university did better in the latest Research Assessment Exercise, with more than a third of its submission rated world-leading or internationally excellent. Philosophy again produced the best results, but dance, social work and social policy, history of art and computer science all did well.

The number of residential places is planned to double in the next few years from the current 1,300 beds. Sports facilities have been improving, particularly following the development of the Hendon campus.

Undergraduate Fees and Bursaries

- Fees for UK/EU students: £3,225
- International student fees: £9,400
- Bursary on full grant: £319
- The university does not award bursaries for students on partial maintenance grants.
- Scholarships based on circumstances or by competition.
- For full details see the university's website: www.mdx.ac.uk/study/undergrad/ugfees/index.asp

Students

Undergraduates:	12,755	(4,120)
Postgraduates:	1,705	(3,045)
Mature students:	38.5%	
Overseas students:	15.5%	
Applications per place:	6.0	
From state-sector schools:	97.8	
From working-class homes:	47.5%	

For detailed information about fees, grants and bursaries and how they work, see chapter 7.

Accommodation

Number of places and costs refer to 2009–10
University-provided places: 1,347
Percentage catered: 0%
Self-catered costs:£86.80–£103.46 a week.
Full-year international students have priority; residential restrictions apply.
International students are guaranteed a room provided requirements are met.
Contact: accomm@mdx.ac.uk

Newcastle University

Twice recently, Newcastle has been named as the best university city in the UK, although the message does not appear to be getting through to applicants. An increase in applications of 2 per cent at the start of 2009 was well below the national average and followed four years of static or falling demand for places.

The university has embarked on a £200-million programme of investment in its campus and facilities. The first phase involves a five-storey, glass-fronted building costing £35 million, which will house all the main student services, as well as a visitor centre, creating a welcoming "front door" to the university. A partnership with a private languages firm will also put £49 million into accommodation and teaching facilities for international students.

Science and engineering laboratories have already been upgraded, disabled access improved and thousands of students provided with internet connections in university owned flats and halls of residence. A new music building, available 24 hours a day, will open in 2009, along with the £24-million Great North Museum: Hancock – a redevelopment of the university's original museum.

Another significant development will be the opening of an international branch campus in Johor, Malaysia, in 2011. Newcastle University Medicine Malaysia (NUMed) will offer degrees in medicine and biomedical science, adding to the courses in naval architecture that are already provided in Singapore.

Originally Durham University's medical school, Newcastle's excellence in that area was confirmed by its selection as a national centre to disseminate best teaching practice in medicine. The school has gone back into partnership with Durham, with about a third of trainees spending their first two years at Durham's Stockton campus.

Newcastle was also chosen to house a national centre of teaching excellence in music. Other academic developments include the creation of nine new research institutes, housed in new buildings costing over £30 million. Research grades improved in the 2008 assessments, although Newcastle entered fewer academics than most members of Russell Group universities. Almost 60 per cent of the work reached the top two categories, with 90 per cent of research in cancer research rated world-leading or internationally excellent. Art and design, music and English also produced outstanding results.

Recent additions to the portfolio of courses have included Britain's first degree in folk and traditional music, and a four-year business and accounting degree, which provides a fast-track to professional

---

Kensington Terrace
Newcastle upon Tyne NE1 7RU
0191 222 5594 (enquiries)
www.ncl.ac.uk/forms/
  enquiries/
www.ncl.ac.uk
www.unionsociety.co.uk

The Times Rankings
Overall Ranking: 21

Student satisfaction:	=28	(77%)
Research quality:	=24	(2.0)
Entry standards:	19	(405)
Student–staff ratio:	=34	(14.9)
Services & facilities/student:	21	(£1,504)
Expected completion rate:	20	(92.2%)
Good honours:	22	(72.2%)
Graduate prospects:	12	(79.4%)

qualifications. Newcastle already had a number of unusual features for a traditional university, such as a fine art degree which attracts up to 15 applicants per place. It also has a longstanding reputation for agriculture, which benefits from two farms in Northumberland.

The campus is spacious and varied, occupying 45 acres close to the main shopping area, civic centre and Newcastle United's ground. The university also boasts an expanded and refurbished theatre, an art gallery and three museums.

The university expanded dramatically in the 1990s, and now has more than 19,000 full-time students. It has become popular with independent schools, whose applicants take three in ten places, but the university has stepped up its contacts with local state schools in order to broaden its intake. Alumni and other friends of the university raised £6 million in two years to add to the bursaries available for students from less affluent backgrounds. Official performance indicators reveal a healthy 92 per cent completion rate – better than anticipated, given the subject mix.

Few students regret choosing Newcastle for a degree, even if southerners can find the winter temperatures a shock. The city's nightlife is legendary – eighth best in the world, according to one survey – and the cost of living is reasonable. Town–gown relations better than in many cities.

Sport is a particular strength, Newcastle claiming to be one of the top ten universities both in terms of performance and facilities. A new £5.5-million sports centre supplements two older centres, which have refurbished fitness suites, massage clinics and all the normal indoor services. The main outdoor pitches are two miles from the university. Over £30,000 is awarded annually in sports bursaries for elite athletes.

Undergraduate Bursaries and Scholarships
- Fees for UK/EU students: £3,225
- International student fees: £10,215–£13,360 £24,735 (medicine)
- Bursary on full grant: £1,280
- Bursaries on partial grant: household income £25K–£32.2K: £640.
- Scholarships based on circumstances or by competition.
- For full details see the university's website: www.ncl.ac.uk/undergraduate/finance

Students		
Undergraduates:	14,165	(220)
Postgraduates:	3,305	(1,360)
Mature students:	10.5%	
Overseas students:	10.2%	
Applications per place:	5.6	
From state-sector schools:	70.0%	
From working-class homes:	20.1%	

For detailed information about fees, grants and bursaries and how they work, see chapter 7.

Accommodation
Number of places and costs refer to 2009–10
University-provided places: 4,278
Percentage catered: 31%
Catered costs: £97.79–£113.19 a week.
Self-catered costs: £68.74–£96.11 a week.
All single undergraduates are guaranteed a room in university-managed accommodation provided requirements are met. Local restrictions apply.
International students: as above.
Contact: accommodation-enquiries@ncl.ac.uk

University of Wales, Newport

Newport saw applications rise by 76 per cent in four years following its change of status from college to university. Growth in the demand for places stalled in 2008, as it did throughout Wales, but the upward trajectory resumed at the start of 2009, with an impressive 12 per cent increase in applications. Students have been attracted by a range of new courses in areas such as creative sound and music, cinema studies and script-writing, computer games design and internet technologies.

Newport had already embarked on an ambitious expansion strategy before attaining full membership of the University of Wales. A futuristic riverside campus that will practically double the number of students has begun to take shape, housing the Business School and part of the School of Art, Media and Design from 2010. At the same time, Newport will pursue closer links with the University of Wales Institute Cardiff, which was already a partner in a number of subjects.

There has been a significant increase in research activity with the launch of a dedicated Research and Enterprise Department. The university entered only 28 staff for the 2008 Research Assessment Exercise, but their work was highly rated compared with most of their peers in similar institutions. More than half of it was considered world-leading or internationally excellent. A joint submission with the University of Wales Institute, Cardiff, in art and design was particularly successful, while mechanical engineering and social work also did well.

Newport also did well in the first National Student Survey, finishing in the top ten, but it has slipped down the table subsequently and was close to the bottom in 2008. Only social work and social studies recorded satisfaction levels of more than 80 per cent. A poll of local employers was particularly positive about the university, however, and Estyn, the Welsh schools inspectorate, gave the best grades in Wales to the teacher-training courses.

The university, which was previously Gwent College of Higher Education, now has over 9,000 students. Virtually all the full-time undergraduates come from state schools and nearly four in ten come from working-class homes. However, the projected dropout rate of 26 per cent is still higher than the benchmark set according to the subject mix. Newport operates a number of access schemes, including a compact agreement with local schools and colleges.

The university is actively involved with a range of local businesses. It was rated the number one university in Wales for

Caerleon Campus
Lodge Road
Newport
South Wales NP18 3QT
01633 432030
admissions@newport.
  ac.uk
www.newport.ac.uk
www.newport
  union.com

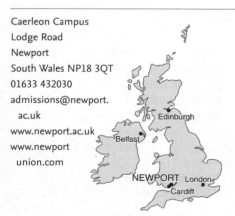

The Times Rankings
Overall Ranking: 107

Student satisfaction:	=78	(73%)
Research quality:	=85	(0.3)
Entry standards:	102	(229)
Student–staff ratio:	114	(25.8)
Services & facilities/student:	89	(£922)
Expected completion rate:	105	(72.1%)
Good honours:	=74	(54.8%)
Graduate prospects:	108	(55.8%)

enterprise education by the Knowledge Exploitation Fund. Among its innovations is the Corus to Campus project for redundant steelworkers (previously employed by Corus), and it is also a leading player in the Community University of the Valleys. The university also hosts the International Film School Wales, whose graduates include double-BAFTA winner Asif Kapadia, and Justin Kerrigan, director of the cult movie *Human Traffic*.

There are currently two campuses. The smaller, Allt-Yr-Yn, campus focuses on engineering and computing, business and professional and social studies. The larger Caerleon campus is further out, with impressive views, and caters for humanities, science, education and art, media and design. This is also where the student village of 661 self-catered study bedrooms is located, and a new building for fashion and the Wales International Study Centre opened in 2008. Free buses link the two sites, which are officially among the safest in Britain: Newport was the first educational establishment to pass an industry-standard security inspection.

A well-equipped sports centre at Caerleon has transformed facilities that previously compared unfavourably with those of other universities. The city of Newport is undergoing a £2-billion regeneration programme and has established a reputation for producing successful rock bands and has plenty of clubs and entertainment venues, but students in search of serious cultural or clubbing activity gravitate to nearby Cardiff.

Undergraduate Fees and Bursaries
- Fees for UK/EU students: £3,225 (grant of up to £1,940 for Welsh students).
- International student fees: £7,750–£8,750
- Bursary of £319 plus £1,000 (limited availability) (household income up to £18,370).
- Bursary of £600 (income up to £30,000) and £300 (household income up to £40,000) (both limited availability).
- Scholarships based on circumstances or by competition.
- For full details see the university's website: www3.newport.ac.uk/ displayPage.aspx?object_id=10496&type=SEC

Students		
Undergraduates:	3,330	(4,265)
Postgraduates:	455	(1,070)
Mature students:	41.0%	
Overseas students:	2.5%	
Applications per place:	3.9	
From state-sector schools:	99.0%	
From working-class homes:	38.2%	

For detailed information about fees, grants and bursaries and how they work, see chapter 7.

Accommodation
Number of places and costs refer to 2009–10
University-provided places: 661
Percentage catered: 0%
Self-catered costs: £59–£79 a week.
First years guaranteed accommodation if requirements met.
International students: same as above.
Contact: accommodation@newport.ac.uk

University of Northampton

Northampton had a university in the thirteenth century, but it took until 2005 to get it back after Henry III dissolved the original version – allegedly because his bishops thought it posed a threat to Oxford. More than 90 places separate the two universities in *The Times* League Table, but Northampton will hope to narrow that gap somewhat in years to come. It has already registered good results in the first four National Student Surveys, finishing in the top half of the table in 2008. Education, psychology, accounting and history had the most satisfied undergraduates.

The modern university has its origins in teacher training, but had developed a wider range of courses, including vocational courses for the leather industry, occupational therapy, nursing and midwifery, by the time university status arrived. All remain in a surprisingly broad portfolio of more than 100 degree and diploma courses. The business school is taking part in a national pilot to develop two-tier degrees and four-year work-based equivalents. Specialisms such as leather technology, fashion and waste management have helped to build up the recruitment of overseas students to some 700 a year from 100 different countries.

The university has two sites: an 80-acre campus on the edge of Northampton, where £73 million has been spent on improvements, and the smaller but more central Avenue campus, which specialises in art and design, media, technology and the performing arts. Both sites have new halls of residence, and the main Park Campus has also seen several new teaching developments, a management centre and a research centre. Another £80 million of investment will be completed in 2010. New arts facilities at Avenue will form the centrepiece of the town's "cultural mile", while an innovative student centre on the Park Campus will provide administrative and support services. Work has started on the conversion of a school next to the Avenue campus, which will house the School of Applied Sciences, as well as a £10-million Technology Realm project featuring the latest 3D visualisation technology and LCD presentation facilities.

Student numbers have been steady for several years, but are expected to rise from the current 11,000 to about 12,000 by 2010. Applications have been rising steadily and were up by another 9 per cent at the start of 2009. Foundation degree students pay £1,125 a year less than the £3,225 fee for honours degrees. Business is the most popular area, but teacher training and health subjects are not far behind. The School of Education was awarded the

Park Campus
Boughton Green Road
Northampton NN2 7AL
0800 358 2232 (courses)
study@northampton.
  ac.uk
www.northampton.ac.uk
www.northampton
union.com

The Times Rankings
Overall Ranking: =92

Student satisfaction:	=54	(75%)
Research quality:	=95	(0.2)
Entry standards:	99	(233)
Student–staff ratio:	100	(20.4)
Services & facilities/student:	97	(£853)
Expected completion rate:	73	(81.3%)
Good honours:	=77	(53.7%)
Graduate prospects:	95	(59.5%)

Training and Development Agency's highest grade for quality, but the university was close to the bottom of the ranking for the 2008 Research Assessment Exercise. There was some world-leading research in four of the ten subject areas, with history producing by far the best results.

Northampton takes its mission to widen participation in higher education seriously: almost all the undergraduates attended state schools or colleges, while more than a third come from working-class homes. The projected dropout rate had improved again in the latest official figures and, at 17 per cent, is now below the national average for the university's courses and entry qualifications. Some of the degrees – such as podiatry and product design – recruit from all over Britain (and farther afield) but in other subjects most of the students are from the region. As a result, the 1,620 residential places are enough to guarantee accommodation for all first years who make Northampton their first choice.

Sports enthusiasts have a Premier League rugby club on their doorstep, as well as a more modest football club and first-class cricket. The university has added a £100,000 gym to its sports facilities, which include a sports hall and outdoor pitches. The town has a number of student-oriented bars, but the two campuses' union bars remain the hub of the social scene. Students receive a free discount card to use in Northampton's high street and independent shops and entertainment and health venues.

Undergraduate Fees and Bursaries
- Fees for UK/EU students: £3,225
- International student fees: £7,950–£8,450
- Bursary on full grant: £1,000
- Bursaries on partial grant: household income up to £30K: £700; household income up to £40K: £500.
- Scholarships based on circumstances or by competition.
- For full details see the university's website: www.northampton.ac.uk/study/fees/

Students		
Undergraduates:	6,885	(2,920)
Postgraduates:	580	(1,200)
Mature students:	46.0%	
Overseas students:	5.6%	
Applications per place:	5.6	
From state-sector schools:	96.9%	
From working-class homes:	35.3%	

For detailed information about fees, grants and bursaries and how they work, see chapter 7.

Accommodation
Number of places and costs refer to 2009–10
University-provided places: 1,620
Percentage catered: 0%
Self-catered costs: £39.00 (small twin) – £86.95 (en-suite single) a week.
First years are guaranteed accommodation provided requirements are met.
International students: guaranteed housing.
Contact:
www.northampton.ac.uk/study/accommodation/

Northumbria University

Northumbria consistently ranks among the leading new universities and a £136-million investment in its city centre campus is producing facilities to match. The first phase was completed in 2007, when 9,000 design, law and business students moved into the new City Campus East development, which is linked to the existing main campus by an iconic new footbridge spanning Newcastle's central motorway. The next phase, which will take until 2010, will turn the main site into the first fully pedestrianised, green campus in a city centre. The library has already been enhanced by a £6-million refurbishment and the new development will include a £20-million sports centre, which is due to open in 2010 and will allow the university to become a pre-Olympics training centre.

There are now over 30,000 UK students and 5,000 more taking franchised courses in other countries, making Northumbria the largest university in the region. About a third of the students are from the northeast of England. Northumbria was one of the few universities to see a significant increase in applications for courses beginning in 2008 and there had been another 12 per cent rise at the start of 2009. The demand for places has been growing for most of the decade.

Entry grades for those with A levels are among the highest in the new universities, but many older students are admitted with other qualifications or on the strength of relevant work experience. Half of the mature students enter through the Higher Education Foundation Certificate, an access course system with modules in more than 30 subjects. Free one-day taster courses run throughout the year to give local people an idea of what studying at Northumbria would be like.

Almost a third of the students come from working-class homes, 15 per cent from areas with little tradition of higher education. The projected dropout rate has been rising but, at almost 18 per cent, is only just above the benchmark for Northumbria's courses and entry grades. Scores have improved in the National Student Survey, taking the university into the top half of that table. Accounting managed 100 per cent satisfaction in the results published in 2008, while psychology, geography and environmental science also did well.

Health subjects have now overtaken business studies in terms of student numbers. Many degrees are available as sandwich courses, with placements of up to a year in business or industry. Education received a glowing report from the Office for Standards in Education, which places it in the top category for primary training and secondary design and technology. The

---

Ellison Terrace
Newcastle upon Tyne NE1 8ST
0191 232 6002 (switchboard)
er.admissions@
    northumbria..ac.uk
www.northumbria.ac.uk
http://mynsu.northumbria
    .ac.uk

The Times Rankings
Overall Ranking: 64

Student satisfaction:	=40	(76%)
Research quality:	=85	(0.3)
Entry standards:	=54	(291)
Student–staff ratio:	=93	(20.0)
Services & facilities/student:	68	(£1,063)
Expected completion rate:	=75	(80.3%)
Good honours:	76	(54.1%)
Graduate prospects:	=36	(73.0%)

university also has a national centre of excellence in assessment, building on Northumbria's attempts to give students more constructive feedback and teaching them how to assess themselves as future professionals. Five of the university's academics have won National Teaching Fellowships.

The majority of subjects will continue to be based in the city centre, with health, education and community studies on the Coach Lane campus on the outskirts of the city, where £18 million has been spent upgrading facilities. Coach Lane now incorporates a learning resources centre with a fully integrated library, a clinical skills centre and new sports facilities, as well as teaching and seminar rooms.

Northumbria's best-known feature is its School of Design, which won the top national award for fashion design in 2006 and produced some of the university's best results in the 2008 Research Assessment Exercise. The university entered a comparatively low proportion of its academics, but more than a third of its submission was considered world-leading or internationally excellent. Architecture and the built environment, general engineering and nursing and midwifery were other high scorers.

Sport plays a growing role: Northumbria is consistently among the top ten in the British Universities and Colleges Sport rankings. The sports scholarship programme has supported over 250 athletes from over 40 sports in the past ten years, some going on to success at the highest level.

All new first years are offered places in university accommodation if they apply "in good time", while others are assisted by the accommodation office. Two large residential developments with en-suite rooms opened in September 2005, bringing the total stock to over 3,500 places, and there is a plentiful supply of privately rented flats and houses.

Undergraduate Fees and Bursaries
- Fees for UK/EU students: £3,225
- International student fees: £8,600–£9,050
- Bursary on full grant: £319
- The university does not award bursaries for students on partial maintenance grants.
- Scholarships based on circumstances or by competition.
- For full details see the university's website: www.northumbria.ac.uk/brochure/studfees/

Students

Undergraduates:	16,760	(6,485)
Postgraduates:	3,045	(3,705)
Mature students:	29.0%	
Overseas students:	11.2%	
Applications per place:	3.5	
From state-sector schools:	91.3%	
From working-class homes:	31.8%	

For detailed information about fees, grants and bursaries and how they work, see chapter 7.

Accommodation

Number of places and costs refer to 2009–10
University-provided places: 3,580
Percentage catered: 8%
Catered costs: £96 or £106 a week.
Self-catered costs: £64–£99 a week.
First years who need accommodation can be offered rooms. Local restrictions apply.
International students: first years are guaranteed accommodation if requirements met.
Contact:
rc.accommodation@northumbria.ac.uk

University of Nottingham

Nottingham is the nearest Britain has to a truly global university, with campuses in China and Malaysia modelled on a headquarters that is among the most attractive in Britain. For many years it has been among the institutions with the stiffest competition for each place, and a striking new campus and extra courses made the university even more fashionable. Growth in applications has resumed after a two-year blip fuelled by media coverage of gun crime early in the decade. The demand for places was up by almost 8 per cent at the start of 2009.

The university enjoyed a spectacular rise up the pecking order of higher education. In less than 20 years, it went from being a solid civic university to a prime alternative to Oxbridge. Currently in the top 90 in the world rankings published by *Times Higher Education*/QS, it seldom stands still.

Nottingham describes itself as "research-led", with work carried out at the university winning two Nobel prizes in 2003. Professor Sir Peter Mansfield, who won the medicine prize for research leading to the development of the MRI scanner, has spent almost all his academic career there. The university's record-breaking research contracts place it among the top four universities for private funding.

About £70 million was spent on a research recruitment initiative in advance of the 2008 Research Assessment Exercise, with 20 new research chairs and the equipment and support posts to accompany them. The investment paid off handsomely with sharply improved results in the RAE, which will bring long-term increases in funding. Almost 60 per cent of a big submission was judged to be world-leading or internationally excellent, with pharmacy and Spanish, Portuguese and Latin American studies producing the best results in the UK and chemistry and physics the second-best.

Physical expansion allowed the university to take almost 1,000 more students in recent years, but new undergraduates' average A-level grades have not dropped. Once in, they tend to stay the course – the dropout rate of 3 per cent is consistently among the best in the country. But the university is trying to broaden an intake which has more independent school students and fewer from working-class homes than the national average for the subjects offered. There is a well-established summer school for state-school teenagers and a bursary scheme, which pre-dated top-up fees, for Nottinghamshire students with no family history of higher education. Consistently good National Student Survey results show chemists, civil engineers and music students the most satisfied.

University Park
Nottingham NG7 2RD
0115 951 5559 (enquiries)
undergraduate-enquiries@
    nottingham.ac.uk
www.nottingham.ac.uk
www.su.nottingham.ac.uk

The Times Rankings
Overall Ranking: 20

Student satisfaction:	=40	(76%)
Research quality:	=19	(2.1)
Entry standards:	16	(408)
Student–staff ratio:	=18	(13.7)
Services & facilities/student:	27	(£1,402)
Expected completion rate:	=8	(95.7%)
Good honours:	17	(74.3%)
Graduate prospects:	24	(76.3%)

The 30-acre Jubilee campus, which cost £50 million and includes 750 residential places, is barely a mile away from the original parkland site. Futuristic buildings clustered around an artificial lake house the schools of management and finance, computer science and education. An additional building for the fast-growing business school was added in 2004 and a new sports hall opened the following year. The campus is undergoing further £200-million expansion to accommodate an innovation park and has acquired a landmark sculpture towering 60 metres over its buildings.

The adjoining medical school is also close to University Park, although its recently established graduate-entry outpost is in Derby. The biosciences and the new veterinary school are at Sutton Bonington, ten miles south of the city. Recent developments include a £7-million biomedical sciences building on the main campus.

Nottingham has long-standing links with the Far East, which provides the majority of its 7,000 overseas students, and has a Chinese physicist, Professor Fujia Yang, as its Chancellor. The university has had a branch in Malaysia since 2000 and launched a new venture in Ningbo, China, in 2004. Purpose-built campuses with echoes of the Nottingham's distinctive clock tower opened in Ningbo and near Kuala Lumpur in September 2005. Students have the opportunity to move between the three countries.

Both main campuses are within three miles of the centre of Nottingham, with a good selection of student-friendly clubs. However, halls of residence and the students' union tend to be the centre of social life for students in both locations. New bars, café facilities and a nightclub were included in a £1-million makeover of student facilities in 2007. Sports facilities are excellent and expanding.

Undergraduate Fees and Bursaries

- Fees for UK/EU students: £3,225
- International student fees: £10,610–£13,910
  £18,980 (veterinary medicine)
  £14,660–£25,480 (medicine)
- Bursary on full grant: £1,080
- Bursaries on partial grant: household income up to £34.5K: £1,080; household income up to £44.5K: sliding scale £810–£270.
- Scholarships based on circumstances or by competition.
- For full details see the university's website: www.nottingham.ac.uk/prospectuses/undergrad/introduction/finance/

Students		
Undergraduates:	20,965	(2,905)
Postgraduates:	5,950	(2,010)
Mature students:	15.4%	
Overseas students:	14.5%	
Applications per place:	5.4	
From state-sector schools:	69.4%	
From working-class homes:	17.4%	

For detailed information about fees, grants and bursaries and how they work, see chapter 7.

Accommodation

Number of places and costs refer to 2009–10
University-provided places: 7,400
Percentage catered: 58%
Catered costs: £106.95–£172.99 a week.
Self-catered costs: £80.00–£101.50 a week (43–44 weeks).
First years are guaranteed housing if conditions are met.
International undergraduates: as above
Contact: www.nottingham.ac.uk/accommodation

Nottingham Trent University

Consistently among the leading new universities in *The Times* League Table, as well as one of the biggest, Nottingham Trent has demonstrated high quality in an unusually wide range of disciplines. Best known for fashion and other creative arts, which have the largest number of students, it also boasts one of the UK's biggest law schools, offering legal practice courses for both solicitors and barristers as well as degrees. A four-year "exempting law degree", launched in 2009, combines both phases with an extended work placement, enabling students to qualify as solicitors without paying postgraduate fees.

Nottingham Trent has among the highest entry grades of any new university and one of the best employment records. It helps that the university has the third highest number of year-long placements in the UK through its working partnerships with more than 6,000 businesses and private sector organisations. More than a third of the undergraduates come from working-class homes and over nine out of ten attended state schools or colleges, while the projected dropout rate of 11 per cent is below the national average for the university's courses and entry grades.

An ambitious research programme attracted a £7.65 million donation – thought to be the largest to a post-1992 university – to advance the university's work in cancer diagnosis and therapy. The university held its own in the 2008 Research Assessment Exercise, although it entered fewer academics than some of the other leading new universities. More than a third of its submission was rated world-leading or internationally excellent, with communication, culture and media studies, social policy, engineering and biomedical sciences producing the best results.

Scores have improved in the National Student Survey, leaving Nottingham Trent in the top half of the table. Chemistry, economics and education produced the best results. The university registered one of the biggest rises in applications at any institution in 2008 and did even better at the start of 2009, with a 13 per cent increase.

There are now nearly 24,000 students, including 5,000 part-timers. The extensive main city site boasts a mixture of Victorian and modern buildings. The schools of science and technology, education, and arts and humanities are five miles away on the Clifton campus.

The Brackenhurst campus, devoted to animal, rural and environmental studies, is 14 miles out of Nottingham and includes an equestrian centre with a purpose-built indoor riding area, a well-equipped veterinary nursing building and animal

---

Burton Street
Nottingham NG1 4BU
0115 848 2814 (admissions)
admissions@ntu.ac.uk
www.ntu.ac.uk
www.trentstudents.org

The Times Rankings
Overall Ranking: 57

Student satisfaction:	=67	(74%)
Research quality:	=71	(0.4)
Entry standards:	65	(276)
Student–staff ratio:	=56	(17.1)
Services & facilities/student:	53	(£1,144)
Expected completion rate:	43	(86.2%)
Good honours:	69	(55.7%)
Graduate prospects:	32	(74.1%)

unit. Another 300 residential places were added there in 2006, following a £3-million renewal of the teaching facilities. A new £1.5-million unit houses state-of-the-art equipment and facilities and will be used to provide veterinary nursing courses

Art and design facilities on the city campus have been upgraded and both the Boots Library and the students' union refurbished. Computing and informatics have a new building on the Clifton campus and the university has launched a bus service linking Clifton and the city. A total of £130 million has been earmarked for building projects over the next six years starting with a £70-million regeneration of the Newton and Arkwright buildings to produce a first-class working environment and student support facilities by the autumn of 2009.

The university was responsible for the largest programme of Foundation degrees when the two-year qualification was launched. Subjects ranging from forensic science to wildlife conservation saw another increase in applications early in 2009.

The student body is diverse, with large numbers of mature and overseas students. The university's residential stock has been increasing, with a £10-million development with 446 beds opening on the City campus in 2004. It still is not sufficient to house all first years, but new students are guaranteed "university-allocated" accommodation, which may be in the private sector, if they make Nottingham Trent their first choice and book by the end of July. Social life varies between campuses, but all have access to the city's lively cultural and clubbing scene. A late-night bus service links the main campuses and the city's new tram system serves the university.

Undergraduate Fees and Bursaries

- Fees for UK/EU students £3,225
- International student fees £8,450–£9,600
- Bursary on full grant: £1,075
- Bursaries on partial grant: household income up to £40K: sliding scale £665–£360.
- Scholarships based on circumstances or by competition.
- For full details see the university's website: www.ntu.ac.uk/prospective_students/ index.html

Students		
Undergraduates:	15,945	(2,805)
Postgraduates:	2,480	(2,275)
Mature students:	16.9%	
Overseas students:	6.1%	
Applications per place:	4.1	
From state-sector schools:	92.7%	
From working-class homes:	35.7%	

For detailed information about fees, grants and bursaries and how they work, see chapter 7.

Accommodation

Number of places and costs refer to 2009–10
University-provided places: 3,800
Percentage catered: 0%
Self-catered costs: £67–111 (42–48 weeks).
First years and new students are guaranteed accommodation if conditions are met.
International students: guaranteed accommodation if conditions are met.
Contact: www.ntu.ac.uk/accommodation
accommodation@ntu.ac.uk
0115 848 2894

University of Oxford

Oxford has topped *The Times* League Table since 2002, when it wrested first place from Cambridge. The oldest and probably the most famous university in the English-speaking world, Oxford remains almost inseparable from Cambridge in terms of overall quality. Both are among the top four universities in the world, according to global rankings published by *Times Higher Education* and QS, and are head and shoulders above the other non-specialist universities in the view of most experts and in *The Times* table. Higher spending on student facilities, marginally better staffing levels and more top degrees keep the university ahead of its ancient rival this year.

Applications were up by 12 per cent at the beginning of 2009, having dipped slightly in the previous year. There are fewer than five applicants to the place – a much more favourable ratio than at some of the top universities – but nearly all are predicted at least three As at A level, or their equivalent. Gradually, there may be more research students and marginally fewer UK undergraduates, making the competition for places still more intense.

The university is still struggling to broaden its intake and shake off allegations of social elitism. The long-term growth in demand for places (which is concentrated in the more job-oriented subjects) is due, at least partly, to more systematic attempts to get the message through to teenagers that Oxford is open to all who can meet the exacting entrance requirements. Student visits to comprehensive schools have been supplemented by summer schools, recruitment fairs and colleges' own initiatives, as well as tireless public statements of intent by the university.

For all the university's efforts to shed its "Brideshead Revisited" stereotype, however, official figures still show 47 per cent of Oxford's students coming from independent schools – the largest proportion at any university. Fewer than one student in ten comes from a working-class home, despite the introduction of bursaries worth £3,225 in 2009–10 for all undergraduates who are eligible for full fee remission. Still higher bursaries introduced in 2006 are yet to broaden the mix further. A projected dropout rate of little more than 2 per cent is the second-lowest in the UK.

Applications must be made by mid-October – a month earlier if you wish to be interviewed overseas. There are written tests for some subjects and you may be asked to submit samples of work. Selection is in the hands of the 30 undergraduate colleges, which vary considerably in their approach to this

---

University Offices
Wellington Square
Oxford OX1 2JD
01865 270000 (main
   switchboard)
undergraduate.admissions
   @admin.ox.ac.uk
www.ox.ac.uk
www.ousu.org

Edinburgh
Belfast
Cardiff
OXFORD
London

The Times Rankings
Overall Ranking: 1

Student satisfaction:	=2	(85%)
Research quality:	2	(3.5)
Entry standards:	2	(524)
Student–staff ratio:	=3	(10.8)
Services & facilities/student:	2	(£3,396)
Expected completion rate:	2	(97.7%)
Good honours:	1	(91.1%)
Graduate prospects:	7	(82.3%)

issue and others. Sound advice on academic strengths and social factors is essential for applicants to give themselves the best chance of winning a place and finding a setting in which they can thrive. Only a minority of candidates opt to go straight into the admissions pool without expressing a preference for a particular college. The choice is particularly important for arts and social science students, whose world-famous individual or small group tuition is based in college. Science and technology, which have benefited from Oxford's phenomenally successful fundraising efforts, are taught mainly in central facilities. All subjects operate on eight-week terms and assess students entirely on final examinations – a system some find too pressurised.

The development of a major new campus on the site of the Radcliffe Infirmary is likely to be the first fruit of a £1-billion fundraising campaign. Recent developments include a £60-million building to house the western world's largest chemistry department, as well as new premises for economics. A £21-million social sciences library followed, while animal research facilities drew bitter (often illegal) protests from animal rights campaigners.

There was never much doubt about the strength of Oxford's research, but the 2008 Research Assessment Exercise found more than 70 per cent of it to be world-leading or internationally excellent. Oxford entered more academics for assessment than any other university – twice as many as some research-based universities of similar size. There were good results in all areas, but the university was pre-eminent in several medical specialisms, statistics, development studies, education and French. Oxford also attracts the largest amount of research income, at more than £200 million.

Undergraduate Fees and Bursaries

- Fees for UK/EU students: £3,225*
- International student fees: £11,750–£13,450†
  £24,500 (medicine)†
- Bursary on full grant: £3,225
- Bursaries on partial grant: household income up to £50K: sliding scale £3,225–£200.
- Scholarships based on circumstances or by competition.
- For full details see the university's website: www.oxfordopportunity.com

* UK & EU students eligible for tuition fee support not liable for College fees
† Plus College fees (£5,212)

Students		
Undergraduates:	11,450	(4,610)
Postgraduates:	6,905	(1,015)
Mature students:	4.1%	
Overseas students:	12.8%	
Applications per place:	4.4	
From state-sector schools:	53.0%	
From working-class homes:	9.8%	

For detailed information about fees, grants and bursaries and how they work, see chapter 7.

Accommodation

See chapter 10 for information about individual colleges.

Oxford Brookes University

Now firmly established as England's leading new university in *The Times* League Table, Oxford Brookes receives almost six applications to the place – a level of competition not unlike that at some Russell Group universities. The demand for places has been steady, although there was only a small increase at the start of 2009 when most universities experienced substantial growth.

Brookes is particularly popular with independent schools, which provide more than a quarter of the undergraduates – by far the highest proportion among the new universities and twice the national average for the university's subjects and entry grades. However, the proportion from working-class homes, at more than 40 per cent, is also considerably ahead of the official benchmark. The university has been trying to attract more students from state schools and has targeted areas in Oxfordshire.

The university's location has always been an advantage in student recruitment, but the quality of provision is the real draw. Its departments feature near the top of *The Times* rankings for several subjects. Ofsted rated primary teacher training outstanding and the university has been in the top 30 in the National Student Survey for the last three years. Education demonstrated 100 per cent satisfaction in 2008, while geography and environmental science also produced good results.

The university houses national centres for hospitality, leisure and tourism, and the teaching of business and undergraduate research, as well as one for teacher training in partnership with Westminster University. The Architect's Journal rated the Department of Architecture the best outside London. Oxford Brookes, which has a consistently excellent record for graduate employment, is also partnering Warwick University in the Government's academy for gifted and talented schoolchildren.

Grades in the 2008 Research Assessment Exercise showed improvement, with more than a third of the work judged to be world-leading or internationally excellent. History, which made headlines in 2001 with a higher grade than its world-renowned neighbour, again produced the best results, but there were good performances, too, in history of art and computer science.

Brookes made a leap in size in 2000, taking in Westminster College, a merger which added 2,000 students, mainly in teacher training and the humanities, and forming a £2.5-million Institute of Education. As a polytechnic, Oxford pioneered the modular degree system that has swept British higher education. After

---

Headington Campus
Gypsy Lane
Oxford OX3 0BP
01865 484848 (enquiries)
query@brookes.ac.uk
www.brookes.ac.uk
www.thesu.com

The Times Rankings
Overall Ranking: 52

Student satisfaction:	=28	(77%)
Research quality:	=60	(0.6)
Entry standards:	53	(301)
Student–staff ratio:	=72	(18.4)
Services & facilities/student:	77	(£997)
Expected completion rate:	=58	(83.9%)
Good honours:	39	(66.1%)
Graduate prospects:	=36	(73.0%)

more than 20 years' experience, the scheme has now trimmed the 2,000 modules it once offered, but undergraduates can pair subjects as diverse as history and biology, or catering management and environmental management. Each subject has compulsory modules in the first year and a list of others that are acceptable later in the course. Students are encouraged to take some subjects outside their main area of study, and there is a range of possible exit points.

There are four main sites, two of which are only a mile from the city centre and linked to each other by a footbridge. Some £150 million has been earmarked for improvements to the Headington, Wheatley and Harcourt Hill campuses over the next few years. Buildings on the original Gipsy Lane site, at Headington, dating from the 1950s and '60s will be replaced with flexible, functional buildings benefiting from the latest technology. A public consultation showed strong support for a contemporary architectural style and more green spaces for the new development. Students starting in 2009 will benefit from the first stages of the project. Maths and engineering have now joined computing and business five miles away at Wheatley. The new engineering building will support the university's status as a Government-designated regional centre for motorsport and high

performance engineering. The Harcourt Hill campus at Botley focuses on teacher education, human development and learning.

A swimming pool and 18-hole golf course have been added to the already impressive sports facilities. Representative teams have a good record, with the rowers particularly successful and the cricketers now combining with Oxford University to take on county teams. The students' union runs the biggest entertainment venue in Oxford, a city that can be expensive, but which offers enough to satisfy most students. The university has 3,500 residential places, all with internet access – enough for all first-year undergraduates.

Undergraduate Fees and Bursaries

- Fees for UK/EU students: £3,225
- International student fees: £9,780–£11,284
- Bursary on full grant: household income up to £5K: £1,800; £5K–£21K: £1,560; £21K–£25K: £1,050.
- Bursaries on partial grant: household income up to £36K: sliding scale £1,050–£150.
- Scholarships based on circumstances or by competition.
- For full details see the university's website: www.brookes.ac.uk/studying/finance

---

Students

Undergraduates:	11,310	(2,785)
Postgraduates:	1,460	(2,480)
Mature students:	33.6%	
Overseas students:	14.0%	
Applications per place:	5.7	
From state-sector schools:	74.0%	
From working-class homes:	41.7%	

For detailed information about fees, grants and bursaries and how they work, see chapter 7.

Accommodation

Number of places and costs refer to 2009–10
University-provided places: 3,500 approx
Percentage catered: 23%
Catered costs: £4,490–£5,218
Self-catered costs: £3,344–£4,902 (for 38 week contract)
All accommodation is allocated to first years by distance from Oxford Brookes.
International students: as above.
Contact: accomm@brookes.ac.uk

University of Plymouth

Now one of the UK's largest universities with nearly 30,000 students, Plymouth has been carrying out major restructuring to concentrate activities in its home city. The original aim was to break into the research elite while still serving the region through teaching, but the new Vice-Chancellor, Professor Wendy Purcell, who graduated from the university in the 1980s, has declared a new mission to make Plymouth the top "enterprise university".

Nevertheless, Plymouth entered by far the largest number of academics of any new university in the 2008 Research Assessment – twice the proportion entered by some of its peer group. More than a third of the submission was rated world-leading or internationally excellent. Computer science produced by far the best results, but civil engineering, geography and environmental science and art and design also did well.

The most controversial element of the restructuring involved the transfer to Plymouth of courses from the Seale-Hayne agricultural campus, near Newton Abbot. The arts and humanities programme has also moved from Exeter and education courses from Exmouth. Plymouth has also seen the opening of a £30-million headquarters and a second teaching building for the Peninsula College of Medicine and Dentistry, a joint enterprise with Exeter University (www.pms.ac.uk).

The library on the main North Hill campus has been extended and upgraded and the students' union refurbished. A £35-million arts complex opened in 2007, housing the Faculty of Arts and the Plymouth Arts Centre. Teaching facilities and residential accommodation for the education courses transferring from Exmouth cost another £40 million, while a £11-million building for the Faculty of Health and Social Work, overlooking the Drake Reservoir, includes sports facilities as well teaching space.

Plymouth opened a £1-million Immersive Vision Theatre, thought to be the first of its kind at a UK university, in 2008. The IVT is used for a variety of subjects in the sciences, arts and medicine, with projection onto the dome giving the audience a strong feeling of being "in", rather than just observing, different types of image. The next development will see the launch in 2009 of the new School of Marine Science and Engineering, building on Plymouth's worldwide reputation in this field. With 1,400 students and 85 staff, the school will be the largest of its kind in Europe.

The Peninsula quickly established itself and was the only successful bidder for a new dental school in the last national competition. The school, which will train

Drake Circus
Plymouth
Devon PL4 8AA
01752 588036 (admissions)
admissions@
plymouth.ac.uk
www.plymouth.ac.uk
www.upsu.com

Edinburgh
Belfast
London
Cardiff
PLYMOUTH

64 dentists a year, opened in 2007. With campuses in Plymouth, Exeter, Truro and Taunton, along with teaching facilities in Bristol, the university's Faculty of Health and Social Work is the largest provider of nurse, midwifery and health professional education and training in the southwest.

The university is a partner in the Combined Universities in Cornwall, which is boosting further and higher education in one of the few counties without its own university. Plymouth has also established a unique relationship with its 16 partner colleges, which spread from Cornwall to Somerset, through a faculty devoted entirely to serving their 5,300 students taking university courses. They have become the University of Plymouth Colleges, sharing £2 million in capital investment.

The intake reflects Plymouth's position as the working-class hub of the southwest, with 95 per cent of students state-educated and a third from the poorest social classes. The projected dropout rate of 14 per cent is below the national average for the courses and entry grades. Plymouth was chosen to house no fewer than four national teaching centres – in health and social care placements, experiential learning in environmental and natural sciences, institutional partnerships and education for sustainable development – as well as a the national subject centre for geography, earth and environmental sciences and the Royal Statistical Society Centre for Statistical Education. No university has exceeded the 11 National Teaching Fellowships won by its academics. It is also taking part in a national pilot of two-year degrees.

The university offers a lively social scene, with excellent and recently upgraded facilities for water sports as well as a thriving nightlife. An £850,000 fitness centre has improved the sports facilities, while a range of sports scholarships and bursaries will help support high-fliers. A £15-million scheme has also seen the construction of a 1,300-bed student village.

Undergraduate Fees and Bursaries

- Fees for UK/EU students: £3,225
- International student fees £8,750
  £20,500 (medicine)*
- Bursary on full grant: £1,010
- Bursaries on partial grant: household income £25K–£40K: £300.
- Scholarships based on circumstances or by competition.
- For full details see the university's website: www.plymouth.ac.uk/ugfees

* Figures for 2008–09

Students		
Undergraduates:	17,750	(7,965)
Postgraduates:	1,060	(2,600)
Mature students:	40.4%	
Overseas students:	5.0%	
Applications per place:	3.9	
From state-sector schools:	94.6%	
From working-class homes:	33.2%	

For detailed information about fees, grants and bursaries and how they work, see chapter 7.

Accommodation

Number of places and costs refer to 2009–10

University-provided places: 2,100

Percentage catered: 0%

Self-catered costs: £80–£125 a week.

First years are not guaranteed university provided accommodation.

International students: overseas students have priority for allocation.

Contact: accommodation@plymouth.ac.uk

University of Portsmouth

Portsmouth registered an extraordinary 25 per cent increase in applications at the start of 2009, attracting almost double the numbers received at the beginning of the decade. It has always been among the leaders of its generation of universities, but a wider portfolio of courses, a modernised campus and new facilities in the city are proving a powerful draw.

Strength in teaching has been recognised with the award of two national centres of excellence and 40 per cent of the work submitted for the 2008 Research Assessment Exercise was considered world-leading or internationally excellent. Applied mathematics and European studies achieved particularly good results, while biomedical and biomolecular sciences also did well. Portsmouth also has the best record of any of the new universities in the National Student Survey. The results published in 2008 showed satisfaction levels of more than 95 per cent in politics, history, geography, mathematics and statistics and management.

Graduate employment is healthy, especially for a university where a high proportion of the students take arts subjects. Languages are Portsmouth's traditional strength – one student in five takes a language course at some level – and the facilities rival those of many traditional universities. About 1,000 Portsmouth students go abroad for part of their course, and at least as many come from the Continent.

However, it is in health subjects that the university's reputation has been growing most obviously. The School of Professionals Complementary to Dentistry is one of the first new dental education facilities in England for 50 years. There is also a Centre for Molecular Design and the UK's first dedicated brain tumour research centre. The £9-million Dental Outreach Centre, operated in partnership with King's College London, will open in 2010.

The main city-centre Guildhall campus has undergone extensive redevelopment. The £11-million library complex, integrated into its 1970s predecessor, was commended in the 2008 Civic Trust awards. Earlier developments included the aluminium-clad St Michael's Building and the eco-friendly Portland Building, with its solar panels. The business school has moved into a new £12-million building on the main campus. Other recent additions include a sports science building that houses laboratories, a swimming flume and two British Olympic Medical Centre accredited climatic chambers. A new £9-million building for the internationally recognised Institute of Cosmology and Gravitation opened in 2009.

Teaching in all subjects is concentrated

University House
Winston Churchill Avenue
Portsmouth
Hampshire PO1 2UP
023 9284 8484
info.centre@port.ac.uk
www.port.ac.uk
www.upsu.net

The Times Rankings
Overall Ranking: 56

Student satisfaction:	=14	(79%)
Research quality:	=63	(0.5)
Entry standards:	67	(271)
Student–staff ratio:	=75	(18.7)
Services & facilities/student:	50	(£1,158)
Expected completion rate:	44	(86.1%)
Good honours:	=85	(52.4%)
Graduate prospects:	78	(63.9%)

on the Guildhall campus, while much of the residential stock is a couple of miles away at Langstone. A £6.5-million student centre caters for the multicultural population of the university with alcohol-free areas, an international students' bar and a family area for students with children. Modernised sport, exercise and fitness facilities include resistance and cardiovascular training gyms, dance studios and a sports hall.

Almost a third of the undergraduates come from working-class homes, although this is still slightly below the national average for the subjects and entry qualifications. Efforts are being made to broaden the intake further through an award-winning membership club that introduces teenagers to higher education through workshops, holiday courses and access to university facilities. The projected dropout rate has improved considerably and, at 13 per cent is now better than the university's benchmark.

Portsmouth has a larger working-class population and more deprivation than some applicants may realise. But the new 170-metre Spinnaker Tower is already a landmark and the city has a vibrant student pub and club scene to supplement a popular students' union. The cost of living is not as high as at many southern universities, and the sea is close at hand. Hall places are offered to 90 per cent of first years and the university runs "secure a home" days at the beginning of September to help the remaining new arrivals with house-hunting. The university is launching a new combined broadband, phone and TV service for students living in private accommodation, mirroring a similar offer for those in halls. Parents will be able to download software allowing them to call students at no cost, using a PC.

Undergraduate Fees and Bursaries
- Fees for UK/EU students: £3,225
- International student fees: £8,750–£10,150
- Bursary on full grant: £900
- Bursaries on partial grant: household income up to £32K: £600.
- Scholarships based on circumstances or by competition.
- For full details see the university's website: www.port.ac.uk/money

Students,		
Undergraduates:	13,330	(2,650)
Postgraduates:	1,270	(2,305)
Mature students:	16.2%	
Overseas students:	9.3%	
Applications per place:	4.0	
From state-sector schools:	94.8%	
From working-class homes:	31.1%	

For detailed information about fees, grants and bursaries and how they work, see chapter 7.

Accommodation
Number of places and costs refer to 2009–10
University-provided places: 2,944
Percentage catered: 25%
Catered costs: £85–£113 a week (36 weeks).
Self-catered costs: £72–£115 a week (36 weeks).
Majority of first years offered university accommodation.
International students: guaranteed university accommodation subject to terms and conditions.
Contact: Student.housing@port.ac.uk

Queen Margaret University

Scotland's first new university of the 21st century got a new campus to match, when Queen Margaret University moved into gleaming new premises in Musselburgh, to the southeast of Edinburgh, in September 2007. The "campus in the park", as it has been dubbed, was designed in consultation with students, and is only six minutes by train from the city centre. Drama courses remain at Edinburgh's Gateway Theatre to ensure that the university retains a foothold in the city centre.

The university is also opening the first UK university campus in Singapore, a joint venture with the East Asia Institute of Management, which has taught Queen Margaret degrees for several years. But all has not been plain sailing for Queen Margaret, which has been struggling with a £20-million deficit and the subject of (hotly denied) merger speculation.

Applications were down by more than 18 per cent at the start of 2009, mainly because of a reorganisation of "conservatoire" drama courses in Scotland, and only one university had a lower average score in the 2008 Research Assessment Exercise.

Named after Saint Margaret, the 11th-century Queen of Scotland, the institution dates back to 1875 and was originally a school of cookery for women. The college had been awarding its own degrees since 1992, but was too small to qualify for university status until 2007. Having achieved that ambition, the university made an auspicious debut in *The Times* League Table and has been outscoring many of the former polytechnics.

Queen Margaret is the smallest university in Scotland and it says that it is likely to remain so. The strategic plan promises that the new university will be "smart, innovative and very clearly focused" to compensate for the limitations of size. Three quarters of the students are female, seven out of ten of them from north of the border. Over 3,000 students are in the health sciences faculty, with social sciences and media, followed in terms of size by business and enterprise, the other main areas. The four drama degrees have been consolidated into one interdisciplinary programme, under the title of Drama and Performance.

Health is an area of particular strength: Queen Margaret offers courses in an unusually broad range of subjects, from dietetics, podiatry and audiology, to art therapy, music therapy and health psychology. There is also a specialism in international health care, with students in Angola, Guatemala, Uganda, Ethiopia, Gambia, India and Cuba. Other international programmes run in Egypt,

---

Queen Margaret University Drive
Musselburgh EH21 6UU
0131 474 0000
admissions@qmu.ac.uk
www.qmu.ac.uk
www.qmusu.org.uk

EDINBURGH
Belfast
London
Cardiff

The Times Rankings
Overall Ranking: 61

Student satisfaction:	–	(–)
Research quality:	=71	(0.4)
Entry standards:	=42	(328)
Student–staff ratio:	=93	(20.0)
Services & facilities/student:	92	(£885)
Expected completion rate:	=83	(78.5%)
Good honours:	42	(65.3%)
Graduate prospects:	54	(69.2%)

Saudi Arabia, Greece and Switzerland, as well as on the new Singapore campus.

The projected dropout rate of over 19 per cent has improved slightly since the last survey, but is still higher than average for the university's courses and entry qualifications. Three undergraduates in ten come from working-class homes and a similar proportion are over the age of 21 on entry.

An impressive learning resource centre, parts of which are open 24 hours a day, offers a variety of study spaces. Specialist laboratories and clinics are well equipped. The nursing simulation lab, for example, is set out exactly like a hospital ward and there are specially equipped rooms for podiatry, radiography, occupational therapy, physiotherapy and art therapy.

There are 800 residential places on the new campus, 500 of them reserved for undergraduates. Other features include a students union building, indoor and outdoor sports facilities, a variety of catering outlets and landscaped gardens with a range of environmental features. Queen Margaret claims that the campus is the "greenest" in Scotland – a high priority among the students. The campus has already won an award for sustainable design and has one of the lowest carbon footprints of any UK higher education establishment.

Undergraduate Fees and Bursaries

- Scottish-domiciled and EU students: no fees payable.
- Non-Scottish UK-domiciled student fees: £1,820 a year.
- International student fees: £8,800–£9,700
- Scholarships based on circumstances or by competition.
- For full details see the university's website: www.qmu.ac.uk/prospective_students/funding.htm

Students

Undergraduates:	2,935	(1,185)
Postgraduates:	385	(825)
Mature students:	32.6%	
Overseas students:	9.6%	
Applications per place:	5.7	
From state-sector schools:	94.7%	
From working-class homes:	30.1%	

For detailed information about fees, grants and bursaries and how they work, see chapter 7.

Accommodation

Number of places and costs refer to 2009–10
University-provided places: 800
Percentage catered: 0%
Self-catered costs: £3,770 (40 weeks) to £4,712.50 (50 weeks).
First years are guaranteed accommodation.
Residential and age restrictions apply.
International students: guaranteed housing.
Contact: accommodation@qmu.ac.uk
www.qmu.ac.uk/services/student_accommodation.htm

Queen Mary, University of London

More than £150 million has been spent developing London University's East End base into a broadly based institution of 14,000 students and strengthening the academic staff. Some of the investment paid off in spectacularly improved grades in the 2008 Research Assessment Exercise, when almost two thirds of the work submitted was rated world-leading or internationally excellent. Linguistics, geography and drama produced the best results in their fields, with dentistry, English and several medical specialisms in the top five, propelling Queen Mary into the top 25 UK universities for research in our Table.

Queen Mary is ranked among the top 200 universities in the world by *Times Higher Education*/QS, and has the capital's most extensive self-contained campus. It includes a state-of-the-art learning resource centre with 24-hour access and an award-winning student village with 2,000 en-suite rooms. An arts quarter, containing research facilities, a conference centre, drama studio and teaching space, was completed in 2006. A £15-million humanities building is due to open in early 2010 and a biosciences innovation centre is also under construction, next door to the

£44-million Blizard Building – the striking new home of Barts and The London School of Medicine and Dentistry, in Whitechapel.

The modern setting is a far cry from the People's Palace, which first used the site to bring education to the Victorian masses, but there is still a community programme as well as conventional teaching and research. The arts-based Westfield College and scientific Queen Mary came together in 1989, but it took time to mould the new institution and overcome financial difficulties. The sale of Westfield's Hampstead base released the necessary capital to begin to modernise the Mile End Road campus.

Already London University's fourth largest unit, Queen Mary is expected to carry on growing. It is one of London's designated points of expansion in the sciences, although its strength is more obvious on the arts side, which boasts a clutch of high-profile academics. The college is leading a national initiative to boost the number of maths graduates.

Applications have risen at the rate of 7 per cent a year for most of the decade and had done so again at the start of 2009. There has been further success in attracting overseas students, who make full use of a unit specialising in English as a foreign language and now fill about one place in six. A strategic alliance with City University covers teaching and research initiatives in

---

Mile End Road
London E1 4NS
0800 376 1800 (prospectus)
admissions@qmul.ac.uk
www.qmul.ac.uk
www.qmsu.org

The Times Rankings
Overall Ranking: 36

Student satisfaction:	=40	(76%)
Research quality:	=24	(2.0)
Entry standards:	40	(346)
Student–staff ratio:	11	(13.0)
Services & facilities/student:	49	(£1,161)
Expected completion rate:	34	(88.5%)
Good honours:	48	(64.2%)
Graduate prospects:	21	(77.3%)

areas such as engineering, health and history.

Results have been consistently good in the National Student Survey, with English, drama, languages and law producing the most satisfied students in 2008. Engineering and materials were also in the national top ten for their subjects in terms of overall satisfaction. The majority of under-graduates take at least one course in departments other than their own, under the modular course system. Most degrees are organised in units to allow maximum flexibility. Interdisciplinary study has always been encouraged: for example, medics can choose selected modules in English and drama. The medical school is to house a national teaching centre for clinical and communications skills. There is a flourishing exchange programme, which includes universities in the United States and Japan, as well as Europe. Each student has an adviser to guide them through the possibilities. Language students can use the University of London Institute, in Paris, while students at Beijing's University of Posts and Telecommunications can take double degrees (awarded by their own institution and Queen Mary) without leaving China.

Queen Mary attracts a socially diverse intake: almost a third of the under-graduates come from the two lowest socio-economic classes, many of them from local ethnic groups. Social life centres on the campus, which features a refurbished students' union with a subsidised health and fitness centre and a new bar, and the West End is easily accessible by tube. Students welcome the relatively low prices (for the capital) in East London, which has more to offer than many expect when they apply.

Undergraduate Fees and Bursaries

- Fees for UK/EU students: £3,225
- International student fees: £9,500–£11,500 £15,350–£24,350 (medicine)
- Bursary on full grant: £1,078
- Bursaries on partial grant: household income up to £34.6K: £861.
- Scholarships based on circumstances or by competition.
- For full details see the university's website: www.qmul.ac.uk/undergraduate/feesfinance

---

Students

Undergraduates:	10,250	(65)
Postgraduates:	2,205	(1,090)
Mature students:	15.7%	
Overseas students:	15.7%	
Applications per place:	6.0	
From state-sector schools:	86.0%	
From working-class homes:	32.5%	

For detailed information about fees, grants and bursaries and how they work, see chapter 7.

Accommodation

Number of places and costs refer to 2008–09
University-provided places: 2,504
Percentage catered: 8.9%
Catered costs: £130 upwards a week.
Self-catered costs: £85.40–£115.64 a week.
First years giving Queen Mary as first choice get priority, if terms and conditions are met. Residential restrictions apply.
International students given priority if conditions are met and includes distance.
Contact: residences@qmul.ac.uk

Queen's University, Belfast

Generally regarded as Northern Ireland's premier university, Queen's became a member of the Russell Group of leading UK research institutions in 2006. The university is investing £259 million in new staff and improved facilities to improve its research performance, raise entry standards and regain the international standing it enjoyed before the Troubles. The 2008 Research Assessment Exercise showed some progress, with more than half of the university's submission rated as world-leading or internationally excellent and Queen's ranked in the UK's top ten in 11 subject areas. Music, English and anthropology produced the highest grades.

Almost £190 million is being spent on capital projects, the centrepiece of which will be a £45-million new library, said to be one of the most ambitious building projects in Northern Ireland, which is due for completion in 2009. The university's vision for the future also includes improvements in student facilities: a student village, also costing £45 million, has replaced the existing tower block residences with three-storey self-catering "villas". A new student guidance centre is bringing services together at the heart of the campus. The students' union has had a £9-million refurbishment and now includes Enterprise SU, an area for students to improve their enterprise and employability skills. Queen's has also introduced Degree Plus; a new award providing official recognition of extra-curricular activities and achievements and to help graduates in the job market.

Consistently high satisfaction levels in the National Student Survey place Queen's among the top 30 universities. Anatomy, physiology and pathology, archaeology, dentistry, pharmacology, toxicology and pharmacy, and subjects allied to medicine produced particularly good results. Strictly non-denominational teaching is enshrined in a charter which has guaranteed student representation and equal rights for women since 1908. The charter even precluded the teaching of theology – this is done through a network of four associated colleges.

Queen's was one of four university colleges for the whole of Ireland in the 19th century, and still draws students from all over the island. Applications were up by more than 6 per cent at the start of 2009. The university has begun to attract more students from Great Britain, as well as boosting the numbers of international students. A variety of international agreements have been forged in the United States, Malaysia, China and India.

The university district, which is among the most attractive in Belfast, is one of the city's main cultural and recreational areas. Queen's runs a highly successful arts

---

University Road
Belfast BT7 1NN
028 9097 2727 (admissions)
admissions@qub.ac.uk
www.qub.ac.uk
www.qubsu.org

Edinburgh
BELFAST
Cardiff
London

The Times Rankings
Overall Ranking: 32

Student satisfaction:	=20	(78%)
Research quality:	=37	(1.7)
Entry standards:	36	(358)
Student–staff ratio:	40	(15.2)
Services & facilities/student:	31	(£1,362)
Expected completion rate:	=51	(85.0%)
Good honours:	30	(69.0%)
Graduate prospects:	=15	(78.3%)

festival each November, opened a new art gallery in 2001 and has the only full-time university cinema in the UK – one of the best in Ireland. Another £2 million has been invested in arts facilities recently, the lion's share of the cash going into a new studio theatre. More teaching accommodation has been added, with better access for the disabled, and the university's great hall has had a £2.5-million refurbishment, courtesy of the university's own foundation.

Students are encouraged to take language programmes from a unique "virtual" language laboratory, which provides online tuition from any computer in the university. IT facilities are good: Queen's was the first institution to meet the national target of providing at least one computer workstation for every five undergraduate students. An unusually large proportion of graduates go on to further study, which does Queen's no harm in the employment league.

The city centre is not short of nightlife, but the social scene is still concentrated on the students' union and the surrounding area. Sports facilities, which include a university hut in the Mourne mountains, are of a high standard. A £7-million extension to the university's physical education centre has helped in Queen's selection as an official training camp for the 2012 Olympics. The university runs academies for rugby and Gaelic sports, which have strong external links. Numerous Queen's players are selected at club, provincial and national levels. First years are have priority for university accommodation and there is plenty of reasonably priced private housing for other years.

Undergraduate Fees and Bursaries
- Fees for UK/EU students: £3,225
- International student fees: £9,418–£11,539 £12,757–£24,066 (medicine)
- Bursary on full grant: household income up to £18.3K: £1,050; household income up to £23.3K £530.*
- The university does not award bursaries for students on partial maintenance grants.
- Scholarships based on circumstances or by competition.
- For full details see the university's website: www.qub.ac.uk/home/TuitionFeesandStudent SupportArrangements200910/

* Figures for 2008–09

Students

Undergraduates:	13,365	(4,250)
Postgraduates:	2,510	(2,100)
Mature students:	18.9%	
Overseas students:	4.9%	
Applications per place:	4.9	
From state-sector schools:	99.1%	
From working-class homes:	35.1%	

For detailed information about fees, grants and bursaries and how they work, see chapter 7.

Accommodation
Number of places and costs refer to 2009–10
University-provided places: over 2,000
Percentage catered: 0%
Self-catered costs: £63.56–£90.65 a week.
First-year students from outside Belfast are guaranteed housing if conditions are met.
International students are given priority.
Contact: accommodation@qub.ac.uk
www.qub.ac.uk/sacc

University of Reading

Reading is another of the medium-sized campus universities that have demonstrated their appeal through the National Student Survey. Consistently in the top 20, it again satisfied almost 90 per cent of its final-year undergraduates in the results published in 2008. Archaeology boasted 100 per cent satisfaction, while architecture, building, business studies, computer science, history, teacher training and geography and environmental science all scored well.

The university was ranked among the top 200 in the world in 2008 and did well in the latest Research Assessment Exercise, despite entering a much higher proportion of its academics than many of its peers. More than half of their work was considered world-leading or internationally excellent, with archaeology and art and design doing particularly well.

There are three main sites within Reading, including the original 320-acre parkland site, and the university also owns 2,000 acres of farmland at nearby Sonning and Shinfield, where the renowned Centre for Dairy Research (CEDAR) is located. To these have been added the former Henley Management College, which became the university's business school in 2008. The Greenlands site, on the banks of the river at Henley-on-Thames, houses postgraduate and executive programmes, while undergraduates are taught at the university's Whiteknights campus.

Reading was the only university established between the two world wars, having been Oxford's extension college for the first part of the last century, but the attractive main campus now has a modern feel. A new School of Pharmacy opened in 2005 and sports facilities have been extended. A multimillion pound student services building, providing a one-stop-shop for student support and welfare, followed in 2007.

Applications were up by more than 11 per cent at the start of 2009, following a healthy increase in the previous year. The university's location, a bus ride away from Heathrow Airport, and an international reputation in key areas for developing countries have always ensured a healthy flow of overseas students.

About one undergraduate in six is from an independent school and fewer than a quarter come from working-class homes, rather less than average for the university's subjects and entry qualifications. However, the retention rate exceeds national norms, with under 7 per cent of undergraduates who started courses in 2006 expected to leave without a qualification.

The university is involved with a number of centres of excellence in teaching and learning, including one focusing on

---

Whiteknights
PO Box 217
Reading RG6 6AH
0118 378 8618/9
student.recruitment@
  reading.ac.uk
www.reading.ac.uk
www.rusu.co.uk

The Times Rankings
Overall Ranking: 31

Student satisfaction:	=14	(79%)
Research quality:	=19	(2.1)
Entry standards:	39	(347)
Student–staff ratio:	52	(16.7)
Services & facilities/student:	69	(£1,062)
Expected completion rate:	24	(91.7%)
Good honours:	12	(75.4%)
Graduate prospects:	58	(68.7%)

career management skills. All undergraduates take career management skills modules that contribute five credits towards their degree classification. The online system, which has 200 web pages of advice, exercises and information, has been bought by 30 other universities and colleges. Sessions are delivered jointly by academics and careers advisors, with input from alumni and leading employers.

The town – only a short walk from the campus – may not be the most fashionable, but it has plenty of nightlife and an award-winning shopping centre. It also offers temporary and part-time employment opportunities for students. London is easily accessible by train, but the cost of living is on a par with the capital. More than 4,500 residential places include a landscaped student village, while first-rate sports provision includes accessible rowing and sailing boathouses, scholarships and an academy. Teams have a good record in inter-university competitions and the campus has been chosen as a possible pre-Olympics training camp for basketball and fencing.

Students praise the social scene, although the high proportion of students from the southeast of England means that many go home at the weekends. The large students' union had a £500,000 refit in 2007, improving and extending its popular main venue. The union has been voted among the best in Britain, and has won numerous awards including Best Bar None status for encouraging safe drinking. Students who live in town can make use of the free night bus service to take them back into Reading.

Undergraduate Fees and Bursaries
- Fees for UK/EU students: £3,225
- International student fees: £9,630–£11,610
- Bursary on full grant: £1,350
- Bursaries on partial grant: household income up to £35K: £900; up to £45K: £450.
- Scholarships based on circumstances or by competition.
- For full details see the university's website: www.rdg.ac.uk/studentfinance/

Students		
Undergraduates:	8,855	(1,855)
Postgraduates:	2,060	(1,705)
Mature students:	12.6%	
Overseas students:	10.2%	
Applications per place:	5.7	
From state-sector schools:	82.4%	
From working-class homes:	23.9%	

For detailed information about fees, grants and bursaries and how they work, see chapter 7.

Accommodation
Number of places and costs refer to 2009–10
University-provided places: about 4,500
Percentage catered: 37%
Catered costs: £105.23–£160.10 (30 weeks).
Self-catered costs: £68.18–£108.68 (38 weeks).
First-year undergraduates are guaranteed a place if conditions are met.
International students: given priority if conditions are met.
Contact: www.reading.ac.uk/life/life-accommodation.asp

The Robert Gordon University

Robert Gordon is again the top new university in *The Times* League Table. It has improved substantially in research quality, one of its weaker areas in previous years, after a much better performance in the 2008 Research Assessment Exercise. Almost a third of its submission was considered world-leading or internationally excellent, with library and information management the star performer.

So close are links with the North Sea oil and gas industries that Robert Gordon used to dub itself the Energy University. But, with nursing and the health sciences now equally important, it has gone for the broader soubriquet of the Professional University. The creative industries are a growth area and there is a full portfolio of courses in business, design and engineering.

Flexible programmes, with credit accumulation and transfer, make for easy movement in and out of the university for an often mobile local workforce. Work placements, lasting up to a year, are the norm, helping an employment record that has been Scotland's best for several years and consistently one of the UK's leaders.

Efforts to extend access beyond the normal higher education catchment have produced a diverse student population,

with a third of the undergraduates coming from working-class homes and almost all attending state schools or colleges. The dropout rate has improved considerably over recent years and, at 14 per cent, is only marginally higher than the UK average for RGU's subjects and entry qualifications.

There are now about 140 degrees, some of which involve collaboration with Aberdeen University. Students from the city's two universities mix easily, and there is healthy academic rivalry in some areas, despite the obvious differences. There is also a partnership with Aberdeen College, which has become an associate college of the university to encourage progression from school to higher education.

Named after an 18th-century philanthropist, Robert Gordon has two sites around the city and an attractive field study centre at Cromarty, in the Highlands. The historic Schoolhill site adjoins Aberdeen Art Gallery in the city centre, while Garthdee, where 70 per cent of undergraduates are taught, is a mile away overlooking the River Dee. The university has spent £100 million on its buildings and facilities, with Norman Foster designing the business school, while other recent developments made room for art, architecture and the faculty of health and social care. Another £110 million of improvements is planned for

---

Schoolhill
Aberdeen AB10 1FR
01224 262728 (enquiries)
admissions@rgu.ac.uk
www.rgu.ac.uk
www.rgunion.co.uk

The Times Rankings
Overall Ranking: 51

Student satisfaction:	–	(–)
Research quality:	=60	(0.6)
Entry standards:	41	(332)
Student–staff ratio:	65	(18.0)
Services & facilities/student:	61	(£1,102)
Expected completion rate:	70	(81.8%)
Good honours:	80	(53.2%)
Graduate prospects:	4	(84.1%)

Garthdee over the next few years.

Like most new universities, especially in Scotland, RGU recruits most of its students locally, 60 per cent of them female. However, overseas recruitment has been growing sharply and the overall demand for places has been stronger than at most universities north of the border. The university offers four-week intensive access programmes in mathematics, engineering, chemistry and computing during August and September for applicants who narrowly miss the entry requirements to top up their qualifications. If they prefer, prospective students may take access units in these subjects by distance learning, using study packs and with the support of an assigned tutor. The scheme, which runs all year round, is recommended for aspiring students without traditional academic backgrounds.

The university is pinning many of its hopes on new technology. An award-winning virtual campus was launched with an online course in e-business for postgraduates. It also enables management undergraduates to receive course materials via an intranet, and other degree and short courses are available. The new Moodle system is used across Robert Gordon's courses for both on-campus and distance learning students.

Aberdeen is a long way to go for English students, but train and air links are excellent, and the city regularly features in the top ten for quality of life. A £12-million sports and leisure centre opened in 2005, provides a centre of excellence for the region in hockey, as well as a 25-metre swimming pool, three gyms, a climbing wall and bouldering room, a café bar, three exercise studios and a large sports hall. Although accommodation can be expensive in the private sector, low prices in the students' union partially compensate, and there are enough residential places to guarantee housing to first years from outside the local area.

Undergraduate Fees and Bursaries
- Scottish-domiciled and EU students: no fees payable.
- Non-Scottish UK-domiciled student fees: £1,820 a year.
- International student fees: £8,400–£10,800.
- Scholarships based on circumstances or by competition.
- For full details see the university's website: www.rgu.ac.uk/stud_finance

Students		
Undergraduates:	6,610	(2,155)
Postgraduates:	1,610	(1,890)
Mature students:	27.5%	
Overseas students:	10.8%	
Applications per place:	3.6	
From state-sector schools:	95.5%	
From working-class homes:	33.1%	

For detailed information about fees, grants and bursaries and how they work, see chapter 7.

Accommodation
Number of places and costs refer to 2009–10
University-provided places: 1,447
Percentage catered: 0%
Self-catered costs: £76.50–£97.50 a week.
All first-year students are eligible to apply for student accommodation. Residential restrictions apply.
International students: given priority for accommodation.
Contact: accommodation@rgu.ac.uk
www.rgu.ac.uk/accommodation

Roehampton University

Fully independent since 2004, Roehampton is now making its mark as a university in its own right, after four years in a federation with Surrey University. There have been record intakes, despite rising entry scores, although the 4 per cent increase at the start of 2009 was half the national average. Successes in the latest Research Assessment Exercise, when Roehampton entered a much higher proportion of its academics than most of its peer group, will add to the university's reputation. A third of the submission was judged to be world-leading or internationally excellent, with the university producing the best results in the country for dance and doing extremely well in anthropology and drama, theatre and performance studies.

Roehampton is a collegiate university with four distinctive colleges, which still maintain some of the traditional ethos of their religious foundations: the Anglican Whitelands, the Roman Catholic Digby Stuart, the Methodist Southlands, and the Froebel, which follows the humanist teachings of Frederick Froebel. Students need not follow any of these denominations to enrol in the colleges. The university also has a Jewish resource centre and Muslim prayer rooms.

All four colleges are based in a 26-hectare campus, with stunning parkland and lakes, on or adjacent to Roehampton Lane. Whitelands moved from Putney in 2004 to the 18th-century mansion, Parkstead House, overlooking Richmond Park, which also houses the School of Human and Life Sciences. The buildings have been refurbished with IT facilities, student accommodation, laboratories and teaching space. The colleges all have their own bars and other leisure facilities, although they are open to all members of the university.

A £6-million building, mainly for dance and PE, opened on the main campus in 2005. Recent projects include a £4-million facility for the School of Arts, which opened in 2006, and a new national centre of excellence for teaching on citizenship education, human rights and social justice. A 15-year programme will bring further improvements, designed to enhance the student experience and provide an environment that can be enjoyed by the local community. The plans include a new library, halls of residence, a university congregation hall, more sports facilities, a new students' union hub, cloisters, piazzas and a performing arts centre.

The four schools of Arts, Education, Human and Life Sciences, and Business and Social Sciences encourage inter-disciplinary work. Themes such as "creativity", "childhood", "wellbeing" and "social justice" are explored in two or more

Erasmus House
Roehampton Lane
London SW15 5PU
020 8392 3232 (enquiries)
enquiries@
  roehampton.ac.uk
www.roehampton.ac.uk
www.roehampton
  student.com

The Times Rankings
Overall Ranking: =92

Student satisfaction:	=99	(71%)
Research quality:	=57	(0.8)
Entry standards:	87	(251)
Student–staff ratio:	=72	(18.4)
Services & facilities/student:	38	(£1,242)
Expected completion rate:	=83	(78.5%)
Good honours:	93	(51.0%)
Graduate prospects:	=105	(56.8%)

schools and permeate many of the university's activities. True to the university's origins, education remains the largest subject area, accounting for more than a quarter of the students.

The Quality Assurance Agency complimented Roehampton on the accessibility of academic staff to students and the positive ways in which they responded to student needs. One example has been the provision of enhanced sports facilities on campus, with a new gym, two football pitches, running track and a multi-use games area. However, this is yet to be reflected in the National Student Survey. Only mass communication and documentation, languages and education had satisfaction levels of more than 85 per cent.

The Sport Performance and Rehabilitation Centre offers students, staff and local people physiotherapy, podiatry and sports massage, as well as access to physiological assessment, biomechanical analysis, sport psychology support and sports nutrition. The university offers four sports scholarships of £3,000 a year and is a High Performance Centre for British Fencing.

More than nine out of ten undergraduates were educated in state schools and over a third come from working-class homes. The projected dropout rate had been coming down, but the latest figures suggest that 21 per cent of students will fail to graduate in the expected time – significantly more than average for the university's courses and entry grades.

About 80 per cent of first years who want a hall place are offered one, with priority going to those who make Roehampton their first preference. Two new residences opened in 2005, adding 300 places to the residential stock. Rents are not cheap for those who miss out on a place or prefer the private sector, but students like the proximity of central London and the lively and attractive suburbs around Roehampton.

Undergraduate Fees and Bursaries

- Fees for UK/EU students: £3,225
- International student fees: £9,360
- Bursary on full grant: £500
- The university does not award bursaries for students on partial maintenance grants.
- Scholarships based on circumstances or by competition.
- For full details see the university's website: www.roehampton.ac.uk/admissions/finance/index.html

Students

Undergraduates:	5,875	(560)
Postgraduates:	1,030	(770)
Mature students:	29.0%	
Overseas students:	6.0%	
Applications per place:	3.7	
From state-sector schools:	96.5%	
From working-class homes:	35.7%	

For detailed information about fees, grants and bursaries and how they work, see chapter 7.

Accommodation

Number of places and costs refer to 2009–10
University-provided places: 1,600
Percentage catered: 12.5%
Catered costs: £126 a week
Self-catered costs: £91 (standard) – £112 (en suite) a week.
First years are given priority if conditions met. Local restrictions apply.
International students: guaranteed for first year
Contact: accommodation@roehampton.ac.uk

Royal Holloway, University of London

Royal Holloway is planning a step change in size and academic character through a merger with St George's, University of London, the capital's last freestanding medical school. If all goes according to plan, a single college of some 13,000 students will encompass biomedicine, science, social sciences, arts and humanities by the start of the 2010–11 academic year. The two intended partners are already collaborating, with Kingston University, in the South West London Academic Network.

As the University of London's "campus in the country", Royal Holloway occupies 135 acres of woodland between Windsor Castle and Heathrow. The 600-bed Founder's Building, modelled on a French chateau and opened by Queen Victoria, is one of Britain's most remarkable university buildings. More than £100 million has been spent on the campus. Recent projects have included a major auditorium, extensions to the School of Management and other academic buildings, an extension to the main library and new student residences, which have been praised for their comfort and eco-friendly features.

Other developments have included expansion of the academic staff, better student services and a portfolio of scholarships and bursaries that predated top-up fees. One offers free places or reduced fees to those who stay on for a postgraduate degree. The conversion of the huge Victorian boilerhouse into a performance space for drama and the establishment of formal links with institutions such as New York, Sydney and Yale universities, demonstrate that progress has not just been a matter of bricks and mortar. Closer to home, another link allows music students to take lessons at the Royal College of Music.

Both Bedford College and Royal Holloway, which amalgamated to form the existing college, were founded for women only, their legacy commemorated in the Bedford Centre for the History of Women. However, the gender balance in the student population is now roughly equal. Royal Holloway is not just about the arts: the college offers a science foundation year at further education colleges in the region, and the balance of disciplines is gradually shifting.

Of the work entered for the Research Assessment Exercise, 60 per cent was rated world-leading or internationally excellent, cementing Royal Holloway's place among the top 25 research universities. Music was ranked top in the UK, with 90 per cent of its research in the top two categories, while biology, drama, earth sciences, economics, geography, German, media arts and

---

University of London
Egham
Surrey TW20 0EX
01784 443350 (admissions)
admissions@rhul.ac.uk
www.rhul.ac.uk
www.surhul.co.uk

The Times Rankings
Overall Ranking: 30

Student satisfaction:	=54	(75%)
Research quality:	16	(2.3)
Entry standards:	=31	(365)
Student–staff ratio:	28	(14.5)
Services & facilities/student:	35	(£1,308)
Expected completion rate:	17	(92.9%)
Good honours:	27	(70.3%)
Graduate prospects:	=50	(69.8%)

psychology were all in the top ten in their fields.

The college has also had consistently good results in the National Student Survey, with 85 per cent of final-year undergraduates satisfied with their courses in 2008. Physics, geography, geology, computer science and classics all produced extremely high levels of satisfaction. All 18 departments encourage interdisciplinary work, which is facilitated by a modular course structure with examinations at the end of every year. An Advanced Skills Programme, covering information technology, communication skills and foreign languages, further encourages breadth of study.

Royal Holloway offers e-degrees in classics, history, business management and postgraduate courses in information security and management. It is also spearheading the development of the University of London Institute in Paris, allowing students to spend part of their course in France.

Applications for courses beginning in 2009 were down by more than 6 per cent, although that followed a big increase in the previous year. The college still draws nearly a quarter of its undergraduates from independent schools, although the proportion coming from working-class homes has been rising. The ethnic mix is above average and the projected dropout rate is back down to 7 per cent – well below the official benchmark.

Over 2,900 students are in halls of residence, many of them in the Founder's Building itself. The college's green belt location at Egham, Surrey, 35 minutes from the centre of London by rail, ensures that social life is concentrated on an extended students' union. However, the West End is close for those determined to seek the high life. Sports facilities are good and have been upgraded recently – Royal Holloway claims to be "the University of London's best sporting college" (although three other colleges performed better in the BUCS league in 2007–08).

A high proportion of students come from London and the Home Counties, so many go home at the weekend, but the lively students' union puts on entertainment and activities seven days a week.

Undergraduate Fees and Bursaries

- Fees for UK/EU students: £3,225
- International student fees: £11,555–£13,120
- Bursary on full grant: £750
- Bursaries on partial grant: household income up to £39.3K: £750.
- Scholarships based on circumstances or by competition.
- For full details see the university's website: www.rhul.ac.uk/prospective-students/finance/ug_Bursaries.html

Students		
Undergraduates:	6,115	(440)
Postgraduates:	1,380	(445)
Mature students:	10.0%	
Overseas students:	25.9%	
Applications per place:	5.0	
From state-sector schools:	78.5%	
From working-class homes:	24.0%	

For detailed information about fees, grants and bursaries and how they work, see chapter 7.

Accommodation

Number of places and costs refer to 2009–10

University-provided places: 2,770

Percentage catered: 6.8%

Catered costs: £124.06 a week (30 weeks).

Self-catered costs: £66.73–£126.43 a week (38–50 weeks).

First years are prioritised for accommodation provided conditions are met.

International students: non-EU students guaranteed accommodation.

Contact: Accommodation-Office@rhul.ac.uk

University of St Andrews

St Andrews has been the leading Scottish university in *The Times* League Table for the last three years, reaping the benefits of outstanding scores in the National Student Survey (NSS). The university already had the highest entry standards, the best staffing levels and the lowest dropout rate north of the border. Now, the distinction of having the most satisfied students in Scotland has taken St Andrews clear of Edinburgh and into the top five overall in our Table.

Scotland's oldest university and the third oldest in the English-speaking world, St Andrews has long been both well known and fashionable among a mainly middle-class clientele. Applications were up by more than 10 per cent at the official deadline for courses beginning in 2009. Previous increases mean that selection is highly competitive in almost all subjects.

With nearly 30 per cent of the students coming from south of the border, St Andrews has earned the nickname of Scotland's English university. But another 26 per cent come from over 100 countries farther afield, giving the university a cosmopolitan feel. Fee concessions and exchange schemes have boosted applications, particularly from the United States, which provides nearly a fifth of first-year students on its own.

Peer assessments have shown that there is top quality behind the prestige. Nearly 60 per cent of the work submitted for the 2008 Research Assessment Exercise was rated as world-leading or internationally excellent. St Andrews was joint top in the UK for philosophy and top in Scotland for physics and astronomy, German, film studies, applied maths, French and psychology.

More than four in ten undergraduates come from independent schools, when the UK average for the university's courses and entry scores is less than a quarter. A dedicated schools liaison service has been trying to broaden the intake, and a fund-raising campaign is building up a bank of £3,000-a-year scholarships for students in need. Only four UK universities have a lower proportion of students from working-class backgrounds. Those who do come could hardly be more satisfied: the 2008 NSS showed 100 per cent satisfaction among chemists and only four of the 23 subjects with published ratings had satisfaction levels of less than 90 per cent.

The town of St Andrews is steeped in history, as well as being the centre of the golfing world. The university at its heart accounts for about a third of the 18,000 inhabitants. There are close cultural and social relations between town and gown. New students ("bejants" and "bejantines") acquire third and fourth-year "parents" to ease them into university life, and on Raisin

---

College Gate
North Street
St Andrews, Fife KY16 9AJ
01334 462150
admissions@
  st-andrews.ac.uk
www.st-andrews.ac.uk
www.yourunion.net

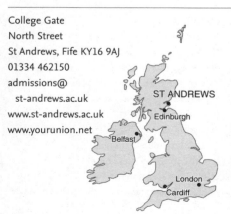

The Times Rankings
Overall Ranking: 4

Student satisfaction:	=5	(84%)
Research quality:	=8	(2.5)
Entry standards:	5	(468)
Student–staff ratio:	=8	(12.4)
Services & facilities/student:	25	(£1,423)
Expected completion rate:	12	(94.2%)
Good honours:	3	(85.1%)
Graduate prospects:	19	(77.8%)

Monday give their academic guardians a bottle of wine in return for a receipt in Latin, which can be written on anything. Another unusual feature is that all humanities students are awarded an MA rather than a BA.

Many of the main buildings date from the 15th and 16th centuries, but sciences are taught at the modern North Haugh site a few streets away. Everything is within walking distance, but bicycles are common. Although small, St Andrews offers a wide range of courses. The university's reputation has always rested on the humanities, which acquired a £1.3-million research centre recently. An £8-million headquarters for the School of International Relations opened in 2006, with Europe's first Centre for Syrian Studies, an Institute of Iranian Studies and a Centre for Peace and Conflict Studies. St Andrews has the largest mediaeval history department in Britain and has now added film studies and sustainable development. A full range of physical sciences is also on offer, with sophisticated lasers and the largest optical telescope in Britain.

A £45-million School of Medicine and the Sciences is due for completion in 2010. This will be one of the first UK medical schools whose research facilities are fully integrated with the other sciences and key university disciplines including physics, chemistry, biology and psychology, offering an important new dimension to medical training and research. A £5-million Bio-medical Sciences Research complex is also planned to lead the fight against superbugs and serious viral, bacterial and parasitic diseases.

Students do not come to St Andrews for the nightclubs, but there is no shortage of parties in a tight-knit community. The sports facilities are excellent and more than half of all students live in halls, the latest of which was opened by Gordon Brown in 2007, providing self-catering accommodation for 920 students during term and three-star accommodation for golfers and other tourists in vacations. Features such as the grass roof made it the first university residence to be awarded the Green Tourism Business Scheme's Gold Award.

Undergraduate Bursaries and Scholarships

- Scottish-domiciled and EU students: no fees payable.
- Non-Scottish UK-domiciled student fees: £1,820 a year (£2,895 medicine).
- International student fees: £11,750 £17,950 (medical science)
- Scholarships based on circumstances or by competition.
- For full details see the university's website: www.st-andrews.ac.uk/admissions/scholarships

Students

Undergraduates:	5,825	(830)
Postgraduates:	1,220	(300)
Mature students:	2.8%	
Overseas students:	26.1%	
Applications per place:	5.8	
From state-sector schools:	58.8%	
From working-class homes:	15.7%	

For detailed information about fees, grants and bursaries and how they work, see chapter 7.

Accommodation

Number of places and costs refer to 2009–10
University-provided places: 3,481
Percentage catered: 49%
Catered costs: £136.13–£200.10 a week (31 weeks).
Self-catered costs: £73.71–£153.58 a week (31 weeks).
First years guaranteed accommodation if conditions are met.
Policy for international students: as above.
Contact: studacc@st-andrews.ac.uk

University of Salford

In the last five years, Salford has slipped below some of the new universities in *The Times* League Table. But consistently good graduate employment rates, carefully targeted courses and an emphasis on the university's location close to the centre of Manchester appeal to students. Applications have been buoyant for several years, although there was only a marginal increase at the start of 2009, when most universities saw strong growth in the demand for places.

The university has embarked on a £500-million investment programme that will take 15 years to complete. It will include a £47-million Arts and Media Centre on campus and a centre at the MediaCityUK development in Salford Quays – home to five BBC departments from 2011. Salford Law School opened in 2007 in a £10-million building featuring a Law Society-approved library. New acoustic laboratories opened in 2008, with a reverberation room capable of transforming the quality of sound and an anechoic chamber, which is said to be the quietest place in the world. Also new is the £22-million Mary Seacole building, which houses the Faculty of Health and Social Care.

Salford stresses its business links and modern portfolio of courses, including two-year Foundation degrees. The university does well on the Government's access measures: four in ten undergraduates come from working-class homes and there is a high proportion from areas sending few students to higher education. The projected dropout rate has improved in the latest statistics but, at 22 per cent, is still well above the national average for the subjects and students' qualifications. A new Student Life Directorate has been charged with improving every aspect of the student experience, even planning events for students staying at Salford over the Christmas holiday closure.

Business and health subjects are now big recruiters. The university's growing involvement in health has seen the establishment of a national centre for prosthetics and orthotics, and Salford has a high reputation for the treatment of sports injuries. Another innovation was the launch of Europe's first nursing course for deaf students. There is also a degree in traditional Chinese medicine, with an acupuncture clinic, and a BA in journalism and war studies – the only undergraduate degree in the UK to combine the two disciplines.

Engineering is the university's traditional strength, attracting many of the 3,000 overseas students. Two thirds of courses offer work placements, half of them abroad and almost all counting towards degree classifications. The tradition of

---

Salford
Greater Manchester M5 4WT
0161 295 4545
course-enquiries@
  salford.ac.uk
www.salford.ac.uk
www.salfordstudents.com

The Times Rankings		
Overall Ranking: =84		
Student satisfaction:	=78	(73%)
Research quality:	56	(0.9)
Entry standards:	84	(253)
Student–staff ratio:	74	(18.6)
Services & facilities/student:	81	(£987)
Expected completion rate:	92	(76.4%)
Good honours:	73	(55.1%)
Graduate prospects:	=82	(62.7%)

sandwich courses always serves Salford well in terms of graduate employment. The Enterprise Academy scheme was commended by the EU after it helped 32 student businesses become established. Students are offered training in entrepreneurship and business skills, as well as a business mentor.

Online degrees have been introduced and the university has also made headlines with more unusual innovations, such as degrees in business economics with gambling studies, not to mention the appointment of Britain's first Professor of Pop Music. The university launched Salford Business School in 2006, formed from the merger of four existing schools and has several areas of expertise such as information management, operational research and gambling studies.

Salford entered a relatively low proportion of its academics for the 2008 Research Assessment Exercise, but still had among the lowest grades of the pre-1992 universities. Architecture and business produced the best results. The university remains committed to research: it has established nine interdisciplinary research centres and a graduate school. It also led the way in formally recognising interaction with business and industry as of equal importance to teaching and research.

The modern landscaped campus, a haven of lawns and shrubberies along the River Irwell, is less than two miles from Manchester city centre and has a mainline railway station. The university also has its own TV and radio studios. The School of Media, Music and Performance plans to take full advantage of the move by the BBC of production facilities to nearby Salford Quays.

There has been some improvement in scores in the National Student Survey, although satisfaction levels are still below the national average. Sociology, English, health and wildlife courses produced the most satisfied undergraduates. Students like the friendly atmosphere and most of the residential places are either on campus or in a student village 15 minutes' walk away.

Undergraduate Fees and Bursaries

- Fees for UK/EU students: £3,225
- International student fees: £8,600–£10,700
- Bursary on full grant: £320
- Bursaries on partial grant: subject and academic bursaries available.
- Scholarships based on circumstances or by competition.
- For full details see the university's website: www.salford.ac.uk/study/undergraduate/money_matters/

Students

Undergraduates:	12,385	(3,265)
Postgraduates:	1,620	(1,910)
Mature students:	38.4%	
Overseas students:	9.0%	
Applications per place:	4.0	
From state-sector schools:	96.7%	
From working-class homes:	40.9%	

For detailed information about fees, grants and bursaries and how they work, see chapter 7.

Accommodation

Number of places and costs refer to 2009–10
University-provided places: 1,307 plus 1,930 managed by specialist providers
Percentage catered: 0%
Self-catered costs:£58.84–£82.47 (en suite); managed accommodation: £74.53– £95.00.
First years are guaranteed accommodation (terms and conditions apply).
International students: as above.
Contact: www.accommodation.salford.ac.uk/

School of Oriental and African Studies, London

As the major national centre for the study of Africa, Asia and the Middle East, SOAS has a global reputation in subjects relating to two thirds of the world's population. Originally only a specialist Oriental college, the school now covers a much wider range of subjects. The library, with more than a million volumes, periodicals and audiovisual materials in 400 languages, attracts scholars from around the world. It is in the top 50 in the *Times Higher Education*/QS world rankings for the arts and humanities and has been strengthening its academic staff in a variety of disciplines.

The 4,600 students on campus, plus 2,200 studying distance learning programmes, come from over 130 countries. However, two thirds are from Britain and the rest of the EU – and the proportion is higher still among the undergraduates.

The school has a much wider portfolio of courses than its name would suggest, with more than 350 degree combinations on offer and 100 postgraduate programmes. Degrees are available in familiar subjects such as law, music, history and the social sciences, but with a different emphasis. There is also a more limited portfolio of foundation programmes and language courses. Over 5,000 students (from inside and outside SOAS) take courses in one of the 50 languages on offer. The school was chosen to house a national teaching centre for languages.

Student recruitment remains healthy, especially among independent school candidates, who account for a quarter of the British entrants to undergraduate courses. Undergraduate applications grew strongly earlier in the decade, but there has been a decline in the last two years. The main growth area is in postgraduate courses, which have helped to tackle a financial deficit.

In addition, more than 2,000 students are now taking distance learning courses, mainly outside the UK. Numbers have risen with the transfer of University of London postgraduate programmes previously taught by Imperial College, making SOAS one of the world's largest providers of distance learning at this level.

Postgraduates are attracted by a research record which saw more than half of the work submitted for the Research Assessment Exercise rated world-leading or internationally excellent. SOAS was ranked top in the UK for Asian studies and did well in anthropology, politics, history and music.

There is an option of spending one, two or three terms of a degree course in one of

Thornhaugh Street
Russell Square
London WC1H 0XG
020 7898 4301/4306
undergradadmissions@
  soas.ac.uk
www.soas.ac.uk
www.soasunion.org

The Times Rankings
Overall Ranking: =33

Student satisfaction:	=90	(72%)
Research quality:	=37	(1.7)
Entry standards:	=27	(378)
Student–staff ratio:	=3	(10.8)
Services & facilities/student:	5	(£1,829)
Expected completion rate:	65	(82.6%)
Good honours:	20	(73.2%)
Graduate prospects:	34	(73.5%)

the school's many partner universities in Africa or Asia. More than a fifth of the British undergraduates come from working-class homes. The dropout rate has fluctuated over recent years, but had risen to more than 17 per cent in the latest statistics, rather more the UK average for the subjects and entry qualifications at SOAS.

The school is located in Bloomsbury, but in 2001 opened a second campus at Vernon Square, Islington. Less than a mile from the main Russell Square site and adjacent to two of the three student residences, it provides student-orientated facilities such as an internet café. The centrepiece of the main campus is an airy, modern building with gallery space as well as teaching accommodation, a gift from the Sultan of Brunei. There is no separate students' union building, although the students do have their own bar and catering facilities. The well-equipped and under-used University of London Union is close at hand, with swimming pool, gym and bars. The West End is also on the doorstep.

Nearly 1,000 residential places accommodate both undergraduates and postgraduates, and are within 15 minutes' walk of the school. Another 119 places are planned in flats in Vernon Square. However, the school has few of its own sports facilities and the outdoor pitches are remote, with no time set aside from lectures. The ethnic and national mix has led to inevitable tensions at times, but SOAS is small enough for most students to know each other, at least by sight, and the atmosphere is normally friendly. Students tend to be highly committed – not surprising since many will return to positions of influence in developing countries – and the variety of cultures makes for lively debate.

Undergraduate Fees and Bursaries

- Fees for UK/EU students: £3,225
- International student fees: £12,000
- Bursary on full grant: £860
- Bursaries on partial grant: household income £25K–£39.3K: £420.
- Scholarships based on circumstances or by competition.
- For full details see the university's website: www.soas.ac.uk/registry/scholarships/

Students

Undergraduates:	2,695	(85)
Postgraduates:	1,495	(460)
Mature students:	26.9%	
Overseas students:	36.9%	
Applications per place:	5.3	
From state-sector schools:	74.7%	
From working-class homes:	20.3%	

For detailed information about fees, grants and bursaries and how they work, see chapter 7.

Accommodation

Number of places and costs refer to 2009–10
University-provided places: 770 (Sanctuary Management Services); 180 (intercollegiate)
Percentage catered: 10%
Catered costs: £108.01–£132.44 a week.
Self-catered costs: £120.89–£143.43 a week.
Priority given to first years on first come basis.
Residential restrictions apply.
International students: as above, although they are a high priority.
Contact: student@sanctuary-housing.co.uk

University of Sheffield

Sheffield has moved back up *The Times* League Table this year with good results in the 2008 Research Assessment Exercise (RAE) and high levels of satisfaction among the students. Student numbers reached 24,000 after 14 per cent growth in three years and there had been another 9 per cent increase in applications at the deadline for courses beginning in 2009. A new student village and a high-tech library have added to the feeling of a university on the move. The £23-million Information Commons operates 24 hours a day, providing 1,300 study spaces and 500 computers linked to the campus network, as well as 110,000 books and periodicals.

More than 60 per cent of the work submitted for the RAE was judged to be world-leading or internationally excellent. Politics and information studies achieved the best results in the country, while town planning, philosophy, Russian, architecture, and mechanical and aeronautical engineering were near the top for their fields.

Sheffield was only just outside the top ten in the National Student Survey in 2008, producing some of the best results among the big city universities. There was 100 per cent satisfaction among civil engineers, with dentistry, philosophy, biology, Hispanic studies and Asian languages not far behind. The university houses national teaching centres for the arts and social sciences and for enterprise learning.

There has been sustained investment in facilities in recent years: £100 million for biological and physical sciences, medicine, engineering and social sciences, and £15 million on an advanced manufacturing research centre in which Boeing is the senior partner, which forms the hub of a technology park. The university is the lead institution for systems engineering, smart materials and stem-cell technology in a research network of European, American and Chinese universities.

The conversion of the former Jessop hospital at the heart of the campus provides a new centre for the arts and humanities, which includes a visitor information centre and café. The new Soundhouse, clad in black rubber, provides ultra-modern music practice studios, rehearsal rooms and recording facilities. Another new site adjacent to the engineering departments will house high-tech multidisciplinary facilities.

The university has always enjoyed a high ratio of applications to places, despite recent expansion. There are more than 3,600 overseas students from 124 countries. Sheffield is in the top 80 universities in the world, according to both the main global rankings.

Academic buildings are concentrated in an area about a mile from the city centre on

---

Western Bank
Sheffield S10 2TN
0114 222 1255 (enquiries)
www.shef.ac.uk/asksheffield
www.shef.ac.uk
www.shef.ac.uk/union

The Times Rankings
Overall Ranking: 18

Student satisfaction:	=20	(78%)
Research quality:	=12	(2.4)
Entry standards:	18	(406)
Student–staff ratio:	=24	(14.2)
Services & facilities/student:	44	(£1,191)
Expected completion rate:	21	(92.1%)
Good honours:	16	(74.5%)
Graduate prospects:	14	(79.1%)

the affluent west side of Sheffield, with most university flats and halls of residence a little further into the suburbs. Recent developments mean that the main university precinct now stretches into an almost unbroken mile-long "campus".

The intake is more diverse than at most leading universities: over 85 per cent of undergraduates come from state schools or colleges and more than one undergraduate in five comes from a working-class home. A famously lively social scene is based on the student union's extended facilities – twice voted the best in Britain – but also takes full advantage of the city's burgeoning club life. In addition to its own popular facilities, the union owns a pub in the western suburb where most students live. Town–gown relations are much better and the crime rate lower than in most big cities. The university claims the highest proportion of graduates staying in the city after completing their studies.

Residential accommodation is plentiful, with most university-owned places within walking distance of lectures, and private housing reasonably priced. First years from outside Sheffield are guaranteed accommodation. The new Endcliffe Village caters for about 3,500 students in a mix of refurbished Victorian houses and new flats. A second development will add another 1,000 places and take spending on accommodation to £200 million.

The university's excellent sports facilities have been the subject of a £6-million makeover, which includes a 170-station fitness centre and a third Astroturf pitch specifically for soccer and rugby. Top-notch facilities were built by the city for the 1991 World Student Games and a £25-million regional centre for the English Institute of Sport opened in 2003. A five-year student sports strategy was launched in 2007, aiming to boost participation at various levels of the sport and recreation.

Undergraduate Fees and Bursaries

- Fees for UK/EU students: £3,225
- International student fees: £10,420–£13,700 £24,760 (medicine)
- Bursary on full grant: household income up to £17.2K: £700; up to £25K: £430.
- Bursaries on partial grant: household income up to £35.5K: £430 (subject and academic bursaries available).
- Scholarships based on circumstances or by competition.
- For full details see the university's website: www.shef.ac.uk/bursaries/

Students		
Undergraduates:	15,980	(1,790)
Postgraduates:	5,285	(1,500)
Mature students:	9.8%	
Overseas students:	9.1%	
Applications per place:	6.2	
From state-sector schools:	85.3%	
From working-class homes:	21.3%	

For detailed information about fees, grants and bursaries and how they work, see chapter 7.

Accommodation

Number of places and costs refer to 2009–10
University-provided places: 6,202
Percentage catered: 16%
Catered costs: £3,875.90–£5,780.44 (35 or 42 weeks).
Self-catered costs: £3,116.40–£4,712.82 (42 weeks).
First years are guaranteed accommodation if conditions are met.
International students: as above.
Contact: www.shef.ac.uk/accommodation

Sheffield Hallam University

Sheffield Hallam has been undergoing a physical transformation designed to alter its image and cater for an even bigger student population. The university has two campuses, one in the heart of the city centre and the other not far away in a leafy inner suburb. Developments have been continuing apace, with almost £100 million already spent on teaching and learning facilities and half as much again earmarked for the next five years.

An atrium provides social space for staff and students, and innovative library developments take pride of place on both campuses. Business and management courses, which account for easily the biggest share of places, have their own city-centre headquarters.

The Collegiate Crescent campus, a former teacher training college, houses education, health and community studies. The students' union has taken over the spectacular but ill-fated National Centre for Popular Music, with facilities described by the former higher education minister Kim Howells as the best he had seen.

While most of the development has been on the main campus, adjoining the main bus and rail stations, the latest stage has seen the opening of a new social centre on the Collegiate Crescent site. A £14-million development that opened in 2005 has allowed the Faculty of Health and Wellbeing to almost double in size, as extra provision is made for nursing, radiotherapy, physiotherapy and social work. The Centre for Sport and Exercise Science, with its £6-million research facility, won glowing praise from inspectors, and is one of Europe's largest centres of its kind, with more than 2,000 students. The Faculty is the biggest provider of health and social care training in the UK and offers the widest range of sports courses.

Another new development, combined with the refurbishment of existing city-centre buildings brought all the departments in the Faculty of Arts, Computing, Engineering and Sciences together on the main campus for the first time, placing them in the heart of Sheffield's thriving cultural industries quarter. The University also launched the Sheffield Business School in May 2009, bringing together academic and professional groups in business, finance, management and languages, with the university's specialisms of facilities management, food and nutrition, tourism, hospitality and events management.

Of the subjects available in 2010, nursing produced the best results in the latest National Student Survey, boasting 100 per cent satisfaction among the undergraduates. Planning, tourism,

---

City Campus
Howard Street
Sheffield S1 1WB
0114 225 5555
enquiries@shu.ac.uk
www.shu.ac.uk
www.hallamunion.com

The Times Rankings
Overall Ranking: 69

Student satisfaction:	=78	(73%)
Research quality:	=71	(0.4)
Entry standards:	71	(268)
Student–staff ratio:	66	(18.1)
Services & facilities/student:	87	(£937)
Expected completion rate:	61	(83.8%)
Good honours:	57	(61.3%)
Graduate prospects:	=75	(64.2%)

nutrition and food and beverage studies also produced high scores. Almost a third of the work submitted for the 2008 Research Assessment Exercise was rated as world-leading or internationally excellent, with planning and art and design achieving the highest grades.

Sheffield Hallam traces its origins in art and design back to the 1840s and celebrated the centenary of education and teacher training in 2005. It is now one of the largest of the new universities, with more than 30,000 students, including high proportions of part-time and mature students, and more than 1,000 taught on franchised courses in further education colleges. Business and industry are closely involved in the development hundreds of courses, with almost half of the students taking sandwich course placements with employers. More than 200 "specialist flexible courses" mix part-time study, distance learning and work-based learning.

The university leads two national teaching centres, one for fostering employability and the other promoting autonomous learning. It is also a partner in a third, led by Coventry University, on e-learning in the professions. A "virtual campus" offers students e-mail accounts and cheap equipment to access the growing volume of online courses, assignments and discussion groups provided by the university, even when they are at home or on work placements.

A third of undergraduates come from working-class homes and almost one in five from areas that send few students to higher education. The projected dropout rate of almost 13 per cent is lower than average for the subjects offered and the students' entry qualifications.

Such is Sheffield Hallam's size that it is not possible to guarantee all first years university-owned accommodation, although the large local intake means that many live at home. Sports facilities are supplemented by those provided by the city for the World Student Games. The impressive swimming complex, for example, is on the university's doorstep.

Undergraduate Fees and Bursaries

- Fees for UK/EU students: £3,225
- International student fees: £8,700–£10,300
- Bursary on full grant: £700
- The university does not award bursaries for students on partial maintenance grants.
- Scholarships based on circumstances or by competition.
- For full details see the university's website: www.shu.ac.uk/study/ug/money.html

---

Students

Undergraduates:	18,410	(5,125)
Postgraduates:	2,575	(4,980)
Mature students:	27.0%	
Overseas students:	6.5%	
Applications per place:	4.2	
From state-sector schools:	95.7%	
From working-class homes:	33.9%	

For detailed information about fees, grants and bursaries and how they work, see chapter 7.

Accommodation

Number of places and costs refer to 2008–09
University-provided places: 4,242
Percentage catered: 10%
Catered costs: £90.53 a week (39 weeks).
Self-catered costs: £49–£92 (42–44 weeks).
All first years offered university owned, managed, partnership or private housing.
International students: as above, providing conditions are met.
Contact: accommodation@shu.ac.uk
www.shu.ac.uk/accommodation

University of Southampton

Southampton saw a big increase in applications at the beginning of 2009, following further investment in campus facilities and more good results in the National Student Survey (NSS). The university is mid-way through a £250-million programme to upgrade its six sites in Southampton and Winchester. The growth of 13.5 per cent in the demand for places was the biggest at any of the 20 Russell Group research-led universities.

The university could not quite repeat its outstanding results in the 2001 Research Assessment Exercise, which took it into the top ten, when the latest RAE took place. However, more than 60 per cent of its work was considered world-leading or internationally excellent and it remained firmly entrenched among the research elite. The best grades came in music, sociology and social policy, computer science and nursing. The proportion of income derived from research at Southampton is among the highest in Britain.

Although the percentages of students from working-class homes and areas with little tradition of university education are lower than the national average for the subjects offered, the statistics agency concluded that this was largely a matter of location. Students act as ambassadors, associates and mentors in local schools and colleges, as part of the university's effort to broaden its intake. A range of Foundation degrees carefully tailored to industry needs offers students flexible ways of learning.

Chemistry and ocean science students gave their courses the highest rating in the country in the 2008 NSS, while the university was also in the top five for medicine, geology, physical geography and environmental science, computer science, and mechanically based, electronic and electrical engineering. The medical school, which features an innovative common core curriculum for the pre-registration programmes of over 3,000 medical, nursing and other health students from entry to internship, again scored well with students.

The main Highfield campus is in an attractive location two miles from the city centre, adjoining Southampton Common. It has been the focus of recent development to cater for a considerable expansion in numbers during this decade. Education, engineering, health sciences, chemistry, electronics and computer science have all benefited. The library has been greatly extended and the campus now has an e-science centre, as well as a commercial services hub. A purpose-built student services centre provides learning support and other advisory facilities – all of which are backed up online for students in other areas of the university. The latest addition is the striking new £55-million

---

University Road
Southampton SO17 1BJ
023 8059 4732 (admissions)
admissns@soton.ac.uk
www.soton.ac.uk
www.susu.org

The Times Rankings
Overall Ranking: 16

Student satisfaction:	=20	(78%)
Research quality:	=24	(2.0)
Entry standards:	17	(407)
Student–staff ratio:	=21	(13.9)
Services & facilities/student:	15	(£1,562)
Expected completion rate:	13	(93.7%)
Good honours:	15	(74.6%)
Graduate prospects:	23	(76.5%)

Mountbatten Building for the School of Electronics and Computer Science and the Optoelectronics Research Centre.

The university has four other sites in Southampton. The Waterside Campus, in the city's revitalised dock area, houses the National Oceanography Centre, Southampton. A £49-million joint project with the Natural Environment Research Council, it is considered Europe's finest. The Avenue campus, near the main site, is home to most of the arts departments. Clinical medicine is based at Southampton General Hospital, where a new research centre opened in 2007.

Winchester School of Art, which has been part of the university since 1996, has also enjoyed significant recent investment in new facilities. The arts are well represented in Southampton, too, with three nationally renowned arts centres: the Turner Sims Concert Hall, the Nuffield Theatre and the John Hansard Gallery all based at Highfield.

Social facilities for students have been expanded and refurbished, with the addition of a popular campus nightclub. Sports facilities are first-class, with an £8.4-million indoor sports complex and swimming pool next to the students' union and £4.5 million of outdoor facilities, with grass and synthetic pitches, a new pavilion, bar and meeting rooms. Student accommodation is plentiful and was improved in 2006 with the £20-million renovation and expansion of three halls of residence.

Undergraduate Fees and Bursaries

- Fees for UK/EU students: £3,225
- International student fees: £9,660–£12,360
  £22,240 (medicine)
- Bursary on full grant: £1,000
- Bursaries on partial grant: household income up to £35K: £500.
- Scholarships based on circumstances or by competition.
- For full details see the university's website: www.soton.ac.uk/study/feesandfunding/

Students

Undergraduates:	14,785	(2,635)
Postgraduates:	4,270	(2,070)
Mature students:	19.1%	
Overseas students:	9.9%	
Applications per place:	6.1	
From state-sector schools:	83.4%	
From working-class homes:	20.0%	

For detailed information about fees, grants and bursaries and how they work, see chapter 7.

Accommodation

Number of places and costs refer to 2008–09
University-provided places: 5,200
Percentage catered: 20%
Catered costs: £101.85–£145.60 a week.
Self-catered costs: £65.45–£109.20 a week (up to £145.95 for a studio flat)
All first years are offered accommodation (conditions apply).
International students: non-EU students are guaranteed accommodation (conditions apply).
Contact: www.soton.ac.uk/accommodation

Southampton Solent University

The largest of the nine new universities created in 2005, Southampton Solent also has the broadest range of programmes, stretching from Foundation courses for those without the qualifications to begin degrees, to PhDs. The 10,600 students embrace civil and mechanical engineering, as well as media, arts and business, with a separate maritime centre capitalising on the coastal location. The subject mix explains why the former Southampton Institute is now one of the few universities with a majority of male students.

The rebranded Solent Curriculum plays to the university's strengths in vocational courses, with an eye to maintaining a good graduate employment record. There is a strong representation of "non-traditional" disciplines, such as yacht and powercraft design, computer and video games, and comedy writing and performance. A new range of courses in 2008 included degrees in fashion management, television and music production, and coaching and sport development. A Graduate Enterprise Centre provides advice and rent-free offices for those hoping to start their own businesses, while the Warsash Maritime Centre is an internationally renowned training and research facility for the shipping and offshore oil industries.

Solent entered fewer academics for the 2008 Research Assessment Exercise than any university in England – less than one in ten of those eligible. But two of the three areas in which it made a submission contained some world-leading research, with art and design achieving much the best results. It was also only three places off the bottom of the student satisfaction table in 2008. Only in sociology and social studies were more than 85 per cent of the students satisfied, and the proportion dropped to less than a third in fine art and the performing arts.

Nevertheless, applications have been healthy and had risen by nearly 12 per cent at the official deadline for courses beginning in 2009. Demand for places remains especially strong in marine-based courses. The university is higher education's premier yachting institution, with a world champion student team that has won the national championships four times in six years. Three new boats will support courses at the new, purpose-built Watersports Centre, where some of the activities are targeted on disadvantaged young people in the area. The centre now boasts seven powerboats, nine dinghies and three keelboats.

Almost a third of the students come from Hampshire and there has been a substantial increase in the proportion with working-class roots, taking it above the national average for the university's

---

East Park Terrace
Southampton SO14 0YN
023 8031 9000
  (main switchboard)
ask@solent.ac.uk
www.solent.ac.uk
www.solentsu.co.uk

The Times Rankings
Overall Ranking: 111

Student satisfaction:	=101	(70%)
Research quality:	=108	(0.1)
Entry standards:	108	(211)
Student–staff ratio:	105	(21.4)
Services & facilities/student:	71	(£1,054)
Expected completion rate:	99	(74.5%)
Good honours:	=110	(45.7%)
Graduate prospects:	107	(56.6%)

subjects and entry qualifications. Solent's projected dropout rate had slipped to over 20 per cent in the latest survey, but is only marginally worse than the university's benchmark. About 12 per cent of undergraduates come from overseas, while a further 100 are enrolled on research degrees. There is a special link with Guernsey, which has no higher education of its own. Colleges on the island (and in various parts of the south of England) bring students for taster courses and provide evidence of academic potential that can lead to entry on criteria other than A level.

The main campus has few architectural pretensions, but is conveniently based in the city centre within walking distance of the station. Recent investment has included a new Centre for Professional Development in Broadcasting and Multimedia Production, which includes an online editing suite, digital television studio and gallery, for use by undergraduates as well as community groups and professionals. Media, arts and society courses now attract almost as many students as the consistently popular business school.

Other recent additions include the Centre for Health, Exercise and Sports Science, which enables sports science students to conduct the latest types of fitness testing, including ergonomic and biomechanical movement analysis. New music studios feature an industry-standard recording complex, while a performance space and dance studio, opened in 2008, includes a dance floor, tiered seating and a technical viewing gallery.

Students like the location, close to the city's growing complement of bars and nightclubs, as well as to the main shopping area. There are more than 2,300 hall places close to the campus, most of which are allocated to first years and almost half of which are en suite. A landlord accreditation scheme helps to guarantee standards of accommodation for those who rely on the private sector. Away from the water, there is the usual range of sports facilities, with a sports hall and fitness suite on campus and outdoor pitches, tennis and netball courts four miles away. Students living in hall and members of university sports clubs get free fitness classes and gym use.

Undergraduate Fees and Bursaries

- Fees for UK/EU students: £3,225
- International student fees: £6,475–£8,400
- Bursary on full grant: household income up to £18.3K: £1,075; up to £23K: £750; up to £28K: £500.
- Bursaries on partial grant: household income up to £39.3K: £250.
- Scholarships based on circumstances or by competition.
- For full details see the university's website: www.solent.ac.uk/fees/info.aspx

Students

Undergraduates:	8,900	(1,230)
Postgraduates:	330	(390)
Mature students:	25.4%	
Overseas students:	12.6%	
Applications per place:	3.2	
From state-sector schools:	96.6%	
From working-class homes:	35.9%	

For detailed information about fees, grants and bursaries and how they work, see chapter 7.

Accommodation

Number of places and costs refer to 2009–10
University-provided places: 2,340 (majority are offered to first years).
Percentage catered: 0%
Self-catered costs: £87.85–£101.85 a week (40 weeks).
First years are guaranteed accommodation if conditions are met.
International students: some accommodation is set aside.
Contact: Accommodation@solent.ac.uk

Staffordshire University

Staffordshire used to describe itself as a "university in the community" but it is increasingly reliant on overseas students, both at home and abroad. There are 6,000 students taking Staffordshire courses outside Britain, almost half of them located around the Pacific Rim, as well as a growing cohort of foreign students in the university's domestic campuses. There are more than 12,000 UK students and, while applications had increased for the first time in three years at the start of 2009, it by less than half the national average.

The university is based on two main sites, in Stoke-on-Trent and 16 miles away in Stafford. Both have modern halls of residence, sports centres and lively Student Union venues.

A quarter of the students taking qualifications either awarded or quality assured by the university are at partner institutions across Europe, in China, India or beyond. There are dedicated admissions offices in Oman, Sri Lanka, Singapore and Macedonia, and enrolment will begin in Slovenia and Kosovo this autumn.

There has been significant investment at the Stafford campus, which features the Octagon Centre, in which lecture theatres, offices and walkways surround one of the largest university computing facilities in Europe. The New Technologies Centre has some of the finest film production facilities at any university. Engineering and technology are based at Stafford, as well as the Faculty of Health, which has branches in Telford and Shrewsbury.

The large business school is based at Stoke, which also hosts the Law School, the Faculty of Arts, Media and Design and courses in sport and exercise. Developments are dominated by a £287-million plan to produce an attractive and thriving University Quarter – one of the largest collaborative project of its kind in the UK. New science facilities are due for completion in 2011, focusing on the university's strengths in forensics, biology and psychology.

A third campus in Lichfield houses an integrated further and higher education centre, developed in partnership with Tamworth and Lichfield College, as well as 26 business start-up units. The Staffordshire University Regional Federation also involves partner colleges in delivering a range of higher education awards to around 3,000 students. A bespoke £520,000 higher education centre will open on the new Newcastle College campus in 2010.

The university is a pioneer of two-year fast-track degrees, which are now offered in accounting, business, English, law, geography and motor sport technology. Staffordshire academics will also be

---

College Road
Stoke-on-Trent ST4 2DE
01782 294000 (main switchboard)
admissions@staffs.ac.uk
www.staffs.ac.uk
www.staffsunion.com

The Times Rankings
Overall Ranking: =74

Student satisfaction:	=40	(76%)
Research quality:	=108	(0.1)
Entry standards:	100	(232)
Student–staff ratio:	=60	(17.5)
Services & facilities/student:	63	(£1,092)
Expected completion rate:	86	78.1%)
Good honours:	=81	(53.0%)
Graduate prospects:	=55	(69.0%)

evaluating the national programme of accelerated degrees. There already was an extensive portfolio of two-year Foundation degrees. Many programmes are available with a January start, a popular arrangement with overseas students who often take English language courses before beginning a degree.

Staffordshire is in the top three universities for secondary teacher training courses. Fine art produced the best results in the 2008 National Student Survey and was the only subject to register more than 90 per cent satisfaction. The university entered only a small proportion of its academics for the latest Research Assessment Exercise. Three of the ten subject areas had some world-leading research, with general engineering and education producing the best results.

With 98 per cent of its undergraduates state-educated and more than a third coming from working-class homes, Staffordshire comfortably exceeds all the benchmarks set by the funding council for widening access to higher education. There is good provision for the 700 students with disabilities. However, the projected dropout rate has risen to more than 21 per cent and is higher than average for the university's courses and entry qualifications.

Stoke is not the liveliest city of its size, but the University Quarter project should attract more social facilities to the area. The campus, which is close to the railway station, is within easy reach of the city centre and has a buzzing union. Stafford is much the more attractive setting and offers the best chance of a residential place, but the town is quiet and the campus is a mile and a half outside it. Sports facilities are good, especially in Stafford, where there is a new £1.4-million sports centre and all-weather pitches. Good coaching has helped attract some outstanding athletes, who have access to a sports performance centre to help with training schedules, psychological support and dietary assessments.

Undergraduate Fees and Bursaries

- Fees for UK/EU students: £3,225
- International student fees: £9,385
- Bursary on full grant: household income up to £20.8K: £1,000; up to £25.5K: £850.
- Bursaries on partial grant: household income up to £30.8K: £500.
- Scholarships based on circumstances or by competition.
- For full details see the university's website: www.staffs.ac.uk/study_here/ fees_and_funding/

Students		
Undergraduates:	8,345	(4,335)
Postgraduates:	965	(2,090)
Mature students:	30.8%	
Overseas students:	5.6%	
Applications per place:	4.0	
From state-sector schools:	97.7%	
From working-class homes:	39.1%	

For detailed information about fees, grants and bursaries and how they work, see chapter 7.

Accommodation

Number of places and costs refer to 2009–10

University-provided places: 1,100 (Stoke); 776 (Stafford)

Percentage catered: 0%

Self-catered accommodation: £55–£90 a week (36 weeks).

First years have priority, if conditions met.

International students: have priority, if conditions are met.

Contact: Accommodation_stoke@staffs.ac.uk
Accommodation_stafford@staffs.ac.uk

University of Stirling

One of the most beautiful campuses in Britain is also one of the best provided for sports facilities. Stirling was designated Scotland's University for Sporting Excellence in 2008 and is home to national swimming and tennis centres, as well as a golf course and a football academy. The university, with its modern buildings in a loch-side setting beneath the Ochil Hills, has twice recently been voted the favourite UK destination of international students.

Stirling remains a relatively small institution of 9,000 students with a strong community feel. There are no faculties, but five "core areas" have been identified: health and well-being, culture and society, environment, enterprise and economy, and sport. Philosophy produced the best results in the 2008 Research Assessment Exercise, but nursing, film, media and journalism, economics, education and history all did well.

The university was the British pioneer of the semester system, which has now become so popular throughout higher education. The academic year is divided into two 15-week terms, with short mid-semester breaks. Students have the option of starting courses in February, rather than September. Successful completion of six semesters will bring a General degree; eight semesters, Honours.

The emphasis on breadth is such that there are no barriers to movement between departments. Undergraduates can switch the whole direction of their studies, in consultation with their academic adviser, as their interests develop. The modular scheme allows students to speed up their progress on a Summer Academic Programme, which squeezes a full semester's teaching into July and August. Full-time students are not allowed to use the programme to reduce the length of their course, but part-timers can use it to make rapid progress.

Applications rose by almost 8 per cent at the beginning of 2009. The intake is surprisingly diverse, with nearly 95 per cent of undergraduates state-educated and almost a third coming from working-class homes. Three-quarters are from Scotland. International exchanges are common, with many students going to American, Asian and European universities each year.

Recent campus developments have included the refurbishment of the School of Biological and Environmental Sciences. Journalism students have the use of a high-tech newsroom. In 2009 the university is launching the UK's first degree in financial journalism. The library is also undergoing major refurbishment, in a £14-million programme that is due to be completed for the start of the 2010–11 academic year. The university has more than 700 computers for

Stirling FK9 4LA
01786 467044 (admissions)
admissions@stir.ac.uk
www.stir.ac.uk
www.susaonline.org.uk

The Times Rankings
Overall Ranking: 48

Student satisfaction:	=40	(76%)
Research quality:	47	(1.3)
Entry standards:	=57	(288)
Student–staff ratio:	=24	(14.2)
Services & facilities/student:	85	(£958)
Expected completion rate:	=71	(81.5%)
Good honours:	47	(64.3%)
Graduate prospects:	=50	(69.8%)

student use, many available 24 hours a day, and all rooms in halls are wired for internet use.

The sports facilities, which include a 50-metre pool and a golf centre with indoor facilities and a synthetic putting green, are used for teaching and research, as well as for training by elite athletes and recreation for the university community. Sports studies are particularly popular, with 56 students in 2008 benefiting from a sports scholarships programme that is open to overseas, as well as UK students. It covers golf, swimming, disability swimming, tennis, triathlon and football.

Students appreciate the individual attention that a small campus university can offer, although some find the atmosphere claustrophobic. Stirling is not the top choice of nightclubbers, but the students' union won "Best Bar None" status for three years in a row and there is a lively social scene. The MacRobert Arts Centre offers a full programme of cultural activities, while the surrounding country-side offers its own attractions for walkers and climbers.

The Highland campus, for nurses and midwives, is based in the modern Centre for Health Science, in Inverness. There is also a Western Isles campus, located in Stornoway, where the teaching accommo-dation is an integral part of the Lewis Hospital.

Undergraduate Fees and Bursaries

- Scottish-domiciled and EU students: no fees payable.
- Non-Scottish UK-domiciled student fees: £1,820 a year.
- International student fees: £9,400–£11,550
- Scholarships based on circumstances or by competition.
- For full details see the university's website: www.external.stir.ac.uk/undergrad/ financial_info/index.php

Students

Undergraduates:	6,370	(840)
Postgraduates:	1,345	(1,250)
Mature students:	27.4%	
Overseas students:	6.3%	
Applications per place:	5.7	
From state-sector schools:	94.3%	
From working-class homes:	32.3%	

For detailed information about fees, grants and bursaries and how they work, see chapter 7.

Accommodation

Number of places and costs refer to 2009–10
University-provided places: 2,577
Percentage catered: 0%
Self-catered costs: £61.50–£92.40 a week.
All first years are guaranteed suitable housing arranged by the university.
International students: as above.
Contact: Accommodation@stir.ac.uk

University of Strathclyde

Even as Anderson's Institution in the 18th century, Strathclyde concentrated on "useful learning". Today's university has set itself the target of being recognised as one of the world's leading technological universities. The new Vice-Chancellor, Professor Jim McDonald, has called for improvements in research to achieve this goal, but has promised not to neglect the student experience.

Strathclyde aims to offer courses that are both innovative and relevant to industry and commerce – hence product design and innovation, or international business with modern languages. Business and law were the main successes in the 2008 Research Assessment Exercise, when almost 60 per cent of the university's submission was rated as world-leading or internationally excellent. Pharmacy and some branches of engineering also achieved good results.

The business school is normally considered Strathclyde's main strength. It is one of the largest in Europe and the only one in Scotland to be accredited by the European Quality Improvement System. Business studies students follow an "integrative studies" programme, which is designed to place them in a realistic business environment from day one and involves work with a range of major companies. The scheme is now being piloted in other faculties.

The engineering faculty is also the largest in Scotland, and has linked with Glasgow University to provide a joint department of naval architecture and marine engineering. There were several joint submissions in the RAE, as part of Scotland's "pooling" arrangement in potentially vulnerable science subjects.

European focus is evident throughout the university, which has encouraged all departments to adapt their courses to the needs of the single market. Many students combine business or engineering with European studies or languages to give themselves an edge in the job market. Mature students account for nearly a fifth of the places and have a special organisation to look after their interests. With nearly 22,000 students, including part-timers, Strathclyde is the third-largest university in Scotland, but its numbers swell to 60,000 including short courses and distance learning programmes.

Strathclyde actively promotes wider access, comfortably exceeding national averages for state-educated students and the share of places going to applicants from working-class homes. Its efforts are underpinned by fundraising for a scholarship programme to aid students from poor homes. The projected dropout rate had fallen to 14 per cent in the latest

---

16 Richmond Street
Glasgow G1 1XQ
0141 552 4400 (main switchboard)
scls@strath.ac.uk
www.strath.ac.uk
www.strathstudents
.com

The Times Rankings
Overall Ranking: 37

Student satisfaction:	=40	(76%)
Research quality:	=41	(1.6)
Entry standards:	23	(393)
Student–staff ratio:	=80	(19.1)
Services & facilities/student:	33	(£1,344)
Expected completion rate:	63	(83.1%)
Good honours:	18	(73.9%)
Graduate prospects:	=17	(78.1%)

survey, but is still higher than the UK average for the university's subjects and entry qualifications.

The main John Anderson campus is in the centre of Glasgow, behind George Square and near Queen Street station. Apart from the Edwardian headquarters, the buildings are mostly modern. The site of a former maternity hospital in the centre of the campus will eventually provide extra teaching accommodation, but a £73-million refurbishment programme is taking priority. Strathclyde has a second campus on the west side of the city, acquired from a merger with Jordanhill College of Education, Scotland's largest teacher training institution, in 1993. The 67-acre parkland site houses the faculty of education, which is breaking new ground with Scotland's first part-time teacher training degree and also offers courses in speech and language pathology, community arts, social work, sport and outdoor education. The university plans to sell the site and move the courses onto the main campus, but this is unlikely to take place in the near future.

Strathclyde has shed its image as a "nine-to-five" university, thanks to a student village on the main campus, complete with pub, which has increased the number of residential places. Over 1,400 of these are on campus, all with network access, and another 500 are

nearby. The Millennium Student project has delivered full network access from every study bedroom on campus and it is planned to make extensive high-speed dial-up facilities into the university network available for all students in the Glasgow area. The ten-floor union building attracts students from all over Glasgow with its reputation for hard-drinking revelry. For those with more sophisticated tastes, there are several theatres and the city's own variety of cultural venues.

Undergraduate Fees and Bursaries

- Scottish-domiciled and EU students: no fees payable.
- Non-Scottish UK-domiciled student fees: £1,820 a year.
- International student fees: £9,500–£12,200
- Scholarships based on circumstances or by competition.
- For full details see the university's website: www.strath.ac.uk/feenews

---

Students

Undergraduates:	11,050	(2,675)
Postgraduates:	4,220	(3,795)
Mature students:	16.7%	
Overseas students:	6.4%	
Applications per place:	5.3	
From state-sector schools:	92.3%	
From working-class homes:	26.7%	

For detailed information about fees, grants and bursaries and how they work, see chapter 7.

Accommodation

Number of places and costs refer to 2009–10

University-provided places: 1,979

Percentage catered: 0%

Self-catered costs: £74–£97 a week.

First years are offered accommodation if they live further than 25 miles from the university.

International students: as above.

Contact:

student.accommodation@mis.strath.ac.uk

www.strath.ac.uk/accommodation/

University of Sunderland

Sunderland already has one of the UK's newest campuses, having taken advantage of urban regeneration programmes to transform its facilities. Now a second phase has been announced, with a £75-million development of the original City Campus to provide new sports and social space, a hotel and conference facility, landscaping and traffic calming measures. The main feature of the campus, right in the city centre, is the Gateway one-stop shop for student services, but there is a well-appointed science complex and design centre.

The university's other campus at St Peter's, an award-winning 24-acre site by the banks of the Wear, houses the business school and the faculties of applied sciences and arts, design and media. The Sir Tom Cowie campus is built around a 7th-century abbey described as one of Britain's first universities and incorporates a working heritage centre for the glass industry. A glass and ceramics design degree maintains a Sunderland tradition, while teaching and research in automotive design and manufacture serve the region's modern industrial base. The large pharmacy department is another strength and the well-equipped Faculty of Applied Sciences is one of the largest in the UK, with over 3,000 students.

Sunderland is making the most of the opportunity to link up with the multinational companies that have arrived on its doorstep. The Institute for Automotive and Manufacturing Advanced Practice has a team of 40 researchers and consultants working with local businesses, while nearby Nissan played an important role in designing a course in automotive product development. The media centre provides students with excellent television and video production facilities.

The university has a determinedly local focus, aiming to double the number of students coming from an area which has little tradition of sending students to higher education. Only one UK university recruits a higher proportion from "low participation neighbourhoods" – at nearly 25 per cent, more than twice the national average for the subjects on offer. A pioneering access scheme offers places to mature students without A levels, as long as they reach the required levels of literacy, numeracy and other basic skills. The Learning North East initiative, based on Sunderland's successful pilot for the University for Industry, even offers free taster courses to take at home.

Almost half the undergraduates have a working-class background, and the projected dropout rate has dropped from more than a quarter to less than one in five in recent years. Provision for disabled

---

Chester Road
Sunderland SR1 3SD
0191 515 3000 (course helpline)
student-helpline@
 sunderland.ac.uk
www.sunderland.ac.uk
www.sunderlandsu
 .co.uk

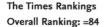

The Times Rankings
Overall Ranking: =84

Student satisfaction:	=28	(77%)
Research quality:	=63	(0.5)
Entry standards:	103	(226)
Student–staff ratio:	=46	(16.1)
Services & facilities/student:	107	(£775)
Expected completion rate:	95	(75.6%)
Good honours:	98	(50.2%)
Graduate prospects:	96	(59.3%)

students is excellent, with award-winning information produced for those with disabilities, trained support staff in every academic school as well as in the libraries and special modules to help dyslexics. The campus also houses the North East Regional Access Centre, which assesses the learning support requirements of students with disabilities and specific learning difficulties. There is special provision among the 2,200 residential places.

The university is in the top half of the table for student satisfaction, with law undergraduates emerging as the most satisfied in the country in the 2008 National Student Survey. English, history and psychology also produced high scores. Sunderland was less successful in the latest Research Assessment Exercise, although more than half of the 16 subject areas contained at least some world-leading work. Communication, cultural and media studies produced by the far best grades, but history and English also did well.

Sunderland itself is fiercely proud of its identity and has the advantage of a coastal location but, despite the city title, with the exception of the impressive new football ground, it has the leisure facilities of a medium-sized town. Those in search of big cultural events or serious nightlife head for Newcastle, which is less than half an hour away by Metro.

Undergraduate Fees and Bursaries

- Fees for UK/EU students: £3,225
- International student fees: £8,300
- Bursary on full grant: £525
- Bursaries on partial grant: household income up to £39.3K: £525.
- Scholarships based on circumstances or by competition.
- For full details see the university's website: www.sunderland.ac.uk/fees/

Students

Undergraduates:	7,530	(7,515)
Postgraduates:	1,595	(1,070)
Mature students:	34.1%	
Overseas students:	14.7%	
Applications per place:	3.9	
From state-sector schools:	98.3%	
From working-class homes:	48.0%	

For detailed information about fees, grants and bursaries and how they work, see chapter 7.

Accommodation

Number of places and costs refer to 2008–09
University provided places: 1,410 beds in Halls, 129 (Managed Houses/Head Tenancy Scheme).
Percentage Catered: 0%
Self Catered Costs: £1,442 (shared twin room; 40 weeks) – £3,500 (en suite; 50 weeks)
First-year undergraduates have priority, followed by all EU students (certain circumstances apply).
International students: as above
Contact: residentialservices@sunderland.ac.uk
www.sunderland.ac.uk/residentialservices

University of Surrey

Surrey has been one of the recent success stories of the university world, remaining true to its technological history while building a strong research base and a degree of financial independence envied by its peers. Even some of the arts degrees carry a BSc and are highly vocational: four out of five undergraduates in all subjects undertake work experience. Placements of one (or two half) years, often taken abroad, mean that most degrees last four years. The format and the subject balance combine to keep Surrey near the top of the graduate employment league, as well as producing a healthy research income. Indeed, it has taken to describing itself as the "University for Jobs" to ram the point home. Recent expansion in healthcare, human sciences and performing arts has added to the traditional strengths in science and engineering.

The mix has been proving popular: applications were down at the beginning of 2009, but this followed growth of 60 per cent over the previous three years while average entry scores rose to 372 points on the UCAS tariff. The increased demand for places has come at an opportune time: the university is planning to boost its numbers further, partly through overseas ventures. An international institute in the Chinese city of Dalian, in partnership with Dongbei

University, is the first of these. Nearer home, Surrey has taking in the Guildford School of Acting, launching its first degree in English literature in 2008.

All students are encouraged to enrol for a course at the European language centre, and a growing number of degrees, including a new range in engineering, have a language component. The cosmopolitan feel is enhanced by one of the largest proportions of overseas students at any university – a feat which won Surrey a Queen's Award for Export Achievement. The 2,700 foreign students come from 140 different countries.

More than half of the work submitted for the 2008 Research Assessment Exercise was considered world-leading or internationally excellent. Electrical and electronic engineering was ranked second in the country, while health and medical sciences, sociology and general engineering were in the top ten in their fields. Another indication of the university's research strength lies in the growing proportion of income derived from sources other than Government grants: up from 10 per cent to about 70 per cent in little over a decade. The Surrey Research Park is one of only three science parks still owned, funded and managed by the university that opened it, helping Surrey to amass one of the highest proportions of private funding at any British university.

Guildford
Surrey GU2 7XH
0800 980 3200 (enquiries)
ug-enquiries@surrey.ac.uk
www.surrey.ac.uk
www.ussu.co.uk

The Times Rankings
Overall Ranking: 38

Student satisfaction:	=40	(76%)
Research quality:	=32	(1.8)
Entry standards:	37	(352)
Student–staff ratio:	53	(16.8)
Services & facilities/student:	42	(£1,202)
Expected completion rate:	33	(88.8%)
Good honours:	44	(65.1%)
Graduate prospects:	11	(80.0%)

Scores in the National Student Survey have improved, with civil engineering, biological subjects, nursing and electronic and electrical engineering producing the highest levels of satisfaction in 2008. The 80 per cent response rate was one of the highest at any university. Both the proportions of undergraduates from working-class homes and from areas without a tradition of higher education are lower than average for the university's subjects and entry standards. But the statistics agency has acknowledged that the explanation lies largely in the university's location. The projected dropout rate of less than 10 per cent is better than the national average.

The compact campus is a ten-minute walk from the centre of Guildford. Most of the buildings date from the late 1960s, but the new business school and the gleaming European Institute of Health and Medical Sciences offer a striking contrast. Shaped like a giant ship's prow, the steel and glass building houses the large nursing and midwifery departments. The campus includes two lakes, playing fields and enough residential accommodation to enable all first-years to live in. A second campus, adjacent to the Stag Hill headquarters, is now being developed.

The new postgraduate medical school is intended to be the first stage in the development of a health campus, which will also contain more residential places for students and staff, as well as other academic buildings, leisure and sporting facilities.

Guildford has plenty of cultural and recreational facilities, but riotous nightclubs are not encouraged. The campus is the centre of social life, and has seen recent improvements to leisure facilities. The proximity of London is an attraction to many students, but also helps account for the high cost of living, which is not mitigated by the allowances available in the capital.

Undergraduate Fees and Bursaries

- Fees for UK/EU students: £3,225
- International student fees: £8,600–£11,000
- Bursary on full grant: household income up to £10K: £2,000; up to £25K: sliding scale.*
- Bursaries on partial grant: household income up to £35K: sliding scale to £0.*
- Scholarships based on circumstances or by competition.
- For full details see the university's website: www.surrey.ac.uk/undergraduate/fees/bursaries/

* Figures for 2008–09

Students		
Undergraduates:	7,845	(1,990)
Postgraduates:	2,960	(2,280)
Mature students:	26.5%	
Overseas students:	13.8%	
Applications per place:	5.0	
From state-sector schools:	90.9%	
From working-class homes:	22.2%	

For detailed information about fees, grants and bursaries and how they work, see chapter 7.

Accommodation

Number of places and costs refer to 2009–10
University-provided places: 4,648
Percentage catered: 0%
Self-catered costs: £58.10–£123.40 a week.
All first years are guaranteed a place.
International non-EU students are guaranteed accommodation for the whole of their course.
Remaining places are allocated to final year students.
Contact: www.surrey.ac.uk/Accommodation

University of Sussex

Sussex is in the top 150 in the world rankings published by *Times Higher Education*/QS, and rates higher still for the arts and social sciences. Its reputation was enhanced by good results in the 2008 Research Assessment Exercise, when almost 60 per cent of an unusually large submission was rated as world-leading or internationally excellent. The university was ranked top in the country for American studies and among the leaders in the history of art and politics. The university now generates more than a third of its income from private sources, largely in research contracts.

There has also been dramatic improvement in Sussex's performance in the National Student Survey over the past two years, propelling the university into the top 30 for satisfaction levels. The results published in 2008 showed 100 per cent satisfaction in physics, with biological subjects, social work, economics and law also doing well. However, previously strong demand for places has stalled in the last two years, with a 4 per cent decline in applications at the start of 2009 following a big drop in 2008.

The university is aiming to improve the student experience with the introduction of the Sussex Plus initiative, which will provide recognition for students' voluntary work and other extra-curricular activities. As part of a focus on flexible learning, the library has introduced 24-hour opening during term time and many lectures are available online for students to download. The interdisciplinary approach that has always been Sussex's trademark has been re-examined to adapt this 1960s concept for the 21st century. An academic restructuring exercise has produced 12 schools of study to improve students' access to support.

Arts and social science students take the biggest share of places, but the life sciences are not far behind. The newly created School of Business, Management and Economics, opening in 2009, will offer a portfolio of undergraduate and postgraduate business and management programmes.

Sussex is committed to taking candidates with no family tradition of higher education and has much larger numbers of mature students than most of its peer group of institutions. The proportion of working-class students is marginally lower than the national average for the university's subjects and entry grades, but this is attributed to the university's south coast location. The projected dropout rate has been improving and, at less than 10 per cent, is below average.

The university is based within the Downs, in a designated Area of

---

Sussex House
Falmer
Brighton BN1 9RH
01273 678416 (admissions)
ug.admissions@
  sussex.ac.uk
www.sussex.ac.uk
www.ussu.info

The Times Rankings
Overall Ranking: 35

Student satisfaction:	=67	(74%)
Research quality:	=17	(2.2)
Entry standards:	=27	(378)
Student–staff ratio:	41	(15.5)
Services & facilities/student:	58	(£1,117)
Expected completion rate:	30	(90.1%)
Good honours:	4	(81.7%)
Graduate prospects:	46	(70.6%)

Outstanding Natural Beauty, four miles from the centre of Brighton. The university is currently completing a £100-million campus development plan, which will refurbish Sir Basil Spence's original buildings and add new ones. Student accommodation has also been upgraded; there are more than 3,000 residential places on campus, including rooms in newly built halls offering en-suite rooms – and there are plans to increase campus accommodation still further. All first-year students are guaranteed a place in university-managed accommodation.

Relations with neighbouring Brighton University are good. The two institutions succeeded in a joint bid for a medical school, which opened in 2003 and has since recorded big increases in applications. The Brighton and Sussex Medical School (www.bsms.ac.uk) is split between the Royal Sussex County Hospital and the two universities' Falmer campuses.

Sussex has always attracted overseas students in large numbers and has seen big increases recently, but a high proportion of the remainder are from the London area, where many return at weekends. As a result, the well-appointed campus can be quiet, although there is no shortage of social events, and Brighton has plenty to offer. Sports facilities are good, and the university has launched initiatives in basketball and hockey to entice top performers.

Undergraduate Fees and Bursaries

- Fees for UK/EU students: £3,225
- International student fees: £9,975–£12,750
  £23,678 (medicine)
- Bursary on full grant: £1,000
- Bursaries on partial grant: subject and academic bursaries available
- Scholarships based on circumstances or by competition.
- For full details see the university's website: www.sussex.ac.uk/ scholarships_and_bursaries.html

Students

Undergraduates:	7,850	(1,940)
Postgraduates:	1,830	(825)
Mature students:	16.2%	
Overseas students:	9.2%	
Applications per place:	4.9	
From state-sector schools:	86.1%	
From working-class homes:	22.3%	

For detailed information about fees, grants and bursaries and how they work, see chapter 7.

Accommodation

Number of places and costs refer to 2008–09

University-provided places: 3,430

Percentage catered: 0%

Self-catered costs: £51–£110 a week.

First-year students are guaranteed accommodation if conditions are met.

International students: given priority providing conditions are met.

Contact: housing@sussex.ac.uk

Swansea University

Swansea's attractive coastal location and easy access from outside Wales have helped to make it a popular choice for students. Applications were up by more than 7 per cent at the start of 2009. Most of those who take up places seem to enjoy their time there: Swansea has won awards for the best student experience in the UK and has become established among the best performers in the National Student Survey. The university has been in and around the top 20 in every year of the survey, with English, sports science, law and geography registering particularly high levels of satisfaction.

Swansea became independent of the University of Wales in 2007 and entrants in 2010 will receive a Swansea degree. Independence is intended to reflect confidence in the future, as well as helping with international recruitment and research partnerships. There are now about 500 degree courses in the modular scheme, and undergraduates are encouraged to stray outside their specialist area in their first year.

The university has links to more than 90 European institutions and offers many degrees that include opportunities to study abroad. It has won European funding for some of its projects, including Graduate Opportunities Wales, which steers students towards small firms through industrial placements and vacation jobs.

The most important academic development, however, has come with the opening of the School of Medicine and the subsequent development of a full four-year graduate entry medical degree to be launched in 2009. Previous entrants have spent half of their course in Cardiff, but the new degree is linked to a new University NHS Trust and the £50-million Institute of Life Science. The institute's six-storey building is home to the IBM "Blue C" Supercomputer, one of the fastest computers in the world dedicated to life science research.

Another recent addition is the £4.3-million Digital Technium Building, housing the media and communication studies department. And the university's commitment to aerospace engineering recently included investment in a £250,000 single-seat flight simulator facility, housed in the School of Engineering.

Despite its international links, Swansea has not forgotten its local responsibilities. The Department of Adult and Community Education teaches mature students in locations throughout the Valleys and elsewhere in South Wales. Compacts with the region's schools encourage students in areas of economic disadvantage to aspire to higher education.

Singleton Park
Swansea SA2 8PP
01792 295111
admissions@swansea.ac.uk
www.swansea.ac.uk
www.swansea-union.co.uk

The Times Rankings
Overall Ranking: 50

Student satisfaction:	=20	(78%)
Research quality:	=43	(1.5)
Entry standards:	51	(304)
Student–staff ratio:	=30	(14.7)
Services & facilities/student:	=56	(£1,122)
Expected completion rate:	38	(87.3%)
Good honours:	97	(50.3%)
Graduate prospects:	85	(62.5%)

Swansea makes a particular effort to cater for disabled students, which are coordinated through a £250,000 assessment and training centre. Other access measures have been successful: almost 10 per cent of the students come from areas of low participation in higher education, while the 93 per cent share of places going to applicants from state schools and colleges is significantly higher than the UK average for the university's courses and entry grades. The projected dropout rate is a respectable 12 per cent.

The attractive parkland campus two miles from the centre of Swansea overlooks the sea and offers ready access to the Gower Peninsula, the UK's first area of outstanding natural beauty. Apart from Singleton Abbey, the neo-Gothic mansion which houses the administration, most of the buildings are modern. The university has recently opened two new halls of residence, providing a further 350 study bedrooms that takes the total to over 3,000.

The University's £20-million Sports Village includes a 50-metre pool, a warm-up pool, athletics track, all-weather pitches, indoor athletics training centre and gym, which attract top performers. The 1,800 computers available for student use represent one of the best ratios at any university. The campus is the focal point of most students' leisure activities, but the city has a good range of leisure facilities, including the new LC2 Leisure Centre, which includes Wales' largest indoor water-park and the world's first deep water standing wave machine – the Boardrider.

Undergraduate Fees and Bursaries
- Fees for UK/EU students: £3,225 (grant of up to £1,940 for Welsh students).
- International student fees: £9,300–£11,900
- Bursary of £319 (household income up to £18,370).
- No other bursaries available.
- Scholarships based on circumstances or by competition.
- For full details see the university's website: www.swansea.ac.uk/scholarships

Students		
Undergraduates:	9,050	(2,685)
Postgraduates:	1,330	(810)
Mature students:	19.5%	
Overseas students:	7.9%	
Applications per place:	3.5	
From state-sector schools:	93.2%	
From working-class homes:	29.2%	

For detailed information about fees, grants and bursaries and how they work, see chapter 7.

Accommodation
Number of places and costs refer to 2008–09
University-provided places: about 3,400
Percentage catered: 11%
Catered costs: £93.50–£104.50 a week.
Self-catered costs: £62–£93 a week.
First-year students holding a firm offer are guaranteed accommodation if conditions are met.
International students: offered up to 3 years.
Contact: accommodation@swansea.ac.uk

Swansea Metropolitan University

Although university status arrived only in 2008, Swansea Met can trace its history back more than 150 years. However, it does not appear in the main League Table or in any of the subject tables because the new university has again instructed the Higher Education Statistics Agency not to release data on its performance. Those figures that are available suggest that it would have appeared in the lower reaches of the table, but not right at the bottom.

The 25 academics entered for the 2008 Research assessment Exercise represented the smallest submission at any UK university, for example. But there was some world-leading research in three of the four subject areas in which the university was assessed. Engineering produced the best results. Every faculty has a research director and a series of research centres is planned.

Similarly, results in the last three National Student Surveys have been disappointing, but Swansea Met would not have been in the bottom 20 universities in 2008. Teacher trainees were extremely satisfied, but no other subject achieved 85 per cent satisfaction levels.

Swansea Met is divided into three faculties: Applied Design and Engineering, Art and Design, and Humanities. Of around 5,500 students, just more than half are full-time undergraduates, almost half of whom are studying education or the humanities, and a third of whom are over 21 on entry. Surprisingly, given the mix of subjects, more of them are male than female. Two thirds of the undergraduates come from within 45 miles of Swansea, but there is also a long-established tradition of overseas recruitment, which accounts for almost 7 per cent of the places.

Based around the centre of Swansea, the new university is gradually developing an urban campus. There are four sites close to the city centre and another high above the city, overlooking Swansea Bay, for education and the humanities. The main Mount Pleasant campus is the largest in terms of student numbers, hosting design and engineering, business and leisure courses. Its automotive engineering degrees – especially those focused on motorsport – are probably now the best-known feature of the university.

The nearby Dynevor site has seen the most recent development, with an impressive new building for art, design and media, which was rated excellent in the now dated teaching quality assessments. All the faculty's students undertake an "external project" with a company or outside organisation, which has improved employment prospects in a

Mount Pleasant
Swansea SA1 6ED
01792 481010
enquiry@smu.ac.uk
www.smu.ac.uk
www.metsu.org

The Times Rankings
Swansea Metropolitan blocked the release of data from the Higher Education Statistics Agency and so we cannot give any ranking information.

notoriously difficult group of subjects. The two smaller sites are the former college of art, which focuses on the university's internationally rated work on architectural stained glass, and the former BBC building, where the music technology degree is located.

University status arrived at an opportune moment for, while other universities in Wales were experiencing a serious downturn in applications at the beginning of 2008, the decline was the smallest in the Principality. However, the demand for places was down by more than 4 per cent at the start of 2009, when most universities saw healthy increases.

Efforts to widen participation in higher education are high on the new university's agenda. More than four undergraduates in ten have a working-class background and a high proportion come from areas with little tradition of higher education. Almost all the students are state-educated. However, the projected dropout rate is well above average for the university's courses and entry grades, with almost a quarter not expected to complete their course in the expected time.

There are fewer than 600 residential places – not enough for all first years – but private housing is plentiful and reasonably priced. The city has seen considerable development recently and has a good range of pubs and clubs. The university's sports facilities are not extensive, but the nearby Gower Peninsula, officially an area of outstanding natural beauty, is a prime location for surfers and walkers.

Undergraduate Fees and Bursaries
- Fees for UK/EU students: £3,225 (grant of up to £1,940 for Welsh students).
- International student fees: £7,500
- Bursary of £319 (household income up to £18,370).
- £500 if living more than 45 miles from University (UK and EU students only).
- Scholarships based on circumstances or by competition.
- For full details see the university's website: www.smu.ac.uk/sihe/bursaries/bursaries.htm

---

Students
From state-sector schools: 98.4%
From working-class homes: 42.4%

For detailed information about fees, grants and bursaries and how they work, see chapter 7.

Accommodation
Number of places and costs refer to 2008–09
University-provided places: 318
Percentage catered: 0%
Self-catered costs: £49 (twin) – £65 (en suite) a week.
First years cannot be guaranteed accommodation. Residential restrictions apply.
International students: guaranteed if conditions met and application received by 31 August.
Contact: accommodation@smu.ac.uk; 01792 482082

Teesside University

Teesside used to describe itself as the Opportunity University, stressing its open access and customer-oriented approach. But its latest mission statement stresses "pursuing excellence" to suggest that there will be no compromise on quality. The formula is popular with undergraduates: the 2008 National Student Survey showed the university's design and media students to be the most satisfied in the country. History, law and English also did well.

Teesside has long been among the leading new universities for the proportion of leavers going into graduate-level jobs or further training. The university also improved its grades in the 2008 Research Assessment Exercise, albeit with only a small proportion of its academics submitting work. Thirty per cent of the research was considered world-leading or internationally excellent, with computer science and history achieving the best results. Five research-led institutes will focus on digital innovation, health, culture, social science and technology.

Official performance indicators also show the university well ahead of the access benchmarks calculated by the Higher Education Statistics Agency. It takes more undergraduates (over a quarter) than any UK university from areas of low participation in higher education, while almost half come from working-class homes. The projected dropout rate has improved, partly because of a programme that supports non-traditional students, funded by the European Union, and is now well below the national average for the courses and entry qualifications.

Over 2,500 students are taking Teesside courses at local further education colleges, which are also involved in the growing range of full-time and part-time two-year Foundation degrees. The university has opened its first higher education centre attached to one of the colleges in Darlington. The Passport scheme offers help and guidance to students considering going to university. However, the university's best-known access initiative targets a much younger age group. The prize-winning Meteor scheme gives primary school children a taste of higher education, with university students acting as mentors while earning some useful extra cash and gaining experience of working in schools.

Although Middlesbrough has never been considered a fashionable student destination, the demand for places has been sustained at a time when some new universities were having recruitment problems. There was a decline in applications in 2008, but the demand for places had recovered at the start of 2009, with a 7 per cent increase. Teesside is also

7 Borough Road
Middlesbrough TS1 3BA
01642 218121 (switchboard)
enquiries@tees.ac.uk
www.tees.ac.uk
www.utsu.org.uk

Edinburgh
Belfast
MIDDLESBROUGH
London
Cardiff

The Times Rankings
Overall Ranking: =81

=		
Student satisfaction:	=28	(77%)
Research quality:	=95	(0.2)
Entry standards:	=80	(257)
Student–staff ratio:	84	(19.3)
Services & facilities/student:	103	(£808)
Expected completion rate:	103	(72.7%)
Good honours:	=85	(52.4%)
Graduate prospects:	63	(67.3%)

becoming more popular with international students with the numbers from outside the EU almost doubling over the last two years.

There are now more than 22,000 undergraduates, over half of them taking part-time courses and more than a third over 21 on entry. The 9,500 health students are now by far the largest group in the university, but Teesside is strong in niche markets such as computer games design and animation, sport and exercise, forensic science and health-related courses like physiotherapy and radiography.

More than £100 million has been spent in recent years on the town-centre campus. A new sport and health sciences building with dentistry training and hydrotherapy facilities is due to open in 2010. Recent developments include a £10-million centre for creative technologies, for computing, media and design students, and a £12-million Institute of Digital Innovation, which supports digital business enterprises. Over 100 new graduate businesses have been incubated on campus since 2001 and Teesside has been awarded £5 million to help it become a leading business-facing university. Computer provision is generous, with 2,500 workstations available for student use. Specialist facilities for those studying computer games design, animation and digital media include a new digital sound and TV studio which can create special effects.

Middlesbrough has more nightlife than sceptics might imagine, and the booming student population has attracted new pubs, cafés and student-orientated shops in and around the Southfield Road area. The cost of living is another attraction: university rents are reasonable and the lively students' union has twice won the title of students' union of the year. Outdoor sports facilities, shared with Durham University, include a £1.5-million watersports centre on the River Tees.

Undergraduate Fees and Bursaries

- Fees for UK/EU students: £3,225
- International student fees: £8,500
- Bursary on full grant: £1,025
- Bursaries on partial grant: n/a
- Scholarships based on circumstances or by competition.
- For full details see the university's website: www.tees.ac.uk/funding

Students

Undergraduates:	8,325	(14,100)
Postgraduates:	1,375	(1,605)
Mature students:	36.5%	
Overseas students:	4.6%	
Applications per place:	3.5	
From state-sector schools:	99.1%	
From working-class homes:	48.6%	

For detailed information about fees, grants and bursaries and how they work, see chapter 7.

Accommodation

Number of places and costs refer to 2009–10

University-provided places: 1,124

Percentage catered: 0%

Self-catered costs: £45.50–£78.00 a week (residences, 37 weeks); £41–£45 a week (managed housing, 38 weeks)

University managed residences are reserved exclusively for first years.

International students: as above.

Contact: 01642 342255; accommodation@tees.ac.uk

Thames Valley University

A series of mergers has altered the scale and character of Thames Valley, which is aiming to become the country's leading university for employer engagement, with an accent on the creative industries and entrepreneurship. The university now has 33,000 students, two thirds of whom are part-timers and more than half taking further education courses. There is even a sixth-form academy.

The three main campuses all have distinctive missions. Reading, where the former college campus is being redeveloped, mainly offers further education with locally focused higher education. In Slough, where there is an award-winning learning resources centre designed by Sir Richard Rogers, the university will concentrate on the needs of the town's large business community, while the Ealing campus, in west London, has a more traditional university feel and is being upgraded at a cost of almost £10 million. In addition, a landmark building in Brentford, not far from the Ealing campus, houses one of the largest healthcare faculty in Britain and contains 850 residential places.

It is all a far cry from the end of the 1990s, when barely 30 degrees were left, after a tumultuous period in which academic standards were criticised and student demand collapsed. The university is virtually unrecognisable from those dark days, but there was a hitch in its development when a failure to hit previous recruitment targets led to cuts of nearly 12 per cent in its budget for 2009–10. Applications were up at the start of 2009 by 4 per cent, but the university was shedding staff to balance the books.

Courses are now concentrated in three faculties – arts, professional studies and health and human sciences. Many further education programmes are being extended into degrees or professional qualifications. Amid the reconstruction, new honours degrees have been launched in areas such as video production, 3D design, entrepreneurship, computing and information systems. The portfolio of two-year Foundation degrees is growing, with employers such as Compaq, Ealing Studios and the Savoy Hotel Group helping to provide courses. Some are run in conjunction with Stratford-upon-Avon College – one of a number of partner institutions.

Nursing courses are popular and well regarded, while the School of Hospitality and Tourism is recognised by the Académie Culinaire de France for its culinary arts programmes. The London College of Music, which is part of TVU, has some of the longest-established music technology courses in the country. The

St Mary's Road
Ealing
London W5 5RF
0800 036 8888 (admissions)
admissions@tvu.ac.uk
www.tvu.ac.uk
www.tvusu.co.uk

The Times Rankings
Overall Ranking: 110

Student satisfaction:	=78	(73%)
Research quality:	=95	(0.2)
Entry standards:	111	(197)
Student–staff ratio:	101	(20.6)
Services & facilities/student:	102	(£827)
Expected completion rate:	113	(63.6%)
Good honours:	96	(50.4%)
Graduate prospects:	93	(59.7%)

university has improved its scores in the National Student Survey, but was still close to the bottom ten in 2008. Only business courses achieved a satisfaction rate of more than 85 per cent, while fewer than half of the final-year undergraduates in film studies, photography and other creative arts were satisfied overall with their course.

A policy of open access puts the university at a disadvantage on other measures in our ranking. For example, the projected dropout rate has been climbing alarmingly and, at almost 29 per cent, is now among the highest in the country. Three quarters of the students are over 24, and about 60 per cent are female. Four undergraduates in ten come from working-class homes.

TVU improved its ratings considerably in the 2008 Research Assessment Exercise, but entered only a small proportion of its academics. Only nursing and midwifery was judged to have world-leading research.

The town-centre sites in Ealing, Brentford and Slough are linked by a free bus service. The busy Ealing base is within easy reach of central London without the metropolitan hassle that students encounter at some institutions in the capital. Almost half of the students are from London or Berkshire, and there is an unexpectedly large contingent of international students.

Residential accommodation is growing and the new Paragon building, in Brentford, won *Building* magazine's Major Housing Project of the Year award. However, students who rely on private housing find the cost of living high. There is a football ground and cricket pitch close to the Ealing campus, but otherwise sports facilities are limited.

Undergraduate Fees and Bursaries
- Fees for UK/EU students: £3,225
- International student fees: £7,600–£8,900*
- Bursary on full grant: £1,060
- Bursaries on partial grant: household income £25K–£40K: £530.
- Scholarships based on circumstances or by competition.
- For full details see the university's website: www.tvu.ac.uk/students/undergraduate/ Scholarships_and_bursaries.jsp

* Figures for 2008–09

Students

Undergraduates:	8,325	(7,785)
Postgraduates:	565	(1,465)
Mature students:	61.5%	
Overseas students:	15.4%	
Applications per place:	3.2	
From state-sector schools:	98.3%	
From working-class homes:	40.2%	

For detailed information about fees, grants and bursaries and how they work, see chapter 7.

Accommodation

Number of places and costs refer to 2007–08
University-provided places: about 911
Percentage catered: 0%
Self-catered costs: £87–£152 a week.
First years are prioritised for accommodation at Ealing if conditions are met; accommodation at Reading is allocated on a distance from campus basis.
International students: same as above.
Contact: uas@tvu.ac.uk
reading.homes@tvu.ac.uk

University of Ulster

Ulster is in the top 20 universities in terms of applications and registered another 6 per cent increase at the start of 2009. One of the best performances of any new university in the 2008 Research Assessment Exercise can only enhance its reputation. Nearly half of its submission was rated as world-leading or internationally excellent, with the university ranked in the top three for bio-medical sciences, nursing and midwifery and Celtic studies. Results improved in almost all areas, leaving Ulster within sight of neighbouring Queen's University in the research tables.

The university is the only one in Britain with a charter stipulating that there should be courses below degree level. Certificates, diplomas and integrated foundation years lead on to honours degrees. Plans to improve and expand all four main sites, at a cost of £200 million, are almost complete. With more Irish students now choosing to stay in the Province to study, there is plenty of scope for expansion, despite the fact that UU already has nearly 24,000 students, including almost 8,000 part-timers.

The main sites in and near Belfast have never been busier, while the Magee campus, in Londonderry, attracts students from both sides of the border. The sites are 80 miles apart at their farthest point and very different in character, although there is extensive use of e-learning. A few courses offer lectures on more than one campus, but for the most part students are based on a single site throughout their university life. The contrasts contribute to bigger variations in satisfaction levels in different subjects than at most universities. The 2008 National Student Survey showed 100 per cent satisfaction in biology and high levels in finance, sports science, geography and English, but relatively low scores in linguistics and subjects allied to medicine.

Jordanstown, seven miles outside Belfast, has the most students, concentrat-ing on engineering, health and social science. New student accommodation has been added recently, with another 350 rooms due to be available for the 2009–10 academic year. About £20 million has been invested in a new sports centre, with the aim of making Ulster Ireland's top univer-sity for sport. Facilities include an indoor sports hall, outdoor and indoor sprint tracks, a strength and conditioning suite, water recovery area and sports science and sports medicine facilities. Jordanstown already hosted the Sports Institute for Northern Ireland and the university's own High Performance Centre. There are no on-site sports facilities at the Belfast campus.

The small Belfast site specialises in art and design but, since a £30-million redevelopment, has added hospitality and tourism with degrees that include

---

Cromore Road
Coleraine
Co. Londonderry BT52 1SA
08700 400 700
enquiry via website
www.ulster.ac.uk
www.uusu.org

The Times Rankings
Overall Ranking: 54

Student satisfaction:	=54	(75%)
Research quality:	=52	(1.0)
Entry standards:	=69	(268)
Student–staff ratio:	45	(15.9)
Services & facilities/student:	17	(£1,548)
Expected completion rate:	88	(77.4%)
Good honours:	56	(61.4%)
Graduate prospects:	72	(65.0%)

international hotel and tourism management; and culinary arts. New student facilities include new lecture theatres and flexible learning spaces, a learning resource centre, conference and gallery facilities and a training restaurant.

The original classic campus is at Coleraine and focuses on science and the humanities. It has an £11-million Centre for Molecular Biosciences and a new learning resource centre opened in 2007. There is now a Learning Resource Centre at each of the University's four campuses. Once the poor relation of the university, confined to adult education, Magee is now a thriving centre. Further expansion is planned in the new schools of performing arts, computing and electronics, as well as improved provision for education, nursing and Irish studies. The Graduate School of Professional Legal Education will allow graduates to train as barristers and solicitors. The historic Foyle Arts Centre has become part of the university and a postgraduate medical school is planned.

Almost half the students come from working-class homes, and the student profile mirrors the religious balance in the wider population. Mature students are well catered for, with access courses for those who lack the necessary entry qualifications, a nursery and three playgroups in the university. The projected dropout rate had improved in the latest survey but, at more than 21 per cent, was still considerably higher than the benchmark calculated according to the university's subjects and entry grades. Over the next three years, the university is making £3 million available to fund "Opportunity Scholarships" across all faculties. There has never been a big representation from mainland Britain, but the university's contingent of international students include those from the Republic of Ireland as well as further afield. The Campus One programme provides an alternative mode of study, offering courses online to students all over the world.

With more than half of Ulster's students home based, the university is not always the focus of social life. The exception is the Coleraine campus, although many gravitate towards the nearby seaside towns of Portrush and Portstewart.

Undergraduate Fees and Bursaries

- Fees for UK/EU students: £3,225
- International student fees: £8,760
- Bursary on full grant: up to £18.2: £1,070; up to £21.5K: £640.
- Bursaries on partial grant: household income up to £40.2K: £320.
- Scholarships based on circumstances or by competition.
- For full details see the university's website: http://prospectus.ulster.ac.uk/geninfo/how-much-does-it-cost.html

---

Students

Undergraduates:	14,675	(4,370)
Postgraduates:	1,245	(3,350)
Mature students:	18.6%	
Overseas students:	8.3%	
Applications per place:	4.8	
From state-sector schools:	100.0%	
From working-class homes:	47.2%	

For detailed information about fees, grants and bursaries and how they work, see chapter 7.

Accommodation

Number of places and costs refer to 2008–09
University-provided places: 2,300
Percentage catered: 0%
Self-catered costs: £50–£130 a week.
First-year students are guaranteed accommodation if conditions are met.
International students: same as above.
Contact: accommodation@ulster.ac.uk

University of the Arts London

The collection of world-famous art, design, fashion and media colleges that constituted the London Institute became a university in 2005. With more nearly 30,000 further and higher education students spread through 20 sites around central London, it is the largest arts university in Europe. Unlike the other new foundations of that year, it has a research remit and is already becoming a powerful "brand".

The five component colleges became six when Wimbledon College of Art joined in 2006, bringing an international reputation in theatre design and the UK's largest school of theatre. The founding members, which continue to use their own names and enjoy considerable autonomy, were Camberwell College of Arts, Central Saint Martins College of Art and Design, Chelsea College of Art and Design, London College of Fashion and London College of Communication (formerly the London College of Printing).

Big changes were already under way before the change of title was agreed: a £70-million development programme has produced prestigious new premises for Chelsea College next door to the Tate Gallery, on Millbank, with extensive workshop facilities, studios and an impressive new library. Another £32 million was spent on new headquarters for the College of Communication at the Elephant and Castle, south of the Thames, where a newly built Special Archives and Collections Centre will include the archives of the filmmaker Stanley Kubrick. The college now has Film Academy status.

London's largest open air art gallery was launched in July 2008 on the Parade Ground at the heart of the Chelsea College of Art and Design, funded by a £1.5-million gift from the Rootstein Hopkins Foundation. Summer 2008 also saw the launch of University's first virtual degree show, showcasing final-year students' work online. The next major project will bring Central Saint Martins together on one site for the first time, when it moves to the new King's Cross development in 2011.

Published assessments have barely done justice to the eminence of the colleges. But the 2008 Research Assessment Exercise saw half of the university's submission rated as world-leading or internationally excellent – albeit one that involved a relatively low proportion of the academics.

Chelsea and London College of Fashion were jointly awarded a national teaching centre for the arts, focusing on practice-based teaching and learning. All the colleges make good use of visiting lecturers, who keep students abreast of current developments in their field. But Arts London has had the lowest score in the last three National Student Surveys, the

---

65 Davies Street
London W1K 5DA
020 7514 6130 (enquiries)
info@arts.ac.uk
www.arts.ac.uk
www.suarts.org

The Times Rankings
Overall Ranking: 96

Student satisfaction:	110	(62%)
Research quality:	=52	(1.0)
Entry standards:	44	(322)
Student–staff ratio:	108	(21.7)
Services & facilities/student:	99	(£849)
Expected completion rate:	47	(85.5%)
Good honours:	54	(61.6%)
Graduate prospects:	80	(63.6%)

level of satisfaction falling in 2008, when there were rises elsewhere. Art and design students are among the least satisfied nationally, but the university was not among the top 15 for those subjects alone.

The figures have not affected applications, which have risen every year since the university was established. There had been another 6 per cent increase at the official deadline for courses beginning in 2009. A number of two-year Foundation degrees have been introduced, including one in interactive games production and another in fashion styling and photography.

The university has been running weekend classes and summer schools in an attempt to broaden the intake, as well as organising a national event to help students with their portfolios, and the proportion of undergraduates from working-class homes is now over a quarter. The projected dropout rate of 14 per cent is slightly higher than average for the subjects on offer.

Students have access to the largest art and design specialist careers information centre in the country, while the pioneering Emerging Artists Programme continues to support graduates in the early years of their careers. A £2-million information technology system links all the sites. The colleges vary considerably in character and facilities, although a single students' union serves them all and a new Student Hub has brought all student services together at the university's central London headquarters. The university is not overprovided with residential accommodation, although there are 11 residences spread around the colleges, providing more than 2,900 beds. House-hunting workshops help those who have to rely on what is inevitably an expensive private housing market. Somewhat stereotypically, the university owns no sports facilities, although it has arranged student discounts with a number of providers.

Undergraduate Fees and Bursaries

- Fees for UK/EU students: £3,225
- International student fees: £11,900
- Bursary on full grant: £319
- Bursaries on partial grant: considered for £1,000 University Access Bursary.
- Scholarships based on circumstances or by competition.
- For full details see the university's website: www.arts.ac.uk/money

Students

Undergraduates:	12,100	(655)
Postgraduates:	1,760	(845)
Mature students:	29.2%	
Overseas students:	31.4%	
Applications per place:	5.4	
From state-sector schools:	95.0%	
From working-class homes:	28.2%	

For detailed information about fees, grants and bursaries and how they work, see chapter 7.

Accommodation

Number of places and costs refer to 2009–10
University-provided places: 2,936
Percentage catered: 0%
Self-catered costs: £81–£208 a week.
First-year students are offered accommodation if conditions are met. Priority for disabled students and those from outside London. International students: guaranteed if conditions met.
Contact: www.arts.ac.uk/housing/ accommodation@arts.ac.uk

University College London

Such is the breadth and quality of provision at University College London (UCL) that, even without being a university in its own right, it can fairly describe itself as one of the top multifaculty institutions in England. Its position in *The Times* rankings has regularly confirmed this and it climbed to seventh place in the world in the global rankings published by *Times Higher Education*/QS in 2008. UCL's excellence is built on a history of pioneering subjects that have become commonplace in higher education: modern languages, geography and fine arts among them.

The 2008 Research Assessment Exercise provided further confirmation of UCL's academic power, with two thirds of its submission judged to be world-leading or internationally excellent. The top scorers were economics, which saw 95 per cent of its work rated in the top two categories, and computer science and informatics, immunology and infection, environmental sciences and history of art, all of which had at least 80 per cent at this level. Architecture, chemical engineering, cancer studies, law, philosophy and psychology also produced outstanding results.

Already comfortably the largest of London University's colleges, UCL took in a number of specialist schools and institutes at the end of the 1990s. Most were medical or dental, and UCL's medical school is now a large and formidable unit. Its credentials have been strengthened still further with the announcement that UCL will be the main university partner in the new national medical research centre to be constructed adjacent to St Pancras Station. The centre will undertake cutting-edge research to advance understanding of health and disease.

The various acquisitions mean that there are now outposts in several parts of central and north London, but the main activity remains centred on the original impressive Bloomsbury site. There have been discussions with Camden Council on the creation of a university quarter, linking UCL's buildings and the neighbouring University College Hospital buildings, together with neighbouring parts of the University of London.

UCL has done better than most London universities in the National Student Survey, with 88 per cent of final-year undergraduates expressing satisfaction in the results published in 2008. English, anthropology and archaeology produced the best scores, but at least 80 per cent of the students in every subject were satisfied. A growing number of degrees take four years, and most are organised on a modular basis.

About 6,600 of UCL's students are from overseas, nearly half of them postgraduates and a third of them from other EU

Gower Street
London WC1E 6BT
020 7679 3000 (Study
   Information Centre)
contact via website
www.ucl.ac.uk
www.uclu.org

The Times Rankings
Overall Ranking: 5

Student satisfaction:	=28	(77%)
Research quality:	=5	(2.7)
Entry standards:	8	(452)
Student–staff ratio:	1	(8.9)
Services & facilities/student:	7	(£1,784)
Expected completion rate:	22	(92.0%)
Good honours:	7	(80.4%)
Graduate prospects:	6	(82.9%)

countries, reflecting the college's high international standing. The proportion is likely to rise further in the coming years. Most departments interview suitably qualified British applicants and, once accepted, many first-year students are helped to make the academic and social adjustment to university life through UCL's Transition Programme, which includes a variety of activities such as peer mentoring and workshops. UCL stresses its commitment to teaching in small groups, especially in the second and subsequent years of degree courses. The approach seems to work: over three quarters leave with a first or upper second. The projected dropout rate of 8 per cent is below the national average for the courses and entry grades.

UCL is conscious of its traditions as a college founded to expand access to higher education, but the 33 per cent share of places going to independent school students is one of the highest in Britain. Less than one undergraduate in five has a working-class background. Concerted attempts are being made to broaden the intake with summer schools for state school students, outreach activities and campus-based programmes. UCL is sponsoring a new academy, which it sees as part of its contribution to the local community.

The academic pace can be frantic but, close to the West End and with its own theatre and recreational facilities, there is no shortage of leisure options. Students also have immediate access to London University's underused central students' union facilities. Residential accommodation is plentiful and of a good standard. Indoor sports facilities are close at hand, but the main outdoor pitches, though good enough to attract professional football clubs, are a (free) coach ride away in Hertfordshire. Hockey players have access to Astroturf pitches at the Old Cranleighans ground, in Thames Ditton.

Undergraduate Fees and Bursaries

- Fees for UK/EU students: £3,225
- International student fees: £12,280–£16,080
  £23,980 (medicine)
- Bursary on full grant: household income up to £11.9K: £2,775; household incomes up to £14.1K: £2,220; household incomes up to £16.2K: £1,650, then at least 50% of maintenance grant.
- Bursaries on partial grant: at least 50% of maintenance grant.
- Scholarships based on circumstances or by competition.
- For full details see the university's website:www.ucl.ac.uk/prospective-students/undergraduate-study/fees-and-costs/www.ucl.ac.uk/scholarships

Students

Undergraduates:	11,275	(645)
Postgraduates:	5,975	(3,090)
Mature students:	16.3%	
Overseas students:	28.0%	
Applications per place:	8.0	
From state-sector schools:	66.6%	
From working-class homes:	18.9%	

For detailed information about fees, grants and bursaries and how they work, see chapter 7.

Accommodation

Number of places and costs refer to 2008–09
University-provided places: 4,197 (including 500 intercollegiate places)
Percentage catered: 30%
Catered costs: £101.71–£144.97 a week.
Self-catered costs: £68.60–£145.18 a week.
First years are guaranteed accommodation if conditions are met.
International students: as above.
Contact: Residences@ucl.ac.uk
www.ucl.ac.uk/admission/accommodation

University for the Creative Arts

England's newest university is the product of a merger between two well-established arts institutes straddling Kent and Surrey. Indeed, the first version of its title was the unwieldy University for the Creative Arts at Canterbury, Epsom, Farnham, Maidstone and Rochester, although the multiple locations have since been dropped. The constituent colleges all date back to Victorian times, but university status arrived only in 2008. The location of each college is given in the map below: Canterbury (1), Epsom (2), Farnham (3), Maidstone (4) and Rochester (5).

With about 6,000 students, UCA is already sizeable by the standards of specialist institutions and it has set itself the ambitious target of becoming the leading university in the field by 2010.

By far the largest enrolment is at Farnham, in Surrey, where more than 2,000 students take courses in art, design, cinematics and communications. There is a purpose-built student village with 350 rooms in the centre of town and two galleries, as well as teaching space and a library and learning centre. The campus boasts Oscar and BAFTA winners in animation in its pre-university days. It is now home to research centres in animation, crafts and sustainable design. Courses range from pre-degree foundation courses in art and design to degrees in film production, motoring journalism and three-dimensional design.

The other four sites are of similar size in terms of student numbers. The second base in Surrey, at Epsom, specialises in fashion, graphics and new media, although it offers general art and design courses at further education level. There is a modern library and learning resource centre for more than 1,200 students, a bar and café on campus and two halls of residence for 120 students. Degrees include music journalism and fashion promotion and imaging.

The largest of the three campuses in Kent is at Rochester, which offers a full range of art and design, including fashion, photography and specialist design courses. The purpose-built campus is set on a hillside overlooking the city centre and River Medway. Halls of residence with 214 places are close to the campus, which has studio space, library and learning resource centre and a gallery.

The Maidstone campus is in parkland, ten minutes from the centre of town, with another gallery and extensive library. The integrated teaching and research facilities include a multi-user video editing facility and video studio, printmaking area, animation resources and a specialist photography resource. Courses for more than 900 students encourage interdisciplinary study.

New Dover Road
Canterbury, Kent CT1 3AN
01227 817302 (enquiries)
contact via website
www.ucreative.ac.uk
www.uccasu.com

The Times Rankings
Overall Ranking: 114

Student satisfaction:	109	(66%)
Research quality:	=63	(0.5)
Entry standards:	91	(247)
Student–staff ratio:	112	(24.3)
Services & facilities/student:	74	(£1,033)
Expected completion rate:	49	(85.3%)
Good honours:	91	(51.2%)
Graduate prospects:	102	(58.2%)

At Canterbury, the accent is on architecture, but there are also degrees in fine art, interior design and more general art and design. The modern site is close to the city centre and contains purpose-built studios, workshops and lecture theatres. The Canterbury School of Architecture is the only such school to remain within a specialist art and design institution, encouraging collaboration between student architects, designers and fine artists.

The university offers four-year degrees, incorporating a foundation year, as well as the three-year format and two-year Foundation degrees, which can be topped up to produce Honours. However, results in the National Student Survey have been poor in all four years of polling. Although there was improvement in the results published in 2008, the university remained in the bottom three, with only mass communications and documentation courses satisfying more than 85 per cent of undergraduates.

Many staff are practitioners as well as academics and the colleges have produced a string of famous graduates, such as Tracy Emin, Karen Millen and Zandra Rhodes. There is also a strong research culture, although UCA had only limited success in the 2008 Research Assessment Exercise. Thirty per cent of the university's submission was considered world-leading or internationally excellent, but this left it well down the ranking for art and design.

Undergraduate Fees and Bursaries

- Fees for UK/EU students: £3,225
- International student fees: £7,406–£9,507
- Bursary on full grant: £319
- Bursaries on partial grant: n/a
- Scholarships based on circumstances or by competition.
- For full details see the university's website: www.ucreative.ac.uk/ index.cfm?articleid=19668

Students

Undergraduates:	4,920	(240)
Postgraduates:	185	(90)
Mature students:	17.2%	
Overseas students:	11.1%	
Applications per place:	3.6	
From state-sector schools:	98.3%	
From working-class homes:	34.6%	

For detailed information about fees, grants and bursaries and how they work, see chapter 7.

Accommodation

Number of places and costs refer to 2008–09

University-provided places: 1,055

Percentage catered: 0%

Self-catered costs: £48.90–£105.30.

New full-time students are eligible to apply and priority is given to those students who live the furthest distance from the relevant university campus.

International students: same as above.

Contact: accommodation@ucreative.ac.uk; www.ucreative.ac.uk

University of Warwick

The most successful of the first wave of new universities, Warwick was derided by many in its early years for its close links with business and industry. Few are critical today. Gordon Brown described it as "one of the great universities, absolutely central to the industrial, scientific and technological future of our country." Research was very highly rated in the 2008 assessments, but the university's mission statement still stresses the extension of access to higher and continuing education and community links.

There is a smaller proportion of independent school students than at most of the leading universities – less than a quarter – although this does not translate into large numbers of working-class undergraduates. The share of places going to students from the lowest social classes and the representation from areas sending few young people to higher education are both lower than the national average for Warwick's subjects and entry qualifications. But the mix helps to produce one of the lowest dropout rates in Britain. Warwick puts almost a third of its income from top-up fees into bursaries and financial support – one of the highest proportions among the old universities.

Almost two thirds of the work submitted for the 2008 Research Assessment Exercise was considered world-leading or internationally excellent, placing Warwick among the top ten universities. Film and television studies achieved one of the top scores for any subject at any university, the Institute of Horticultural Studies was ranked top for agriculture, while pure maths, French and Italian were in the top three. There were particularly high grades, too, for economics, applied maths and theatre, performance and cultural studies.

The university was a late starter in the National Student Survey, due to opposition from the students' union, but is now in the top 20. Literary studies, biology, French, physics and astronomy, area studies and maths, operational research, statistics and economics also produced good scores. Warwick was awarded a national teaching centre in theatrical performance, in partnership with the Royal Shakespeare Company, and is collaborating with Oxford Brookes University on another centre to "reinvent" undergraduate research.

The science park, one of the first in Britain, is among the most successful.

The university invested shrewdly in business, science and engineering and there is now a thriving graduate entry medical school, with more than 2,000 students and new professional courses in implant dentistry. Warwick is also one of the few leading universities to embrace two-year Foundation degrees, running

Coventry CV4 7AL
024 7652 3723 (admissions)
ugadmissions@warwick.ac.uk
www.warwick.ac.uk
www.warwicksu.com/
Default.aspx

The Times Rankings
Overall Ranking: 6

Student satisfaction:	=28	(77%)
Research quality:	=12	(2.4)
Entry standards:	6	(463)
Student–staff ratio:	=12	(13.1)
Services & facilities/student:	4	(£2,118)
Expected completion rate:	=6	(96.0%)
Good honours:	8	(79.7%)
Graduate prospects:	13	(79.2%)

courses in education and community enterprise, the latter taught by a local further education college.

With nearly nine applicants for every place on conventional degree courses, many departments stick rigidly to offers averaging more than an A and two Bs at A level. Applications have been buoyant, showing a 4 per cent increase at the start of 2009. Warwick has been building up its numbers in science and engineering, as other universities have struggled to fill their places. The business school has also been growing rapidly, with a new £15-million extension now complete, while computer science has acquired new, upgraded facilities.

Hundreds of millions of pounds have been spent on the campus, which has often resembled a building site. However, a second significant extension to student union facilities will open in time for start of the 2009–10 academic year. A £7-million extension to the university's already extensive Warwick Arts Centre, which attracts over 250,000 visitors a year, is almost complete. There is also a new £12.5-million building to house a "digital laboratory" for manufacturing and engineering research, and a new indoor tennis centre opened in 2008.

The 750-acre campus is three miles south of Coventry, where many students choose to live, and three times as far from Warwick. University accommodation is plentiful and the sports facilities are both extensive and conveniently placed on campus, where there is a new sports centre with 25-metre swimming pool and a range of other facilities. In summer 2009 the university will host the UK Transplant Games.

Undergraduate Fees and Bursaries

- Fees for UK/EU students: £3,225
- International student fees: £10,900–£13,950
- Bursary on full grant: £1,800
- Bursaries on partial grant: household income up to £36K: £1,800.
- Scholarships based on circumstances or by competition.
- For full details see the university's website: www.warwick.ac.uk/go/WUAP

Students		
Undergraduates:	10,990	(8,760)
Postgraduates:	3,605	(5,090)
Mature students:	10.6%	
Overseas students:	16.0%	
Applications per place:	8.7	
From state-sector schools:	76.4%	
From working-class homes:	17.6%	

For detailed information about fees, grants and bursaries and how they work, see chapter 7.

Accommodation

Number of places and costs refer to 2009–10
University-provided places: 5,779 (on campus); 1,680 (head leasing)
Percentage catered: 0%
Self-catered costs: £74–£122 a week (30, 39, 50 week contracts).
All first-year undergraduates are guaranteed accommodation (terms and conditions apply). International students as above (terms and conditions apply).
Contact: www.warwick.ac.uk/accommodation

University of the West of England, Bristol (UWE)

West of England (UWE) is the largest provider of higher education in the south-west of England and one of the most popular post-1992 universities, both in terms of total applications and the proportion – one in four – who subsequently choose to study there. Applications were up by another 7.5 per cent at the official deadline for courses beginning in 2009, following several years of increases earlier in the decade.

UWE has sometimes found itself in trouble for missing its benchmarks for widening access to higher education, but official reports now accept that this is largely due to its location. The proportion of independent school entrants has dropped to 11 per cent – still a figure exceeded by only one new university – while the share of places going to students from working-class homes is approaching three in ten. UWE has one of England's largest bursary schemes, with annual bursaries of £1,000 going to about a third of its students. At nearly 20 per cent, the projected dropout rate had been coming down, but is now well above the national average for the university's subjects and entry qualifications.

The university has improved its scores in the National Student Survey and is now in the top half of the table. There were particularly high levels of satisfaction in biology, film studies and photography, forensic sciences and physical sciences in the results published in 2008. Unusually, the university trains and pays its 900 student representatives – the biggest such network in the country. More than half of the students come from the West Country and there are close links with local business and industry. These provide guest lecturers, professors involved in practice and thousands of part-time jobs and work placements for students.

A tradition of vocational education regularly helps the university to a healthy graduate employment record. The entrance system credits vocational qualifications and practical experience equally with traditional academic results. Law received a commendation from the Legal Practice Board and the degree in architecture and planning won a similar accolade from the Royal Town Planning Institute for bringing together the two disciplines in one joint-honours course giving dual professional qualifications. UWE is one of just four universities recognised by the Forensic Science Society for the quality of courses in the subject.

Only two new universities entered more academics than UWE in the 2008 Research Assessment Exercise. More than

Frenchay Campus
Coldharbour Lane
Bristol BS16 1QY
0117 328 3333 (admissions)
admissions@uwe.ac.uk
www.uwe.ac.uk
www.uwesu.org

The Times Rankings
Overall Ranking: 62

Student satisfaction:	=40	(76%)
Research quality:	=63	(0.5)
Entry standards:	66	(275)
Student–staff ratio:	83	(19.2)
Services & facilities/student:	79	(£995)
Expected completion rate:	82	(78.8%)
Good honours:	50	(63.2%)
Graduate prospects:	66	(66.1%)

a third of the work was judged to be world-leading or internationally excellent, with physiotherapy and other health subjects, media studies and general engineering producing the best results.

There are four sites in Bristol itself, mainly around the north of the city. Only Bower Ashton, which has new studio space and media suites for its art, media and design students, is in the south. The main campus at Frenchay, close to Bristol Parkway station but four miles out of the city centre, has by far the largest number of students and includes the Student Services Department, which brings together the various non-academic services. The university has purchased land to double the size of the Frenchay campus. The St Matthias campus (for social sciences and humanities) and Glenside (for midwifery, nursing, physiotherapy and radiography) are more attractive but less lively.

A network of 15 colleges stretches into Somerset and Wiltshire, offering UWE programmes. Hartpury College, near Gloucester, has become an associate faculty of the university, specialising in agriculture, equine studies and other land-based courses, and there are university centres in hospitals in Bath and Swindon that concentrate nursing and allied health professions.

Bristol is a hugely popular student centre: an attractive and lively city, but not cheap. University accommodation has become more plentiful in recent years, with over 4,000 places available, including nearly 2,000 in a new £80-million student village on the Frenchay campus. Sports facilities were a bone of contention for students, but a new sports complex opened in 2006 as part of a £300-million investment programme, which is one of the largest in UK higher education. It has been chosen as a pre-Olympics training site for badminton, fencing, table tennis, indoor volleyball and wrestling.

Undergraduate Fees and Bursaries

- Fees for UK/EU students: £3,225
- International student fees: £8,250–£8,700
- Bursary on full grant: £1,000
- Bursaries on partial grant: n/a
- Scholarships based on circumstances or by competition.
- For full details see the university's website: www.uwe.ac.uk/money

---

Students

Undergraduates:	18,235	(7,185)
Postgraduates:	1,965	(4,315)
Mature students:	26.2%	
Overseas students:	6.6%	
Applications per place:	3.9	
From state-sector schools:	89.0%	
From working-class homes:	29.0%	

For detailed information about fees, grants and bursaries and how they work, see chapter 7.

Accommodation

Number of places and costs refer to 2008–09
University-provided places: 4,079
Percentage catered: 0%
Self-catered costs: £85.00–£125.20 a week.
First-year students are guaranteed accommodation provided requirements are met.
International students are offered accommodation where possible.
Contact: accommodation@uwe.ac.uk

University of the West of Scotland

A merger between Paisley University and Bell College, in Hamilton, has produced Scotland's largest new university, with more than 18,000 students and the largest School of Health, Nursing and Midwifery north of the border. The university is planning £150 million of improvements to its four campuses, with local provision within reach of 40 per cent of Scots. However, it is not possible to monitor its progress in *The Times* league table since the university has blocked the release of data.

Since last year's placing just outside the bottom ten, which was based on the Paisley campus alone, UWS has improved its research grades, but did not receive the boost in applications that new universities normally enjoy. The demand for places was down by 4.5 per cent when there were rises elsewhere in Scotland. A quarter of the work in a comparatively small submission was rated as world-leading or internationally excellent, with biomedical sciences and social policy and social work producing the best results.

Paisley had enjoyed surges in popularity in the early years of the decade as students flocked to a new range of degree subjects such as computer animation, commercial music, computer games technology, sports studies and music technology.

The two parent institutions had proud records in attracting under-represented groups onto courses. More than a third of Paisley's entrants in the year before the merger were from working-class homes the proportion at Bell was close to half. Unfortunately, however, projected dropout rates on both campuses have been high. Paisley introduced a range of measures to address the problem, including a personal tutor system, strengthened counselling support and attendance monitoring. Access measures are continuing, with hundreds of youngsters aged 14 and 15 attending the "University Experience" and sampling a week of student life.

The new university's four bases are in Paisley, Ayr, Dumfries and Hamilton. Among the first developments will be a new campus in Ayr, costing more than £75 million, to be completed by 2010; £5.5 million of library and student support services in Dumfries; and a £2-million engineering centre at Hamilton. A new computing laboratory and an employment centre for students have already opened at Paisley.

Paisley is Scotland's largest town, while Hamilton is the fifth-largest. Both are within a dozen miles of Glasgow and draw a high proportion of the students from the

---

Paisley Campus
Paisley
Renfrewshire PA1 2BE
0141 848 3000
  (switchboard)
info@uws.ac.uk
www.uws.ac.uk
www.sauws.org.uk

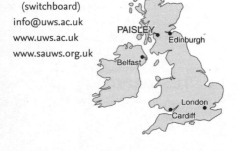

The Times Rankings
West of Scotland blocked the release of data from the Higher Education Statistics Agency and so we cannot give any ranking information.

local area, many on part-time courses. Numbers at Paisley have grown rapidly in recent years, but staffing levels compare favourably with most new universities. There are around 1,100 international students, thanks to long-established links with over 40 EU institutions and a growing number of Chinese and Indian nationals.

Courses are strongly vocational, with business, multimedia and health subjects by far the most popular choices. There are close links with business and industry and all students are offered hands-on computer training. Paisley was the first UK university approved by Microsoft, Macromedia and Cisco, and has the status of Microsoft Academic Professional Development Centre. A games development laboratory, supported by Sony, is part of a £300,000 package of investment in multimedia and games facilities.

Paisley pioneered credit transfer in Scotland, including credit for non-academic achievement, and the modular course system covers day, evening and weekend classes. Most students either take sandwich degrees or have work placements built into their courses, earning an average of £10,000 in the process, but the impact on graduate employment has not been as great as in some other universities.

Over £9 million has been invested in student facilities in Paisley in recent years.

The main campus, 20 acres in the town centre, has seen substantial development, including a new library and learning resource centre. There is a £5-million union building and recently upgraded indoor and outdoor sports facilities to improve the student experience. At Ayr, a management centre has been established in an 18th-century mansion and a new students' union has opened. The Dumfries (Crichton) campus, operated in partnership with Glasgow University, has over 400 students.

The Hamilton campus, in the town centre, contains teaching facilities, a students' union, an upgraded leisure centre and some accommodation. The Centre for Engineering Excellence is the newest addition to the campus.

Undergraduate Fees and Bursaries
- Scottish-domiciled and EU students: no fees payable.
- Non-Scottish UK-domiciled student fees: £1,820 a year.
- International student fees: £9,300–£10,050
- Scholarships based on circumstances or by competition.
- For full details see the university's website: www.uws.ac.uk/schoolsdepts/studentservices/fundingadvice/index.asp

---

Students
From state-sector schools: 99.1%
From working-class homes: 37.1%

For detailed information about fees, grants and bursaries and how they work, see chapter 7.

Accommodation
Number of places and costs refer to 2008–09
University-provided places: 884 (628 at Paisley; 100 at Ayr; 156 at Hamilton)
Percentage catered: 0%
Self-catered costs: £64 a week.
First-year students have priority (conditions apply).
International students: single students guaranteed accommodation if conditions are met.
Contact: www.uws.ac.uk/about/facilities/accommodation.asp

University of Westminster

Westminster hit the headlines in the 2008 Research Assessment Exercise, when it was rated top in the UK for media studies with one of the highest proportions of world-leading research (60 per cent) in any subject. More than a third of all the work submitted by the university was rated in the top two categories, resulting a doubling of Westminster's research grants. Art and design, architecture and biomedical sciences all achieved good grades.

The university has completed a ten-year modernisation of its four sites, costing £130 million, and has since added new gym facilities, a £1-million venue and a vast underground exhibition space. The £33-million transformation of the former Harrow College, in north London was Europe's largest university construction project and the redevelopment of one of the three central sites, opposite Madame Tussauds, was even more costly. The large business school acquired a "cloistered environment" creating more space for teaching and research. The last phase saw the redevelopment of the New Cavendish Street site, near the BT Tower.

The greenfield Harrow campus boasts a high-tech information resources centre with good facilities for the highly rated media studies courses. Computing and design are also based on a site designed for 7,500 students. The West End sites provide the perfect catchment area for part-time undergraduates, who account for about a third of the 17,000 undergraduate places. By no means all the students are Londoners, however: over 5,000 come from overseas – among the highest proportions among the new universities – and Westminster has the largest number of ethnic minority students in Britain. Westminster courses are also taught in nine overseas countries, from Sri Lanka to Uzbekistan, a characteristic which won the university a Queen's Award for Enterprise.

The historic headquarters building, near Broadcasting House, in central London, houses social sciences and languages. Westminster claims to offer the largest number of languages of any British university, while science and health courses are concentrated on the Cavendish campus. The university's growing interest in health includes degrees from the British College of Naturopathy and Osteopathy and a range of courses in complementary medicine, including a BSc in acupuncture. There are degrees in herbal medicine, naturopathy and nutritional therapy, and a diploma in the traditional Chinese massage technique of Qigong.

The university weaves work-related skills into its degree programmes and the dropout rate is now below 20 per cent – just better than average for the university's

309 Regent Street
London W1B 2UW
020 7911 5000 (enquiries)
course-enquiries@
   wmin.ac.uk
www.wmin.ac.uk
www.uwsu.com

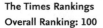

The Times Rankings
Overall Ranking: 100

Student satisfaction:	105	(69%)
Research quality:	=63	(0.5)
Entry standards:	88	(249)
Student–staff ratio:	48	(16.4)
Services & facilities/student:	=105	(£800)
Expected completion rate:	87	(77.5%)
Good honours:	90	(51.5%)
Graduate prospects:	111	(54.1%)

subjects and entry standards. But scores in the 2008 National Student Survey were among the lowest in the country for the third successive year. Only biology, psychology and some social sciences had satisfaction rates of more than 85 per cent among final-year undergraduates.

More than four out of ten undergraduates are from working-class homes – a much higher proportion than the national average for the subjects offered. The university also exceeds its benchmark for the admission of students from state schools and colleges. The scholarship programme is the largest of its kind, with three As at A level securing a "gold level" award of £4,000 a year in tuition fees and cash, while three Bs merit a "silver level" of £2,000 a year fee remission. Other scholarships are available to both home and overseas students, while all those receiving a maintenance grant qualify for a £319 bursary.

Westminster's students, like those at all the London universities, complain of the high cost of living, particularly for accommodation. The university has added considerably to its residential stock in recent years, with the opening of a £6-million block of halls in Harrow and the refurbishment of its Marylebone halls, but there is no way round the capital's inflated housing market at some stage. The Harrow campus is lively socially, but those based on

the other sites tend to be spread around the capital. Sports facilities are also dispersed, with playing fields and a boathouse in Chiswick, west London.

Undergraduate Fees and Bursaries

- Fees for UK/EU students: £3,225
- International student fees: £9,830
- Bursary on full grant: £319
- Bursaries on partial grant: £319
- Scholarships based on circumstances or by competition.
- For full details see the university's website: www.wmin.ac.uk/funding

Students		
Undergraduates:	11,190	(5,845)
Postgraduates:	2,885	(3,305)
Mature students:	29.5%	
Overseas students:	16.5%	
Applications per place:	4.5	
From state-sector schools:	95.6%	
From working-class homes:	44.4%	

For detailed information about fees, grants and bursaries and how they work, see chapter 7.

Accommodation

Number of places and costs refer to 2009–10

University-provided places: nearly 1,500

Percentage catered: 0%

Self-catered costs: £73.50 (small single) – £147.00 (en suite) a week.

First-year students have priority. Residential restrictions apply.

International students: as above.

Contact: www.wmin.ac.uk/unilet

University of Winchester

Winchester stresses its "human scale", with fewer than 6,000 students and an emphasis on providing a supportive community for students to unlock their potential. Successive finishes around the top 30 in the National Student Survey suggest that the approach has struck a chord. Sports science had the second-highest satisfaction levels in the UK in 2008, when education, business and history also did well. Applications were up again the official deadline for courses beginning in 2009.

The university traces its history as an Anglican foundation back to 1840 and has occupied its King Alfred campus since 1862. The compact site is on a wooded hillside overlooking the cathedral city, ten minutes walk away, with views of the surrounding countryside. A second centre, which opened in 2003, occupies a large 18th-century rectory in nearby Basingstoke and concentrates on lifelong learning. It offers Foundation degrees in community and creative industries, cultural studies, education and social sciences.

Known as King Alfred's College until 2004, the university is still best-known for teacher training, which accounts for about a third of the places. It is one of the largest providers of primary school training in England, but courses on the main campus also span business, arts, health and social care, and social sciences. Degrees range from choreography and dance, through social work, business, accounting, law, media and teacher training to ethics and spirituality. Street arts, global tourism, sustainable development management, philosophy, and health and wellbeing were added in 2009. Ancient, classical and medieval studies, modern liberal arts, and vocal and choral studies are among the innovations planned for 2010.

Winchester improved on already respectable grades in the 2008 Research Assessment Exercise, when it was ranked second among the new universities in history, with over half of its submission considered world-leading or internationally excellent. Overall, more than a third of the university's work reached the top two categories and there was some world-leading research in four of the six subject areas.

The university is particularly proud of its low dropout rate. At less than 12 per cent, the last official projection was below the national average for the subjects and entry grades, although the university puts the true figure lower still. Nearly 97 per cent of the British students are state-educated and about a third are from working-class homes. Male undergraduates are heavily outnumbered and there are about 150 overseas students from a range of countries. Winchester students can take

---

Winchester
Hampshire SO22 4NR
01962 827234
course.enquiries@
  winchester.ac.uk
www.winchester.ac.uk
www.winchester
  students.co.uk

The Times Rankings
Overall Ranking: 73

Student satisfaction:	=28	(77%)
Research quality:	=71	(0.4)
Entry standards:	=77	(261)
Student–staff ratio:	59	(17.2)
Services & facilities/student:	95	(£867)
Expected completion rate:	46	(85.6%)
Good honours:	=69	(55.7%)
Graduate prospects:	109	(55.6%)

advantage of exchange schemes with American universities in Maine, Oregon and Wisconsin, as well as with Beppu University in Japan.

The main campus is well equipped, with its own theatre, sports hall and fitness suite now supplemented by the £3.5-million Winchester Sports Stadium, which opened in 2008. Open to local people as well as students, the stadium has an Olympic standard 400-metre eight-lane athletics track with supporting facilities for field events and also a floodlit all-weather pitch.

A four-storey University Centre opened in September 2007, transforming the students' union, adding a nightclub, cinema, catering facilities, a bookshop and a supermarket at a cost of £9 million. A "learning café" creates an informal working space with networked PCs and wireless internet access. An award-winning extension to the library made room for 200,000 books, 450 study spaces and 150 computers.

A £12-million student village provides nearly 1,000 residential places – enough to guarantee accommodation for all first years, as well as those from overseas. Another hall of residence, with en-suite rooms arranged in cluster flats with shared kitchen facilities, is under construction. Students value the close-knit atmosphere and find the city livelier than its staid image might suggest, with a number of bars

catering to their tastes. London is only an hour away by train and Southampton less than half that for those who hanker after the attractions of a bigger city.

Undergraduate Fees and Bursaries
- Fees for UK/EU students: £3,225
- International student fees: £7,890
- Bursary on full grant: £820
- Bursaries on partial grant: household income up to £39.3K: £410.
- Scholarships based on circumstances or by competition.
- For full details see the university's website: www.winchester.ac.uk/?page=6891

Students		
Undergraduates:	3,595	(735)
Postgraduates:	120	(790)
Mature students:	19.6%	
Overseas students:	4.5%	
Applications per place:	3.9	
From state-sector schools:	96.9%	
From working-class homes:	32.0%	

For detailed information about fees, grants and bursaries and how they work, see chapter 7.

Accommodation
Number of places and costs refer to 2008–09
University-provided places: 956; 130 spaces off campus managed by the university.
Percentage catered: 21%
Catered costs: £107.59 a week (31 weeks).
Self-catered costs: £82.25–£90.09 a week (40 weeks).
First years are guaranteed accommodation if conditions are met.
International students: non EU, as above.
Contact: housing@winchester.ac.uk

University of Wolverhampton

Wolverhampton's success in widening participation in higher education is such that it is the only university in Britain where a majority of undergraduates come from working-class homes. Almost all the students are from state schools and almost one in five comes from an area of low participation in higher education. Strongly regional in outlook, the university draws two thirds of its 21,000 students from the West Midlands, although there is a growing contingent from overseas – the university has offices in China, India, Poland and Nigeria. A third of the places are filled by mature students and its four campuses have a cosmopolitan feel, with about the same proportion coming from the region's ethnic minorities.

Wolverhampton pioneered the high street "higher education shop" and more recently, a dedicated Student Finance Support Unit and Student Gateway Service, bringing all student support together in one convenient location. Big outreach programmes take courses into the workplace. The four campuses each have their own learning centres and are linked by a free bus service. Two are in the city, while sport and performance, education and part of the School of Health are based in Walsall. The original site is in the heart of the city centre. A purpose-built campus at

Telford in Shropshire focuses on business and engineering for a county with no higher education institution of its own.

The university has been investing millions of pounds in an infrastructure programme known as "New Horizons", which is almost complete. The project has seen £26 million spent on the City Campus, notably on the flagship Millennium City Building, an extension of the Harrison Learning Centre, a new technology centre with 600 PCs and a teaching and administration building. A 350-bed student village has opened on the Walsall campus, together with a Lottery-supported sports hall offering elite training facilities for judo and a Sports Science and Medicine Centre that are being used to train Olympic contenders. A £12-million building for the School of Education and the Institute for Learning Enhancement opened in 2008. At Telford the £7-million e-Innovation Centre has already won awards for the incubation and support it offers to e-businesses.

The latest statistics show an improvement in the projected dropout rate, but still more than one in five of those who entered in 2005 may fail to complete their courses in the expected time. Wolverhampton insists that the actual dropout rate is much lower. The university runs a national teaching centre focusing on retention, progression and achievement. Teacher training courses are rated in the top four in

---

Wulfruna Street
Wolverhampton WV1 1LY
01902 321000
enquiries@wlv.ac.uk
www.wlv.ac.uk
www.wolvesunion.org

Edinburgh
Belfast
WOLVERHAMPTON
Cardiff
London

The Times Rankings
Overall Ranking: 102

Student satisfaction:	=90	(72%)
Research quality:	=85	(0.3)
Entry standards:	110	(204)
Student–staff ratio:	=78	(19.0)
Services & facilities/student:	67	(£1,078)
Expected completion rate:	101	(73.4%)
Good honours:	113	(44.6%)
Graduate prospects:	89	(60.9%)

the country by Ofsted, and Wolverhampton academics have been awarded five National Teaching Fellowships by the Higher Education Academy. But the university was in the bottom 20 in the 2008 National Student Survey. Only building, languages and mass communications and documentation satisfied more than 85 per cent of the students.

The university claims a number of firsts for its academic programmes, pioneering interactive multimedia communication degrees, as well as offering the only degree in British sign language and one of the first in virtual reality design and manufacturing. It was the first university to be registered under the British Standard for the quality of its all-round provision. Wolverhampton was also the first to open a student employment bureau with an online jobs vacancy service that has since been adopted by many other institutions. The university stresses innovation and enterprise in its work with students and businesses, encouraging student "start up" companies and leading a project to develop student placements in their own companies for those who wish to become entrepreneurs.

Research is mainly applied, serving the needs of business and industry, as well as underpinning teaching at all levels. The main strengths are in applications of computing and biomedical science, including ground-breaking work on brain tumours. In the 2008 Research Assessment Exercise, Wolverhampton was ranked fourth in the UK for statistical cybermetrics (the analysis of web content and traffic) and sixth for computational linguistics. A relatively low proportion of the academics were entered for assessment, but 30 per cent of their research was considered world-leading or internationally excellent.

Social facilities vary considerably between sites. Wolverhampton has a growing nightlife and the university has been voted the friendliest in the West Midlands. The cost of living is reasonable and the attractions of Birmingham are now only a metro tramride away.

Undergraduate Fees and Bursaries

- Fees for UK/EU students: £3,145
- International student fees: £8,850
- Bursary on full grant: £500
- Bursaries on partial grant: household income up to £35K: £300.
- Scholarships based on circumstances or by competition.
- For full details see the university's website: www.wlv.ac.uk/default.aspx?page=6949

Students

Undergraduates:	12,080	(5,465)
Postgraduates:	1,250	(2,510)
Mature students:	34.4%	
Overseas students:	10.9%	
Applications per place:	3.8	
From state-sector schools:	98.9%	
From working-class homes:	51.6%	

For detailed information about fees, grants and bursaries and how they work, see chapter 7.

Accommodation

Number of places and costs refer to 2009–10
University-provided places: 2,048
Percentage catered: 0%
Self-catered costs: £2,357–£3,430 (37 weeks).
First-year students are offered accommodation provided requirements are met. Residential restrictions apply.
International students: same as above.
Contact: residences@wlv.ac.uk

University of Worcester

Worcester has the most ambitious development plans of all the new universities created in 2005. It is spending £120 million on a second campus in the city centre and another £60 million on a unique library and history centre that will be the first joint public and university library in Britain. Work is already under way on the second campus to cater for an additional 4,000 students over the next five years. Some 200 student residences are due to open in September 2009 in restored Georgian buildings and the project is due for completion by 2011.

At the start of 2009, applications were up by almost 9 per cent , following an even bigger increase in the previous year. The demand for places grew in each of the last five years before university status arrived. Business courses have been particularly popular and there have been big increases, too, in physical education, sports studies, forensic science, marketing, pre-hospital and emergency care, journalism, social work and advertising.

First as a post-war emergency teacher training college and later as a university college, the institution has always been the only provider of higher education in Hereford and Worcester. The university remains strong in education and also in nursing and midwifery – a mix that explains an overwhelmingly female student population. Jacqui Smith, the Home Secretary, trained as a teacher there. But the six academic departments also cover applied sciences, geography and archaeology, a business school and arts, humanities and social sciences. Degrees range from animal biology to sports coaching and computing.

The 23 academics entered for the 2008 Research Assessment Exercise represented the smallest contingent from any university in England. Only English had any world-leading research, although there are pockets of excellence such as the National Pollen and Aerobiology Research Unit, which produces all Britain's pollen forecasts. Results in the first four National Student Surveys have been more positive, placing Worcester in the top 40 in 2008. The most satisfied students were in English, history and teacher training.

Almost 40 per cent of the undergraduates come from working-class homes. The projected dropout rate has improved and, at 15 per cent, is below average for the university's subjects and entry grades. As well as the normal range of bursaries, the university offers £1,000 scholarships for academic achievement in the first year of a course and extra-curricular activities such as voluntary work.

The existing campus occupies a parkland site ten minutes walk from the

Henwick Grove
Worcester WR2 6AJ
01905 855111 (admissions)
admissions@worc.ac.uk
www.worc.ac.uk
www.worcsu.com

The Times Rankings

Overall Ranking: =81

Student satisfaction:	=40	(76%)
Research quality:	=108	(0.1)
Entry standards:	=96	(236)
Student–staff ratio:	=93	(20.0)
Services & facilities/student:	94	(£869)
Expected completion rate:	=58	(83.9%)
Good honours:	103	(48.4%)
Graduate prospects:	59	(68.2%)

city centre. Recent improvements have included a £1-million digital arts centre and drama studio, and another 182 residential places will be added in a £10-million development that is due to open in September 2009. Sport plays an important part in university life: a well-appointed sports centre also provides employment opportunities for students, while competitive teams are successful and the facilities for casual participants extensive. A mobile 3-D motion analysis laboratory has been used by the England Cricket Board. Modest sports scholarships are offered in partnership with Worcestershire County Cricket Club, Worcester Wolves Basketball Club and Worcester Hockey Club. The basketball team have been national champions for three years in succession.

The new campus, which is being developed with the aid of regional and central Government grants, will occupy the site of the old Worcester Royal Infirmary. It will include teaching, residential and conference facilities, as well as the new library and learning centre. The university has undertaken to continue improving the existing St John's campus, which will still be the place of study for two thirds of the university when the new development is completed. It contains three halls of residence with a total of 589 rooms, most of which are allocated to first years. There will be shuttle buses and a cycle route between the two sites. The university also has a number of partner colleges around the region offering Worcester courses.

Social life revolves around the students' union, which also has a "job pod" to help members find work experience and part-time jobs. The cathedral city is not large, but is safer than many university locations and has its share of pubs and clubs that cater for a growing student clientele.

Undergraduate Fees and Bursaries
- Fees for UK/EU students: £3,225
- International student fees: £8,400
- Bursary on full grant: £750
- Bursaries on partial grant: £625; if not eligible for maintenance grant: £500.
- Scholarships based on circumstances or by competition.
- For full details see the university's website: www.worc.ac.uk/student/finance/

Students		
Undergraduates:	4,255	(1,920)
Postgraduates:	465	(1,125)
Mature students:	44.9%	
Overseas students:	4.9%	
Applications per place:	4.1	
From state-sector schools:	97.1%	
From working-class homes:	38.8%	

For detailed information about fees, grants and bursaries and how they work, see chapter 7.

Accommodation

Number of places and costs refer to 2009–10
University-provided places: 947 university-owned; 119 university-managed
Percentage catered: 0%
Self-catered costs: £69–£115 a week.
First-year students are guaranteed accommodation, on a first come, first served basis, if they have accepted an offer by 1 May. International students are accommodated provided requirements are met.
Contact: accommodation@worc.ac.uk

University of York

Although just missing the top ten in *The Times* League Table this year for the first time, York has built a reputation in less than half a century that places it among the top 30 universities in Europe. But the university has decided that, with just over 13,000 students, it is too small to maintain that standing, play a leading role in the economy of the region and contribute to the national agenda for higher education. In an audacious move for a highly selective university, York is developing a second campus to accommodate a 50 per cent increase in student numbers.

The first buildings on the Heslington East site, close to the existing campus, are now under construction. They are due to be ready before the start of the 2010–11 academic year, but the development will take 10 to 15 years to complete. The first cluster of buildings will include computer science and a new department of theatre, film and television, as well as residential accommodation and a central "hub" providing social facilities and teaching space. Eventually, the new campus will contain housing for 3,300 students, as well as more academic buildings, sports facilities and a performing arts and community complex.

Expansion into new subjects has already started. The first intake of undergraduates in writing, directing and performance in theatre, film and television and in law arrived in 2008. The university believes that, with eight applicants for every place, other departments can grow at the same time as retaining or achieving a place in the top ten for their subject. Applications were up by 16 per cent at the start of 2009, following two years of declining numbers.

Medicine was introduced in 2003 in partnership with Hull University (hyms.ac.uk). York also runs its own nursing and midwifery programmes, which came fourth in our table for these subjects this year. The university has also done well in the National Student Survey, finishing in the top 30 in all four years of polling. Chemistry, biology and archaeology produced particularly high levels of satisfaction in the 2008 results.

Entrance requirements are high and the dropout rate of only 4 per cent is among the lowest in the country. Although eight out of ten undergraduates are state educated, only 17 per cent come from working-class homes. Every student has a supervisor responsible for their academic and personal welfare. Extra-curricular courses include language and computer literacy training, as well as courses on personal effectiveness, financial management, active citizenship and an introduction to accounting. The business community is involved at every level. Undergraduates can

---

Heslington
York YO10 5DD
01904 433533 (admissions)
admissions@york.ac.uk
www.york.ac.uk
www.yusu.org

The Times Rankings
Overall Ranking: 11

Student satisfaction:	=14	(79%)
Research quality:	=8	(2.5)
Entry standards:	12	(434)
Student–staff ratio:	=12	(13.1)
Services & facilities/student:	18	(£1,534)
Expected completion rate:	=6	(96.0%)
Good honours:	14	(74.9%)
Graduate prospects:	52	(69.4%)

also take the "York Award", comprising a range of courses, work placements and voluntary activities which aim to prepare students for the world of work. Over 600 students work as volunteer teaching assistants in local schools.

York was among the top ten institutions in the 2008 Research Assessment Exercise, when more than 60 per cent of the work submitted was judged to be world-leading or internationally excellent. The university was ranked top in the UK for English and health services research, joint top for sociology and among the leaders for linguistics and nursing and midwifery.

The current campus occupies 200 acres of parkland, a mile outside the picturesque city centre. Students join one of eight colleges – soon to be nine – which mix academic and social roles. Most departments have their headquarters in one of the colleges, but the student community is a deliberate mixture of disciplines, years and sexes. Nursing apart, only archaeology and medieval studies are located off campus, sharing a medieval building in the centre of the city.

Social life on campus is lively. There are two newspapers, television and radio stations, as well as several magazines, to keep students abreast of campus issues. Sports facilities are good, and include a 50-station fitness suite, four sports halls, and dance studio. Extensive playing fields are on campus and the River Ouse fosters a strong rowing tradition. Cultural events abound in the city, which is also famous for a high concentration of pubs. The club scene has improved, but students still head for Leeds for the top names.

Undergraduate Fees and Bursaries
- Fees for UK/EU students: £3,225
- International student fees: £10,271–£13,811
- £21,600 (medicine)
- Bursary on full grant: £1,436
- Bursaries on partial grant: household income up to £35.9K: £718; up to £41K: £360.
- Scholarships based on circumstances or by competition.
- For full details see the university's website: www.york.ac.uk/studentmoney/

Students		
Undergraduates:	8,010	(1,340)
Postgraduates:	2,915	(915)
Mature students:	11.4%	
Overseas students:	10.3%	
Applications per place:	5.8	
From state-sector schools	80.0%	
From working-class homes:	16.8%	

For detailed information about fees, grants and bursaries and how they work, see chapter 7.

Accommodation
Number of places and costs refer to 2009–10
University-provided places: 4,656
Percentage catered: 0%
Self-catered costs: £82.18–£99.40 a week.
First-year single undergraduates are provided with accommodation if terms and conditions are met.
International students: as above.
Contact: accommodation@york.ac.uk
www.york.ac.uk/admin/accom

York St John University

One of the four universities designated in 2006, York St John is a Church of England foundation that dates back almost 170 years. The eight-acre site faces York Minster across the city walls and is a five-minute walk from the city centre. Now serving over 6,000 students, the campus has seen £60 million of development in recent years and more is planned. The Fountains Learning Centre, which has 500 computer workstations, an internet café and lecture theatre, provides a striking entrance to the university. Another new teaching development, mainly for health and life sciences, opened at the end of 2008 and is intended to be a signature building linking the university quarter with the city centre.

York Diocesan Training School opened in 1841 with one pupil on the register, in whose honour the current students' union is named. Divided between York and Ripon for most of its existence, the institution diversified beyond teacher training in the 1980s and decided at the start of this decade to concentrate all its teaching on York. Almost three quarters of the students are female and only about half come straight from school.

Education and theology remains the biggest faculty, with 1,700 students taking programmes in teacher education, education studies, theology and religious studies. Health and life sciences are not far behind in terms of size, with 1,600 full-time students and 200 part-timers studying health courses such as physiotherapy and occupational therapy, as well as psychology and sport. The large faculty of business and communication has a high proportion of joint honours, while the faculty of arts, which was established in 2001, is expanding, particularly in media subjects such as film and television production, one of the university's most popular degrees.

The university was awarded a national centre for excellence in creativity, based on its work in English and theatre studies, which is working an enriched curriculum in the creative arts. The C4C Centre, based in a renovated Victorian Gothic chapel situated on campus, provides facilities for students, staff, and creative partners to work together. Another music technology suite has been added, and a refurbishment programme has begun in the design and technology block.

Satisfaction levels varied widely in the National Student Survey published in 2008. More than 90 per cent of final-year undergraduates in theology and religious studies, education and teacher training were satisfied with their courses, but the proportion was little more than 40 per cent in cinematics and photography. Drama,

---

New Mayor's Walk
York YO31 7EX
01904 876598 (enquiries)
admissions@yorksj.ac.uk
www.yorksj.ac.uk
www.ysjsu.com

The Times Rankings
Overall Ranking: 80

Student satisfaction:	=54	(75%)
Research quality:	=95	(0.2)
Entry standards:	=57	(288)
Student–staff ratio:	=93	(20.0)
Services & facilities/student:	73	(£1,042)
Expected completion rate:	54	(84.5%)
Good honours:	83	(52.9%)
Graduate prospects:	=100	(58.8%)

dance and performing arts was the most successful field in the 2008 Research Assessment Exercise and the only one to contain world-leading research.

Applications were up by more than 10 per cent at the official deadline for entry in 2009, following a run of good figures since university status was announced. More than 93 per cent of students attended state schools or colleges, while almost three in ten are from working-class homes. The projected dropout rate had improved considerably in the latest survey and, at less than 11 per cent, is significantly below the national average for York St John's courses and entry qualifications.

The university was one of a handful that set undergraduate charges below the £3,000 maximum when top-up fees were introduced. It charged £2,560 a year for degrees in 2007, but it has since joined almost all other universities on the top level of fees. Charges for Foundation degrees have been set at the standard level of £1,285 a year in 2009–10.

Relatively high numbers of locally based mature students ease the pressure on residential accommodation. As a result, first years who want to live in university-owned accommodation are usually able to do so. More self-catering accommodation for 230 students, costing £10 million, opened in September 2008 and another 200 places are planned. Sports facilities are not extensive, but York is popular as a student city with a growing range of clubs as well as, supposedly, a pub for every day of the year.

Undergraduate Fees and Bursaries

- Fees for UK/EU students: £3,225
- International student fees: £8,100–£11,100
- Bursary on full grant: household income up to £18,360: £1,610; up to £20,970: £1,075; up to £25K: £540.
- The university does not award bursaries for students on partial maintenance grants.• Scholarships based on circumstances or by competition.
- For full details see the university's website: www2.yorksj.ac.uk/default.asp?Page_ID=5737

Students		
Undergraduates:	4,250	(1,120)
Postgraduates:	200	(635)
Mature students:	23.5%	
Overseas students:	2.2%	
Applications per place:	4.0	
From state-sector schools:	93.2%	
From working-class homes:	28.9%	

For detailed information about fees, grants and bursaries and how they work, see chapter 7.

Accommodation

Number of places and costs refer to 2009–10
University-provided places: 1,124
Percentage catered: 14.5%
Catered costs: £107.50 (10-meal package) a week.
Self-catered costs: £69–£125 a week (44–48 weeks).
First years are guaranteed accommodation.
Residential and age restrictions apply.
International students: guaranteed housing.
Contact: accommodation@yorksj.ac.uk

Colleges of Higher Education

This listing gives contact details for higher education institutions not mentioned elsewhere within the book. All the institutions of the University of London which do not have their own entry are listed under the main entry for the University of London. All the institutions listed below offer degree courses, some providing a wide range of courses while others are specialist colleges with a limited range of courses and a small intake. Those marked with a * are members of GuildHE (www.guildhe.ac.uk).

The Arts Institute at Bournemouth*
Wallisdown
Poole
Dorset BH12 5HH
01202 533011
general@aib.ac.uk
www.aib.ac.uk

Bishop Grosseteste University College, Lincoln*
Lincoln LN1 3DY
01522 527347
info@bishopg.ac.uk
www.bishopg.ac.uk

Conservatoire for Dance and Drama
1–7 Woburn Walk
London WC1H 0JJ
020 7387 5101
info@cdd.ac.uk
www.cdd.ac.uk
and **Royal Academy of Dramatic Arts**
62–64 Gower Street
London WC1E 6ED
020 7636 7076
www.rada.org

Edinburgh College of Art
Lauriston Place, Edinburgh EH3 9DF
0131 221 6000
enquiries@eca.ac.uk
www.eca.ac.uk

Glasgow School of Art
167 Renfrew Street,
Glasgow G3 6RQ
0141 353 4500
registry@gsa.ac.uk
www.gsa.ac.uk

Harper Adams University College*
Newport, Shropshire TF10 8NB
01952 820280
admissions@harper-adams.ac.uk
www.harper-adams.ac.uk

Leeds Trinity and All Saints College*
Brownberrie Lane, Horsforth,
Leeds LS18 5HD
0113 283 7100
enquiries@leedstrinity.ac.uk
www.leedstrinity.ac.uk

Liverpool Institute of Performing Arts*
Mount Street
Liverpool LI 9HF
0151 330 3000
admissions@lipa.ac.uk
www.lipa.ac.uk

Newman University College*
Genners Lane, Bartley Green,
Birmingham B32 3NT
0121 476 1181
admissions@newman.ac.uk
www.newman.ac.uk

Northern School of Contemporary Dance
98 Chapeltown Road
Leeds LS7 4BH
0113 219 3000
info@nscd.ac.uk
www.nscd.ac.uk

Norwich University College of the Arts*
Francis House, 3–7 Redwell Street
Norwich, Norfolk NR2 4SN
01603 610561
info@nuca.ac.uk
www.nuca.ac.uk

Ravensbourne College of Design and Communication*
Walden Road
Chislehurst, Kent BR7 5SN
020 8289 4900
info@rave.ac.uk
www.rave.ac.uk

Rose Bruford College*
Burnt Oak Lane
Sidcup, Kent DA15 9DF
020 8308 2600
contact from website
www.bruford.ac.uk

Royal Agricultural College*
Stroud Road, Cirencester
Gloucestershire GL7 6JS
01285 652531
admissions@rac.ac.uk
www.rac.ac.uk

Royal College of Art
Kensington Gore
London SW7 2EU
020 7590 4444
admissions@rca.ac.uk
www.rca.ac.uk

Royal College of Music
Prince Consort Road
London SW7 2BS
020 7589 3643
admissions@rcm.ac.uk
www.rcm.ac.uk

Royal College of Nursing
20 Cavendish Square
London W1G 0RN
020 7409 3333
contact from website
www.rcn.org.uk

Royal Northern College of Music
124 Oxford Road
Manchester M13 9RD
0161 907 5200

info@rncm.ac.uk
www.rncm.ac.uk

Royal Scottish Academy of Music and Drama
100 Renfrew Street
Glasgow G2 3DB
0141 332 4101
music.admissions@rsamd.ac.uk
drama.admissions@rsamd.ac.uk
www.rsamd.ac.uk

Royal Welsh College of Music and Drama
Castle Grounds
Cathays Park
Cardiff CF10 3ER
029 2034 2854
music.admissions@rwcmd.ac.uk
drama.admissions@rwcmd.ac.uk
www.rwcmd.ac.uk

St Mary's University College*
Waldegrave Road, Strawberry Hill
Twickenham, Middlesex TW1 4SX
020 8240 4000
enquiry@smuc.ac.uk
www.smuc.ac.uk

St Mary's University College
191 Falls Road
Belfast BT12 6FE
028 9032 7678
contact via website
www.stmarys-belfast.ac.uk

Stranmillis University College
Stranmillis Road
Belfast BT9 5DY
028 9038 1271
registry@stran.ac.uk
www.stran.ac.uk

Trinity University College
College Road, Carmarthen
Wales SA31 3EP
01267 676767
registry@trinity-cm.ac.uk
www.trinity-cm.ac.uk

Trinity Laban
King Charles Court, Old Royal Naval Court,
Greenwich, London SE10 9JF
020 8305 4300
info@trinitylaban.ac.uk
www.trinitylaban.ac.uk

University College Birmingham*
Summer Row
Birmingham B3 1JB
0121 604 1000
marketing@ucb.ac.uk
www.ucb.ac.uk

University College Falmouth*
Woodlane
Falmouth
Cornwall TR11 4RH
01326 211077
admissions@falmouth.ac.uk
www.falmouth.ac.uk
and **Dartington Campus**
Dartington Hall Estate
Totnes
Devon TQ9 6EJ
0180362224
enquiries@dartington.ac.uk
www.dartinton.ac.uk

**University College Plymouth St Mark and
St John* (Marjon)**
Derriford Road
Plymouth
Devon PL6 8BH
01752 636700
admissions@marjon.ac.uk
www.marjon.ac.uk

University of the Highlands and Islands
UHI Millennium Institute
Ness Walk
Inverness IV3 5SQ
01463 279000
info@uhi.ac.uk
www.uhi.ac.uk

Writtle College*
Chelmsford
Essex CM1 3RR
01245 424200
info@writtle.ac.uk
www.writtle.ac.uk

Index

1994 Group 32
A levels 7
  choosing 19
  future of 11
  those not accepted 18, 19
  and UCAS tariff 17
Aberdeen, University of 284–5
Abertay, University of 286–7
Aberystwyth University 288–9
academic subjects 22
access courses 27
Access to Learning Fund 219
accommodation 186–97
  after first year 190–91
  choices 187–8
  costs 33, 34, 186–7
  private sector 189–90, 191–5
  university 189–91
  useful websites 196–7
accommodation agreements, university 191
accounting and finance 51–3, 244
Adjustment period 7, 175, 179, 234
admissions tests 20
adult dependent's grant 219
Advanced Highers, and UCAS tariff 17, 19
aeronautical and manufacturing
  engineering 53–5, 247
African studies 139–40
agriculture and forestry 55–6
American studies 56–8
anatomy and physiology 58–9
Anglia Ruskin University 290–91
anthropology 59–60
application deadlines 177, 179, 180
application process 175–85
  international students 241
  parental involvement 233–4
application timetable 179
application trends, 2009 8
applications
  decisions on 179, 180, 181
  decreases in 29
  increases in 8, 29
  most popular universities 30
  useful websites 185
Apply 175–80
archaeology 60–62
architecture 62–4, 247
architecture, history of 117–19
art and design 64–7, 244
  Foundation courses 27
  Route B, end of 172, 173, 175

art, history of 117–19
Arts, University of, London 500–01
Assembly Learning Grant, Wales 216
assured shorthold tenancy 193
Aston University 292–3
astronomy 152–4
Athletic Union 202
audiology 145–8
Australia, studying in 33
Balliol College, Oxford 254
Bangor University 294–5
banks, and student accounts 220
Bath, University of 10, 49, 296–7
  and sport 198, 199, 203
Bath Spa University 298–9
Bedfordshire, University of 300–01
biological sciences 67–9, 245
BioMedical Admissions Test (BMAT) 20
Birkbeck College 283, 414
Birmingham, University of 302–3
  and sport 201, 203
Birmingham City University 304–5
Bishop Grosseteste University College
  89, 100
Bolton, University of 306–7
Bournemouth University 308–9
Bradford, University of 310–11
Brasenose College, Oxford 254
Brighton, University of 312–13
Brighton and Sussex Medical School 137,
  138, 312, 489
Bristol, University of 314–15
British Council 237
British Universities and Colleges Sport
  (BUCS) 199, 203
Brunel University 316–17
  and sport 199
Buckingham, University of 27, 318–19
Buckinghamshire New University 9,
  320–21
budget, student 222, 235
building 70–71
bursaries 33, 216–17
  by university 223–31
business studies 71–4, 244
Cambridge, University of 10, 322–3
  A levels not fully accepted 18, 19
  applications and acceptances by subject
    251
  application process 177, 248, 252–3
  choosing a college 249–52
  college fees 33

college profiles 268–81
　IBs not fully accepted 18, 19
　and sport 199
　state school applicants 248–9
　and subject tables 48
　Tompkins Table 249
campus universities 31
Canada, studying in 33
Canterbury Christ Church University
　324–5
Cardiff University 10, 326–7
Cardiff, University of Wales Institute
　(UWIC) 328–9
Career Development Loan 219
catered accommodation, university 190
Celtic studies 74–5
Central Lancashire, University of (UCLan)
　330–31
Central School of Speech and Drama 415
Certificate of Acceptance for Study 242
chemical engineering 75–7, 247
chemistry 77–8
Chester University 332–3
Chichester, University of 334–5
Child Tax Credits 214
childcare grant 219
choices of university courses 15–36
　checklist 35
　and graduate recruitment 22
　making 32
　number of 32, 177
　and UCAS Apply 177
　useful websites 35–6
Christ Church College, Oxford 255
Christ's College, Cambridge 268
Churchill College, Cambridge 268–9
cinematics 89–92, 247
Citizen's Advice Bureau 193
city universities 31
City University London 336–7
civil engineering 79–80, 246
Clare College, Cambridge 269
Clarke, Charles, and The Times Table 10
classics and ancient history 80–81
Clearing 32, 182, 183–4, 234, 235
Combined Honours 22
communication and media studies 82–4,
　246
Community Service Volunteers 184
complementary therapies 145–8
completion measure 40–41
computer facilities, and league table 40
computer science 85–8, 244
conditional acceptance (CF) 181

conditional offer (C) 181
Conservatoires UK Admissions Service 175
contracts, accommodation 193–4
Corpus Christi College, Cambridge 269–70
Corpus Christi College, Oxford 255
cost of accommodation 186–7, 188
cost of university 210–31
Council Tax 195
counselling 145–8
course, choosing 15–29
　and graduate recruitment 22
　and professional qualifications 21
courses, full-time 23
courses, modular 22–3
Courtauld Institute of Art 415
Coventry University 338–9
Cranfield University 283
Creative Arts, University for the 10, 504–5
Cumbria University 340–41
dance 89–92, 247
deadline for applications 177, 179, 180
deferred place 177, 185
degree results, and league table 41
De Montfort University 342–3
dentistry 88–9
deposit, accommodation 194
Derby, University of 344–5
design 64–7, 244
design, history of 117–19
destinations, graduate 28
disabled student allowance 219
distance learning 23
Downing College, Cambridge 270
drama, dance and cinematics 89–92, 247
Dundee, University of 346–7
Durham University 348–9
East and South Asian studies 92–3
East Anglia, University 350–51
　and sport 199
East European languages 159–60
East London, University of 352–3
economics 93–5, 244
Edge Hill University 354–5
Edinburgh, University of 356–7
Edinburgh Napier University 358–9
education 95–8
Education and Library Board, Northern
　Ireland 214
Education UK 237
education, teaching quality 49
electrical engineering 98–100, 245
electronic engineering 98–100, 245
Emmanuel College, Cambridge 270–71
employability, and league table 41

employers
　　and knowledge of universities 12
　　most favoured universities 31
employment agencies, student 219
employment prospects, graduate 8, 24–9
employment regulations, international
　　students 242
employment, part–time, and choice 33
engineering courses, length of 28
England, financial support for students
　　212–14, 215, 217
England, tuition fees for students 211–12
English 100–03, 247
English language requirements,
　　international students 240
English Literature Admissions Test (ELAT)
　　20
entry regulations, international students
　　241–2
entry standards 10, 29–30
　　and league table 40
　　and subject tables 49
environmental sciences 108–11
Erasmus 28, 33
Essex, University of 10, 360–61
EU students
　　fees 238
　　financial support 218
Europe, studying in 33
exam grades, lower than offer 182
exchange programmes 28
Exeter, University of 362–3
Exeter College, Oxford 255–6
expenditure, student 222–22
facilities spend see services and facilities
　　spend measure
facilities, and university choice 33–4
fee remission 217
fees, by university 223–31
finance 51–3, 244
Financial Contingency Fund, Wales 219
financial support for students
　　between different UK countries 217–18
　　England 215
　　EU students 218
　　Northern Ireland 216
　　Scotland 216
　　timetable for applications 215
　　Wales 208
　　websites 222–3, 216–17
firm acceptance (UF) 181
Fitzwilliam College, Cambridge 271
flat sharing 192–3
flats, renting 192–5

food science 103–5
forestry 55–6
Foundation degree 11, 15, 23, 55, 119, 141,
　　143, 211
French 105–7
Fresh Talent scheme, Scotland 242
full maintenance grant 223
full–time course 23
funding help 210–11, 228
gap year 184, 218–19
　　income from 218
　　useful websites 185
gas safety certificate 194
general engineering 107–8, 247
geography and environmental sciences
　　108–11
geology 111–12
German 112–14
Girton College, Cambridge 271
Glamorgan, University of 364–5
Glasgow, University of 366–7
Glasgow Caledonian University 368–9
Gloucestershire, University of 370–71
　　tuition fee discount 212
Glyndŵr University 10, 372–3
Goldsmiths, University of London 374–5
Gonville and Caius College, Cambridge 272
good honours measure 41
graduate destinations 28
graduate endowment, Scotland, abolition
　　of 212
Graduate Medical School Admissions Test
　　(GAMSAT) 20
graduate prospects measure
　　and main league table 41
　　and subject tables 49
graduate recruitment, and course choice 22
Graduate Teacher Training Registry 175
grants 9, 214–16
Greenwich, University of 376–7
　　reduced tuition fees 212
guild of students 34
Guild HE 32
hall of residence 190
Hardship Fund, Scotland 219
Harper Adams University College 35, 134
Harris Manchester College, Oxford 256
Health Professions Admissions Test
　　(HPAT) 20
health sciences 145–8
health services management 145–8
HEFCE and league tables 8
helicopter parent 232, 235
Heriot-Watt University 378–9

Hertford College, Oxford 256–7
Hertfordshire, University of 380–81
HESA 28, 38, 41, 48
Heythrop College 415
Higher Education, Colleges of 525–7
higher education,
  options in 12
  percentage entering 11
  value of 12, 13, 15
Higher Education Act 2004 13
Higher National Diploma 23
Highers, and UCAS tariff 17, 19
history 114–17
History Aptitude Test (HAT) 20
history of art, architecture and design 117–19
HMOs 193
home, living at 8, 30, 189
Homerton College, Cambridge 272–3
honours, good, measure 41
hospitality, leisure, recreation and tourism
  119–21, 245
hostel accommodation 191
household income 215, 223
Houses in Multiple Occupation (HMO) 193
Housing Act 2004 193
Huddersfield, University of 382–3
Hughes Hall, Cambridge 273
Hull, University of 384–5
Hull York Medical School 137, 138, 385, 520
Iberian languages 121–2
Imperial College of Science, Technology
  and Medicine 10, 48, 386–7
income support, from government 219
information management 128–9
Institute of Education, University of
  London 415
insurance 196–7, 222
insurance choice (CI) 30, 181
International Baccalaureate 17, 19
  acceptability of 18
  and UCAS tariff 17
International Graduate Scheme 242
international students 237–47
  application process 241
  employment regulations 242
  English language requirements 240–41
  entry regulations 241–2
  family members 242
  most popular subjects studied 238–41
  tuition fees, by university 223–31
  university support 242–3
  what to study 240, 244–7
  where coming from 238
  where to study 237–9

internet, reliability of information on 34
interviews 137, 175, 178, 180–81, 249, 253
inventory, rented flat 194
Italian 123–4
Jesus College, Cambridge 273
Jesus College, Oxford 257
job prospects 24–9
Joint Honours 22
Keble College, Oxford 257–8
Keele, University of 388–9
Kent, University of 390–91
King's College London 392–3
King's College, Cambridge 274
Kingston University 394–5
Lady Margaret Hall, Oxford 258
Lampeter, University of Wales 396–7
Lancaster University 398–9
land and property management 124–5
landscape 172–3
law 21–2, 125–8, 244
Law Advice Centre 193
league tables 37–41
  changes in measures used 37
  measures used 38–41, 48–9
  and universities 8
  value of 37
  weighting in 38
lease 193–4
Leeds, University of 400–01
Leeds Metropolitan University 402–3
  and reduced tuition fees 32–3, 212
  and sport 199
Leicester, University of 404–5
leisure 119–21, 245
librarianship and information management
  128–9
library facilities, and league table 40
Lincoln, University of 406–7
Lincoln College, Oxford 258–9
linguistics 129–30
Liverpool, University of 408–9
Liverpool Hope University 410–11
  and blocked data 10
Liverpool John Moores University (LJMU)
  412–13
living at home 8, 30, 189
living costs 220–21
loans, student 212–14
  interest on 214
  maintenance loan 213
  repayment of 214
  tuition fees loan 213
Local Education Authority (LEA) 215
location, university 30–31

lodging accommodation 191
London, cost of living 33, 187
London, University of 277, 414–15
London Business School 283, 415
London Metropolitan University 416–7
  and blocked data 10
London School of Economics and Political
  Science (LSE) 10, 48, 418–9
  A levels not accepted 18, 19
London School of Hygiene and Tropical
  Medicine 415
London South Bank University 420–21
Loughborough University 48, 422–3
  and sport 199, 203
LSE 418–9
Lucy Cavendish College, Cambridge 274
Magdalen College, Oxford 259
Magdalene College, Cambridge 274–5
maintenance grant 214–16
maintenance loan 213, 208
Manchester, University of 424–5
Manchester Business School 283
Manchester Metropolitan University 426–7
Mansfield College, Oxford 259–60
manufacturing engineering 53–5, 247
Marjon, University College Plymouth 109
Masters courses 28
materials technology 130–31
mathematics 131–4, 245
mature students, loan support 214
measures,
  league table 37–41
  subject tables 49
mechanical engineering 134–6, 245
media studies 82–4, 246
medicine 21–2, 136–9, 245
medicine, other subjects allied to 145–8, 246
Merton College, Oxford 260
Middle Eastern and African studies 140
Middlesex University 428–9
Million + Group 32
mobile phone costs 221
Modern and Medieval Languages Test
  (MML) 20
modular degrees 22–3
Murray Edwards College, Cambridge 275
music 141–3
Napier University (now Edinburgh Napier)
  358–9
National Admissions Test for Law (LNAT)
  20
National Student Survey 9, 16
  and campus size 31
  and league table 37, 39

most satisfied students 32
  and subject tables 48, 47
National Tenancy Deposit Scheme 194
NatWest Student Living Index 2008 186,
  187
New College, Oxford 260–61
Newcastle University 430–31
NEWI see Glyndŵr University
Newman University College 109, 168
Newnham College, Cambridge 275–6
Newport, University of Wales 432–3
Norrington Table, Oxford 250
Northampton, University of 434–5
Northern Ireland
  financial support 216
  tuition fees 211–12
Northumbria University 436–7
Nottingham, University of 438–9
Nottingham Trent University 440–41
nursing 143–5, 241
nursing and midwifery, Scotland, and
  UCAS 175
nutrition 145–8
occupational therapy 145–8
offers 181
Office for Fair Access 217
Ofsted 49
Olympic Games 2012 198, 200
online application, UCAS 175
open days 31, 234
Open University 23, 283
ophthalmology 145–8
optometry 145–8
Oriel College, Oxford 251
orthoptics 145–8
osteopathy 145–8
other subjects allied to medicine 145–8,
  246
Oxbridge 248–81
Oxford, University of 10, 442–3
  application and acceptance by subject
  252–3
  application process 177
  choosing a college 249–52
  college fees 33
  college profiles 254–67
  Norrington Table 250
  and sport 199
  state school applicants 248–9
  and subject tables 48
Oxford Brookes University 444–5
parents, their role 232–6
Parents' Learning Allowance 214
partial maintenance grant 223

part-time course 23, 184
part-time work 219–20
Pembroke College, Cambridge 276
Pembroke College, Oxford 261–2
Peninsula College of Medicine and
    Dentistry 88, 137, 138, 363, 446
performance indicators 36
personal statement, UCAS 177–9
Peterhouse College, Cambridge 276–7
pharmacology 148–50, 246
pharmacy 148–50, 246
philosophy 150–52
Philosophy, Politics and Economics
    (PPE) Admissions Test 19
physics 152–4
physiology 58–9
physiotherapy 145–8
places, availability of in 2010 9, 13
planning 172–3
Plymouth, University of 446–7
podiatry 145–8
politics 154–6, 246
polytechnic 32
Portsmouth, University of 448–9
positive destinations 28, 48
private accommodation 189–90, 191–5
private sector, renting 192–5
professional qualifications 21
property management 124–5
prospectus 34
psychology 156–9, 246
Queen Margaret University 450–51
Queen Mary, University of London
    452–3
Queen's College, Oxford 262
Queens' College, Cambridge 277
Queen's University, Belfast 454–5
radiography 145–8
RAE see Research Assessment Exercise
Reading, University of 48, 456–7
recession, and student numbers 7
recreation 119–21, 245
recreational facilities, and choice 34
recruiting universities 9
reference, UCAS 179
rejection (R) 181
religious studies 170–72
rental agreement 193–4
rents, average student 186
repayment of loans 214
Research Assessment Exercise 2008
    10, 38–40, 41, 48
    and staff numbers involved 38–9, 41
research quality measure 39–40, 41, 49

residence, hall of 190
resits 184
results day 182–3
    and parents 234–5
    Scotland 183
Robert Gordon University 458–9
Robinson College, Cambridge 277–8
Roehampton University 460–61
Route B, UCAS, end of 175
Royal Academy of Music 141, 415
Royal and Ancient scholarships 201
Royal College of Art 283
Royal College of Music, London 141,
    462
Royal Holloway, University of London
    462–3
Royal Scottish Academy of Music and
    Drama 141
Royal Veterinary College 174, 415
Russell Group 19, 32
Russian 159–60
safety, student 195
St Andrews, University of 10, 464–5
St Anne's College, Oxford 262–3
St Catharine's College, Cambridge 278
St Catherine's College, Oxford 263
St Edmund Hall, Oxford 263
St Edmund's College, Cambridge 278
St George's Hospital Medical School,
    University of London 283, 415
St Hilda's College, Oxford 264
St Hugh's College, Oxford 264
St John's College, Cambridge 279
St John's College, Oxford 264–5
St Mary's College, Twickenham 115,
    165, 171, 217
St Peter's College, Oxford 265
Salford, University of 466–7
sandwich course 22
scholarships 216–17
School of Oriental and African Studies,
    London 468–9
School of Pharmacy, London 415
science courses, length of 28
Scotland
    financial support 216
    and National Student Survey 38, 48
    tuition fees 212
    universities in 30
Scottish exam results, and Clearing 183
Scottish qualifications, and UCAS tariff
    17, 19
Scottish students 8, 216
    studying outside Scotland 217–18

security, student 195
selecting universities 9
self-catering accommodation, university 190
Selwyn College, Cambridge 279–80
services and facility spend measure 40
Sheffield, University of 49, 470–71
Sheffield Hallam University 472–3
Sidney Sussex College, Cambridge 280
Sixth Term Examination Papers (STEP) 20
SOAS 468–9
social policy 160–62
social work 162–5
sociology 165–7
Sodexo University Lifestyle Survey 2008 16, 28, 188, 189, 191, 195, 210, 218, 233
Somerville College, Oxford 265–6
South Asian studies 92–3
Southampton, University of 474–5
Southampton Solent University 476–7
Special Support Grant, Northern Ireland 216
speech therapy 145–8
sports, at university 198–209
  cost of 200–01
  increasing importance in university choice 198
  facilities 200, 203–9
  location of 201
  and part-time jobs 202
  scholarships 201–2
  useful websites 202, 205, 207, 209
sports science 10, 168–70, 201
Staffordshire University 478–9
standard offers 30
Stanford Test 22
Stirling, University of 480–81
  and sport 199
Strathclyde, University of 482–3
student accommodation accreditation schemes 193
Student Awards Agency for Scotland 212, 213, 214
student budget 222, 235
student bursaries 33, 216–17
  by university 223–31
student credit card 221–2
student debt 210
student expenditure 220–22
student facilities, and league table 40
Student Finance England 214
Student Finance Northern Ireland 214

Student Finance Wales 214
student finance, and parents 232
student grants 214–16
student income 218–20
student loans 212–14
  interest on 214
Student Loans Company 210, 214
student overdraft 212–2
student satisfaction measure 39, 49
student-staff ratio measure 40
Student Visitor entry route 242
students' union 16–17, 34
studying abroad 33
studying, cost of 32–3, 221
studying, most popular place for 189
subject selection 8, 15–29
  earnings prospects 26–7, 28–9
  employment prospects 24–5, 28
  by international students 240, 244–7
  most applications for 21
  most popular 21
Sunderland, University of 484–5
Supplementary Application Questionnaire, Cambridge 253
Support Funds, Northern Ireland 219
Surrey, University of 486–7
Sussex, University of 488–9
Swansea, University of 490–91
Swansea Metropolitan University 492–3
  and blocked data 10
Talented Athletes Training Scheme 202
tariff, UCAS 17, 18–19
teaching quality 37,
  Ofsted 49
Teesside, University of 494–5
Thames Valley University 496–7
The Times League Table 9, 37–47
theology and religious studies 170–72
Thinking Skills Assessment (TSA) 20
third semester 27
Tier 4 approved colleges and international students 241–2
timetable, application 179
timetable, financial support 215
Tompkins Table, Cambridge 249
top up fees 7, 9, 13, 32–3, 211–12
  and parents 232
tourism 119–21, 245
town and country planning and landscape 172–3
Track 180
travel time to university 188
Trinity College, Cambridge 280–81

Trinity College, Oxford 266
Trinity Hall, Cambridge 281
Trinity Saint David, University of Wales 396
tuition fees 7, 9, 13, 32–3, 211–12
    review 13, 211
tuition fees grant, Wales 212
tuition fees loan 213
two-year degrees 27
UCAS application process 175–83
    form, importance of 175
    personal statement 177–9
    reference 179
UCAS *Apply* 175–80
UCAS course code 177
UCAS Extra 32, 182
UCAS Route B, end of 175
UCAS tariff 11, 17, 18–19
    and league table 40
UCAS *Track* 180, 184
UCAS website 18, 32
    and Clearing 183
    and financial information 216
UCL 502–3
UCLan 330–31
UK Clinical Aptitude Test (UKCAT) 20
Ulster, University of 498–9
unconditional acceptance (UF) 181
unconditional offer (U) 181
unemployment, and graduates 24–5, 28, 29
UNITE 189
United States of America, studying in 33
universities
    accommodation provided by 189–91
    fees and bursaries 211–12, 223–31
    growth of 11–12
    hierarchy of 11
    league table 8, 37–47
    most favoured by employers 31
    most popular with international students 239
    and openness of information 12
    recruiting 9
    selecting 9
    support for international students 242–3
    top for applications 30
    value of 12, 13, 15

university choice 15–16, 23, 29–3
    and cost 32–3, 210–31
    and the countries of the UK 30
    and facilities 33–4
    and location 30–31
    non-academic factors in 28
    and university reputation 32
University College London 502–3
University College, Oxford 266–7
University for the Creative Arts 504–5
University of the Arts, London 500–01
University of the Creative Arts 10
University of Wales, Newport 432–3
university profiles, definitions 282–3
UWE, Bristol 508–9
UWIC 199, 328–9
vacation work 220
veterinary medicine 173–4
virtual university 13
visa fees 241
visa regulations 241–2
vocational diplomas 18, 19
vocational subjects 8, 19–20, 22
voluntary work 219
Wadham College, Oxford 267
Wales
    financial support 216
    tuition fees 212
Wales, University of 283
Warwick, University of 48, 506–7
websites, financial support 222–3
Welsh National Bursary 216, 218, 231
Welsh students 8
    studying outside Wales 218
West of England, Bristol, University of 508–9
West of Scotland, University of 510–11
    and blocked data 10
Westminster, University of 512–13
Winchester, University of 514–15
Wolfson College, Cambridge 281
Wolverhampton, University of 516–17
Worcester, University of 518–19
Worcester College, Oxford 267
work placements 219
work, part–time 219–20
work, vacation 220
York, University of 10, 520–21
York St John University 522–3
Young Student's Bursary, Scotland 216, 218
Z–scores 38